PENGUIN CLASSICS

APOLOGIA PRO VITA SUA

JOHN HENRY NEWMAN was born in 1801 and educated privately at Ealing School and Trinity College, Oxford. Elected a Fellow of Oriel in 1822, he became vicar of the university church of St Mary's in 1828. In 1833 he began the *Tracts for the Times*; but after his controversial Tract 90, which attempted to interpret the 39 Articles of the Church of England in a Catholic sense, he retired in 1842 to monastic seclusion at Littlemore. Without completing his *Essay on the Development of Christian Doctrine*, he was received in 1845 into the Roman Catholic Church. Ordained a priest in 1847, he founded the Birmingham Oratory in 1848. In 1851 he was appointed first rector of the Catholic University of Ireland (resigning in 1858), and his Dublin lectures and articles were eventually published as *The Idea of a University*. His theological autobiography, *Apologia pro Vita Sua*, appeared in 1864 in response to a public attack by Charles Kingsley. His poem on the afterlife, *The Dream of Gerontius*, was published in 1865 and later inspired Elgar's musical masterpiece. In 1870 he finally completed his philosophical justification of religious faith in *An Essay in Aid of a Grammar of Assent*. Created a cardinal in 1879, he died in 1890. He was declared 'Venerable' in 1991.

IAN KER teaches theology at Oxford, having previously taught both theology and English at universities in Britain and the United States. He is the author and editor of twenty books, mostly on Newman, including *John Henry Newman: A Biography* (1988) and *The Catholic Revival in English Literature 1845–1961* (2003).

D0057692

JOHN HENRY NEWMAN

Apologia pro Vita Sua

Edited by IAN KER

PENGUIN BOOKS

PENGUIN BOOKS

Published by the Penguin Group
Penguin Books Ltd, 80 Strand, London WC2R ORL, England
Penguin Putnam Inc., 375 Hudson Street, New York, New York 10014, USA
Penguin Books Australia Ltd, 250 Camberwell Road, Camberwell, Victoria 3124, Australia
Penguin Books Canada Ltd, 10 Alcorn Avenue, Toronto, Ontario, Canada M4V 3B2
Penguin Books India (P) Ltd, 11 Community Centre, Panchsheel Park, New Delhi – 110 017, India
Penguin Books (NZ) Ltd, Cnr Rosedale and Airborne Roads, Albany, Auckland, New Zealand
Penguin Books (South Africa) (Pty) Ltd, 24 Sturdee Avenue, Rosebank 2196, South Africa

Penguin Books Ltd, Registered Offices: 80 Strand, London WC2R ORL, England

www.penguin.com

First published 1994
Reprinted 2004
11

Introduction and Notes copyright © Ian Ker, 1994
All rights reserved

The moral right of the editor has been asserted

Filmset by Datix International Limited, Bungay, Suffolk
Printed in England by Clays Ltd, St Ives plc
Set in 10/11.5 pt Monophoto Garamond

JOHN HENRY NEWMAN

Apologia pro Vita Sua

Edited by IAN KER

CONTENTS

ABBREVIATIONS

Newman collected his works in a uniform edition of thirty-six volumes (1868–81). Until his death in 1890 he continued making minor textual changes in reprints of individual volumes, all of which from 1886 were published by Longmans, Green and Co. of London. Unless otherwise stated, all references are to volumes in the uniform edition published after 1890 by Longmans, except that references to the *Apologia* are to this Penguin edition.

Apo.	*Apologia pro Vita Sua*
Ari.	*The Arians of the Fourth Century*
Ath. i, ii	*Select Treatises of St Athanasius*, 2 vols.
AW	*John Henry Newman: Autobiographical Writings*, ed. H. Tristram (London and New York: Sheed and Ward, 1956)
Corr.	*Correspondence of John Henry Newman with John Keble and Others, 1839–1845*, ed. at the Birmingham Oratory (London: Longmans, 1917)
DA	*Discussions and Arguments on Various Subjects*
Dev.	*An Essay on the Development of Christian Doctrine*
Diff. i, ii	*Certain Difficulties felt by Anglicans in Catholic Teaching*, 2 vols.
Ess. i, ii	*Essays Critical and Historical*, 2 vols.
HS i, ii, iii	*Historical Sketches*, 3 vols.
Jfc.	*Lectures on the Doctrine of Justification*
LD	*The Letters and Diaries of John Henry Newman*, ed. C. S. Dessain et al., vols. i–vi (Oxford: Clarendon Press, 1978–84), xi–xxii (Edinburgh: Nelson, 1961–72), xxiii–xxxi (Oxford: Clarendon Press, 1973–7)
Mir.	*Two Essays on Biblical and Ecclesiastical Miracles*
Moz. i, ii	*Letters and Correspondence of John Henry Newman*

	during his Life in the English Church, ed. A. Mozley, 2 vols. (London: Longmans, 1891)
MD	*Meditations and Devotions of the Late Cardinal Newman* (London: Longmans, 1893)
OS	*Sermons Preached on Various Occasions*
PS i–viii	*Parochial and Plain Sermons*, 8 vols.
US	*Fifteen Sermons Preached before the University of Oxford*
VM i, ii	*The Via Media*, 2 vols.
VV	*Verses on Various Occasions*
Ker	Ian Ker, *John Henry Newman: A Biography* (Oxford: Clarendon Press, 1988)

INTRODUCTION

1   The Background, Composition, and Reception of the Apologia

On 30 December 1863 Newman received in the post a copy of the January number of *Macmillan's Magazine*. It was sent (anonymously) by William Pope, a Catholic priest in Yorkshire and a former Anglican clergyman who had himself been converted by Newman's writings (curiously enough, he was a nephew of Richard Whately, the fellow of Oriel whose formative influence on Newman is generously acknowledged in the *Apologia* but who was to become an inveterate opponent of all that his former disciple stood for). The issue contained an enthusiastic review by Charles Kingsley of J. A. Froude's anti-Catholic *History of England* in which various passages had been marked in pencil, including the following words that have become celebrated because of the book they inspired, or rather provoked:

> Truth, for its own sake, had never been a virtue with the Roman clergy. Father Newman informs us that it need not, and on the whole ought not to be; that cunning is the weapon which Heaven has given to the saints wherewith to withstand the brute male force of the wicked world which marries and is given in marriage. Whether his notion be doctrinally correct or not, it is at least historically so.[1]

The accusation that unscrupulous cunning was the hallmark of Roman Catholics was familiar enough to Newman: after all, he had shared it to some extent himself as an Anglican, and even as a Catholic he was not unaware of a temptation to doctor historical facts if the defence of the Church seemed to require it. What may seem rather more startling is Kingsley's sarcastic reference to celibacy. To understand this, one needs to bear in mind the deep suspicion that the Victorian Protestant mind entertained on the subject of clerical and religious celibacy, a suspicion which in the case of Kingsley, who before finding a resolution in marriage had been violently torn between the attractions of the flesh and the spirit, had become a neurotic obsession.[1]

After Newman had written to the publishers to complain, he received a letter from Kingsley claiming that his charge could be justified by a number of passages in Newman's writings, but particularly by one of his Anglican sermons. The publisher himself, Alexander Macmillan, wrote politely to say that it had not occurred to him that Newman or any other Roman Catholic would object to being criticized for what he assumed was the accepted Catholic strategy towards so-called heretics, namely, the proverbial craft of the serpent. In spite of his ostensible indignation at such an assumption, Newman could hardly have been too surprised at Macmillan's reaction. After all, it only reflected the prevailing view of Roman Catholics in a country whose national and cultural identity was ineluctably bound up with that peculiarly English version of the Protestant Reformation, the Elizabethan settlement, which had apparently established for all time that the integrity and well-being of England depended on its freeing itself from the shackles of papal tyranny and on its having its own national church, independent of Catholic Europe and particularly of its traditional rivals France and Spain, as befitted an insular power whose greatness was held practically to date from the break with Rome.

Kingsley's response to Newman's protest was to send him a draft of an 'apology' he proposed to publish, which clearly only added insult to injury. It included these two smoothly equivocal paragraphs:

> No man knows the use of words better than Dr Newman. No man, therefore, has a better right to define what he does, or does not, mean by them.
>
> It only remains, therefore, for me to express my hearty regret at having so seriously mistaken him; and my hearty pleasure at finding him on the side of Truth, in this, or any other matter.[2]

After Newman had sarcastically sent back a witty paraphrase of

1. See Martin J. Svaglic, ed., *Apologia* (Oxford: Clarendon Press, 1967), xxxi–v.
2. *Apo.* 366–7.

the 'apology', Kingsley agreed to omit the second sentence quoted, and the second half of the last sentence, but refused to withdraw the objectionable first sentence (this truncated version was published in the February number of *Macmillan's Magazine*). Since Kingsley had also failed to provide any evidence for his insinuations, apart from making a general reference to one sermon as though its meaning were self-evidently what he alleged it to be, Newman decided to print the correspondence in the form of a pamphlet, with some concluding reflections.

Newman certainly did not see Kingsley's attack in a personal light: it was simply yet another, if glaring, example of the kind of hostility – and fear – that his name aroused in so many of his compatriots. To appreciate the contemporary significance of the *Apologia*, we need to realize two things: first, the contempt and hatred with which English people had been brought up to regard Roman Catholicism, a religion they saw both as the antithesis of the true Christianity which the Reformation had recovered for them and as the embodiment of all that was foreign and anti-English; second, the incredulous dismay that anyone with Newman's ability and position at Oxford (then not only the intellectual centre of England but also the hub of its religious life) could not only have inspired and led a movement deliberately calculated to subvert the Protestant character of the established Church, but could also have actually been converted to the very religion that represented the epitome of all that was repugnant to a patriotic Englishman. For Catholicism was not simply a false and superstitious religion, it was manifestly out of date and an affront to all the progressive beliefs of the most advanced and powerful nation in the world, convinced of its divinely appointed duty to spread the enlightened civilization of the British empire all over the globe – a mission in which of course the Protestant Church of England had its own privileged place.

For thirty years, ever since the beginning of the Oxford or Tractarian movement in 1833, Newman had been used to being a national object of suspicion. But the present attack on him was more significant, he was starting to realize, than the kind of slander to which he was accustomed. Not that it was as libellous or offensive as some of the things he was used to reading in the newspapers – like a recent report that the famous 'clerical pervert' was now a sceptic living in Paris (for the respectable Victorian middle class the symbol of immorality and irreligion).[1] Because of Newman's known opposition to the growing influence in the Catholic Church of extreme right-wing papal Ultramontanism, there were many rumours at this time that he was about to leave the Church of Rome and return disillusioned to the Church of England, and he had already taken advantage of a categorical announcement to that effect in one influential newspaper to issue a no less categorical denial. Kingsley, however, was an important figure, who was not only Regius Professor of Modern History at Cambridge but a well-known popular novelist. Moreover, by issuing the kind of challenge that his pamphlet represented, Newman could expect Kingsley to reply in kind, quite possibly by publicizing every passage that he could conceivably drag out of Newman's works to support his charge. This in turn would mean that Newman would have to respond with a full-scale defence of his integrity:

> This would lead me to a survey of my whole course, which I should not be sorry for, tho' I dread the wear and tear of it. The chance that such a task is sooner or later in store for me, is what makes me wish to get about me as many letters and memoranda as I can. I have never defended myself . . .[2]

He even told a friend that he had 'prepared' himself 'from the first' for this eventuality, and indeed had 'always looked forward to the possibility' of 'an opening to defend myself as to various passages in my life and writings'.[3] This was partly why he had been concerned to have all his letters and papers in order, although so far he had only got as far as 1836, whereas the documents he would have most need of were those covering the vital years (1841–5) leading up to his conversion to Rome.

The controversy with Kingsley occurred at a time in Newman's life when he had never been so depressed and when it seemed as if he had nothing more to look forward to in the way of achievement. He was now sixty-three years old. His fateful

1. See Ker, 508.   2. *LD* xxi. 70.   3. *LD* xxi. 69.

involvement in the affairs of the liberal Catholic *Rambler* that led to his publishing what is one of his most famous theological writings, his lengthy article 'On Consulting the Faithful in Matters of Doctrine' (1859), had resulted in his falling under the suspicion and disapproval of the ecclesiastical authorities in Rome as well as England. His first real experience of the authoritarian clericalism of the nineteenth-century Catholic Church had come with his disappointing and frustrating association with the ill-fated Catholic University of Ireland which he had struggled to launch as its first president (1851–8). It seemed not only to him but to most Catholics who counted that he had nothing more to contribute and that he was lucky to have avoided a formal censure for the offending article. The Oratory he had founded in Birmingham in 1848 was hardly thriving: in fact it was so depleted that much of the community and pastoral work now had to be done by Newman himself. The daughter house that had been founded in London under the flamboyant Father (F. W.) Faber was now not only much better known and successful, but was in active opposition both to Newman's idea of the nature of an Oratory and to the kind of moderate Catholicism he was trying to promote in an increasingly polarized church. So low had Newman been feeling for so long that on 13 March 1864 he actually wrote down a last profession of faith 'in prospect of death'.[1] He really was beginning to think that he was close to death, even though there was nothing actually wrong with his health. It was his lowest point, and he could hardly have dreamed how dramatic and sudden the reversal in his fortunes would be. But as he began writing around to friends, asking for their help and advice, we can sense in the new excited tempo a return of the old creative impulse; at last that essential 'external stimulus', without which he said he had 'scarcely written any' of his books, had come again. But he was only too well aware that the 'pain' of writing would be 'a mental child-bearing'.[2]

On 20 March Kingsley countered with his own pamphlet *What, Then, Does Dr Newman Mean?*, in which he hurled angry aspersions and insinuations against the deceitful cunning of

---

1. *MD* 437.   2. *LD* xxi. 69.

Newman and Catholics in general. Newman now knew what he had to do. As he put it to his old Anglican curate, W. J. Copeland:

> The whole strength of what he says, *as directed rhetorically* to the popular mind, is in the antecedent prejudice that *I was a Papist while I was an Anglican* . . . The only way in which I can destroy this, is to give my history, and the history of my mind, from 1822 or earlier, down to 1845. I wish I had my papers properly about me.[1]

On 10 April Newman's diary reads, 'beginning of my hard work for my Apologia'.[2] The educated world of London knew he was not a liar, but the average Protestant or 'Brummagem' really did assume he was 'a clever knave', so strong and pervasive was the anti-Catholic prejudice. By writing a 'History of my Opinions', he would be able at last to show that he had been sincere in his Anglo-Catholicism, and not an agent in the pay of Rome, as so many of his contemporaries automatically assumed. He had now abandoned the idea of giving a series of lectures in self-defence as they would not be suitable for a personal account of his life. But the *Apologia* was not to be only about his Anglican life: in the last chapter he was to touch on some of the most controverted aspects of contemporary Roman Catholicism. Probably it was a letter from the liberal Catholic Lord Acton that first suggested the idea. For on the same day that Newman began work in earnest, Acton wrote to say that brilliantly as he had justified himself in the duel with Kingsley, the fact that he had not attempted to defend the integrity of the Catholic clergy as a whole against Kingsley's aspersions had been noticed and accounted for by the fact that a defence of the Catholic Church's commitment to truth would be hard to sustain; to this extent, the controversy had inadvertently shown the Church up in as bad a light as it had shown Newman in a good light. Newman immediately accepted the challenge – 'you may be sure I shall go as far as ever I can'.[3]

Newman had decided to bring out the book in weekly pam-

1. *LD* xxi. 90–1.   2. *LD* xxi. 92.   3. *LD* xxi. 94.

phlets, which the publisher wanted to appear as soon as possible
while the controversy was still news. A complete book would
reach fewer people because of its length and because there would
be less interest by the time it was published. The first of the
pamphlets was published on Thursday 21 April, followed by six
more on consecutive Thursdays, the series being concluded by
an appendix which appeared two weeks later. It was truly an
astonishing feat, which Newman himself called 'the most arduous
work . . . I ever had in my life', and which was also 'one of the
most terrible trials that I have had'.[1] As Newman wrote, he
consulted old Anglican friends, warning that he was not attempting to write a history of the Oxford movement – it was a purely
personal account to prove his honesty. As he composed the part
which dealt with his early life up to the beginning of the
movement in 1833, he was in tears and unable to read it aloud.
He was warned that the first two pamphlets which dealt with
Kingsley might provoke an unfavourable reaction if it was felt
that he was striking a man already down (eventually both parts
would be consigned to appendices). However, he felt he had to
'speak strongly', otherwise people would not think he was
serious. He had been attacked often enough, but the attacks on
the whole had been anonymous (Kingsley had put his initials to
the offending review), 'or else a sentence or two on some
particular point has been the whole'. But he had already decided
that if anyone well known 'made an elaborate charge on me, I
was bound to speak'.[2] Now his only concern was 'to tell the
truth, and to leave the matter in God's hands'. He was 'writing
from morning till night, hardly having time for my meals'.[3] He
expected friends to be amazed by what they read: he had certainly
never before written in this kind of intimate, autobiographical
way. It was hard to write the letters he had to send out asking
for criticism and information: 'My fingers have been *walking*
nearly 20 miles a day.' It was not that what he was writing would
be a particularly long book, but he was continually revising and
rewriting 'from the necessity of digesting and compressing'.[4] It
was a strange irony that Kingsley's attack had brought him into

1. *LD* xxi. 96–7.   2. *LD* xxi. 97–100.   3. *LD* xxi. 103.   4. *LD* xxi. 105.

contact with old Anglican friends, who were now helping him to write a book that was ultimately critical of Anglicanism, at least to the extent that it was a defence of his own conversion to Catholicism.

On 20 May Newman's diary records that he actually worked on the manuscript 'for 22 hours running'.[1] By now five parts or pamphlets had been published, and the sixth and seventh appeared the two following weeks. Then, after another fortnight, the eighth appeared on 16 June, an appendix called 'Answer in Detail to Mr Kingsley's Accusations'. No other writing had cost Newman so much, both because of the speed with which he had had to write and because of the emotional pain involved. He had had to work continuously and at such pressure that he had been afraid of seriously damaging his health. No one indeed could describe the pains of authorship more graphically and vividly than Newman. Sometimes, he recorded, he had 'to sweep away . . . ruthlessly' what he had composed, with the next deadline 'yawning close upon me'. Nor was it at all easy to conclude each separate part as his material piled up, with the result that 'manuscript and proof got jammed together, as in a stoppage in the streets of London – and the proof almost got ahead of the manuscript, if that can be'.[2] It was true that he had had to write pamphlets in the course of a single day or night at critical moments during the Oxford movement, but never before a substantial book 'all at a heat'. It was as if he were 'ploughing in a very stiff clay. It was moving on at the rate of a mile an hour, when I had to write and print and correct a hundred miles by the next day's post.' Every week another pamphlet had to be ready for publication – 'and Thursday would come round once a week – so I was like a man who had fallen overboard and had to swim to land, and found the distance he had to go greater and greater. At last I am ashore, and have crawled upon the beach, and there I lie . . .'[3]

The eight parts or pamphlets were published together in one volume in 1864 under the title *Apologia pro Vita Sua: Being a Reply to a Pamphlet entitled 'What, Then, Does Dr Newman Mean?'* The second edition, which appeared in 1865, was simply entitled

1. *LD* xxi. 111.   2. *LD* xxi. 126.   3. *LD* xxi. 131–2.

History of my Religious Opinions; a brief preface was substituted for the first two polemical parts, and the appendix was shortened and recast in the form of a series of notes, in which all reference to Kingsley was dropped and additional matter was provided. In 1873 Newman restored the original – and by now famous – title, while retaining as a subtitle 'Being a History of his Religious Opinions'; in the course of various revisions, the preface was also enlarged with further extracts from the first two pamphlets, while additional notes were inserted at the end. It is this definitive text which Newman included in the uniform edition of his works and which is reproduced here. Where this edition differs from the original 1873 edition is in including all the minor textual changes that Newman introduced into later reprints before his death. It also contains extra appendices comprising the two original pamphlets by Newman and Kingsley and also the first two parts and the appendix of the 1864 edition. Not only does this material have historical interest and provide useful background information for the modern reader, but the polemical satire has an enduring literary value.

It was, in fact, the satire of Newman's original pamphlet that had attracted the extremely favourable attention of Richard Holt Hutton, the prominent literary critic, who had written a review of it entitled 'Father Newman's Sarcasm', in which he called Newman 'not only one of the greatest of English writers, but, perhaps the very greatest master of . . . sarcasm in the English language'.[1] The review was important not just because of the recognition of Newman's literary powers, but because it represented a turning-point in the public perception of Newman, with Hutton dismissing as absurd Kingsley's intemperate attack. Indeed, it was the first of many favourable reviews. There was some support for Kingsley (inevitably), but the overwhelming view was that Newman had defeated Kingsley and proved his integrity. The most favourable response came surprisingly from the then powerful Nonconformist constituency, although Anglicans appreciated how generously Newman had written about the Church of England. It was also the first time since the Reformation that Roman Catholicism had received such sympathetic

1. *LD* xxi. 61 n. 2.

attention: simply from a cultural and religious point of view the *Apologia*, which was an immediate best-seller, was of enormous importance in breaking down deep-grained prejudices. As a result of its success, English Roman Catholics may be said to have won a new respectability as well as a quite unprecedented respect for their religion. Kingsley himself, however, remained quite unrepentant. Bitterly resentful of Newman's public victory, he wrote to Alexander Macmillan to say that while he had deliberately 'struck as hard' as he could, he had no intention of putting himself 'a second time, by any fresh act of courtesy, into the power of one who, like a treacherous ape, lifts to you meek and suppliant eyes, till he thinks he has you within his reach, and then springs, gibbering and biting, at your face'.[1]

2 What Kind of a Book is the Apologia?

As we have seen, Newman was anxious to disclaim any suggestion that the *Apologia* was a history of the Oxford movement. And yet it obviously is, to some extent at least, a historical account, and seen from the point of view of the man who in effect inspired and led the movement until he began to be assailed by serious doubts. But it is this very fact that may easily be disguised by Newman's modest narrative, in which he does not make clear how crucial was his own role and influence. So closely documented is his account by letters and quotations from published writings that there is little room for any serious factual errors, while the author's comments on and interpretation of the facts tend to be carefully expressed as simply his own personal opinions, thus disarming any complaints about their lack of objectivity. After all, the point of the *Apologia* was to try and describe as far as possible the development of the narrator's theological views leading to his conversion to Rome. As such a subjective account, which is fully supported by the wealth of autobiographical materials (now partially published), the book has never been challenged, although of course the actual ideas and their evolution have been held up to plenty of critical scrutinies, especially from apologists for the Church of England.[1]

The fact is that the *Apologia* is essentially an autobiography. But unlike that other Victorian classic, John Ruskin's *Praeterita*, the *Apologia* is an austerely intellectual work, purporting to be merely what its subtitle 'A History of his Religious Opinions' indicates. Certainly it is often called a 'spiritual' autobiography, but in the strict sense of the word it is very far from being a spiritual work like St Augustine's *Confessions*, with which it is indeed often compared. If it is at all confessional, it is virtually only in its theological revelations, and such disclosures as there are of the writer's soul are almost incidental to the account of his theological development. Thus, for example, Newman tells us nothing of his prayer life, there is no mention of his Anglican confirmation and first communion, nor is his ordination ever referred to, or the parochial work he did as a curate in the Oxford parish of St Clement's, or his strongly held convictions about the pastoral responsibilities of a college tutor. Central autobiographical themes like these, of great importance for understanding Newman's spiritual life, are simply ignored.

In at least two cases the silence may be misleading, as there were important effects on his theological development. I refer in the first place to Newman's gradual deconversion from Evangelicalism. In his 'Autobiographical Memoir' which he wrote in the 1870s, he records that after receiving Anglican orders he discovered from 'personal experience' that the kind of Christianity he had imbibed from reading books by Evangelicals like John Newton and Thomas Scott 'would not work in a parish; that it was unreal; that this he had actually found as a fact ... that Calvinism was not a key to the phenomena of human nature, as they occur in the world'. In other words, it was not only through the kind of theological discussion and study which he records in the *Apologia* that he became disenchanted with Evan-

1. Sometimes without regard to what Newman actually says, as when Owen Chadwick claims that he was in search of 'an ideal' church, to which he believed the Roman Catholic Church to be the closest (Introduction to Susan Foister, *Cardinal Newman 1801–90: A Centenary Exhibition* (London: National Portrait Gallery Publications, 1990), 7). In *Newman* (Oxford: Oxford University Press, 1983), 14, Chadwick virtually attributes his conversion to intellectual isolation at Littlemore.

gelicalism, but also as a result of the actual pastoral work he undertook in the working-class parish of St Clement's. But to this practical experience – 'the teaching of facts'[1] – he makes no reference at all in the *Apologia*.

That the silence was quite deliberately self-imposed can be shown by the even more glaring omission of any real description of the effect on his religious imagination of his momentous Mediterranean cruise of 1832–3, immediately prior to the formal beginning of the Oxford movement. Newman's visits to Italy, Malta and the Greek islands are dismissed in six paragraphs in the first chapter in the *Apologia*, and yet the letters and verses he wrote on his travels, as well as the extraordinarily vivid account he later wrote of his near-fatal illness in Sicily, show how crucial this intense period was for his subsequent religious development. In this regard too, then, the *Apologia* is quite misleading autobiographically.

Actually, in a later passage in the second chapter of the *Apologia*, Newman does let drop a hint that his earlier brief account of his foreign travels was less than complete. In the course of discussing his theological position in 1833, he alludes to his ingrained prejudice that the pope was the Antichrist predicted in Scripture, which he had acquired through his adolescent Evangelical reading. When he noted in the first chapter, 'My imagination was stained by the effects of this doctrine up to the year 1843', he had qualified this by adding, 'it had been obliterated from my reason and judgment at an earlier date'.[2] This contrast reappears in the second chapter when he traces the gradual diminution of his antipathy to the papacy. But this time it is his imagination which becomes less anti-papal than his reason. When he went abroad for the first time to Catholic countries, 'the sight of so many great places, venerable shrines, and noble churches, much impressed my imagination'. His 'heart was touched also', he recalled, by Catholic devotions and worship, and although his 'reason was not affected at all', for his 'judgment was against her, when viewed as an institution, as truly as it ever had been', nevertheless he 'learned to have tender feelings towards her'.[3]

1. *A W* 79.   2. *Apo.* 27.   3. *Apo.* 65.

The contradiction between these two passages seems obvious, but the discrepancy is more apparent than real. Keenly sensitive as he always was to the complex interaction of the imaginative and the rational elements in the human mind, Newman was well aware that just as the imagination may anticipate ideas only later embraced by the reason, so too the imagination may refuse to keep up with the intellect's progress. Thus, while a view of the pope as the Antichrist may leave a 'stain' on the imagination which the intellect finds itself unable to expunge, so too the imagination may be impressed by ideas which are not yet entertained by the reason.

As Newman's great philosophical work the *Grammar of Assent* (1870) shows so profoundly, the intellect and imagination are in his view integrally connected; nevertheless, the *Apologia*, in its scrupulous concentration on the intellectual development of its author's religious views, downplays the impressions he received during those eventful months abroad before the inception of the movement. It is of course true that Newman's two traumatic experiences in the summer of 1839 could be called as much imaginative as intellectual, as they are described in the *Apologia*. But such is the force of those celebrated pages that a reader would conclude that Newman's deconversion from Anglicanism only really began in that fateful long vacation. In fact, what the travel letters of 1832–3 reveal so graphically is that the imaginative seeds of Newman's eventual conversion to Rome were sown during his visits to the countries of southern Europe, where he experienced at first hand for the first time the two forms of Christianity which had never been 'reformed' by the events of the sixteenth century and which could trace back their origins directly and uninterruptedly to the primitive Church of apostles and martyrs. There was a sense in which eastern Orthodoxy interested him more than Roman Catholicism, as after all it was the Greek rather than the Latin Fathers who were his real theological mentors, especially his hero St Athanasius. Witnessing Orthodox devotion to the Virgin Mary – more prominent in their liturgy than in the Latin Mass – and to the saints clearly disconcerted Newman, as such idolatry and superstition were supposed to be the peculiar marks of the Church of Rome. It also seemed that the various Protestant sects with which

Newman was familiar in England were far more heretical than either Constantinople or Rome. Most perplexing of all were his very mixed emotions on reaching Rome – the city of the Antichrist but also the city where Peter and Paul were martyred; the city to which England owed its Christian faith but also the city where the most famous church in Christendom, St Peter's, had been built partly by the sale of indulgences; the city full of superstition but also full of churches and shrines conspicuous for their devotion. It was all very confusing when he had been taught to believe that Rome was one of the four beasts of the Apocalypse. He was impressed by the devoutness of the seminarians he saw, and yet he knew (as all Protestants knew) that the Roman Catholic priesthood was deeply corrupt – but then again he found himself wondering if the pompous Anglican chaplain in Rome was really closer to Christian truth than were the Italian priests he saw. In the end he came to the somewhat contradictory conclusion that while Roman Catholicism itself was hopelessly corrupt, nevertheless individual Roman Catholics could be very impressive indeed. But what, he dared wonder, if this in reality was an example of the principle that the corruption of the best is the worst? He was beginning to glimpse that the argument from corruption was a two-edged weapon. As he waited in Palermo for a ship to take him home he put into verse his new attitude to Roman Catholicism, full of ambivalence and of significance for a decision that was still twelve years away:

> Oh that thy creed were sound!
> For thou dost soothe the heart, Thou Church of Rome,
>   By thy unwearied watch and varied round
> Of service, in thy Saviour's holy home.[1]

In both Newman's deconversion from Evangelicalism, then, and in his conversion to Roman Catholicism personal experience of a very concrete kind was a key factor, reinforcing the more theological aspects to which the *Apologia* largely confines itself.[2]

---

1. *VV* 153.

2. For a fuller account of these experiential factors in Newman's religious development, see Ian Ker, 'Newman's Conversion to the Catholic Church: Another Perspective', *Renascence*, xliii (1990–91), pp. 17–27.

It is time now to look at what kind of autobiography the *Apologia* is, rather than what it is not.

First of all, it stands clearly within a recognizable genre, as its author indicates when he acknowledges his enormous debt to the Evangelical Thomas Scott (1747–1821), who recounted his own religious pilgrimage in his best-selling little autobiography *The Force of Truth* (1779), a work which Newman says deeply impressed him because it showed how Scott 'followed truth wherever it led him, beginning with Unitarianism, and ending in a . . . faith in the Holy Trinity'.[1] Scott's book, of course, belonged to the English Protestant autobiographical tradition that originated with John Bunyan's *Grace Abounding to the Chief of Sinners* (1666). The autobiography of conversion was especially dear to Evangelicals, whose spirituality and theology were so overwhelmingly centred on personal conversion to Christ. The typical Evangelical pattern of conversion was to be found, for example, in the extremely popular *Rise and Progress of Religion in the Soul* (1745) by Philip Doddridge (1702–51), which Newman lent to his parishioners.[2] It was a book that his own Evangelical mentor, Walter Mayers, had recommended to him after Newman's conversion in 1816 in a letter which accompanied the gift of a copy of *Private Thoughts upon Religion* and *Private Thoughts upon a Christian Life* by William Beveridge (1637–1708). It is significant that nearly sixty years later Newman himself testified to the exclusively intellectual nature of his own autobiography when he noted that he had not mentioned Beveridge's *Private Thoughts* in the *Apologia*, because he was 'speaking there of the formation of my doctrinal opinions, and I do not think they were influenced by it. I had fully and eagerly taken up Calvinism into my religion before it came into my hands [.] But no book was more dear to me, or exercised a more powerful influence over my devotion and my habitual thoughts. In my private memoranda I even wrote in its style.'[3]

Unlike the autobiographies of Bunyan, Cowper, Newton and Whitefield, Scott's *The Force of Truth* was, like the *Apologia*, devoid of emotional introspection, being wholly concerned with giving a strictly theological account of the author's religious development. Scott also avoided the personal details of his life –

---

1. *Apo.* 26.   2. *LD* i. 196.   3. *LD* i. 30 n. 1.

although in this reticence he was only following Bunyan and Newton. Again, as if to prove that his conversion was based on intellectual rather than merely emotional grounds, Scott emphasized that the Trinitarian Christianity he eventually embraced was derived ultimately from his reading of orthodox Anglican divines. Similarly, as if to show that he was not influenced by subjective considerations, Newman stressed that his conversion had little or nothing to do with reading or meeting Roman Catholics. Whereas the Protestant autobiographical tradition naturally depended on biblical motifs, particularly that of the exodus of the Israelites, Newman is influenced by the analogies he finds in his study of the primitive Church and the early heresies.

As has recently been shown,[1] Newman's autobiography was not only the culmination of the English Protestant tradition but also bears marked resemblances to the most famous of all spiritual autobiographies, the *Confessions* of St Augustine. Indeed, it was, Newman tells us, a sentence from another of Augustine's writings that triggered off his own eventual conversion to Catholicism, just as, he reminds us, Augustine himself had been converted to Catholic Christianity from Manichaeism by hearing some chance words of a child – an event which is also the dramatic turning-point of the *Confessions*. Rather as with Augustine's depiction of his conversion, in terms of a transition from death to life, so Newman finds himself on his Anglican death-bed, an image which in effect replaces the traditional Protestant idea of the religious seeker wandering in the desert like the Israelites in search of the promised land. Like Augustine, too, Newman has to recant his misconceptions of Catholicism. And again rather like Augustine, who commends his mother St Monica to the prayers of his readers at the end of book IX, so Newman prays

1 Linda H. Peterson, *Victorian Autobiography: The Tradition of Self-Interpretation* (New Haven and London: Yale University Press, 1986), 93–119; a study to which I am indebted for the foregoing and following remarks, although I cannot agree with the unconvincing parallel she attempts to draw (on the basis of a flimsy and unpersuasive piece of secondary evidence) between Augustine's mother, who was profoundly involved in his conversion, and Newman's mother, who (unlike his grandmother and aunt) can safely be said to have had no significant effect whatsoever on his religious development nor indeed any sympathy with it.

at the end of chapter V for all his old Oxford friends, a finale
which contrasts with the traditional Protestant closure that concerns the salvation of the individual Christian. Finally, just as,
with the achievement of conversion, the last four books (X–
XIII) of the *Confessions* abandon narrative for reflective exposition, so too the last chapter of the *Apologia* turns to a different
kind of 'apologia' where Newman defends Catholicism against
the traditional Protestant charges, in the same way that Augustine
ends by defending the Catholic doctrine of creation against the
Manichaean heresy he himself had previously held.

But if it is true that in the *Apologia* Newman has drawn,
however unconsciously, from a Catholic model, thus modifying
the Protestant or Evangelical tradition from within which he is
clearly and more or less consciously writing, it is also the case, as
I have already indicated, that the *Apologia* is much more drily
theological, like Scott's *The Force of Truth*, than the introspective,
spiritual *Confessions*. So, it may be asked, how is it that the
Apologia has continued to grip readers even in the latter part of
the twentieth century when ecumenism on the one hand and
secularization on the other may seem to have combined to rob so
much of Newman's theological pilgrimage of the compelling
interest it once had?

First of all, the austere, largely documentary form that
Newman employs paradoxically serves to highlight the few personal details that are divulged. In the first chapter, for instance, a
large number of people appear whom Newman acknowledges as
formative influences, but because he wishes for his own apolo-
getic reasons to confine himself to their theological significance,
such description of them as his uncompromising narrative con-
cedes is tantalizingly fleeting and elusive. For example, in his
generously detailed account of the influence of the provost of
Oriel, Edward Hawkins, he alludes with extreme politeness to
the fact that 'he provoked me very much from time to time,
though I am perfectly certain that I have provoked him a great
deal more'.[1] This is all that he says about the celebrated row over
the college office of tutor, which was not only germane to future
developments of the famous Oxford tutorial system but also

1. *Apo.* 28.

highly relevant to the formation of Newman's own views on education which would achieve their classic expression in *The Idea of a University* (1873). The sparsity of the text gives a certain dramatic resonance to the narrative as the reader picks up the vibrations of the carefully controlled voice of the narrator. Similarly, there is no attempt to convey the actual atmosphere of the famous Oriel common room, but small details are allowed to escape: for example, it was on a walk round Christ Church meadow that the Rev. William James taught Newman the doctrine of apostolical succession, while on another but solitary walk as a new, shy fellow of Oriel, he encountered the then provost, Edward Copleston, who 'turned round, and with the kind courteousness which sat so well on him, made me a bow and said "that one was never less alone than when alone"'.[1] It is little, apparently incidental touches like these that give the narrative a personal immediacy which is the more strongly felt precisely because of the sense of suppressed emotion. Moreover, the reader is affected by the sense that it is only the author's overriding desire to present as frankly and squarely as possible his developing doctrinal views that restrains him from more personal revelations. And it is this very impression of severe self-restraint that enhances the dramatic tension of the theological story, as our attention is focused relentlessly on the pressure of ideas on a mind both alertly responsive to new problems and questions and keenly aware of its own moral responsibility to follow the truth wherever it might lead.

It was, as we have seen, this single-minded pursuit of the truth which had so impressed Newman in Scott's *The Force of Truth*. However, it would be quite misleading to imply that the only passion to be found in the *Apologia* lies in a kind of repressed intellectual excitement. Perhaps the great triumph of the book is the way in which Newman not only holds our attention by the detached documentary report of his theological pilgrimage but also draws us into the dim historical events of the early Church, against the background of which he resolves his own religious identity. We find ourselves as surprised at our own interest in the Monophysites ('I saw my face in that mirror, and I was a

Monophysite')[1] as Newman himself was astonished that a particularly unsavoury episode in the history of the early Church should have caused his first really serious doubt about the Anglican position. The dramatic passage that he then quotes from a later controversial writing in which he revisited this moment of crisis reminds us that the *Apologia* consists to a very great extent of lengthy quotations from private letters as well as published works, and that this sets in relief the limpid tone of the narrative which itself is a kind of connecting commentary on those documents. For there is plenty of excitement in the *Apologia*, but the difference from Newman's other writings is that the argument and polemic are now recollected at a distance – if not exactly in tranquillity, at least in relative detachment.

It is a curious anomaly that the book on which Newman's literary reputation is presumed principally to rest should differ strikingly from his other works of controversy, which give him so distinctive a place in the history of English literature. Much of its power lies in the (almost) disconcertingly calm tone of the author's conversational, sometimes even colloquial, voice. Flashes of eloquence are rare (and all the more effective for their rarity), for eloquence is excluded nearly as rigorously as explicit self-defence: 'I am not setting myself up as a pattern of good sense or of any thing else: I am but giving a history of my opinions, and that, with the view of showing that I have come by them through intelligible processes of thought and honest external means.'[2] Nor is there any claim that his history will be of any great human interest – 'I have no romantic story to tell.'[3] Indeed, the *Apologia* is unique among Newman's published works not only in its form and content, but also in its style and tone. Nearly all Newman's writings were 'occasional' in the sense of being responses to particular occasions, and of course the *Apologia* is no exception, for it is an extended answer to the attack of Kingsley, which itself was representative of many others. But what makes the *Apologia* so different is that, with the exception of the last chapter, the actual argument, debate and polemic are now all in the recorded past tense. And the main 'apologia'

1. *Apo.* 114.   2. *Apo.* 46.   3. *Apo.* 51.

persuades not by overt argument but by the narration of facts, albeit largely of past controversies and polemic.

As we have already seen, it is to those parts of the original *Apologia* that Newman later omitted or drastically abridged that we must turn for the polemic that makes Newman probably the greatest controversialist in the English language. Newman was certainly right to omit what would not only have looked vindictive to an audience that had already recognized his victory over Kingsley, but would have been at best irrelevant and at worst prejudicial to the purpose of the history he had decided to tell in refutation of Kingsley in particular and of the prejudiced Protestant public in general. However, from the literary point of view we cannot but regret the loss of writing that recalls the exuberant satire that flowered in the years after Newman's conversion, preeminently in *Lectures on Certain Difficulties felt by Anglicans in submitting to the Catholic Church* (1850) and *Lectures on the Present Position of Catholics in England* (1851). Newman not only echoes ideas from the latter work, but employs similar imagery to express the blind power of prejudice:

> He [Kingsley] need not commit himself to a definite accusation against me, such as requires definite proof and admits of definite refutation; for he has two strings to his bow; – when he is thrown off his balance on the one leg, he can recover himself by the use of the other. If I demonstrate that I am not a knave, he may exclaim, 'Oh, but you are a fool!' and when I demonstrate that I am not a fool, he may turn round and retort, 'Well, then, you are a knave.'[1]

The superb invective of some of the passages that Newman eventually omitted may startle, even shock, modern readers unused to the kind of hard-hitting religious controversy that came naturally to the Victorians. We should notice, however, that Newman explicitly makes the point that it is 'very difficult to get up resentment towards persons whom one has never seen', and so 'I wish to impute nothing worse to Mr Kingsley than that he has been furiously carried away by his feeling'.[2] When Kingsley died ten years later, Newman felt he could honestly say he had never felt angry personally with him. But at the time he was

1. *Apo.* 414.   2. *Apo.* 421, 422

so convinced that it was only by speaking out strongly that people would believe him, that he had decided 'it would not do to be tame, and not to show indignation'. Anyway, the fact was that by his 'passionate attack' on him Kingsley had inadvertently become one of his 'best friends, whom I always wished to shake hands with when living, and towards whose memory I have much tenderness'.[1] This claim is supported by an examination of Newman's satirical method which invariably (except in one very serious and justifiable instance that Newman always acknowledged) avoided the kind of moral personalizing that is usually the stock-in-trade of the satirist. Instead, what Newman's satire fastens upon here (as elsewhere) is the absurdity of the inconsistency and incoherence of Kingsley's blustering indictment. It is not Kingsley's moral character that is under sarcastic scrutiny but the superficiality of his intelligence and understanding.[2]

Finally, the *Apologia* is not only an autobiography that grew out of controversy and satire; it is a theological record and, more than that, at least in its last chapter, a very important contribution to ecclesiology, that is, the theology of the Church. The modern development or revival of Catholic understanding of the nature of the Church, to which Newman contributed so significantly, would culminate in the great reforming Second Vatican Council (1962–5) that effectively closed the Tridentine era and opened a new chapter in the history of Christianity. It would be impossible and inappropriate here to attempt to offer any close study of the key issue that Newman examines with such sensitivity and subtlety in chapter V, a rhetorical *tour de force* which may be read as an essay in its own right.[3]

What Newman is considering in his general defence of the Roman Catholic Church is really the question of authority and freedom. As against the modern assumption that freedom by definition means the absence of checks and limitations (except such as may incidentally be imposed by conflict between opposing freedoms), Newman's case is that freedom demands boundaries,

1. *LD* xxvii. 219; xxix. 388.

2. For a fuller consideration of Newman's satire, see Ian Ker, 'Newman the Satirist', *Newman after a Hundred Years*, ed. Ian Ker and Alan G. Hill (Oxford: Clarendon Press, 1990), 1–20.

3. For a full discussion, see Ker, 549–59.

because these actually define its nature; otherwise it degenerates into anarchy and thus destroys itself. The post-Enlightenment outlook assumes the validity of the individual mind seeking truth in a kind of splendid isolation both from tradition and the community of other minds. Now although Newman did not live to see philosophers of science 'cast doubt upon the credentials of science itself as an avenue to truth',[1] he did seriously challenge the epistemology of the Enlightenment in other areas of human knowledge. And in this last chapter of the *Apologia* he insists that the authority of an infallible church, far from destroying reason, actually sustains it by protecting it from its own 'suicidal excesses'.[2] Not only that, he argues, but paradoxically the 'energy of the human intellect ... thrives and is joyous, with a tough elastic strength, under the terrible blows of the divinely-fashioned weapon [infallibility], and is never so much itself as when it has lately been overthrown'.[3] Newman claims that the reason for the vitality of Catholic theology is precisely that it has to work within the constraints and discipline of an authoritative church, and that the resulting tension, indeed conflict, far from being debilitating or frustrating, is actually creative and liberating:

> ... it is the vast Catholic body itself, and it only, which affords an arena for both combatants in that awful, never-dying duel. It is necessary for the very life of religion, viewed in its large operations and its history, that the warfare should be incessantly carried on. Every exercise of infallibility is brought out into act by an intense and varied operation of the Reason, both as its ally and as its opponent, and provokes again, when it has done its work, a re-action of Reason against it; and, as in a civil polity the State exists and endures by means of the rivalry and collision, the encroachments and defeats of its constituent parts, so in like manner Catholic Christendom is no simple exhibition of religious absolutism, but presents a continuous picture of Authority and Private Judgment alternately advancing and retreating as the ebb and flow of the tide . . .[4]

1. Basil Mitchell, 'Newman as a Philosopher', *Newman after a Hundred Years*, 237.
2. *Apo.* 220.
3. *Apo.* 225.
4. *Apo.* 225.

Newman does not purport to be able to provide any kind of schematic theology for the relation between authority and freedom in the Church, and indeed the whole implication of his rhetoric is that no such blueprint is possible for what, after all, is a living rather than a static relationship. But he does proceed, with pointed examples from church history, to show, as against the authoritarianism of the Ultramontanes – at whom this chapter is aimed at least as much as at Kingsley – how important theology is for the life of the Church. And it is the careful balance with which he asserts both the right of theologians to free inquiry and at the same time the prerogatives of the hierarchical teaching authority that still makes his discussion highly pertinent to the perennial problem of reconciling the conservative and the innovative elements in the Church.

SELECT BIBLIOGRAPHY

Between 1868 and 1881 Newman collected most of his works in a uniform edition (thirty-six volumes) which was published by Longmans, Green and Co. of London from 1886 until the destruction of the stock in World War II. Second-hand copies of works in this edition (and others) are fairly easy to find and most of the volumes have been photographically reprinted (in a limited edition) by Christian Classics, Westminster, Maryland, USA. Reprints of the more popular works appear regularly. A number of other volumes of writings have been, and are being, published posthumously. The complete edition (in thirty-one volumes) of *The Letters and Diaries of John Henry Newman*, begun by Charles Stephen Dessain (who edited all the volumes for the Catholic period) in 1961, is nearing completion. Several anthologies of Newman's writings have been published, including most recently *The Genius of John Henry Newman: Selections from His Writings* (ed. Ian Ker, 1989) and *Newman the Theologian: A Reader* (ed. Ker, 1990).

The best short introduction to Newman's life is Meriol Trevor's *Newman's Journey* (1974), an abridged version of her two-volume personal biography *Newman: The Pillar of the Cloud* and *Newman: Light in Winter* (1962). Dessain's excellent short life *John Henry Newman* (1966) is the best introduction to his thought, especially his theology. Ian Ker's *John Henry Newman: A Biography* (1988) is a full-length life as well as an intellectual and literary biography. Sheridan Gilley's *Newman and His Age* (1990) is good on the historical background of the Anglican period, although he makes no use of the many still unpublished letters for the crucial years leading up to Newman's conversion.

C. F. Harold's *John Henry Newman: An Expository and Critical Study of His Mind, Thought and Art* (1945) is a useful survey of the writings. Ker's *The Achievement of John Henry Newman* (1990) focuses on the five main areas of Newman's genius, including the literary. *Newman after a Hundred Years* (ed. Ian Ker and Alan

G. Hill, 1990) is an interdisciplinary revaluation of Newman's significance.

There is a critical edition of the *Apologia* by Martin J. Svaglic (1967), to which I am greatly indebted in the preparation of this edition. The only book devoted solely to a study of it is Walter E. Houghton's *The Art of Newman's* Apologia (1945). David J. DeLaura's edition (1968) includes a selection of essays in criticism. Recent studies are also to be found in A. O. J. Cockshut's *The Art of Autobiography in 19th and 20th century England* (1984), Linda Peterson's *Victorian Autobiography: The Tradition of Self-Interpretation* (1986), and Steven Helmling's *The Esoteric Comedies of Carlyle, Newman, and Yeats* (1988).

A CHRONOLOGY OF
JOHN HENRY NEWMAN

1845   3 October: resigns Oriel fellowship.
        9 October: received into the Roman Catholic Church.
        Essay on the Development of Christian Doctrine.

1846   23 February: leaves Oxford for Maryvale, near
        Birmingham.

1847   30 May: ordained priest in Rome.
        Writes *Loss and Gain.*

1848   1 February: founds the Oratory of St Philip Neri at
        Birmingham.

1849   *Discourses Addressed to Mixed Congregations.*

1850   *Lectures on Certain Difficulties felt by Anglicans in submit-
        ting to the Catholic Church.*
        Restoration of Catholic hierarchy to England.

1851   *Lectures on the Present Position of Catholics in England.*
        Appointed rector of the Catholic University of Ireland
        (resigns 1858).

1852   *Discourses on the Scope and Nature of University Education.*

1856   *Callista: A Sketch of the Third Century.*

1857   *Sermons Preached on Various Occasions.*

1859   *Lectures and Essays on University Subjects.*
        Publishes *On Consulting the Faithful in Matters of Doctrine*
        as article in *Rambler* magazine.

1864   *Apologia pro Vita Sua.*

1865   *The Dream of Gerontius.*

1866   *A Letter to the Rev. E. B. Pusey.*

1868   Collected poetry published as *Verses on Various
        Occasions.*

1870   *An Essay in Aid of a Grammar of Assent.*
        Papal infallibility defined by Vatican Council.

1873   *The Idea of a University.*

1875   *A Letter to the Duke of Norfolk.*

1877   *Via Media.*
        Elected honorary fellow of Trinity College, Oxford.

1879   Created cardinal.

1890   11 August: died.

APOLOGIA PRO VITA SUA

PREFACE

The following History of my Religious Opinions, now that it is detached from the context in which it originally stood, requires some preliminary explanation; and that, not only in order to introduce it generally to the reader, but specially to make him understand, how I came to write a whole book about myself, and about my most private thoughts and feelings. Did I consult indeed my own impulses, I should do my best simply to wipe out of my Volume, and consign to oblivion, every trace of the circumstances to which it is to be ascribed; but its original title of *Apologia* is too exactly borne out by its matter and structure, and these again are too suggestive of correlative circumstances, and those circumstances are of too grave a character, to allow of my indulging so natural a wish. And therefore, though in this new Edition I have managed to omit nearly a hundred pages of my original Volume, which I could safely consider to be of merely ephemeral importance, I am even for that very reason obliged, by way of making up for their absence, to prefix to my Narrative some account of the provocation out of which it arose.

It is now more than twenty years that a vague impression to my disadvantage has rested on the popular mind, as if my conduct towards the Anglican Church, while I was a member of it, was inconsistent with Christian simplicity and uprightness. An impression of this kind was almost unavoidable under the circumstances of the case, when a man, who had written strongly against a cause, and had collected a party round him by virtue of such writings, gradually faltered in his opposition to it, unsaid his words, threw his own friends into perplexity and their proceedings into confusion, and ended by passing over to the side of those whom he had so vigorously denounced. Sensitive then as I have ever been of the imputations which have been so freely cast upon me, I have never felt much impatience under them, as considering them to be a portion of the penalty which I naturally and justly incurred by my change of religion, even though they were to continue as long as I lived. I left their removal to a future day, when personal feelings would have died out, and documents would see the light, which were as yet buried in closets or scattered through the country.

This was my state of mind, as it had been for many years, when, in the beginning of 1864, I unexpectedly found myself publicly put upon my defence, and furnished with an opportunity of pleading my cause before the world, and, as it so happened, with a fair prospect of an impartial hearing. Taken indeed by surprise, as I was, I had much reason to be anxious how I should be able to acquit myself in so serious a matter; however, I had long had a tacit understanding with myself, that, in the improbable event of a challenge being formally made to me, by a person of name, it would be my duty to meet it. That opportunity had now occurred; it never might occur again; not to avail myself of it at once would be virtually to give up my cause; accordingly, I took advantage of it, and, as it has turned out, the circumstance that no time was allowed me for any studied statements has compensated, in the equitable judgment of the public, for such imperfections in composition as my want of leisure involved.

It was in the number for January 1864, of a magazine of wide circulation, and in an Article upon Queen Elizabeth, that a popular writer took occasion formally to accuse me by name of thinking so lightly of the virtue of Veracity, as in set terms to have countenanced and defended that neglect of it which he at the same time imputed to the Catholic Priesthood. His words were these: –

'Truth, for its own sake, had never been a virtue with the Roman clergy. Father Newman informs us that it need not, and on the whole ought not to be; that cunning is the weapon which heaven has given to the Saints wherewith to withstand the brute male force of the wicked world which marries and is given in marriage. Whether his notion be doctrinally correct or not, it is at least historically so.'

These assertions, going far beyond the popular prejudice entertained against me, had no foundation whatever in fact. I never had said, I never had dreamed of saying, that truth for its own sake, need not, and on the whole ought not to be, a virtue with the Roman Clergy; or that cunning is the weapon which heaven has given to the Saints wherewith to withstand the wicked world. To what work of mine then could the writer be referring? In a correspondence which ensued upon the subject between him and myself, he rested his charge against me on a Sermon of mine, preached, before I was a Catholic, in the pulpit of my Church at Oxford; and he gave me to understand, that, after having done as much as this, he was not bound, over and above such a general reference to my Sermon, to specify the passages of it, in which the doctrine, which he imputed to me, was contained. On my part I considered this not enough; and I demanded of him to bring out his proof of his accusation in form and in detail, or to confess he was unable to do so. But he persevered in his refusal to cite any distinct passages from any writing of mine; and, though he consented to withdraw his charge, he would not do so on the issue of its truth or falsehood, but simply on the ground that I assured him that I had had no intention of incurring it. This did not satisfy my sense of justice. Formally to charge me with committing a fault is one thing; to allow that I did not intend to commit it, is another; it is no satisfaction to me, if a man accuses me of *this* offence, for him to profess that he does not accuse me *of that*; but he thought differently. Not being able to gain redress in the quarter, where I had a right to ask it, I appealed to the public. I published the correspondence in the shape of a Pamphlet, with some remarks of my own at the end, on the course which that correspondence had taken.

This Pamphlet, which appeared in the first weeks of February, received a reply from my accuser towards the end of March, in another Pamphlet of 48 pages, entitled, *What then does Dr. Newman mean?* in which he professed to do that which I had called upon him to do; that is, he brought together a number of extracts from various works of mine, Catholic and Anglican, with the object of showing that, if I was to be acquitted of the crime of teaching and practising deceit and dishonesty, according to his first supposition, it was at the price of my being considered no longer responsible for my actions; for, as he expressed it, 'I had a human reason once, no doubt, but I had gambled it away,' and I had 'worked my mind into that morbid state, in which nonsense was the only food for which it hungered;' and that it could not be called 'a hasty or far-fetched or unfounded mistake, when he concluded that I did not care for truth for its own sake, or teach my disciples to regard it as a virtue;' and, though 'too many prefer the charge of insincerity to that of insipience, Dr. Newman seemed not to be of that number.'

He ended his Pamphlet by returning to his original imputation against me, which he had professed to abandon. Alluding by anticipation to my probable answer to what he was then publishing, he professed his heartfelt embarrassment how he was to believe any thing I might say in my exculpation, in the plain and literal sense of the words. 'I am henceforth,' he said, 'in doubt and fear, as much as an honest man can be, concerning every word Dr. Newman may write. How can I tell, that I shall not be the dupe of some cunning equivocation, of one of the three kinds laid down as permissible by the blessed St. Alfonso da Liguori[1] and his pupils, even when confirmed with an oath, because "then we do not deceive our neighbour, but allow him to deceive himself"? . . . How can I tell, that I may not in this Pamphlet have made an accusation, of the truth of which Dr. Newman is perfectly conscious; but that, as I, a heretic Protestant, have no business to make it, he has a full right to deny it?'

Even if I could have found it consistent with my duty to my own reputation to leave such an elaborate impeachment of my moral nature unanswered, my duty to my Brethren in the Catholic Priesthood, would have forbidden such a course. *They* were involved in the charges which this writer, all along, from the original passage in the Magazine, to the very last paragraph of the Pamphlet, had so confidently, so pertinaciously made. In exculpating myself, it was plain I should be pursuing no mere personal quarrel; – I was offering my humble service to a sacred cause. I was making my protest in behalf of a large body of men of high character, of honest and religious minds, and of sensitive honour – who had their place and their rights in this world, though they were ministers of the world unseen, and who were insulted by my Accuser, as the above extracts from him sufficiently show, not only in my person, but directly and pointedly in their own. Accordingly, I at once set about writing the *Apologia pro vitâ suâ*, of which the present Volume is a New

Edition; and it was a great reward to me to find, as the controversy proceeded, such large numbers of my clerical brethren supporting me by their sympathy in the course which I was pursuing, and, as occasion offered, bestowing on me the formal and public expression of their approbation. These testimonials in my behalf, so important and so grateful to me, are, together with the Letter, sent to me with the same purpose, from my Bishop, contained in the last pages of this Volume.

This Edition differs from the first form of the *Apologia* as follows: – The original work consisted of seven Parts, which were published in series on consecutive Thursdays, between April 21 and June 2. An Appendix, in answer to specific allegations urged against me in the Pamphlet of Accusation, appeared on June 16. Of these Parts 1 and 2, as being for the most part directly controversial, are omitted in this Edition, excepting certain passages in them, which are subjoined to this Preface, as being necessary for the due explanation of the subsequent five Parts. These, (being 3, 4, 5, 6, 7, of the *Apologia*,) are here numbered as Chapters 1, 2, 3, 4, 5 respectively. Of the Appendix, about half has been omitted, for the same reason as has led to the omission of Parts 1 and 2. The rest of it is thrown into the shape of Notes of a discursive character, with two new ones on *Liberalism* and the *Lives of the English Saints of 1843–4*, and another, new in part, on *Ecclesiastical Miracles*. In the body of the work, the only addition of consequence is the letter which is found at p. 206, a copy of which has recently come into my possession.

I should add that, since writing the *Apologia* last year, I have seen for the first time Mr. Oakeley's[2] *Notes on the Tractarian Movement*. This work remarkably corroborates the substance of my Narrative, while the kind terms in which he speaks of me personally, call for my sincere gratitude.

May 2, 1865

I make these extracts from the first edition of my Apologia, Part

1. pp. 3, 20–25, and Part 2, pp. 29–31 and pp. 41–51, in order to set before the reader the drift I had in writing my Volume: –

I cannot be sorry to have forced my Accuser to bring out in fulness his charges against me. It is far better that he should discharge his thoughts upon me in my lifetime, than after I am dead. Under the circumstances I am happy in having the opportunity of reading the worst that can be said of me by a writer who has taken pains with his work and is well satisfied with it. I account it a gain to be surveyed from without by one who hates the principles which are nearest to my heart, has no personal knowledge of me to set right his misconceptions of my doctrine, and who has some motive or other to be as severe with me as he can possibly be. . . .

But I really feel sad for what I am obliged now to say. I am in warfare with him, but I wish him no ill; – it is very difficult to get up resentment towards persons whom one has never seen. It is easy enough to be irritated with friends or foes *vis-à-vis*; but, though I am writing with all my heart against what he has said of me, I am not conscious of personal unkindness towards himself. I think it necessary to write as I am writing, for my own sake, and for the sake of the Catholic Priesthood; but I wish to impute nothing worse to him than that he has been furiously carried away by his feelings. Yet what shall I say of the upshot of all his talk of my economies[3] and equivocations and the like? What is the precise *work* which it is directed to effect? I am at war with him; but there is such a thing as legitimate warfare: war has its laws; there are things which may fairly be done, and things which may not be done. I say it with shame and with stern sorrow; – he has attempted a great transgression; he has attempted (as I may call it) to *poison the wells*. I will quote him and explain what I mean . . . He says, –

'I am henceforth in doubt and fear, as much as any honest man can be, *concerning every word* Dr. Newman may write. *How can I tell that I shall not be the dupe of some cunning equivocation*, of one of the three kinds laid down as permissible by the blessed Alfonso da Liguori and his pupils, even when confirmed by an oath, because "then we do not deceive our neighbour, but allow him to deceive himself"? . . . It is admissible, therefore, to use words and sentences which have a double signification, and leave the hapless hearer to take which of them he may choose. *What proof have I, then, that by "mean it? I never said it!" Dr. Newman does not signify*, I did not say it, but I did mean it?' – pp. 44, 45.

Now these insinuations and questions shall be answered in their proper places; here I will but say that I scorn and detest lying, and quibbling, and double-tongued practice, and slyness, and cunning, and smoothness, and cant, and pretence, quite as much as any Protestants hate them; and I pray to be kept from the snare of them. But all this is just now by the bye; my present subject is my Accuser; what I insist upon here is this unmanly attempt of his, in his concluding pages, to cut the ground from under my feet; – to poison by anticipation the public mind against me, John Henry Newman, and to infuse into the imaginations of my readers, suspicion and mistrust of everything that I may say in reply to him. This I call *poisoning the wells*.

'I am henceforth in *doubt and fear*,' he says, 'as much as any *honest* man can be, *concerning every word* Dr. Newman may write. *How can I tell that I shall not be the dupe of some cunning equivocation?*' . . .

Well, I can only say, that, if his taunt is to take effect, I am but wasting my time in saying a word in answer to his calumnies; and this is precisely what he knows and intends to be its fruit. I can hardly get myself to protest against a method of controversy so base and cruel, lest in doing so, I should be violating my self-respect and self-possession; but most base and most cruel it is. We all know how our imagination runs away with us, how suddenly and at what a pace; – the saying, 'Caesar's wife should not be suspected,' is an instance of what I mean. The habitual prejudice, the humour of the moment, is the turning-point which leads us to read a defence in a good sense or a bad. We interpret it by our antecedent impressions. The very same sentiments, according as our jealousy is or is not awake, or our aversion stimulated, are tokens of truth or of dissimulation and pretence. There is a story of a sane person being by mistake shut up in the wards of a Lunatic Asylum, and that, when he pleaded his cause to some strangers visiting the establishment, the only remark he elicited in answer was, 'How naturally he talks! you would think he was in his senses.' Controversies should be decided by the reason; is it legitimate warfare to appeal to the misgivings of the public mind and to its dislikings? Any how, if my accuser is able thus to practise upon my readers, the more I succeed, the less will be my success. If I am natural, he will tell them 'Ars est celare artem;'[4] if I am convincing, he will suggest that I am an able logician; if I show warmth, I am acting the indignant innocent; if

I am calm, I am thereby detected as a smooth hypocrite; if I clear up difficulties, I am too plausible and perfect to be true. The more triumphant are my statements, the more certain will be my defeat.

So will it be if my Accuser succeeds in his manoeuvre; but I do not for an instant believe that he will. Whatever judgment my readers may eventually form of me from these pages, I am confident that they will believe me in what I shall say in the course of them. I have no misgiving at all, that they will be ungenerous or harsh towards a man who has been so long before the eyes of the world; who has so many to speak of him from personal knowledge; whose natural impulse it has ever been to speak out; who has ever spoken too much rather than too little; who would have saved himself many a scrape, if he had been wise enough to hold his tongue; who has ever been fair to the doctrines and arguments of his opponents; who has never slurred over facts and reasonings which told against himself; who has never given his name or authority to proofs which he thought unsound, or to testimony which he did not think at least plausible; who has never shrunk from confessing a fault when he felt that he had committed one; who has ever consulted for others more than for himself; who has given up much that he loved and prized and could have retained, but that he loved honesty better than name, and Truth better than dear friends. . . .

What then shall be the special imputation, against which I shall throw myself in these pages, out of the thousand and one which my Accuser directs upon me? I mean to confine myself to one, for there is only one about which I much care, – the charge of Untruthfulness. He may cast upon me as many other imputations as he pleases, and they may stick on me, as long as they can, in the course of nature. They will fall to the ground in their season.

And indeed I think the same of the charge of Untruthfulness, and select it from the rest, not because it is more formidable but because it is more serious. Like the rest, it may disfigure me for a time, but it will not stain: Archbishop Whately[5] used to say, 'Throw dirt enough, and some will stick;' well, will stick, but not, will stain. I think he used to mean 'stain,' and I do not agree with him. Some dirt sticks longer than other dirt; but no dirt is immortal. According to the old saying, Praevalebit Veritas.[6] There are virtues indeed, which the world is not fitted to judge of or to uphold, such as faith, hope, and charity: but it can judge about Truthfulness; it can judge about the natural virtues, and Truthfulness is one of them. Natural virtues may also become supernatural; Truthfulness is such; but that does not withdraw it from the jurisdiction of mankind at large. It may be more difficult in this or that particular case for men to take cognizance of it, as it may be difficult for the Court of Queen's Bench at Westminster to try a case fairly which took place in Hindoostan: but that is a question of capacity, not of right. Mankind has the right to judge of Truthfulness in a Catholic, as in the case of a Protestant, of an Italian, or of a Chinese. I have never doubted, that in my hour, in God's hour, my avenger will appear, and the world will acquit me of untruthfulness, even though it be not while I live.

Still more confident am I of such eventual acquittal, seeing that my judges are my own countrymen. I consider, indeed, Englishmen the most suspicious and touchy of mankind; I think them unreasonable, and unjust in their seasons of excitement; but I had rather be an Englishman, (as in fact I am,) than belong to any other race under heaven. They are as generous, as they are hasty and burly; and their repentance for their injustice is greater than their sin.

For twenty years and more I have borne an imputation, of which I am at least as sensitive, who am the object of it, as they can be, who are only the judges. I have not set myself to remove it, first, because I never have had an opening to speak, and, next, because I never saw in them the disposition to hear. I have wished to appeal from Philip drunk to Philip sober. When shall I pronounce him to be himself again? If I may judge from the tone of the public press, which represents the public voice, I have great reason to take heart at this time. I have been treated by contemporary critics in this controversy with great fairness and gentleness, and I am grateful to them for it. However, the decision of the time and mode of my defence has been taken out of my hands; and I am thankful that it has been so. I am bound now as a duty to myself, to the Catholic cause, to the Catholic Priesthood, to give account of myself without any delay, when I am so rudely and circumstantially charged with Untruthfulness. I accept the challenge; I shall do my best to meet it, and I shall be content when I have done so.

It is not my present accuser alone who entertains, and has entertained, so dishonourable an opinion of me and of my writings. It is the impression of large classes of men; the impression twenty years ago and the impression now. There has been a general feeling that I was for years where I had no right to be; that I was a 'Romanist' in Protestant livery and service; that I was doing the work of a hostile Church in the bosom of the English Establishment, and knew it, or ought to have known it. There was no need of arguing about particular passages in my writings, when the fact was so patent, as men thought it to be.

First it was certain, and I could not myself deny it, that I scouted[7] the name 'Protestant.' It was certain again, that many of the doctrines which I professed were popularly and generally known as badges of the Roman Church, as distinguished from the faith of the Reformation. Next, how could I have come by them? Evidently, I had certain friends and advisers who did not appear; there was some underground communication between Stonyhurst[8] or Oscott[9] and my rooms at Oriel. Beyond a doubt, I was advocating certain doctrines, not by accident, but on an understanding with ecclesiastics of the old religion. Then men went further, and said that I had actually been received into that religion, and withal had leave given me to profess myself a Protestant still. Others went even further, and gave it out to the world, as a matter of fact, of which they themselves had the proof in their hands, that I was actually a Jesuit. And when the opinions which I advocated spread, and younger men went further than I, the feeling against me waxed stronger and took a wider range.

And now indignation arose at the knavery of a conspiracy such as this: – and it became of course all the greater in consequence of its being the received belief of the public at large, that craft and intrigue, such as they fancied they beheld with their eyes, were the very instruments to which the Catholic Church has in these last centuries been indebted for her maintenance and extension.

There was another circumstance still, which increased the irritation and aversion felt by the large classes, of whom I have been speaking, against the preachers of doctrines, so new to them and so unpalatable; and that was, that they developed them in so measured a way. If they were inspired by Roman theologians, (and this was taken for granted,) why did they not speak out at once? Why did they keep the world in such suspense and anxiety as to what was coming next, and what was to be the upshot of the whole? Why this reticence, and half-speaking, and apparent indecision? It was plain that the plan of operations had been carefully mapped out from the first, and that these men were cautiously advancing towards its accomplishment, as far as was safe at the moment; that their aim and their hope was to carry off a large body with them of the young and the ignorant; that they meant gradually to leaven the minds of the rising generation, and to open the gates of that city, of which they were the sworn defenders, to the enemy who lay in ambush outside of it. And when in spite of the many protestations of the party to the contrary, there was at length an actual movement among their disciples, and one went over to Rome, and then another, the worst anticipations and the worst judgments which had been formed of them received their justification. And, lastly, when men first had said of me, 'You will see, *he* will go, he is only biding his time, he is waiting the word of command from Rome,' and, when after all, after my arguments and denunciations of former years, at length I did leave the Anglican Church for the Roman, then they said to each other, 'It is just as we said: we knew it would be so.'

This was the state of mind of masses of men twenty years ago, who took no more than an external and common sense view of what was going on. And partly the tradition, partly the effect of that feeling, remains to the present time. Certainly I consider that, in my own case, it is the great obstacle in the way of my being favourably heard, as at present, when I have to make my defence. Not only am I now a member of a most un-English communion, whose great aim is considered to be the extinction of Protestantism and the Protestant Church, and whose means of attack are popularly supposed to be unscrupulous cunning and deceit, but how came I originally to have any relations with the Church of Rome at all? did I, or my opinions, drop from the sky? how came I, in Oxford, *in gremio Universitatis*,[10] to present myself to the eyes of men in that full blown investiture of Popery? How could I dare, how could I have the conscience, with warnings, with prophecies, with accusations against me, to persevere in a path which steadily advanced towards, which ended in, the religion of Rome? And how am I now to be trusted, when long ago I was trusted, and was found wanting?

It is this which is the strength of the case of my Accuser against me; – not the articles of impeachment which he has framed from my writings, and which I shall easily crumble into dust, but the bias of the court. It is the state of the atmosphere; it is the vibration all around, which will echo his bold assertion of my dishonesty; it is that prepossession against me, which takes it for granted that, when my reasoning is convincing it is only ingenious, and that when my statements are unanswerable, there is always something put out of sight or hidden in my sleeve; it is that plausible, but cruel conclusion to which men are apt to jump, that when much is imputed, much must be true, and that it is more likely that one should be to blame, than that many should be mistaken in blaming; – these are the real foes which I have to fight, and the auxiliaries to whom my Accuser makes his advances.

Well, I must break through this barrier of prejudice against me if I can; and I think I shall be able to do so. When first I read the Pamphlet of Accusation, I almost despaired of meeting effectively such a heap of misrepresentations and such a vehemence of animosity. What was the good of answering first one point, and then another, and going through the whole circle of its abuse; when my answer to the first point would be forgotten, as soon as I got to the second? What was the use of bringing out half a hundred separate principles or views for the refutation of the separate counts in the Indictment, when rejoinders of this sort would but confuse and torment the reader by their number and their diversity? What hope was there of condensing into a pamphlet of a readable length, matter which ought freely to expand itself into half a dozen volumes? What means was there, except the expenditure of interminable pages, to set right even one of that series of 'single passing hints,' to use my Assailant's own language, which, 'as with his finger tip he had delivered' against me?

All those separate charges had their force in being illustrations of one and the same great imputation. He had already a positive idea to illuminate his whole matter, and to stamp it with a force, and to quicken it with an interpretation. He called me a *liar*, – a simple, a broad, an intelligible, to the English public a plausible arraignment; but for me, to answer in detail charge one by reason one, and charge two by reason two, and charge three by reason three, and so on through the whole string both of accusations and replies, each of which was to be independent of the rest, this would be certainly labour lost as regards any effective result. What I needed was a corresponding antagonist unity in my defence, and where was that to be found? We see, in the case of commentators on the prophecies of Scripture, an exemplification of the principle on which I am insisting; viz. how much more powerful even a false interpretation of the sacred text is than none at all; – how a certain key to the visions of the Apocalypse, for instance, may cling to the mind (I have found it so in the case of my own), because the view, which it opens on us, is positive and objective, in spite of the fullest demonstration that it really has no claim upon our reception. The reader says, 'What else can the prophecy mean?' just as my Accuser asks, *What, then, does Dr. Newman mean?* ... I reflected, and I saw a way out of my perplexity.

Yes, I said to myself, his very question is about my *meaning*; 'What does Dr. Newman mean?' It pointed in the very same direction as that into which my musings had turned me already. He asks what I *mean*; not about my words, not about my arguments, not about my actions, as his ultimate point, but about that living intelligence, by which I write, and argue, and act. He asks about my Mind and its Beliefs and its sentiments; and he shall be answered; – not for his own sake, but for mine, for the sake of the Religion which I profess, and of the Priesthood in which I am unworthily included, and of my friends and of my foes, and of that general public which consists of neither one nor the other, but of well-wishers, lovers of fair play, sceptical cross-questioners, interested inquirers, curious lookers-on, and simple strangers, unconcerned yet not careless about the issue, – for the sake of all these he shall be answered.

My perplexity had not lasted half an hour. I recognized what I had to do, though I shrank from both the task and the exposure which it would entail. I must, I said, give the true key to my whole life; I must show what I am, that it may be seen what I am not, and that the phantom may be extinguished which gibbers instead of me. I wish to be known as a living man, and not as a scarecrow which is dressed up in my clothes. False ideas may be refuted indeed by argument, but by true ideas alone are they expelled. I will vanquish, not my Accuser, but my judges. I will indeed answer his charges and criticisms on me one by one,* lest any one should say that they are unanswerable, but such a work shall not be the scope nor the substance of my reply. I will draw out, as far as may be, the history of my mind; I will state the point at which I began, in what external suggestion or accident each opinion had its rise, how far and how they developed from within, how they grew, were modified, were combined, were in

* This was done in the Appendix, of which the more important parts are preserved in the Notes.

collision with each other, and were changed; again how I conducted myself towards them, and how, and how far, and for how long a time, I thought I could hold them consistently with the ecclesiastical engagements which I had made and with the position which I held. I must show, – what is the very truth, – that the doctrines which I held, and have held for so many years, have been taught me (speaking humanly) partly by the suggestions of Protestant friends, partly by the teaching of books, and partly by the action of my own mind: and thus I shall account for that phenomenon which to so many seems so wonderful, that I should have left 'my kindred and my father's house'[11] for a Church from which once I turned away with dread; – so wonderful to them! as if forsooth a Religion which has flourished through so many ages, among so many nations, amid such varieties of social life, in such contrary classes and conditions of men, and after so many revolutions, political and civil, could not subdue the reason and overcome the heart, without the aid of fraud in the process and the sophistries of the schools.

What I had proposed to myself in the course of half-an-hour, I determined on at the end of ten days. However, I have many difficulties in fulfilling my design. How am I to say all that has to be said in a reasonable compass? And then as to the materials of my narrative; I have no autobiographical notes to consult, no written explanations of particular treatises or of tracts which at the time gave offence, hardly any minutes of definite transactions or conversations, and few contemporary memoranda, I fear, of the feelings or motives under which from time to time I acted. I have an abundance of letters from friends with some copies or drafts of my answers to them, but they are for the most part unsorted; and, till this process has taken place, they are even too numerous and various to be available at a moment for my purpose. Then, as to the volumes which I have published, they would in many ways serve me, were I well up in them: but though I took great pains in their composition, I have thought little about them, when they were once out of my hands, and for the most part the last time I read them has been when I revised their last proof sheets.

Under these circumstances my sketch will of course be incomplete. I now for the first time contemplate my course as a whole; it is a first essay, but it will contain, I trust, no serious or substantial mistake, and so far will answer the purpose for which I write it. I purpose to set nothing down in it as certain, of which

I have not a clear memory, or some written memorial, or the corroboration of some friend. There are witnesses enough up and down the country to verify, or correct, or complete it; and letters moreover of my own in abundance, unless they have been destroyed.

Moreover, I mean to be simply personal and historical: I am not expounding Catholic doctrine, I am doing no more than explaining myself, and my opinions and actions. I wish, as far as I am able, simply to state facts, whether they are ultimately determined to be for me or against me. Of course there will be room enough for contrariety of judgment among my readers, as to the necessity, or appositeness, or value, or good taste, or religious prudence, of the details which I shall introduce. I may be accused of laying stress on little things, of being beside the mark, of going into impertinent or ridiculous details, of sounding my own praise, of giving scandal; but this is a case above all others, in which I am bound to follow my own lights and to speak out my own heart. It is not at all pleasant for me to be egotistical; nor to be criticized for being so. It is not pleasant to reveal to high and low, young and old, what has gone on within me from my early years. It is not pleasant to be giving to every shallow or flippant disputant the advantage over me of knowing my most private thoughts, I might even say the intercourse between myself and my Maker. But I do not like to be called to my face a liar and a knave; nor should I be doing my duty to my faith or to my name, if I were to suffer it. I know I have done nothing to deserve such an insult, and if I prove this, as I hope to do, I must not care for such incidental annoyances as are involved in the process.

CONTENTS

ADDITIONAL NOTES

MY RELIGIOUS OPINIONS

CHAPTER I

It may easily be conceived how great a trial it is to me to write
the following history of myself; but I must not shrink from the
task. The words, 'Secretum meum mihi,'[1] keep ringing in my
ears; but as men draw towards their end, they care less for
disclosures. Nor is it the least part of my trial, to anticipate that,
upon first reading what I have written, my friends may consider
much in it irrelevant to my purpose; yet I cannot help thinking
that, viewed as a whole, it will effect what I propose to myself in
giving it to the public.

I was brought up from a child to take great delight in reading
the Bible; but I had no formed religious convictions till I was
fifteen. Of course I had a perfect knowledge of my Catechism.

After I was grown up, I put on paper my recollections of the
thoughts and feelings on religious subjects, which I had at the
time that I was a child and a boy, – such as had remained on my
mind with sufficient prominence to make me then consider them
worth recording. Out of these, written in the Long Vacation of
1820, and transcribed with additions in 1823, I select two, which
are at once the most definite among them, and also have a
bearing on my later convictions.

1. 'I used to wish the Arabian Tales were true: my imagination
ran on unknown influences, on magical powers, and talismans.
. . . I thought life might be a dream, or I an Angel, and all this
world a deception, my fellow-angels by a playful device concealing themselves from me, and deceiving me with the semblance of
a material world.'

Again: 'Reading in the Spring of 1816 a sentence from [Dr.
Watts's] *Remnants of Time*,[2] entitled "the Saints unknown to the
world," to the effect, that "there is nothing in their figure or

countenance to distinguish them," &c., &c., I supposed he spoke of Angels who lived in the world, as it were disguised.'

2. The other remark is this: 'I was very superstitious, and for some time previous to my conversion' [when I was fifteen] 'used constantly to cross myself on going into the dark.'

Of course I must have got this practice from some external source or other; but I can make no sort of conjecture whence; and certainly no one had ever spoken to me on the subject of the Catholic religion, which I only knew by name. The French master was an *émigré* Priest, but he was simply made a butt, as French masters too commonly were in that day, and spoke English very imperfectly. There was a Catholic family in the village,[3] old maiden ladies we used to think; but I knew nothing about them. I have of late years heard that there were one or two Catholic boys in the school;[4] but either we were carefully kept from knowing this, or the knowledge of it made simply no impression on our minds. My brother[5] will bear witness how free the school was from Catholic ideas.

I had once been into Warwick Street Chapel,[6] with my father, who, I believe, wanted to hear some piece of music; all that I bore away from it was the recollection of a pulpit and a preacher, and a boy swinging a censer.

When I was at Littlemore,[7] I was looking over old copy-books of my school days, and I found among them my first Latin verse-book; and in the first page of it there was a device which almost took my breath away with surprise. I have the book before me now, and have just been showing it to others. I have written in the first page, in my school-boy hand, 'John H. Newman, February 11th, 1811, Verse Book;' then follow my first Verses. Between 'Verse' and 'Book' I have drawn the figure of a solid cross upright, and next to it is, what may indeed be meant for a necklace, but what I cannot make out to be anything else than a set of beads suspended, with a little cross attached. At this time I was not quite ten years old. I suppose I got these ideas from some romance, Mrs Radcliffe's[8] or Miss Porter's;[9] or from some religious picture; but the strange thing is, how, among the thousand objects which meet a boy's eyes, these in particular should so have fixed themselves in my mind, that I made them thus practically my own. I am certain there was nothing in the churches I attended, or the prayer books I read, to suggest them. It must be recollected that Anglican churches and prayer books were not decorated in those days as I believe they are now.

When I was fourteen, I read Paine's[10] *Tracts against the Old Testament*, and found pleasure in thinking of the objections which were contained in them. Also, I read some of Hume's *Essays*; and perhaps that on *Miracles*.[11] So at least I gave my Father to understand; but perhaps it was a brag. Also, I recollect copying out some French verses, perhaps Voltaire's, in denial of the immortality of the soul, and saying to myself something like 'How dreadful, but how plausible!'

When I was fifteen, (in the autumn of 1816,)[12] a great change of thought took place in me. I fell[13] under the influences of a definite Creed, and received into my intellect impressions of dogma, which, through God's mercy, have never been effaced or obscured. Above and beyond the conversations and sermons of the excellent man, long dead, the Rev. Walter Mayers,[14] of Pembroke College, Oxford, who was the human means of this beginning of divine faith in me, was the effect of the books which he put into my hands, all of the school of Calvin. One of the first books I read was a work of Romaine's;[15] I neither recollect the title nor the contents, except one doctrine, which of course I do not include among those which I believe to have come from a divine source, viz. the doctrine of final perseverance. I received it at once, and believed that the inward conversion of which I was conscious, (and of which I still am more certain than that I have hands and feet,)would last into the next life, and that I was elected to eternal glory. I have no consciousness that this belief had any tendency whatever to lead me to be careless about pleasing God. I retained it till the age of twenty-one, when it gradually faded away: but I believe that it had some influence on my opinions, in the direction of those childish imaginations which I have already mentioned, viz. in isolating me from the objects which surrounded me, in confirming me in my mistrust of the reality of material phenomena, and making me rest in the thought of two and two only absolute and luminously self-evident beings, myself and my Creator; – for while I considered myself predestined to salvation, my mind did not dwell upon others, as fancying them simply passed over, not predestined to eternal death. I only thought of the mercy to myself.

The detestable doctrine last mentioned is simply denied and abjured, unless my memory strangely deceives me, by the writer who made a deeper impression on my mind than any other, and to whom (humanly speaking) I almost owe my soul, – Thomas Scott[16] of Aston Sandford. I so admired and delighted in his writings, that, when I was an Under-graduate, I thought of making a visit to his Parsonage, in order to see a man whom I so deeply revered. I hardly think I could have given up the idea of this expedition, even after I had taken my degree; for the news of his death in 1821 came upon me as a disappointment as well as a sorrow. I hung upon the lips of Daniel Wilson,[17] afterwards Bishop of Calcutta, as in two sermons at St. John's Chapel he gave the history of Scott's life and death. I had been possessed of his *Force of Truth* and *Essays* from a boy; his *Commentary* I bought when I was an Under-graduate.

What, I suppose, will strike any reader of Scott's history and writings, is his bold unworldliness and vigorous independence of mind. He followed truth wherever it led him, beginning with Unitarianism, and ending in a zealous faith in the Holy Trinity. It was he who first planted deep in my mind that fundamental truth of religion. With the assistance of Scott's *Essays*, and the admirable work of Jones[18] of Nayland, I made a collection of Scripture texts in proof of the doctrine, with remarks (I think) of my own upon them, before I was sixteen; and a few months later I drew up a series of texts in support of each verse of the Athanasian Creed.[19] These papers I have still.

Besides his unworldliness, what I also admired in Scott was his resolute opposition to Antinomianism,[20] and the minutely practical character of his writings. They show him to be a true Englishman, and I deeply felt his influence; and for years I used almost as proverbs what I considered to be the scope and issue of his doctrine, *Holiness rather than peace*, and *Growth the only evidence of life*.

Calvinists make a sharp separation between the elect and the world; there is much in this that is cognate or parallel to the Catholic doctrine; but they go on to say, as I understand them, very differently from Catholicism, – that the converted and the unconverted can be discriminated by man, that the justified are conscious of their state of justification, and that the regenerate cannot fall away. Catholics on the other hand shade and soften the awful antagonism between good and evil, which is one of their dogmas, by holding that there are different degrees of justification, that there is a great difference in point of gravity between sin and sin, that there is the possibility and the danger of falling away, and that there is no certain knowledge given to anyone that he is simply in a state of grace, and much less that he is to persevere to the end: — of the Calvinistic tenets the only one which took root in my mind was the fact of heaven and hell, divine favour and divine wrath, of the justified and the unjustified. The notion that the regenerate and the justified[21] were one and the same, and that the regenerate, as such, had the gift of perseverance, remained with me not many years, as I have said already.

This main Catholic doctrine of the warfare between the city of God and the powers of darkness was also deeply impressed upon my mind by a work of a character very opposite to Calvinism, Law's[22] Serious Call.

From this time I have held with a full inward assent and belief the doctrine of eternal punishment, as delivered by our Lord Himself, in as true a sense as I hold that of eternal happiness; though I have tried in various ways to make that truth less terrible to the imagination.

Now I come to two other works, which produced a deep impression on me in the same Autumn of 1816, when I was fifteen years old, each contrary to each, and planting in me the seeds of an intellectual inconsistency which disabled me for a long course of years. I read Joseph Milner's Church History,[23] and was nothing short of enamoured of the long extracts from St. Augustine, St. Ambrose, and the other Fathers which I found there. I read them as being the religion of the primitive Christians: but simultaneously with Milner I read Newton On the Prophecies,[24] and in consequence became most firmly convinced that the Pope was the Antichrist predicted[25] by Daniel, St. Paul, and St. John. My imagination was stained by the effects of this doctrine up to the year 1843; it had been obliterated from my reason and judgment at an earlier date; but the thought remained upon me as a sort of false conscience. Hence came that conflict of mind, which so many have felt besides myself; – leading some men to make a compromise between two ideas, so inconsistent with each other, – driving others to beat out the one idea or the other from their minds, – and ending in my own case, after many years of intellectual unrest, in the gradual decay and extinction of one of them, – I do not say in its violent death, for why should I not have murdered it sooner, if I murdered it at all?

I am obliged to mention, though I do it with great reluctance, another deep imagination, which at this time, the autumn of 1816, took possession of me, – there can be no mistake about the fact; viz. that it would be the will of God that I should lead a single life. This anticipation, which has held its ground almost continuously ever since, – with the break of a month now and a month then, up to 1829, and, after that date, without any break at all, – was more or less connected in my mind with the notion, that my calling in life would require such a sacrifice as celibacy involved; as, for instance, missionary work among the heathen, to which I had a great drawing for some years. It also strengthened my feeling of separation from the visible world, of which I have spoken above.

In 1822[26] I came under very different influences from those to which I had hitherto been subjected. At that time, Mr. Whately,[27] as he was then, afterwards Archbishop of Dublin, for the few months he remained in Oxford, which he was leaving for good, showed great kindness to me. He renewed it in 1825, when he became Principal of Alban Hall, making me his Vice-Principal and Tutor. Of Dr. Whately I will speak presently: for from 1822 to 1825 I saw most of the present Provost of Oriel, Dr. Hawkins,[28] at that time Vicar of St. Mary's; and, when I took orders in 1824 and had a curacy[29] in Oxford, then, during the Long Vacations, I was especially thrown into his company. I can say with a full heart that I love him, and have never ceased to love him; and I thus preface what otherwise might sound rude, that in the course of the many years in which we were together afterwards, he provoked[30] me very much from time to time, though I am perfectly certain that I have provoked him a great deal more. Moreover, in me such provocation was unbecoming, both because he was the Head of my College, and because, in the first years that I knew him, he had been in many ways of great service to my mind.

He was the first who taught me to weigh my words, and to be cautious in my statements. He led me to that mode of limiting and clearing my sense in discussion and in controversy, and of distinguishing between cognate ideas, and of obviating mistakes by anticipation, which to my surprise has been since considered, even in quarters friendly to me, to savour of the polemics of Rome. He is a man of most exact mind himself, and he used to snub me severely, on reading, as he was kind enough to do, the first Sermons that I wrote, and other compositions which I was engaged upon.

Then as to doctrine, he was the means of great additions to my belief. As I have noticed elsewhere, he gave me the *Treatise on Apostolical Preaching*, by Sumner,[31] afterwards Archbishop of Canterbury, from which I was led to give up my remaining Calvinism, and to receive the doctrine of Baptismal Regeneration. In many other ways too he was of use to me, on subjects semi-religious and semi-scholastic.

It was Dr. Hawkins too who taught me to anticipate that, before many years were over, there would be an attack made upon the books and the canon of Scripture. I was brought to the same belief by the conversation of Mr Blanco White,[32] who also led me to have freer views on the subject of inspiration than were usual in the Church of England at the time.

There is one other principle, which I gained from Dr. Hawkins, more directly bearing upon Catholicism, than any that I have mentioned; and that is the doctrine of Tradition. When I was an Under-graduate, I heard him preach in the University Pulpit his celebrated sermon[33] on the subject, and recollect how long it appeared to me, though he was at that time a very striking preacher; but, when I read it and studied it as his gift, it made a most serious impression upon me. He does not go one step, I think, beyond the high Anglican doctrine, nay he does not reach it; but he does his work thoroughly, and his view was in him original, and his subject was a novel one at the time. He lays down a proposition, self-evident as soon as stated, to those who have at all examined the structure of Scripture, viz. that the sacred text was never intended to teach doctrine, but only to prove it, and that, if we would learn doctrine, we must have recourse to the formularies of the Church; for instance to the Catechism, and to the Creeds. He considers, that, after learning from them the doctrines of Christianity, the inquirer must verify them by Scripture. This view, most true in its outline, most fruitful in its consequences, opened upon me a large field of thought. Dr. Whately held it too. One of its effects was to strike at the root of the principle on which the Bible Society[34] was set up. I belonged to its Oxford Association; it became a matter of time when I should withdraw my name from its subscription-list, though I did not do so at once.

It is with pleasure that I pay here a tribute to the memory of the Rev. William James,[35] then Fellow of Oriel; who, about the year 1823, taught me the doctrine of Apostolical Succession,[36] in the course of a walk, I think, round Christ Church meadow; I recollect being somewhat impatient of the subject at the time.

It was at about this date, I suppose, that I read Bishop Butler's Analogy;[37] the study of which has been to so many, as it was to me, an era in their religious opinions. Its inculcation of a visible Church, the oracle of truth and a pattern of sanctity, of the duties of external religion, and of the historical character of Revelation, are characteristics of this great work which strike the reader at once; for myself, if I may attempt to determine what I most gained from it, it lay in two points, which I shall have an opportunity of dwelling on in the sequel; they are the underlying principles of a great portion of my teaching. First, the very idea of an analogy between the separate works of God leads to the conclusion that the system which is of less importance is economically or sacramentally connected with the more momentous system,* and of this conclusion the theory, to which I was inclined as a boy, viz. the unreality of material phenomena, is an ultimate resolution. At this time I did not make the distinction between matter itself and its phenomena, which is so necessary and so obvious in discussing the subject. Secondly, Butler's doctrine that Probability is the guide of life, led me, at least under the teaching to which a few years later I was introduced, to the question of the logical

---

* It is significant that Butler begins his work with a quotation from Origen.[38]

cogency of Faith, on which I have written so much. Thus to Butler I trace those two principles of my teaching, which have led to a charge against me both of fancifulness and of scepticism.

And now as to Dr. Whately. I owe him a great deal. He was a man of generous and warm heart. He was particularly loyal to his friends, and to use the common phrase, 'all his geese were swans.' While I was still awkward and timid in 1822, he took me by the hand, and acted towards me the part of a gentle and encouraging instructor. He, emphatically, opened my mind, and taught me to think and to use my reason. After being first noticed by him in 1822, I became very intimate with him in 1825, when I was his Vice-Principal at Alban Hall. I gave up that office in 1826, when I became Tutor of my College, and his hold upon me gradually relaxed. He had done his work towards me or nearly so, when he had taught me to see with my own eyes and to walk with my own feet. Not that I had not a good deal to learn from others still, but I influenced them as well as they me, and co-operated rather than merely concurred with them. As to Dr. Whately, his mind was too different from mine for us to remain long on one line. I recollect how dissatisfied he was with an Article[39] of mine in the London Review, which Blanco White, good-humouredly, only called Platonic. When I was diverging from him in opinion (which he did not like), I thought of dedicating my first book to him, in words to the effect that he had not only taught me to think, but to think for myself. He left Oxford in 1831; after that, as far as I can recollect, I never saw him but twice, – when he visited the University; once in the street in 1834, once in a room in 1838. From the time that he left, I have always felt a real affection for what I must call his memory; for, at least from the year 1834, he made himself dead to me. He had practically indeed given me up from the time that he became Archbishop in 1831; but in 1834 a correspondence[40] took place between us, which, though conducted especially on his side in a friendly spirit, was the expression of differences of opinion which acted as a final close to our intercourse. My reason told me that it was impossible we could have got on together longer, had he stayed in Oxford; yet I loved him too much to bid him farewell without pain. After a few years had passed, I began to believe that his influence on me in a higher respect than intellectual advance, (I will not say through his fault,) had not been satisfactory. I believe that he has inserted sharp things in his later works about me. They have never come in my way, and I have not thought it necessary to seek out what would pain me so much in the reading.

What he did for me in point of religious opinion, was, first, to teach me the existence of the Church, as a substantive body or corporation; next to fix in me those anti-Erastian[41] views of Church polity, which were one of the most prominent features of the Tractarian movement. On this point, and, as far as I know, on this point alone, he and Hurrell Froude[42] intimately sympathized, though Froude's development of opinion here was of a later date. In the year 1826, in the course of a walk, he said much to me about a work then just published, called *Letters on the Church by an Episcopalian*. He said that it would make my blood boil. It was certainly a most powerful composition. One of our common friends told me, that, after reading it, he could not keep still, but went on walking up and down his room. It was ascribed at once to Whately; I gave eager expression to the contrary opinion; but I found the belief of Oxford in the affirmative to be too strong for me; rightly or wrongly I yielded to the general voice; and I have never heard, then or since, of any disclaimer of authorship on the part of Dr. Whately.

The main positions of this able essay are these; first that Church and State should be independent of each other: – he speaks of the duty of protesting 'against the profanation of Christ's kingdom, by that *double usurpation*, the interference of the Church in temporals, of the State in spirituals,' p. 191; and, secondly, that the Church may justly and by right retain its property, though separated from the State. 'The clergy,' he says, p. 133, 'though they ought not to be the hired servants of the Civil Magistrate, may justly retain their revenues; and the State, though it has no right of interference in spiritual concerns, not only is justly entitled to support from the ministers of religion, and from all other Christians, but would, under the system I am recommending, obtain it much more effectually.' The author of this work, whoever he may be, argues out both these points with great force and ingenuity, and with a thoroughgoing vehemence, which perhaps we may refer to the circumstance, that he wrote, not *in propriâ personâ*, and as thereby answerable for every sentiment that he advanced, but in the professed character of a Scotch Episcopalian. His work had a gradual, but a deep effect on my mind.

I am not aware of any other religious opinion which I owe to Dr. Whately. In his special theological tenets[43] I had no sympathy. In the next year, 1827, he told me he considered that I was Arianizing.[44] The case was this: though at that time I had not read Bishop Bull's *Defensio*[45] nor the Fathers, I was just then very strong for that ante-Nicene view of the Trinitarian doctrine, which some writers, both Catholic and non-Catholic, have accused of wearing a sort of Arian exterior. This is the meaning of a passage in Froude's *Remains*,[46] in which he seems to accuse me of speaking against the Athanasian Creed. I had contrasted the two aspects of the Trinitarian doctrine, which are respectively presented by the Athanasian Creed and the Nicene. My criticisms were to the effect that some of the verses of the former Creed were unnecessarily scientific. This is a specimen of a certain disdain for Antiquity which had been growing on me now for several years. It showed itself in some flippant language[47] against the Fathers in the Encyclopaedia Metropolitana, about whom I knew little at the time, except what I had learnt as a boy from Joseph Milner. In writing on the Scripture Miracles in 1825–6, I had read Middleton[48] *On the Miracles of the early Church*, and had imbibed a portion of his spirit.

The truth is, I was beginning to prefer intellectual excellence to moral; I was drifting in the direction of the Liberalism of the day.* I was rudely awakened from my dream at the end of 1827 by two great blows – illness and bereavement.[49]

In the beginning of 1829, came the formal break between Dr. Whately and me; the affair[50] of Mr. Peel's re-election was the occasion of it. I think in 1828 or 1827 I had voted in the minority, when the Petition[51] to Parliament against the Catholic Claims was brought into Convocation.[52] I did so mainly on the views suggested to me in the Letters of an Episcopalian. Also I shrank from the bigoted 'two-bottle-orthodox,'[53] as they were

* Vide Note A, *Liberalism*, at the end of the volume.

invidiously called. When then I took part against Mr. Peel, it was on an academical, not at all an ecclesiastical or a political ground; and this I professed at the time. I considered that Mr. Peel had taken the University by surprise; that his friends had no right to call upon us to turn round on a sudden, and to expose ourselves to the imputation of time-serving; and that a great University ought not to be bullied even by a great Duke of Wellington. Also by this time I was under the influence of Keble[54] and Froude; who, in addition to the reasons I have given, disliked the Duke's change of policy as dictated by Liberalism.

Whately was considerably annoyed at me, and he took a humorous revenge, of which he had given me due notice beforehand. As head of a house he had duties of hospitality to men of all parties; he asked a set of the least intellectual men in Oxford to dinner, and men most fond of port; he made me one of this party; placed me between Provost This and Principal That, and then asked me if I was proud of my friends. However, he had a serious meaning in his act; he saw, more clearly than I could do, that I was separating from his own friends for good and all.

Dr. Whately attributed my leaving his *clientela* to a wish on my part to be the head of a party myself. I do not think that this charge was deserved. My habitual feeling then and since has been, that it was not I who sought friends, but friends who sought me. Never man had kinder or more indulgent friends than I have had; but I expressed my own feeling as to the mode in which I gained them, in this very year 1829, in the course of a copy of verses.[55] Speaking of my blessings, I said, 'Blessings of friends, which to my door *unasked, unhoped*, have come.' They have come, they have gone; they came to my great joy, they went to my great grief. He who gave took away. Dr. Whately's impression about me, however, admits of this explanation: –

During the first years of my residence at Oriel, though proud of my College, I was not quite at home there. I was very much alone, and I used often to take my daily walk by myself. I recollect once meeting Dr. Copleston,[56] then Provost, with one of the Fellows. He turned round, and with the kind courteousness which sat so well on him, made me a bow and said, 'Nunquam minus solus, quàm cùm solus.'[57] At that time indeed (from 1823) I had the intimacy of my dear and true friend Dr. Pusey,[58] and could not fail to admire and revere a soul so devoted to the cause of religion, so full of good works, so faithful in his affections; but he left residence when I was getting to know him well. As to Dr. Whately himself, he was too much my superior to allow of my being at my ease with him; and to no one in Oxford at this time did I open my heart fully and familiarly. But things changed in 1826. At that time I became one of the Tutors of my College, and this gave me position; besides, I had written one or two Essays[59] which had been well received. I began to be known. I preached my first University Sermon.[60] Next year I was one of the Public Examiners for the B.A. degree. In 1828 I became Vicar of St. Mary's. It was to me like the feeling of spring weather after winter; and, if I may so speak, I came out of my shell; I remained out of it till 1841.

The two persons[61] who knew me best at that time are still alive, beneficed clergymen, no longer my friends. They could tell better than any one else what I was in those years. From this time my tongue was, as it were, loosened, and I spoke spontaneously and without effort. One of the two, Mr. Rickards, said of me, I have been told, 'Here is a fellow who, when he is silent, will never begin to speak; and when he once begins to speak, will never stop.' It was at this time that I began to have influence, which steadily increased for a course of years. I gained upon my pupils, and was in particular intimate and affectionate with two of our probationer Fellows,[62] Robert Isaac Wilberforce[63] (afterwards Archdeacon) and Richard Hurrell Froude. Whately then, an acute man, perhaps saw around me the signs of an incipient party, of which I was not conscious myself. And thus we discern the first elements of that movement afterwards called Tractarian.

The true and primary author of it, however, as is usual with great motive-powers, was out of sight. Having carried off as a mere boy the highest honours of the University, he had turned from the admiration which haunted his steps, and sought for a better and holier satisfaction in pastoral work in the country. Need I say that I am speaking of John Keble? The first time that I was in a room with him was on occasion of my election to a fellowship at Oriel, when I was sent for into the Tower,[64] to shake hands with the Provost and Fellows. How is that hour fixed in my memory after the changes of forty-two years, forty-two this very day[65] on which I write! I have lately had a letter in my hands, which I sent at the time to my great friend, John William Bowden,[66] with whom I passed almost exclusively my Under-graduate years. 'I had to hasten to the Tower,' I say to him, 'to receive the congratulations of all the Fellows. I bore it till Keble took my hand, and then felt so abashed and unworthy of the honour done me, that I seemed desirous of quite sinking into the ground.' His had been the first name which I had heard spoken of, with reverence rather than admiration, when I came up to Oxford. When one day I was walking in High Street with my dear earliest friend just mentioned, with what eagerness did he cry out, 'There's Keble!' and with what awe did I look at him! Then at another time I heard a Master of Arts of my College give an account how he had just then had occasion to introduce himself on some business to Keble, and how gentle, courteous, and unaffected Keble had been, so as almost to put him out of countenance. Then too it was reported, truly or falsely, how a rising man of brilliant reputation, the present Dean of St. Paul's, Dr. Milman,[67] admired and loved him, adding, that somehow he was strangely unlike any one else. However, at the time when I was elected Fellow of Oriel he was not in residence,[68] and he was shy of me for years in consequence of the marks which I bore upon me of the evangelical and liberal schools. At least so I have ever thought. Hurrell Froude brought us together about 1828: it is one of the sayings preserved in his *Remains*,[69] – 'Do you know the story of the murderer who had done one good thing in his life? Well; if I was ever asked what good deed I had ever done, I should say that I had brought Keble and Newman to understand each other.'

The *Christian Year*[70] made its appearance in 1827. It is not necessary, and scarcely becoming, to praise a book which has already become one of the classics of the language. When the general tone of religious literature was so nerveless and impotent, as it was at that time, Keble struck an original note and woke up in the hearts of thousands a new music, the music of a school, long unknown in England. Nor can I pretend to analyze, in my own instance, the effect of religious teaching so deep, so pure, so beautiful. I have never till now tried to do so; yet I think I am

not wrong in saying, that the two main intellectual truths which
it brought home to me, were the same two, which I had learned
from Butler, though recast in the creative mind of my new
master. The first of these was what may be called, in a large
sense of the word, the Sacramental system; that is, the doctrine
that material phenomena are both the types and the instruments
of real things unseen, – a doctrine, which embraces in its fulness,
not only what Anglicans, as well as Catholics, believe about
Sacraments properly so called; but also the article[71] of 'the
Communion of Saints;' and likewise the Mysteries of the faith.
The connexion of this philosophy of religion with what is
sometimes called 'Berkeleyism' has been mentioned above; I
knew little of Berkeley[72] at this time except by name; nor have I
ever studied him.

On the second intellectual principle which I gained from Mr.
Keble, I could say a great deal; if this were the place for it. It
runs through very much that I have written, and has gained for
me many hard names. Butler teaches us that probability is the
guide of life. The danger of this doctrine, in the case of many
minds, is, its tendency to destroy in them absolute certainty,
leading them to consider every conclusion as doubtful, and
resolving truth into an opinion, which it is safe indeed to obey
or to profess, but not possible to embrace with full internal
assent. If this were to be allowed, then the celebrated saying,[73]
'O God, if there be a God, save my soul, if I have a soul!' would
be the highest measure of devotion: – but who can really pray to
a Being, about whose existence he is seriously in doubt?

I considered that Mr. Keble met this difficulty by ascribing the
firmness of assent which we give to religious doctrine, not to the
probabilities which introduced it, but to the living power of faith
and love which accepted it. In matters of religion, he seemed to
say, it is not merely probability which makes us intellectually
certain, but probability as it is put to account by faith and love.
It is faith and love which give to probability a force which it has
not in itself. Faith and love are directed towards an Object; in
the vision of that Object they live; it is that Object, received in
faith and love, which renders it reasonable to take probability as
sufficient for internal conviction. Thus the argument from Probability, in the matter of religion, became an argument from

Personality, which in fact is one form of the argument from Authority.

In illustration, Mr. Keble used to quote the words of the Psalm:[74] 'I will guide thee with mine *eye*. Be ye not like to horse and mule, which have no understanding; whose mouths must be held with bit and bridle, lest they fall upon thee.' This is the very difference, he used to say, between slaves, and friends or children. Friends do not ask for literal commands; but, from their knowledge of the speaker, they understand his half-words, and from love of him they anticipate his wishes. Hence it is, that in his Poem[75] for St. Bartholomew's Day, he speaks of the 'Eye of God's word;' and in the note quotes Mr. Miller,[76] of Worcester College, who remarks in his Bampton Lectures, on the special power of Scripture, as having 'this Eye, like that of a portrait, uniformly fixed upon us, turn where we will.' The view thus suggested by Mr. Keble, is brought forward in one of the earliest of the *Tracts for the Times*. In No. 8 I say, 'The Gospel is a Law of Liberty. We are treated as sons, not as servants; not subjected to a code of formal commandments, but addressed as those who love God, and wish to please Him.'

I did not at all dispute this view of the matter, for I made use of it myself; but I was dissatisfied, because it did not go to the root of the difficulty. It was beautiful and religious, but it did not even profess to be logical; and accordingly I tried to complete it by considerations of my own, which are to be found[77] in my University Sermons, Essay on Ecclesiastical Miracles, and Essay on Development of Doctrine. My argument is in outline as follows: that that absolute certitude which we were able to possess, whether as to the truths of natural theology, or as to the fact of a revelation, was the result of an *assemblage* of concurring and converging probabilities, and that, both according to the constitution of the human mind and the will of its Maker; that certitude was a habit of mind, that certainty was a quality of propositions; that probabilities which did not reach to logical certainty, might suffice for a mental certitude; that the certitude thus brought about might equal in measure and strength the certitude which was created by the strictest scientific demonstration; and that to possess such certitude might in given cases and to given individuals be a plain duty, though not to others in other circumstances: –

Moreover, that as there were probabilities which sufficed for certitude, so there were other probabilities which were legitimately adapted to create opinion; that it might be quite as much a matter of duty in given cases and to given persons to have about a fact an opinion of a definite strength and consistency, as in the case of greater or of more numerous probabilities it was a duty to have a certitude; that accordingly we were bound to be more or less sure, on a sort of (as it were) graduated scale of assent, viz. according as the probabilities attaching to a professed fact were brought home to us, and as the case might be, to entertain about it a pious belief, or a pious opinion, or a religious conjecture, or at least, a tolerance of such belief, or opinion or conjecture in others; that on the other hand, as it was a duty to have a belief, of more or less strong texture, in given cases, so in other cases it was a duty not to believe, not to opine, not to conjecture, not even to tolerate the notion that a professed fact was true, inasmuch as it would be credulity or superstition, or some other moral fault, to do so. This was the region of Private Judgment in religion; that is, of a Private Judgment, not formed arbitrarily and according to one's fancy or liking, but conscientiously, and under a sense of duty.

Considerations such as these throw a new light on the subject of Miracles, and they seem to have led me to reconsider the view which I had taken of them in my Essay in 1825–6. I do not know what was the date of this change in me, nor of the train of ideas on which it was founded. That there had been already great miracles, as those of Scripture, as the Resurrection, was a fact establishing the principle that the laws of nature had sometimes been suspended by their Divine Author, and since what had happened once might happen again, a certain probability, at least no kind of improbability, was attached to the idea taken in itself, of miraculous intervention in later times, and miraculous accounts were to be regarded in connexion with the verisimilitude, scope, instrument, character, testimony, and circumstances, with which they presented themselves to us; and, according to the final result of those various considerations, it was our duty to be sure, or to believe, or to opine, or to surmise, or to tolerate, or to reject, or to denounce. The main difference between my Essay on Miracles in 1826 and my Essay[78] in 1842 is this: that in 1826 I considered that miracles were sharply divided into two classes, those which were to be received, and those which were to be rejected; whereas in 1842 I saw that they were to be regarded according to their greater or less probability, which was in some cases sufficient to create certitude about them, in other cases only belief or opinion.

Moreover, the argument from Analogy, on which this view of the question was founded, suggested to me something besides, in recommendation of the Ecclesiastical Miracles. It fastened itself upon the theory of Church History which I had learned as a boy from Joseph Milner. It is Milner's doctrine, that upon the visible Church come down from above, at certain intervals, large and temporary *Effusions* of divine grace. This is the leading idea of his work. He begins by speaking of the Day of Pentecost, as marking 'the first of those *Effusions* of the Spirit of God, which from age to age have visited the earth since the coming of Christ.' Vol. i. p. 3. In a note he adds that 'in the term "Effusion" there is *not* here included the idea of the miraculous or extraordinary operations of the Spirit of God;' but still it was natural for me, admitting Milner's general theory, and applying to it the principle of analogy, not to stop short at his abrupt *ipse dixit*, but boldly to pass forward to the conclusion, on other grounds plausible, that as miracles accompanied the first effusion of grace, so they might accompany the later. It is surely a natural and on the whole, a true anticipation (though of course there are exceptions in particular cases), that gifts and graces go together; now, according to the ancient Catholic doctrine, the gift of miracles was viewed as the attendant and shadow of transcendent sanctity: and moreover, since such sanctity was not of every day's occurrence, nay further, since one period of Church history differed widely from another, and, as Joseph Milner would say, there have been generations or centuries of degeneracy or dis-order, and times of revival, and since one region might be in the mid-day of religious fervour, and another in twilight or gloom, there was no force in the popular argument, that, because we did not see miracles with our own eyes, miracles had not happened in former times, or were not now at this very time taking place in distant places: – but I must not dwell longer on a subject, to which in a few words it is impossible to do justice.*

Hurrell Froude was a pupil of Keble's, formed by him, and in turn reacting upon him. I knew him first in 1826, and was in the closest and most affectionate friendship with him from about 1829 till his death in 1836. He was a man of the highest gifts, – so truly many-sided, that it would be presumptuous in me to attempt to describe him, except under those aspects in which he came before me. Nor have I here to speak of the gentleness and tenderness of nature, the playfulness, the free elastic force and graceful versatility of mind, and the patient winning considerateness in discussion, which endeared him to those to whom he opened his heart; for I am all along engaged upon matters of belief and opinion, and am introducing others into my narrative, not for their own sake, or because I love and have loved them, so much as because, and so far as, they have influenced my theological views. In this respect then, I speak of Hurrell Froude, – in his intellectual aspect, – as a man of high genius, brimful and overflowing with ideas and views, in him original, which were too many and strong even for his bodily strength, and which crowded and jostled against each other in their effort after distinct shape and expression. And he had an intellect as critical and logical as it was speculative and bold. Dying prematurely, as he did, and in the conflict and transition-state of opinion, his religious views never reached their ultimate conclusion, by the very reason of their multitude and their depth. His opinions arrested and influenced me, even when they did not gain my assent. He professed openly his admiration of the Church of Rome, and his hatred of the Reformers. He delighted in the notion of an hierarchical system, of sacerdotal power, and of full ecclesiastical liberty. He felt scorn of the maxim,[79] 'The Bible and the Bible only is the religion of Protestants;' and he gloried in accepting Tradition as a main instrument of religious teaching. He had a high severe idea of the intrinsic excellence of Virginity; and he considered the Blessed Virgin its great Pattern. He delighted in thinking of the Saints; he had a vivid appreciation of

* Vide Note B, *Ecclesiastical Miracles*, at the end of the volume.

the idea of sanctity, its possibility and its heights; and he was more than inclined to believe a large amount of miraculous interference as occurring in the early and middle ages. He embraced the principle of penance and mortification. He had a deep devotion to the Real Presence,[80] in which he had a firm faith. He was powerfully drawn to the Medieval Church, but not to the Primitive.

He had a keen insight into abstract truth; but he was an Englishman to the backbone in his severe adherence to the real and the concrete. He had a most classical taste, and a genius for philosophy and art; and he was fond of historical inquiry, and the politics of religion. He had no turn for theology as such. He set no sufficient value on the writings of the Fathers, on the detail or development of doctrine, on the definite traditions of the Church viewed in their matter, on the teaching of the Ecumenical Councils, or on the controversies out of which they arose. He took an eager courageous view of things on the whole. I should say that his power of entering into the minds of others did not equal his other gifts; he could not believe, for instance, that I really held the Roman Church to be Antichristian. On many points he would not believe but that I agreed with him, when I did not. He seemed not to understand my difficulties. His were of a different kind, the contrariety between theory and fact. He was a high Tory of the Cavalier stamp, and was disgusted with the Toryism of the opponents of the Reform Bill.[81] He was smitten with the love of the Theocratic Church; he went abroad and was shocked by the degeneracy which he thought he saw in the Catholics of Italy.

It is difficult to enumerate the precise additions to my theological creed which I derived from a friend to whom I owe so much. He taught me to look with admiration towards the Church of Rome, and in the same degree to dislike the Reformation. He fixed deep in me the idea of devotion to the Blessed Virgin, and he led me gradually to believe in the Real Presence.

There is one remaining source of my opinions to be mentioned, and that far from the least important. In proportion as I moved out of the shadow of that Liberalism which had hung over my course, my early devotion towards the Fathers returned; and in the Long Vacation of 1828 I set about to read them chronologic-ally, beginning with St. Ignatius[82] and St. Justin.[83] About 1830[84] a proposal was made to me by Mr. Hugh Rose, who with Mr. Lyall (afterwards Dean of Canterbury) was providing writers for a Theological Library, to furnish them with a History of the Principal Councils. I accepted it, and at once set to work on the Council of Nicaea. It was to launch myself on an ocean with currents innumerable; and I was drifted back first to the ante-Nicene history, and then to the Church of Alexandria. The work at last appeared under the title of *The Arians of the Fourth Century*;[85] and of its 422 pages, the first 117[86] consisted of introductory matter, and the Council of Nicaea did not appear till the 254th, and then occupied at most twenty pages.

I do not know when I first learnt to consider that Antiquity was the true exponent of the doctrines of Christianity and the basis of the Church of England; but I take it for granted that the works[87] of Bishop Bull, which at this time I read, were my chief introduction to this principle. The course of reading, which I pursued in the composition of my volume, was directly adapted to develop it in my mind. What principally attracted me in the ante-Nicene period was the great Church of Alexandria, the historical centre of teaching in those times. Of Rome for some centuries comparatively little is known. The battle of Arianism was first fought in Alexandria; Athanasius,[88] the champion of the truth, was Bishop of Alexandria; and in his writings he refers to the great religious names of an earlier date, to Origen,[89] Diony-sius,[90] and others, who were the glory of its see, or of its school. The broad philosophy of Clement[91] and Origen carried me away; the philosophy, not the theological doctrine; and I have drawn out some features of it in my volume, with the zeal and freshness, but with the partiality, of a neophyte. Some portions of their teaching, magnificent in themselves, came like music to my inward ear, as if the response to ideas, which, with little external to encourage them, I had cherished so long. These were based on the mystical or sacramental principle, and spoke of the various Economies or Dispensations of the Eternal. I understood these passages to mean that the exterior world, physical and historical, was but the manifestion to our senses of realities greater than itself. Nature was a parable: Scripture was an allegory: pagan literature, philosophy, and mythology, properly understood, were but a preparation for the Gospel. The Greek poets and sages were in a certain sense prophets; for 'thoughts beyond their thought to those high bards were given.'[92] There had been a directly divine dispensation granted to the Jews; but there had been in some sense a dispensation carried on in favour of the Gentiles. He who had taken the seed of Jacob for His elect people had not therefore cast the rest of mankind out of His sight. In the fulness of time both Judaism and Paganism had come to nought; the outward framework, which concealed yet suggested the Living Truth, had never been intended to last, and it was dissolving under the beams of the Sun of Justice which shone behind it and through it. The process of change had been slow; it had been done not rashly, but by rule and measure, 'at sundry times and in divers manners,'[93] first one disclosure and then another, till the whole evangelical doctrine was brought into full manifestation. And thus room was made for the anticipation of further and deeper disclosures, of truths still under the veil of the letter, and in their season to be revealed. The visible world still remains without its divine interpretation; Holy Church in her sacraments and her hierarchical appointments, will remain, even to the end of the world, after all but a symbol of those heavenly facts which fill eternity. Her mysteries are but the expressions in human language of truths to which the human mind is unequal. It is evident how much there was in all this in correspondence with the thoughts which had attracted me when I was young, and with the doctrine which I have already associated with the *Analogy* and the *Christian Year*.

It was, I suppose, to the Alexandrian school and to the early Church, that I owe in particular what I definitely held about the Angels. I viewed them, not only as the ministers employed by the Creator in the Jewish and Christian dispensations, as we find on the face of Scripture, but as carrying on, as Scripture also implies, the Economy of the Visible World. I considered them as the real causes of motion, light, and life, and of those elementary principles of the physical universe, which, when offered in their developments to our senses, suggest to us the notion of cause and effect, and of what are called the laws of nature. This doctrine I have drawn out in my Sermon[94] for Michaelmas day, written in 1831. I say of the Angels, 'Every breath of air and ray of light and heat, every beautiful prospect, is, as it were, the skirts of their garments, the waving of the robes of those whose faces see God.' Again, I ask what would be the thoughts of a man who, 'when examining a flower, or a herb, or a pebble, or a ray of light, which he treats as something so beneath him in the scale of existence, suddenly discovered that he was in the presence of some powerful being who was hidden behind the visible things he was inspecting, – who, though concealing his wise hand, was giving them their beauty, grace, and perfection, as being God's instrument for the purpose, – nay, whose robe and ornaments those objects were, which he was so eager to analyze?' and I therefore remark that 'we may say with grateful and simple hearts with the Three Holy Children,[95] "O all ye works of the Lord, &c., &c., bless ye the Lord, praise Him, and magnify Him for ever."'

Also, besides the hosts of evil spirits, I considered there was a middle race, δαιμόνια,[96] neither in heaven, nor in hell; partially fallen, capricious, wayward; noble or crafty, benevolent or malicious, as the case might be. These beings gave a sort of inspiration or intelligence to races, nations, and classes of men. Hence the action of bodies politic and associations, which is often so different from that of the individuals who compose them. Hence the character and the instinct of states and governments, of religious communities and communions. I thought these assemblages had their life in certain unseen Powers. My preference of the Personal to the Abstract would naturally lead me to this view. I thought it countenanced by the mention of 'the Prince of Persia' in the Prophet Daniel;[97] and I think I considered that it was of such intermediate beings that the Apocalypse[98] spoke, in its notice of 'the Angels of the Seven Churches.'

In 1837 I made a further development of this doctrine. I said to an intimate and dear friend, Samuel Francis Wood,[99] in a letter which came into my hands on his death, 'I have an idea. The mass of the Fathers (Justin, Athenagoras, Irenaeus, Clement, Tertullian, Origen, Lactantius, Sulpicius, Ambrose, Nazianzen,) hold that, though Satan fell from the beginning, the Angels[100] fell before the deluge, falling in love with the daughters of men. This has lately come across me as a remarkable solution of a notion which I cannot help holding. Daniel speaks as if each nation had its guardian Angel. I cannot but think that there are beings with a great deal of good in them, yet with great defects, who are the animating principles of certain institutions, &c., &c. ... Take England with many high virtues, and yet a low Catholicism. It seems to me that John Bull is a spirit neither of heaven nor hell. ... Has not the Christian Church, in its parts, surrendered itself to one or other of these simulations of the truth? ... How are we to avoid Scylla and Charybdis and go straight on to the very image of Christ?' &c., &c.

I am aware that what I have been saying will, with many men, be doing credit to my imagination at the expense of my judgment − 'Hippoclides doesn't care;'[101] I am not setting myself up as a pattern of good sense or of any thing else: I am but giving a history of my opinions, and that, with the view of showing that I have come by them through intelligible processes of thought and honest external means. The doctrine indeed of the Economy has in some quarters been itself condemned as intrinsically pernicious, − as if leading to lying and equivocation, when applied, as I have applied it in my remarks upon it in my History of the Arians,[102] to matters of conduct. My answer to this imputation I postpone to the concluding pages of my Volume.

While I was engaged in writing my work upon the Arians, great events were happening at home and abroad, which brought out into form and passionate expression the various beliefs which had so gradually been winning their way into my mind. Shortly before, there had been a Revolution[103] in France; the Bourbons had been dismissed: and I held that it was unchristian for nations to cast off their governors, and, much more, sovereigns who had the divine right of inheritance. Again, the great Reform[104] Agitation was going on around me as I wrote. The Whigs had come into power; Lord Grey had told the Bishops to set their house in order, and some of the Prelates had been insulted and threatened in the streets of London. The vital question was, how were we to keep the Church from being liberalized? there was such apathy on the subject in some quarters, such imbecile alarm in others; the true principles of Churchmanship seemed so radically decayed, and there was such distraction in the councils of the Clergy. Blomfield[105] the Bishop of London of the day, an active and open-hearted man, had been for years engaged in diluting the high orthodoxy of the Church by the introduction of members of the Evangelical body into places of influence and trust. He had deeply offended men who agreed in opinion with myself, by an off-hand saying (as it was reported) to the effect that belief in the Apostolical succession had gone out with the Nonjurors.[106] 'We can count you,' he said to some of the gravest and most venerated persons of the old school. And the Evangelical party itself, with their late successes, seemed to have lost that simplicity and unworldliness which I admired so much in Milner and Scott. It was not that I did not venerate such men as Ryder,[107] the then Bishop of Lichfield, and others of similar sentiments, who were not yet promoted out of the ranks of the Clergy, but I thought little of the Evangelicals as a class. I thought they played into the hands of the Liberals. With the Establishment thus divided and threatened, thus ignorant of its true strength, I compared that fresh vigorous Power of which I was reading in the first centuries. In her triumphant zeal on behalf of that Primeval Mystery,[108] to which I had had so great a devotion from my youth, I recognized the movement of my Spiritual Mother. 'Incessu patuit Dea.'[109] The self-conquest of her Ascetics, the patience of her Martyrs, the irresistible determination of her Bishops, the joyous swing of her advance, both exalted and abashed me. I said to myself, 'Look on this picture and on that;'[110] I felt affection for my own Church, but not tenderness; I felt dismay at her prospects, anger and scorn at her do-nothing perplexity. I thought that if Liberalism once got a footing within her, it was sure of the victory in the event. I saw that Reformation principles were powerless to rescue her. As to leaving her, the thought never crossed my imagination; still I ever kept before me that there was something greater than the Established Church, and that that was the Church Catholic and Apostolic, set up from the beginning, of which she was but the local presence and the organ. She was nothing, unless she was this. She must be dealt with strongly, or she would be lost. There was need of a second reformation.

At this time I was disengaged from College duties,[111] and my health had suffered from the labour involved in the composition of my Volume. It was ready for the Press in July, 1832, though not published till the end of 1833. I was easily persuaded to join Hurrell Froude and his Father,[112] who were going to the south of Europe for the health of the former.

We set out in December, 1832. It was during this expedition that my Verses which are in the Lyra Apostolica[113] were written; – a few indeed before it, but not more than one or two of them after it. Exchanging, as I was, definite Tutorial work, and the literary quiet and pleasant friendships of the last six years, for foreign countries and an unknown future, I naturally was led to think that some inward changes, as well as some larger course of action, were coming upon me. At Whitchurch, while waiting for the down mail to Falmouth, I wrote the verses[114] about my Guardian Angel, which begin with these words: 'Are these the tracks of some unearthly Friend?' and which go on to speak of 'the vision' which haunted me: – that vision is more or less brought out in the whole series of these compositions.

I went to various coasts of the Mediterranean; parted with my friends at Rome; went down for the second time to Sicily without companion, at the end of April; and got back to England by Palermo in the early part of July. The strangeness of foreign life threw me back into myself; I found pleasure in historical sites and beautiful scenes, not in men and manners. We kept clear of Catholics throughout our tour. I had a conversation with the Dean[115] of Malta, a most pleasant man, lately dead; but it was about the Fathers, and the Library of the great church. I knew the Abbate Santini[116], at Rome, who did no more than copy for me the Gregorian tones. Froude and I made two calls upon Monsignore (now Cardinal) Wiseman[117] at the Collegio Inglese, shortly before we left Rome. Once we heard him preach at a church in the Corso. I do not recollect being in a room with any other ecclesiastics, except a Priest[118] at Castro-Giovanni in Sicily, who called on me when I was ill, and with whom I wished to hold a controversy. As to Church Services, we attended the Tenebrae,[119] at the Sestine, for the sake of the Miserere; and that was all. My general feeling was, 'All save the spirit of man, is divine.'[120] I saw nothing but what was external; of the hidden life of Catholics I knew nothing. I was still more driven back into myself, and felt my isolation. England was in my thoughts solely, and the news from England came rarely and imperfectly.

The Bill[121] for the Suppression of the Irish Sees was in progress, and filled my mind. I had fierce thoughts against the Liberals.

It was the success of the Liberal cause which fretted me inwardly. I became fierce against its instruments and its manifestations. A French vessel was at Algiers; I would not even look at the tricolour. On my return, though forced to stop twenty-four hours at Paris, I kept indoors the whole time, and all that I saw of that beautiful city was what I saw from the Diligence. The Bishop of London had already sounded me as to my filling one of the Whitehall preacherships,[122] which he had just then put on a new footing; but I was indignant at the line which he was taking, and from my Steamer I had sent home a letter declining the appointment by anticipation, should it be offered to me. At this time I was specially annoyed with Dr. Arnold,[123] though it did not last into later years. Some one, I think, asked, in conversation[124] at Rome, whether a certain interpretation of Scripture was Christian? It was answered that Dr. Arnold took it; I interposed, 'But is *he* a Christian?' The subject went out of my head at once; when afterwards I was taxed with it, I could say no more in explanation, than (what I believe was the fact) that I must have had in mind some free views of Dr. Arnold about the Old Testament: – I thought I must have meant, 'Arnold answers for the interpretation, but who is to answer for Arnold?' It was at Rome, too, that we began[125] the *Lyra Apostolica* which appeared monthly in the *British Magazine*. The motto shows the feeling of both Froude and myself at the time: we borrowed from M. Bunsen[126] a Homer, and Froude chose the words[127] in which Achilles, on returning to the battle, says, 'You shall know the difference, now that I am back again.'

Especially when I was left by myself, the thought came upon me that deliverance is wrought, not by the many but by the few, not by bodies but by persons. Now it was, I think, that I repeated to myself the words, which had ever been dear to me from my school days, 'Exoriare aliquis!'[128] – now too, that Southey's beautiful poem of Thalaba,[129] for which I had an immense liking, came forcibly to my mind. I began to think that I had a mission. There are sentences of my letters to my friends to this effect, if they are not destroyed. When we took leave[130] of Monsignore Wiseman, he had courteously expressed a wish that we might make a second visit to Rome; I said with great gravity, 'We have a work to do in England.' I went down at once to Sicily,[131] and the presentiment grew stronger. I struck into the middle of the island, and fell ill of a fever at Leonforte.[132] My servant thought that I was dying, and begged for my last directions.[133] I gave them, as he wished; but I said, 'I shall not die.' I repeated, 'I shall not die, for I have not sinned against light, I have not sinned against light.' I never have been able quite to make out what I meant.

I got to Castro-Giovanni,[134] and was laid up there for nearly three weeks. Towards the end of May[135] I left for Palermo, taking three days for the journey. Before starting from my inn[136] in the morning of May 26th or 27th, I sat down on my bed, and began to sob violently. My servant, who had acted as my nurse, asked what ailed me. I could only answer him, 'I have a work to do in England.'

I was aching to get home; yet for want of a vessel I was kept at Palermo for three weeks. I began to visit the Churches, and they calmed my impatience,[137] though I did not attend any services. I knew nothing of the Presence of the Blessed Sacrament there. At last[138] I got off in an orange boat, bound for Marseilles. Then it was that I wrote the lines,[139] 'Lead, kindly light,' which have since become well known. We were becalmed a whole week in the Straits of Bonifacio. I was writing verses the whole time of my passage. At length I got to Marseilles, and set off for England. The fatigue of travelling was too much for me, and I was laid up for several days at Lyons. At last[140] I got off again, and did not stop night or day, (except a compulsory delay at Paris,) till I reached England, and my mother's house. My brother had arrived from Persia only a few hours before. This was on the Tuesday. The following Sunday, July 14th, Mr. Keble preached the Assize Sermon[141] in the University Pulpit. It was published under the title of 'National Apostasy.' I have ever considered and kept the day, as the start of the religious movement of 1833.

CHAPTER II

In spite of the foregoing pages, I have no romantic story to tell; but I have written them, because it is my duty to tell things as they took place. I have not exaggerated the feelings with which I returned to England, and I have no desire to dress up the events which followed, so as to make them in keeping with the narrative which has gone before. I soon relapsed into the every-day life which I had hitherto led; in all things the same, except that a new object was given me. I had employed myself in my own rooms in reading and writing, and in the care of a Church, before I left England, and I returned to the same occupations when I was back again. And yet perhaps those first vehement feelings which carried me on, were necessary for the beginning of the Movement; and afterwards, when it was once begun, the special need of me was over.

When I got home from abroad, I found that already a movement had commenced, in opposition to the specific danger which at that time was threatening the religion of the nation and its Church. Several zealous and able men had united their counsels, and were in correspondence with each other. The principal of these were Mr. Keble, Hurrell Froude, who had reached home long before me, Mr. William Palmer[1] of Dublin and Worcester College (not Mr. William Palmer of Magdalen,[2] who is now a Catholic), Mr. Arthur Perceval,[3] and Mr. Hugh Rose.[4]

To mention Mr. Hugh Rose's name is to kindle in the minds of those who knew him a host of pleasant and affectionate remembrances. He was the man above all others fitted by his cast of mind and literary powers to make a stand, if a stand could be made, against the calamity of the times. He was gifted with a high and large mind, and a true sensibility of what was great and beautiful; he wrote with warmth and energy; and he had a cool head and cautious judgment. He spent his strength and shortened his life, Pro Ecclesia Dei,[5] as he understood that sovereign idea. Some years earlier he had been the first to give warning, I think from the University Pulpit at Cambridge, of the perils to England which lay in the biblical and theological speculations of Germany. The Reform agitation followed, and the Whig Government came into power; and he anticipated in their distribution of Church patronage the authoritative introduction of liberal opinions into the country. He feared that by the Whig party a door would be opened in England to the most grievous of heresies, which never could be closed again. In order under such grave circumstances to unite Churchmen together, and to make a front against the coming danger, he had in 1832 commenced the British Magazine, and in the same year he came to Oxford in the summer term, in order to beat up for writers for his publication; on that occasion I became known to him through Mr. Palmer. His reputation and position came in aid of his obvious fitness, in point of character and intellect, to become the centre of an ecclesiastical movement, if such a movement were to depend on the action of a party. His delicate health, his premature death, would have frustrated the expectation, even though the new school of opinion had been more exactly thrown into the shape of a party, than in fact was the case. But he zealously backed up the first efforts of those who were principals in it; and, when he went abroad to die, in 1838, he allowed me the solace of expressing my feelings of attachment and gratitude to him by addressing him, in the dedication of a volume of my Sermons, as the man 'who, when hearts were failing, bade us stir up the gift that was in us, and betake ourselves to our true Mother.'

But there were other reasons, besides Mr. Rose's state of health, which hindered those who so much admired him from availing themselves of his close co-operation in the coming fight. United as both he and they were in the general scope of the Movement, they were in discordance with each other from the first in their estimate of the means to be adopted for attaining it. Mr. Rose had a position in the Church, a name, and serious responsibilities; he had direct ecclesiastical superiors; he had intimate relations with his own University, and a large clerical connexion through the country. Froude and I were nobodies; with no characters to lose, and no antecedents to fetter us. Rose could not go a-head across country, as Froude had no scruples in doing. Froude was a bold rider, as on horseback, so also in his speculations. After a long conversation with him on the logical bearing of his principles, Mr. Rose said of him with quiet humour, that 'he did not seem to be afraid of inferences.' It was simply the truth; Froude had that strong hold of first principles, and that keen perception of their value, that he was comparatively indifferent to the revolutionary action which would attend on their application to a given state of things; whereas in the thoughts of Rose, as a practical man, existing facts had the precedence of every other idea, and the chief test of the soundness of a line of policy lay in the consideration whether it would work. This was one of the first questions, which, as it seemed to me, on every occasion occurred to his mind. With Froude, Erastianism, – that is, the union (so he viewed it) of Church and State, – was the parent, or if not the parent, the serviceable and sufficient tool, of liberalism. Till that union was snapped, Christian doctrine never could be safe; and, while he well knew how high and unselfish was the temper of Mr. Rose, yet he used to apply to him an epithet, reproachful in his own mouth; – Rose was a 'conservative.' By bad luck, I brought out this word to Mr. Rose in a letter[6] of my own, which I wrote to him in criticism of something he had inserted in his Magazine: I got a vehement rebuke for my pains, for though Rose pursued a conservative line, he had as high a disdain, as Froude could have, of a worldly ambition, and an extreme sensitiveness of such an imputation.

But there was another reason still, and a more elementary one, which severed Mr. Rose from the Oxford Movement. Living movements do not come of committees, nor are great ideas worked out through the post, even though it had been the penny post.[7] This principle deeply penetrated both Froude and myself from the first, and recommended to us the course which things soon took spontaneously, and without set purpose of our own. Universities are the natural centres of intellectual movements. How could men act together, whatever was their zeal, unless they were united in a sort of individuality? Now, first, we had no unity of place. Mr. Rose was in Suffolk, Mr. Perceval in Surrey,

Mr. Keble in Gloucestershire;[8] Hurrell Froude had to go for his health to Barbadoes. Mr. Palmer was indeed in Oxford; this was an important advantage, and told well in the first months of the Movement; – but another condition, besides that of place, was required.

A far more essential unity was that of antecedents, – a common history, common memories, an intercourse of mind with mind in the past, and a progress and increase in that intercourse in the present. Mr. Perceval, to be sure, was a pupil of Mr. Keble's; but Keble, Rose, and Palmer, represented distinct parties, or at least tempers, in the Establishment. Mr. Palmer had many conditions of authority and influence. He was the only really learned man among us. He understood theology as a science; he was practised in the scholastic mode of controversial writing; and, I believe, was as well acquainted, as he was dissatisfied, with the Catholic schools. He was as decided in his religious views, as he was cautious and even subtle in their expression, and gentle in their enforcement. But he was deficient in depth; and besides, coming from a distance, he never had really grown into an Oxford man, nor was he generally received as such; nor had he any insight into the force of personal influence and congeniality of thought in carrying out a religious theory, – a condition which Froude and I considered essential to any true success in the stand which had to be made against Liberalism. Mr. Palmer had a certain connexion, as it may be called, in the Establishment, consisting of high Church dignitaries, Archdeacons, London Rectors, and the like, who belonged to what was commonly called the high-and-dry school. They were far more opposed than even he was to the irresponsible action of individuals. Of course their *beau idéal* in ecclesiastical action was a board of safe sound, sensible men. Mr. Palmer was their organ and representative; and he wished for a Committee, an Association, with rules and meetings, to protect the interests of the Church in its existing peril. He was in some measure supported by Mr. Perceval.

I, on the other hand, had out of my own head begun the Tracts;[9] and these, as representing the antagonist principle of personality, were looked upon by Mr. Palmer's friends with considerable alarm. The great point at the time with these good men in London, – some of them men of the highest principle,

and far from influenced by what we used to call Erastianism, –
was to put down the Tracts. I, as their editor, and mainly their
author, was of course willing to give way. Keble and Froude
advocated their continuance strongly, and were angry with me
for consenting to stop them. Mr. Palmer shared the anxiety of his
own friends; and, kind as were his thoughts of us, he still not
unnaturally felt, for reasons of his own, some fidget and nervous-
ness at the course which his Oriel friends were taking. Froude,
for whom he had a real liking, took a high tone in his project of
measures for dealing with bishops and clergy, which must have
shocked and scandalized him considerably. As for me, there was
matter enough in the early Tracts to give him equal disgust; and
doubtless I much tasked his generosity, when he had to defend
me, whether against the London dignitaries or the country
clergy. Oriel, from the time of Dr. Copleston to Dr. Hampden,[10]
had had a name far and wide for liberality of thought; it had
received a formal recognition from the *Edinburgh Review*,[11] if my
memory serves me truly, as the school of speculative philosophy
in England; and on one occasion, in 1833, when I presented
myself, with some of the first papers of the Movement, to a
country clergyman in Northamptonshire, he paused awhile, and
then, eyeing me with significance, asked, 'Whether Whately was
at the bottom of them?'

Mr. Perceval wrote to me in support of the judgment of Mr.
Palmer and the dignitaries. I replied in a letter,[12] which he
afterwards published. 'As to the Tracts,' I said to him (I quote my
own words from his Pamphlet), 'every one has his own taste.
You object to some things, another to others. If we altered to
please every one, the effect would be spoiled. They were not
intended as symbols *ê cathedrâ*,[13] but as the expression of individual minds; and individuals, feeling strongly, while on the one
hand, they are incidentally faulty in mode or language, are still
peculiarly effective. No great work was done by a system;
whereas systems rise out of individual exertions. Luther was an
individual. The very faults of an individual excite attention; he
loses, but his cause (if good and he powerful-minded) gains. This
is the way of things; we promote truth by a self-sacrifice.'

The visit which I made to the Northamptonshire Rector was
only one of a series of similar expedients, which I adopted

during the year 1833. I called upon clergy in various parts of the country, whether I was acquainted with them or not, and I attended at the houses of friends where several of them were from time to time assembled. I do not think that much came of such attempts, nor were they quite in my way. Also I wrote various letters to clergymen, which fared not much better, except that they advertised the fact, that a rally in favour of the Church was commencing. I did not care whether my visits were made to high Church or low Church; I wished to make a strong pull in union with all who were opposed to the principles of liberalism, whoever they might be. Giving my name to the Editor, I commenced a series[14] of letters in the *Record* Newspaper: they ran to a considerable length; and were borne by him with great courtesy and patience. The heading given to them was, 'Church Reform.' The first was on the revival of Church Discipline; the second, on its Scripture proof; the third, on the application of the doctrine; the fourth was an answer to objections; the fifth was on the benefits of discipline. And then the series was abruptly brought to a termination. I had said what I really felt, and what was also in keeping with the strong teaching of the Tracts, but I suppose the Editor discovered in me some divergence from his own line of thought; for at length he sent a very civil letter, apologising for the non-appearance of my sixth communication, on the ground that it contained an attack upon 'Temperance Societies,'[15] about which he did not wish a controversy in his columns. He added, however, his serious regret at the theological views of the Tracts. I had subscribed a small sum in 1828 towards the first start of the *Record*.

Acts of the officious character, which I have been describing, were uncongenial to my natural temper, to the genius of the Movement, and to the historical mode of its success: – they were the fruit of that exuberant and joyous energy with which I had returned from abroad, and which I never had before or since. I had the exultation of health restored, and home regained. While I was at Palermo and thought of the breadth of the Mediterranean, and the wearisome journey across France, I could not imagine how I was ever to get to England; but now I was amid familiar scenes and faces once more. And my health and strength came back to me with such a rebound, that some friends at

Oxford, on seeing me, did not well know that it was I, and hesitated before they spoke to me. And I had the consciousness that I was employed in that work which I had been dreaming about, and which I felt to be so momentous and inspiring. I had a supreme confidence in our cause; we were upholding that primitive Christianity which was delivered for all time by the early teachers of the Church, and which was registered and attested in the Anglican formularies and by the Anglican divines. That ancient religion had well-nigh faded away out of the land, through the political changes of the last 150 years, and it must be restored. It would be in fact a second Reformation: – a better reformation, for it would be a return not to the sixteenth century, but to the seventeenth.[16] No time was to be lost, for the Whigs had come to do their worst, and the rescue might come too late. Bishopricks were already in course of suppression; Church property was in course of confiscation; Sees would soon be receiving unsuitable occupants. We knew enough to begin preaching upon, and there was no one else to preach. I felt as on board a vessel, which first gets under weigh, and then the deck is cleared out, and luggage and live stock stowed away into their proper receptacles.

Nor was it only that I had confidence in our cause, both in itself, and in its polemical force, but also, on the other hand, I despised every rival system of doctrine and its arguments too. As to the high[17] Church and the low Church, I thought that the one had not much more of a logical basis than the other; while I had a thorough contempt for the controversial position of the latter. I had a real respect for the character of many of the advocates of each party, but that did not give cogency to their arguments; and I thought, on the contrary, that the Apostolical form of doctrine was essential and imperative, and its grounds of evidence impregnable. Owing to this supreme confidence, it came to pass at that time, that there was a double aspect in my bearing towards others, which it is necessary for me to enlarge upon. My behaviour had a mixture in it both of fierceness and of sport; and on this account, I dare say, it gave offence to many; nor am I here defending it.

I wished men to agree with me, and I walked with them step by step, as far as they would go; this I did sincerely; but if they would stop, I did not much care about it, but walked on, with some satisfaction that I had brought them so far. I liked to make them preach the truth without knowing it, and encouraged them to do so. It was a satisfaction to me that the *Record* had allowed me to say so much in its columns, without remonstrance. I was amused to hear of one of the Bishops, who, on reading an early Tract on the Apostolical Succession, could not make up his mind whether he held the doctrine or not. I was not distressed at the wonder or anger of dull and self-conceited men, at propositions which they did not understand. When a correspondent, in good faith, wrote to a newspaper, to say that the 'Sacrifice of the Holy Eucharist,' spoken of in the Tract, was a false print for 'Sacrament,' I thought the mistake too pleasant to be corrected before I was asked about it. I was not unwilling to draw an opponent on step by step, by virtue of his own opinions, to the brink of some intellectual absurdity, and to leave him to get back as he could. I was not unwilling to play with a man, who asked me impertinent questions. I think I had in my mouth the words of the Wise man,[18] 'Answer a fool according to his folly,' especially if he was prying or spiteful. I was reckless of the gossip which was circulated about me; and, when I might easily have set it right, did not deign to do so. Also I used irony in conversation, when matter-of-fact men would not see what I meant.

This kind of behaviour was a sort of habit with me. If I have ever trifled with my subject, it was a more serious fault. I never used arguments which I saw clearly to be unsound. The nearest approach which I remember to such conduct, but which I consider was clear of it nevertheless, was in the case of Tract 15.[19] The matter of this Tract was furnished to me by a friend, to whom I had applied for assistance, but who did not wish to be mixed up with the publication. He gave it me, that I might throw it into shape, and I took his arguments as they stood. In the chief portion of the Tract I fully agreed; for instance, as to what it says about the Council of Trent; but there were arguments, or some argument, in it which I did not follow; I do not recollect what it was. Froude, I think, was disgusted with the whole Tract, and accused me of *economy* in publishing it. It is principally through Mr Froude's *Remains* that this word has got into our language. I think, I defended myself with arguments such as these: – that, as every one knew, the Tracts were written by various persons who agreed together in their doctrine, but not always in the arguments by which it was to be proved; that we must be tolerant of difference of opinion among ourselves; that the author of the Tract had a right to his own opinion, and that the argument in question was ordinarily received; that I did not give my own name or authority, nor was asked for my personal belief, but only acted instrumentally, as one might translate a friend's book into a foreign language. I account these to be good arguments; nevertheless I feel also that such practices admit of easy abuse and are consequently dangerous; but then, again, I feel also this – that if all such mistakes were to be severely visited, not many men in public life would be left with a character for honour and honesty.

This absolute confidence in my cause, which led me to the negligence or wantonness which I have been instancing, also laid me open, not unfairly, to the opposite charge of fierceness in certain steps which I took, or words which I published. In the *Lyra Apostolica*,[20] I have said that before learning to love, we must 'learn to hate;' though I had explained my words by adding 'hatred of sin.' In one of my first Sermons[21] I said, 'I do not shrink from uttering my firm conviction that it would be a gain to the country were it vastly more superstitious, more bigoted, more gloomy, more fierce in its religion than at present it shows itself to be.' I added, of course, that it would be an absurdity to suppose such tempers of mind desirable in themselves. The corrector of the press bore these strong epithets till he got to 'more fierce,' and then he put in the margin a *query*. In the very first page of the first Tract, I said of the Bishops, that, 'black event though it would be for the country, yet we could not wish them a more blessed termination of their course, than the spoiling of their goods and martyrdom.' In consequence of a passage[22] in my work upon the Arian History, a Northern dignitary[23] wrote to accuse me of wishing to re-establish the blood and torture of the Inquisition. Contrasting heretics and heresiarchs, I had said, 'The latter should meet with no mercy: he assumes the office of the Tempter; and, so far forth as his error goes, must be dealt with by the competent authority, as if he were embodied evil. To spare him is a false and dangerous pity. It is to endanger the souls of thousands, and it is uncharitable towards himself.' I cannot deny that this is a very fierce passage; but Arius[24] was banished, not burned;[25] and it is only fair to myself to say that neither at this, nor any other time of my life, not even when I was fiercest, could I have even cut off a Puritan's ears, and I think the sight of a Spanish *auto-da-fè* would have been the death of me. Again, when one[26] of my friends, of liberal and evangelical opinions, wrote to expostulate with me on the course I was taking, I said that we would ride over him and his, as Othniel[27] prevailed over Chushan-rishathaim, king of Mesopotamia. Again, I would have no dealings[28] with my brother, and I put my conduct upon a syllogism. I said, 'St. Paul[29] bids us avoid those who cause divisions; you cause divisions: therefore I must avoid you.' I dissuaded a lady from attending the marriage of a sister who had seceded from the Anglican Church. No wonder that Blanco White, who had known me under such different circumstances, now hearing the general course that I was taking, was amazed at the change which he recognized in me. He speaks bitterly and unfairly of me in his letters contemporaneously with the first years of the Movement; but in 1839, on looking back, he uses terms of me, which it would be hardly modest in me to quote, were it not that what he says of me in praise occurs in the midst of blame. He says: 'In this party [the anti-Peel, in 1829] I found, to my great surprise, my dear friend, Mr. Newman of Oriel. As he had been one of the annual Petitioners to Parliament for Catholic Emancipation, his sudden union with the most violent bigots was inexplicable to me. That change was the first manifestation of the mental revolution, which has suddenly made him one of the leading persecutors of Dr. Hampden,[30] and the most active and influential member of that association called the Puseyite party, from which we have those very strange productions, entitled, *Tracts for the Times*. While stating these public facts, my heart feels a pang at the recollection of the affectionate and mutual friendship between that excellent man and myself; a friendship, which his principles of orthodoxy could not allow him to continue in regard to one, whom he now regards as inevitably doomed to eternal perdition. Such is the venomous character of orthodoxy. What mischief must it create in a bad heart and narrow mind, when it can work so effectually for evil, in one of the most benevolent of bosoms, and one of the ablest of minds, in the amiable, the intellectual, the refined John Henry Newman!' (Vol. iii. p. 131.)[31] He adds that I would have nothing to do with him, a circumstance which I do not recollect, and very much doubt.

I have spoken of my firm confidence in my position; and now let me state more definitely what the position was which I took up, and the propositions about which I was so confident. These were three: –

1. First was the principle of dogma: my battle was with liberalism; by liberalism I mean the anti-dogmatic principle and its developments. This was the first point on which I was certain. Here I make a remark: persistence in a given belief is no sufficient test of its truth: but departure from it is at least a slur upon the man who has felt so certain about it. In proportion, then, as I had in 1832 a strong persuasion of the truth of opinions which I have since given up, so far a sort of guilt attaches to me, not only for that vain confidence, but for all the various proceedings which were the consequence of it. But under this first head I have the satisfaction of feeling that I have nothing to retract, and nothing to repent of. The main principle of the movement is as dear to me now, as it ever was. I have changed in many things: in this I have not. From the age of fifteen, dogma has been the fundamental principle of my religion: I know no other religion; I cannot enter into the idea of any other sort of religion; religion, as a mere sentiment, is to me a dream and a mockery. As well can there be filial love without the fact of a father, as devotion without the fact of a Supreme Being. What I held in 1816, I held in 1833, and I hold in 1864. Please God, I shall hold it to the end. Even when I was under Dr. Whately's influence, I had no temptation to be less zealous for the great dogmas of the faith, and at various times I used to resist such trains of thought on his part as seemed to me (rightly or wrongly) to obscure them. Such was the fundamental principle of the Movement of 1833.

2. Secondly, I was confident in the truth of a certain definite religious teaching, based upon this foundation of dogma; viz. that

there was a visible Church, with sacraments and rites which are the channels of invisible grace. I thought that this was the doctrine of Scripture, of the early Church, and of the Anglican Church. Here again, I have not changed in opinion; I am as certain now on this point as I was in 1833, and have never ceased to be certain. In 1834 and the following years I put this ecclesiastical doctrine on a broader basis, after reading Laud,[32] Bramhall[33] and Stillingfleet[34] and other Anglican divines on the one hand, and after prosecuting the study of the Fathers on the other; but the doctrine of 1833 was strengthened in me, not changed. When I began the *Tracts for the Times* I rested the main doctrine, of which I am speaking, upon Scripture, on the Anglican Prayer Book, and on St. Ignatius's Epistles.[35] (1) As to the existence of a visible Church, I especially argued out the point from Scripture, in Tract 11,[36] viz. from the Acts of the Apostles and the Epistles. (2) As to the Sacraments and Sacramental rites, I stood on the Prayer Book. I appealed to the Ordination Service, in which the Bishop says, 'Receive the Holy Ghost;' to the Visitation Service, which teaches confession and absolution; to the Baptismal Service, in which the Priest speaks of the child after baptism as regenerate; to the Catechism, in which Sacramental Communion is receiving 'verily and indeed the Body and Blood of Christ;' to the Commination Service,[37] in which we are told to do 'works of penance;' to the Collects, Epistles, and Gospels, to the calendar and rubrics, portions of the Prayer Book, wherein we find the festivals of the Apostles, notice of certain other Saints, and days of fasting and abstinence.

(3) And further, as to the Episcopal system, I founded it upon the Epistles of St. Ignatius, which inculcated it in various ways. One passage[38] especially impressed itself upon me: speaking of cases of disobedience to ecclesiastical authority, he says, 'A man does not deceive that Bishop whom he sees, but he practises rather with the Bishop Invisible, and so the question is not with flesh, but with God, who knows the secret heart.' I wished to act on this principle to the letter, and I may say with confidence that I never consciously transgressed it. I loved to act as feeling myself in my Bishop's sight, as if it were the sight of God. It was one of my special supports and safeguards against myself; I could not go very wrong while I had reason to believe that I was in no

respect displeasing him. It was not a mere formal obedience to
rule that I put before me, but I desired to please him personally,
as I considered him set over me by the Divine Hand. I was
strict in observing my clerical engagements, not only because
they *were* engagements, but because I considered myself simply
as the servant and instrument of my Bishop. I did not care
much for the Bench of Bishops, except as they might be the
voice of my Church: nor should I have cared much for a
Provincial Council; nor for a Diocesan Synod presided over by
my Bishop; all these matters seemed to me to be *jure ecclesiastico*,[39]
but what to me was *jure divino*[40] was the voice of my Bishop in
his own person. My own Bishop was my Pope; I knew no
other; the successor of the Apostles, the Vicar of Christ. This
was but a practical exhibition of the Anglican theory of Church
Government, as I had already drawn it out myself, after various
Anglican Divines. This continued all through my course; when
at length, in 1845, I wrote to Bishop Wiseman, in whose Vicariate[41] I found myself, to announce my conversion, I could find
nothing better to say to him than that I would obey the Pope as
I had obeyed my own Bishop in the Anglican Church. My duty
to him was my point of honour; his disapprobation was the one
thing which I could not bear. I believe it to have been a
generous and honest feeling; and in consequence I was rewarded
by having all my time for ecclesiastical superior a man, whom,
had I had a choice, I should have preferred, out and out, to any
other Bishop on the Bench, and for whose memory I have a
special affection, Dr. Bagot[42] – a man of noble mind, and as
kind-hearted and as considerate as he was noble. He ever sympathized with me in my trials which followed; it was my own
fault, that I was not brought into more familiar personal relations
with him, than it was my happiness to be. May his name be ever
blessed!

And now in concluding my remarks on the second point on
which my confidence rested, I repeat that here again I have no
retractation to announce as to its main outline. While I am now
as clear in my acceptance of the principle of dogma, as I was in
1833 and 1816, so again I am now as firm in my belief of a
visible Church, of the authority of Bishops, of the grace of the
sacraments, of the religious worth of works of penance, as I was

in 1833. I have added Articles to my Creed; but the old ones, which I then held with a divine faith, remain.

3. But now, as to the third point on which I stood in 1833, and which I have utterly renounced and trampled upon since, – my then view of the Church of Rome; – I will speak about it as exactly as I can. When I was young, as I have said already, and after I was grown up, I thought the Pope to be Antichrist. At Christmas 1824–5 I preached a sermon to that effect. But in 1827 I accepted eagerly the stanza[43] in the *Christian Year*, which many people thought too charitable, 'Speak *gently* of thy sister's fall.' From the time that I knew Froude I got less and less bitter on the subject. I spoke (successively, but I cannot tell in what order or at what dates) of the Roman Church as being bound up with 'the *cause* of Antichrist,' as being *one* of the '*many* antichrists' foretold by St. John, as being influenced by 'the *spirit* of Antichrist,' and as having something 'very Antichristian' or 'unchristian' about her. From my boyhood and in 1824 I considered, after Protestant authorities, that St. Gregory I.[44] about A.D. 600 was the first Pope that was Antichrist, though, in spite of this, he was also a great and holy man; but in 1832–3 I thought the Church of Rome was bound up with the cause of Antichrist by the Council of Trent.[45] When it was that in my deliberate judgment I gave up the notion altogether in any shape, that some special reproach was attached to her name, I cannot tell; but I had a shrinking from renouncing it, even when my reason so ordered me, from a sort of conscience or prejudice, I think up to 1843. Moreover, at least during the Tract Movement, I thought the essence of her offence to consist in the honours which she paid to the Blessed Virgin and the Saints; and the more I grew in devotion, both to the Saints and to our Lady, the more impatient was I at the Roman practices, as if those glorified creations of God must be gravely shocked, if pain could be theirs, at the undue veneration of which they were the objects.

On the other hand, Hurrell Froude in his familiar conversations was always tending to rub the idea out of my mind. In a passage of one of his letters from abroad, alluding, I suppose, to what I used to say in opposition to him, he observes: "I think people are injudicious who talk against the Roman Catholics for worshipping Saints, and honouring the Virgin and images, &c. These things may perhaps be idolatrous; I cannot make up my mind about it; but to my mind it is the Carnival that is real practical idolatry, as it is written, "the people sat down to eat and drink, and rose up to play".' The Carnival, I observe in passing, is, in fact, one of those very excesses, to which, for at least three centuries, religious Catholics have ever opposed themselves, as we see in the life of St. Philip,[46] to say nothing of the present day; but this we did not then know. Moreover, from Froude I learned to admire the great medieval Pontiffs; and, of course, when I had come to consider the Council of Trent to be the turning-point of the history of Christian Rome, I found myself as free, as I was rejoiced, to speak in their praise. Then, when I was abroad, the sight of so many great places, venerable shrines, and noble churches, much impressed my imagination. And my heart was touched also. Making an expedition on foot across some wild country in Sicily, at six in the morning, I came upon a small church; I heard voices, and I looked in. It was crowded, and the congregation was singing. Of course it was the mass, though I did not know it at the time. And, in my weary days at Palermo, I was not ungrateful for the comfort which I had received in frequenting the churches; nor did I ever forget it. Then, again, her zealous maintenance of the doctrine and the rule of celibacy, which I recognized as Apostolic, and her faithful agreement with Antiquity in so many other points which were dear to me, was an argument as well as a plea in favour of the great Church of Rome. Thus I learned to have tender feelings towards her; but still my reason was not affected at all. My judgment was against her, when viewed as an institution, as truly as it ever had been.

This conflict between reason and affection I expressed in one of the early Tracts, published July, 1834. 'Considering the high gifts and the strong claims of the Church of Rome and its dependencies on our admiration, reverence, love, and gratitude; how could we withstand it, as we do, how could we refrain from being melted into tenderness, and rushing into communion with it, but for the words of Truth itself, which bid us prefer It to the whole world? "He that loveth father or mother more than Me, is not worthy of Me." How could "we learn to be severe, and execute judgment," but for the warning of Moses against even a divinely-gifted teacher, who should preach new gods; and the anathema of St. Paul even against Angels and Apostles, who should bring in a new doctrine?' – *Records, No. 24.*[47] My feeling was something like that of a man, who is obliged in a court of justice to bear witness against a friend; or like my own now, when I have said, and shall say, so many things on which I had rather be silent.

As a matter, then, of simple conscience, though it went against my feelings, I felt it to be a duty to protest against the Church of Rome. But besides this, it was a duty, because the prescription of such a protest was a living principle of my own Church, as expressed not simply in a *catena*[48] but by a *consensus* of her divines, and by the voice of her people. Moreover, such a protest was necessary as an integral portion of her controversial basis; for I adopted the argument of Bernard Gilpin,[49] that Protestants 'were *not able* to give any *firm and solid* reason of the separation besides this, to wit, that the Pope is Antichrist.' But while I thus thought such a protest to be based upon truth, and to be a religious duty, and a rule of Anglicanism, and a necessity of the case, I did not at all like the work. Hurrell Froude attacked me for doing it; and, besides, I felt that my language had a vulgar and rhetorical look about it. I believed, and really measured, my words, when I used them; but I knew that I had a temptation, on the other hand, to say against Rome as much as ever I could, in order to protect myself against the charge of Popery.

And now I come to the very point, for which I have introduced the subject of my feelings about Rome. I felt such confidence in the substantial justice of the charges which I advanced against her, that I considered them to be a safeguard and an assurance that no harm could ever arise from the freest exposition of what I used to call Anglican principles. All the world was astounded at what Froude and I were saying: men said that it was sheer Popery. I answered, 'True, we seem to be making straight for it; but go on awhile, and you will come to a deep chasm across the path, which makes real approximation impossible.' And I urged in addition, that many Anglican divines had been accused of Popery, yet had died in their Anglicanism; – now, the ecclesiastical principles which I professed, they had professed also; and the judgment against Rome which they had formed, I had formed also. Whatever deficiencies then had to be supplied in the existing

Anglican system, and however boldly I might point them out, any how that system would not in the process be brought nearer to the special creed of Rome, and might be mended in spite of her. In that very agreement of the two forms of faith, close as it might seem, would really be found, on examination, the elements and principles of an essential discordance.

It was with this absolute persuasion on my mind that I fancied that there could be no rashness in giving to the world in fullest measure the teaching and the writings of the Fathers. I thought that the Church of England was substantially founded upon them. I did not know all that the Fathers had said, but I felt that, even when their tenets happened to differ from the Anglican, no harm could come of reporting them. I said out what I was clear they had said; I spoke vaguely and imperfectly, of what I thought they said, or what some of them had said. Any how, no harm could come of bending the crooked stick the other way, in the process of straightening it; it was impossible to break it. If there was anything in the Fathers of a startling character, this would be only for a time; it would admit of explanation, or it might suggest something profitable to Anglicans; it could not lead to Rome. I express this view of the matter in a passage of the Preface[50] to the first volume, which I edited, of the *Library of the Fathers*. Speaking of the strangeness at first sight, in the judgment of the present day, of some of their principles and opinions, I bid the reader go forward hopefully, and not indulge his criticism till he knows more about them, than he will learn at the outset. 'Since the evil,' I say, 'is in the nature of the case itself, we can do no more than have patience, and recommend patience to others, and with the racer in the Tragedy, look forward steadily and hopefully to the *event*, τῷ τέλει πίστιν φέρων,[51] when, as we trust, all that is inharmonious and anomalous in the details, will at length be practically smoothed.'

Such was the position, such the defences, such the tactics, by which I thought that it was both incumbent on us, and possible for us, to meet that onset of Liberal principles, of which we were all in immediate anticipation, whether in the Church or in the University. And during the first year of the Tracts, the attack[52] upon the University began. In November, 1834, was sent to me by Dr. Hampden[53] the second edition of his Pamphlet, entitled,

Observations on Religious Dissent, with particular reference to the use of religious tests in the University. In this Pamphlet it was maintained, that 'Religion is distinct from Theological Opinion,' pp. 1, 28, 30, &c.; that it is but a common prejudice to identify theological propositions methodically deduced and stated, with the simple religion of Christ, p. 1; that under Theological Opinion were to be placed the Trinitarian doctrine, p. 27, and the Unitarian, p. 19; that a dogma was a theological opinion formally insisted on, pp. 20, 21; that speculation always left an opening for improvement, p. 22; that the Church of England was not dogmatic in its spirit, though the wording of its formularies might often carry the sound of dogmatism, p. 23.

I acknowledged the receipt of this work in the following letter[54]: –

'The kindness which has led to your presenting me with your late Pamphlet, encourages me to hope that you will forgive me, if I take the opportunity it affords of expressing to you my very sincere and deep regret that it has been published. Such an opportunity I could not let slip without being unfaithful to my own serious thoughts on the subject.

'While I respect the tone of piety which the Pamphlet displays, I dare not trust myself to put on paper my feelings about the principles contained in it; tending as they do, in my opinion, altogether to make shipwreck of Christian faith. I also lament, that, by its appearance, the first step has been taken towards interrupting that peace and mutual good understanding which has prevailed so long in this place, and which, if once seriously disturbed, will be succeeded by dissensions the more intractable, because justified in the minds of those who resist innovation by a feeling of imperative duty.'

Since that time Phaeton has got into the chariot of the sun;[55] we, alas! can only look on, and watch him down the steep of heaven. Meanwhile, the lands, which he is passing over, suffer from his driving.

Such was the commencement of the assault of Liberalism upon the old orthodoxy of Oxford and England; and it could not have been broken,[56] as it was, for so long a time, had not a great change taken place in the circumstances of that counter-movement which had already started with the view of resisting it. For myself, I was not the person to take the lead of a party; I never was, from first to last, more than a leading author of a school; nor did I ever wish to be anything else. This is my own account of the matter; and I say it, neither as intending to disown the responsibility of what was done, or as if ungrateful to those who at that time made more of me than I deserved, and did more for my sake and at my bidding than I realized myself. I am giving my history from my own point of sight, and it is as follows: – I had lived for ten years among my personal friends; the greater part of the time, I had been influenced, not influencing; and at no time have I acted on others, without their acting upon me. As is the custom of a University, I had lived with my private, nay, with some of my public, pupils, and with the junior fellows of my College, without form or distance, on a footing of equality. Thus it was through friends, younger, for the most part, than myself, that my principles were spreading. They heard what I said in conversation, and told it to others. Under-graduates in due time took their degree, and became private tutors themselves. In their new *status*, they in turn preached the opinions, with which they had already become acquainted. Others went down to the country, and became curates of parishes. Then they had down from London parcels, of the Tracts, and other publications. They placed them in the shops of local booksellers, got them into newspapers, introduced them to clerical meetings, and converted more or less their Rectors and their brother curates. Thus the Movement, viewed with relation to myself, was but a floating opinion; it was not a power. It never would have been a power, if it had remained in my hands. Years after, a friend,[57] writing to me in remonstrance at the excesses, as he thought them, of my disciples, applied to me my own verse about St. Gregory Nazianzen,[58] 'Thou couldst a people raise, but couldst not rule.' At the time that he wrote to me, I had special impediments in the way of such an exercise of power; but at no time could I exercise over others that authority, which under the circumstances was imperatively required. My great principle ever was, Live and let live. I never had the staidness or dignity necessary for a leader. To the last I never recognised the hold I had over young men. Of late years I have read and heard that they even imitated me in various ways. I was quite unconscious of it, and I think my immediate friends knew too well how disgusted I should be at such proceedings, to have the heart to tell me. I felt great impatience at our being called a party, and would not allow that we were such. I had a lounging, free-and-easy way of carrying things on. I exercised no sufficient censorship upon the Tracts. I did not confine them to the writings of such persons as agreed in all things with myself; and, as to my own Tracts, I printed on them a notice to the effect, that any one who pleased, might make what use he would of them, and reprint them with alterations if he chose, under the conviction that their main scope could not be damaged by such a process. It was the same with me afterwards, as regards other publications. For two years I furnished a certain number of sheets for the *British Critic*[59] from myself and my friends, while a gentleman was editor, a man of splendid talent, who, however, was scarcely an acquaintance of mine, and had no sympathy with the Tracts. When I was Editor myself, from 1838 to 1841, in my very first number I suffered to appear a critique unfavourable to my work on Justification, which had been published a few months before, from a feeling of propriety, because I had put the book into the hands of the writer[60] who so handled it. Afterwards I suffered an article[61] against the Jesuits to appear in it, of which I did not like the tone. When I had to provide a curate for my new church at Littlemore, I engaged a friend[62], by no fault of his, who, before he had entered into his charge, preached a sermon, either in depreciation of baptismal regeneration, or of Dr. Pusey's view of it. I showed a similar easiness as to the Editors[63] who helped me in the separate volumes of Fleury's *Church History*; they were able, learned, and excellent men, but their after-history has shown how little my choice of them was influenced by any notion I could have had of any intimate agreement of opinion between them and myself. I shall have to make the same remark in its place concerning the *Lives of the English Saints*, which subsequently appeared. All this may seem inconsistent with what I have said of my fierceness. I am not bound to account for it; but there have been men before me, fierce in act, yet tolerant and moderate in their reasonings; at least, so I read history. However, such was the case, and such its effect upon the Tracts. These at first starting were short, hasty, and some of them ineffective; and at the end of the year, when collected into a volume, they had a slovenly appearance.

It was under these circumstances, that Dr. Pusey joined us. I had known him well since 1827–8, and had felt for him an enthusiastic admiration. I used to call him ὁ μέγας.[64] His great learning, his immense diligence, his scholarlike mind, his simple devotion to the cause of religion, overcame me; and great of course was my joy, when in the last days of 1833 he showed a disposition to make common cause with us. His Tract *On Fasting*[65] appeared as one of the series with the date of December 21. He was not, however, I think, fully associated in the Movement till 1835 and 1836, when he published his Tract *On Baptism*[66] and started[67] the *Library of the Fathers*. He at once gave to us a position and a name. Without him we should have had little chance, especially at the early date of 1834, of making any serious resistance to the Liberal aggression. But Dr. Pusey was a Professor and Canon of Christ Church; he had a vast influence in consequence of his deep religious seriousness, the munificence of his charities, his Professorship, his family connexions,[68] and his easy relations with University authorities. He was to the Movement all that Mr. Rose might have been, with that indispensable addition, which was wanting to Mr. Rose, the intimate friendship and the familiar daily society of the persons who had commenced it. And he had that special claim on their attachment, which lies in the living presence of a faithful and loyal affectionateness. There was henceforth a man who could be the head and centre of the zealous people in every part of the country, who were adopting the new opinions; and not only so, but there was one who furnished the Movement with a front to the world, and gained for it a recognition from other parties in the University. In 1829, Mr. Froude, or Mr. Robert Wilberforce, or Mr. Newman were but individuals; and, when they ranged themselves in the contest of that year on the side of Sir Robert Inglis,[69] men on either side only asked with surprise how they got there, and attached no significancy to the fact; but Dr. Pusey was, to use the common expression, a host in himself; he was able to give a name, a form, and a personality, to what was without him a sort of mob; and when various parties had to meet together in order to resist the liberal acts of the Government, we of the Movement took our place by right among them.

Such was the benefit which he conferred on the Movement externally; nor were the internal advantages at all inferior to it. He was a man of large designs; he had a hopeful, sanguine mind; he had no fear of others; he was haunted by no intellectual perplexities. People are apt to say that he was once nearer to the Catholic Church than he is now; I pray God that he may be one day far nearer to the Catholic Church than he was then; for I believe that, in his reason and judgment, all the time that I knew him, he never was near to it at all. When I became a Catholic, I was often asked, 'What of Dr. Pusey?' When I said that I did not see symptoms of his doing as I had done, I was sometimes thought uncharitable. If confidence in his position is (as it is,) a first essential in the leader of a party, this Dr. Pusey possessed pre-eminently. The most remarkable instance of this, was his statement, in one of his subsequent defences of the Movement, when moreover it had advanced a considerable way in the direction of Rome, that among its more hopeful peculiarities was its 'stationariness.' He made it in good faith; it was his subjective view of it.

Dr. Pusey's influence was felt at once. He saw that there ought to be more sobriety, more gravity, more careful pains, more sense of responsibility in the Tracts and in the whole Movement. It was through him that the character of the Tracts was changed. When he gave to us his Tract *On Fasting*, he put his initials[70] to it. In 1835 he published his elaborate *Treatise on Baptism*, which was followed by other Tracts from different authors, if not of equal learning, yet of equal power and appositeness. The Catenas[71] of Anglican divines, projected by me, which occur in the Series, were executed with a like aim at greater accuracy and method. In 1836 he advertised his great project for a Translation of the Fathers: – but I must return to myself. I am not writing the history either of Dr. Pusey or of the Movement; but it is a pleasure to me to have been able to introduce here reminiscences of the place which he held in it, which have so direct a bearing on myself, that they are no digression from my narrative.

I suspect it was Dr. Pusey's influence and example which set me, and made me set others, on the larger and more careful works in defence of the principles of the Movement which followed in a course of years, – some of them demanding and receiving from their authors, such elaborate treatment that they did not make their appearance till both its temper and its fortunes had changed. I set about a work at once; one in which was brought out with precision the relation in which we stood to the Church of Rome. We could not move a step in comfort, till this was done. It was of absolute necessity and a plain duty from the first, to provide as soon as possible a large statement, which would encourage and reassure our friends, and repel the attacks of our opponents. A cry was heard on all sides of us, that the Tracts and the writings of the Fathers would lead us to become Catholics, before we were aware of it. This was loudly expressed by members of the Evangelical party, who in 1836 had joined us in making a protest in Convocation against a memorable appointment[72] of the Prime Minister. These clergymen even then avowed their desire, that the next time they were brought up to Oxford to give a vote, it might be in order to put down the Popery of the Movement. There was another reason still, and quite as important. Monsignore Wiseman, with the acuteness and zeal which might be expected from that great Prelate, had anticipated what was coming, had returned to England by 1836, had delivered Lectures[73] in London on the doctrines of Catholicism, and created an impression through the country, shared in by ourselves, that we had for our opponents in controversy, not only our brethren, but our hereditary foes. These were the circumstances, which led to my publication of '*The Prophetical Office of the Church viewed relatively to Romanism and Popular Protestantism.*'

This work[74] employed me for three years, from the beginning of 1834 to the end of 1836, and was published in 1837. It was composed, after a careful consideration and comparison of the principal Anglican divines of the 17th century. It was first written in the shape of controversial correspondence with a learned French Priest; then it was re-cast, and delivered in Lectures at St. Mary's; lastly, with considerable retrenchments and additions, it was re-written for publication.

It attempts to trace out the rudimental lines on which Christian faith and teaching proceed, and to use them as means of determining the relation of the Roman and Anglican systems to each other. In this way it shows that to confuse the two together is impossible, and that the Anglican can be as little said to tend to the Roman, as the Roman to the Anglican. The spirit of the Volume is not so gentle to the Church of Rome, as Tract 71[75] published the year before; on the contrary, it is very fierce; and this I attribute to the circumstance that the Volume is theological and didactic, whereas the Tract, being controversial, assumes as little and grants as much as possible on the points in dispute, and insists on points of agreement as well as of difference. A further and more direct reason is, that in my Volume I deal with 'Romanism' (as I call it), not so much in its formal decrees and in the substance of its creed, as in its traditional action and its authorized teaching as represented by its prominent writers; – whereas the Tract is written as if discussing the differences of the Churches with a view to a reconciliation between them. There is a further reason too, which I will state presently.

But this Volume had a larger scope than that of opposing the Roman system. It was an attempt at commencing a system of theology on the Anglican idea, and based upon Anglican authorities. Mr. Palmer, about the same time, was projecting a work of a similar nature in his own way. It was published, I think, under the title,[76] *A Treatise on the Christian Church*. As was to be expected from the author, it was a most learned, most careful composition; and in its form, I should say, polemical. So happily at least did he follow the logical method of the Roman Schools, that Father Perrone[77] in his Treatise on dogmatic theology, recognized in him a combatant of the true cast, and saluted him as a foe worthy of being vanquished. Other soldiers in that field he seems to have thought little better than the *Lanzknechts*[78] of the middle ages, and, I dare say, with very good reason. When I knew that excellent and kind-hearted man at Rome at a later time, he allowed me to put him to ample penance for those light thoughts of me, which he had once had, by encroaching on his valuable time with my theological questions. As to Mr. Palmer's book, it was one which no Anglican could write but himself, – in no sense, if I recollect aright, a tentative work. The ground of controversy was cut into squares, and then every objection had its answer. This is the proper method to adopt in teaching authoritatively young men; and the work in fact was intended for students in theology. My own book, on the other hand, was of a directly tentative and empirical character. I wished to build up an Anglican theology out of the stores which already lay cut and hewn upon the ground, the past toil of great divines. To do this could not be the work of one man; much less, could it be at once received into Anglican theology, however well it was done. This I fully recognized; and, while I trusted that my statements of doctrine would turn out to be true and important, still I wrote, to use the common phrase, 'under correction.'

There was another motive for my publishing, of a personal nature, which I think I should mention. I felt then, and all along felt, that there was an intellectual cowardice in not finding a basis in reason for my belief, and a moral cowardice in not avowing that basis. I should have felt myself less than a man, if I did not bring it out, whatever it was. This is one principal reason why I wrote and published the *Prophetical Office*. It was from the same feeling, that in the spring of 1836, at a meeting of residents on the subject of the struggle then proceeding against a Whig appointment,[79] when some one wanted us all merely to act on college and conservative grounds (as I understood him), with as few published statements as possible, I answered, that the person whom we were resisting had committed himself in writing, and that we ought to commit ourselves too. This again was a main reason for the publication of Tract 90.[80] Alas! it was my portion for whole years to remain without any satisfactory basis for my religious profession, in a state of moral sickness, neither able to acquiesce in Anglicanism, nor able to go to Rome. But I bore it, till in course of time my way was made clear to me. If here it be objected to me, that as time went on, I often in my writings hinted at things which I did not fully bring out, I submit for consideration whether this occurred except when I was in great difficulties, how to speak, or how to be silent, with due regard for the position of mind or the feelings of others. However, I may have an opportunity to say more on this subject. But to return to the *Prophetical Office*.

I thus speak in the Introduction to my Volume: –

'It is proposed,' I say, 'to offer helps towards the formation of a recognized Anglican theology in one of its departments. The present state of our divinity is as follows: the most vigorous, the clearest, the most fertile minds, have through God's mercy been employed in the service of our Church: minds too as reverential and holy, and as fully imbued with Ancient Truth, and as well versed in the writings of the Fathers, as they were intellectually gifted. This is God's great mercy indeed, for which we must ever be thankful. Primitive doctrine has been explored for us in every direction, and the original principles of the Gospel and the Church patiently brought to light. But one thing is still wanting: our champions and teachers have lived in stormy times: political and other influences have acted upon them variously in their day, and have since obstructed a careful consolidation of their judgments. We have a vast inheritance, but no inventory of our treasures. All is given us in profusion; it remains for us to catalogue, sort, distribute, select, harmonize, and complete. We have more than we know how to use; stores of learning, but little that is precise and serviceable; Catholic truth and individual opinion, first principles and the guesses of genius, all mingled in the same works, and requiring to be discriminated. We meet with truths overstated or misdirected, matters of detail variously taken, facts incompletely proved or applied, and rules inconsistently urged or discordantly interpreted. Such indeed is the state of every deep philosophy in its first stages, and therefore of theological knowledge. What we need at present for our Church's well-being, is not invention, nor originality, nor sagacity, nor even learning in our divines, at least in the first place, though all gifts of God are in a measure needed, and never can be unseasonable when used religiously, but we need peculiarly a sound judgment, patient thought, discrimination, a comprehensive mind, an abstinence from all private fancies and caprices and personal tastes, – in a word, Divine Wisdom.'

The subject of the Volume is the doctrine of the *Via Media*[81] a name which had already been applied to the Anglican system by writers of repute. It is an expressive title, but not altogether satisfactory, because it is at first sight negative. This had been the reason of my dislike to the word 'Protestant;' viz. it did not denote the profession of any particular religion at all, and was compatible with infidelity. A *Via Media* was but a receding from extremes, – therefore it needed to be drawn out into a definite shape and character: before it could have claims on our respect, it must first be shown to be one, intelligible, and consistent. This was the first condition of any reasonable treatise on the *Via Media*. The second condition, and necessary too, was not in my power. I could only hope that it would one day be fulfilled. Even if the *Via Media* were ever so positive a religious system, it was not as yet objective and real; it had no original anywhere of which it was the representative. It was at present a paper religion. This I confess in my Introduction; I say, 'Protestantism and Popery are real religions . . . but the *Via Media*, viewed as an integral system, has scarcely had existence except on paper.' I grant the objection, though I endeavour to lessen it: – 'It still remains to be tried, whether what is called Anglo-Catholicism, the religion of Andrewes,[82] Laud, Hammond,[83] Butler, and Wilson,[84] is capable of being professed, acted on, and maintained on a large sphere of action, or whether it be a mere modification or transition-state of either Romanism or popular Protestantism.' I trusted that some day it would prove to be a substantive religion.

Lest I should be misunderstood, let me observe that this hesitation about the validity of the theory of the *Via Media* implied no doubt of the three fundamental points on which it was based, as I have described them above, dogma, the sacramental system, and anti-Romanism.

Other investigations which had to be followed up were of a still more tentative character. The basis of the *Via Media*, consisting of the three elementary points, which I have just mentioned, was clear enough; but, not only had the house itself to be built upon them, but it had also to be furnished, and it is not wonderful if, after building it, both I and others erred in detail in determining what its furniture should be, what was consistent with the style of building, and what was in itself desirable. I will explain what I mean.

I had brought out in the *Prophetical Office* in what the Roman and the Anglican systems differed from each other, but less distinctly in what they agreed. I had indeed enumerated the Fundamentals, common to both, in the following passage: – 'In both systems the same Creeds are acknowledged. Besides other points in common, we both hold, that certain doctrines are necessary to be believed for salvation; we both believe in the doctrines of the Trinity, Incarnation, and Atonement; in original sin; in the necessity of regeneration; in the supernatural grace of the Sacraments; in the Apostolical succession; in the obligation of faith and obedience, and in the eternity of future punishment,' – pp. 55, 56. So much I had said, but I had not said enough. This enumeration implied a great many more points of agreement than were found in those very Articles which were fundamental. If the two Churches were thus the same in fundamentals, they were also one and the same in such plain consequences as were contained in those fundamentals and in such natural observances as outwardly represented them. It was an Anglican principle that 'the abuse of a thing doth not take away the lawful use of it;' and an Anglican Canon in 1603 had declared that the English Church had no purpose to forsake all that was held in the Churches of Italy, France, and Spain, and reverenced those ceremonies and particular points which were Apostolic. Excepting then such exceptional matters, as are implied in this avowal, whether they were many or few, all these Churches were evidently to be considered as one with the Anglican. The Catholic Church in all lands had been one from the first for many centuries; then, various portions had followed their own way to the injury, but not to the destruction, whether of truth or of charity. These portions or branches were mainly three: – the Greek, Latin, and Anglican. Each of these inherited the early undivided Church *in solido*[85] as its own possession. Each branch was identical with that early undivided Church, and in the unity of that Church it had unity with the other branches. The three branches agreed together in *all but* their later accidental errors. Some branches had retained in detail portions of Apostolical truth and usage, which the others had not; and these portions might be and should be appropriated again by the others which had let them slip. Thus, the middle age belonged to the Anglican Church, and much more did the middle age of England. The Church of the 12th century was the Church of the 19th. Dr. Howley[86] sat in the seat of St. Thomas the Martyr; Oxford was a medieval University. Saving our engagements to Prayer Book and Articles, we might breathe and live and act and speak, as in the atmosphere and climate of Henry III.'s day, or the Confessor's, or of Alfred's. And we ought to be indulgent to all that Rome taught now, as to what Rome taught then, saving our protest. We might boldly welcome, even what we did not ourselves think right to adopt. And, when we were obliged on the contrary boldly to denounce, we should do so with pain, not with exultation. By very reason of our protest, which we had made, and made *ex animo*,[87] we could agree to differ. What the members of the Bible Society did on the basis of Scripture, we could do on the basis of the Church; Trinitarian and Unitarian were further apart than Roman and Anglican. Thus we had a real wish to co-operate with Rome in all lawful things, if she would let us, and if the rules of our own Church let us; and we thought there was no better way towards the restoration of doctrinal purity and unity. And we thought that Rome was not committed by her formal decrees to all that she actually taught: and again, if her disputants had been unfair to us, or her rulers tyrannical, we bore in mind that on our side too there had been rancour and slander in our controversial attacks upon her, and violence in our political measures. As to ourselves being direct instruments in improving her belief or practice, I used to say, 'Look at home; let us first (or at least let us the while,) supply our own shortcomings, before we attempt to be physicians to any one else.' This is very much the spirit of Tract 71, to which I referred just now. I am well aware that there is a paragraph[88] inconsistent with it in the Prospectus to the *Library of the Fathers*; but I do not consider myself responsible for it. Indeed, I have no intention whatever of implying that Dr. Pusey concurred in the ecclesiastical theory, which I have been now drawing out; nor that I took it up myself except by degrees in the course of ten years. It was necessarily the growth of time. In fact, hardly any two persons, who took part in the Movement, agreed in their view of the limit to which our general principles might religiously be carried.

And now I have said enough on what I consider to have been the general objects of the various works, which I wrote, edited, or prompted in the years which I am reviewing. I wanted to bring out in a substantive form a living Church of England, in a position proper to herself, and founded on distinct principles; as far as paper could do it, as far as earnestly preaching it and influencing others towards it, could tend to make it a fact; – a living Church, made of flesh and blood, with voice, complexion, and motion and action, and a will of its own. I believe I had no private motive, and no personal aim. Nor did I ask for more than 'a fair stage and no favour,' nor expect the work would be accomplished in my days; but I thought that enough would be secured to continue it in the future, under, perhaps, more hopeful circumstances and prospects than the present.

I will mention in illustration some of the principal works, doctrinal and historical, which originated in the object which I have stated.

I wrote my *Essay on Justification*, in 1837; it was aimed at the Lutheran dictum that justification by faith only was the cardinal doctrine of Christianity. I considered that this doctrine was either a paradox[89] or a truism, – a paradox in Luther's mouth, a truism in Melanchthon's.[90] I thought that the Anglican Church followed Melanchthon, and that in consequence between Rome and Anglicanism, between high Church and low Church, there was no real intellectual difference on the point. I wished to fill up a ditch, the work of man. In this Volume again, I express my desire to build up a system of theology out of the Anglican divines, and imply that my dissertation was a tentative Inquiry. I speak in the Preface of 'offering suggestions towards a work, which must be uppermost in the mind of every true son of the English Church at this day, – the consolidation of a theological system, which, built upon those formularies, to which all clergymen are bound, may tend to inform, persuade, and absorb into itself religious minds, which hitherto have fancied, that, on the peculiar Protestant questions, they were seriously opposed to each other.' – P. vii.

In my *University Sermons*[91] there is a series of discussions upon the subject of Faith and Reason; these again were the tentative commencement of a grave and necessary work, viz. an inquiry into the ultimate basis of religious faith, prior to the distinction into Creeds.

In like manner in a Pamphlet,[92] which I published in the summer of 1838, is an attempt at placing the doctrine of the Real Presence on an intellectual basis. The fundamental idea is consonant to that to which I had been so long attached: it is the denial of the existence of space except as a subjective idea of our minds.

The *Church of the Fathers*[93] is one of the earliest productions of the Movement, and appeared in numbers in the *British Magazine*,

being written with the aim of introducing the religious sentiments, views, and customs of the first ages into the modern
Church of England.

The Translation of Fleury's *Church History* was commenced
under these circumstances: – I was fond of Fleury for a reason
which I express in the Advertisement; because it presented a sort
of photograph of ecclesiastical history without any comment
upon it. In the event, that simple representation of the early
centuries had a good deal to do with unsettling me in my
Anglicanism; but how little I could anticipate this, will be seen in
the fact that the publication of Fleury was a favourite scheme
with Mr. Rose. He proposed it to me twice, between the years
1834 and 1837; and I mention it as one out of many particulars
curiously illustrating how truly my change of opinion arose, not
from foreign influences, but from the working of my own mind,
and the accidents around me. The date, from which the portion
actually translated began, was determined by the Publisher on
reasons with which we were not concerned.

Another historical work, but drawn from original sources, was
given to the world by my old friend Mr. Bowden, being a *Life*[94]
of Pope Gregory VII. I need scarcely recall to those who have read
it, the power and the liveliness of the narrative. This composition
was the author's relaxation, on evenings and in his summer
vacations, from his ordinary engagements in London. It had
been suggested to him originally by me, at the instance of
Hurrell Froude.

The Series of the *Lives of the English Saints* was projected at
a later period, under circumstances which I shall have in the sequel to describe. Those beautiful compositions have nothing in
them, as far as I recollect, simply inconsistent with the general
objects which I have been assigning to my labours in these years,
though the immediate occasion which led to them, and the tone in
which they were written, had little that was congenial with
Anglicanism.

At a comparatively early date I drew up the Tract[95] *On the
Roman Breviary*. It frightened my own friends on its first appearance; and several years afterwards, when younger men[96] began to
translate for publication the four volumes *in extenso*, they were
dissuaded from doing so by advice to which from a sense of duty

they listened. It was an apparent accident, which introduced me to the knowledge of that most wonderful and most attractive monument of the devotion of saints. On Hurrell Froude's death, in 1836, I was asked to select one of his books as a keepsake. I selected Butler's *Analogy*; finding that it had been already chosen, I looked with some perplexity along the shelves as they stood before me, when an intimate friend[97] at my elbow said, 'Take that.' It was the Breviary which Hurrell had had with him at Barbadoes. Accordingly I took it, studied it, wrote my Tract from it, and have it on my table in constant use till this day.

That dear and familiar companion, who thus put the Breviary into my hands, is still in the Anglican Church. So, too, is that early venerated long-loved friend, together with whom I edited a work which, more perhaps than any other, caused disturbance and annoyance in the Anglican world, – Froude's *Remains*; yet, however judgments might run as to the prudence of publishing it, I never heard any one impute to Mr. Keble the very shadow of dishonesty or treachery towards his Church in so acting.

The annotated Translation[98] of the *Treatises of St. Athanasius* was of course in no sense of a tentative character; it belongs to another order of thought. This historico-dogmatic work employed me for years. I had made preparations for following it up with a doctrinal history of the heresies which succeeded to the Arian.

I should make mention also of the *British Critic*. I was Editor of it for three years, from July 1838 to July 1841. My writers belonged to various schools, some to none at all. The subjects are various, – classical, academical, political, critical, and artistic, as well as theological, and upon the Movement none are to be found which do not keep quite clear of advocating the cause of Rome.

So I went on for years up to 1841. It was, in a human point of view, the happiest time of my life. I was truly at home. I had in one of my volumes appropriated to myself the words[99] of Bramhall, 'Bees, by the instinct of nature, do love their hives, and birds their nests.' I did not suppose that such sunshine would last, though I knew not what would be its termination. It was the time of plenty, and, during its seven years, I tried to lay up as much as I could for the dearth which was to follow it. We prospered and spread. I have spoken of the doings of these years since I was a Catholic, in a passage,[100] part of which I will here quote:

'From beginnings so small,' I said, 'from elements of thought so fortuitous, with prospects so unpromising, the Anglo-Catholic party suddenly became a power in the National Church, and an object of alarm to her rulers and friends. Its originators would have found it difficult to say what they aimed at of a practical kind: rather, they put forth views and principles for their own sake, because they were true, as if they were obliged to say them; and, as they might be themselves surprised at their earnestness in uttering them, they had as great cause to be surprised at the success which attended their propagation. And, in fact, they could only say that those doctrines were in the air; that to assert was to prove, and that to explain was to persuade; and that the Movement in which they were taking part was the birth of a crisis rather than of a place. In a very few years a school of opinion was formed, fixed in its principles, indefinite and progressive in their range; and it extended itself into every part of the country. If we inquire what the world thought of it, we have still more to raise our wonder; for, not to mention the excitement it caused in England, the Movement and its party-names were known to the police of Italy and to the back-woodmen of America. And so it proceeded, getting stronger and stronger every year, till it came into collision with the Nation, and that Church of the Nation, which it began by professing especially to serve.'

The greater its success, the nearer was that collision at hand. The first threatenings of what was coming were heard in 1838. At that time, my Bishop in a Charge[101] made some light animadversions, but they *were* animadversions, on the *Tracts for the Times*. At once I offered to stop them. What took place on the occasion I prefer to state in the words in which I related it in a Pamphlet[102] addressed to him in a later year, when the blow actually came down upon me.

'In your Lordship's *Charge* for 1838,' I said, 'an allusion was made to the *Tracts for the Times*. Some opponents of the Tracts said that you treated them with undue indulgence. . . . I wrote to the Archdeacon on the subject, submitting the Tracts entirely to your Lordship's disposal. What I thought about your Charge will appear from the words I then used to him. I said, "A Bishop's lightest word *ex cathedrâ* is heavy. His judgment on a book cannot be light. It is a rare occurrence." And I offered to withdraw any of the Tracts over which I had control, if I were informed which were those to which your Lordship had objections. I afterwards wrote to your Lordship to this effect that "I trusted I might say sincerely, that I should feel a more lively pleasure in knowing that I was submitting myself to your Lordship's expressed judgment in a matter of that kind, than I could have even in the widest circulation of the volumes in question." Your Lordship did not think it necessary to proceed to such a measure, but I felt, and always have felt, that, if ever you determined on it, I was bound to obey.'

That day at length came, and I conclude this portion of my narrative, with relating the circumstances of it.

From the time that I had entered upon the duties of Public Tutor at my College, when my doctrinal views were very different from what they were in 1841, I had meditated a comment upon the Articles.[103] Then, when the Movement was in its swing, friends had said to me, 'What will you make of the Articles?' but I did not share the apprehension which their question implied. Whether, as time went on, I should have been forced, by the necessities of the original theory of the Movement, to put on paper the speculations which I had about them, I am not able to conjecture. The actual cause of my doing so, in the beginning of 1841, was the restlessness, actual and prospective, of those who neither liked the *Via Media*, nor my strong judgment against Rome. I had been enjoined, I think by my Bishop, to keep these men straight, and I wished so to do: but their tangible difficulty was subscription to the Articles; and thus the question of the Articles came before me. It was thrown in our teeth; 'How can you manage to sign the Articles? they are directly against Rome.' 'Against Rome?' I made answer, 'What do you mean by "Rome"?' and then I proceeded to make distinctions, of which I shall now give an account.

By 'Roman doctrine' might be meant one of three things: 1, the *Catholic teaching* of the early centuries; or 2, the *formal dogmas of Rome* as contained in the later Councils, especially the Council of Trent, and as condensed in the Creed of Pope Pius IV.; [104] 3, the *actual popular beliefs and usages* sanctioned by Rome in the countries in communion with it, over and above the dogmas; and these I called 'dominant errors.' Now Protestants commonly thought that in all three senses, 'Roman doctrine' was condemned in the Articles: I thought that the *Catholic teaching* was not condemned; that the *dominant errors* were; and as to the *formal dogmas* that some were, some were not, and that the line had to be drawn between them. Thus, 1. The use of Prayers for the dead was a Catholic doctrine, – not condemned in the Articles; 2. The prison of Purgatory was a Roman dogma, – which was condemned in them; but the infallibility of Ecumenical Councils was a Roman dogma, – not condemned; and 3. The fire of Purgatory was an authorized and popular error, not a dogma, – which was condemned.

Further, I considered that the difficulties, felt by the persons whom I have mentioned, mainly lay in their mistaking, 1, Catholic teaching, which was not condemned in the Articles, for Roman dogma which was condemned; and 2, Roman dogma, which was not condemned in the Articles, for dominant error which was. If they went further than this, I had nothing more to say to them.

A further motive which I had for my attempt, was the desire to ascertain the ultimate points of contrariety between the Roman and Anglican creeds, and to make them as few as possible. I thought that each creed was obscured and misrepresented by a dominant circumambient 'Popery' and 'Protestantism.'

The main thesis then of my Essay was this: – the Articles do not oppose Catholic teaching; they but partially oppose Roman dogma; they for the most part oppose the dominant errors of Rome. And the problem was, as I have said, to draw the line as to what they allowed and what they condemned.

Such being the object which I had in view, what were my prospects of widening and of defining their meaning? The prospect was encouraging; there was no doubt at all of the elasticity of the Articles: to take a palmary instance, the seventeenth[105] was assumed by one party to be Lutheran, by another Calvinistic, though the two interpretations were contradictory of each other;

why then should not other Articles be drawn up with a vagueness of an equally intense character? I wanted to ascertain what was the limit of that elasticity in the direction of Roman dogma. But next, I had a way of inquiry of my own, which I state without defending. I instanced it afterwards in my *Essay on Doctrinal Development*. That work, I believe, I have not read since I published it, and I do not doubt at all I have made many mistakes in it; − partly, from my ignorance of the details of doctrine, as the Church of Rome holds them, but partly from my impatience to clear as large a range for the *principle* of doctrinal Development (waiving the question of historical *fact*) as was consistent with the strict Apostolicity and identity of the Catholic Creed. In like manner, as regards the 39 Articles, my method of inquiry was to leap *in medias res*.[106] I wished to institute an inquiry how far, in critical fairness, the text *could* be opened; I was aiming far more at ascertaining what a man who subscribed it might hold than what he must, so that my conclusions were negative rather than positive. It was but a first essay. And I made it with the full recognition and consciousness, which I had already expressed in my *Prophetical Office*, as regards the *Via Media*, that I was making only 'a first approximation to the required solution;' − 'a series of illustrations supplying hints for the removal' of a difficulty, and with full acknowledgment 'that in minor points, whether in question of fact or of judgment, there was room for difference or error of opinion,' and that I 'should not be ashamed to own a mistake, if it were proved against me, nor reluctant to bear the just blame of it.' − *Proph. Off.* p. 31.

I will add, I was embarrassed in consequence of my wish to go as far as was possible in interpreting the Articles in the direction of Roman dogma, without disclosing what I was doing to the parties whose doubts I was meeting; who, if they understood at once the full extent of the licence which the Articles admitted, might be thereby encouraged to proceed still further than at present they found in themselves any call to go.

1. But in the way of such an attempt comes the prompt objection that the Articles were actually drawn up against 'Popery,' and therefore it was transcendently absurd and dishonest to suppose that Popery, in any shape, − patristic belief,

Tridentine dogma, or popular corruption authoritatively sanctioned, – would be able to take refuge under their text. This premiss I denied. Not any religious doctrine at all, but a political principle, was the primary English idea of 'Popery' at the date of the Reformation. And what was that political principle, and how could it best be suppressed in England? What was the great question in the days of Henry and Elizabeth? The *Supremacy*; – now, was I saying one single word in favour of the Supremacy of the Holy See, in favour of the foreign jurisdiction? No, I did not believe in it myself. Did Henry VIII. religiously hold Justification by faith only? did he disbelieve Purgatory? Was Elizabeth zealous for the marriage of the Clergy? or had she a conscience against the Mass? The Supremacy of the Pope was the essence of the 'Popery' to which, at the time of the composition of the Articles, the Supreme Head or Governor of the English Church was so violently hostile.

2. But again I said this: – let 'Popery' mean what it would in the mouths of the compilers of the Articles, let it even, for argument's sake, include the doctrines of that Tridentine Council, which was not yet over when the Articles were drawn up, and against which they could not be simply directed, yet, consider, what was the object of the Government in their imposition? merely to get rid of 'Popery'? No; it had the further object of gaining the 'Papists.' What then was the best way to induce reluctant or wavering minds, and these, I supposed, were the majority, to give in their adhesion to the new symbol? how had the Arians drawn up their Creeds? was it not on the principle of using vague ambiguous language, which to the subscribers would seem to bear a Catholic sense, but which, when worked out on the long run, would prove to be heterodox? Accordingly, there was great antecedent probability, that, fierce as the Articles might look at first sight, their bark would prove worse than their bite. I say antecedent probability, for to what extent that surmise might be true, could only be ascertained by investigation.

3. But a consideration came up at once, which threw light on this surmise: – what if it should turn out that the very men who drew up the Articles, in the very act of doing so, had avowed, or rather in one of those very Articles themselves had imposed on

subscribers, a number of those very 'Papistical' doctrines, which they were now thought to deny, as part and parcel of that very Protestantism, which they were now thought to consider divine? and this was the fact, and I showed it in my Essay.

Let the reader observe: – the 35th Article says: 'The second Book of Homilies doth contain *a godly and wholesome doctrine, and necessary for* these times, as doth the former Book of Homilies.' Here the *doctrine* of the Homilies[107] is recognised as godly and wholesome, and concurrence in that recognition is imposed on all subscribers of the Articles. Let us then turn to the Homilies, and see what this godly doctrine is: I quoted from them to the following effect:

i. They declare that the so-called 'apocryphal' book of Tobit is the teaching of the Holy Ghost, and is Scripture.

ii. That the so-called 'apocryphal' book of Wisdom is Scripture, and the infallible and undeceivable word of God.

iii. That the Primitive Church, next to the Apostles' time, and, as they imply, for almost 700 years, is no doubt most pure.

iv. That the Primitive Church is specially to be followed.

v. That the Four first General Councils belong to the Primitive Church.

vi. That there are Six Councils which are allowed and received by all men.

vii. Again, they speak of a certain truth, and say that it is declared by God's word, the sentences of the ancient doctors, and judgment of the Primitive Church.

viii. Of the learned and holy Bishops and doctors of the Church of the first eight centuries being of great authority and credit with the people.

ix. Of the declaration of Christ and His Apostles and all the rest of the Holy Fathers.

x. Of the authority both of Scripture and also of Augustine.

xi. Of Augustine, Chrysostom, Ambrose, Jerome, and about thirty other Fathers, to some of whom they give the title of 'Saint,' to others of 'ancient Catholic Fathers and doctors, &c.'

xii. They declare that, not only the holy Apostles and disciples of Christ, but the godly Fathers also, before and since Christ, were endued without doubt with the Holy Ghost.

xiii. That the ancient Catholic Fathers say that the 'Lord's

Supper' is the salve of immortality, the sovereign preservative against death, the food of immortality, the healthful grace.

xiv. That the Lord's Blessed Body and Blood are received under the form of bread and wine.

xv. That the meat in the Sacrament is an invisible meat and a ghostly substance.

xvi. That the holy Body and Blood of thy God ought to be touched with the mind.

xvii. That Ordination is a Sacrament.

xviii. That Matrimony is a Sacrament.

xix. That there are other Sacraments besides 'Baptism and the Lord's Supper,' though not 'such as' they.

xx. That the souls of the Saints are reigning in joy and in heaven with God.

xxi. That alms-deeds purge the soul from the infection and filthy spots of sin, and are a precious medicine, an inestimable jewel.

xxii. That mercifulness wipes out and washes away sins, as salves and remedies to heal sores and grievous diseases.

xxiii. That the duty of fasting is a truth more manifest than it should need to be proved.

xxiv. That fasting, used with prayer, is of great efficacy and weigheth much with God; so the Angel Raphael told Tobias.

xxv. That the puissant and mighty Emperor Theodosius was, in the Primitive Church which was most holy and godly, excommunicated by St. Ambrose.

xxvi. That Constantine, Bishop of Rome, did condemn Philippicus, then Emperor, not without a cause indeed, but very justly.

Putting altogether aside the question how far these separate theses came under the matter to which subscription was to be made, it was quite plain, that in the minds of the men who wrote the Homilies, and who thus incorporated them into the Anglican system of doctrine, there was no such nice discrimination between the Catholic and the Protestant faith, no such clear recognition of formal Protestant principles and tenets, no such accurate definition of 'Roman doctrine,' as is received at the present day: – hence great probability accrued to my presentiment, that the Articles were tolerant, not only of what I called 'Catholic teaching,' but of much that was 'Roman.'

4. And here was another reason against the notion that the
Articles directly attacked the Roman dogmas as declared at Trent
and as promulgated by Pius the Fourth: – the Council of Trent
was not over, nor its Canons promulgated at the date when the
Articles were drawn up,* so that those Articles must be aiming
at something else? What was that something else? The Homilies
tell us: the Homilies are the best comment upon the Articles. Let
us turn to the Homilies, and we shall find from first to last that,
not only is not the Catholic teaching of the first centuries, but
neither again are the dogmas of Rome, the objects of the protest
of the compilers of the Articles, but the dominant errors, the
popular corruptions, authorized or suffered by the high name of
Rome. The eloquent declamation of the Homilies finds its matter
almost exclusively in the dominant errors. As to Catholic teaching, nay as to Roman dogma, of such theology those Homilies,
as I have shown, contained no small portion themselves.

5. So much for the writers of the Articles and Homilies; – they
were witnesses, not authorities, and I used them as such; but in
the next place, who were the actual authorities imposing them? I
reasonably considered the authority *imponens*[108] to be the Convocation of 1571; but here again, it would be found that the very
Convocation, which received and confirmed the 39 Articles, also
enjoined by Canon that 'preachers should be *careful*, that they
should *never* teach aught in a sermon, to be religiously held and
believed by the people, except that which is agreeable to the
doctrine of the Old and New Testament, and *which the Catholic
Fathers and ancient Bishops have collected* from that very doctrine.'
Here, let it be observed, an appeal is made by the Convocation
imponens to the very same ancient authorities, as had been mentioned with such profound veneration by the writers of the
Homilies and the Articles, and thus, if the Homilies contained
views of doctrine which now would be called Roman, there
seemed to me to be an extreme probability that the Convocation
of 1571 also countenanced and received, or at least did not reject,
those doctrines.

6. And further, when at length I came actually to look into the

* The Pope's Confirmation of the Council, by which its Canons became *de fide*,
and his Bull *super confirmatione* by which they were promulgated to the world, are
dated January 26, 1564. The Articles are dated 1562.

text of the Articles, I saw in many cases a patent justification of all that I had surmised as to their vagueness and indecisiveness, and that, not only on questions which lay between Lutherans, Calvinists, and Zuinglians,[109] but on Catholic questions also; and I have noticed them in my Tract.[110] In the conclusion of my Tract I observe: The Articles are 'evidently framed on the principle of leaving open large questions on which the controversy hinges. They state broadly extreme truths, and are silent about their adjustment. For instance, they say that all necessary faith must be proved from Scripture; but do not say *who* is to prove it. They say, that the Church has authority in controversies; they do not say *what* authority. They say that it may enforce nothing beyond Scripture, but do not say *where* the remedy lies when it does. They say that works *before* grace *and* justification are worthless and worse, and that works *after* grace *and* justification are acceptable, but they do not speak at all of works *with* God's aid *before* justification. They say that men are lawfully called and sent to minister and preach, who are chosen and called by men who have public authority *given* them in the Congregation; but they do not add *by whom* the authority is to be given. They say that Councils called by *princes* may err; they do not determine whether Councils called in the name of Christ may err.'

Such were the considerations which weighed with me in my inquiry how far the Articles were tolerant of a Catholic, or even a Roman interpretation; and such was the defence which I made in my Tract for having attempted it. From what I have already said, it will appear that I have no need or intention at this day to maintain every particular interpretation[111] which I suggested in the course of my Tract, nor indeed had I then. Whether it was prudent or not, whether it was sensible or not, any how I attempted only a first essay of a necessary work, an essay which, as I was quite prepared to find, would require revision and modification by means of the lights which I should gain from the criticism of others. I should have gladly withdrawn any statement, which could be proved to me to be erroneous; I considered my work to be faulty and open to objection in the same sense in which I now consider my Anglican interpretations of Scripture to be erroneous; but in no other sense. I am surprised that men do not apply to the interpreters of Scripture generally the hard

names which they apply to the author of Tract 90. He held a
large system of theology, and applied it to the Articles: Episcopa-
lians, or Lutherans, or Presbyterians, or Unitarians, hold a large
system of theology and apply it to Scripture. Every theology has
its difficulties; Protestants hold justification by faith only, though
there is no text in St. Paul[112] which enunciates it, and though St.
James[113] expressly denies it; do we therefore call Protestants
dishonest? they deny that the Church has a divine mission,
though St. Paul says that it is 'the Pillar and ground of Truth;'[114]
they keep the Sabbath, though St. Paul says, 'Let no man judge
you in meat or drink or in respect of . . . the sabbath days.'[115]
Every creed has texts in its favour, and again texts which run
counter to it: and this is generally confessed. And this is what I
felt keenly: – how had I done worse in Tract 90 than Anglicans,
Wesleyans, and Calvinists did daily in their Sermons and their
publications? how had I done worse, than the Evangelical party
in their *ex animo* reception of the Services for Baptism and
Visitation of the Sick?* Why was I to be dishonest and they
immaculate? There was an occasion on which our Lord gave an
answer, which seemed to be appropriate to my own case, when
the tumult broke out against my Tract: – 'He that is without sin
among you, let him first cast a stone at him.'[116] I could have
fancied that a sense of their own difficulties of interpretation
would have persuaded the great party I have mentioned to some
prudence, or at least moderation, in opposing a teacher of an

* For instance, let candid men consider the form of Absolution contained in that
Prayer Book, of which all clergymen, Evangelical and Liberal as well as high
Church, and (I think) all persons in University office declare that 'it containeth
nothing contrary to the Word of God.'

I challenge, in the sight of all England, Evangelical clergymen generally, to
put on paper an interpretation of this form of words, consistent with their
sentiments, which shall be less forced than the most objectionable of the
interpretations which Tract 90 puts upon any passage in the Articles.

'Our Lord Jesus Christ, who hath left *power* to His Church to absolve all
sinners who truly repent and believe in Him, of His great mercy forgive thee
thine offences; and by *His authority committed to me, I absolve thee from all thy sins*, in
the Name of the Father, and of the Son, and of the Holy Ghost. Amen.'

I subjoin the Roman form, as used in England and elsewhere: 'Dominus noster
Jesus Christus te absolvat; et ego auctoritate ipsius te absolvo, ab omni vinculo
excommunicationis et interdicti, in quantum possum et tu indiges. Deinde ego te
absolvo à peccatis tuis, in nomine Patris et Filii et Spiritûs Sancti. Amen.'

opposite school. But I suppose their alarm and their anger overcame their sense of justice.

In the sudden storm of indignation with which the Tract was received throughout the country on its appearance, I recognize much of real religious feeling, much of honest and true principle, much of straightforward ignorant common sense. In Oxford there was genuine feeling too; but there had been a smouldering, stern, energetic animosity, not at all unnatural, partly rational, against its author. A false step had been made; now was the time for action. I am told that, even before the publication of the Tract, rumours of its contents had got into the hostile camp in an exaggerated form; and not a moment was lost in proceeding to action, when I was actually fallen into the hands of the Philistines. I was quite unprepared for the outbreak, and was startled at its violence. I do not think I had any fear. Nay, I will add, I am not sure that it was not in one point of view a relief to me.

I saw indeed clearly that my place in the Movement was lost; public confidence was at an end; my occupation was gone.[117] It was simply an impossibility that I could say anything henceforth to good effect, when I had been posted up by the marshal on the buttery-hatch of every College of my University, after the manner of discommoned pastry-cooks, and when in every part of the country and every class of society, through every organ and opportunity of opinion, in newspapers, in periodicals, at meetings, in pulpits, at dinner-tables, in coffee-rooms, in railway carriages, I was denounced as a traitor who had laid his train and was detected in the very act of firing it against the time-honoured Establishment. There were indeed men, besides my own immediate friends, men of name and position, who gallantly took my part, as Dr. Hook,[118] Mr. Palmer,[119] and Mr. Perceval; it must have been a grievous trial for themselves; yet what after all could they do for me? Confidence in me was lost; – but I had already lost full confidence in myself. Thoughts had passed over me a year and a half before in respect to the Anglican claims, which for the time had profoundly troubled me. They had gone: I had not less confidence in the power and the prospects of the Apostolical movement than before; not less confidence than before in the grievousness of what I called the 'dominant errors' of Rome: but how was I any more to have absolute confidence in myself? how was I to have confidence in my present confidence? how was I to be sure that I should always think as I thought now? I felt that by this event a kind Providence had saved me from an impossible position in the future.

First, if I remember right, they wished me to withdraw the Tract. This I refused to do: I would not do so for the sake of those who were unsettled or in danger of unsettlement. I would not do so for my own sake; for how could I acquiesce in a mere Protestant interpretation of the Articles? how could I range myself among the professors of a theology, of which it put my teeth on edge even to hear the sound?

Next they said, 'Keep silence; do not defend the Tract;' I answered, 'Yes, if you will not condemn it, – if you will allow it to continue on sale.' They pressed on me whenever I gave way; they fell back when they saw me obstinate. Their line of action was to get out of me as much as they could; but upon the point of their tolerating the Tract I *was* obstinate. So they let me continue it on sale; and they said they would not condemn it. But they said that this was on condition that I did not defend it, that I stopped the series, and that I myself published my own condemnation in a letter[120] to the Bishop of Oxford. I impute nothing whatever to him, he was ever most kind to me. Also, they said they could not answer for what some individual Bishops might perhaps say about the Tract in their own charges. I agreed to their conditions. My one point was to save the Tract.

Not a line in writing was given me, as a pledge of the observance of the main article on their side of the engagement. Parts of letters from them were read to me, without being put into my hands. It was an 'understanding.' A clever man[121] had warned me against 'understandings' some thirteen years before: I have hated them ever since.

In the last words of my letter to the Bishop of Oxford I thus resigned my place in the Movement: –

'I have nothing to be sorry for,' I say to him, 'except having made your Lordship anxious, and others whom I am bound to revere. I have nothing to be sorry for, but everything to rejoice in and be thankful for. I have never taken pleasure in seeming to be able to move a party, and whatever influence I have had, has been found, not sought after. I have acted because others did not act, and have sacrificed a quiet which I prized. May God be with me in time to come, as He has been hitherto! and He will be if I can but keep my hand clean and my heart pure. I think I can bear, or at least will try to bear, any personal humiliation, so that I am preserved from betraying sacred interests, which the Lord of grace and power has given into my charge.'*

* To the Pamphlets published in my behalf at this time I should add 'One Tract more,' an able and generous defence of Tractarianism and No. 90, by the present Lord Houghton.[122]

CHAPTER III

And now that I am about to trace, as far as I can, the course of that
great revolution of mind, which led me to leave my own home, to
which I was bound by so many strong and tender ties, I feel
overcome with the difficulty of satisfying myself in my account of
it, and have recoiled from the attempt, till the near approach of the
day, on which these lines must be given to the world, forces me to
set about the task. For who can know himself, and the multitude
of subtle influences which act upon him? And who can recollect,
at the distance of twenty-five years, all that he once knew about
his thoughts and his deeds, and that, during a portion of his life,
when, even at the time, his observation, whether of himself or of
the external world, was less than before or after, by very reason of
the perplexity and dismay which weighed upon him, – when, in
spite of the light given to him according to his need amid his
darkness, yet a darkness it emphatically was? And who can
suddenly gird himself to a new and anxious undertaking, which he
might be able indeed to perform well, were full and calm leisure
allowed him to look through every thing that he had written,
whether in published works or private letters? yet again, granting
that calm contemplation of the past, in itself so desirable, who
could afford to be leisurely and deliberate, while he practises on
himself a cruel operation, the ripping up of old griefs, and the
venturing again upon the 'infandum dolorem'[1] of years, in which
the stars of this lower heaven were one by one going out? I could
not in cool blood, nor except upon the imperious call of duty,
attempt what I have set myself to do. It is both to head and heart
an extreme trial, thus to analyze what has so long gone by, and to
bring out the results of that examination. I have done various bold
things in my life: this is the boldest: and, were I not sure I should
after all succeed in my object, it would be madness to set about it.

*

In the spring of 1839 my position in the Anglican Church was at its height. I had supreme confidence in my controversial *status*, and I had a great and still growing success, in recommending it to others. I had in the foregoing autumn been somewhat sore at the Bishop's Charge, but I have a letter which shows that all annoyance had passed from my mind. In January, if I recollect aright, in order to meet the popular clamour against myself and others, and to satisfy the Bishop, I had collected into one all the strong things which they, and especially I, had said against the Church of Rome, in order to their insertion among the advertisements appended to our publications. Conscious as I was that my opinions in religion were not gained, as the world said, from Roman sources, but were, on the contrary, the birth of my own mind and of the circumstances in which I had been placed, I had a scorn of the imputations which were heaped upon me. It was true that I held a large bold system of religion, very unlike the Protestantism of the day, but it was the concentration and adjustment of the statements of great Anglican authorities, and I had as much right to hold it, as the Evangelical, and more right than the Liberal party could show, for asserting their own respective doctrines. As I declared[2] on occasion of Tract 90, I claimed, in behalf of who would in the Anglican Church, the right of holding with Bramhall a comprecation[3] with the Saints, and the Mass all but Transubstantiation[4] with Andrewes, or with Hooker[5] that Transubstantiation itself is not a point for Churches to part communion upon, or with Hammond[6] that a General Council, truly such, never did, never shall err in a matter of faith, or with Bull[7] that man had in paradise, and lost on the fall, a supernatural habit of grace, or with Thorndike[8] that penance is a propitiation for post-baptismal sin, or with Pearson[9] that the all-powerful name of Jesus is no otherwise given than in the Catholic Church. 'Two can play at that,' was often in my mouth, when men of Protestant sentiments appealed to the Articles, Homilies, or Reformers; in the sense that, if they had a right to speak loud, I had the liberty to speak out as well as they, and had the means, by the same or parallel appeals, of giving them tit for tat. I thought that the Anglican Church was tyrannized over by a mere party, and I aimed at bringing into effect the promise contained in the motto to the Lyra, 'They shall know the difference now.' I only asked to be allowed to show them the difference.

What will best describe my state of mind at the early part of 1839, is an Article[10] in the *British Critic* for that April. I have looked over it now, for the first time since it was published; and have been struck by it for this reason: – it contains the last words which I ever spoke as an Anglican to Anglicans. It may now be read as my parting address and valediction, made to my friends. I little knew it at the time. It reviews the actual state of things, and it ends by looking towards the future. It is not altogether mine;[11] for my memory goes to this, – that I had asked a friend to do the work; that then, the thought came on me, that I would do it myself: and that he was good enough to put into my hands what he had with great appositeness written, and that I embodied it in my Article. Every one, I think, will recognize the greater part of it as mine. It was published two years before the affair of Tract 90, and was entitled *The State of Religious Parties*.

In this Article, I begin by bringing together testimonies from our enemies to the remarkable success of our exertions. One writer[12] said: 'Opinions and views of a theology of a very marked and peculiar kind have been extensively adopted and strenuously upheld, and are daily gaining ground among a considerable and influential portion of the members, as well as ministers of the Established Church.' Another:[13] The Movement has manifested itself 'with the most rapid growth of the hot-bed of these evil days.' Another:[14] 'The *Via Media* is crowded with young enthusiasts, who never presume to argue, except against the propriety of arguing at all.' Another:[15] 'Were I to give you a full list of the works, which they have produced within the short space of five years, I should surprise you. You would see what a task it would be to make yourself complete master of their system, even in its present probably immature state. The writers have adopted the motto, "In quietness and confidence shall be your strength." With regard to confidence, they have justified their adopting it; but as to quietness, it is not very quiet to pour forth such a succession of controversial publications.' Another:[16] 'The spread of these doctrines is in fact now having the effect of rendering all other distinctions obsolete, and of severing the religious community into two portions, fundamentally and vehemently opposed one to the other. Soon there will be no middle ground left; and every man, and especially every clergyman, will be compelled to make his choice between the two.' Another:[17] 'The time has gone by, when those unfortunate and deeply regretted publications can be passed over without notice, and the hope that their influence would fail is now dead.' Another:[18] 'These doctrines had already made fearful progress. One of the largest churches in Brighton is crowded to hear them; so is the church at Leeds. There are few towns of note, to which they have not extended. They are preached in small towns in Scotland. They obtain in Elginshire, 600 miles north of London. I found them myself in the heart of the highlands of Scotland. They are advocated in the newspaper and periodical press. They have even insinuated themselves into the House of Commons.' And, lastly, a bishop[19] in a charge: – It 'is daily assuming a more serious and alarming aspect. Under the specious pretence of deference to Antiquity and respect for primitive models, the foundations of the Protestant Church are undermined by men who dwell within her walls, and those who sit in the Reformers' seat are traducing the Reformation.'

After thus stating the phenomenon of the time, as it presented itself to those who did not sympathize in it, the Article proceeds to account for it; and this it does by considering it as a re-action from the dry and superficial character of the religious teaching and the literature of the last generation, or century, and as a result of the need which was felt both by the hearts and the intellects of the nation for a deeper philosophy, and as the evidence and as the partial fulfilment of that need, to which even the chief authors[20] of the then generation had borne witness. First, I mentioned the literary influence of Walter Scott, who turned men's minds in the direction of the middle ages. 'The general need,' I said, 'of something deeper and more attractive, than what had offered itself elsewhere, may be considered to have led to his popularity; and by means of his popularity he re-acted on his readers, stimulating their mental thirst, feeding their hopes, setting before them visions, which, when once seen, are not easily forgotten, and silently indoctrinating them with nobler ideas, which might afterwards be appealed to as first principles.'

Then I spoke of Coleridge, thus: 'While history in prose and verse was thus made the instrument of Church feelings and opinions, a philosophical basis for the same was laid in England by a very original thinker, who, while he indulged a liberty of speculation, which no Christian can tolerate, and advocated conclusions which were often heathen rather than Christian, yet after all installed a higher philosophy into inquiring minds, than they had hitherto been accustomed to accept. In this way he made trial of his age, and succeeded in interesting its genius in the cause of Catholic truth.'

Then come Southey and Wordsworth, 'two living poets, one of whom in the department of fantastic fiction, the other in that of philosophical meditation, have addressed themselves to the same high principles and feelings, and carried forward their readers in the same direction.'

Then comes the prediction of this re-action hazarded by 'a sagacious observer withdrawn from the world, and surveying its movements from a distance,' Mr. Alexander Knox.[21] He had said twenty years before the date of my Article: 'No Church on earth has more intrinsic excellence than the English Church, yet no Church probably has less practical influence. . . . The rich provision, made by the grace and providence of God, for habits of a noble kind, is evidence that men shall arise, fitted both by nature and ability, to discover for themselves, and to display to others, whatever yet remains undiscovered, whether in the words or works of God.' Also I referred to 'a much venerated clergyman[22] of the last generation,' who said shortly before his death, 'Depend on it, the day will come, when those great doctrines, now buried, will be brought out to the light of day, and then the effect will be fearful.' I remarked upon this, that they who 'now blame the impetuosity of the current, should rather turn their animadversions upon those who have dammed up a majestic river, till it has become a flood.'

These being the circumstances under which the Movement began and progressed, it was absurd to refer it to the act of two or three individuals. It was not so much a movement as a 'spirit afloat;' it was within us, 'rising up in hearts where it was least suspected, and working itself, though not in secret, yet so subtly and impalpably, as hardly to admit of precaution or encounter on any ordinary human rules of opposition. It is,' I continued, 'an adversary in the air, a something one and entire, a whole wherever it is, unapproachable and incapable of being grasped, as being the result of causes far deeper than political or other visible agencies, the spiritual awakening of spiritual wants.'

To make this clear, I proceed to refer to the chief preachers of the revived doctrines at that moment, and to draw attention to the variety of their respective antecedents. Dr. Hook and Mr. Churton[23] represented the high Church dignitaries of the last century; Mr. Perceval, the Tory aristocracy; Mr. Keble came from a country parsonage; Mr. Palmer from Ireland; Dr. Pusey from the Universities of Germany,[24] and the study of Arabic MSS.;[25] Mr. Dodsworth[26] from the study of Prophecy; Mr. Oakeley[27] had gained his views, as he himself expressed it, 'partly by study, partly by reflection, partly by conversation with one or two friends, inquirers like himself:' while I speak of myself as being 'much indebted to the friendship of Archbishop Whately.' And thus I am led on to ask, 'What head of a sect is there? What march of opinions can be traced from mind to mind among preachers such as these? They are one and all in their degree the organs of one Sentiment, which has risen up simultaneously in many places very mysteriously.'

My train of thought next led me to speak of the disciples of the Movement, and I freely acknowledged and lamented that they needed to be kept in order. It is very much to the purpose to draw attention to this point now, when such extravagances as then occurred, whatever they were, are simply laid to my door, or to the charge of the doctrines which I advocated. A man cannot do more than freely confess what is wrong, say that it need not be, that it ought not to be, and that he is very sorry that it should be. Now I said in the Article, which I am reviewing, that the great truths themselves, which we were preaching, must not be condemned on account of such abuse of them. 'Aberrations there must ever be, whatever the doctrine is, while the human heart is sensitive, capricious, and wayward. A mixed multitude went out of Egypt with the Israelites.' 'There will ever be a number of persons,' I continued, 'professing the opinions of a movement party, who talk loudly and strangely, do odd or fierce things, display themselves unnecessarily, and disgust other people; persons, too young to be wise, too generous to be cautious, too warm to be sober, or too intellectual to be humble. Such persons will be very apt to attach themselves to particular persons, to use particular names, to say things merely because others do, and to act in a party-spirited way.'

While I thus republish what I then said about such extravagances as occurred in these years, at the same time I have a very strong conviction that those extravagances furnished quite as much the welcome excuse for those who were jealous or shy of us, as the stumbling-blocks of those who were well inclined to our doctrines. This too we felt at the time; but it was our duty to see that our good should not be evil-spoken of; and accordingly, two or three of the writers of the Tracts for the Times had commenced a Series[28] of what they called *Plain Sermons* with the avowed purpose of discouraging and correcting whatever was uppish or extreme in our followers: to this Series I contributed a volume myself.

Its conductors say in their Preface: 'If therefore as time goes on, there shall be found persons, who admiring the innate beauty and majesty of the fuller system of Primitive Christianity, and seeing the transcendent strength of its principles, *shall become loud and voluble advocates* in their behalf, speaking the more freely, *because they do not feel them deeply as founded* in divine and eternal truth, of such persons *it is our duty to declare plainly*, that, as we should contemplate their condition with serious misgiving, *so would they be the last persons from whom we should* seek support.

'But if, on the other hand, there shall be any, who, in the silent humility of their lives, and in their unaffected reverence for holy things, show that they in truth accept these principles as real and substantial, and by habitual purity of heart and serenity of temper, give proof of their deep veneration for sacraments and sacramental ordinances, those persons, *whether our professed adherents or not*, best exemplify the kind of character which the writers of the *Tracts for the Times* have wished to form.'

These clergymen had the best of claims to use these beautiful words, for they were themselves, all of them, important writers in the Tracts, the two Mr. Kebles[29] and Mr. Isaac Williams.[30] And this passage, with which they ushered their Series into the world, I quoted in the Article, of which I am giving an account, and I added, 'What more can be required of the preachers of neglected truth, than that they should admit that some, who do not assent to their preaching, are holier and better men than some who do?' They were not answerable for the intemperance of those who dishonoured a true doctrine, provided they protested, as they did, against such intemperance. 'They were not answerable for the dust and din which attends any great moral movement. The truer doctrines are, the more liable they are to be perverted.'

The notice of these incidental faults of opinion or temper in adherents of the Movement, led on to a discussion of the secondary causes, by means of which a system of doctrine may be embraced, modified, or developed, of the variety of schools which may all be in the One Church, and of the succession of one phase of doctrine to another, while that doctrine is ever one and the same. Thus I was brought on to the subject of Antiquity, which was the basis of the doctrine of the *Via Media*, and by which was not to be understood a servile imitation of the past, but such a reproduction of it as is really new, while it is old. 'We have good hope,' I say, 'that a system will be rising up, superior to the age, yet harmonizing with, and carrying out its higher points, which will attract to itself those who are willing to make a venture and to face difficulties, for the sake of something higher in prospect. On this, as on other subjects, the proverb will apply, "Fortes fortuna adjuvat." '[31]

Lastly, I proceeded to the question of that future of the Anglican Church, which was to be a new birth of the Ancient Religion. And I did not venture to pronounce upon it. 'About the future, we have no prospect before our minds whatever, good or bad. Ever since that great luminary, Augustine, proved to be the last bishop of Hippo, Christians have had a lesson against attempting to foretell, *how* Providence will prosper and' [or ?] 'bring to an end, what it begins.' Perhaps the lately-revived principles would prevail in the Anglican Church; perhaps they would be lost in 'some miserable schism, or some more miserable compromise; but there was nothing rash in venturing to predict that 'neither Puritanism nor Liberalism had any permanent inheritance within her.'

Then I went on: 'As to Liberalism,[32] we think the formularies of the Church will ever, with the aid of a good Providence, keep it from making any serious inroads upon the clergy. Besides, it is too cold a principle to prevail with the multitude.' But as regarded what was called Evangelical Religion or Puritanism, there was more to cause alarm. I observed upon its organization; but on the other hand it had no intellectual basis; no internal idea, no principle of unity, no theology. 'Its adherents,' I said, 'are already separating from each other; they will melt away like a snow-drift. It has no straightforward view on any one point, on which it professes to teach, and to hide its poverty, it has dressed itself out in a maze of words. We have no dread of it at all; we only fear what it may lead to. It does not stand on intrenched ground, or make any pretence to a position; it does but occupy the space between contending powers, Catholic Truth and Rationalism. Then indeed will be the stern encounter, when two real and living principles, simple, entire, and consistent, one in the Church, the other out of it, at length rush upon each other, contending not for names and words, or half-views, but for elementary notions and distinctive moral characters.'

Whether the ideas of the coming age upon religion were true or false, at least they would be real. 'In the present day,' I said, 'mistiness is the mother of wisdom. A man who can set down a half-a-dozen general propositions, which escape from destroying one another only by being diluted into truisms, who can hold the balance between opposites so skilfully as to do without fulcrum or beam, who never enunciates a truth without guarding himself against being supposed to exclude the contradictory, – who holds that Scripture is the only authority, yet that the Church is to be deferred to, that faith only justifies, yet that it does not justify without works, that grace does not depend on the sacraments, yet is not given without them, that bishops are a divine ordinance, yet those who have them not are in the same religious condition as those who have, – this is your safe man and the hope of the Church; this is what the Church is said to want, not party men, but sensible, temperate, sober, well-judging persons, to guide it through the channel of no-meaning, between the Scylla and Charybdis of Aye and No.'

This state of things, however, I said, could not last, if men were to read and think. They 'will not keep in that very attitude which you call sound Church-of-Englandism or orthodox Protestantism. They cannot go on for ever standing on one leg, or sitting without a chair, or walking with their feet tied, or like Tityrus's stags[33] grazing in the air. They will take one view or another, but it will be a consistent view. It may be Liberalism, or Erastianism, or Popery, or Catholicity; but it will be real.'

I concluded the Article by saying, that all who did not wish to be 'democratic, or pantheistic, or popish,' must 'look out for *some* Via Media which will preserve us from what threatens, though it cannot restore the dead. The spirit of Luther is dead; but Hildebrand[34] and Loyola[35] are alive. Is it sensible, sober, judicious, to be so very angry with those writers of the day, who point to the fact, that our divines of the seventeenth century have occupied a ground which is the true and intelligible mean between extremes? Is it wise to quarrel with this ground, because it is not exactly what we should choose, had we the power of choice? Is it true moderation, instead of trying to fortify a middle doctrine, to fling stones at those who do? . . . Would you rather have your sons and daughters members of the Church of England or of the Church of Rome?'

And thus I left the matter. But, while I was thus speaking of the future of the Movement, I was in truth winding up my accounts with it, little dreaming that it was so to be; – while I was still, in some way or other, feeling about for an available *Via Media*, I was soon to receive a shock which was to cast out of my imagination all middle courses and compromises for ever. As I have said, this Article appeared in the April number of the *British Critic*; in the July number, I cannot tell why, there is no Article of mine; before the number for October, the event had happened to which I have alluded.

But before I proceed to describe what happened to me in the summer of 1839, I must detain the reader for a while, in order to describe the *issue* of the controversy between Rome and the Anglican Church, as I viewed it. This will involve some dry discussion; but it is as necessary for my narrative, as plans of buildings and homesteads are at times needed in the proceedings of our law courts.

I have said already that, though the object of the Movement was to withstand the Liberalism of the day, I found and felt this could not be done by mere negatives. It was necessary for us to have a positive Church theory erected on a definite basis. This took me to the great Anglican divines; and then of course I found at once that it was impossible to form any such theory, without cutting across the teaching of the Church of Rome. Thus came in the Roman controversy.

When I first turned myself to it, I had neither doubt on the subject, nor suspicion that doubt would ever come upon me. It was in this state of mind that I began to read up Bellarmine[36] on the one hand, and numberless Anglican writers on the other. But I soon found, as others had found before me, that it was a tangled and manifold controversy, difficult to master, more difficult to put out of hand with neatness and precision. It was easy to make points, not easy to sum up and settle. It was not easy to find a clear issue for the dispute, and still less by a logical process to decide it in favour of Anglicanism. This difficulty, however, had no tendency whatever to harass or perplex me: it was a matter which bore not on convictions, but on proofs.

First I saw, as all see who study the subject, that a broad distinction had to be drawn between the actual state of belief and of usage in the countries which were in communion with the Roman Church, and her formal dogmas; the latter did not cover the former. Sensible pain, for instance, is not implied in the Tridentine decree upon Purgatory; but it was the tradition of the Latin Church, and I had seen the pictures of souls in flames in the streets of Naples. Bishop Lloyd[37] had brought this distinction out strongly in an Article in the *British Critic* in 1825; indeed, it was one of the most common objections made to the Church of Rome, that she dared not commit herself by formal decree, to what nevertheless she sanctioned and allowed. Accordingly, in my *Prophetical Office*, I view as simply separate ideas, Rome quiescent, and Rome in action. I contrasted her creed on the one hand, with her ordinary teaching, her controversial tone, her political and social bearing, and her popular beliefs and practices, on the other.

While I made this distinction between the decrees and the traditions of Rome, I drew a parallel distinction between Anglicanism quiescent, and Anglicanism in action. In its formal creed Anglicanism was not at a great distance from Rome: far otherwise, when viewed in its insular space, the traditions of its establishment, its historical characteristics, its controversial ran-cour, and its private judgment. I disavowed and condemned those excesses, and called them 'Protestantism' or 'Ultra-Protestantism:' I wished to find a parallel disclaimer, on the part of Roman controversialists, of that popular system of beliefs and usages in their own Church, which I called 'Popery.' When that hope was a dream, I saw that the controversy lay between the book-theology of Anglicanism on the one side, and the living system of what I called Roman corruption on the other. I could not get further than this; with this result I was forced to content myself.

These then were the *parties* in the controversy: – the Anglican *Via Media* and the popular religion of Rome. And next, as to the *issue*, to which the controversy between them was to be brought, it was this: – the Anglican disputant took his stand upon Antiquity or Apostolicity, the Roman upon Catholicity. The Anglican said to the Roman: 'There is but One Faith, the Ancient, and you have not kept to it;' the Roman retorted: 'There is but One Church, the Catholic, and you are out of it.' The Anglican urged 'Your special beliefs, practices, modes of action, are nowhere in Antiquity;' the Roman objected: 'You do not communicate with any one Church besides your own and its offshoots, and you have discarded principles, doctrines, sacra-ments, and usages, which are and ever have been received in the East and the West.' The true Church, as defined in the Creeds, was both Catholic and Apostolic; now, as I viewed the contro-versy in which I was engaged, England and Rome had divided these notes or prerogatives between them: the cause lay thus, Apostolicity *versus* Catholicity.

However, in thus stating the matter, of course I do not wish it supposed that I allowed the note of Catholicity really to belong to Rome, to the disparagement of the Anglican Church; but I considered that the special point or plea of Rome in the contro-versy was Catholicity, as the Anglican plea was Antiquity. Of course I contended that the Roman idea of Catholicity was not ancient and apostolic. It was in my judgment at the utmost only natural, becoming, expedient, that the whole of Christendom should be united in one visible body; while such a unity might, on the other hand, be nothing more than a mere heartless and political combination. For myself, I held with the Anglican divines, that, in the Primitive Church, there was a very real mutual independence between its separate parts, though, from a dictate of charity, there was in fact a close union between them. I considered that each See and Diocese might be compared to a crystal, and that each was similar to the rest, and that the sum total of them all was only a collection of crystals. The unity of the Church lay, not in its being a polity, but in its being a family, a race, coming down by apostolical descent from its first founders and bishops. And I considered this truth brought out, beyond the possibility of dispute, in the Epistles of St. Ignatius, in which the Bishop is represented as the one supreme authority in the Church, that is, in his own place, with no one above him, except as, for the sake of ecclesiastical order and expedience, arrangements had been made by which one was put over or under another. So much for our own claim to Catholicity, which was so perversely appropriated by our opponents to themselves: – on the other hand, as to our special strong point, Antiquity, while, of course, by means of it, we were able to condemn most emphatically the novel claim of Rome to domineer over other Churches, which were in truth her equals, further than that, we thereby especially convicted her of the intolerable offence of having added to the Faith. This was the critical head of accusation urged against her by the Anglican disputant; and as he referred to St. Ignatius in proof that he himself was a true Catholic, in spite of being separated from Rome, so he triumphantly referred to the Treatise of Vincentius of Lerins[38] upon the 'Quod semper, quod ubique, quod ab omnibus,' in proof that the controversialists of Rome, in spite of their possession of the Catholic name, were separated in their creed from the Apostolical and primitive faith.

Of course those controversialists had their own mode of answering him, with which I am not concerned in this place; here I am only concerned with the issue itself, between the one party and the other – Antiquity *versus* Catholicity.

Now I will proceed to illustrate what I have been saying of the *status* of the controversy, as it presented itself to my mind, by extracts from my writings of the dates of 1836, 1840, and 1841. And I introduce them with a remark, which especially applies to the paper, from which I shall quote first, of the date of 1836. That paper[39] appeared in the March and April numbers of the *British Magazine* of that year, and was entitled *Home Thoughts Abroad*. Now it will be found, that, in the discussion which it contains, as in various other writings of mine, when I was in the Anglican Church, the argument in behalf of Rome is stated with considerable perspicuity and force. And at the time my friends and supporters cried out, 'How imprudent!' and, both at the time, and especially at a later date, my enemies have cried out, 'How insidious!' Friends and foes virtually agreed in their criticism; I had set out the cause which I was combating to the best advantage: this was an offence; it might be from imprudence, it might be with a traitorous design. It was from neither the one nor the other; but for the following reasons. First, I had a great impatience, whatever was the subject, of not bringing out the whole of it, as clearly as I could; next I wished to be as fair to my adversaries as possible; and thirdly I thought that there was a great deal of shallowness among our own friends, and that they undervalued the strength of the argument in behalf of Rome, and that they ought to be roused to a more exact apprehension of the position of the controversy. At a later date, (1841,) when I really felt the force of the Roman side of the question myself, as a difficulty which had to be met, I had a fourth reason for such frankness in argument, and that was, because a number of persons were unsettled far more than I was, as to the Catholicity of the Anglican Church. It was quite plain that, unless I was perfectly candid in stating what could be said against it, there was no chance that any representations, which I felt to be in its favour, or at least to be adverse to Rome, would have had any success with the persons in question. At all times I had a deep conviction, to put the matter on the lowest ground, that 'honesty was the best policy.' Accordingly, in July 1841,[40] I expressed myself thus on the Anglican difficulty: 'This is an objection which we must honestly say is deeply felt by many people, and not inconsiderable ones; and the more it is openly avowed to be a difficulty, the better; for there is then the chance of its being acknowledged, and in the course of time obviated, as far as may be, by those who have the power. Flagrant evils cure themselves by being flagrant; and we are sanguine that the time is come when so great an evil as this is, cannot stand its ground against the good feeling and common sense of religious persons. It is the very strength of Romanism against us; and, unless the proper persons take it into their serious consideration, they may look for certain to undergo the loss, as time goes on, of some whom they would least like to be lost to our Church.' The measure which I had especially in view in this passage, was the project of a Jerusalem Bishopric, which the then Archbishop of Canterbury was at that time concocting with M. Bunsen, and of which I shall speak more in the sequel. And now to return to the *Home Thoughts Abroad* of the spring of 1836: –

The discussion contained in this composition runs in the form of a dialogue. One of the disputants says: 'You say to me that the Church of Rome is corrupt. What then? to cut off a limb is a strange way of saving it from the influence of some constitutional ailment. Indigestion may cause cramp in the extremities; yet we spare our poor feet notwithstanding. Surely there is such a religious *fact* as the existence of a great Catholic body, union with which is a Christian privilege and duty. Now, we English are separate from it.'

The other answers: 'The present is an unsatisfactory, miserable state of things, yet I can grant no more. The Church is founded on a doctrine, – on the gospel of Truth; it is a means to an end. Perish the Church, (though, blessed be the promise! this cannot be,) yet let it perish *rather* than the Truth should fail. Purity of faith is more precious to the Christian than unity itself. If Rome has erred grievously in doctrine, then it is a duty to separate even from Rome.'

His friend, who takes the Roman side of the argument, refers to the image of the Vine and its branches, which is found, I think, in St. Cyprian,[41] as if a branch cut from the Catholic Vine must necessarily die. Also he quotes a passage from St. Augustine[42] in controversy with the Donatists to the same effect; viz. that, as being separated from the body of the Church, they were *ipso facto* cut off from the heritage of Christ. And he quotes St. Cyril's argument[43] drawn from the very title Catholic, which no body or communion of men has ever dared or been able to appropriate, besides one. He adds, 'Now I am only contending for the fact, that the communion of Rome constitutes the main body of the Church Catholic, and that we are split off from it, and in the condition of the Donatists.'

The other replies by denying the fact that the present Roman communion is like St. Augustine's Catholic Church, inasmuch as there must be taken into account the large Anglican and Greek communions. Presently he takes the offensive, naming distinctly the points in which Rome has departed from Primitive Christ-ianity, viz. 'the practical idolatry, the virtual worship of the Virgin and Saints, which are the offence of the Latin Church, and the degradation of moral truth and duty, which follows from these.' And again: 'We cannot join a Church, did we wish it ever so much, which does not acknowledge our orders, refuses us the Cup,[44] demands our acquiescence in image-worship, and excom-municates us, if we do not receive it and all other decisions of the Tridentine Council.'

His opponent answers these objections by referring to the doctrine of 'developments of gospel truth.' Besides 'The Anglican system itself is not found complete in those early centuries; so that the [Anglican] principle [of Antiquity] is self-destructive.' 'When a man takes up this *Via Media*, he is a mere *doctrinaire*;' he is like those, 'who, in some matter of business, start up to suggest their own little crotchet, and are ever measuring moun-tains with a pocket ruler, or improving the planetary courses.' 'The *Via Media* has slept in libraries; it is a substitute of infancy for manhood.'

It is plain, then, that at the end of 1835 or beginning of 1836, I had the whole state of the question before me, on which, to my mind, the decision between the Churches depended. It is observ-able that the question of the position of the Pope, whether as the centre of unity, or as the source of jurisdiction, did not come into my thoughts at all; nor did it, I think I may say, to the end. I doubt whether I ever distinctly held any of his powers to be *de jure divino*, while I was in the Anglican Church; – not that I saw any difficulty in the doctrine; not that in connexion with the history of St. Leo, of which I shall speak by and by, the idea of his infallibility did not cross my mind, for it did, – but after all, in my view the controversy did not turn upon it; it turned upon the Faith and the Church. This was my issue of the controversy from the beginning to the end. There was a contrariety of claims between the Roman and Anglican religions, and the history of my conversion is simply the process of working it out to a solution. In 1838[45] I illustrated it by the contrast presented to us between the Madonna and Child, and a Calvary. The peculiarity of the Anglican theology was this, – that it 'supposed the Truth to be entirely objective and detached, not' (as in the theology of Rome) 'lying hid in the bosom of the Church as if one with her, clinging to and (as it were) lost in her embrace, but as being sole and unapproachable, as on the Cross or at the Resurrection, with the Church close by, but in the background.'

As I viewed the controversy in 1836 and 1838, so I viewed it in 1840 and 1841. In the *British Critic*[46] of January 1840, after gradually investigating how the matter lies between the Churches by means of a dialogue, I end thus: 'It would seem, that, in the above discussion, each disputant has a strong point: our strong point is the argument from Primitiveness, that of Romanists from Universality. It is a fact, however it is to be accounted for, that Rome has added to the Creed; and it is a fact, however we justify ourselves, that we are estranged from the great body of Christians over the world. And each of these two facts is at first sight a grave difficulty in the respective systems to which they belong.' Again, 'While Rome, though not deferring to the Fathers, recognizes them, and England, not deferring to the large body of the Church, recognizes it, both Rome and England have a point to clear up.'

And still more strongly, in July, 1841:[47]

'If the Note of schism, on the one hand, lies against England, an antagonist disgrace lies upon Rome, the Note of idolatry. Let us not be mistaken here; we are neither accusing Rome of idolatry nor ourselves of schism; we think neither charge tenable; but still the Roman Church practises what is so like idolatry, and the English Church makes much of what is so very like schism, that without deciding what is the duty of a Roman Catholic towards the Church of England in her present state, we do seriously think that members of the English Church have a providential direction given them, how to comport themselves towards the Church of Rome, while she is what she is.'

One remark more about Antiquity and the *Via Media*. As time went on, without doubting the strength of the Anglican argument from Antiquity, I felt also that it was not merely our special plea, but our only one. Also I felt that the *Via Media*, which was to represent it, was to be a sort of remodelled and adapted Antiquity. This I advanced both in *Home Thoughts Abroad* and in the Article of the *British Critic* which I have analyzed above. But this circumstance, that after all we must use private judgment upon Antiquity, created a sort of distrust of my theory altogether, which in the conclusion[48] of my Volume on the *Prophetical Office* (1836-7) I express thus: 'Now that our discussions draw to a close, the thought, with which we entered on the subject, is apt to recur, when the excitement of the inquiry has subsided, and weariness has succeeded, that what has been said is but a dream, the wanton exercise, rather than the practical conclusions of the intellect.' And I conclude the paragraph by anticipating a line of thought into which I was, in the event, almost obliged to take refuge: 'After all,' I say, 'the Church is ever invisible in its day, and faith only apprehends it.' What was this, but to give up the Notes of a visible Church altogether, whether the Catholic Note or the Apostolic?

The Long Vacation of 1839 began early. There had been a great many visitors to Oxford from Easter to Commemoration;[49] and Dr. Pusey's party had attracted attention, more, I think, than in any former year. I had put away from me the controversy with Rome for more than two years. In my Parochial Sermons the subject had at no time been introduced: there had been nothing for two years, either in my Tracts or in the British Critic, of a polemical character. I was returning, for the Vacation, to the course of reading which I had many years before chosen as especially my own. I have no reason to suppose that the thoughts of Rome came across my mind at all. About the middle of June I began to study and master the history of the Monophysites.[50] I was absorbed in the doctrinal question. This was from about June 13th to August 30th. It was during this course of reading that for the first time a doubt came upon me of the tenableness of Anglicanism. I recollect on the 30th of July mentioning to a friend, whom I had accidentally met, how remarkable the history was; but by the end of August I was seriously alarmed.

I have described in a former work,[51] how the history affected me. My stronghold was Antiquity; now here, in the middle of the fifth century, I found, as it seemed to me, Christendom of the sixteenth and the nineteenth centuries reflected. I saw my face in that mirror, and I was a Monophysite. The Church of the *Via Media* was in the position of the Oriental communion, Rome was where she now is; and the Protestants were the Eutychians.[52] Of all passages of history, since history has been, who would have thought of going to the sayings and doings of old Eutyches, that *delirus senex*, as (I think) Petavius[53] calls him, and to the enormities of the unprincipled Dioscorus, in order to be converted to Rome!

Now let it be simply understood that I am not writing controversially, but with the one object of relating things as they happened to me in the course of my conversion. With this view I will quote a passage[54] from the account, which I gave in 1850, of my reasonings and feelings in 1839:

'It was difficult to make out how the Eutychians or Monophysites were heretics, unless Protestants and Anglicans were heretics also; difficult to find arguments against the Tridentine Fathers, which did not tell against the Fathers of Chalcedon; difficult to condemn the Popes of the sixteenth century, without condemning the Popes of the fifth. The drama of religion, and the combat of truth and error, were ever one and the same. The principles and proceedings of the Church now, were those of the Church then; the principles and proceedings of heretics then, were those of Protestants now. I found it so, – almost fearfully; there was an awful similitude, more awful, because so silent and unimpassioned, between the dead records of the past and the feverish chronicle of the present. The shadow of the fifth century was on the sixteenth. It was like a spirit rising from the troubled waters of the old world, with the shape and lineaments of the new. The Church then, as now, might be called peremptory and stern, resolute, overbearing, and relentless; and heretics were shifting, changeable, reserved, and deceitful, ever courting civil power, and never agreeing together, except by its aid; and the civil power was ever aiming at comprehensions, trying to put the invisible out of view, and substituting expediency for faith. What was the use of continuing the controversy, or defending my position, if, after all, I was forging arguments for Arius or Eutyches, and turning devil's advocate against the much-enduring Athanasius and the majestic Leo?[55] Be my soul with the Saints! and shall I lift up my hand against them? Sooner may my right hand[56] forget her cunning, and wither outright, as his who once stretched it out against a prophet of God![57] anathema to a whole tribe of Cranmers,[58] Ridleys,[59] Latimers,[60] and Jewels![61] perish the names of Bramhall, Ussher,[62] Taylor,[63] Stillingfleet, and Barrow[64] from the face of the earth, ere I should do ought but fall at their feet in love and in worship, whose image was continually before my eyes, and whose musical words were ever in my ears and on my tongue!'

Hardly had I brought my course of reading to a close, when the *Dublin Review* of that same August was put into my hands, by friends[65] who were more favourable to the cause of Rome than I was myself. There was an article[66] in it on the 'Anglican Claim' by Dr. Wiseman. This was about the middle of September. It was on the Donatists, with an application to Anglicanism. I read it, and did not see much in it. The Donatist controversy was known to me for some years, as has appeared already. The case was not parallel to that of the Anglican Church. St. Augustine in Africa wrote against the Donatists in Africa. They were a furious party who made a schism within the African Church, and not beyond its limits. It was a case of Altar against Altar, of two occupants of the same See, as that between the Non-jurors in England and the Established Church; not the case of one Church against another, as of Rome against the Oriental Monophysites. But my friend, an anxiously religious man, now, as then, very dear to me, a Protestant still, pointed out the palmary words[67] of St. Augustine, which were contained in one of the extracts made in the *Review*, and which had escaped my observation. 'Securus judicat orbis terrarum.' He repeated these words again and again, and, when he was gone, they kept ringing in my ears. 'Securus judicat orbis terrarum;' they were words which went beyond the occasion of the Donatists: they applied to that of the Monophysites. They gave a cogency to the Article, which had escaped me at first. They decided ecclesiastical questions on a simpler rule than that of Antiquity; nay, St. Augustine was one of the prime oracles of Antiquity; here then Antiquity was deciding against itself. What a light was hereby thrown upon every

controversy in the Church! not that, for the moment, the multitude may not falter in their judgment, – not that, in the Arian
hurricane, Sees more than can be numbered did not bend before
its fury, and fall off from St. Athanasius, – not that the crowd of
Oriental Bishops did not need to be sustained during the contest
by the voice and the eye of St. Leo; but that the deliberate
judgment, in which the whole Church at length rests and acqui-
esces, is an infallible prescription and a final sentence against
such portions of it as protest and secede. Who can account for
the impressions which are made on him? For a mere sentence,
the words of St. Augustine, struck me with a power which I
never had felt from any words before. To take a familiar instance,
they were like the 'Turn again Whittington'[68] of the chime; or,
to take a more serious one, they were like the 'Tolle, lege, –
Tolle, lege,'[69] of the child, which converted St. Augustine himself.
'Securus judicat orbis terrarum!' By those great words of the
ancient Father, interpreting and summing up the long and varied
course of ecclesiastical history, the theory of the *Via Media* was
absolutely pulverized.

I became excited at the view thus opened upon me. I was just
starting on a round of visits; and I mentioned my state of mind
to two most intimate friends:[70] I think to no others. After a
while, I got calm, and at length the vivid impression upon my
imagination faded away. What I thought about it on reflection, I
will attempt to describe presently. I had to determine its logical
value, and its bearing upon my duty. Meanwhile, so far as this
was certain, – I had seen the shadow of a hand upon the wall.[71] It
was clear that I had a good deal to learn on the question of the
Churches, and that perhaps some new light was coming upon
me. He who has seen a ghost, cannot be as if he had never seen
it. The heavens[72] had opened and closed again. The thought for
the moment had been, 'The Church of Rome will be found right
after all;' and then it had vanished. My old convictions remained
as before.

At this time, I wrote my Sermon on Divine Calls, which I
published in my volume of *Plain Sermons*. It ends[73] thus: –

'O that we could take that simple view of things, as to feel
that the one thing which lies before us is to please God! What
gain is it to please the world, to please the great, nay even to

please those whom we love, compared with this? What gain is it to be applauded, admired, courted, followed, – compared with this one aim, of not being disobedient to a heavenly vision? What can this world offer comparable with that insight into spiritual things, that keen faith, that heavenly peace, that high sanctity, that everlasting righteousness, that hope of glory, which they have, who in sincerity love and follow our Lord Jesus Christ? Let us beg and pray Him day by day to reveal Himself to our souls more fully, to quicken our senses, to give us sight and hearing, taste and touch of the world to come; so to work within us, that we may sincerely say, "Thou shalt guide me with Thy counsel, and after that receive me with glory. Whom have I in heaven but Thee? and there is none upon earth that I desire in comparison of Thee. My flesh and my heart faileth, but God is the strength of my heart, and my portion for ever."'

Now to trace the succession of thoughts, and the conclusions, and the consequent innovations on my previous belief, and the general conduct, to which I was led upon this sudden visitation. And first, I will say, whatever comes of saying it, for I leave inferences to others, that for years I must have had something of an habitual notion, though it was latent, and had never led me to distrust my own convictions, that my mind had not found its ultimate rest, and that in some sense or other I was on journey. During the same passage across the Mediterranean in which I wrote *Lead, kindly light*, I also wrote the verses, which are found in the *Lyra* under the head of *Providences*, beginning, 'When I look back.'[74] This was in 1833; and, since I have begun this narrative, I have found memorandum[75] under the date of September 7, 1829, in which I speak of myself, as 'now in my rooms in Oriel College, slowly advancing, &c. and led on by God's hand blindly, not knowing whither He is taking me.' But, whatever this presentiment be worth, it was no protection against the dismay and disgust which I felt, in consequence of the dreadful misgiving, of which I have been relating the history. The one question was, what was I to do? I had to make up my mind for myself, and others could not help me. I determined to be guided, not by my imagination, but by my reason. And this I said over and over again in the years which followed, both in conversation and in private letters. Had it not been for this severe resolve, I should have been a Catholic sooner than I was. Moreover, I felt on consideration a positive doubt, on the other hand, whether the suggestion did not come from below. Then I said to myself, Time alone can solve that question. It was my business to go on as usual, to obey those convictions to which I had so long surrendered myself, which still had possession of me, and on which my new thoughts had no direct bearing. That new conception of things should only so far influence me, as it had a logical claim to do so. If it came from above, it would come again; – so I trusted, – and with more definite outlines and greater cogency and consistency of proof. I thought of Samuel, before 'he knew the word of the Lord;'[76] and therefore I went, and lay down to sleep again. This was my broad view of the matter, and my *primâ facie* conclusion.

However, my new historical fact had already to a certain point a logical force. Down had come the *Via Media* as a definite theory or scheme, under the blows of St. Leo.[77] My *Prophetical Office* had come to pieces; not indeed as an argument against 'Roman errors,' nor as against Protestantism, but as in behalf of England. I had no longer a distinctive plea for Anglicanism, unless I would be a Monophysite. I had, most painfully, to fall back upon my three original points of belief, which I have spoken so much of in a former passage, – the principle of dogma, the sacramental system, and anti-Romanism. Of these three, the first two were better secured in Rome than in the Anglican Church. The Apostolical Succession, the two prominent sacraments, and the primitive Creeds, belonged, indeed, to the latter; but there had been and was far less strictness on matters of dogma and ritual in the Anglican system than in the Roman: in consequence, my main argument for the Anglican claims lay in the positive and special charges, which I could bring against Rome. I had no positive Anglican theory. I was very nearly a pure Protestant. Lutherans had a sort of theology, so had Calvinists; I had none.

However, this pure Protestantism, to which I was gradually left, was really a practical principle. It was a strong, though it was only a negative ground, and it still had great hold on me. As a boy of fifteen, I had so fully imbibed it, that I had actually erased in my *Gradus ad Parnassum*,[78] such titles, under the word 'Papa,' as 'Christi Vicarius,' 'sacer interpres,' and 'sceptra gerens,' and substituted epithets so vile that I cannot bring myself to write them down here. The effect of this early persuasion remained as, what I have already called it, a 'stain upon my imagination.' As regards my reason, I began in 1833 to form theories on the subject, which tended to obliterate it; yet by 1838 I had got no further than to consider Antichrist, as not the Church of Rome, but the spirit of the old pagan city, the fourth monster of Daniel[79] which was still alive, and which had corrupted the Church which was planted there. Soon after this indeed, and before my attention was directed to the Monophysite controversy, I underwent a great change of opinion. I saw that, from the nature of the case, the true Vicar of Christ must ever to the world seem like Antichrist, and be stigmatized as such, because a resemblance must ever exist between an original and a forgery; and thus the fact of such a calumny was almost one of the notes of the Church. But we cannot unmake ourselves or change our habits in a moment. Though my reason was convinced, I did not throw off, for some time after, – I could not have thrown off, – the unreasoning prejudice and suspicion, which I cherished about her at least by fits and starts, in spite of this conviction of my reason. I cannot prove this, but I believe it to have been the case from what I recollect of myself. Nor was there any thing in the history of St. Leo and the Monophysites to undo the firm belief I had in the existence of what I called the practical abuses and excesses of Rome.

To her inconsistencies then, to her ambition and intrigue, to her sophistries (as I considered them to be) I now had recourse in my opposition to her, both public and personal. I did so by way of a relief. I had a great and growing dislike, after the summer of 1839, to speak against the Roman Church herself or her formal doctrines. I was very averse to speaking against doctrines, which might possibly turn out to be true, though at the time I had no reason for thinking they were; or against the Church, which had preserved them. I began to have misgivings, that, strong as my own feelings had been against her, yet in some things which I had said, I had taken the statements of Anglican divines for granted without weighing them for myself. I said to a friend in 1840, in a letter,[80] which I shall use presently, 'I am troubled by doubts whether as it is, I have not, in what I have published, spoken too strongly against Rome, though I think I did it in a kind of faith, being determined to put myself into the English system, and say all that our divines said, whether I had fully weighed it or not.' I was sore about the great Anglican divines, as if they had taken me in, and made me say strong things, which facts did not justify. Yet I *did* still hold in substance all that I had said against the Church of Rome in my *Prophetical Office*. I felt the force of the usual Protestant objections against her; I believed that we had the Apostolical succession in the Anglican Church, and the grace of the sacraments; I was not sure that the difficulty of its isolation might not be overcome, though I was far from sure that it could. I did not see any clear proof that it had committed itself to any heresy, or had taken part against the truth; and I was not sure that it would not revive into full Apostolic purity and strength, and grow into union with Rome herself (Rome explaining her doctrines and guarding against their abuse), that is, if we were but patient and hopeful. I began to wish for union between the Anglican Church and Rome, if, and when, it was possible; and I did what I could to gain weekly prayers for that object. The ground which I felt to be good against her was the moral ground: I felt I could not be wrong in striking at her political and social line of action. The alliance of a dogmatic religion with liberals, high or low, seemed to me a providential direction against moving towards Rome, and a better 'Preservative against Popery,' than the three volumes[81] in folio, in which, I think, that prophylactic is to be found. However, on occasions which demanded it, I felt it a duty to give out plainly all that I thought, though I did not like to do so. One such instance occurred, when I had to publish a Letter[82] about Tract 90. In that Letter, I said, 'Instead of setting before the soul the Holy Trinity, and heaven and hell, the Church of Rome does seem to me, as a popular system, to preach the Blessed Virgin and the Saints, and purgatory.' On this occasion I recollect expressing to a friend the distress it gave me thus to speak; but, I said, 'How can I help saying it, if I think it? and I *do* think it; my Bishop calls on me to say out what I think; and that is the long and the short of it.' But I recollected Hurrell Froude's words[83] to me, almost his dying words, 'I must enter another protest against your cursing and swearing. What good can it do? and I call it uncharitable to an excess. How mistaken we may ourselves be on many points that are only gradually opening on us!'

Instead then of speaking of errors in doctrine, I was driven, by my state of mind, to insist upon the political conduct, the controversial bearing, and the social methods and manifestations of Rome. And here I found a matter ready to my hand, which affected me the more sensibly for the reason that it lay at our very doors. I can hardly describe too strongly my feeling upon it. I had an unspeakable aversion to the policy and acts of Mr. O'Connell,[84] because, as I thought, he associated himself with men of all religions and no religion against the Anglican Church, and advanced Catholicism by violence and intrigue. When then I found him taken up by the English Catholics, and, as I supposed, at Rome, I considered I had a fulfilment before my eyes how the Court of Rome played fast and loose, and justified the serious charges which I had seen put down in books against it. Here we saw what Rome was in action, whatever she might be when quiescent. Her conduct was simply secular and political.

This feeling led me into the excess of being very rude to that zealous and most charitable man, Mr. Spencer,[85] when he came to Oxford in January, 1840, to get Anglicans to set about praying for Unity. I myself, at that time, or soon after, drew up such prayers; their desirableness was one of the first thoughts which came upon me after my shock; but I was too much annoyed with the political action of the Catholic body in these islands to wish to have any thing to do with them personally. So glad in my heart was I to see him, when he came to my rooms with Mr. Palmer of Magdalen, that I could have laughed for joy; I think I did laugh; but I was very rude to him, I would not meet him at dinner, and that, (though I did not say so,) because I considered him 'in loco apostatae'[86] from the Anglican Church, and I hereby beg his pardon for it. I wrote afterwards with a view to apologize, but I dare say he must have thought that I made the matter worse, for these were my words to him: –

'The news that you are praying for us is most touching, and raises a variety of indescribable emotions. . . . May their prayers return abundantly into their own bosoms. . . . Why then do I not meet you in a manner conformable with these first feelings? For this single reason, if I may say it, that your acts are contrary to your words. You invite us to a union of hearts, at the same time that you are doing all you can, not to restore, not to reform, not to re-unite, but to destroy our Church. You go further than your principles require. You are leagued with our enemies. "The voice is Jacob's voice, but the hands are the hands of Esau."[87] This is what especially distresses us; this is what we cannot understand; how Christians, like yourselves, with the clear view you have that a warfare is ever waging in the world between good and evil, should, in the present state of England, ally yourselves with the side of evil against the side of good. . . . Of parties now in the country, you cannot but allow, that next to yourselves we are nearest to revealed truth. We maintain great and holy principles; we profess Catholic doctrines. . . . So near are we as a body to yourselves in modes of thinking, as even to have been taunted with the nicknames which belong to you; and, on the other hand, if there are professed infidels, scoffers, sceptics, unprincipled men, rebels, they are found among our opponents. And yet you take part with them against us. . . . You consent to act hand in hand [with these and others] for our overthrow. Alas! all this it is that impresses us irresistibly with the notion that you are a political, not a religious party; that in order to gain an end on which you set your hearts, – an open stage for yourselves in England, – you ally yourselves with those who hold nothing against those who hold something. This is what distresses my own mind so greatly, to speak of myself, that, with limitations which need not now be mentioned, I cannot meet familiarly any leading persons of the Roman Communion, and least of all when they come on a religious errand. Break off, I would say, with Mr. O'Connell in Ireland and the liberal party in England, or come not to us with overtures for mutual prayer and religious sympathy.'

And here came in another feeling, of a personal nature, which had little to do with the argument against Rome, except that, in my prejudice, I viewed what happened to myself in the light of my own ideas of the traditionary conduct of her advocates and instruments. I was very stern in the case of any interference in our Oxford matters on the part of charitable Catholics, and of any attempt to do me good personally. There was nothing, indeed, at the time more likely to throw me back. 'Why do you meddle? why cannot you let me alone? You can do me no good: you know nothing on earth about me; you may actually do me harm; I am in better hands than yours. I know my own sincerity of purpose; and I am determined upon taking my time.' Since I have been a Catholic, people have sometimes accused me of backwardness in making converts; and Protestants have argued from it that I have no great eagerness to do so. It would be against my nature to act otherwise than I do; but besides, it would be to forget the lessons which I gained in the experience of my own history in the past.

This is the account which I have to give of some savage and ungrateful words in the *British Critic*[88] of 1840 against the controversialists of Rome: 'By their fruits ye shall know them. . . . We see it attempting to gain converts among us by unreal representations of its doctrines, plausible statements, bold assertions, appeals to the weaknesses of human nature, to our fancies, our eccentricities, our fears, our frivolities, our false philosophies. We see its agents, smiling and nodding and ducking to attract attention, as gipsies make up to truant boys, holding out tales for the nursery, and pretty pictures, and gilt gingerbread, and physic concealed in jam, and sugar-plums for good children. Who can but feel shame when the religion of Ximenes,[89] Borromeo,[90] and Pascal,[91] is so overlaid? Who can but feel sorrow, when its devout and earnest defenders so mistake its genius and its capabilities? We Englishmen like manliness, openness, consistency, truth. Rome will never gain on us, till she learns these virtues, and uses them; and then she *may* gain us, but it will be by ceasing to be what we now mean by Rome, by having a right, not to "have dominion over our faith,"[92] but to gain and possess our affections in the bonds of the gospel. Till she ceases to be what she practically is, a union is impossible between her and England; but, if she does reform, (and who can presume to say that so large a part of Christendom never can?) then it will be our Church's duty at once to join in communion with the continental Churches, whatever politicians at home may say to it, and whatever steps the civil power may take in consequence.

And though we may not live to see that day, at least we are
bound to pray for it; we are bound to pray for our brethren
that they and we may be led together into the pure light of
the gospel, and be one as we once were one. It was most
touching news[93] to be told, as we were lately, that Christians
on the Continent were praying together for the spiritual well-
being of England. May they gain light, while they aim at
unity, and grow in faith while they manifest their love! We
too have our duties to them; not of reviling, not of slandering,
not of hating, though political interests require it; but the duty
of loving brethren still more abundantly in spirit, whose faces,
for our sins and their sins, we are not allowed to see in the
flesh.'

No one ought to indulge in insinuations; it certainly diminishes
my right to complain of slanders uttered against myself, when, as
in this passage, I had already spoken in disparagement of the
controversialists of that religious body, to which I myself now
belong.

I have thus put together, as well as I can, what has to be said
about my general state of mind from the autumn of 1839 to the
summer of 1841; and, having done so, I go on to narrate how
my new misgivings affected my conduct, and my relations towards the Anglican Church.

When I got back to Oxford in October, 1839, after the visits
which I had been paying, it so happened, there had been, in my
absence, occurrences[94] of an awkward character, compromising
me both with my Bishop and also with the authorities of the
University; and this drew my attention at once to the state of the
Movement party there, and made me very anxious for the future.
In the spring of the year, as has been seen in the Article analyzed
above, I had spoken of the excesses which were to be found
among persons commonly included in it: – at that time I thought
little of such an evil, but the new views, which had come on me
during the Long Vacation, on the one hand made me comprehend
it, and on the other took away my power of effectually meeting
it. A firm and powerful control was necessary to keep men
straight; I never had a strong wrist, but at the very time, when it
was most needed, the reins had broken in my hands. With an

anxious presentiment on my mind of the upshot of the whole inquiry, which it was almost impossible for me to conceal from men who saw me day by day, who heard my familiar conversation, who came perhaps for the express purpose of pumping me, and having a categorical *yes* or *no* to their questions, – how could I expect to say any thing about my actual, positive, present belief, which would be sustaining or consoling to such persons as were haunted already by doubts of their own? Nay, how could I, with satisfaction to myself, analyze my own mind, and say what I held and what I did not hold? or how could I say with what limitations, shades of difference, or degrees of belief, I still held that body of Anglican opinions which I had openly professed and taught? how could I deny or assert this point or that, without injustice to the new light, in which the whole evidence for those old opinions presented itself to my mind?

However, I had to do what I could, and what was best, under the circumstances; I found a general talk on the subject of the Article in the *Dublin Review*; and, if it had affected me, it was not wonderful, that it affected others also. As to myself, I felt no kind of certainty that the argument in it was conclusive. Taking it at the worst, granting that the Anglican Church had not the Note of Catholicity; yet there were many Notes of the Church. Some belonged to one age or place, some to another. Bellarmine[95] had reckoned Temporal Prosperity among the Notes of the Church; but the Roman Church had not any great popularity, wealth, glory, power, or prospects, in the nineteenth century. It was not at all certain as yet, even that we had not the Note of Catholicity; but, if not this, we had others. My first business then, was to examine this question carefully, and see, whether a great deal could not be said after all for the Anglican Church, in spite of its acknowledged short-comings. This I did in an Article[96] 'on the Catholicity of the English Church,' which appeared in the *British Critic* of January, 1840. As to my personal distress on the point, I think it had gone by February 21st in that year, for I wrote then to Mr. Bowden about the important Article in the Dublin, thus: 'It made a great impression here [Oxford]; and, I say what of course I would only say to such as yourself, it made me for a while very uncomfortable in my own mind. The great speciousness of his argument is one of the things which have made me despond so much,' that is, as anticipating its effect upon others.

But, secondly, the great stumbling-block lay in the 39 Articles. It was urged that here was a positive Note *against* Anglicanism: – Anglicanism claimed to hold, that the Church of England was nothing else than a continuation in this country, (as the Church of Rome might be in France or Spain,) of that one Church of which in old times Athanasius and Augustine were members. But, if so, the doctrine must be the same; the doctrine of the Old Church must live and speak in Anglican formularies, in the 39 Articles. Did it? Yes, it did; that is what I maintained; it did in substance, in a true sense. Man had done his worst to disfigure, to mutilate, the old Catholic Truth; but there it was, in spite of them, in the Articles still. It was there, – but this must be shown. It was a matter of life and death to us to show it. And I believed that it could be shown; I considered that those grounds of justification, which I gave above, when I was speaking of Tract 90, were sufficient for the purpose; and therefore I set about showing it at once. This was in March, 1840, when I went up to Littlemore. And, as it was a matter of life and death with us, all risks must be run to show it. When the attempt was actually made, I had got reconciled to the prospect of it, and had no apprehensions as to the experiment; but in 1840, while my purpose was honest, and my grounds of reason satisfactory, I did nevertheless recognize that I was engaged in an *experimentum crucis*.[97] I have no doubt that then I acknowledged to myself that it would be a trial of the Anglican Church, which it had never undergone before, – not that the Catholic sense of the Articles had not been held or at least suffered by their framers and promulgators, not that it was not implied in the teaching of Andrewes or Beveridge,[98] but that it had never been publicly recognized, while the interpretation of the day was Protestant and exclusive. I observe also, that, though my Tract was an experiment, it was, as I said at the time, 'no *feeler*'; the event showed this; for, when my principle was not granted, I did not draw back, but gave up. I would not hold office in a Church which would not allow my sense of the Articles. My tone was, 'This is necessary for us, and have it we must and will, and, if it tends to bring men to look less bitterly on the Church of Rome so much the better.'

This then was the second work to which I set myself; though when I got to Littlemore, other things interfered to prevent my accomplishing it at the moment. I had in mind to remove all such obstacles as lay in the way of holding the Apostolic and Catholic character of the Anglican teaching; to assert the right of all who chose, to say in the face of day, 'Our Church teaches the Primitive Ancient faith.' I did not conceal this: in Tract 90, it is put forward as the first principle of all, 'It is a duty which we owe both to the Catholic Church, and to our own, to take our reformed confessions in the most Catholic sense they will admit: we have no duties towards their framers.' And still more point-edly in my Letter,[99] explanatory of the Tract, addressed to Dr. Jelf,[100] I say: 'The only peculiarity of the view I advocate, if I must so call it, is this – that whereas it is usual at this day to make the *particular belief of their writers* their true interpretation, I would make the *belief of the Catholic Church such*. That is, as it is often said that infants are regenerated in Baptism, not on the faith of their parents, but of the Church, so in like manner I would say that the Articles are received, not in the sense of their framers, but (as far as the wording will admit or any ambiguity requires it) in the one Catholic sense.'

A third measure which I distinctly contemplated, was the resignation of St. Mary's, whatever became of the question of the 39 Articles; and as a first step I meditated a retirement to Littlemore.[101] Littlemore was an integral part of St. Mary's Parish, and between two and three miles distant from Oxford. I had built a Church there several years before; and I went there to pass the Lent of 1840, and gave myself up to teaching in the Parish School, and practising the choir. At the same time, I had in view a monastic house there. I bought ten acres of ground and began planting; but this great design was never carried out. I mention it, because it shows how little I had really the idea at that time of ever leaving the Anglican Church. That I contem-plated as early as 1839 the further step of giving up St. Mary's, appears from a letter[102] which I wrote in October, 1840, to Mr. Keble, the friend whom it was most natural for me to consult on such a point. It ran as follows: –

'For a year past a feeling has been growing on me that I ought to give up St. Mary's, but I am no fit judge in the matter. I cannot ascertain accurately my own impressions and convictions, which are the basis of the difficulty, and though you cannot of course do this for me, yet you may help me generally, and perhaps supersede the necessity of my going by them at all.

'First, it is certain that I do not know my Oxford parishioners; I am not conscious of influencing them, and certainly I have no insight into their spiritual state. I have no personal, no pastoral acquaintance with them. To very few have I any opportunity of saying a religious word. Whatever influence I exert on them is precisely that which I may be exerting on persons out of my parish. In my excuse I am accustomed to say to myself that I am not adapted to get on with them, while others are. On the other hand, I am conscious that by means of my position at St. Mary's, I do exert a considerable influence on the University, whether on Undergraduates or Graduates. It seems, then, on the whole that I am using St. Mary's, to the neglect of its direct duties, for objects not belonging to it; I am converting a parochial charge into a sort of University office.

'I think I may say truly that I have begun scarcely any plan but for the sake of my parish, but every one has turned, independently of me, into the direction of the University. I began[103] Saints'-days Services, daily Services, and Lectures in Adam de Brome's Chapel, for my parishioners: but they have not come to them. In consequence I dropped the last mentioned, having, while it lasted, been naturally led to direct it to the instruction of those who did come, instead of those who did not. The Weekly Communion, I believe, I did begin for the sake of the University.

'Added to this the authorities of the University, the appointed guardians of those who form great part of the attendants on my Sermons, have shown a dislike of my preaching. One dissuades men from coming; – the late[104] Vice-Chancellor threatens to take his own children away from the Church; and the present,[105] having an opportunity last spring of preaching in my parish pulpit, gets up and preaches against doctrine with which I am in good measure identified. No plainer proof can be given of the feeling in these quarters, than the absurd myth, now a second time put forward, "that Vice-Chancellors cannot be got to take the office on account of Puseyism."

'But further than this, I cannot disguise from myself that my preaching is not calculated to defend that system of religion which has been received for 300 years, and of which the Heads of Houses are the legitimate maintainers in this place. They exclude me, as far as may be, from the University Pulpit; and, though I never have preached strong doctrine in it, they do so rightly, so far as this, that they understand that my sermons are calculated to undermine things established. I cannot disguise from myself that they are. No one will deny that most of my sermons are on moral subjects, not doctrinal; still I am leading my hearers to the Primitive Church, if you will, but not to the Church of England. Now, ought one to be disgusting the minds of young men with the received religion, in the exercise of a sacred office, yet without a commission, and against the wish of their guides and governors?

'But this is not all. I fear I must allow that, whether I will or no, I am disposing them towards Rome. First, because Rome is the only representative of the Primitive Church besides ourselves; in proportion then as they are loosened from the one, they will go to the other. Next, because many doctrines which I have held have far greater, or their only scope, in the Roman system. And, moreover, if, as is not unlikely, we have in process of time heretical Bishops or teachers among us, an evil which *ipso facto* infects the whole community to which they belong, and if, again (what there are at this moment symptoms of), there be a movement in the English Roman Catholics to break the alliance of O'Connell and of Exeter Hall,[106] strong temptations will be placed in the way of individuals, already imbued with a tone of thought congenial to Rome, to join her Communion.

'People tell me, on the other hand, that I am, whether by sermons or otherwise, exerting at St. Mary's a beneficial influence on our prospective clergy; but what if I take to myself the credit of seeing further than they, and of having in the course of the last year discovered that what they approve so much is very likely to end in Romanism?

'The *arguments* which I have published against Romanism seem to myself as cogent as ever, but men go by their sympathies, not by argument; and if I feel the force of this influence myself, who bow to the arguments, why may not others still more, who never have in the same degree admitted the arguments?

'Nor can I counteract the danger by preaching or writing against Rome. I seem to myself almost to have shot my last arrow in the Article on English Catholicity. It must be added, that the very circumstance that I have committed myself against Rome has the effect of setting to sleep people suspicious about me, which is painful now that I begin to have suspicions about myself. I mentioned my general difficulty to Rogers[107] a year since, than whom I know no one of a more fine and accurate conscience, and it was his spontaneous idea that I should give up St. Mary's, if my feelings continued. I mentioned it again to him lately, and he did not reverse his opinion, only expressed great reluctance to believe it must be so.'

Mr. Keble's judgment was in favour of my retaining my living; at least for the present; what weighed with me most was his saying, 'You must consider, whether your retiring either from the Pastoral Care only, or from writing and printing and editing in the cause, would not be a sort of scandalous thing, unless it were done very warily. It would be said, "You see he can go on no longer with the Church of England, except in mere Lay Communion;" or people might say you repented of the cause altogether. Till you see [your way to mitigate, if not remove this evil] I certainly should advise you to stay.' I answered[108] as follows: –

'Since you think I *may* go on, it seems to follow that, under the circumstances, I *ought* to do so. There are plenty of reasons for it, directly it is allowed to be lawful. The following considerations have much reconciled my feelings to your conclusion.

'1. I do not think that we have yet made fair trial how much the English Church will bear. I know it is a hazardous experiment, – like proving cannon. Yet we must not take it for granted that the metal will burst in the operation. It has borne at various times, not to say at this time, a great infusion of Catholic truth without damage. As to the result, viz. whether this process will not approximate the whole English Church, as a body, to Rome, that is nothing to us. For what we know, it may be the providential means of uniting the whole Church in one, without fresh schismatizing or use of private judgment.'

Here I observe, that, what was contemplated was the bursting of the *Catholicity* of the Anglican Church, that is, my *subjective idea* of that Church. Its bursting would not hurt her with the world, but would be a discovery that she was purely and essentially Protestant, and would be really the 'hoisting of the engineer with his own petard.'[109] And this was the result. I continue: –

'2. Say, that I move sympathies for Rome: in the same sense does Hooker, Taylor, Bull, &c. Their *arguments* may be against Rome, but the sympathies they raise must be towards Rome, *so far* as Rome maintains truths which our Church does not teach or enforce. Thus it is a question of *degree* between our divines and me. I may, if so be, go further; I may raise sympathies *more*; but I am but urging minds in the same direction as they do. I am doing just the very thing which all our doctors have ever been doing. In short, would not Hooker, if Vicar of St. Mary's, be in my difficulty?' – Here it may be objected, that Hooker could preach against Rome and I could not; but I doubt whether he could have preached effectively against Transubstantiation better than I, though neither he nor I held that doctrine.

'3. Rationalism is the great evil of the day. May not I consider my post at St. Mary's as a place of protest against it? I am more certain that the Protestant [spirit], which I oppose, leads to infidelity, than that which I recommend, leads to Rome. Who knows what the state of the University may be, as regards Divinity Professors in a few years hence? Any how, a great battle may be coming on, of which Milman's book[110] is a sort of earnest. The whole of *our* day may be a battle with this spirit. May we not leave to another age *its own* evil, – to settle the question of Romanism?'

I may add that from this time I had a curate[111] at St. Mary's, who gradually took more and more of my work.

Also, this same year, 1840, I made arrangements for giving up the *British Critic*, in the following July, which were carried into effect at that date.

Such was about my state of mind, on the publication of Tract 90 in February 1841. I was indeed in prudence taking steps towards eventually withdrawing from St. Mary's, and I was not confident about my permanent adhesion to the Anglican creed; but I was in no actual perplexity or trouble of mind. Nor did the immense commotion consequent upon the publication of the Tract unsettle me again: for I fancied I had weathered the storm, as far as the Bishops were concerned: the Tract had not been condemned: that was the great point, and I made much of it.

To illustrate my feelings during this trial, I will make extracts from my letters addressed severally to Mr. Bowden and another friend,[112] which have come into my possession.

1. March 15. – 'The Heads, I believe, have just done a violent act: they have said that my interpretation of the Articles is an *evasion*. Do not think that this will pain me. You see, no *doctrine* is censured, and my shoulders shall manage to bear the charge. If you knew all, or were here, you would see that I have asserted a great principle, and I *ought* to suffer for it: – that the Articles are to be interpreted, not according to the meaning of the writers, but (as far as the wording will admit) according to the sense of the Catholic Church.'

2. March 25. – 'I do trust I shall make no false step, and hope my friends will pray for me to this effect. If, as you say, a destiny hangs over us, a single false step may ruin all. I am very well and comfortable; but we are not yet out of the wood.'

3. April 1. – 'The Bishop sent me word on Sunday to write a Letter[113] to him *'instanter.'* So I wrote it on Monday: on Tuesday it passed through the press: on Wednesday it was out: and to-day [Thursday] it is in London.

'I trust that things are smoothing now; and that we have made a *great step* is certain. It is not right to boast, till I am clear out of the wood, i.e. till I know how the Letter is received in London. You know, I suppose, that I am to stop the Tracts; but you will see in the Letter, though I speak *quite* what I feel, yet I have managed to take out on *my* side my snubbing's worth. And this makes me anxious how it will be received in London.

'I have not had a misgiving for five minutes from the first: but I do not like to boast, lest some harm come.'

4. April 4. – 'Your letter of this morning was an exceedingly great gratification to me: and it is confirmed, I am thankful to say, by the opinion of others. The Bishop sent me a message that

my Letter had his unqualified approbation; and since that, he has sent me a note to the same effect, only going more into detail. It is most pleasant too to my feelings, to have such a testimony to the substantial truth and importance of No. 90, as I have had from so many of my friends, from those who, from their cautious turn of mind, I was least sanguine about. I have not had one misgiving myself about it throughout; and I do trust that what has happened will be overruled to subserve the great cause we all have at heart.'

5. May 9. – 'The Bishops are very desirous of hushing the matter up: and I certainly have done my utmost to co-operate with them, on the understanding that the Tract is not to be withdrawn or condemned.'

Upon this occasion several Catholics wrote to me; I answered one[114] of my correspondents in the same tone: –

'April 8. – You have no cause to be surprised at the discontinuance of the Tracts. We feel no misgivings about it whatever, as if the cause of what we hold to be Catholic truth would suffer thereby. My letter to my Bishop has, I trust, had the effect of bringing the preponderating *authority* of the Church on our side. No stopping of the Tracts can, humanly speaking, stop the spread of the opinions which they have inculcated.

'The Tracts are not *suppressed*. No doctrine or principle has been conceded by us, or condemned by authority. The Bishop has but said that a certain Tract is "objectionable," no reason being stated. I have no intention whatever of yielding any one point which I hold on conviction; and that the authorities of the Church know full well.'

In the summer of 1841, I found myself at Littlemore without any harass or anxiety on my mind. I had determined to put aside all controversy, and I set myself down to my translation of St. Athanasius; but, between July and November, I received three blows which broke me.

1. I had got but a little way in my work, when my trouble returned on me. The ghost had come a second time. In the *Arian History* I found the very same phenomenon, in a far bolder shape, which I had found in the Monophysite. I had not observed it in 1832. Wonderful that this should come upon me! I had not

sought it out; I was reading and writing in my own line of study, far from the controversies of the day, on what is called a 'metaphysical' subject; but I saw clearly, that in the history of Arianism, the pure Arians were the Protestants, the semi-Arians were the Anglicans, and that Rome now was what it was then. The truth lay, not with the *Via Media*, but with what was called 'the extreme party.' As I am not writing a work of controversy, I need not enlarge upon the argument; I have said something on the subject in a Volume,[115] from which I have already quoted.

2. I was in the misery of this new unsettlement, when a second blow came upon me. The Bishops one after another began to charge against me. It was a formal, determinate movement. This was the real 'understanding;' that, on which I had acted on the first appearance of Tract 90, had come to nought. I think the words, which had then been used to me, were, that 'perhaps two or three of them might think it necessary to say something in their charges;' but by this time they had tided over the difficulty of the Tract, and there was no one to enforce the 'understanding.' They went on in this way, directing charges at me, for three whole years. I recognized it as a condemnation; it was the only one that was in their power. At first I intended to protest; but I gave up the thought in despair.

On October 17th, I wrote thus to a friend[116]: 'I suppose it will be necessary in some shape or other to re-assert Tract 90; else, it will seem, after these Bishop's Charges, as if it were silenced, which it has not been, nor do I intend it should be. I wish to keep quiet; but if Bishops speak, I will speak too. If the view were silenced, I could not remain in the Church, nor could many others; and therefore, since it is *not* silenced, I shall take care to show that it isn't.'

A day or two after, Oct. 22, a stranger[117] wrote to me to say, that the *Tracts for the Times* had made a young friend of his a Catholic, and to ask, 'would I be so good as to convert him back;' I made answer: –

'If conversions to Rome take place in consequence of the *Tracts for the Times*, I do not impute blame to them, but to those who, instead of acknowledging such Anglican principles of theology and ecclesiastical polity as they contain, set themselves to oppose them. Whatever be the influence of the Tracts, great or small, they may become just as powerful for Rome, if our Church refuses them, as they would be for our Church if she accepted them. If our rulers speak either against the Tracts, or not at all, if any number of them, not only do not favour, but even do not suffer the principles contained in them, it is plain that our members may easily be persuaded either to give up those principles, or to give up the Church. If this state of things goes on, I mournfully prophesy, not one or two, but many secessions to the Church of Rome.'

Two years afterwards, looking back on what had passed, I said, 'There were no converts to Rome, till after the condemnation of No. 90.'

3. As if all this were not enough, there came the affair of the Jerusalem Bishopric;[118] and, with a brief mention of it, I shall conclude.

I think I am right in saying that it had been long a desire with the Prussian Court to introduce Episcopacy into the new Evangelical Religion, which was intended in that country to embrace both the Lutheran and Calvinistic bodies. I almost think I heard of the project, when I was at Rome in 1833, at the Hotel of the Prussian Minister, M. Bunsen, who was most hospitable and kind, as to other English visitors, so also to my friends and myself. The idea of Episcopacy, as the Prussian king[119] understood it, was, I suppose, very different from that taught in the Tractarian School: but still, I suppose also, that the chief authors of that school would have gladly seen such a measure carried out in Prussia, had it been done without compromising those principles which were necessary to the being of a Church. About the time of the publication of Tract 90, M. Bunsen and the then Archbishop[120] of Canterbury were taking steps for its execution, by appointing and consecrating a Bishop for Jerusalem. Jerusalem, it would seem, was considered a safe place for the experiment; it was too far from Prussia to awaken the susceptibilities of any party at home; if the project failed, it failed without harm to any one; and, if it succeeded, it gave Protestantism a *status* in the East, which, in association with the Monophysite or Jacobite[121] and the Nestorian[122] bodies, formed a political instrument for England, parallel to that which Russia had in the Greek Church, and France in the Latin.

Accordingly, in July 1841, full of the Anglican difficulty on the question of Catholicity, I thus spoke of the Jerusalem scheme in an Article in the *British Critic*[123]: 'When our thoughts turn to the East, instead of recollecting that there are Christian Churches there, we leave it to the Russians to take care of the Greeks, and the French to take care of the Romans, and we content ourselves with erecting a Protestant Church at Jerusalem, or with helping the Jews to rebuild their Temple there, or with becoming the august protectors of Nestorians, Monophysites, and all the heretics we can hear of, or with forming a league with the Mussulman against Greeks and Romans together.'

I do not pretend, so long after the time, to give a full or exact account of this measure in detail. I will but say that in the Act of Parliament, under date of October 5, 1841, (if the copy, from which I quote, contains the measure as it passed the Houses,) provision is made for the consecration of 'British subjects, or the subjects or citizens of any foreign state, to be Bishops in any foreign country, whether such foreign subjects or citizens be or be not subjects or citizens of the country in which they are to act, and . . . without requiring such of them as may be subjects or citizens of any foreign kingdom or state to take the oaths of allegiance and supremacy, and the oath of due obedience to the Archbishop for the time being' . . . also 'that such Bishop or Bishops, so consecrated, may exercise within such limits, as may from time to time be assigned for that purpose in such foreign countries by her Majesty, spiritual jurisdiction over the ministers of British congregations of the United Church of England and Ireland, and over *such other Protestant* Congregations, as may be desirous of placing themselves under his or their authority.'

Now here, at the very time that the Anglican Bishops were directing their censure upon me for avowing an approach to the Catholic Church not closer than I believed the Anglican formularies would allow, they were on the other hand, fraternizing, by their act or by their sufferance, with Protestant bodies, and allowing them to put themselves under an Anglican Bishop, without any renunciation of their errors or regard to their due reception of baptism and confirmation; while there was great reason to suppose that the said Bishop was intended to make converts from the orthodox Greeks, and the schismatical Oriental bodies, by means of the influence of England. This was the third blow, which finally shattered my faith in the Anglican Church. That Church was not only forbidding any sympathy or concurrence with the Church of Rome, but it actually was courting an intercommunion with Protestant Prussia and the heresy of the Orientals. The Anglican Church might have the Apostolical succession, as had the Monophysites; but such acts as were in progress led me to the gravest suspicion, not that it would soon cease to be a Church, but that, since the 16th century, it had never been a Church all along.

On October 12th, I thus wrote to Mr. Bowden: – 'We have not a single Anglican in Jerusalem; so we are sending a Bishop to *make* a communion, not to govern our own people. Next, the excuse is, that there are converted Anglican Jews there who require a Bishop; I am told there are not half-a-dozen. But for *them* the Bishop is sent out, and for them he is a Bishop of the *circumcision*' (I think he was a converted Jew,[124] who boasted of his Jewish descent), 'against the Epistle[125] to the Galatians pretty nearly. Thirdly, for the sake of Prussia, he is to take under him all the foreign Protestants who will come; and the political advantages will be so great, from the influence of England, that there is no doubt they *will* come. They are to sign the Confession of Augsburg,[126] and there is nothing to show that they hold the doctrine of Baptismal Regeneration.

'As to myself, I shall do nothing whatever publicly, unless indeed it were to give my signature to a Protest; but I think it would be out of place in *me* to agitate, having been in a way silenced; but the Archbishop is really doing most grave work, of which we cannot see the end.'

I did make a solemn Protest, and sent it to the Archbishop of Canterbury, and also sent it to my own Bishop with the following letter: –

'It seems as if I were never to write to your Lordship, without giving you pain, and I know that my present subject does not specially concern your Lordship; yet, after a great deal of anxious thought, I lay before you the enclosed Protest.

'Your Lordship will observe that I am not asking for any notice of it, unless you think that I ought to receive one. I do this very serious act in obedience to my sense of duty.

'If the English Church is to enter on a new course, and assume a new aspect, it will be more pleasant to me hereafter to think, that I did not suffer so grievous an event to happen, without bearing witness against it.

'May I be allowed to say, that I augur nothing but evil, if we in any respect prejudice our title to be a branch of the Apostolic Church? That Article of the Creed, I need hardly observe to your Lordship, is of such constraining power, that, if *we* will not claim it, and use it for ourselves, *others* will use it in their own behalf against us. Men who learn whether by means of documents or measures, whether from the statements or the acts of persons in authority, that our communion is not a branch of the One Church, I foresee with much grief, will be tempted to look out for that Church elsewhere.

'It is to me a subject of great dismay, that, as far as the Church has lately spoken out, on the subject of the opinions which I and others hold, those opinions are, not merely not *sanctioned* (for that I do not ask), but not even *suffered*.

'I earnestly hope that your Lordship will excuse my freedom in thus speaking to you of some members of your Most Rev. and Right Rev. Body. With every feeling of reverent attachment to your Lordship,

'I am, &c.'

PROTEST

'Whereas the Church of England has a claim on the allegiance of Catholic believers only on the ground of her own claim to be considered a branch of the Catholic Church:

'And whereas the recognition of heresy, indirect as well as direct, goes far to destroy such claim in the case of any religious body:

'And whereas to admit maintainers of heresy to communion, without formal renunciation of their errors, goes far towards recognizing the same:

'And whereas Lutheranism and Calvinism are heresies, repugnant to Scripture, springing up three centuries since, and anathematized by East as well as West:

'And whereas it is reported that the Most Reverend Primate and other Right Reverend Rulers of our Church have consecrated a Bishop with a view to exercising spiritual jurisdiction over Protestant, that is, Lutheran and Calvinist congregations in the East (under the provisions of an Act made in the last session of Parliament to amend an Act made in the 26th year of the reign of his Majesty King George the Third, intituled, "An Act to empower the Archbishop of Canterbury, or the Archbishop of York for the time being, to consecrate to the office of Bishop persons being subjects or citizens of countries out of his Majesty's dominions"), dispensing at the same time, not in particular cases and accidentally, but as if on principle and universally, with any abjuration of error on the part of such congregations, and with any reconciliation to the Church on the part of the presiding Bishop; thereby giving some sort of formal recognition to the doctrines which such congregations maintain:

'And whereas the dioceses in England are connected together by so close an intercommunion, that what is done by authority in one, immediately affects the rest:

'On these grounds, I in my place, being a priest of the English Church and Vicar of St. Mary the Virgin's, Oxford, by way of relieving my conscience, do hereby solemnly protest against the measure aforesaid, and disown it, as removing our Church from her present ground and tending to her disorganization.

'JOHN HENRY NEWMAN.

'*November 11, 1841.*'

Looking back two years afterwards on the above-mentioned and other acts, on the part of Anglican Ecclesiastical authorities, I observed[127]: 'Many a man might have held an abstract theory about the Catholic Church, to which it was difficult to adjust the Anglican, – might have admitted a suspicion, or even painful doubts about the latter, – yet never have been impelled onwards, had our Rulers preserved the quiescence of former years; but it is the corroboration of a present, living, and energetic heterodoxy, that realizes and makes such doubts practical; it has been the recent speeches and acts of authorities, who had so long been tolerant of Protestant error, which has given to inquiry and to theory its force and its edge.'

As to the project of a Jerusalem Bishopric, I never heard of any good or harm it has ever done, except what it has done for me; which many think a great misfortune, and I one of the greatest of mercies. It brought me on to the beginning of the end.

CHAPTER IV

HISTORY OF MY RELIGIOUS OPINIONS FROM
1841 TO 1845

I

From the end of 1841, I was on my death-bed, as regards my membership with the Anglican Church, though at the time I became aware of it only by degrees. I introduce what I have to say with this remark, by way of accounting for the character of this remaining portion of my narrative. A death-bed has scarcely a history; it is a tedious decline, with seasons of rallying and seasons of falling back; and since the end is foreseen, or what is called a matter of time, it has little interest for the reader, especially if he has a kind heart. Moreover, it is a season when doors are closed and curtains drawn, and when the sick man neither cares nor is able to record the stages of his malady. I was in these circumstances, except so far as I was not allowed to die in peace, – except so far as friends, who had still a full right to come in upon me, and the public world which had not, have given a sort of history to those last four years. But in consequence, my narrative must be in great measure documentary, as I cannot rely on my memory, except for definite particulars, positive or negative. Letters of mine to friends since dead have come into my hands; others have been kindly lent me for the occasion; and I have some drafts of others, and some notes which I made, though I have no strictly personal or continuous memoranda to consult, and have unluckily mislaid some valuable papers.

And first as to my position in the view of duty; it was this: – 1. I had given up my place in the Movement in my letter to the Bishop of Oxford in the spring of 1841; but 2. I could not give up my duties towards the many and various minds who had more or less been brought into it by me; 3. I expected or intended gradually to fall back into Lay Communion; 4. I never contemplated leaving the Church of England; 5. I could not hold office in its service, if I were not allowed to hold the Catholic sense of the Articles; 6. I could not go to Rome, while she suffered honours to be paid to the Blessed Virgin and the Saints which I thought in my conscience to be incompatible with the Supreme, Incommunicable Glory of the One Infinite and Eternal; 7. I desired a union with Rome under conditions, Church with Church; 8. I called Littlemore my Torres Vedras,[1] and thought that some day we might advance again within the Anglican Church, as we had been forced to retire; 9. I kept back all persons who were disposed to go to Rome with all my might.

And I kept them back for three or four reasons; 1. because what I could not in conscience do myself, I could not suffer them to do; 2. because I thought that in various cases they were acting under excitement; 3. because I had duties to my Bishop and to the Anglican Church; and 4. in some cases, because I had received from their Anglican parents or superiors direct charge of them.

This was my view of my duty from the end of 1841 to my resignation of St. Mary's in the autumn of 1843. And now I shall relate my view, during that time, of the state of the controversy between the Churches.

As soon as I saw the hitch in the Anglican argument, during my course of reading in the summer of 1839, I began to look about, as I have said, for some ground which might supply a controversial basis for my need. The difficulty in question had affected my view both of Antiquity and Catholicity; for, while the history of St. Leo showed me that the deliberate and eventual consent of the great body of the Church ratified a doctrinal decision as a part of revealed truth, it also showed that the rule of Antiquity was not infringed, though a doctrine had not been publicly recognized as so revealed, till centuries after the time of the Apostles. Thus, whereas the Creeds tell us that the Church is One, Holy, Catholic, and Apostolic, I could not prove that the Anglican communion was an integral part of the One Church, on the ground of its teaching being Apostolic or Catholic, without reasoning in favour of what are commonly called the Roman corruptions; and I could not defend our separation from Rome and her faith without using arguments prejudicial to those great doctrines concerning our Lord, which are the very foundation of the Christian religion. The *Via Media* was an impossible idea; it was what I had called 'standing on one leg'; and it was necessary, if my old issue of the controversy was to be retained, to go further either one way or the other.

Accordingly, I abandoned that old ground and took another. I deliberately quitted the old Anglican ground as untenable; though I did not do so all at once, but as I became more and more convinced of the state of the case. The Jerusalem Bishopric was the ultimate condemnation of the old theory of the *Via Media*: – if its establishment did nothing else, at least it demolished the sacredness of diocesan rights. If England could be in Palestine, Rome might be in England. But its bearing upon the controversy, as I have shown in the foregoing chapter, was much more serious than this technical ground. From that time the Anglican Church was, in my mind, either not a normal portion of that One Church to which the promises were made, or at least in an abnormal state; and from that time I said boldly (as I did in my Protest, and as indeed I had even intimated in my Letter to the Bishop of Oxford), that the Church in which I found myself had no claim on me, except on condition of its being a portion of the One Catholic Communion, and that that condition must ever be borne in mind as a practical matter, and had to be distinctly proved. All this is not inconsistent with my saying above that, at this time, I had no thought of leaving the Church of England; because I felt some of my old objections against Rome as strongly as ever. I had no right, I had no leave, to act against my conscience. That was a higher rule than any argument about the Notes of the Church.

Under these circumstances I turned for protection to the Note of Sanctity, with a view of showing that we had at least one of the necessary Notes, as fully as the Church of Rome; or, at least, without entering into comparisons, that we had in such a sufficient sense as to reconcile us to our position, and to supply full evidence, and a clear direction, on the point of practical duty. We had the Note of Life, – not any sort of life, not such only as can come of nature, but a supernatural Christian life, which could only come directly from above. Thus, in my Article[2] in the *British Critic*, to which I have so often referred, in January, 1840 (before the time of Tract 90), I said of the Anglican Church that 'she has the note of possession, the note of freedom from party titles, the note of life, – a tough life and a vigorous; she has ancient descent, unbroken continuance, agreement in doctrine with the Ancient Church.' Presently I go on to speak of sanctity: 'Much as Roman Catholics may denounce us at present as schismatical, they could not resist us if the Anglican communion had but that one note of the Church upon it, – sanctity. The Church of the day [4th century] could not resist Meletius;[3] his enemies were fairly overcome by him, by his meekness and holiness, which melted the most jealous of them.' And I continue, 'We are almost content to say to Romanists, account us not yet as a branch of the Catholic Church, though we be a branch, till we are like a branch, provided that when we do become like a branch, then you consent to acknowledge us,' &c. And so I was led on in the Article to that sharp attack on English Catholics, for their shortcomings as regards this Note, a good portion of which I have already quoted in another place. It is there that I speak of the great scandal which I took at their political, social, and controversial bearing; and this was a second reason why I fell back upon the Note of Sanctity, because it took me away from the necessity of making any attack upon the doctrines of the Roman Church, nay, from the consideration of her popular beliefs, and brought me upon a ground on which I felt I could not make a mistake; for what is a higher guide for us in speculation and in practice, than that conscience of right and wrong, of truth and falsehood, those sentiments of what is decorous, consistent, and noble, which our Creator has made a part of our original nature? Therefore I felt I could not be wrong in attacking what I fancied was a fact, – the unscrupulousness, the deceit, and the intriguing spirit of the agents and representatives of Rome.

This reference to Holiness as the true test of a Church was steadily kept in view in what I wrote in connexion with Tract 90. I say[4] in its Introduction, 'The writer can never be party to forcing the opinions or projects of one school upon another; religious changes should be the act of the whole body. No good can come of a change which is not a development of feelings springing up freely and calmly within the bosom of the whole body itself; every change in religion' must be 'attended by deep repentance; changes' must be 'nurtured in mutual love; we cannot agree without a supernatural influence;' we must come 'together to God to do for us what we cannot do for ourselves.' In my Letter to the Bishop I said,[5] 'I have set myself against suggestions for considering the differences between ourselves and the foreign Churches with a view to their adjustment.' (I meant in the way of negotiation, conference, agitation, or the like.) 'Our business is with ourselves, – to make ourselves more holy, more self-denying, more primitive, more worthy of our high calling. To be anxious for a composition of differences is to begin at the end. Political reconciliations are but outward and hollow, and fallacious. And till Roman Catholics renounce political efforts, and manifest in their public measures the light of holiness and truth, perpetual war is our only prospect.'

According to this theory, a religious body is part of the One Catholic and Apostolic Church, if it has the succession and the creed of the Apostles, with the note of holiness of life; and there is much in such a view to approve itself to the direct common sense and practical habits of an Englishman. However, with the events consequent upon Tract 90, I sunk my theory to a lower level. For what could be said in apology, when the Bishops and the people of my Church, not only did not suffer, but actually rejected primitive Catholic doctrine, and tried to eject from their communion all who held it? after the Bishops' charges? after the Jerusalem 'abomination'?* Well, this could be said; still we were not nothing: we could not be as if we never had been a Church; we were 'Samaria.'[6] This then was that lower level on which I placed myself, and all who felt with me, at the end of 1841.

To bring out this view was the purpose of *Four Sermons*[7] *preached at St. Mary's* in December of that year. Hitherto I had not introduced the exciting topics of the day into the Pulpit;† on this occasion I did. I did so, for the moment was urgent; there was great unsettlement of mind among us, in consequence of those

* Matt. xxiv 15.
† Vide Note C, *Sermon on Wisdom and Innocence.*

same events which had unsettled me. One special anxiety, very
obvious, which was coming on me now, was, that what was 'one
man's meat was another man's poison.' I had said even of Tract
90, 'It was addressed to one set of persons, and has been used
and commented on by another;' still more was it true now, that
whatever I wrote for the service of those whom I knew to be in
trouble of mind, would become on the one hand matter of
suspicion and slander in the mouths of my opponents, and of
distress and surprise to those on the other hand who had no
difficulties of faith at all. Accordingly, when I published these
Four Sermons at the end of 1843, I introduced them with a
recommendation that none should read them who did not need
them. But in truth the virtual condemnation of Tract 90, after
that the whole difficulty seemed to have been weathered, was an
enormous disappointment and trial. My Protest also against the
Jerusalem Bishopric was an unavoidable cause of excitement in
the case of many; but it calmed them too, for the very fact of a
Protest was a relief to their impatience. And so, in like manner,
as regards the Four Sermons, of which I speak, though they
acknowledged freely the great scandal which was involved in the
recent episcopal doings, yet at the same time they might be said
to bestow upon the multiplied disorders and shortcomings of the
Anglican Church a sort of place in the Revealed Dispensation,
and an intellectual position in the controversy, and the dignity of
a great principle, for unsettled minds to take and use, – a
principle which might teach them to recognize their own consistency, and to be reconciled to themselves, and which might
absorb and dry up a multitude of their grudgings, discontents,
misgivings, and questionings, and lead the way to humble,
thankful, and tranquil thoughts; – and this was the effect which
certainly it produced on myself.

The point[8] of these Sermons is, that, in spite of the rigid
character of the Jewish law, the formal and literal force of its
precepts, and the manifest schism, and worse than schism, of the
Ten Tribes, yet in fact they were still recognized as a people by
the Divine Mercy; that the great prophets Elias and Eliseus[9]
were sent to them; and not only so, but were sent to preach to
them and reclaim them, without any intimation that they must be
reconciled to the line of David and the Aaronic priesthood, or

go up to Jerusalem to worship. They were not in the Church, yet they had the means of grace and the hope of acceptance with their Maker. The application of all this to the Anglican Church was immediate; – whether, under the circumstances, a man could assume or exercise ministerial functions, or not, might not clearly appear (though it must be remembered that England had the Apostolic Priesthood, whereas Israel had no priesthood at all), but so far was clear, that there was no call at all for an Anglican to leave his Church for Rome, though he did not believe his own to be part of the One Church: – and for this reason, because it was a fact that the kingdom of Israel was cut off from the Temple; and yet its subjects, neither in a mass, nor as individuals, neither the multitudes on Mount Carmel,[10] nor the Shunammite[11] and her household, had any command given them, though miracles were displayed before them, to break off from their own people, and to submit themselves to Judah.*

It is plain, that a theory such as this, – whether the marks of a divine presence and life in the Anglican Church were sufficient to prove that she was actually within the covenant, or only sufficient to prove that she was at least enjoying extraordinary and uncovenanted mercies, – not only lowered her level in a religious point of view, but weakened her controversial basis. Its very novelty made it suspicious; and there was no guarantee that the process of subsidence might not continue, and that it might not end in a submersion. Indeed, to many minds, to say that England was wrong was even to say that Rome was right; and no ethical or casuistic reasoning whatever could overcome in their case the argument from prescription and authority. To this objection, as made to my new teaching, I could only answer that I did not make my circumstances. I fully acknowledged the force and effectiveness of the genuine Anglican theory, and that it was all but proof against the disputants of Rome; but still like Achilles, it had a vulnerable point, and that St. Leo had found it out for me, and that I could not help it; – that, were it not for matter of fact, the theory would be great indeed; it would be

* As I am not writing controversially, I will only here remark upon this argument, that there is a great difference between a command, which presupposes physical, material, and political conditions, and one which is moral. To go to Jerusalem was a matter of the body, not of the soul.

irresistible, if it were only true. When I became a Catholic, the Editor of the *Christian Observer*, Mr. Wilkes,[12] who had in former days accused me, to my indignation, of tending towards Rome, wrote to me to ask, which of the two was now right, he or I? I answered him in a letter, part of which I here insert, as it will serve as a sort of leave-taking of the great theory, which is so specious to look upon, so difficult to prove, and so hopeless to work.

'Nov. 8, 1845. I do not think, at all more than I did, that the Anglican principles which I advocated at the date you mention, lead men to the Church of Rome. If I must specify what I mean by "Anglican principles," I should say, e.g. taking *Antiquity*, not the *existing Church*, as the oracle of truth; and holding that the *Apostolical Succession* is a sufficient guarantee of Sacramental Grace, *without union with the Christian Church throughout the world*. I think these still the firmest, strongest ground against Rome – that is, *if they can be held*' [as truths or facts]. 'They *have* been held by many, and are far more difficult to refute in the Roman controversy, than those of any other religious body.

'For myself, I found I *could not* hold them. I left them. From the time I began to suspect their unsoundness, I ceased to put them forward. When I was fairly sure of their unsoundness, I gave up my Living. When I was fully confident that the Church of Rome was the only true Church, I joined her.

'I have felt all along that Bp. Bull's theology was the only theology on which the English Church could stand. I have felt, that opposition to the Church of Rome was *part* of that theology; and that he who could not protest against the Church of Rome was no true divine in the English Church. I have never said, nor attempted to say, that any one in office in the English Church, whether Bishop or incumbent, could be otherwise than in hostility to the Church of Rome.'

The *Via Media* then disappeared for ever, and a Theory, made expressly for the occasion, took its place. I was pleased with my new view. I wrote to an intimate friend, Samuel F. Wood, Dec. 13, 1841: 'I think you will give me the credit, Carissime, of not undervaluing the strength of the feelings which draw one [to

Rome], and yet I am (I trust) quite clear about my duty to remain where I am; indeed, much clearer than I was some time since. If it is not presumptuous to say, I have . . . a much more definite view of the promised inward Presence of Christ with us in the Sacraments now that the outward notes of it are being removed. And I am content to be with Moses in the desert, or with Elijah excommunicated from the Temple. I say this, putting things at the strongest.'

However, my friends of the moderate Apostolical party, who were my friends for the very reason of my having been so moderate and Anglican myself in general tone in times past, who had stood up for Tract 90 partly from faith in me, and certainly from generous and kind feeling, and had thereby shared an obloquy which was none of theirs, were naturally surprised and offended at a line of argument, novel, and, as it appeared to them, wanton, which threw the whole controversy into confusion, stultified my former principles, and substituted, as they would consider, a sort of methodistic self-contemplation, especially abhorrent both to my nature and to my past professions, for the plain and honest tokens, as they were commonly received, of a divine mission in the Anglican Church. They could not tell whither I was going: and were still further annoyed when I persisted in viewing the condemnation of Tract 90 by the public and the Bishops as so grave a matter, and when I threw about what they considered mysterious hints of 'eventualities,' and would not simply say, 'An Anglican I was born, and an Anglican I will die.' One of my familiar friends, Mr. Church,[13] who was in the country at Christmas, 1841-2, reported to me the feeling that prevailed about me; and how I felt towards it will appear in the following letter of mine, written in answer: –

'Oriel, Dec. 24, 1841. Carissime, you cannot tell how sad your account of Moberly[14] has made me. His view of the sinfulness of the decrees of Trent is as much against union of Churches as against individual conversions. To tell the truth, I never have examined those decrees with this object, and have no view; but that is very different from having a deliberate view against them. Could not he say *which* they are? I suppose Transubstantiation is one. Charles Marriott,[15] though of course he would not like to have it repeated* does not scruple at that. I have not my mind clear. Moberly must recollect that Palmer [of Worcester] thinks they all bear a Catholic interpretation. For myself, this only I see, that there is indefinitely more in the Fathers against our own state of alienation from Christendom than against the Tridentine Decrees.

'The only thing I can think of,' [that I can have said of a startling character,] 'is this, that there were persons who, if our Church committed herself to heresy, *sooner* than think that there was no Church any where, would believe the Roman to be the Church; and therefore would on faith accept what they could not otherwise acquiesce in. I suppose, it would be no relief to him to insist upon the circumstance that there is no immediate danger. Individuals can never be answered for of course; but I should think lightly of that man, who, for some act of the Bishops, should all at once leave the Church. Now, considering how the Clergy really are improving, considering that this row is even making them read the Tracts, is it not possible we may all be in a better state of mind seven years hence to consider these matters? and may we not leave them meanwhile to the will of Providence? I *cannot* believe this work has been of man: God has a right to His own work, to do what He will with it. May we not try to leave it in His hands, and be content?

'If you learn any thing about Barter,[16] which leads you to think that I can relieve him by a letter, let me know. The truth is this, – our good friends do not read the Fathers; they assent to us from the common sense of the case: then, when the Fathers, and we, say *more* than their common sense, they are dreadfully shocked.

'The Bishop of London has rejected a man,[17] 1. For holding *any* Sacrifice in the Eucharist. 2. The Real Presence. 3. That there is a grace in ordination.†

'Are we quite sure that the Bishops will not be drawing up

---

* As things stand now, I do not think he would have objected to his opinion being generally known.

† I cannot prove this at this distance of time; but I do not think it wrong to introduce here the passage containing it, as I am imputing to the Bishop nothing which the world would think disgraceful, but, on the contrary, what a large religious body would approve.

some stringent declarations of faith? Is this what Moberly fears? Would the Bishop of Oxford accept them? If so, I should be driven into the Refuge for the Destitute [Littlemore]. But I promise Moberly, I would do my utmost to catch all dangerous persons and clap them into confinement there.'

Christmas Day, 1841. 'I have been dreaming of Moberly all night. Should not he and the like see, that it is unwise, unfair, and impatient to ask others, What will you do under circumstances, which have not, which may never come? Why bring fear, suspicion, and disunion into the camp about things which are merely *in posse*?[18] Natural, and exceedingly kind as Barter's and another friend's letters were, I think they have done great harm. I speak most sincerely when I say, that there are things which I neither contemplate, nor wish to contemplate; but, when I am asked about them ten times, at length I begin to contemplate them.

'He surely does not mean to say, that *nothing* could separate a man from the English Church, e.g. its avowing Socinianism;[19] its holding the Holy Eucharist in a Socinian sense. Yet, he would say, it was not *right* to contemplate such things.

'Again, our case is [diverging] from that of Ken's.[20] To say nothing of the last miserable century,[21] which has given us to *start* from a much lower level and with much less to *spare* than a Churchman in the 17th century, questions of *doctrine* are now coming in; with him, it was a question of discipline.

'If such dreadful events were realized, I cannot help thinking we should all be vastly more agreed than we think now. Indeed, is it possible (humanly speaking) that those, who have so much the same heart, should widely differ? But let this be considered, as to alternatives. *What* communion could we join? Could the Scotch or American sanction the presence of its Bishops and congregations in England, without incurring the imputation of schism, unless indeed (and is that likely?) they denounced the English as heretical?

'Is not this a time of strange providences? is it not our safest course, without looking to consequences, to do simply *what we think right* day by day? shall we not be sure to go wrong, if we attempt to trace by anticipation the course of divine Providence?

'Has not all our misery, as a Church, arisen from people being afraid to look difficulties in the face? They have palliated acts, when they should have denounced them. There is that good fellow, Worcester Palmer, can whitewash the Ecclesiastical Commission[22] and the Jerusalem Bishopric. And what is the consequence? that our Church has, through centuries, ever been sinking lower and lower, till good part of its pretensions and professions is a mere sham, though it be a duty to make the best of what we have received. Yet, though bound to make the best of other men's shams, let us not incur any of our own. The truest friends of our Church are they, who say boldly when her rulers are going wrong, and the consequences; and (to speak catachrestically)[23] *they* are most likely to die in the Church, who are, under these black circumstances, most prepared to leave it.

'And I will add, that, considering the traces of God's grace which surround us, I am very sanguine, or rather confident (if it is right so to speak,) that our prayers and our alms will come up as a memorial before God, and that all this miserable confusion tends to good.

'Let us not then be anxious, and anticipate differences in prospect, when we agree in the present.

'P.S. I think when friends' [i.e. the extreme party] 'get over their first unsettlement of mind and consequent vague apprehensions, which the new attitude of the Bishops, and our feelings upon it, have brought about, they will get contented and satisfied. They will see that they exaggerated things. . . . Of course it would have been wrong to anticipate what one's feelings would be under such a painful contingency as the Bishops' charging as they have done, – so it seems to me nobody's fault. Nor is it wonderful that others' [moderate men] 'are startled' [i.e. at my Protest, &c., &c.]; 'yet they should recollect that the more implicit the reverence one pays to a Bishop, the more keen will be one's perception of heresy in him. The cord is binding and compelling, till it snaps.

'Men of reflection would have seen this, if they had looked that way. Last spring, a very high churchman[24] talked to me of resisting my Bishop, of asking him for the Canons under which he acted, and so forth; but those, who have cultivated a loyal feeling towards their superiors, are the most loving servants, or the most zealous protestors. If others became so too, if the clergy of Chester denounced the heresy of their diocesan,[25] they would be doing their duty, and relieving themselves of the share which they otherwise have in any possible defection of their brethren.'

'St. Stephen's [Day, December 26]. How I fidget! I now fear that the note I wrote yesterday only makes matters worse by *disclosing* too much. This is always my great difficulty.

'In the present state of excitement on both sides, I think of leaving out altogether my reassertion of No. 90 in my Preface to Volume 6 [of Parochial Sermons], and merely saying, "As many false reports are at this time in circulation about him, he hopes his well-wishers will take this Volume as an indication of his real thoughts and feelings: those who are not, he leaves in God's hand to bring them to a better mind in His own time." What do you say to the logic, sentiment, and propriety of this?'

An old friend, at a distance from Oxford, Archdeacon Robert I. Wilberforce, must have said something to me at this time, I do not know what, which challenged a frank reply;[26] for I disclosed to him, I do not know in what words, my frightful suspicion, hitherto only known to two persons, viz. his brother Henry[27] and Mr. Frederic Rogers,* that, as regards my Anglicanism, perhaps I might break down in the event, – that perhaps we were both out of the Church. I think I recollect expressing my difficulty, as derived from the Arian and Monophysite history, in a form in which it would be most intelligible to him, as being in fact an admission of Bishop Bull's; viz. that in the controversies of the early centuries the Roman Church was ever on the right side, which was of course a *primâ facie* argument in favour of Rome and against Anglicanism now. He answered me thus, under date of Jan. 29, 1842: 'I don't think that I ever was so shocked by any communication, which was ever made to me, as by your letter of this morning. It has quite unnerved me. . . . I cannot but write to you, though I am at a loss where to begin. . . . I know of no act by which we have dissevered ourselves from the communion of the Church Universal. . . . The more I study Scripture, the more am I impressed with the resemblance between the Romish principle in the Church and the Babylon of St. John. . . . I am ready to grieve that I ever directed my

* Now Lord Blachford.

thoughts to theology, if it is indeed so uncertain, as your doubts seem to indicate.'

While my old and true friends were thus in trouble about me, I suppose they felt not only anxiety but pain, to see that I was gradually surrendering myself to the influence of others, who had not their own claims upon me, younger men, and of a cast of mind in no small degree uncongenial to my own. A new school of thought was rising, as is usual in doctrinal inquiries, and was sweeping the original party of the Movement aside, and was taking its place. The most prominent person in it, was a man of elegant genius, of classical mind, of rare talent in literary composition: – Mr. Oakeley. He was not far from my own age; I had long known him, though of late years he had not been in residence at Oxford; and quite lately, he has been taking several signal[28] occasions of renewing that kindness, which he ever showed towards me when we were both in the Anglican Church. His tone of mind was not unlike that which gave a character to the early Movement; he was almost a typical Oxford man, and, as far as I recollect, both in political and ecclesiastical views, would have been of one spirit with the Oriel party of 1826–1833. But he had entered late into the Movement; he did not know its first years; and, beginning with a new start, he was naturally thrown together with that body of eager, acute, resolute minds who had begun their Catholic life about the same time as he, who knew nothing about the *Via Media*, but had heard much about Rome. This new party rapidly formed and increased, in and out of Oxford, and, as it so happened, contemporaneously with that very summer, when I received so serious a blow to my ecclesiastical views from the study of the Monophysite controversy. These men cut into the original Movement at an angle, fell across its line of thought, and then set about turning that line in its own direction. They were most of them keenly religious men, with a true concern for their souls as the first matter of all, with a great zeal for me, but giving little certainty at the time as to which way they would ultimately turn. Some in the event have remained firm to Anglicanism, some have become Catholics, and some have found a refuge in Liberalism. Nothing was clearer concerning them, than that they needed to be kept in order; and on me

who had had so much to do with the making of them, that duty
was as clearly incumbent; and it is equally clear, from what I
have already said, that I was just the person, above all others,
who could not undertake it. There are no friends like old friends;
but of those old friends, few could help me, few could understand
me, many were annoyed with me, some were angry, because I
was breaking up a compact party, and some, as a matter of
conscience, could not listen to me. When I looked round for
those whom I might consult in my difficulties, I found the very
hypothesis of those difficulties acting as a bar to their giving me
their advice. Then I said, bitterly, 'You are throwing me on
others, whether I will or no.' Yet still I had good and true
friends around me of the old sort, in and out of Oxford too, who
were a great help to me. But on the other hand, though I neither
was so fond (with a few exceptions) of the persons, nor of the
methods of thought, which belonged to this new school, as of
the old set, though I could not trust in their firmness of purpose,
for, like a swarm of flies, they might come and go, and at length
be divided and dissipated, yet I had an intense sympathy in their
object and in the direction in which their path lay, in spite of my
old friends, in spite of my old life-long prejudices. In spite of my
ingrained fears of Rome, and the decision of my reason and
conscience against her usages, in spite of my affection for Oxford
and Oriel, yet I had a secret longing love of Rome the Mother of
English Christianity, and I had a true devotion to the Blessed
Virgin, in whose College I lived, whose Altar I served, and
whose Immaculate Purity I had in one[29] of my earliest printed
Sermons made much of. And it was the consciousness of this
bias in myself, if it is so to be called, which made me preach so
earnestly against the danger of being swayed in religious inquiry
by our sympathy rather than by our reason. And moreover, the
members of this new school looked up to me, as I have said, and
did me true kindnesses, and really loved me, and stood by me in
trouble, when others went away, and for all this I was grateful;
nay, many of them were in trouble themselves, and in the same
boat with me, and that was a further cause of sympathy between
us; and hence it was, when the new school came on in force, and
into collision with the old, I had not the heart, any more than the
power, to repel them; I was in great perplexity, and hardly knew

where I stood; I took their part; and, when I wanted to be in peace and silence, I had to speak out, and I incurred the charge of weakness from some men, and of mysteriousness, shuffling, and underhand dealing from the majority.

Now I will say here frankly, that this sort of charge is a matter which I cannot properly meet, because I cannot duly realize it. I have never had any suspicion of my own honesty; and, when men say that I was dishonest, I cannot grasp the accusation as a distinct conception, such as it is possible to encounter. If a man said to me, 'On such a day and before such persons you said a thing was white, when it was black,' I understand what is meant well enough, and I can set myself to prove an *alibi* or to explain the mistake; or if a man said to me, 'You tried to gain me over to your party, intending to take me with you to Rome, but you did not succeed,' I can give him the lie, and lay down an assertion of my own as firm and as exact as his, that not from the time that I was first unsettled, did I ever attempt to gain any one over to myself or to my Romanizing opinions, and that it is only his own coxcombical fancy which has bred such a thought in him: but my imagination is at a loss in presence of those vague charges, which have commonly been brought against me, charges, which are made up of impressions, and understandings, and inferences, and hearsay, and surmises. Accordingly, I shall not make the attempt, for, in doing so, I should be dealing blows in the air; what I shall attempt is to state what I know of myself and what I recollect, and leave to others its application.

While I had confidence in the *Via Media*, and thought that nothing could overset it, I did not mind laying down large principles, which I saw would go further than was commonly perceived. I considered that to make the *Via Media* concrete and substantive, it must be much more than it was in outline; that the Anglican Church must have a ceremonial, a ritual, and a fulness of doctrine and devotion, which it had not at present, if it were to compete with the Roman Church with any prospect of success. Such additions would not remove it from its proper basis, but would merely strengthen and beautify it: such, for instance, would be confraternities, particular devotions, reverence for the Blessed Virgin, prayers for the dead, beautiful churches, munifi-

cent offerings to them and in them, monastic houses, and many
other observances and institutions, which I used to say belonged
to us as much as to Rome, though Rome had appropriated them
and boasted of them, by reason of our having let them slip from
us. The principle, on which all this turned, is brought out in
one[30] of the Letters I published on occasion of Tract 90. 'The
age is moving,' I said, 'towards something; and most unhappily
the one religious communion among us, which has of late years
been practically in possession of this something, is the Church of
Rome. She alone, amid all the errors and evils of her practical
system, has given free scope to the feelings of awe, mystery,
tenderness, reverence, devotedness, and other feelings which
may be especially called Catholic. The question then is, whether
we shall give them up to the Roman Church or claim them for
ourselves. . . . But if we do give them up, we must give up the
men who cherish them. We must consent either to give up the
men, or to admit their principles.' With these feelings I frankly
admit, that, while I was working simply for the sake of the
Anglican Church, I did not at all mind, though I found myself
laying down principles in its defence, which went beyond that
particular kind of defence which high-and-dry men thought
perfection, and even though I ended in framing a kind of
defence, which they might call a revolution, while I thought it a
restoration. Thus, for illustration, I might discourse upon the
'Communion of Saints' in such a manner (though I do not
recollect doing so,) as might lead the way towards devotion to
the Blessed Virgin and the Saints on the one hand, and towards
prayers for the dead on the other. In a memorandum of the year
1844 or 1845, I thus speak on this subject: 'If the Church be not
defended on establishment grounds, it must be upon principles,
which go far beyond their immediate object. Sometimes I saw
these further results, sometimes not. Though I saw them, I
sometimes did not say that I saw them: – so long as I thought
they were inconsistent, *not* with our Church, but only with the
existing opinions, I was not unwilling to insinuate truths into
our Church, which I thought had a right to be there.'

To so much I confess; but I do not confess, I simply deny that
I ever said any thing which secretly bore against the Church of
England, knowing it myself, in order that others might unwarily

accept it. It was indeed one of my great difficulties and causes of reserve, as time went on, that I at length recognized in principles which I had honestly preached as if Anglican, conclusions favourable to the cause of Rome. Of course I did not like to confess this; and, when interrogated, was in consequence in perplexity. The prime instance of this was the appeal to Antiquity; St. Leo had overset, in my own judgment, its force as the special argument for Anglicanism; yet I was committed to Antiquity, together with the whole Anglican school; what then was I to say, when acute minds urged this or that application of it against the *Via Media*? it was impossible that, in such circumstances, any answer could be given which was not unsatisfactory, or any behaviour adopted which was not mysterious. Again, sometimes in what I wrote I went just as far as I saw, and could as little say more, as I could see what is below the horizon; and therefore, when asked as to the consequences of what I had said, I had no answer to give. Again, sometimes when I was asked, whether certain conclusions did not follow from a certain principle, I might not be able to tell at the moment, especially if the matter were complicated; and for this reason, if for no other, because there is great difference between a conclusion in the abstract and a conclusion in the concrete, and because a conclusion may be modified in fact by a conclusion from some opposite principle. Or it might so happen that my head got simply confused, by the very strength of the logic which was administered to me, and thus I gave my sanction to conclusions which really were not mine; and when the report of those conclusions came round to me through others, I had to unsay them. And then again, perhaps I did not like to see men scared or scandalized by unfeeling logical inferences, which would not have troubled them to the day of their death, had they not been forced to recognize them. And then I felt altogether the force of the maxim of St. Ambrose,[31] 'Non in dialecticâ complacuit Deo salvum facere populum suum;' — I had a great dislike of paper logic. For myself, it was not logic that carried me on; as well might one say that the quicksilver in the barometer changes the weather. It is the concrete being that reasons; pass a number of years, and I find my mind in a new place; how? the whole man moves; paper logic is but the record of it. All the logic in the world would not have made me move faster towards Rome than I did; as well might you say that I have arrived at the end of my journey, because I see the village church before me, as venture to assert that the miles, over which my soul had to pass before it got to Rome, could be annihilated, even though I had been in possession of some far clearer view than I then had, that Rome was my ultimate destination. Great acts take time. At least this is what I felt in my own case; and therefore to come to me with methods of logic had in it the nature of a provocation, and, though I do not think I ever showed it, made me somewhat indifferent how I met them, and perhaps led me, as a means of relieving my impatience, to be mysterious or irrelevant, or to give in because I could not meet them to my satisfaction. And a greater trouble still than these logical mazes, was the introduction of logic into every subject whatever, so far, that is, as this was done. Before I was at Oriel, I recollect an acquaintance saying to me that 'the Oriel Common Room stank of Logic.' One is not at all pleased when poetry, or eloquence, or devotion, is considered as if chiefly intended to feed syllogisms. Now, in saying all this, I am saying nothing against the deep piety and earnestness which were characteristics of this second phase of the Movement, in which I had taken so prominent a part. What I have been observing is, that this phase had a tendency to bewilder and to upset me; and, that, instead of saying so, as I ought to have done, perhaps from a sort of laziness I gave answers at random, which have led to my appearing close or inconsistent.

I have turned up two letters of this period, which in a measure illustrate what I have been saying. The first was written to the Bishop of Oxford on occasion of Tract 90: –

'March 20, 1841. No one can enter into my situation but myself. I see a great many minds working in various directions and a variety of principles with multiplied bearings; I act for the best. I sincerely think that matters would not have gone better for the Church, had I never written. And if I write I have a choice of difficulties. It is easy for those who do not enter into those difficulties to say, "He ought to say this and not say that," but things are wonderfully linked together, and I cannot, or rather I would not be dishonest. When persons too interrogate me, I am obliged in many cases to give an opinion, or I seem to be underhand. Keeping silence looks like artifice. And I do not like people to consult or respect me, from thinking differently of my opinions from what I know them to be. And again (to use the proverb) what is one man's food is another man's poison. All these things make my situation very difficult. But that collision must at some time ensue between members of the Church of opposite sentiments, I have long been aware. The time and mode have been in the hand of Providence; I do not mean to exclude my own great imperfections in bringing it about; yet I still feel obliged to think the Tract necessary.'

The second is taken from the notes of a letter which I sent to Dr. Pusey in the next year: –

'October 16, 1842. As to my being entirely with Ward,[32] I do not know the limits of my own opinions. If Ward says that this or that is a development from what I have said, I cannot say Yes or No. It is plausible, it *may* be true. Of course the fact that the Roman Church *has* so developed and maintained, adds great weight to the antecedent plausibility. I cannot assert that it is not true; but I cannot, with that keen perception which some people have, appropriate it. It is a nuisance to me to be *forced* beyond what I can fairly accept.'

There was another source of the perplexity with which at this time I was encompassed, and of the reserve and mysteriousness, of which that perplexity gained for me the credit. After Tract 90 the Protestant world would not let me alone; they pursued me in the public journals to Littlemore. Reports of all kinds were circulated about me. 'Imprimis, why did I go up to Littlemore at all? For no good purpose certainly; I dared not tell why.' Why, to be sure, it was hard that I should be obliged to say to the Editors of newspapers that I went up there to say my prayers; it was hard to have to tell the world in confidence, that I had a certain doubt about the Anglican system, and could not at that moment resolve it, or say what would come of it; it was hard to have to confess that I had thought of giving up my Living a year or two before, and that this was a first step to it. It was hard to have to plead, that, for what I knew, my doubts would vanish, if the newspapers would be so good as to give me time and let me alone. Who would ever dream of making the world his confidant?

Yet I was considered insidious, sly, dishonest, if I would not open my heart to the tender mercies of the world. But they persisted: 'What was I doing at Littlemore?' Doing there! have I not retreated from you? have I not given up my position and my place? am I alone, of Englishmen, not to have the privilege to go where I will, no questions asked? am I alone to be followed about by jealous prying eyes, which take note whether I go in at a back door or at the front, and who the men are who happen to call on me in the afternoon? Cowards! if I advanced one step, you would run away; it is not you that I fear: 'Di me terrent, et Jupiter hostis.'[33] It is because the Bishops still go on charging against me, though I have quite given up: it is that secret misgiving of heart which tells me that they do well, for I have neither lot nor part with them: this it is which weighs me down. I cannot walk into or out of my house, but curious eyes are upon me. Why will you not let me die in peace? Wounded brutes creep into some hole to die in, and no one grudges it them. Let me alone, I shall not trouble you long. This was the keen feeling which pierced me, and, I think, these are the very words in which I expressed it to myself. I asked, in the words of a great motto,[34] 'Ubi lapsus? quid feci?' One day when I entered my house, I found a flight of Undergraduates inside. Heads[35] of Houses, as mounted patrols, walked their horses round those poor cottages. Doctors of Divinity dived into the hidden recesses of that private tenement uninvited, and drew domestic conclusions from what they saw there. I had thought that an Englishman's house was his castle; but the newspapers thought otherwise, and at last the matter came before my good Bishop. I insert his letter, and a portion of my reply to him: –

'April 12, 1842. So many of the charges against yourself and your friends which I have seen in the public journals have been, within my own knowledge, false and calumnious, that I am not apt to pay much attention to what is asserted with respect to you in the newspapers.

'In' [a newspaper] 'however, of April 9, there appears a paragraph in which it is asserted, as a matter of notoriety, that a "so-called Anglo-Catholic Monastery is in process of erection at Littlemore, and that the cells of dormitories, the chapel, the refectory, the cloisters all may be seen advancing to perfection, under the eye of a Parish Priest of the Diocese of Oxford."

'Now, as I have understood that you really are possessed of some tenements at Littlemore, – as it is generally believed that they are destined for the purposes of study and devotion, – and as much suspicion and jealousy are felt about the matter, I am anxious to afford you an opportunity of making me an explanation on the subject.

'I know you too well not to be aware that you are the last man living to attempt in my Diocese a revival of the Monastic orders (in any thing approaching to the Romanist sense of the term) without previous communication with me, – or indeed that you should take upon yourself to originate any measure of importance without authority from the heads of the Church, – and therefore I at once exonerate you from the accusation brought against you by the newspaper I have quoted, but I feel it nevertheless a duty to my Diocese and myself, as well as to you, to ask you to put it in my power to contradict what, if uncontradicted, would appear to imply a glaring invasion of all ecclesiastical discipline on *your* part, or of inexcusable neglect and indifference to my duties on *mine*.'

I wrote in answer as follows: –

'April 14, 1842. I am very much obliged by your Lordship's kindness in allowing me to write to you on the subject of my house at Littlemore; at the same time I feel it hard both on your Lordship and myself that the restlessness of the public mind should oblige you to require an explanation of me.

'It is now a whole year that I have been the subject of incessant misrepresentation. A year since I submitted entirely to your Lordship's authority; and, with the intention of following out the particular act enjoined upon me, I not only stopped the series of Tracts, on which I was engaged, but withdrew from all public discussion of Church matters of the day, or what may be called ecclesiastical politics. I turned myself at once to the preparation for the Press of the translations of St. Athanasius to which I had long wished to devote myself, and I intended and intend to employ myself in the like theological studies, and in the concerns of my own parish and in practical works.

'With the same view of personal improvement I was led more seriously to a design which had been long on my mind. For many years, at least thirteen, I have wished to give myself to a life of greater religious regularity than I have hitherto led; but it is very unpleasant to confess such a wish even to my Bishop, because it seems arrogant, and because it is committing me to a profession which may come to nothing. For what have I done that I am to be called to account by the world for my private actions, in a way in which no one else is called? Why may I not have that liberty which all others are allowed? I am often accused of being underhand and uncandid in respect to the intentions to which I have been alluding: but no one likes his own good resolutions noised about, both from mere common delicacy and from fear lest he should not be able to fulfil them. I feel it very cruel, though the parties in fault do not know what they are doing, that very sacred matters between me and my conscience are made a matter of public talk. May I take a case parallel though different? suppose a person in prospect of marriage; would he like the subject discussed in newspapers, and parties, circumstances, &c., &c., publicly demanded of him, at the penalty of being accused of craft and duplicity?

'The resolution I speak of has been taken with reference to myself alone, and has been contemplated quite independent of the co-operation of any other human being, and without reference to success or failure other than personal, and without regard to the blame or approbation of man. And being a resolution of years, and one to which I feel God has called me, and in which I am violating no rule of the Church any more than if I married, I should have to answer for it, if I did not pursue it, as a good Providence made openings for it. In pursuing it then I am thinking of myself alone, not aiming at any ecclesiastical or external effects. At the same time of course it would be a great comfort to me to know that God had put it into the hearts of others to pursue their personal edification in the same way, and unnatural not to wish to have the benefit of their presence and encouragement, or not to think it a great infringement on the rights of conscience if such personal and private resolutions were interfered with. Your Lordship will allow me to add my firm conviction that such religious resolutions are most necessary for keeping a certain class of minds firm in their allegiance to our Church; but still I can as truly say that my own reason for any thing I have done has been a personal one, without which I should not have entered upon it, and which I hope to pursue whether with or without the sympathies of others pursuing a similar course. . . .

'As to my intentions, I purpose to live there myself a good deal, as I have a resident curate in Oxford. In doing this, I believe I am consulting for the good of my parish, as my population at Littlemore is at least equal to that of St. Mary's in Oxford, and the *whole* of Littlemore is double of it. It has been very much neglected; and in providing a parsonage-house at Littlemore, as this will be, and will be called, I conceive I am doing a very great benefit to my people. At the same time it has appeared to me that a partial or temporary retirement from St. Mary's Church might be expedient under the prevailing excitement.

'As to the quotation from the [newspaper], which I have not seen, your Lordship will perceive from what I have said, that no "monastery is in process of erection;" there is no "chapel;" no "refectory," hardly a dining-room or parlour. The "cloisters" are my shed connecting the cottages. I do not understand what "cells of dormitories" means. Of course I can repeat your Lordship's words that "I am not attempting a revival of the Monastic Orders, in any thing approaching to the Romanist sense of the term," or "taking on myself to originate any measure of importance without authority from the Heads of the Church." I am attempting nothing ecclesiastical, but something personal and private, and which can only be made public, not private, by newspapers and letter-writers, in which sense the most sacred and conscientious resolves and acts may certainly be made the objects of an unmannerly and unfeeling curiosity.'

One calumny there was which the Bishop did not believe, and of which of course he had no idea of speaking. It was that I was actually in the service of the enemy. I had forsooth been already received into the Catholic Church, and was rearing at Littlemore a nest of Papists, who, like me, were to take the Anglican oaths which they disbelieved, by virtue of a dispensation from Rome, and thus in due time were to bring over to that unprincipled Church great numbers of the Anglican Clergy and Laity. Bishops gave their countenance to this imputation against me. The case was simply this: – as I made Littlemore a place of retirement for myself, so did I offer it to others. There were young men in Oxford, whose testimonials for Orders had been refused by their Colleges; there were young clergymen, who had found themselves unable from conscience to go on with their duties, and had thrown up their parochial engagements. Such men were already going straight to Rome, and I interposed; I interposed for the reasons I have given in the beginning of this portion of my narrative. I interposed from fidelity to my clerical engagements, and from duty to my Bishop; and from the interest which I was bound to take in them, and from belief that they were premature or excited. Their friends besought me to quiet them, if I could. Some of them came to live with me at Littlemore. They were laymen, or in the place of laymen. I kept some of them back for several years from being received into the Catholic Church. Even when I had given up my living, I was still bound by my duty to their parents or friends, and I did not forget still to do what I could for them. The immediate occasion of my resigning St. Mary's, was the unexpected conversion[36] of one of them. After that, I felt it was impossible to keep my post there, for I had been unable to keep my word with my Bishop.

The following letters refer, more or less, to these men, whether they were actually with me at Littlemore or not: –

1. 'March 6, 1842. Church doctrines are a powerful weapon; they were not sent into the world for nothing. God's word does not return unto Him void: If I have said, as I have, that the doctrines of the Tracts for the Times would build up our Church and destroy parties, I meant, if they were used, not if they were denounced. Else, they will be as powerful against us, as they might be powerful for us.

'If people who have a liking for another, hear him called a Roman Catholic, they will say, "Then after all Romanism is no such bad thing." All these persons, who are making the cry, are fulfilling their own prophecy. If all the world agree in telling a man, he has no business in our Church, he will at length begin to think he has none. How easy is it to persuade a man of any thing, when numbers affirm it! so great is the force of imagination. Did every one who met you in the streets look hard at you, you would think you were somehow in fault. I do not know any thing so irritating, so unsettling, especially in the case of young persons, as, when they are going on calmly and unconsciously, obeying their Church and following its divines (I am speaking from facts,) as suddenly to their surprise to be conjured not to make a leap, of which they have not a dream and from which they are far removed.'

2. 1843 or 1844. 'I did not explain to you sufficiently the state of mind of those who were in danger. I only spoke of those who were convinced that our Church was external to the Church Catholic, though they felt it unsafe to trust their own private convictions; but there are two other states of mind; 1. that of those who are unconsciously near Rome, and whose *despair* about our Church would at once develope into a state of conscious approximation, or a *quasi*-resolution to go over; 2. those who feel they can with a safe conscience remain with us *while* they are allowed to *testify* in behalf of Catholicism, i.e. as if by such acts they were putting our Church, or at least that portion of it in which they were included, in the position of catechumens.'

3. 'June 20, 1843. I return the very pleasing letter you have permitted me to read. What a sad thing it is, that it should be a plain duty to restrain one's sympathies, and to keep them from boiling over; but I suppose it is a matter of common prudence.

'Things are very serious here; but I should not like you to say so, as it might do no good. The Authorities find, that, by the Statutes, they have more than military power; and the general impression seems to be, that they intend to exert it, and put down Catholicism at any risk. I believe that by the Statutes, they can pretty nearly suspend a Preacher, as *seditiosus* or causing dissension, without assigning their grounds in the particular case, nay, banish him, or imprison him. If so, all holders of preferment in the University should make as quiet an *exit* as they can. There is more exasperation on both sides at this moment, as I am told, than ever there was.'

4. 'July 16, 1843. I assure you that I feel, with only too much sympathy, what you say. You need not be told that the whole subject of our position is a subject of anxiety to others beside yourself. It is no good attempting to offer advice, when perhaps I might raise difficulties instead of removing them. It seems to

me quite a case, in which you should, as far as may be, make up your mind for yourself. Come to Littlemore by all means. We shall all rejoice in your company; and, if quiet and retirement are able, as they very likely will be, to reconcile you to things as they are, you shall have your fill of them. How distressed poor Henry Wilberforce must be! Knowing how he values you,[37] I feel for him; but, alas! he has his own position, and every one else has his own, and the misery is that no two of us have exactly the same.

'It is very kind of you to be so frank and open with me, as you are; but this is a time which throws together persons who feel alike. May I without taking a liberty sign myself, yours affectionately, &c.'

5. 'August 30, 1843. A. B. has suddenly conformed to the Church of Rome. He was away for three weeks. I suppose I must say in my defence, that he promised me distinctly to remain in our Church three years, before I received him here.'

6. 'June 17, 1845. I am concerned to find you speak of me in a tone of distrust. If you knew me ever so little, instead of hearing of me from persons who do not know me at all, you would think differently of me, whatever you thought of my opinions. Two years since, I got your son to tell you my intention of resigning St. Mary's, before I made it public, thinking you ought to know it. When you expressed some painful feeling upon it, I told him I could not consent to his remaining here, painful as it would be to me to part with him, without your written sanction. And this you did me the favour to give.

'I believe you will find that it has been merely a delicacy on your son's part, which has delayed his speaking to you about me for two months past; a delicacy, lest he should say either too much or too little about me. I have urged him several times to speak to you.

'Nothing can be done after your letter, but to recommend him to go to A. B. (his home) at once. I am very sorry to part with him.'

7. The following letter is addressed to Cardinal Wiseman, then Vicar Apostolic, who accused me of coldness in my conduct towards him: –

'April 16, 1845. I was at that time in charge of a ministerial office in the English Church, with persons entrusted to me, and a Bishop to obey; how could I possibly write otherwise than I did without violating sacred obligations and betraying momentous interests which were upon me? I felt that my immediate, undeniable duty, clear if any thing was clear, was to fulfil that trust. It might be right indeed to give it up, that was another thing; but it never could be right to hold it, and to act as if I did not hold it. . . . If you knew me, you would acquit me, I think, of having ever felt towards your Lordship in an unfriendly spirit, or ever having had a shadow on my mind (as far as I dare witness about myself) of what might be called controversial rivalry or desire of getting the better, or fear lest the world should think I had got the worse, or irritation of any kind. You are too kind indeed to imply this, and yet your words lead me to say it. And now in like manner, pray believe, though I cannot explain it to you, that I am encompassed with responsibilities, so great and so various, as utterly to overcome me, unless I have mercy from Him, who all through my life has sustained and guided me, and to whom I can now submit myself, though men of all parties are thinking evil of me.'

Such fidelity, however, was taken *in malam partem*[38] by the high Anglican authorities; they thought it insidious. I happen still to have a correspondence which took place in 1843, in which the chief place is filled by one of the most eminent Bishops of the day, a theologian and reader of the Fathers, a moderate man, who at one time was talked of as likely on a vacancy to succeed to the Primacy. A young clergyman[39] in his diocese became a Catholic; the papers at once reported on authority from 'a very high quarter,' that, after his reception, 'the Oxford men had been recommending him to retain his living.' I had reasons for thinking that the allusion was made to me, and I authorized the Editor[40] of a Paper, who had inquired of me on the point, to 'give it, as far as I was concerned, an unqualified contradiction;' – when from a motive of delicacy he hesitated, I added 'my direct and indignant contradiction.' 'Whoever is the author of it,' I continued to the Editor, 'no correspondence or intercourse of any kind, direct or indirect, has passed between Mr. S. and myself, since his conforming to the Church of Rome, except my formally and merely acknowledging the receipt of his letter, in which he informed me of the fact, without, as far as I recollect, my expressing any opinion upon it. You may state this as broadly as I have set it down.' My denial was told to the Bishop; what took place upon it is given in a letter from which I copy. 'My father showed the letter to the Bishop, who, as he laid it down, said, "Ah, those Oxford men are not ingenuous." "How do you mean?" asked my father. "Why," said the Bishop, "they advised Mr. B. S. to retain his living after he turned Catholic. I know that to be a fact, because A. B. told me so."' 'The Bishop,' continues the letter, 'who is perhaps the most influential man in reality on the bench, evidently believes it to be the truth.' Upon this Dr. Pusey wrote in my behalf to the Bishop; and the Bishop instantly beat a retreat. 'I have the honour,' he says in the autograph which I transcribe, 'to acknowledge the receipt of your note, and to say in reply that it has not been stated by me, (though such a statement has, I believe, appeared in some of the Public Prints,) that Mr. Newman had advised Mr. B. S. to retain his living, after he had forsaken our Church. But it has been stated to me, that Mr. Newman was in close correspondence with Mr. B. S., and, being fully aware of his state of opinions and feelings, yet advised him to continue in our communion. Allow me to add,' he says to Dr. Pusey, 'that neither your name, nor that of Mr. Keble, was mentioned to me in connexion with that of Mr. B. S.'

I was not going to let the Bishop off on this evasion, so I wrote[41] to him myself. After quoting his Letter to Dr. Pusey, I continued, 'I beg to trouble your Lordship with my own account of the two allegations' [*close correspondence* and *fully aware*, &c] 'which are contained in your statement, and which have led to your speaking of me in terms which I hope never to deserve. 1. Since Mr. B. S. has been in your Lordship's diocese, I have seen him in Common rooms or private parties in Oxford two or three times, when I never (as far as I can recollect) had any conversation with him. During the same time I have, to the best of my memory, written to him three letters. One was lately, in acknowledgment of his informing me of his change of religion. Another was last summer, when I asked him (to no purpose) to come and stay with me in this place. The earliest of the three letters was written just a year since, as far as I recollect, and it certainly was on the subject of his joining the Church of Rome. I wrote this letter at the earnest wish of a friend of his. I cannot be sure that, on his replying, I did not send him a brief note in explanation of points in my letter which he had misapprehended. I cannot recollect any other correspondence between us.

'2. As to my knowledge of his opinions and feelings, as far as I remember, the only point of perplexity which I knew, the only point which to this hour I know, as pressing upon him, was that of the Pope's supremacy. He professed to be searching Antiquity whether the see of Rome had formerly that relation to the whole Church which Roman Catholics now assign to it. My letter was directed to the point, that it was his duty not to perplex himself with arguments on [such] a question, . . . and to put it altogether aside. . . . It is hard that I am put upon my memory, without knowing the details of the statement made against me, considering the various correspondence in which I am from time to time unavoidably engaged. . . . Be assured, my Lord, that there are very definite limits, beyond which persons like me would never urge another to retain preferment in the English Church, nor would retain it themselves; and that the censure which has been directed against them by so many of its Rulers has a very grave bearing upon those limits.' The Bishop replied in a civil letter, and sent my own letter to his original informant,[42] who wrote to me the letter of a gentleman. It seems that an anxious lady had said something or other which had been misinterpreted, against her real meaning, into the calumny which was circulated, and so the report vanished into thin air. I closed the correspondence with the following Letter to the Bishop: —

'I hope your Lordship will believe me when I say, that statements about me, equally incorrect with that which has come to your Lordship's ears, are from time to time reported to me as credited and repeated by the highest authorities in our Church, though it is very seldom that I have the opportunity of denying them. I am obliged by your Lordship's letter to Dr. Pusey as giving me such an opportunity.' Then I added, with a purpose, 'Your Lordship will observe that in my Letter I had no occasion to proceed to the question, whether a person holding Roman Catholic opinions can in honesty remain in our Church. Lest then any misconception should arise from my silence, I here take the liberty of adding, that I see nothing wrong in such a person's continuing in communion with us, provided he holds no preferment or office, abstains from the management of ecclesiastical matters and is bound by no subscription or oath to our doctrines.'

This was written on March 8, 1843, and was in anticipation of my own retirement into lay communion. This again leads me to a remark: – for two years I was in lay communion, not indeed being a Catholic in my convictions, but in a state of serious doubt, and with the probable prospect of becoming some day, what as yet I was not. Under these circumstances I thought the best thing I could do was to give up duty and to throw myself into lay communion, remaining an Anglican. I could not go to Rome, while I thought what I did of the devotions she sanctioned to the Blessed Virgin and the Saints. I did not give up my fellowship, for I could not be sure that my doubts would not be reduced or overcome, however unlikely I might consider such an event. But I gave up my living; and, for two years before my conversion, I took no clerical duty. My last Sermon[43] was in September, 1843; then I remained at Littlemore in quiet for two years. But it was made a subject of reproach to me at the time, and is at this day, that I did not leave the Anglican Church sooner. To me this seems a wonderful charge; why, even had I been quite sure that Rome was the true Church, the Anglican Bishops would have had no just subject of complaint against me, provided I took no Anglican oath, no clerical duty, no ecclesiastical administration. Do they force all men who go to their Churches to believe in the 39 Articles, or to join in the Athanasian Creed? However, I was to have other measure dealt to me; great authorities ruled it so; and a great controversialist, Mr. Stanley Faber,[44] thought it a shame that I did not leave the Church of England as much as ten years sooner than I did. He said this in print between the years 1847 and 1849. His nephew,[45] an Anglican clergyman, kindly wished to undeceive him on this point. So, in the latter year, after some correspondence, I wrote the following letter, which will be of service to this narrative, from its chronological notes: –

'Dec. 6, 1849. Your uncle says, "If he (Mr. N.) will declare, *sans phrase*,[46] as the French say, that I have laboured under an entire mistake, and that he was not a concealed Romanist during the ten years in question," (I suppose, the last ten years of my membership with the Anglican Church,) "or during any part of the time, my controversial antipathy will be at an end, and I will readily express to him that I am truly sorry that I have made such a mistake."

'So candid an avowal is what I should have expected from a mind like your uncle's. I am extremely glad he has brought it to this issue.

'By a "concealed Romanist" I understand him to mean one, who, professing to belong to the Church of England, in his heart and will intends to benefit the Church of Rome, at the expense of the Church of England. He cannot mean by the expression merely a person who in fact is benefiting the Church of Rome, while he is intending to benefit the Church of England, for that is no discredit to him morally, and he (your uncle) evidently means to impute blame.

'In the sense in which I have explained the words, I can simply and honestly say that I was not a concealed Romanist during the whole, or any part of, the years in question.

'For the first four years of the ten, (up to Michaelmas, 1839,) I honestly wished to benefit the Church of England, at the expense of the Church of Rome:

'For the second four years I wished to benefit the Church of England without prejudice to the Church of Rome:

'At the beginning of the ninth year (Michaelmas, 1843) I began to despair of the Church of England, and gave up all clerical duty; and then, what I wrote and did was influenced by a mere wish not to injure it, and not by the wish to benefit it:

'At the beginning of the tenth year I distinctly contemplated leaving it, but I also distinctly told my friends that it was in my contemplation.

'Lastly, during the last half of that tenth year I was engaged in writing a book (*Essay on Development*) in favour of the Roman Church, and indirectly against the English; but even then, till it was finished, I had not absolutely intended to publish it, wishing to reserve to myself the chance of changing my mind when the argumentative views which were actuating me had been distinctly brought out before me in writing.

'I wish this statement, which I make from memory, and without consulting any document, severely tested by my writings and doings, as I am confident it will, on the whole, be borne out, whatever real or apparent exceptions (I suspect none) have to be allowed by me in detail.

'Your uncle is at liberty to make what use he pleases of this explanation.'

I have now reached an important date in my narrative, the year 1843; but before proceeding to the matters which it contains, I will insert portions of my letters from 1841 to 1843, addressed to Catholic acquaintances.

1. 'April 8, 1841. . . . The unity of the Church Catholic is very near my heart, only I do not see any prospect of it in our time; and I despair of its being effected without great sacrifices on all hands. As to resisting the Bishop's will, I observe that no point of doctrine or principle was in dispute, but a course of action, the publication of certain works. I do not think you sufficiently understood our position. I suppose you would obey the Holy See in such a case; now, when we were separated from the Pope, his authority reverted to our Diocesans. Our Bishop is our Pope. It is our theory, that each diocese is an integral Church, intercommunion being a duty, (and the breach of it a sin,) but not essential to Catholicity. To have resisted my Bishop, would have been to place myself in an utterly false position, which I never could have recovered. Depend upon it, the strength of any party lies in its being *true to its theory*. Consistency is the life of a movement.

'I have no misgivings whatever that the line I have taken can be other than a prosperous one: that is, in itself, for of course Providence may refuse to us its legitimate issues for our sins.

'I am afraid, that in one respect you may be disappointed. It is my trust, though I must not be too sanguine, that we shall not have individual members of our communion going over to yours. What one's duty would be under other circumstances, what our duty ten or twenty years ago, I cannot say; but I do think that there is less of private judgment in going with one's Church, than in leaving it. I can earnestly desire a union between my Church and yours. I cannot listen to the thought of your being joined by individuals among us.'

2. 'April 26, 1841. My only anxiety is lest your branch of the Church should not meet us by those reforms which surely are *necessary*. It never could be, that so large a portion of Christendom should have split off from the communion of Rome, and kept up a protest for 300 years for nothing. I think I never shall believe that so much piety and earnestness would be found among Protestants, if there were not some very grave errors on the side of Rome. To suppose the contrary is most unreal, and violates all one's notions of moral probabilities. All aberrations are founded on, and have their life in, some truth or other – and Protestantism, so widely spread and so long enduring, must have in it, and must be witness for, a great truth or much truth. That I am an advocate for Protestantism, you cannot suppose; – but I am forced into a *Via Media*, short of Rome, as it is at present.'

3. 'May 5, 1841. While I most sincerely hold that there is in the Roman Church a traditionary system which is not necessarily connected with her essential formularies, yet, were I ever so much to change my mind on this point, this would not tend to bring me from my present position, providentially appointed in the English Church. That your communion was unassailable, would not prove that mine was indefensible. Nor would it at all affect the sense in which I receive our Articles; they would still speak against certain definite errors, though you had reformed them.

'I say this lest any lurking suspicion should be left in the mind of your friends that persons who think with me are likely, by the growth of their present views, to find it imperative on them to pass over to your communion. Allow me to state strongly, that if you have any such thoughts, and proceed to act upon them, your friends will be committing a fatal mistake. We have (I trust) the principle and temper of obedience too intimately wrought into us to allow of our separating ourselves from our ecclesiastical superiors because in many points we may sympathize with others. We have too great a horror of the principle of private judgment to trust it in so immense a matter as that of changing from one communion to another. We may be cast out of our communion, or it may decree heresy to be truth, – you shall say whether such contingencies are likely; but I do not see other conceivable causes of our leaving the Church in which we were baptized.

'For myself, persons must be well acquainted with what I have written before they venture to say whether I have much changed my main opinions and cardinal views in the course of the last eight years. That my *sympathies* have grown towards the religion of Rome I do not deny; that my *reasons* for *shunning* her communion have lessened or altered it would be difficult perhaps to prove. And I wish to go by reason, not by feeling.'

4. 'June 18, 1841. You urge persons whose views agree with mine to commence a movement in behalf of a union between the Churches. Now in the letters I have written, I have uniformly said that I did not expect that union in our time, and have discouraged the notion of all sudden proceedings with a view to it. I must ask your leave to repeat on this occasion most distinctly, that I cannot be party to any agitation, but mean to remain quiet in my own place, and to do all I can to make others take the same course. This I conceive to be my simple duty; but, over and above this, I will not set my teeth on edge with sour grapes.[47] I know it is quite within the range of possibilities that one or another of our people should go over to your communion; however, it would be a greater misfortune to you than grief to us. If your friends wish to put a gulf between themselves and us, let them make converts, but not else. Some months ago, I ventured to say that I felt it a painful duty to keep aloof from all Roman Catholics who came with the intention of opening negotiations for the union of the Churches: when you now urge us to petition our Bishops for a union, this, I conceive, is very like an act of negotiation.'

5. I have the first sketch or draft of a letter, which I wrote to a zealous Catholic layman:[48] it runs as follows, as far as I have preserved it, but I think there were various changes and additions:– 'September 12, 1841. It would rejoice all Catholic minds among us, more than words can say, if you could persuade members of the Church of Rome to take the line in politics which you so earnestly advocate. Suspicion and distrust are the main causes at present of the separation between us, and the nearest approaches in doctrine will but increase the hostility, which, alas, our people feel towards yours, while these causes

continue. Depend upon it, you must not rely upon our Catholic tendencies till they are removed. I am not speaking of myself, or of any friends of mine; but of our Church generally. Whatever *our* personal feelings may be, we shall but tend to raise and spread a *rival* Church to yours in the four quarters of the world, unless *you* do what none but you *can* do. Sympathies, which would flow over to the Church of Rome, as a matter of course, did she admit them, will but be developed in the consolidation of our own system, if she continues to be the object of our suspicions and fears. I wish, of course I do, that our own Church may be built up and extended, but still, not at the cost of the Church of Rome, not in opposition to it. I am sure, that, while you suffer, we suffer too from the separation; *but we cannot remove the obstacles*; it is with you to do so. You do not fear us; we fear you. Till we cease to fear you, we cannot love you.

'While you are in your present position, the friends of Catholic unity in our Church are but fulfilling the prediction of those of your body who are averse to them, viz. that they will be merely strengthening a rival communion to yours. Many of you say that *we* are your greatest enemies; we have said so ourselves: so we are, so we shall be, as things stand at present. We are keeping people from you, by supplying their wants in our own Church. We *are* keeping persons from you: do you wish us to keep them from you for a time or for ever? It rests with you to determine. I do not fear that you will succeed among us; you will not supplant our Church in the affections of the English nation; only through the English Church can you act upon the English nation. I wish of course our Church should be consolidated, with and through and in your communion, for its sake, and your sake, and for the sake of unity.

'Are you aware that the more serious thinkers among us are used, as far as they dare form an opinion, to regard the spirit of Liberalism as the characteristic of the destined Antichrist? In vain does any one clear the Church of Rome from the badges of Antichrist, in which Protestants would invest her, if she deliberately takes up her position in the very quarter, whither we have cast them, when we took them off from her. Antichrist is described as the ἄνομος,[49] as exalting himself above the yoke of religion and law. The spirit of lawlessness came in with the Reformation, and Liberalism is its offspring.

'And now I fear I am going to pain you by telling you, that you consider the approaches in doctrine on our part towards you, closer than they really are. I cannot help repeating what I have many times said in print, that your services and devotions to St. Mary in matter of fact do most deeply pain me. I am only stating it as a fact.

'Again, I have nowhere said that I can accept the decrees of Trent throughout, nor implied it. The doctrine of Transubstantiation is a great difficulty with me, as being, as I think, not primitive. Nor have I said that our Articles in all respects admit of a Roman interpretation; the very word "Transubstantiation" is disowned in them.

'Thus, you see, it is not merely on grounds of expedience that we do not join you. There are positive difficulties in the way of it. And, even if there were not, we shall have no divine warrant for doing so, while we think that the Church of England is a branch of the true Church, and that intercommunion with the rest of Christendom is necessary, not for the life of a particular Church, but for its health only. I have never disguised that there are actual circumstances in the Church of Rome, which pain me much; of the removal of these I see no chance, while we join you one by one; but if our Church were prepared for a union, she might make her terms; she might gain the cup; she might protest against the extreme honours paid to St. Mary; she might make some explanation of the doctrine of Transubstantiation. I am not prepared to say that a reform in other branches of the Roman Church would be necessary for our uniting with them, however desirable in itself, so that we were allowed to make a reform in our own country. We do not look towards Rome as believing that its communion is infallible, but that union is a duty.'

6. The following letter was occasioned by the present made to me of a book by the friend to whom it is written; more will be said on the subject of it presently: —

'Nov. 22, 1842. I only wish that your Church were more known among us by such writings. You will not interest us in her, till we see her, not in politics, but in her true functions of exhorting, teaching, and guiding. I wish there were a chance of making the leading men among you understand, what I believe is no novel thought to yourself. It is not by learned discussions, or acute arguments, or reports of miracles, that the heart of England can be gained. It is by men "approving themselves," like the Apostle, "ministers of Christ."[50]

'As to your question, whether the Volume you have sent is not calculated to remove my apprehensions that another gospel is substituted for the true one in your practical instructions, before I can answer it in any way, I ought to know how far the Sermons which it comprises are *selected* from a number, or whether they are the whole, or such as the whole, which have been published of the author's. I assure you, or at least I trust, that, if it is ever clearly brought home to me that I have been wrong in what I have said on this subject, my public avowal of that conviction will only be a question of time with me.

'If, however, you saw our Church as we see it, you would easily understand that such a change of feeling, did it take place, would have no necessary tendency, which you seem to expect, to draw a person from the Church of England to that of Rome. There is a divine life among us, clearly manifested, in spite of all our disorders, which is as great a note of the Church, as any can be. Why should we seek our Lord's presence elsewhere, when He vouchsafes it to us where we are? What *call* have we to change our communion?

'Roman Catholics will find this to be the state of things in time to come, whatever promise they may fancy there is of a large secession to their Church. This man or that may leave us, but there will be no general movement. There is, indeed, an incipient movement of our *Church* towards yours, and this your leading men are doing all they can to frustrate by their unwearied efforts at all risks to carry off individuals. When will they know their position, and embrace a larger and wiser policy?'

2

The letter which I have last inserted, is addressed to my dear friend, Dr. Russell,[51] the present President of Maynooth. He had, perhaps, more to do with my conversion than any one else. He called upon me, in passing through Oxford in the summer of

1841, and I think I took him over some of the buildings of the University. He called again another summer, on his way from Dublin to London. I do not recollect that he said a word on the subject of religion on either occasion. He sent me at different times several letters; he was always gentle, mild, unobtrusive, uncontroversial. He let me alone. He also gave me one or two books. Veron's Rule of Faith[52] and some Treatises[53] of the Wallenburghs was one; a volume of St. Alfonso Liguori's Sermons was another; and it is to those Sermons that my letter to Dr. Russell relates.

Now it must be observed that the writings of St. Alfonso, as I knew them by the extracts commonly made from them, prejudiced me as much against the Roman Church as any thing else, on account of what was called their 'Mariolatry;' but there was nothing of the kind in this book. I wrote to ask Dr. Russell whether any thing had been left out in the translation; he answered that there certainly were omissions in one Sermon about the Blessed Virgin. This omission, in the case of a book intended for Catholics, at least showed that such passages as are found in the works of Italian Authors were not acceptable to every part of the Catholic world. Such devotional manifestations in honour of our Lady had been my great *crux* as regards Catholicism; I say frankly, I do not fully enter into them now; I trust I do not love her the less, because I cannot enter into them. They may be fully explained and defended; but sentiment and taste do not run with logic: they are suitable for Italy, but they are not suitable for England. But, over and above England, my own case was special; from a boy I had been led to consider that my Maker and I, His creature, were the two beings luminously such, *in rerum naturâ*.[54] I will not here speculate, however, about my own feelings. Only this I know full well now, and did not know then, that the Catholic Church allows no image of any sort, material or immaterial, no dogmatic symbol, no rite, no sacrament, no Saint, not even the Blessed Virgin herself, to come between the soul and its Creator. It is face to face, 'solus cum solo,' in all matters between man and his God. He alone creates; He alone has redeemed; before His awful eyes we go in death; in the vision of Him is our eternal beatitude.

1. Solus cum solo: – I recollect but indistinctly what I gained

from the Volume of which I have been speaking; but it must have been something considerable. At least I had got a key to a difficulty; in these Sermons, (or rather heads of sermons, as they seem to be, taken down by a hearer,) there is much of what would be called legendary illustration; but the substance of them is plain, practical, awful preaching upon the great truths of salvation. What I can speak of with greater confidence is the effect produced on me a little later by studying the Exercises[55] of St. Ignatius. For here again, in a matter consisting in the purest and most direct acts of religion, – in the intercourse between God and the soul, during a season of recollection, of repentance, of good resolution, of inquiry into vocation, – the soul was 'sola cum solo;' there was no cloud interposed between the creature and the Object of his faith and love. The command practically enforced was, 'My son, give Me thy heart.' The devotions then to Angels and Saints as little interfered with the incommunicable glory of the Eternal, as the love which we bear our friends and relations, our tender human sympathies, are inconsistent with that supreme homage of the heart to the Unseen, which really does but sanctify and exalt, not jealously destroy, what is of earth. At a later date Dr. Russell sent me a large bundle of penny or half-penny books of devotion, of all sorts, as they are found in the booksellers' shops at Rome; and, on looking them over, I was quite astonished to find how different they were from what I had fancied, how little there was in them to which I could really object. I have given an account[56] of them in my *Essay on the Development of Doctrine*. Dr. Russell sent me St. Alfonso's book at the end of 1842; however, it was still a long time before I got over my difficulty, on the score of the devotions paid to the Saints; perhaps, as I judge from a letter I have turned up, it was some way into 1844 before I could be said fully to have got over it.

2. I am not sure that I did not also at this time feel the force of another consideration. The idea of the Blessed Virgin was as it were *magnified* in the Church of Rome, as time went on, – but so were all the Christian ideas; as that of the Blessed Eucharist. The whole scene of pale, faint, distant Apostolic Christianity is seen in Rome, as through a telescope or magnifier. The harmony of the whole, however, is of course what it was. It is unfair then to

take one Roman idea, that of the Blessed Virgin, out of what may be called its context.

3. Thus I am brought to the principle of development of doctrine in the Christian Church, to which I gave my mind at the end of 1842. I had made mention[57] of it in the passage, which I quoted many pages back (vide p. 111), in *Home Thoughts Abroad*, published in 1836; and even at an earlier date I had introduced[58] it into my *History of the Arians* in 1832; nor had I ever lost sight of it in my speculations. And it is certainly recognized in the *Treatise of Vincent of Lerins*, which has so often been taken as the basis of Anglicanism. In 1843 I began to consider it attentively; I made it the subject of my last University Sermon[59] on February 2; and the general view to which I came is stated thus in a letter to a friend[60] of the date of July 14, 1844; – it will be observed that, now as before, my *issue* is still Creed *versus* Church: –

'The kind of considerations which weighs with me are such as the following: – 1. I am far more certain (according to the Fathers) that we *are* in a state of culpable separation, *than* that developments do *not* exist under the Gospel, and that the Roman developments are not the true ones. 2. I am far more certain, that *our* (modern) doctrines are wrong, *than* that the *Roman* (modern) doctrines are wrong. 3. Granting that the Roman (special) doctrines are not found drawn out in the early Church, yet I think there is sufficient trace of them in it, to recommend and prove them, *on the hypothesis* of the Church having a divine guidance, though not sufficient to prove them by itself. So that the question simply turns on the nature of the promise of the Spirit, made to the Church. 4. The proof of the Roman (modern) doctrine is as strong (or stronger) in Antiquity, as that of certain doctrines which both we and Romans hold: e.g. there is more of evidence in Antiquity for the necessity of Unity, than for the Apostolical Succession; for the Supremacy of the See of Rome, than for the Presence in the Eucharist; for the practice of Invocation, than for certain books in the present Canon of Scripture, &c., &c. 5. The analogy of the Old Testament, and also of the New, leads to the acknowledgment of doctrinal developments.'

4. And thus I was led on to a further consideration. I saw that the principle of development not only accounted for certain

facts, but was in itself a remarkable philosophical phenomenon, giving a character to the whole course of Christian thought. It was discernible from the first years of the Catholic teaching up to the present day, and gave to that teaching a unity and individuality. It served as a sort of test, which the Anglican could not exhibit, that modern Rome was in truth ancient Antioch, Alexandria, and Constantinople, just as a mathematical curve has its own law and expression.

5. And thus again I was led on to examine more attentively what I doubt not was in my thoughts long before, viz. the concatenation of argument by which the mind ascends from its first to its final religious idea; and I came to the conclusion that there was no medium, in true philosophy, between Atheism and Catholicity, and that a perfectly consistent mind, under those circumstances in which it finds itself here below, must embrace either the one or the other. And I hold this still: I am a Catholic by virtue of my believing in a God; and if I am asked why I believe in a God, I answer that it is because I believe in myself, for I feel it impossible to believe in my own existence (and of that fact I am quite sure) without believing also in the existence of Him, who lives as a Personal, All-seeing, All-judging Being in my conscience. Now, I dare say, I have not expressed myself with philosophical correctness, because I have not given myself to the study of what metaphysicians have said on the subject; but I think I have a strong true meaning in what I say which will stand examination.

6. Moreover, I found a corroboration of the fact of the logical connexion of Theism with Catholicism in a consideration parallel to that which I had adopted on the subject of development of doctrine. The fact of the operation from first to last of that principle of development in the truths of Revelation, is an argument in favour of the identity of Roman and Primitive Christianity; but as there is a law which acts upon the subject-matter of dogmatic theology, so is there a law in the matter of religious faith. In the first chapter of this Narrative I spoke of certitude as the consequence, divinely intended and enjoined upon us, of the accumulative force of certain given reasons which, taken one by one, were only probabilities. Let it be recollected that I am historically relating my state of mind, at the

period of my life which I am surveying. I am not speaking theologically, nor have I any intention of going into controversy, or of defending myself; but speaking historically of what I held in 1843–4, I say, that I believed in a God on a ground of probability, that I believed in Christianity on a probability, and that I believed in Catholicism on a probability, and that these three grounds of probability, distinct from each other of course in subject matter, were still all of them one and the same in nature of proof, as being probabilities – probabilities of a special kind, a cumulative, a transcendent probability but still probability; inasmuch as He who made us has so willed, that in mathematics indeed we should arrive at certitude by rigid demonstration, but in religious inquiry we should arrive at certitude by accumulated probabilities; – He has willed, I say, that we should so act, and, as willing it, He co-operates with us in our acting, and thereby enables us to do that which He wills us to do, and carries us on, if our will does but co-operate with His, to a certitude which rises higher than the logical force of our conclusions. And thus I came to see clearly, and to have a satisfaction in seeing, that, in being led on into the Church of Rome, I was not proceeding on any secondary or isolated grounds of reason, or by controversial points in detail, but was protected and justified, even in the use of those secondary or particular arguments, by a great and broad principle. But, let it be observed, that I am stating a matter of fact, not defending it; and if any Catholic says in consequence that I have been converted in a wrong way, I cannot help that now.

I have nothing more to say on the subject of the change in my religious opinions. On the one hand I came gradually to see that the Anglican Church was formally in the wrong, on the other that the Church of Rome was formally in the right: then, that no valid reasons could be assigned for continuing in the Anglican, and again that no valid objections could be taken to joining the Roman. Then, I had nothing more to learn; what still remained for my conversion, was, not further change of opinion, but to change opinion itself into the clearness and firmness of intellectual conviction.

Now I proceed to detail the acts, to which I committed myself during this last stage of my inquiry.

*

In 1843, I took two very significant steps: – 1. In February, I made a formal Retractation[61] of all the hard things which I had said against the Church of Rome. 2. In September, I resigned the Living of St. Mary's, Littlemore included: – I will speak of these two acts separately.

1. The words, in which I made my Retractation, have given rise to much criticism. After quoting a number of passages from my writings against the Church of Rome, which I withdrew, I ended thus: – 'If you ask me how an individual could venture, not simply to hold, but to publish such views of a communion so ancient, so widespreading, so fruitful in Saints, I answer that I said to myself, "I am not speaking my own words, I am but following almost a *consensus* of the divines of my own Church. They have ever used the strongest language against Rome, even the most able and learned of them. I wish to throw myself into their system. While I say what they say, I am safe. Such views, too, are necessary for our position." Yet I have reason to fear still, that such language is to be ascribed, in no small measure, to an impetuous temper, a hope of approving myself to persons I respect, and a wish to repel the charge of Romanism.'

These words have been, and are, again and again cited against me, as if a confession that, when in the Anglican Church, I said things against Rome which I did not really believe.

For myself, I cannot understand how any impartial man can so take them; and I have explained them in print several times. I trust that by this time their plain meaning has been satisfactorily brought out by what I have said in former portions of this Narrative; still I have a word or two to say in addition to my former remarks upon them.

In the passage in question I apologize for *saying out* in controversy charges against the Church of Rome, which withal I affirm that I fully *believed* at the time when I made them. What is wonderful in such an apology? There are surely many things a man may hold, which at the same time he may feel that he has no right to say publicly, and which it may annoy him that he has said publicly. The law recognizes this principle. In our own time, men have been imprisoned and fined for saying true things of a bad king. The maxim has been held, that, 'The greater the truth, the greater is the libel.' And so as to the judgment of society, a just indignation would be felt against a writer who brought forward wantonly the weaknesses of a great man, though the whole world knew that they existed. No one is at liberty to speak ill of another without a justifiable reason, even though he knows he is speaking truth, and the public knows it too. Therefore, though I believed what I said against the Roman Church, nevertheless I could not religiously speak it out, unless I was really justified, not only in believing ill, but in speaking ill. I did believe what I said on what I thought to be good reasons; but had I also a just cause for saying out what I believed? I thought I had, and it was this, viz. that to say out what I believed was simply necessary in the controversy for self-defence. It was impossible to let it alone: the Anglican position could not be satisfactorily maintained, without assailing the Roman. In this, as in most cases of conflict, one party was right or the other, not both; and the best defence was to attack. Is not this almost a truism in the Roman controversy? Is it not what every one says, who speaks on the subject at all? does any serious man abuse the Church of Rome, for the sake of abusing her, or because that abuse justifies his own religious position? What is the meaning of the very word 'Protestantism,' but that there is a call to speak out? This then is what I said; 'I know I spoke strongly against the Church of Rome; but it was no mere abuse, for I had a serious reason for doing so.'

But, not only did I think such language necessary for my Church's religious position, but I recollected that all the great Anglican divines had thought so before me. They had thought so, and they had acted accordingly. And therefore I observe in the passage in question, with much propriety, that I had not used strong language simply out of my own head, but that in doing so I was following the track, or rather reproducing the teaching, of those who had preceded me.

I was pleading guilty to using violent language, but I was pleading also that there were extenuating circumstances in the case. We all know the story of the convict who on the scaffold bit off his mother's ear. By doing so he did not deny the fact of his own crime, for which he was to hang; but he said that his mother's indulgence when he was a boy, had a good deal to do with it. In like manner I had made a charge, and I had made it *ex animo*; but I accused others of having, by their own example, led me into believing it and publishing it.

I was in a humour, certainly, to bite off their ears. I will freely confess, indeed I said it some pages back, that I was angry with the Anglican divines. I thought they had taken me in; I had read the Fathers with their eyes; I had sometimes trusted their quotations or their reasonings; and from reliance on them, I had used words or made statements, which by right I ought rigidly to have examined myself. I had thought myself safe, while I had their warrant for what I said. I had exercised more faith than criticism in the matter. This did not imply any broad misstatements on my part, arising from reliance on their authority, but it implied carelessness in matters of detail. And this of course was a fault.

But there was a far deeper reason for my saying what I said in this matter, on which I have not hitherto touched; and it was this: – The most oppressive thought, in the whole process of my change of opinion, was the clear anticipation, verified by the event, that it would issue in the triumph of Liberalism. Against the Anti-dogmatic principle I had thrown my whole mind; yet now I was doing more than any one else could do, to promote it. I was one of those who had kept it at bay in Oxford for so many years; and thus my very retirement was its triumph. The men who had driven me from Oxford were distinctly the Liberals; it was they who had opened the attack upon Tract 90, and it was they who would gain a second benefit, if I went on to abandon the Anglican Church. But this was not all. As I have already said, there are but two alternatives, the way to Rome, and the way to Atheism: Anglicanism is the halfway house on the one side, and Liberalism is the halfway house on the other. How many men were there, as I knew full well, who would not follow me now in my advance from Anglicanism to Rome, but would at once leave Anglicanism and me for the Liberal camp. It is not at all easy (humanly speaking) to wind up an Englishman to a dogmatic level. I had done so in good measure, in the case both of young men and of laymen, the Anglican *Via Media* being the representative of dogma. The dogmatic and the Anglican principle were one, as I had taught them; but I was breaking the *Via Media* to pieces, and would not dogmatic faith altogether be broken up, in the minds of a great number, by the demolition of the *Via Media*? Oh! how unhappy this made me! I heard once from an eye-witness the account of a poor sailor whose legs were shattered by a ball, in the action off Algiers in 1816, and who was taken below for an operation. The surgeon and the chaplain persuaded him to have a leg off; it was done and the tourniquet applied to the wound. Then, they broke it to him that he must have the other off too. The poor fellow said, "You should have told me that, gentlemen,' and deliberately unscrewed the instrument and bled to death. Would not that be the case with many friends of my own? How could I ever hope to make them believe in a second theology, when I had cheated them in the first? with what face could I publish a new edition of a dogmatic creed, and ask them to receive it as gospel? Would it not be plain to them that no certainty was to be found any where? Well, in my defence I could but make a lame apology; however, it was the true one, viz. that I had not read the Fathers cautiously enough; that in such nice points, as those which determine the angle of divergence between the two Churches, I had made considerable miscalculations. But how came this about? why, the fact was, unpleasant as it was to avow, that I had leaned too much upon the assertions of Ussher, Jeremy Taylor, or Barrow, and had been deceived by them. Valeat quantum,[62] – it was all that *could* be said. This then was a chief reason of that wording of the Retractation, which has given so much offence, because the bitterness, with which it was written, was not understood; – and the following letter will illustrate it: –

'April 3, 1844. I wish to remark on William's[63] chief distress, that my changing my opinion seemed to unsettle one's confidence in truth and falsehood as external things, and led one to be suspicious of the new opinion as one became distrustful of the old. Now in what I shall say, I am not going to speak in favour of my second thoughts in comparison of my first, but against such scepticism and unsettlement about truth and falsehood generally, the idea of which is very painful.

'The case with me, then, was this, and not surely an unnatural one: – as a matter of feeling and of duty I threw myself into the system which I found myself in. I saw that the English Church had a theological idea or theory as such, and I took it up. I read

Laud on Tradition,[64] and thought it (as I still think it) very masterly. The Anglican Theory was very distinctive. I admired it and took it on faith. It did not (I think) occur to me to doubt it; I saw that it was able, and supported by learning, and I felt it was a duty to maintain it. Further, on looking into Antiquity and reading the Fathers, I saw such portions of it as I examined, fully confirmed (e.g. the supremacy of Scripture). There was only one question about which I had a doubt, viz. whether it would *work*, for it has never been more than a paper system. . . .

'So far from my change of opinion having any fair tendency to unsettle persons as to truth and falsehood viewed as objective realities, it should be considered whether such change is not *necessary*, if truth be a real objective thing, and be made to confront a person who has been brought up in a system *short of* truth. Surely the *continuance* of a person, who wishes to go right, in a wrong system, and not his *giving it up*, would be that which militated against the objectiveness of Truth, leading, as it would, to the suspicion, that one thing and another were equally pleasing to our Maker, where men were sincere.

'Nor surely is it a thing I need be sorry for, that I defended the system in which I found myself, and thus have had to unsay my words. For is it not one's duty, instead of beginning with criticism, to throw oneself generously into that form of religion which is providentially put before one? Is it right, or is it wrong, to begin with private judgment? May we not, on the other hand, look for a blessing *through* obedience even to an erroneous system, and a guidance even by means of it out of it? Were those who were strict and conscientious in their Judaism, or those who were lukewarm and sceptical, more likely to be led into Christianity, when Christ came? Yet in proportion to their previous zeal, would be their appearance of inconsistency. Certainly, I have always contended that obedience even to an erring conscience was the way to gain light, and that it mattered not where a man began, so that he began on what came to hand, and in faith; and that any thing might become a divine method of Truth; that to the pure all things are pure, and have a self-correcting virtue and a power of germinating. And though I have no right at all to assume that this mercy is granted to me, yet the fact, that a person in my situation *may* have it granted to him, seems to me to remove the perplexity which my change of opinion may occasion.

'It may be said, – I have said it to myself, – "Why, however, did you *publish*? had you waited quietly, you would have changed your opinion without any of the misery, which now is involved in the change, of disappointing and distressing people." I answer, that things are so bound up together, as to form a whole, and one cannot tell what is or is not a condition of what. I do not see how possibly I could have published the Tracts, or other works professing to defend our Church, without accompanying them with a strong protest or argument against Rome. The one obvious objection against the whole Anglican line is, that it is Roman; so that I really think there was no alternative between silence altogether, and forming a theory and attacking the Roman system.'

2. And now, in the next place, as to my Resignation of St. Mary's, which was the second of the steps which I took in 1843. The ostensible, direct, and sufficient reason for my doing so was the persevering attack of the Bishops on Tract 90. I alluded to it in the letter which I have inserted above, addressed to one of the most influential among them. A series of their *ex cathedra* judgments, lasting through three years, and including a notice of no little severity in a Charge of my own Bishop, came as near to a condemnation of my Tract, and, so far, to a repudiation of the ancient Catholic doctrine, which was the scope of the Tract, as was possible in the Church of England. It was in order to shield the Tract from such a condemnation, that I had at the time of its publication in 1841 so simply put myself at the disposal of the higher powers in London. At that time, all that was distinctly contemplated in the way of censure, was contained in the message which my Bishop sent me, that the Tract was 'objectionable.' That I thought was the end of the matter. I had refused to suppress it, and they had yielded that point. Since I published the former portions of this Narrative, I have found what I wrote to Dr. Pusey on March 24, while the matter was in progress. 'The more I think of it,' I said, 'the more reluctant I am to suppress Tract 90, though *of course* I will do it if the Bishop wishes it; I cannot, however, deny that I shall feel it a severe act.' According to the notes which I took of the letters or messages which I sent

to him on that and the following days, I wrote successively, 'My first feeling was to obey without a word; I will obey still; but my judgment has steadily risen against it ever since.' Then in the Postscript, 'If I have done any good to the Church, I do ask the Bishop this favour, as my reward for it, that he would not insist on a measure, from which I think good will not come. However, I will submit to him.' Afterwards, I got stronger still and wrote: 'I have almost come to the resolution, if the Bishop publicly intimates that I must suppress the Tract, or speaks strongly in his charge against it, to suppress it indeed, but to resign my living also. I could not in conscience act otherwise. You may show this in any quarter you please.'

All my then hopes, all my satisfaction at the apparent fulfilment of those hopes was at an end in 1843. It is not wonderful then, that in May of that year, when two out of the three years were gone, I wrote on the subject of my retiring from St. Mary's to the same friend,[65] whom I had consulted upon it in 1840. But I did more now; I told him my great unsettlement of mind on the question of the Churches. I will insert portions of two of my letters: –

'May 4, 1843. . . . At present I fear, as far as I can analyze my own convictions, I consider the Roman Catholic Communion to be the Church of the Apostles, and that what grace is among us (which, through God's mercy, is not little) is extraordinary, and from the overflowings of His dispensation. I am very far more sure that England is in schism, than that the Roman additions to the Primitive Creed may not be developments, arising out of a keen and vivid realizing of the Divine Depositum of Faith.

'You will now understand what gives edge to the Bishops' Charges, without any undue sensitiveness on my part. They distress me in two ways: – first, as being in some sense protests and witnesses to my conscience against my own unfaithfulness to the English Church, and next, as being samples of her teaching, and tokens how very far she is from even aspiring to Catholicity.

'Of course my being unfaithful to a trust is my great subject of dread, – as it has long been, as you know.'

When he wrote to make natural objections to my purpose, such as the apprehension that the removal of clerical obligations might have the indirect effect of propelling me towards Rome, I answered: –

'May 18, 1843. . . . My office or charge at St. Mary's is not a mere *state*, but a continual *energy*. People assume and assert certain things of me in consequence. With what sort of sincerity can I obey the Bishop? how am I to act in the frequent cases, in which one way or another the Church of Rome comes into consideration? I have to the utmost of my power tried to keep persons from Rome, and with some success; but even a year and a half since, my arguments, though more efficacious with the persons I aimed at than any others could be, were of a nature to infuse great suspicion of me into the minds of lookers-on.

'By retaining St. Mary's, I am an offence and a stumbling-block. Persons are keen-sighted enough to make out what I think on certain points, and then they infer that such opinions are compatible with holding situations of trust in our Church. A number of younger men take the validity of their interpretation of the Articles, &c. from me on *faith*. Is not my present position a cruelty, as well as a treachery towards the Church?

'I do not see how I can either preach or publish again, while I hold St. Mary's; – but consider again the following difficulty in such a resolution, which I must state at some length.

'Last Long Vacation the idea suggested itself to me of publishing the Lives of the English Saints;[66] and I had a conversation with (a publisher)[67] upon it. I thought it would be useful, as employing the minds of men who were in danger of running wild, bringing them from doctrine to history, and from speculation to fact; – again, as giving them an interest in the English soil, and the English Church, and keeping them from seeking sympathy in Rome, as she is; and further, as tending to promote the spread of right views.

'But, within the last month, it has come upon me, that, if the scheme goes on, it will be a practical carrying out of No. 90, from the character of the usages and opinions of ante-reformation times.

'It is easy to say, "Why *will* you do *any* thing? why won't you keep quiet? what business had you to think of any such plan at all?" But I cannot leave a number of poor fellows in the lurch. I am bound to do my best for a great number of people both in

Oxford and elsewhere. If *I* did not act, others would find means to do so.

'Well, the plan has been taken up with great eagerness and interest. Many men are setting to work. I set down the names of men, most of them engaged, the rest half engaged and probable, some actually writing.' About thirty names follow, some of them at that time of the school of Dr. Arnold, others of Dr. Pusey's, some my personal friends and of my own standing, others whom I hardly knew, while of course the majority were of the party of the new Movement. I continue: –

'The plan has gone so far, that it would create surprise and talk, were it now suddenly given over. Yet how is it compatible with my holding St. Mary's, being what I am?'

Such was the object and the origin of the projected Series of the English Saints; and, since the publication was connected, as has been seen, with my resignation of St. Mary's, I may be allowed to conclude what I have to say on the subject here, though it may read like a digression. As soon then as the first of the Series got into print, the whole project broke down. I had already anticipated that some portions of the Series would be written in a style inconsistent with the professions of a beneficed clergyman, and therefore I had given up my Living; but men of great weight went further in their misgivings than I, when they saw the *Life of St. Stephen Harding*,[68] and decided that it was of a character inconsistent even with its proceeding from an Anglican publisher: and so the scheme was given up at once. After the two first numbers, I retired from the Editorship, and those Lives only were published in addition, which were then already finished or in advanced preparation. The following passages from what I or others wrote at the time will illustrate what I have been saying: –

In November, 1844, I wrote thus to the author[69] of one of them: 'I am not Editor, I have no direct control over the Series. It is T.'s[70] work; he may admit what he pleases; and exclude what he pleases. I was to have been Editor. I did edit the two first numbers. I was responsible for them, in the way in which an Editor is responsible. Had I continued Editor, I should have exercised a control over all. I laid down in the Preface that doctrinal subjects were, if possible, to be excluded. But even

then, I also set down that no writer was to be held answerable
for any of the Lives but his own. When I gave up the Editorship,
I had various engagements with friends for separate Lives remaining on my hands. I should have liked to have broken from them
all, but there were some from which I could not break, and I let
them take their course. Some have come to nothing; others like
yours have gone on. I have seen such, either in MS. or Proof. As
time goes on, I shall have less and less to do with the Series. I
think the engagement between you and me should come to an
end. I have any how abundant responsibility on me, and too
much. I shall write to T. that if he wants the advantage of your
assistance, he must write to you direct.'

In accordance with this letter, I had already advertised in
January 1844, ten months before it, that 'other Lives,' after St.
Stephen Harding, would 'be published by their respective authors
on their own responsibility.' This notice was repeated in February, in the advertisement to the second number entitled *The
Family of St. Richard*, though to this number, for some reason
which I cannot now recollect, I also put my initials. In the *Life of
St. Augustine*, the author, a man of nearly my own age, says in like
manner, 'No one but himself is responsible for the way in which
these materials have been used.' I have in MS. another advertisement to the same effect, but I cannot tell whether it ever
appeared in print.

I will add, since the authors have been considered[71] 'hot-
headed fanatic young men,' whom I was in charge of, and whom
I suffered to do intemperate things, that, while the writer of *St.
Augustine* was in 1844 past forty, the author of the proposed *Life
of St. Boniface*, Mr. Bowden, was forty-six; Mr. Johnson,[72] who
was to write *St. Aldhelm*, forty-three; and most of the others were
on one side or other of thirty. Three, I think, were under
twenty-five. Moreover, of these writers some became Catholics,
some remained Anglicans, and others have professed what are
called free or liberal opinions.*

The immediate cause of the resignation of my Living is stated in
the following letter, which I wrote to my Bishop: –

* Vide Note D, *Lives of the English Saints*.

'August 29, 1843. It is with much concern that I inform your Lordship, that Mr. A. B.,[73] who has been for the last year an inmate of my house here, has just conformed to the Church of Rome. As I have ever been desirous, not only of faithfully discharging the trust, which is involved in holding a living in your Lordship's diocese, but of approving myself to your Lordship, I will for your information state one or two circumstances connected with this unfortunate event. ... I received him on condition of his promising me, which he distinctly did, that he would remain quietly in our Church for three years. A year has passed since that time, and, though I saw nothing in him which promised that he would eventually be contented with his present position, yet for the time his mind became as settled as one could wish, and he frequently expressed his satisfaction at being under the promise which I had exacted of him.'

I felt it impossible to remain any longer in the service of the Anglican Church, when such a breach of trust, however little I had to do with it, would be laid at my door. I wrote in a few days to a friend:[74] –

'September 7, 1843. I this day ask the Bishop leave to resign St. Mary's. Men whom you little think, or at least whom I little thought, are in almost a hopeless way. Really we may expect any thing. I am going to publish a Volume[75] of Sermons, including those Four against moving.'

I resigned my living on September the 18th. I had not the means of doing it legally at Oxford. The late Mr. Goldsmid[76] was kind enough to aid me in resigning it in London. I found no fault with the Liberals; they had beaten me in a fair field. As to the act of the Bishops, I thought, to borrow a Scriptural image from Walter Scott,[77] that they had 'seethed the kid in his mother's milk.'

I said to a friend:

'Victrix causa diis placuit, sed victa Catoni.'[78]

And now I may be almost said to have brought to an end, as far as is necessary for a sketch such as this is, the history both of my changes of religious opinion and of the public acts which they involved.

I had one final advance of mind to accomplish, and one final step to take. That further advance of mind was to be able honestly to say that I was *certain* of the conclusions at which I had already arrived. That further step, imperative when such certitude was attained, was my *submission* to the Catholic Church.

This submission did not take place till two full years after the resignation of my living in September 1843; nor could I have made it at an earlier day, without doubt and apprehension, that is, with any true conviction of mind or certitude.

In the interval, of which it remains to speak, viz. between the autumns of 1843 and 1845, I was in lay communion with the Church of England, attending its services as usual, and abstaining altogether from intercourse with Catholics, from their places of worship, and from those religious rites and usages, such as the Invocation of Saints, which are characteristics of their creed. I did all this on principle; for I never could understand how a man could be of two religions at once.

What I have to say about myself between these two autumns I shall almost confine to this one point, – the difficulty I was in, as to the best mode of revealing the state of my mind to my friends and others, and how I managed to reveal it.

Up to January, 1842, I had not disclosed my state of unsettlement to more than three persons, as has been mentioned above, and as is repeated in the course of the letters which I am now about to give to the reader. To two of them, intimate and familiar companions, in the Autumn of 1839: to the third, an old friend too, whom I have also named above, I suppose, when I was in great distress of mind upon the affair of the Jerusalem Bishopric. In May, 1843, I made it known, as has been seen, to the friend, by whose advice I wished, as far as possible, to be guided. To mention it on set purpose to any one, unless indeed I was asking advice, I should have felt to be a crime. If there is any thing that was abhorrent to me, it was the scattering doubts, and unsettling consciences without necessity. A strong presentiment that my existing opinions would ultimately give way, and that the grounds of them were unsound, was not a sufficient warrant for disclosing the state of my mind. I had no guarantee yet, that that presentiment would be realized. Supposing I were crossing ice, which came right in my way, which I had good reasons for considering sound, and which I saw numbers before me crossing in safety, and supposing a stranger from the bank, in a voice of authority, and in an earnest tone, warned me that it was dangerous, and then was silent, I think I should be startled, and should look about me anxiously, but I think too that I should go on, till I had better grounds for doubt; and such was my state, I believe, till the end of 1842. Then again, when my dissatisfaction became greater, it was hard at first to determine the point of time, when it was too strong to suppress with propriety. Certitude of course is a point, but doubt is a progress; I was not near certitude yet. Certitude is a reflex action; it is to know that one knows. Of that I believe I was not possessed, till close upon my reception into the Catholic Church. Again, a practical, effective doubt is a point too, but who can easily ascertain it for himself? Who can determine when it is, that the scales in the balance of opinion begin to turn, and what was a greater probability in behalf of a belief becomes a positive doubt against it?

In considering this question in its bearing upon my conduct in 1843, my own simple answer to my great difficulty had been, *Do what your present state of opinion requires in the light of duty, and let that doing tell: speak by acts*. This I had done; my first *act* of the year had been in February. After three months' deliberation I had published my retractation of the violent charges which I had made against Rome: I could not be wrong in doing so much as this; but I did no more at the time: I did not retract my Anglican teaching. My second *act* had been in September in the same year; after much sorrowful lingering and hesitation, I had resigned my Living. I tried indeed, before I did so, to keep Littlemore for myself, even though it was still to remain an integral part of St. Mary's. I had given to it a Church and a sort of Parsonage; I had made it a Parish, and I loved it; I thought in 1843 that perhaps I need not forfeit my existing relations towards it. I could indeed submit to become the curate at will of another, but I hoped an arrangement was possible, by which, while I had the curacy, I might have been my own master in serving it. I had hoped an exception might have been made in my favour, under the circumstances; but I did not gain my request.[79] Perhaps I was asking what was impracticable, and it is well for me that it was so.

These had been my two acts of the year, and I said, 'I cannot be wrong in making them; let that follow which must follow in the thoughts of the world about me, when they see what I do.' And, as time went on, they fully answered my purpose. What I felt it a simple duty to do, did create a general suspicion about me, without such responsibility as would be involved in my initiating any direct act for the sake of creating it. Then, when friends wrote me on the subject, I either did not deny or I confessed my state of mind, according to the character and need of their letters. Sometimes in the case of intimate friends, whom I should otherwise have been leaving in ignorance of what others knew on every side of them, I invited the question.

And here comes in another point for explanation. While I was fighting in Oxford for the Anglican Church, then indeed I was very glad to make converts, and, though I never broke away from that rule of my mind, (as I may call it,) of which I have already spoken, of finding disciples rather than seeking them, yet, that I made advances to others in a special way, I have no doubt; this came to an end, however, as soon as I fell into misgivings as to the true ground to be taken in the controversy. For then, when I gave up my place in the Movement, I ceased from any such proceedings: and my utmost endeavour was to tranquillize such persons, especially those who belonged to the new school, as were unsettled in their religious views, and, as I judged, hasty in their conclusions. This went on till 1843; but, at that date, as soon as I turned my face Romeward, I gave up, as far as ever was possible, the thought of in any respect and in any shape acting upon others. Then I myself was simply my own concern. How could I in any sense direct others, who had to be guided in so momentous a matter myself? How could I be considered in a position, even to say a word to them one way or the other? How could I presume to unsettle them, as I was unsettled, when I had no means of bringing them out of such unsettlement? And, if they were unsettled already, how could I point to them a place of refuge, when I was not sure that I should choose it for myself? My only line, my only duty, was to keep simply to my own case. I recollected Pascal's words,[80] 'Je mourrai seul.' I deliberately put out of my thoughts all other works and claims, and said nothing to any one, unless I was obliged.

But this brought upon me a great trouble. In the newspapers there were continual reports about my intentions; I did not answer them; presently strangers or friends wrote, begging to be allowed to answer them; and, if I still kept to my resolution and said nothing, then I was thought to be mysterious, and a prejudice was excited against me. But, what was far worse, there were a number of tender, eager hearts, of whom I knew nothing at all, who were watching me, wishing to think as I thought, and to do as I did, if they could but find it out; who in consequence were distressed, that, in so solemn a matter, they could not see what was coming, and who heard reports about me this way or that, on a first day and on a second; and felt the weariness of waiting, and the sickness of delayed hope, and did not understand that I was as perplexed as they were, and, being of more sensitive complexion of mind than myself, were made ill by the suspense. And they too of course for the time thought me mysterious and inexplicable. I ask their pardon as far as I was really unkind to them. There was a gifted and deeply earnest lady,[81] who in a parabolical account of that time, has described both my conduct as she felt it, and her own feelings upon it. In a singularly graphic, amusing vision of pilgrims, who were making their way across a bleak common in great discomfort, and who were ever warned against, yet continually nearing, 'the king's highway,' on the right, she says, 'All my fears and disquiets were speedily renewed by seeing the most daring of our leaders, (the same who had first forced his way through the palisade, and in whose courage and sagacity we all put implicit trust,) suddenly stop short, and declare that he would go on no further. He did not, however, take the leap at once, but quietly sat down on the top of the fence with his feet hanging towards the road, as if he meant to take his time about it, and let himself down easily.' I do not wonder at all that I thus seemed so unkind to a lady, who at that time had never seen me. We were both in trial in our different ways. I am far from denying that I was acting selfishly both in her case and in that of others; but it was a religious selfishness. Certainly to myself my own duty seemed clear. They that are whole can heal others; but in my case it was, 'Physician, heal thyself.' My own soul was my first concern, and it seemed an absurdity to my reason to be converted in partnership. I wished to go to my Lord by myself, and in my own way, or rather His way. I had neither wish, nor, I may say, thought of taking a number with me. Moreover, it is but the truth to say, that it had ever been an annoyance to me to seem to be the head of a party; and that even from fastidiousness of mind, I could not bear to find a thing done elsewhere, simply or mainly because I did it myself, and that, from distrust of myself, I shrank from the thought, whenever it was brought home to me that I was influencing others. But nothing of this could be known to the world.

The following three letters are written to a friend, who had every claim upon me to be frank with him, Archdeacon Manning:[82] – it will be seen that I disclose the real state of my mind in proportion as he presses me.

1. 'October 14, 1843. I would tell you in a few words why I have resigned St. Mary's, as you seem to wish, were it possible to do so. But it is most difficult to bring out in brief, or even *in extenso*, any just view of my feelings and reasons.

'The nearest approach I can give to a general account of them is to say, that it has been caused by the general repudiation of the view, contained in No. 90, on the part of the Church. I could not stand against such an unanimous expression of opinion from the Bishops, supported, as it has been, by the concurrence, or at least silence, of all classes in the Church, lay and clerical. If there ever was a case, in which an individual teacher has been put aside and virtually put away by a community, mine is one. No decency has been observed in the attacks upon me from authority; no protests have been offered against them. It is felt, – I am far from denying, justly felt, – that I am a foreign material, and cannot assimilate with the Church of England.

'Even my own Bishop has said that my mode of interpreting the Articles makes them mean *any thing or nothing*. When I heard this delivered, I did not believe my ears. I denied to others that it was said. . . . Out came the charge,[83] and the words could not be mistaken. This astonished me the more, because I published that Letter to him, (how unwillingly you know,) on the understanding that *I* was to deliver his judgment on No. 90 *instead* of him. A year elapses, and a second and heavier judgment came forth. I did not bargain for this, – nor did he, but the tide was too strong for him.

'I fear that I must confess, that, in proportion as I think the English Church is showing herself intrinsically and radically alien from Catholic principles, so do I feel the difficulties of defending her claims to be a branch of the Catholic Church. It seems a dream to call a communion Catholic, when one can neither appeal to any clear statement of Catholic doctrine in its formularies, nor interpret ambiguous formularies by the received and living Catholic sense, whether past or present. Men of Catholic views are too truly but a party in our Church. I cannot deny that many other independent circumstances, which it is not worth while entering into, have led me to the same conclusion.

'I do not say all this to every body, as you may suppose; but I do not like to make a secret of it to you.'

2. 'Oct. 25, 1843. You have engaged in a dangerous correspondence; I am deeply sorry for the pain I shall give you.

'I must tell you then frankly, (but I combat arguments which to me, alas, are shadows,) that it is not from disappointment, irritation, or impatience, that I have, whether rightly or wrongly, resigned St. Mary's: but because I think the Church of Rome the Catholic Church, and ours not part of the Catholic Church, because not in communion with Rome; and because I feel that I could not honestly be a teacher in it any longer.

'This thought came to me last summer four years. ... I mentioned it to two friends in the autumn. ... It arose in the first instance from the Monophysite and Donatist controversies, the former of which I was engaged with in the course of theological study to which I had given myself. This was at a time when no Bishop, I believe, had declared against us,* and when all was progress and hope. I do not think I have ever felt disappointment or impatience, certainly not then; for I never looked forward to the future, nor do I realize it now.

'My first effort was to write that article on the Catholicity of the English Church; for two years it quieted me. Since the

---

* I think Sumner, Bishop of Chester, must have done so already.

summer of 1839 I have written little or nothing on modern controversy. . . . You know how unwillingly I wrote my letter to the Bishop in which I committed myself again, as the safest course under circumstances. The article I speak of quieted me till the end of 1841, over the affair of No. 90, when that wretched Jerusalem Bishopric (no personal matter) revived all my alarms. They have increased up to this moment. At that time I told my secret to another person in addition.

'You see then that the various ecclesiastical and quasi-ecclesiastical acts, which have taken place in the course of the last two years and a half, are not the *cause* of my state of opinion, but are keen stimulants and weighty confirmations of a conviction forced upon me, while engaged in the *course of duty*, viz. that theological reading to which I had given myself. And this last-mentioned circumstance is a fact, which has never, I think, come before me till now that I write to you.

'It is three years since, on account of my state of opinion, I urged the Provost in vain to let St. Mary's be separated from Littlemore; thinking I might with a safe conscience serve the latter, though I could not comfortably continue in so public a place as a University. This was before No. 90.

'Finally, I have acted under advice, and that, not of my own choosing, but what came to me in the way of duty, nor the advice of those only who agree with me, but of near friends who differ from me.

'I have nothing to reproach myself with, as far as I see, in the matter of impatience; i.e. practically or in conduct. And I trust that He, who has kept me in the slow course of change hitherto, will keep me still from hasty acts, or resolves with a doubtful conscience.

'This I am sure of, that such interposition as yours, kind as it is, only does what *you* would consider harm. It makes me realize my own views to myself; it makes me see their consistency; it assures me of my own deliberateness; it suggests to me the traces of a Providential Hand; it takes away the pain of disclosures; it relieves me of a heavy secret.

'You may make what use of my letters you think right.'

3. My correspondent wrote to me once more, and I replied thus: 'October 31, 1843. Your letter has made my heart ache

more, and caused me more and deeper sighs than any I have had
a long while, though I assure you there is much on all sides of
me to cause sighing and heartache. On all sides: − I am quite
haunted by the one dreadful whisper repeated from so many
quarters, and causing the keenest distress to friends. You know
but a part of my present trial, in knowing that I am unsettled
myself.

'Since the beginning of this year I have been obliged to tell the
state of my mind to some others; but never, I think, without
being in a way obliged, as from friends writing to me as you did,
or guessing how matters stood. No one in Oxford knows it or
here' [Littlemore], 'but one near friend[84] whom I felt I could not
help telling the other day. But, I suppose, many more suspect it.'

On receiving these letters, my correspondent, if I recollect
rightly, at once communicated the matter of them to Dr. Pusey,
and this will enable me to describe, as nearly as I can, the way in
which he first became aware of my changed state of opinion.

I had from the first a great difficulty in making Dr. Pusey
understand such differences of opinion as existed between himself
and me. When there was a proposal about the end of 1838 for a
subscription for a Cranmer Memorial,[85] he wished us both to
subscribe together to it. I could not, of course, and wished him
to subscribe by himself. That he would not do; he could not bear
the thought of our appearing to the world in separate positions,
in a matter of importance. And, as time went on, he would not
take any hints, which I gave him, on the subject of my growing
inclination to Rome. When I found him so determined, I often
had not the heart to go on. And then I knew, that, from
affection to me, he so often took up and threw himself into what
I said, that I felt the great responsibility I should incur, if I put
things before him just as I might view them myself. And, not
knowing him so well as I did afterwards, I feared lest I should
unsettle him. And moreover, I recollected well, how prostrated
he had been with illness in 1832, and I used always to think that
the start of the Movement had given him a fresh life. I fancied
that his physical energies even depended on the presence of a
vigorous hope and bright prospects for his imagination to feed
upon; so much so, that when he was so unworthily treated by
the authorities[86] of the place in 1843, I recollect writing to the

late Mr. Dodsworth[87] to state my anxiety, lest, if his mind became dejected in consequence, his health should suffer seriously also. These were difficulties in my way; and then again, another difficulty was, that, as we were not together under the same roof, we only saw each other at set times; others indeed, who were coming in or out of my rooms freely, and according to the need of the moment, knew all my thoughts easily; but for him to know them well, formal efforts were necessary. A common friend[88] of ours broke it all to him in 1841, as far as matters had gone at that time, and showed him clearly the logical conclusions which must lie in propositions to which I had committed myself; but somehow or other in a little while, his mind fell back into its former happy state, and he could not bring himself to believe that he and I should not go on pleasantly together to the end. But that affectionate dream needs must have been broken at last; and two years afterwards, that friend to whom I wrote the letters which I have just now inserted, set himself, as I have said, to break it. Upon that, I too begged Dr. Pusey to tell in private to any one he would, that I thought in the event I should leave the Church of England. However, he would not do so; and at the end of 1844 had almost relapsed into his former thoughts about me, if I may judge from a letter of his which I have found. Nay, at the Commemoration of 1845, a few months before I left the Anglican Church, I think he said about me to a friend, 'I trust after all we shall keep him.'

In that autumn of 1843, at the time that I spoke to Dr. Pusey, I asked another friend also to communicate in confidence, to whom he would, the prospect which lay before me.

To another friend, Mr. James Hope, now Mr. Hope Scott,[89] I gave the opportunity of knowing it, if he would, in the following Postscript to a letter[90]: —

'While I write, I will add a word about myself. You may come near a person or two who, owing to circumstances, know more exactly my state of feeling than you do, though they could not tell you. Now I do not like that you should not be aware of this, though I see no *reason* why you should know what they happen to know. Your wishing it would *be* a reason.'

I had a dear and old friend,[91] near his death; I never told him my state of mind. Why should I unsettle that sweet calm tranquility, when I had nothing to offer him instead? I could not say, 'Go to Rome;' else I should have shown him the way. Yet I offered myself for his examination. One day he led the way to my speaking out; but, rightly or wrongly, I could not respond. My reason was, 'I have no certainty on the matter myself. To say "I think" is to tease and to distress, not to persuade.'

I wrote to him on Michaelmas Day, 1843: 'As you may suppose, I have nothing to write to you about, pleasant. I *could* tell you some very painful things; but it is best not to anticipate trouble, which after all can but happen, and, for what one knows, may be averted. You are always so kind, that sometimes, when I part with you, I am nearly moved to tears, and it would be a relief to be so, at your kindness and at my hardness. I think no one ever had such kind friends as I have.'

The next year, January 22, I wrote to him: 'Pusey has quite enough on him, and generously takes on himself more than enough, for me to add burdens when I am not obliged; particularly too, when I am very conscious, that there *are* burdens, which I am or shall be obliged to lay upon him some time or other, whether I will or no.'

And on February 21: 'Half-past ten. I am just up, having a bad cold; the like has not happened to me (except twice in January) in my memory. You may think you have been in my thoughts, long before my rising. Of course you are so continually, as you well know. I could not come to see you; I am not worthy of friends. With my opinions, to the full of which I dare not confess, I feel like a guilty person with others, though I trust I am not so. People kindly think that I have much to bear externally, disappointment, slander, &c. No, I have nothing to bear, but the anxiety which I feel for my friends' anxiety for me, and their perplexity. This is a better Ash-Wednesday than birthday present;' [his birthday was the same day as mine; it was Ash-Wednesday that year;] 'but I cannot help writing about what is uppermost. And now, my dear B., all kindest and best wishes to you, my oldest friend, whom I must not speak more about, and with reference to myself, lest you should be angry.' It was not in his nature to have doubts: he used to look at me with anxiety, and wonder what had come over me.

On Easter Monday: 'All that is good and gracious descend

upon you and yours from the influences of this Blessed Season; and it will be so, (so be it!) for what is the life of you all, as day passes after day, but a simple endeavour to serve Him, from whom all blessing comes? Though we are separated in place, yet this we have in common, that you are living a calm and cheerful time, and I am enjoying the thought of you. It is your blessing to have a clear heaven, and peace around, according to the blessing pronounced on Benjamin.* So it is, my dear B., and so may it ever be.'

He was in simple good faith. He died in September of the same year. I had expected that his last illness would have brought light to my mind, as to what I ought to do. It brought none. I made a note, which runs thus: 'I sobbed bitterly over his coffin, to think that he left me still dark as to what the way of truth was, and what I ought to do in order to please God and fulfil His will.' I think I wrote[92] to Charles Marriott to say, that at that moment, with the thought of my friend before me, my strong view in favour of Rome remained just what it was. On the other hand, my firm belief that grace was to be found within the Anglican Church remained too.† I wrote to another friend[93] thus: —

'Sept. 16, 1844. I am full of wrong and miserable feelings, which it is useless to detail, so grudging and sullen, when I should be thankful. Of course, when one sees so blessed an end, and that, the termination of so blameless a life, of one who really fed on our ordinances and got strength from them, and sees the same continued in a whole family, the little children finding quite a solace of their pain in the Daily Prayer, it is impossible not to feel more at ease in our Church, as at least a sort of Zoar,[94] a place of refuge and temporary rest, because of the steepness of the way. Only, may we be kept from unlawful security, lest we have Moab and Ammon[95] for our progeny, the enemies of Israel.'

I could not continue in this state, either in the light of duty or of reason. My difficulty was this: I had been deceived greatly once; how could I be sure that I was not deceived a second time?

* Deut. xxxiii. 12.

† On this subject, vide my Third Lecture on 'Anglican Difficulties,' also Note E, *Anglican Church*.

I thought myself right then; how was I to be certain that I was right now? How many years had I thought myself sure of what I now rejected? how could I ever again have confidence in myself? As in 1840 I listened to the rising doubt in favour of Rome, now I listened to the waning doubt in favour of the Anglican Church. To be certain is to know that one knows; what inward test had I, that I should not change again, after that I had become a Catholic? I had still apprehension of this, though I thought a time would come, when it would depart. However, some limit ought to be put to these vague misgivings; I must do my best and then leave it to a higher Power to prosper it. So, at the end of 1844, I came to the resolutions of writing an Essay on Doctrinal Development; and then, if, at the end of it, my convictions in favour of the Roman Church were not weaker, of taking the necessary steps for admission into her fold.

By this time the state of my mind was generally known, and I made no great secret of it. I will illustrate it by letters of mine which have been put into my hands.

'November 16, 1844. I am going through what must be gone through; and my trust only is that every day of pain is so much taken from the necessary draught which must be exhausted. There is no fear (humanly speaking) of my moving for a long time yet. This had got out without my intending it; but it is all well. As far as I know myself, my one great distress is the perplexity, unsettlement, alarm, scepticism, which I am causing to so many; and the loss of kind feeling and good opinion on the part of so many, known and unknown, who have wished well to me. And of these two sources of pain it is the former that is the constant, urgent unmitigated one. I had for days a literal ache all about my heart; and from time to time all the complaints of the Psalmist seemed to belong to me.

'And as far as I know myself, my one paramount reason for contemplating a change is my deep, unvarying conviction that our Church is in schism, and that my salvation depends on my joining the Church of Rome. I may use *argumenta ad hominem* to this person or that;* but I am not conscious of resentment, or disgust, at any thing that has happened to me. I have no visions

---

* Vide supr. p. 199, &c. Letter of Oct. 14, 1843, compared with that of Oct. 25.

whatever of hope, no schemes of action, in any other sphere more suited to me. I have no existing sympathies with Roman Catholics; I hardly ever, even abroad, was at one of their services; I know none of them, I do not like what I hear of them.

'And then, how much I am giving up in so many ways! and to me sacrifices irreparable, not only from my age, when people hate changing, but from my especial love of old associations and the pleasures of memory. Nor am I conscious of any feeling, enthusiastic or heroic, of pleasure in the sacrifice; I have nothing to support me here.

'What keeps me yet is what has kept me long; a fear that I am under a delusion; but the conviction remains firm under all circumstances, in all frames of mind. And this most serious feeling is growing on me; viz. that the reasons for which I believe as much as our system teaches, *must* lead me to believe more, and that not to believe more is to fall back into scepticism.

'A thousand thanks for your most kind and consoling letter; though I have not yet spoken of it, it was a great gift.'

Shortly after I wrote to the same friend[96] thus: 'My intention is, if nothing comes upon me, which I cannot foresee, to remain quietly *in statu quo* for a considerable time, trusting that my friends will kindly remember me and my trial in their prayers. And I should give up my fellowship some time before any thing further took place.'

There was a lady,[97] now a nun of the Visitation, to whom at this time I wrote the following letters: –

1. 'November 7, 1844. I am still where I was; I am not moving. Two things, however, seem plain, that every one is prepared for such an event, next, that every one expects it of me. Few, indeed, who do not think it suitable, fewer still, who do not think it likely. However, I do not think it either suitable or likely. I have very little reason to doubt about the issue of things, but the when and the how are known to Him, from whom, I trust, both the course of things and the issue come. The expression of opinion, and the latent and habitual feeling about me, which is on every side and among all parties, has great force. I insist upon it, because I have a great dread of going by my own feelings, lest they should mislead me. By one's sense of duty one must go; but external facts support one in doing so.'

2. 'January 8, 1845. What am I to say in answer to your letter? I know perfectly well, I ought to let you know more of my feelings and state of mind than you do know. But how is that possible in a few words? Any thing I say must be abrupt; nothing can I say which will not leave a bewildering feeling, as needing so much to explain it, and being isolated, and (as it were) unlocated, and not having any thing with it to show its bearings upon other parts of the subject.

'At present, my full belief is, in accordance with your letter, that, if there is a move in our Church, very few persons indeed will be partners to it. I doubt whether one or two at the most among residents at Oxford. And I don't know whether I can wish it. The state of the Roman Catholics is at present so unsatisfactory. This I am sure of, that nothing but a simple, direct call of duty is a warrant for any one leaving our Church; no preference of another Church, no delight in its services, no hope of greater religious advancement in it, no indignation, no disgust, at the persons and things, among which we may find ourselves in the Church of England. The simple question is, Can *I* (it is personal, not whether another, but can *I*) be saved in the English Church? am *I* in safety, were I to die to-night? Is it a mortal sin in *me*, not joining another communion?

'P.S. I hardly see my way to concur in attendance, though occasional, in the Roman Catholic chapel, unless a man has made up his mind pretty well to join it eventually. Invocations are not *required* in the Church of Rome; somehow, I do not like using them except under the sanction of the Church, and this makes me unwilling to admit them in members of our Church.'

3. 'March 30. Now I will tell you more than any one knows except two friends. My own convictions are as strong as I suppose they can become: only it is so difficult to know whether it is a call of *reason* or of conscience. I cannot make out, if I am impelled by what seems *clear*, or by a sense of *duty*. You can understand how painful this doubt is; so I have waited, hoping for light, and using the words of the Psalmist,[98] 'Show some token upon me.' But I suppose I have no right to wait for ever for this. Then I am waiting, because friends are most considerately bearing me in mind, and asking guidance for me; and, I trust, I should attend to any new feelings which came upon me,

should that be the effect of their kindness. And then this waiting subserves the purpose of preparing men's minds. I dread shocking, unsettling people. Any how, I can't avoid giving incalculable pain. So, if I had my will, I should like to wait till the summer of 1846, which would be a full seven years from the time that my convictions first began to fall on me. But I don't think I shall last so long.

'My present intention is to give up my Fellowship in October, and to publish some work or treatise between that and Christmas. I wish people to know *why* I am acting, as well as *what* I am doing; it takes off that vague and distressing surprise, "What *can* have made him?"'

4. 'June 1. What you tell me of yourself makes it plain that it is your duty to remain quietly and patiently, till you see more clearly where you are; else you are leaping in the dark.'

In the early part of this year, if not before, there was an idea afloat that my retirement from the Anglican Church was owing to my distress that I had been so thrust aside, without any one's taking my part. Various measures[99] were, I believe, talked of in consequence of this surmise. Coincidently with it appeared an exceedingly kind article about me in a Quarterly,[100] in its April number. The writer praised me in kind and beautiful language far above my deserts. In the course of his remarks, he said, speaking of me as Vicar of St. Mary's: 'He had the future race of clergy hearing him. Did he value and feel tender about, and cling to his position? . . . Not at all. . . . No sacrifice to him perhaps, he did not care about such things.'

There was a censure implied, however covertly, in these words; and it is alluded to in the following letter, addressed to a very intimate friend: –

'April 3, 1845. . . . Accept this apology, my dear Church, and forgive me. As I say so, tears come into my eyes; – that arises from the accident of this time, when I am giving up so much I love. Just now I have been overset by James Mozley's article in the Remembrancer; yet really, my dear Church, I have never for an instant had even the temptation of repenting my leaving Oxford. The feeling of repentance has not even come into my mind. How could it? How could I remain at St. Mary's a hypocrite? how could I be answerable for souls, (and life so uncertain,) with the convictions, or at least persuasions, which I had upon me? It is indeed a responsibility to act as I am doing; and I feel His hand heavy on me without intermission, who is all Wisdom and Love, so that my heart and mind are tired out, just as the limbs might be from a load on one's back. That sort of dull aching pain is mine; but my responsibility really is nothing to what it would be, to be answerable for souls, for confiding loving souls, in the English Church, with my convictions. My love to Marriott, and save me the pain of sending him a line.'

I am now close upon the date of my reception into the Catholic Church; at the beginning of the year a letter had been addressed to me by a very dear friend, now no more, Charles Marriott. I quote some sentences from it, for the love which I bear him and the value that I set on his good word.

'January 15, 1845. You know me well enough to be aware, that I never see through any thing at first. Your letter to Badeley[101] casts a gloom over the future, which you can understand, if you have understood me, as I believe you have. But I may speak out at once, of what I see and feel at once, and doubt not that I shall ever feel: that your whole conduct towards the Church of England and towards us, who have striven and are still striving to seek after God for ourselves, and to revive true religion among others, under her authority and guidance, has been generous and considerate, and, were that word appropriate, dutiful, to a degree that I could scarcely have conceived possible, more unsparing of self than I should have thought nature could sustain. I have felt with pain every link that you have severed, and I have asked no questions, because I felt that you ought to measure the disclosure of your thoughts according to the occasion, and the capacity of those to whom you spoke. I write in haste, in the midst of engagements engrossing in themselves, but partly made tasteless, partly embittered by what I have heard; but I am willing to trust even you, whom I love best on earth, in God's Hand, in the earnest prayer that you may be so employed as is best for the Holy Catholic Church.'

In July, a Bishop thought it worth while to give out to the world that 'the adherents of Mr. Newman are few in number. A short time will now probably suffice to prove this fact. It is well known that he is preparing for secession; and, when that event takes place, it will be seen how few will go with him.'

I had begun my *Essay on the Development of Doctrine* in the beginning of 1845, and I was hard at it all through the year till October. As I advanced, my difficulties so cleared away that I ceased to speak of 'the Roman Catholics,' and boldly called them Catholics. Before I got to the end, I resolved to be received, and the book remains in the state in which it was then, unfinished.

One[102] of my friends at Littlemore had been received into the Church on Michaelmas Day, at the Passionist House at Aston, near Stone, by Father Dominic,[103] the Superior. At the beginning of October the latter was passing through London to Belgium; and, as I was in some perplexity what steps to take for being received myself, I assented to the proposition made to me that the good priest should take Littlemore in his way, with a view to his doing for me the same charitable service as he had done to my friend.

On October the 8th I wrote to a number of friends the following letter: —

'Littlemore, October 8th, 1845. I am this night expecting Father Dominic, the Passionist, who, from his youth, has been led to have distinct and direct thoughts, first of the countries of the North, then of England. After thirty years' (almost) waiting, he was without his own act sent here. But he has had little to do with conversions. I saw him here for a few minutes on St. John Baptist's day last year.

'He is a simple, holy man; and withal gifted with remarkable powers. He does not know of my intention; but I mean to ask of him admission into the One Fold of Christ. . . .

'I have so many letters to write, that this must do for all who choose to ask about me. With my best love to dear Charles Marriott, who is over your head, &c., &c.

'P.S. This will not go till all is over. Of course it requires no answer.'

For a while after my reception, I proposed to betake myself to some secular calling. I wrote thus in answer to a very gracious letter of congratulation sent me by Cardinal Acton:[104] —

'Nov. 25, 1845. I hope you will have anticipated, before I

express it, the great gratification which I received from your Eminence's letter. That gratification, however, was tempered by the apprehension, that kind and anxious well-wishers at a distance attach more importance to my step than really belongs to it. To me indeed personally it is of course an inestimable gain; but persons and things look great at a distance, which are not so when seen close; and, did your Eminence know me, you would see that I was one, about whom there has been far more talk for good and bad than he deserves, and about whose movements far more expectation has been raised than the event will justify.

'As I never, I do trust, aimed at any thing else than obedience to my own sense of right, and have been magnified into the leader of a party without my wishing it or acting as such, so now, much as I may wish to the contrary, and earnestly as I may labour (as is my duty) to minister in a humble way to the Catholic Church, yet my powers will, I fear, disappoint the expectations of both my own friends, and of those who pray for the peace of Jerusalem.

'If I might ask of your Eminence a favour, it is that you would kindly moderate those anticipations. Would it were in my power to do, what I do not aspire to do! At present certainly I cannot look forward to the future, and, though it would be a good work if I could persuade others to do as I have done, yet it seems as if I had quite enough to do in thinking of myself.'

Soon, Dr. Wiseman, in whose Vicariate Oxford lay, called me to Oscott;[105] and I went there with others; afterwards he sent me to Rome,[106] and finally placed me in Birmingham.[107]

I wrote to a friend[108]: —

'January 20, 1846. You may think how lonely I am. "Obliviscere populum tuum et domum patris tui,"[109] has been in my ears for the last twelve hours. I realize more that we are leaving Littlemore, and it is like going on the open sea.'

I left Oxford for good on Monday, February 23, 1846. On the Saturday and Sunday before, I was in my house at Littlemore simply by myself, as I had been for the first day or two when I had originally taken possession of it. I slept on Sunday night at my dear friend's, Mr. Johnson's, at the Observatory.[110] Various friends came to see the last of me; Mr. Copeland,[111] Mr. Church, Mr. Buckle,[112] Mr. Pattison,[113] and Mr. Lewis.[114] Dr. Pusey too came up to take leave of me; and I called on Dr. Ogle,[115] one of my very oldest friends, for he was my private Tutor, when I was an Undergraduate. In him I took leave of my first College, Trinity, which was so dear to me, and which held on its foundation so many who had been kind to me both when I was a boy, and all through my Oxford life. Trinity had never been unkind to me. There used to be much snap-dragon growing on the walls opposite my freshman's rooms there, and I had for years taken it as the emblem of my own perpetual residence even unto death in my University.

On the morning of the 23rd I left the Observatory. I have never seen Oxford since, excepting its spires, as they are seen from the railway.*

* At length I revisited Oxford on February 26th, 1878, after an absence of just 32 years. Vide Additional Note at the end of the volume.

CHAPTER V

From the time that I became a Catholic, of course I have no further history of my religious opinions to narrate. In saying this, I do not mean to say that my mind has been idle, or that I have given up thinking on theological subjects; but that I have had no variations to record, and have had no anxiety of heart whatever. I have been in perfect peace and contentment; I never have had one doubt. I was not conscious to myself, on my conversion, of any change, intellectual or moral, wrought in my mind. I was not conscious of firmer faith in the fundamental truths of Revelation, or of more self-command; I had not more fervour; but it was like coming into port after a rough sea; and my happiness on that score remains to this day without interruption.

Nor had I any trouble about receiving those additional articles, which are not found in the Anglican Creed. Some of them I believed already, but not any one of them was a trial to me. I made a profession of them upon my reception with the greatest ease, and I have the same ease in believing them now. I am far of course from denying that every article of the Christian Creed, whether as held by Catholics or by Protestants, is beset with intellectual difficulties; and it is simple fact, that, for myself, I cannot answer those difficulties. Many persons are very sensitive of the difficulties of Religion; I am as sensitive of them as any one; but I have never been able to see a connexion between apprehending those difficulties, however keenly, and multiplying them to any extent, and on the other hand doubting the doctrines to which they are attached. Ten thousand difficulties do not make one doubt, as I understand the subject; difficulty and doubt are incommensurate. There of course may be difficulties in the evidence; but I am speaking of difficulties intrinsic to the doctrines themselves, or to their relations with each other. A man may be annoyed that he cannot work out a mathematical problem, of which the answer is or is not given to him, without doubting that it admits of an answer, or that a certain particular answer is the true one. Of all points of faith, the being of a God is, to my own apprehension, encompassed with most difficulty, and yet borne in upon our minds with most power.

People say that the doctrine of Transubstantiation is difficult to believe; I did not believe the doctrine till I was a Catholic. I had no difficulty in believing it, as soon as I believed that the Catholic Roman Church was the oracle of God, and that she had declared this doctrine to be part of the original revelation. It is difficult, impossible, to imagine, I grant; – but how is it difficult to believe? Yet Macaulay[1] thought it so difficult to believe, that he had need of a believer in it of talents as eminent as Sir Thomas More, before he could bring himself to conceive that the Catholics of an enlightened age could resist 'the overwhelming force of the argument against it.' 'Sir Thomas More,' he says, 'is one of the choice specimens of wisdom and virtue; and the doctrine of transubstantiation is a kind of proof charge. A faith which stands that test, will stand any test.' But for myself, I cannot indeed prove it, I cannot tell *how* it is; but I say, 'Why should it not be? What's to hinder it? What do I know of substance or matter? just as much as the greatest philosophers, and that is nothing at all;' – so much is this the case, that there is a rising school of philosophy now, which considers phenomena to constitute the whole of our knowledge in physics. The Catholic doctrine leaves phenomena alone. It does not say that the phenomena go; on the contrary, it says that they remain; nor does it say that the same phenomena are in several places at once. It deals with what no one on earth knows any thing about, the material substances themselves. And, in like manner, of that majestic Article of the Anglican as well as of the Catholic Creed, – the doctrine of the Trinity in Unity. What do I know of the Essence of the Divine Being? I know that my abstract idea of three is simply incompatible with my idea of one; but when I come to the question of concrete fact, I have no means of proving that there is not a sense in which one and three can equally be predicated of the Incommunicable God.

But I am going to take upon myself the responsibility of more than the mere Creed of the Church; as the parties accusing me are determined I shall do. They say, that now, in that I am a Catholic, though I may not have offences of my own against honesty to answer for, yet, at least, I am answerable for the offences of others, of my co-religionists, of my brother priests, of the Church herself. I am quite willing to accept the responsibility; and, as I have been able, as I trust, by means of a few words, to dissipate, in the minds of all those who do not begin with disbelieving me, the suspicion with which so many Protestants start, in forming their judgment of Catholics, viz. that our Creed is actually set up in inevitable superstition and hypocrisy, as the original sin of Catholicism; so now I will proceed, as before, identifying myself with the Church and vindicating it, – not of course denying the enormous mass of sin and error which exists of necessity in that world-wide multiform Communion, – but going to the proof of this one point, that its system is in no sense dishonest, and that therefore the upholders and teachers of that system, as such, have a claim to be acquitted in their own persons of that odious imputation.

Starting then with the being of a God, (which, as I have said, is as certain to me as the certainty of my own existence, though when I try to put the grounds of that certainty into logical shape I find a difficulty in doing so in mood and figure to my satisfaction,) I look out of myself into the world of men, and there I see a sight which fills me with unspeakable distress. The world seems simply to give the lie to that great truth, of which my whole being is so full; and the effect upon me is, in consequence, as a matter of necessity, as confusing as if it denied that I am in existence myself. If I looked into a mirror, and did not see my face, I should have the sort of feeling which actually comes upon me, when I look into this living busy world, and see no reflexion of its Creator. This is, to me, one of those great difficulties of this absolute primary truth, to which I referred just now. Were it not for this voice, speaking so clearly in my conscience and my heart, I should be an atheist, or a pantheist, or a polytheist when I looked into the world. I am speaking for myself only; and I am far from denying the real force of the arguments in proof of a God, drawn from the general facts of human society and the course of history, but these do not warm me or enlighten me; they do not take away the winter of my desolation, or make the buds unfold and the leaves grow within me, and my moral being rejoice. The sight of the world is nothing else than the prophet's scroll,[2] full of 'lamentations, and mourning, and woe.'

To consider the world in its length and breadth, its various history, the many races of man, their starts, their fortunes, their mutual alienation, their conflicts; and then their ways, habits, governments, forms of worship; their enterprises, their aimless courses, their random achievements and acquirements, the impotent conclusion of long-standing facts, the tokens so faint and broken of a superintending design, the blind evolution of what turn out to be great powers or truths, the progress of things, as if from unreasoning elements, not towards final causes, the greatness and littleness of man, his far-reaching aims, his short duration, the curtain hung over his futurity, the disappointments of life, the defeat of good, the success of evil, physical pain, mental anguish, the prevalence and intensity of sin, the pervading idolatries, the corruptions, the dreary hopeless irreligion, that condition of the whole race, so fearfully yet exactly described in the Apostle's words,[3] 'having no hope and without God in the world,' – all this is a vision to dizzy and appal; and inflicts upon the mind the sense of a profound mystery, which is absolutely beyond human solution.

What shall be said to this heart-piercing, reason-bewildering fact? I can only answer, that either there is no Creator, or this living society of men is in a true sense discarded from His presence. Did I see a boy of good make and mind, with the tokens on him of a refined nature, cast upon the world without provision, unable to say whence he came, his birth-place or his family connexions, I should conclude that there was some mystery connected with his history, and that he was one, of whom, from one cause or other, his parents were ashamed. Thus only should I be able to account for the contrast between the promise and the condition of his being. And so I argue about the world; – *if* there be a God, *since* there is a God, the human race is implicated in some terrible aboriginal calamity. It is out of joint with the purposes of its Creator. This is a fact, a fact as true as the fact of its existence; and thus the doctrine of what is theologically called original sin becomes to me almost as certain as that the world exists, and as the existence of God.

And now, supposing it were the blessed and loving will of the Creator to interfere in this anarchical condition of things, what are we to suppose would be the methods which might be necessarily or naturally involved in His purpose of mercy? Since the world is in so abnormal a state, surely it would be no surprise to me, if the interposition were of necessity equally extraordinary – or what is called miraculous. But that subject does not directly come into the scope of my present remarks. Miracles as evidence, involve a process of reason, or an argument; and of course I am thinking of some mode of interference which does not immediately run into argument. I am rather asking what must be the face-to-face antagonist, by which to withstand and baffle the fierce energy of passion and the all-corroding, all-dissolving scepticism of the intellect in religious inquiries? I have no intention at all of denying, that truth is the real object of our reason, and that, if it does not attain to truth, either the premiss or the process is in fault; but I am not speaking here of right reason, but of reason as it acts in fact and concretely in fallen man. I know that even the unaided reason, when correctly exercised, leads to a belief in God, in the immortality of the soul, and in a future retribution; but I am considering the faculty of reason actually and historically; and in this point of view, I do not think I am wrong in saying that its tendency is towards a simple unbelief in matters of religion. No truth, however sacred, can stand against it, in the long run; and hence it is that in the pagan world, when our Lord came, the last traces of the religious knowledge of former times were all but disappearing from those portions of the world in which the intellect had been active and had had a career.

And in these latter days, in like manner, outside the Catholic Church things are tending, – with far greater rapidity than in that old time from the circumstance of the age, – to atheism in one shape or other. What a scene, what a prospect, does the whole of Europe present at this day! and not only Europe, but every government and every civilization through the world, which is under the influence of the European mind! Especially, for it most concerns us, how sorrowful, in the view of religion, even taken in its most elementary, most attenuated form, is the spectacle presented to us by the educated intellect of England, France, and Germany! Lovers of their country and of their race, religious men, external to the Catholic Church, have attempted various expedients to arrest fierce wilful human nature in its onward course, and to bring it into subjection. The necessity of some form of religion for the interests of humanity, has been generally acknowledged: but where was the concrete representative of things invisible, which would have the force and the toughness necessary to be a breakwater against the deluge? Three centuries ago the establishment of religion, material, legal, and social, was generally adopted as the best expedient for the purpose, in those countries which separated from the Catholic Church; and for a long time it was successful; but now the crevices of those establishments are admitting the enemy. Thirty years ago, education was relied upon: ten years ago there was a hope that wars would cease for ever, under the influence of commercial enterprise and the reign of the useful and fine arts; but will any one venture to say that there is any thing any where on this earth, which will afford a fulcrum for us, whereby to keep the earth from moving onwards?

The judgment, which experience passes whether on establishments or on education, as a means of maintaining religious truth in this anarchical world, must be extended even to Scripture, though Scripture be divine. Experience proves surely that the Bible does not answer a purpose for which it was never intended. It may be accidentally the means of the conversion of individuals; but a book, after all, cannot make a stand against the wild living intellect of man, and in this day it begins to testify, as regards its own structure and contents, to the power of that universal solvent, which is so successfully acting upon religious establishments.

Supposing then it to be the Will of the Creator to interfere in human affairs, and to make provisions for retaining in the world a knowledge of Himself, so definite and distinct as to be proof against the energy of human scepticism, in such a case, – I am far from saying that there was no other way, – but there is nothing to surprise the mind, if He should think fit to introduce a power into the world invested with the prerogative of infallibility in religious matters. Such a provision would be a direct, immediate, active, and prompt means of withstanding the difficulty; it would be an instrument suited to the need; and, when I find that this is the very claim of the Catholic Church, not only do I feel no difficulty in admitting the idea, but there is a fitness in it, which recommends it to my mind. And thus I am brought to speak of the Church's infallibility, as a provision, adapted by the mercy of the Creator, to preserve religion in the world, and to restrain that freedom of thought, which of course in itself is one of the greatest of our natural gifts, and to rescue it from its own suicidal excesses. And let it be observed that, neither here nor in what follows, shall I have occasion to speak directly of Revelation in its subject-matter, but in reference to the sanction which it gives to truths which may be known independently of it, – as it bears upon the defence of natural religion. I say, that a power, possessed of infallibility in religious teaching, is happily adapted to be a working instrument, in the course of human affairs, for smiting hard and throwing back the immense energy of the aggressive, capricious, untrustworthy intellect: – and in saying this, as in the other things that I have to say, it must still be recollected that I am all along bearing in mind my main purpose, which is a defence of myself.

I am defending myself here from a plausible charge brought against Catholics, as will be seen better as I proceed. The charge is this: – that I, as a Catholic, not only make profession to hold doctrines which I cannot possibly believe in my heart, but that I also believe in the existence of a power on earth, which at its own will imposes upon men any new set of *credenda*,[4] when it pleases, by a claim to infallibility; in consequence, that my own thoughts are not my own property; that I cannot tell that to-morrow I may not have to give up what I hold to-day, and that the necessary effect of such a condition of mind must be a degrading bondage, or a bitter inward rebellion relieving itself in secret infidelity, or the necessity of ignoring the whole subject of religion in a sort of disgust, and of mechanically saying every thing that the Church says, and leaving to others the defence of it. As then I have above spoken of the relation of my mind towards the Catholic Creed, so now I shall speak of the attitude which it takes up in the view of the Church's infallibility.

And first, the initial doctrine of the infallible teacher must be an emphatic protest against the existing state of mankind. Man had rebelled against his Maker. It was this that caused the divine interposition: and to proclaim it must be the first act of the divinely-accredited messenger. The Church must denounce rebellion as of all possible evils the greatest. She must have no terms with it; if she would be true to her Master, she must ban and anathematize it. This is the meaning of a statement of mine, which has furnished matter for one of those special accusations to which I am at present replying: I have, however, no fault at all to confess in regard to it; I have nothing to withdraw, and in consequence I here deliberately repeat it. I said,[5] 'The Catholic Church holds it better for the sun and moon to drop from heaven, for the earth to fail, and for all the many millions on it to die of starvation in extremest agony, as far as temporal affliction goes, than that one soul, I will not say, should be lost, but should commit one single venial sin, should tell one wilful untruth, or should steal one poor farthing without excuse.' I think the principle here enunciated to be the mere preamble in the formal credentials of the Catholic Church, as an Act of Parliament might begin with a '*Whereas*.' It is because of the intensity of the evil which has possession of mankind, that a suitable antagonist has been provided against it; and the initial act of that divinely-commissioned power is of course to deliver her challenge and to defy the enemy. Such a preamble then gives a meaning to her position in the world, and an interpretation to her whole course of teaching and action.

In like manner she has ever put forth, with most energetic distinctness, those other great elementary truths, which either are an explanation of her mission or give a character to her work. She does not teach that human nature is irreclaimable, else wherefore should she be sent? not, that it is to be shattered and reversed, but to be extricated, purified, and restored; not, that it is a mere mass of hopeless evil, but that it has the promise upon it of great things, and even now, in its present state of disorder and excess, has a virtue and a praise proper to itself. But in the next place she knows and she preaches that such a restoration, as she aims at effecting in it, must be brought about, not simply through certain outward provisions of preaching and teaching, even though they be her own, but from an inward spiritual power or grace imparted directly from above, and of which she is the channel. She has it in charge to rescue human nature from its misery, but not simply by restoring it on its own level, but by lifting it up to a higher level than its own. She recognizes in it real moral excellence though degraded, but she cannot set it free from earth except by exalting it towards heaven. It was for this end that a renovating grace was put into her hands; and therefore from the nature of the gift, as well as from the reasonableness of the case, she goes on, as a further point, to insist, that all true conversion must begin with the first springs of thought, and to teach that each individual man must be in his own person one whole and perfect temple of God, while he is also one of the living stones which build up a visible religious community. And thus the distinctions between nature and grace, and between outward and inward religion, become two further articles in what I have called the preamble of her divine commission.

Such truths as these she vigorously reiterates, and pertinaciously inflicts upon mankind; as to such she observes no halfmeasures, no economical reserve, no delicacy or prudence. 'Ye must be born again,'[6] is the simple, direct form of words which she uses after her Divine Master: 'your whole nature must be reborn; your passions, and your affections, and your aims, and your conscience, and your will, must all be bathed in a new element, and reconsecrated to your Maker, – and, the last not the least, your intellect.' It was for repeating these points of her teaching in my own way, that certain passages of one of my Volumes have been brought into the general accusation which has been made against my religious opinions. The writer has said that I was demented if I believed, and unprincipled if I did not believe, in my own statement,[7] that a lazy, ragged, filthy, storytelling beggar-woman, if chaste, sober, cheerful, and religious, had a prospect of heaven, such as was absolutely closed to an accomplished statesman, or lawyer, or noble, be he ever so just, upright, generous, honourable, and conscientious, unless he had also some portion of the divine Christian graces; – yet I should have thought myself defended from criticism by the words which our Lord used to the chief priests, 'The publicans and harlots go into the kingdom of God before you.'[8] And I was subjected again to the same alternative of imputations, for having ventured to say that consent to an unchaste wish was indefinitely more heinous than any lie viewed apart from its causes, its motives, and its consequences: though a lie, viewed under the limitation of these conditions, is a random utterance, an almost outward act, not directly from the heart, however disgraceful and despicable it may be, however prejudicial to the social contract, however deserving of public reprobation; whereas we have the express words of our Lord to the doctrine that 'whoso looketh on a woman to lust after her, hath committed adultery with her already in his heart.'[9] On the strength of these texts, I have surely as much right to believe in these doctrines which have caused so much surprise, as to believe in original sin, or that there is a supernatural revelation, or that a Divine Person suffered, or that punishment is eternal.

Passing now from what I have called the preamble of that grant of power, which is made to the Church, to that power itself, Infallibility, I premise two brief remarks: – 1. on the one hand, I am not here determining any thing about the essential seat[10] of that power, because that is a question doctrinal, not historical and practical; 2. nor, on the other hand, am I extending the direct subject-matter, over which that power of Infallibility has jurisdiction, beyond religious opinion: – and now as to the power itself.

This power, viewed in its fulness, is as tremendous as the giant evil which has called for it. It claims, when brought into exercise but in the legitimate manner, for otherwise of course it is but quiescent, to know for certain the very meaning of every portion of that Divine Message in detail, which was committed by our Lord to His Apostles. It claims to know its own limits, and to decide what it can determine absolutely and what it cannot. It claims, moreover, to have a hold upon statements not directly religious, so far as this, – to determine whether they indirectly relate to religion, and, according to its own definitive judgment, to pronounce whether or not, in a particular case, they are simply consistent with revealed truth. It claims to decide magisterially, whether as within its own province or not, that such and such statements are or are not prejudicial to the *Depositum* of faith, in their spirit or in their consequences, and to allow them, or condemn and forbid them, accordingly. It claims to impose silence at will on any matters, or controversies, of doctrine, which on its own *ipse dixit*, it pronounces to be dangerous, or inexpedient, or inopportune. It claims that, whatever may be the judgment of Catholics upon such acts, these acts should be received by them with those outward marks of reverence, submission, and loyalty, which Englishmen, for instance, pay to the presence of their sovereign, without expressing any criticism on them on the ground that in their matter they are inexpedient, or in their manner violent or harsh. And lastly, it claims to have the right of inflicting spiritual punishment, of cutting off from the ordinary channels of the divine life, and of simply excommunicating, those who refuse to submit themselves to its formal declarations. Such is the infallibility lodged in the Catholic Church, viewed in the concrete, as clothed and surrounded by the appendages of its high sovereignty: it is, to repeat what I said above, a supereminent prodigious power sent upon earth to encounter and master a giant evil.

And now, having thus described it, I profess my own absolute submission to its claim. I believe the whole revealed dogma as taught by the Apostles, as committed by the Apostles to the Church, and as declared by the Church to me. I receive it, as it is infallibly interpreted by the authority to whom it is thus committed, and (implicitly) as it shall be, in like manner, further interpreted by that same authority till the end of time. I submit, moreover, to the universally received traditions of the Church, in which lies the matter of those new dogmatic definitions which are from time to time made, and which in all times are the clothing and the illustration of the Catholic dogma as already defined. And I submit myself to those other decisions of the Holy See, theological or not, through the organs which it has itself appointed, which, waiving the question of their infallibility, on the lowest ground come to me with a claim to be accepted and obeyed. Also, I consider that, gradually and in the course of ages, Catholic inquiry has taken certain definite shapes, and has thrown itself into the form of a science, with a method and a phraseology of its own, under the intellectual handling of great minds, such as St. Athanasius, St. Augustine, and St. Thomas;[11] and I feel no temptation at all to break in pieces the great legacy of thought thus committed to us for these latter days.

All this being considered as the profession which I make *ex animo*, as for myself, so also on the part of the Catholic body, as far as I know it, it will at first sight be said that the restless intellect of our common humanity is utterly weighed down, to the repression of all independent effort and action whatever, so that, if this is to be the mode of bringing it into order, it is brought into order only to be destroyed. But this is far from the result, far from what I conceive to be the intention of that high Providence who has provided a great remedy for a great evil, – far from borne out by the history of the conflict between Infallibility and Reason in the past, and the prospect of it in the future. The energy of the human intellect 'does from opposition grow;'[12] it thrives and is joyous, with a tough elastic strength, under the terrible blows of the divinely-fashioned weapon, and is never so much itself as when it has lately been overthrown. It is the custom with Protestant writers to consider that, whereas there are two great principles in action in the history of religion, Authority and Private Judgment, they have all the Private Judgment to themselves, and we have the full inheritance and the superincumbent oppression of Authority. But this is not so; it is the vast Catholic body itself, and it only, which affords an arena for both combatants in that awful, never-dying duel. It is necessary for the very life of religion, viewed in its large operations and its history, that the warfare should be incessantly carried on. Every exercise of Infallibility is brought out into act by an intense and varied operation of the Reason, both as its ally and as its opponent, and provokes again, when it has done its work, a re-action of Reason against it; and, as in a civil polity the State exists and endures by means of the rivalry and collision, the encroachments and defeats of its constituent parts, so in like manner Catholic Christendom is no simple exhibition of religious absolutism but presents a continuous picture of Authority and Private Judgment alternately advancing and retreating as the ebb and flow of the tide; – it is a vast assemblage of human beings with wilful intellects and wild passions, brought together into one by the beauty and the Majesty of a Superhuman Power,

– into what may be called a large reformatory or training-school, not as if into a hospital or into a prison, not in order to be sent to bed, not to be buried alive, but (if I may change my metaphor) brought together as if into some moral factory, for the melting, refining, and moulding, by an incessant, noisy process, of the raw material of human nature, so excellent, so dangerous, so capable of divine purposes.

St Paul[13] says in one place that his Apostolical power is given him to edification, and not to destruction. There can be no better account of the Infallibility of the Church. It is a supply for a need, and it does not go beyond that need. Its object is, and its effect also, not to enfeeble the freedom or vigour of human thought in religious speculation, but to resist and control its extravagance. What have been its great works? All of them in the distinct province of theology: – to put down Arianism, Eutychianism, Pelagianism,[14] Manichaeism,[15] Lutheranism, Jansenism.[16] Such is the broad result of its action in the past; – and now as to the securities which are given us that so it ever will act in time to come.

First, Infallibility cannot act outside of a definite circle of thought, and it must in all its decisions, or *definitions*, as they are called, profess to be keeping within it. The great truths of the moral law, of natural religion, and of Apostolical faiths, are both its boundary and its foundation. It must not go beyond them, and it must ever appeal to them. Both its subject-matter, and its articles in that subject-matter, are fixed. And it must ever profess to be guided by Scripture and by tradition. It must refer to the particular Apostolic truth which it is enforcing, or (what is called) *defining*. Nothing, then, can be presented to me, in time to come, as part of the faith, but what I ought already to have received, and hitherto have been kept from receiving, (if so,) merely because it has not been brought home to me. Nothing can be imposed upon me different in kind from what I hold already, – much less contrary to it. The new truth which is promulgated, if it is to be called new, must be at least homogeneous, cognate, implicit, viewed relatively to the old truth. It must be what I may even have guessed, or wished, to be included in the Apostolic revelation; and at least it will be of such a character, that my thoughts readily concur in it or coalesce with it, as soon as I hear it. Perhaps I and others actually have always believed it, and the only question which is now decided in my behalf, is, that I have henceforth the satisfaction of having to believe, that I have only been holding all along what the Apostles held before me.

Let me take the doctrine which Protestants consider our greatest difficulty, that of the Immaculate Conception. Here I entreat the reader to recollect my main drift, which is this. I have no difficulty in receiving the doctrine; and that, because it so intimately harmonizes with that circle of recognized dogmatic truths, into which it has been recently received; – but if I have no difficulty, why may not another have no difficulty also? why may not a hundred? a thousand? Now I am sure that Catholics in general have not any intellectual difficulty at all on the subject of the Immaculate Conception; and that there is no reason why they should. Priests have no difficulty. You tell me that they *ought* to have a difficulty; – but they have not. Be large-minded enough to believe, that men may reason and feel very differently from yourselves; how is it that men, when left to themselves, fall into such various forms of religion, except that there are various types of mind among them, very distinct from each other? From my testimony then about myself, if you believe it, judge of others also who are Catholics: we do not find the difficulties which you do in the doctrines which we hold; we have no intellectual difficulty in that doctrine in particular, which you call a novelty of this day. We priests need not be hypocrites, though we be called upon to believe in the Immaculate Conception. To that large class of minds, who believe in Christianity after our manner, – in the particular temper, spirit, and light, (whatever word is used,) in which Catholics believe it, – there is no burden at all in holding that the Blessed Virgin was conceived without original sin; indeed, it is a simple fact to say, that Catholics have not come to believe it because it is defined, but that it was defined because they believed it.

So far from the definition[17] in 1854 being a tyrannical infliction on the Catholic world, it was received every where on its promulgation with the greatest enthusiasm. It was in consequence of the unanimous petition, presented from all parts of the Church to the Holy See, in behalf of an *ex cathedrâ* declaration that the doctrine was Apostolic, that it was declared so to be. I never heard of one Catholic having difficulties in receiving the doctrine, whose faith on other grounds was not already suspicious. Of course there were grave and good men, who were made anxious by the doubt whether it could be formally proved to be Apostolical either by Scripture or tradition, and who accordingly, though believing it themselves, did not see how it could be defined by authority and imposed upon all Catholics as a matter of faith; but this is another matter. The point in question is, whether the doctrine is a burden. I believe it to be none. So far from it being so, I sincerely think that St. Bernard[18] and St. Thomas, who scrupled at it in their day, had they lived into this, would have rejoiced to accept it for its own sake. Their difficulty, as I view it, consisted in matters of words, ideas, and arguments. They thought the doctrine inconsistent with other doctrines; and those who defended it in that age had not that precision in their view of it, which had been attained by means of the long disputes of the centuries which followed. And in this want of precision lay the difference of opinion, and the controversy.

Now the instance which I have been taking suggests another remark; the number of those (so called) new doctrines will not oppress us, if it takes eight centuries to promulgate even one of them. Such is about the length of time through which the preparation has been carried on for the definition of the Immaculate Conception. This of course is an extraordinary case; but it is difficult to say what is ordinary, considering how few are the formal occasions on which the voice of Infallibility has been solemnly lifted up. It is to the Pope in Ecumenical Council that we look, as to the normal seat of Infallibility: now there have been only eighteen such Councils since Christianity was, – an average of one to a century, – and of these Councils some passed no doctrinal decree at all, others were employed on only one, and many of them were concerned with only elementary points of the Creed. The Council of Trent embraced a large field of doctrine certainly; but I should apply to its Canons a remark contained in that University Sermon[19] of mine, which has been so ignorantly criticized in the Pamphlet which has been the occasion of this Volume; – I there have said that the various verses of the Athanasian Creed are only repetitions in various shapes of one and the same idea; and in like manner, the Tridentine Decrees are not isolated from each other, but are occupied in bringing out in detail, by a number of separate declarations, as if into bodily form, a few necessary truths. I should make the same remark on the various theological censures, promulgated by Popes, which the Church has received, and on their dogmatic decisions generally. I own that at first sight those decisions seem from their number to be a greater burden on the faith of individuals than are the Canons of Councils; still I do not believe that in matter of fact they are so at all, and I give this reason for it: – it is not that a Catholic, layman or priest, is indifferent to the subject, or, from a sort of recklessness, will accept any thing that is placed before him, or is willing, like a lawyer, to speak according to his brief, but that in such condemnations the Holy See is engaged, for the most part, in repudiating one or two great lines of error, such as Lutheranism or Jansenism, principally ethical not doctrinal, which are divergent from the Catholic mind, and that it is but expressing what any good Catholic, of fair abilities, though unlearned, would say himself, from common and sound sense, if the matter could be put before him.

Now I will go on in fairness to say what I think *is* the great trial to the Reason, when confronted with that august prerogative of the Catholic Church, of which I have been speaking. I enlarged just now upon the concrete shape and circumstances, under which pure infallible authority presents itself to the Catholic. That authority has the prerogative of an indirect jurisdiction on subject-matters which lie beyond its own proper limits, and it most reasonably has such a jurisdiction. It could not act in its own province, unless it had a right to act out of it. It could not properly defend religious truth, without claiming for that truth what may be called its *pomoeria*;[20] or, to take another illustration, without acting as we act, as a nation, in claiming as our own, not only the land on which we live, but what are called British waters. The Catholic Church claims, not only to judge infallibly on religious questions, but to animadvert on opinions in secular matters which bear upon religion, on matters of philosophy, of science, of literature, of history, and it demands our submission to her claim. It claims to censure books, to silence authors, and to forbid discussions. In this province, taken as a whole, it does not so much speak doctrinally, as enforce measures of discipline. It must of course be obeyed without a word, and perhaps in process of time it will tacitly recede from its own injunctions. In such cases the question of faith does not come in at all; for what is matter of faith is true for all times, and never can be unsaid. Nor does it at all follow, because there is a gift of infallibility in the Catholic Church, that therefore the parties who are in possession of it are in all their proceedings infallible. 'O, it is excellent,' says the poet,[21] 'to have a giant's strength, but tyrannous, to use it like a giant.' I think history supplies us with instances in the Church, where legitimate power has been harshly used. To make such admission is no more than saying that the divine treasure, in the words of the Apostle,[22] is 'in earthen vessels;' nor does it follow that the substance of the acts of the ruling power is not right and expedient, because its manner may have been faulty. Such high authorities act by means of instruments; we know how such instruments claim for themselves the name of their principals, who thus get the credit of faults which really are not theirs. But granting all this to an extent greater than can with any show of reason be imputed to the ruling power in the Church, what difficulty is there in the fact of this want of prudence or moderation more than can be urged, with far greater justice, against Protestant communities and institutions? What is there in it to make us hypocrites, if it has not that effect upon Protestants? We are called upon, not to profess any thing, but to submit and be silent, as Protestant Churchmen have before now obeyed the royal command to abstain from certain theological questions. Such injunctions as I have been contemplating are laid merely upon our actions, not upon our thoughts. How, for instance, does it tend to make a man a hypocrite, to be forbidden to publish a libel? his thoughts are as free as before: authoritative prohibitions may tease and irritate, but they have no bearing whatever upon the exercise of reason.

So much at first sight; but I will go on to say further, that, in spite of all that the most hostile critic may urge about the encroachments or severities of high ecclesiastics, in times past, in the use of their power, I think that the event has shown after all, that they were mainly in the right, and that those whom they were hard upon were mainly in the wrong. I love, for instance, the name of Origen: I will not listen to the notion that so great a soul was lost; but I am quite sure that, in the contest between his doctrine and followers and the ecclesiastical power, his opponents were right, and he was wrong. Yet who can speak with patience of his enemy and the enemy of St. John Chrysostom, that Theophilus,[23] bishop of Alexandria? who can admire or revere Pope Vigilius?[24] And here another consideration presents itself to my thoughts. In reading ecclesiastical history, when I was an Anglican, it used to be forcibly brought home to me, how the initial error of what afterwards became heresy was the urging forward some truth against the prohibition of authority at an unseasonable time. There is a time for every thing, and many a man desires a reformation of an abuse, or the fuller development of a doctrine, or the adoption of a particular policy, but forgets to ask himself whether the right time for it is come: and, knowing that there is no one who will be doing any thing towards its accomplishment in his own lifetime unless he does it himself, he will not listen to the voice of authority, and he spoils a good work in his own century, in order that another man, as yet unborn, may not have the opportunity of bringing it happily to perfection in the next. He may seem to the world to be nothing else than a bold champion for the truth and a martyr to free opinion, when he is just one of those persons whom the competent authority ought to silence; and, though the case may not fall within that subject-matter in which that authority is infallible, or the formal conditions of the exercise of that gift may be wanting, it is clearly the duty of authority to act vigorously in the case. Yet its act will go down to posterity as an instance of a tyrannical interference with private judgment, and of the silencing of a reformer, and of a base love of corruption or error; and it will show still less to advantage, if the ruling power happens in its proceedings to evince any defect of prudence or consideration. And all those who take the part of that ruling authority will be considered as time-servers, or indifferent to the cause of uprightness and truth; while, on the other hand, the said authority may be accidentally supported by a violent ultra party,[25] which exalts opinions into dogmas, and has it principally at heart to destroy every school of thought but its own.

Such a state of things may be provoking and discouraging at the time, in the case of two classes of persons; of moderate men who wish to make differences in religious opinion as little as they fairly can be made; and of such as keenly perceive, and are honestly eager to remedy, existing evils, – evils, of which divines in this or that foreign country know nothing at all, and which even at home, where they exist, it is not every one who has the means of estimating. This is a state of things both of past time and of the present. We live in a wonderful age; the enlargement of the circle of secular knowledge just now is simply a bewilderment, and the more so, because it has the promise of continuing, and that with greater rapidity, and more signal results. Now these discoveries, certain or probable, have in matter of fact an indirect bearing upon religious opinions, and the question arises how are the respective claims of revelation and of natural science to be adjusted. Few minds in earnest can remain at ease without some sort of rational grounds for their religious belief; to reconcile theory and fact is almost an instinct of the mind. When then a flood of facts, ascertained or suspected, comes pouring in upon us, with a multitude of others in prospect, all believers in Revelation, be they Catholic or not, are roused to consider their bearing upon themselves, both for the honour of God, and from tenderness for those many souls who, in consequence of the confident tone of the schools of secular knowledge, are in danger of being led away into a bottomless liberalism of thought.

I am not going to criticize here that vast body of men, in the mass, who at this time would profess to be liberals in religion; and who look towards the discoveries of the age, certain or in progress, as their informants, direct or indirect, as to what they shall think about the unseen and the future. The Liberalism which gives a colour to society now, is very different from that character of thought which bore the name thirty or forty years ago. Now it is scarcely a party; it is the educated lay world. When I was young, I knew the word first as giving name to a periodical,[26] set up by Lord Byron and others. Now, as then, I have no sympathy with the philosophy of Byron. Afterwards, Liberalism was the badge of a theological school,[27] of a dry and repulsive character, not very dangerous in itself, though dangerous as opening the door to evils which it did not itself either anticipate or comprehend. At present it is nothing else than that deep, plausible scepticism, of which I spoke above, as being the development of human reason, as practically exercised by the natural man.

The Liberal religionists of this day are a very mixed body, and therefore I am not intending to speak against them. There may be, and doubtless is, in the hearts of some or many of them a real antipathy or anger against revealed truth, which it is distressing to think of. Again; in many men of science or literature there may be an animosity arising from almost a personal feeling; it being a matter of party, a point of honour, the excitement of a game, or a satisfaction to the soreness or annoyance occasioned by the acrimony or narrowness of apologists for religion, to prove that Christianity or that Scripture is untrustworthy. Many scientific and literary men, on the other hand, go on, I am confident, in a straightforward impartial way, in their own province and on their own line of thought, without any disturbance from religious difficulties in themselves, or any wish at all to give pain to others by the result of their investigations. It would ill become me, as if I were afraid of truth of any kind, to blame those who pursue secular facts, by means of the reason which God has given them, to their logical conclusions: or to be angry with science, because religion is bound in duty to take cognizance of its teaching. But putting these particular classes of men aside, as having no special call on the sympathy of the Catholic, of course he does most deeply enter into the feelings of a fourth and large class of men, in the educated portions of society, of religious and sincere minds, who are simply perplexed, – frightened or rendered desperate, as the case may be, – by the utter confusion into which late discoveries or speculations have thrown their most elementary ideas of religion. Who does not feel for such men? who can have one unkind thought of them? I take up in their behalf St. Augustine's beautiful words[28] 'Illi in vos saeviant,' &c. Let them be fierce with you who have no experience of the difficulty with which error is discriminated from truth, and the way of life is found amid the illusions of the world. How many a Catholic has in his thoughts followed such men, many of them so good, so true, so noble! how often has the wish risen in his heart that some one from among his own people should come forward as the champion of revealed truth against its opponents! Various persons, Catholic and Protestant, have asked me to do so myself; but I had several strong difficulties in the way. One of the greatest is this, that at the moment it is so difficult to say precisely what it is that is to be encountered and overthrown. I am far from denying that scientific knowledge is really growing, but it is by fits and starts; hypotheses rise and fall; it is difficult to anticipate which of them will keep their ground, and what the state of knowledge in relation to them will be from year to year. In this condition of things, it has seemed to me to be very undignified for a Catholic to commit himself to the work of chasing what might turn out to be phantoms, and, in behalf of some special objections, to be ingenious in devising a theory, which, before it was completed, might have to give place to some theory newer still, from the fact that those former objections had already come to nought under the uprising of others. It seemed to be especially a time, in which Christians had a call to be patient, in which they had no other way of helping those who were alarmed, than that of exhorting them to have a little faith and fortitude, and to 'beware,' as the poet[29] says, 'of dangerous steps.' This seemed so clear to me, the more I thought of the matter, as to make me surmise, that, if I attempted what had so little promise in it, I should find that the highest Catholic Authority was against the attempt, and that I should have spent my time and my thought, in doing what either it would be imprudent to bring before the public at all, or what, did I do so, would only complicate matters further which were already complicated, without my interference, more than enough. And I interpret recent acts[30] of that authority as fulfilling my expectation; I interpret them as tying the hands of a controversialist, such as I should be, and teaching us that true wisdom, which Moses inculcated on his people, when the Egyptians were pursuing them, 'Fear ye not, stand still; the Lord shall fight for you, and ye shall hold your peace.'[31] And so far from finding a difficulty in obeying in this case, I have cause to be thankful and to rejoice to have so clear a direction in a matter of difficulty.

But if we would ascertain with correctness the real course of a principle, we must look at it at a certain distance, and as history represents it to us. Nothing carried on by human instruments, but has its irregularities, and affords ground for criticism, when minutely scrutinized in matters of detail. I have been speaking of that aspect of the action of an infallible authority, which is most open to invidious criticism from those who view it from without; I have tried to be fair, in estimating what can be said to its disadvantage, as witnessed at a particular time in the Catholic Church, and now I wish its adversaries to be equally fair in their judgment upon its historical character. Can, then, the infallible authority, with any show of reason, be said in fact to have destroyed the energy of the Catholic intellect? Let it be observed, I have not here to speak of any conflict which ecclesiastical authority has had with science, for this simple reason, that conflict there has been none; and that, because the secular sciences, as they now exist, are a novelty in the world, and there has been no time yet for a history of relations between theology and these new methods of knowledge, and indeed the Church may be said to have kept clear of them, as is proved by the constantly cited case of Galileo.[32] Here 'exceptio probat regulam:'[33] for it is the one stock argument. Again, I have not to speak of any relations of the Church to the new sciences, because my simple question all along has been whether the assumption of infallibility by the proper authority is adapted to make me a hypocrite, and till that authority passes decrees on pure physical subjects and calls on me to subscribe them, (which it will never do, because it has not the power,) it has no tendency to interfere by any of its acts with my private judgment on those points. The simple question is, whether authority has so acted upon the reason of individuals, that they can have no opinion of their own, and have but an alternative of slavish superstition or secret rebellion of heart; and I think the whole history of theology puts an absolute negative upon such a supposition.

It is hardly necessary to argue out so plain a point. It is individuals, and not the Holy See, that have taken the initiative, and given the lead to the Catholic mind, in theological inquiry. Indeed, it is one of the reproaches urged against the Roman Church, that it has originated nothing, and has only served as a sort of *remora* or break in the development of doctrine. And it is an objection which I really embrace as a truth; for such I conceive to be the main purpose of its extraordinary gift. It is said, and truly, that the Church of Rome possessed no great mind in the whole period of persecution. Afterwards for a long while, it has not a single doctor to show; St. Leo, its first, is the teacher of one point[34] of doctrine; St. Gregory, who stands at the very extremity of the first age of the Church, has no place in dogma or philosophy. The great luminary of the western world is, as we know, St. Augustine; he, no infallible teacher, has formed the intellect of Christian Europe; indeed to the African Church generally we must look for the best early exposition of Latin ideas. Moreover, of the African divines, the first in order of time, and not the least influential, is the strong-minded and heterodox Tertullian.[35] Nor is the Eastern intellect, as such, without its share in the formation of the Latin teaching. The free thought of Origen is visible in the writings of the Western Doctors, Hilary[36] and Ambrose;[37] and the independent mind of Jerome[38] has enriched his own vigorous commentaries on Scripture, from the stores of the scarcely orthodox Eusebius.[39] Heretical questionings have been transmuted by the living power of the Church into salutary truths. The case is the same as regards the Ecumenical Councils. Authority in its most imposing exhibition, grave Bishops, laden with the traditions and rivalries of particular nations or places, have been guided in their decisions by the commanding genius of individuals, sometimes young and of inferior rank. Not that uninspired intellect overruled the superhuman gift which was committed to the Council, which would be a self-contradictory assertion, but that in that process of inquiry and deliberation, which ended in an infallible enunciation, individual reason was paramount. Thus Malchion,[40] a mere presbyter, was the instrument of the great Council of Antioch in the third century in meeting and refuting, for the assembled Fathers, the heretical Patriarch of that see. Parallel to this instance is the influence, so well known, of a young deacon, St. Athanasius, with the 318 Fathers at Nicaea. In mediaeval times we read of St. Anselm[41] at Bari, as the champion of the Council there held, against the Greeks. At Trent, the writings of St. Bonaventura,[42] and, what is more to the point, the address of a Priest and theologian, Salmeron,[43] had a critical effect on some of the definitions of dogma. In some of these cases the influence might be partly moral, but in others it was that of a discursive knowledge of ecclesiastical writers, a scientific acquaintance with theology, and a force of thought in the treatment of doctrine.

There are of course intellectual habits which theology does not tend to form, as for instance the experimental, and again the philosophical; but that is because it *is* theology, not because of the gift of infallibility. But, as far as this goes, I think it could be shown that physical science on the other hand, or again mathematical, affords but an imperfect training for the intellect. I do not see then how any objection about the narrowness of theology comes into our question, which simply is, whether the belief in an infallible authority destroys the independence of the mind; and I consider that the whole history of the Church, and especially the history of the theological schools, gives a negative to the accusation. There never was a time when the intellect of the educated class was more active, or rather more restless, than in the middle ages. And then again all through Church history from the first, how slow is authority in interfering! Perhaps a local teacher, or a doctor in some local school, hazards a proposition, and a controversy ensues. It smoulders or burns in one place, no one interposing; Rome simply lets it alone. Then it comes before a Bishop; or some priest, or some professor in some other seat of learning takes it up; and then there is a second stage of it. Then it comes before a University, and it may be condemned by the theological faculty. So the controversy proceeds year after year, and Rome is still silent. An appeal perhaps is next made to a seat of authority inferior to Rome; and then at last after a long while it comes before the supreme power. Meanwhile, the question has been ventilated and turned over and over again, and viewed on every side of it, and authority is called upon to pronounce a decision, which has already been arrived at by reason. But even then, perhaps the supreme authority hesitates to do so, and nothing is determined on the point for years: or so generally and vaguely, that the whole controversy has to be gone through again, before it is ultimately determined. It is manifest how a mode of proceeding, such as this, tends not only to the liberty, but to the courage, of the individual theologian or controversialist. Many a man has ideas, which he hopes are true, and useful for his day, but he is not confident about them, and wishes to have them discussed. He is willing, or rather would be thankful, to give them up, if they can be proved to be erroneous or dangerous, and by means of controversy he obtains his end. He is answered, and he yields; or on the contrary he finds that he is considered safe. He would not dare to do this, if he knew an authority, which was supreme and final, was watching every word he said, and made signs of assent or dissent to each sentence, as he uttered it. Then indeed he would be fighting, as the Persian soldiers, under the lash, and the freedom of his intellect might truly be said to be beaten out of him. But this has not been so: – I do not mean to say that, when controversies run high, in schools or even in small portions of the Church, an interposition may not advisably take place; and again, questions may be of that urgent nature, that an appeal must, as a matter of duty, be made at once to the highest authority in the Church; but if we look into the history of controversy, we shall find, I think, the general run of things to be such as I have represented it. Zosimus[44] treated Pelagius and Coelestius with extreme forbearance; St. Gregory VII. was equally indulgent with Berengarius:[45] – by reason of the very power of the Popes they have commonly been slow and moderate in their use of it.

And here again is a further shelter for the legitimate exercise of the reason: – the multitude of nations which are within the fold of the Church will be found to have acted for its protection, against any narrowness, on the supposition of narrowness, in the various authorities at Rome, with whom lies the practical decision of controverted questions. How have the Greek traditions been respected and provided for in the later Ecumenical Councils, in spite of the countries that held them being in a state of schism! There are important points of doctrine which have been (humanly speaking) exempted from the infallible sentence, by the tenderness with which its instruments, in framing it, have treated the opinions of particular places. Then, again, such national influences have a providential effect in moderating the bias which the local influences of Italy may exert upon the See of St. Peter. It stands to reason that, as the Gallican Church has in it a French element, so Rome must have in it an element of Italy; and it is no prejudice to the zeal and devotion with which we submit ourselves to the Holy See to admit this plainly. It seems to me, as I have been saying, that Catholicity is not only one of the notes of the Church, but, according to the divine purposes, one of its securities. I think it would be a very serious evil, which Divine Mercy avert! that the Church should be contracted in Europe within the range of particular nationalities. It is a great idea to introduce Latin civilization into America, and to improve the Catholics there by the energy of French devotedness; but I trust that all European races will ever have a place in the Church, and assuredly I think that the loss of the English, not to say the German element, in its composition has been a most serious misfortune. And certainly, if there is one consideration more than another which should make us English grateful to Pius the Ninth, it is that, by giving us a Church of our own,[46] he has prepared the way for our own habits of mind, our own manner of reasoning, our own tastes, and our own virtues, finding a place and thereby a sanctification, in the Catholic Church.

There is only one other subject, which I think it necessary to introduce here, as bearing upon the vague suspicions which are attached in this country to the Catholic Priesthood. It is one of which my accusers have before now said much, – the charge of reserve and economy. They found it in no slight degree on what I have said on the subject in my History of the Arians,[47] and in a note upon one of my Sermons[48] in which I refer to it. The principle of Reserve is also advocated by an admirable writer[49] in two numbers of the *Tracts for the Times*, and of these I was the Editor.

Now, as to the Economy itself,* it is founded upon the words of our Lord, 'Cast not your pearls before swine;'[50] and it was observed by the early Christians, more or less, in their intercourse with the heathen populations among whom they lived. In the midst of the abominable idolatries and impurities of that fearful time, the Rule of the Economy was an imperative duty. But that rule, at least as I have explained and recommended it, in anything that I have written, did not go beyond (1) the concealing the truth when we could do so without deceit, (2) stating it only partially, and (3) representing it under the nearest form possible to a learner or inquirer, when he could not possibly understand

---

* Vide Note F, *The Economy*.

it exactly. I conceive that to draw Angels with wings is an instance of the third of these economical modes; and to avoid the question, 'Do Christians believe in a Trinity?' by answering, 'They believe in only one God,' would be an instance of the second. As to the first, it is hardly an Economy, but comes under what is called the *Disciplina Arcani*.[51] The second and third economical modes Clement[52] calls *lying*; meaning that a partial truth is in some sense a lie, as is also a representative truth. And this, I think, is about the long and the short of the ground of the accusation which has been so violently urged against me, as being a patron of the Economy.

Of late years I have come to think, as I believe most writers do, that Clement meant more than I have said. I used to think he used the word 'lie' as an hyperbole, but I now believe that he, as other early Fathers, thought that, under certain circumstances, it was lawful to tell a lie. This doctrine I never maintained, though I used to think, as I do now, that the theory of the subject is surrounded with considerable difficulty; and it is not strange that I should say so, considering that great English writers declare without hesitation that in certain extreme cases, as to save life, honour, or even property, a lie is allowable. And thus I am brought to the direct question of truth, and of the truthfulness of Catholic priests generally in their dealings with the world, as bearing on the general question of their honesty, and of their internal belief in their religious professions.

It would answer no purpose, and it would be departing from the line of writing which I have been observing all along, if I entered into any formal discussion on this question; what I shall do here, as I have done in the foregoing pages, is to give my own testimony on the matter in question, and there to leave it. Now first I will say, that, when I became a Catholic, nothing struck me more at once than the English out-spoken manner of the Priests. It was the same at Oscott, at Old Hall Green,[53] at Ushaw;[54] there was nothing of that smoothness, or mannerism, which is commonly imputed to them, and they were more natural and unaffected than many an Anglican clergyman. The many years, which have passed since, have only confirmed my first impression. I have ever found it in the priests of this

Diocese; did I wish to point out a straightforward Englishman, I should instance the Bishop,[55] who has, to our great benefit, for so many years presided over it.

And next, I was struck, when I had more opportunity of judging of the Priests, by the simple faith in the Catholic Creed and system, of which they always gave evidence, and which they never seemed to feel, in any sense at all, to be a burden. And now that I have been in the Church nineteen years, I cannot recollect hearing of a single instance in England of an infidel priest. Of course there are men from time to time, who leave the Catholic Church for another religion, but I am speaking of cases, when a man keeps a fair outside to the world and is a hollow hypocrite in his heart.

I wonder that the self-devotion of our priests does not strike a Protestant in this point of view. What do they gain by professing a Creed, in which, if their enemies are to be credited, they really do not believe? What is their reward for committing themselves to a life of self-restraint and toil, and perhaps to a premature and miserable death? The Irish fever[56] cut off between Liverpool and Leeds thirty priests and more, young men in the flower of their days, old men who seemed entitled to some quiet time after their long toil. There was a bishop[57] cut off in the North; but what had a man of his ecclesiastical rank to do with the drudgery and danger of sick calls, except that Christian faith and charity constrained him? Priests volunteered for the dangerous service. It was the same with them on the first coming of the cholera,[58] that mysterious awe-inspiring infliction. If they did not heartily believe in the Creed of the Church, then I will say that the remark of the Apostle had its fullest illustration: – 'If in this life only we have hope in Christ, we are of all men most miserable.'[59] What could support a set of hypocrites in the presence of a deadly disorder, one of them following another in long order up the forlorn hope, and one after another perishing? And such, I may say, in its substance, is every Mission-Priest's life. He is ever ready to sacrifice himself for his people. Night and day, sick or well himself, in all weathers, off he is, on the news of a sick call. The fact of a parishioner dying without the Sacraments through his fault is terrible to him; why terrible, if he has not a deep absolute faith, which he acts upon with a free service? Protestants admire this, when they see it; but they do not seem to see as clearly, that it excludes the very notion of hypocrisy.

Sometimes, when they reflect upon it, it leads them to remark on the wonderful discipline of the Catholic priesthood; they say that no Church has so well ordered a clergy, and that in that respect it surpasses their own; they wish they could have such exact discipline among themselves. But is it an excellence which can be purchased? is it a phenomenon which depends on nothing else than itself, or is it an effect which has a cause? You cannot buy devotion at a price. 'It hath never been heard of in the land of Chanaan, neither hath it been seen in Theman. The children of Agar, the merchants of Meran, none of these have known its way.'[60] What then is that wonderful charm, which makes a thousand men act all in one way, and infuses a prompt obedience to rule, as if they were under some stern military compulsion? How difficult to find an answer, unless you will allow the obvious one, that they believe intensely what they profess!

I cannot think what it can be, in a day like this, which keeps up the prejudice of this Protestant country against us, unless it be the vague charges which are drawn from our books of Moral Theology; and with a short notice of the work in particular which by our accusers is especially thrown into our teeth, I shall bring these observations to a close.

St. Alfonso Liguori,[61] then, it cannot be denied, lays down that an equivocation, (that is, a play upon words, in which one sense is taken by the speaker, and another sense intended by him for the hearer,) is allowable, if there is a just cause, that is, in an extraordinary case, and may even be confirmed by an oath. I shall give my opinion on this point as plainly as any Protestant can wish; and therefore I avow at once that in this department of morality, much as I admire the high points of the Italian character, I like the English rule of conduct better; but, in saying so, I am not, as will shortly be seen, saying any thing disrespectful to St. Alfonso, who was a lover of truth, and whose intercession I trust I shall not lose, though, on the matter under consideration, I follow other guidance in preference to his.

Now I make this remark first: – great English authors, Jeremy Taylor,[62] Milton,[63] Paley,[64] Johnson,[65] men of very different schools of thought, distinctly say, that under certain extraordinary circumstances it is allowable to tell a lie. Taylor says: 'To tell a lie for charity, to save a man's life, the life of a friend, of a husband, of a prince, of a useful and a public person, hath not only been done at all times, but commended by great and wise and good men. Who would not save his father's life, at the charge of a harmless lie, from persecutors or tyrants?' Again, Milton says: 'What man in his senses would deny, that there are those whom we have the best grounds for considering that we ought to deceive, – as boys, madmen, the sick, the intoxicated, enemies, men in error, thieves? I would ask, by which of the commandments is a lie forbidden? You will say, by the ninth. If then my lie does not injure my neighbour, certainly it is not forbidden by this commandment.' Paley says: 'There are falsehoods, which are not lies,' that is, which are not criminal.' Johnson: 'The general rule is, that truth should never be violated; there must, however, be some exceptions. If, for instance, a murderer should ask you which way a man is gone.'

Now, I am not using these instances as an *argumentum ad hominem*; but the purpose to which I put them is this: –

1. First, I have set down the distinct statements of Taylor, Milton, Paley, and Johnson: – now, would any one give ever so little weight to these statements, in forming a real estimate of the veracity of the writers, if they now were alive? Were a man, who is so fierce with St. Alfonso, to meet Paley or Johnson to-morrow in society, would he look upon him as a liar, a knave, as dishonest and untrustworthy? I am sure he would not. Why then does he not deal out the same measure to Catholic priests? If a copy of Scavini,[66] which speaks of equivocation as being in a just cause allowable, be found in a student's room at Oscott, not Scavini himself, but even the unhappy student, who has what a Protestant calls a bad book in his possession, is judged to be for life unworthy of credit. Are all Protestant text-books, which are used at the University, immaculate? Is it necessary to take for gospel every word of Aristotle's Ethics, or every assertion of Hey[67] or Burnett[68] on the Articles? Are text-books the ultimate authority, or rather are they not manuals in the hands of a lecturer, and the groundwork of his remarks? But, again, let us suppose, not the case of a student, or of a professor, but of

Scavini himself, or of St. Alfonso; now here again I ask, since you would not scruple in holding Paley for an honest man, in spite of his defence of lying, why do you scruple at holding St. Alfonso honest? I am perfectly sure that you would not scruple at Paley personally; you might not agree with him, but you would not go further than to call him a bold thinker: then why should St. Alfonso's person be odious to you, as well as his doctrine?

Now I wish to tell you why you are not afraid of Paley; because, you would say, when he advocated lying, he was taking *extreme* or *special cases*. You would have no fear of a man who you knew had shot a burglar dead in his own house, because you know you are *not* a burglar: so you would not think that Paley had a habit of telling lies in society, because in the case of a cruel alternative he thought it the lesser evil to tell a lie. Then why do you show such suspicion of a Catholic theologian, who speaks of certain extraordinary cases in which an equivocation in a penitent cannot be visited by his confessor as if it were a sin? for this is the exact point of the question.

But again, why does Paley, why does Jeremy Taylor, when no practical matter is actually before him, lay down a maxim about the lawfulness of lying, which will startle most readers? The reason is plain. He is forming a theory of morals, and he must treat every question in turn as it comes. And this is just what St. Alfonso or Scavini is doing. You only try your hand yourself at a treatise on the rules of morality, and you will see how difficult the work is. What is the *definition* of a lie? Can you give a better than that it is a sin against justice, as Taylor and Paley consider it? but, if so, how can it be a sin at all, if your neighbour is not injured? If you do not like this definition, take another; and then, by means of that, perhaps you will be defending St. Alfonso's equivocation. However, this is what I insist upon; that St. Alfonso, as Paley, is considering the different portions of a large subject, and he must, on the subject of lying, give his judgment, though on that subject it is difficult to form any judgment which is satisfactory.

But further still: you must not suppose that a philosopher or moralist uses in his own case the licence which his theory itself would allow him. A man in his own person is guided by his own conscience; but in drawing out a system of rules he is obliged to go by logic, and follow the exact deduction of conclusion from conclusion, and must be sure that the whole system is coherent and one. You hear of even immoral or irreligious books being written by men of decent character; there is a late writer[69] who says that David Hume's sceptical works are not at all the picture of the man. A priest might write a treatise which was really lax on the subject of lying, which might come under the condemnation of the Holy See, as some treatises on that score have already been condemned, and yet in his own person be a rigorist. And, in fact, it is notorious from St. Alfonso's Life,[70] that he, who has the repute of being so lax a moralist, had one of the most scrupulous and anxious of consciences himself. Nay, further than this, he was originally in the Law, and on one occasion he was betrayed into the commission of what seemed like a deceit, though it was an accident; and that was the very occasion of his leaving the profession and embracing the religious life.

The account of this remarkable occurrence is told us in his Life: –

'Notwithstanding he had carefully examined over and over the details of the process, he was completely mistaken regarding the sense of one document, which constituted the right of the adverse party. The advocate of the Grand Duke perceived the mistake, but he allowed Alfonso to continue his eloquent address to the end without interruption; as soon, however, as he had finished, he rose, and said with cutting coolness, "Sir, the case is not exactly what you suppose it to be; if you will review the process, and examine this paper attentively, you will find there precisely the contrary of all you have advanced." "Willingly," replied Alfonso, without hesitating; "the decision depends on this question – whether the fief were granted under the law of Lombardy, or under the French Law." The paper being examined, it was found that the Grand Duke's advocate was in the right. "Yes," said Alfonso, holding the paper in his hand, "I am wrong, I have been mistaken." A discovery so unexpected, and the fear of being accused of unfair dealing filled him with consternation, and covered him with confusion, so much so, that every one saw his emotion. It was in vain that the President Caravita, who loved him, and knew his integrity, tried to console him, by telling him that such mistakes were not uncommon, even among the first men at the bar. Alfonso would listen to nothing, but, overwhelmed with confusion, his head sunk on his breast, he said to himself, "World, I know you now; courts of law, never shall you see me again!" And turning his back on the assembly, he withdrew to his own house, incessantly repeating to himself, "World, I know you now." What annoyed him most was, that having studied and re-studied the process during a whole month, without having discovered this important flaw, he could not understand how it had escaped his observation.'

And this is the man, so easily scared at the very shadow of trickery, who is so flippantly pronounced to be a patron of lying.

But, in truth, a Catholic theologian has objects in view which men in general little compass; he is not thinking of himself, but of a multitude of souls, sick souls, sinful souls, carried away by sin, full of evil, and he is trying with all his might to rescue them from their miserable state; and, in order to save them from more heinous sins, he tries, to the full extent that his conscience will allow him to go, to shut his eyes to such sins, as are, though sins, yet lighter in character or degree. He knows perfectly well that, if he is as strict as he would wish to be, he shall be able to do nothing at all with the run of men; so he is as indulgent with them as ever he can be. Let it not be for an instant supposed, that I allow of the maxim of doing evil that good may come; but, keeping clear of this, there is a way of winning men from greater sins by winking for the time at the less, or at mere improprieties or faults; and this is the key to the difficulty which Catholic books of moral theology so often cause to the Protestant. They are intended for the Confessor, and Protestants view them as intended for the Preacher.

2. And I observe upon Taylor, Milton, and Paley thus: What would a Protestant clergyman say to me, if I accused him of teaching that a lie was allowable; and if, when he asked for my proof, I said in reply that such was the doctrine of Taylor and Milton? Why, he would sharply retort, '*I* am not bound by Taylor or Milton;' and if I went on urging that 'Taylor was one of his authorities,' he would answer that Taylor was a great writer, but great writers were not therefore infallible. This is

pretty much the answer which I make, when I am considered in this matter a disciple of St. Alfonso.

I plainly and positively state, and without any reserve, that I do not at all follow this holy and charitable man in this portion of his teaching. There are various schools of opinion allowed in the Church: and on this point I follow others. I follow Cardinal Gerdil,[71] and Natalis Alexander,[72] nay, St. Augustine. I will quote one passage from Natalis Alexander: – 'They certainly lie, who utter the words of an oath, without the will to swear or bind themselves: or who make use of mental reservations and *equivocations* in swearing, since they signify by words what they have not in mind, contrary to the end for which language was instituted, viz. as signs of ideas. Or they mean something else than the words signify in themselves and the common custom of speech.' And, to take an instance: I do not believe any priest in England would dream of saying, 'My friend is not here;' meaning, 'He is not in my pocket or under my shoe.' Nor should any consideration make me say so myself. I do not think St. Alfonso would in his own case have said so; and he would have been as much shocked at Taylor and Paley, as Protestants are at him.*

And now, if Protestants wish to know what our real teaching is, as on other subjects, so on that of lying, let them look, not at our books of casuistry, but at our catechisms. Works on pathology do not give the best insight into the form and the harmony of the human frame; and, as it is with the body, so is it with the mind. The Catechism of the Council of Trent was drawn up for the express purpose of providing preachers with subjects for their Sermons; and, as my whole work has been a defence of myself, I may here say that I rarely preach a Sermon, but I go to this beautiful and complete Catechism to get both my matter and my doctrine. There we find the following notices[73] about the duty of Veracity: –

'"Thou shalt not bear false witness," &c.: let attention be drawn to two laws contained in this commandment: – the one, forbidding false witness; the other bidding, that removing all pretence and deceits, we should measure our words and deeds by

* Vide Note G, *Lying and Equivocation.*

simple truth, as the Apostle admonished the Ephesians of that duty in these words: "Doing truth in charity, let us grow in Him through all things."

'To deceive by a lie in joke or for the sake of compliment, though to no one there accrues loss or gain in consequence, nevertheless is altogether unworthy: for thus the Apostle admonishes, "Putting aside lying, speak ye truth." For therein is great danger of lapsing into frequent and more serious lying, and from lies in joke men gain the habit of lying, whence they gain the character of not being truthful. And thence again, in order to gain credence to their words, they find it necessary to make a practice of swearing.

'Nothing is more necessary [for us] than truth of testimony, in those things, which we neither know ourselves, nor can allowably be ignorant of, on which point there is extant that maxim of St. Augustine's; Whoso conceals the truth, and whoso puts forth a lie, each is guilty; the one because he is not willing to do a service, the other because he has a wish to do a mischief.

'It is lawful at times to be silent about the truth, but out of a court of law; for in court, when a witness is interrogated by the judge according to law, the truth is wholly to be brought out.

'Witnesses, however, must beware, lest, from overconfidence in their memory, they affirm for certain, what they have not verified.

'In order that the faithful may with more good will avoid the sin of lying, the Parish Priest shall set before them the extreme misery and turpitude of this wickedness. For, in holy writ, the devil is called the father of a lie; for, in that he did not remain in Truth, he is a liar, and the father of a lie. He will add, with the view of ridding men of so great a crime, the evils which follow upon lying; and, whereas they are innumerable, he will point out [at least] the sources and the general heads of these mischiefs and calamities, viz. 1. How great is God's displeasure and how great His hatred of a man who is insincere and a liar. 2. What little security there is that a man who is specially hated by God may not be visited by the heaviest punishments. 3. What more unclean and foul, as St. James says, than ... that a fountain by the same jet should send out sweet water and bitter? 4. For that tongue, which just now praised God, next, as far as in it lies, dishonours Him by lying. 5. In consequence, liars are shut out from the possession of heavenly beatitude. 6. That too is the worst evil of lying, that that disease of the mind is generally incurable.

'Moreover, there is this harm too, and one of vast extent, and touching men generally, that by insincerity and lying faith and truth are lost, which are the firmest bonds of human society, and, when they are lost, supreme confusion follows in life, so that men seem in nothing to differ from devils.

'Lastly, the Parish Priest will set those right who excuse their insincerity and allege the example of wise men, who, they say, are used to lie for an occasion. He will tell them, what is most true, that the wisdom of the flesh is death. He will exhort his hearers to trust in God, when they are in difficulties and straits, nor to have recourse to the expedient of a lie.

'They who throw the blame of their own lie on those who have already by a lie deceived them, are to be taught that men must not revenge themselves, nor make up for one evil by another.' . . .

There is much more in the Catechism to the same effect, and it is of universal obligation; whereas the decision of a particular author in morals need not be accepted by any one.

To one other authority I appeal on this subject, which commands from me attention of a special kind, for it is the teaching of a Father. It will serve to bring my work to a conclusion.

'St. Philip,' says the Roman Oratorian[74] who wrote his Life, 'had a particular dislike of affectation both in himself and others, in speaking, in dressing, or in any thing else.

'He avoided all ceremony which savoured of worldly compliment, and always showed himself a great stickler for Christian simplicity in every thing; so that, when he had to deal with men of worldly prudence, he did not very readily accommodate himself to them.

'And he avoided, as much as possible, having any thing to do with *two-faced persons*, who did not go simply and straightforwardly to work in their transactions.

'*As for liars, he could not endure them*, and he was *continually reminding* his spiritual children, *to avoid them as they would a pestilence.*'

These are the principles on which I have acted before I was a Catholic; these are the principles which, I trust, will be my stay and guidance to the end.

I have closed this history of myself with St. Philip's name upon St. Philip's feast-day; and, having done so, to whom can I more suitably offer it, as a memorial of affection and gratitude, than to St. Philip's sons, my dearest brothers of this House, the Priests of the Birmingham Oratory, AMBROSE ST. JOHN,[75] HENRY AUSTIN MILLS,[76] HENRY BITTLESTON,[77] EDWARD CASWALL,[78] WILLIAM PAINE NEVILLE,[79] and HENRY IGNATIUS DUDLEY RYDER?[80] who have been so faithful to me; who have been so sensitive of my needs; who have been so indulgent to my failings; who have carried me through so many trials; who have grudged no sacrifice, if I asked for it; who have been so cheerful under discouragements of my causing; who have done so many good works, and let me have the credit of them; – with whom I have lived so long, with whom I hope to die.

And to you especially, dear AMBROSE ST. JOHN; whom God gave me, when He took every one else away; who are the link between my old life and my new; who have now for twenty-one years been so devoted to me, so patient, so zealous, so tender; who have let me lean so hard upon you; who have watched me so narrowly; who have never thought of yourself, if I was in question.

And in you I gather up and bear in memory those familiar affectionate companions and counsellors, who in Oxford were given to me, one after another, to be my daily solace and relief; and all those others, of great name and high example, who were my thorough friends, and showed me true attachment in times long past; and also those many younger men, whether I knew them or not, who have never been disloyal to me by word or deed; and of all these, thus various in their relations to me, those more especially who have since joined the Catholic Church.

And I earnestly pray for this whole company, with a hope

against hope, that all of us, who once were so united, and so happy in our union, may even now be brought at length, by the Power of the Divine Will, into One Fold and under One Shepherd.

May 26, 1864.
In Festo Corp. Christ.

NOTES

Note A. On Page 33

LIBERALISM

I have been asked to explain more fully what it is I mean by 'Liberalism,' because merely to call it the Anti-dogmatic Principle is to tell very little about it. An explanation is the more necessary, because such good Catholics and distinguished writers as Count Montalembert and Father Lacordaire use the word in a favourable sense, and claim to be Liberals themselves. 'The only singularity,' says the former of the two in describing his friend, 'was his Liberalism. By a phenomenon, at that time unheard of, this convert, this seminarist, this confessor of nuns, was just as stubborn a liberal, as in the days when he was a student and a barrister.' – *Life* (transl.), p. 19.

I do not believe that it is possible for me to differ in any important matter from two men whom I so highly admire. In their general line of thought and conduct I enthusiastically concur, and consider them to be before their age. And it would be strange indeed if I did not read with a special interest, in M. de Montalembert's beautiful volume, of the unselfish aims, the thwarted projects, the unrequited toils, the grand and tender resignation of Lacordaire. If I hesitate to adopt their language about Liberalism, I impute the necessity of such hesitation to some differences between us in the use of words or in the circumstances of country; and thus I reconcile myself to remaining faithful to my own conception of it, though I cannot have their voices to give force to mine. Speaking then in my own way, I proceed to explain what I meant as a Protestant by Liberalism, and to do so in connexion with the circumstances under which that system of opinion came before me at Oxford.

If I might presume to contrast Lacordaire and myself, I should say, that we had been both of us inconsistent; – he, a Catholic, in calling himself a Liberal; I, a Protestant, in being an Anti-liberal; and moreover, that the cause of this inconsistency had been in both cases one and the same. That is, we were both of us such good conservatives, as to take up with what we happened to find established in our respective countries, at the time when we came into active life. Toryism was the creed of Oxford; he inherited, and made the best of, the French Revolution.

When, in the beginning of the present century, not very long before my own time, after many years of moral and intellectual declension, the University of Oxford woke up to a sense of its duties, and began to reform itself, the first instruments of this change, to whose zeal and courage we all owe so much, were naturally thrown together for mutual support, against the numerous obstacles which lay in their path, and soon stood out in relief from the body of residents, who, though many of them men of talent themselves, cared little for the object which the others had at heart. These Reformers, as they may be called, were for some years members of scarcely more than three or four Colleges; and their own Colleges, as being under their direct influence, of course had the benefit of those stricter views of discipline and teaching, which they themselves were urging on the University. They had, in no long time, enough of real progress in their several spheres of exertion, and enough of reputation out of doors, to warrant them in considering themselves the *élite* of the place; and it is not wonderful if they were in consequence led to look down upon the majority of Colleges, which had not kept pace with the reform, or which had been hostile to it. And, when those rivalries of one man with another arose, whether personal or collegiate, which befall literary and scientific societies, such disturbances did but tend to raise in their eyes the value which they had already set upon academical distinction, and increase their zeal in pursuing it. Thus was formed an intellectual circle or class in the University, – men, who felt they had a career before them, as soon as the pupils, whom they were forming, came into public life; men, whom non-residents, whether country parsons or preachers of the Low Church, on coming up from time to time to the old place, would look at, partly with admiration, partly with suspicion, as being an honour indeed to Oxford, but withal exposed to the temptation of ambitious views, and to the spiritual evils signified in what is called the 'pride of reason.'

Nor was this imputation altogether unjust; for, as they were following out the proper idea of a University, of course they suffered more or less from the moral malady incident to such a pursuit. The very object of such great institutions lies in the cultivation of the mind and the spread of knowledge: if this object, as all human objects, has its dangers at all times, much more would these exist in the case of men, who were engaged in a work of reformation, and had the opportunity of measuring themselves, not only with those who were their equals in intellect, but with the many, who were below them. In this select circle or class of men, in various Colleges, the direct instruments and the choice fruit of real University Reform, we see the rudiments of the Liberal party.

Whenever men are able to act at all, there is the chance of extreme and intemperate action; and therefore, when there is exercise of mind, there is the chance of wayward or mistaken exercise. Liberty of thought is in itself a good; but it gives an opening to false liberty. Now by Liberalism I mean false liberty of thought, or the exercise of thought upon matters, in which, from the constitution of the human mind, thought cannot be brought to any successful issue, and therefore is out of place. Among such matters are first principles of whatever kind; and of these the most sacred and momentous are especially to be reckoned the truths of Revelation. Liberalism then is the mistake of subjecting to human judgment those revealed doctrines which are in their nature beyond and independent of it, and of claiming to determine on intrinsic grounds the truth and value of propositions which rest for their reception simply on the external authority of the Divine Word.

Now certainly the party of whom I have been speaking, taken as a whole, were of a character of mind out of which Liberalism might easily grow up, as in fact it did; certainly they breathed around an influence which made men of religious seriousness shrink into themselves. But, while I say as much as this, I have no intention whatever of implying that the talent of the University, in the years before and after 1820, was liberal in its theology, in the sense in which the bulk of the educated classes through the country are liberal now. I would not for the world be supposed to detract from the Christian earnestness, and the activity in religious works, above the average of men, of many of the persons in question. They would have protested against their being supposed to place reason before faith, or knowledge before devotion; yet I do consider that they unconsciously encouraged and successfully introduced into Oxford a licence of opinion which went far beyond them. In their day they did little more than take credit to themselves for enlightened views, largeness of mind, liberality of sentiment, without drawing the line between what was just and what was inadmissible in speculation, and without seeing the tendency of their own principles; and engrossing, as they did, the mental energy of the University, they met for a time with no effectual hindrance to the spread of their influence, except (what indeed at the moment was most effectual, but not of an intellectual character) the thorough-going Toryism and traditionary Church-of-England-ism of the great body of the Colleges and Convocation.

Now and then a man of note appeared in the Pulpit or Lecture Rooms of the University, who was a worthy representative of the more religious and devout Anglicans. These belonged chiefly to the High-Church party; for the party called Evangelical never has been able to breathe freely in the atmosphere of Oxford, and at no time has been conspicuous, as a party, for talent or learning. But of the old High Churchmen several exerted some sort of Anti-liberal influence in the place, at least from time to time, and that influence of an intellectual nature. Among these especially may be mentioned Mr. John Miller, of Worcester College, who preached the Bampton Lecture in the year 1817. But, as far as I know, he who turned the tide, and brought the talent of the University round to the side of the old theology, and against what was familiarly called 'march-of-mind,' was Mr. Keble. In and from Keble the mental activity of Oxford took that contrary direction which issued in what was called Tractarianism.

Keble was young in years, when he became a University celebrity, and younger in mind. He had the purity and simplicity of a child. He had few sympathies with the intellectual party, who sincerely welcomed him as a brilliant specimen of young Oxford. He instinctively shut up before literary display, and pomp and donnishness of manner, faults which always will beset academical notabilities. He did not respond to their advances. His collision with them (if it may be so called) was thus described by Hurrell Froude in his own way. 'Poor Keble!' he used gravely to say, 'he was asked to join the aristocracy of talent, but he soon found his level.' He went into the country, but his instance serves to prove that men need not, in the event, lose that influence which is rightly theirs, because they happen to be thwarted in the use of the channels natural and proper to its exercise. He did not lose his place in the minds of men because he was out of their sight.

Keble was a man who guided himself and formed his judgments, not by processes of reason, by inquiry or by argument, but, to use the word in a broad sense, by authority. Conscience is an authority; the Bible is an authority; such is the Church; such is Antiquity; such are the words of the wise; such are hereditary lessons; such are ethical truths; such are historical memories, such are legal saws and state maxims; such are proverbs; such are sentiments, presages, and prepossessions. It seemed to me as if he ever felt happier, when he could speak or act under some such primary or external sanction; and could use argument mainly as a means of recommending or explaining what had claims on his reception prior to proof. He even felt a tenderness, I think, in spite of Bacon, for the Idols of the Tribe and the Den, of the Market and the Theatre. What he hated instinctively was heresy, insubordination, resistance to things established, claims of independence, disloyalty, innovation, a critical, censorious spirit. And such was the main principle of the school which in the course of years was formed around him; nor is it easy to set limits to its influence in its day; for multitudes of men, who did not profess its peculiar doctrines, were willing nevertheless, or found it to their purpose, to act in company with it.

Indeed for a time it was practically the champion and advocate of the political doctrines of the great clerical interest through the country, who found in Mr. Keble and his friends an intellectual, as well as moral support to their cause, which they looked for in vain elsewhere. His weak point, in their eyes, was his consistency; for he carried his love of authority and old times so far, as to be more than gentle towards the Catholic Religion, with which the

Toryism of Oxford and of the Church of England had no sympathy. Accordingly, if my memory be correct, he never could get himself to throw his heart into the opposition made to Catholic Emancipation, strongly as he revolted from the politics and the instruments by means of which that Emancipation was won. I fancy he would have had no difficulty in accepting Dr. Johnson's saying about 'the first Whig;' and it grieved and offended him that the 'Via prima salutis' should be opened to the Catholic body from the Whig quarter. In spite of his reverence for the Old Religion, I conceive that on the whole he would rather have kept its professors beyond the pale of the Constitution with the Tories, than admit them on the principles of the Whigs. Moreover, if the Revolution of 1688 was too lax in principle for him and his friends, much less, as is very plain, could they endure to subscribe to the revolutionary doctrines of 1776 and 1789, which they felt to be absolutely and entirely out of keeping with theological truth.

The old Tory or Conservative party in Oxford had in it no principle or power of development, and that from its very nature and constitution: it was otherwise with the Liberals. They represented a new idea, which was but gradually learning to recognize itself, to ascertain its characteristics and external relations, and to exert an influence upon the University. The party grew, all the time that I was in Oxford, even in numbers, certainly in breadth and definiteness of doctrine, and in power. And, what was a far higher consideration, by the accession of Dr. Arnold's pupils, it was invested with an elevation of character which claimed the respect even of its opponents. On the other hand, in proportion as it became more earnest and less self-applauding, it became more free-spoken; and members of it might be found who, from the mere circumstance of remaining firm to their original professions, would in the judgment of the world, as to their public acts, seem to have left it for the Conservative camp. Thus, neither in its component parts nor in its policy, was it the same in 1832, 1836, and 1841, as it was in 1845.

These last remarks will serve to throw light upon a matter personal to myself, which I have introduced into my Narrative, and to which my attention has been pointedly called, now that my Volume is coming to a second edition.

It has been strongly urged upon me to re-consider the following passages which occur in it: 'The men who had driven me from Oxford were distinctly the Liberals, it was they who had opened the attack upon Tract 90,' p. 186, and 'I found no fault with the Liberals; they had beaten me in a fair field,' p. 194.

I am very unwilling to seem ungracious, or to cause pain in any quarter; still I am sorry to say I cannot modify these statements. It is surely a matter of historical fact that I left Oxford upon the University proceedings of 1841; and in those proceedings, whether we look to the Heads of Houses or the resident Masters, the leaders, if intellect and influence make men such, were members of the Liberal party. Those who did not lead, concurred or acquiesced in them, – I may say, felt a satisfaction. I do not recollect any Liberal who was on my side on that occasion. Excepting the Liberal, no other party, as a party, acted against me. I am not complaining of them; I deserved nothing else at their hands. They could not undo in 1845, even had they wished it, (and there is no proof they did,) what they had done in 1841. In 1845, when I had already given up the contest for four years, and my part in it had passed into the hands of others, then some of those who were prominent against me in 1841, feeling (what they had not felt in 1841) the danger of driving a number of my followers to Rome, and joined by younger friends who had come into University importance since 1841 and felt kindly towards me, adopted a course more consistent with their principles, and proceeded to shield from the zeal of the Hebdomadal Board, not me, but, professedly, all parties through the country, – Tractarians, Evangelicals, Liberals in general, – who had to subscribe to the Anglican formularies, on the ground that those formularies, rigidly taken, were, on some point or other, a difficulty to all parties alike.

However, besides the historical fact, I can bear witness to my own feeling at the time, and my feeling was this: – that those who in 1841 had considered it to be a duty to act against me, had then done their worst. What was it to me what they were now doing in opposition to the New Test proposed by the Hebdomadal Board? I owed them no thanks for their trouble. I took no interest at all, in February, 1845, in the proceedings of the Heads of Houses and of the Convocation. I felt myself *dead* as regarded my relations to the Anglican Church. My leaving it was all but a matter of time. I believe I did not even thank my real friends, the two Proctors, who in Convocation stopped by their Veto the condemnation of Tract 90; nor did I make any acknowledgment to Mr. Rogers, nor to Mr. James Mozley, nor, as I think, to Mr. Hussey, for their pamphlets on my behalf. My frame of mind is best described by the sentiment of the passage in Horace, which at the time I was fond of quoting, as expressing my view of the relation that existed between the Vice-Chancellor and myself.

> 'Penthen,
> Rector Thebarum, quid me perferre patique
> Indignum cogas?' 'Adimam bona.' 'Nempe pecus, rem,
> Lectos, argentum; tollas licet.' 'In manicis et
> Compedibus, saevo te sub custode tenebo.' (*viz. the 39 Articles.*)
> '*Ipse Deus, simul atque volam, me solvet.*' Opinor,
> Hoc sentit: *Moriar. Mors ultima linea rerum est.*

I conclude this notice of Liberalism in Oxford, and the party which was antagonistic to it, with some propositions in detail, which, as a member of the latter, and together with the High Church, I earnestly denounced and abjured.

1. No religious tenet is important, unless reason shows it to be so.

Therefore, e.g. the doctrine of the Athanasian Creed is not to be insisted on, unless it tends to convert the soul; and the doctrine of the Atonement is to be insisted on, if it does convert the soul.

2. No one can believe what he does not understand.

Therefore, e.g. there are no mysteries in true religion.

3. No theological doctrine is any thing more than an opinion which happens to be held by bodies of men.

Therefore, e.g. no creed, as such, is necessary for salvation.

4. It is dishonest in a man to make an act of faith in what he has not had brought home to him by actual proof.

Therefore, e.g. the mass of men ought not absolutely to believe in the divine authority of the Bible.

5. It is immoral in a man to believe more than he can spontaneously receive as being congenial to his moral and mental nature.

Therefore, e.g. a given individual is not bound to believe in eternal punishment.

6. No revealed doctrines or precepts may reasonably stand in the way of scientific conclusions.

Therefore, e.g. Political Economy may reverse our Lord's declarations about poverty and riches, or a system of Ethics may teach that the highest condition of body is ordinarily essential to the highest state of mind.

7. Christianity is necessarily modified by the growth of civilization, and the exigencies of times.

Therefore, e.g. the Catholic priesthood, though necessary in the Middle Ages, may be superseded now.

8. There is a system of religion more simply true than Christianity as it has ever been received.

Therefore, e.g. we may advance that Christianity is the 'corn of wheat' which has been dead for 1800 years, but at length will bear fruit; and that Mahometanism is the manly religion, and existing Christianity the womanish.

9. There is a right of Private Judgment: that is, there is no existing authority on earth competent to interfere with the liberty of individuals in reasoning and judging for themselves about the Bible and its contents, as they severally please.

Therefore, e.g. religious establishments requiring subscription are Anti-christian.

10. There are rights of conscience such, that every one may lawfully advance a claim to profess and teach what is false and wrong in matters, religious, social, and moral, provided that to his private conscience it seems absolutely true and right.

Therefore, e.g. individuals have a right to preach and practise fornication and polygamy.

11. There is no such thing as a national or state conscience.

Therefore, e.g. no judgments can fall upon a sinful or infidel nation.

12. The civil power has no positive duty, in a normal state of things, to maintain religious truth.

Therefore, e.g. blasphemy and sabbath-breaking are not rightly punishable by law.

13. Utility and expedience are the measure of political duty.

Therefore, e.g. no punishment may be enacted, on the ground that God commands it: e.g. on the text, 'Whoso sheddeth man's blood, by man shall his blood be shed.'

14. The Civil Power may dispose of Church property without sacrilege.

Therefore, e.g. Henry VIII. committed no sin in his spoliations.

15. The Civil Power has the right of ecclesiastical jurisdiction and administration.

Therefore, e.g. Parliament may impose articles of faith on the Church or suppress Dioceses.

16. It is lawful to rise in arms against legitimate princes.

Therefore, e.g. the Puritans in the 17th century, and the French in the 18th, were justifiable in their Rebellion and Revolution respectively.

17. The people are the legitimate source of power.

Therefore, e.g. Universal Suffrage is among the natural rights of man.

18. Virtue is the child of knowledge, and vice of ignorance.

Therefore, e.g. education, periodical literature, railroad travelling, ventilation, drainage, and the arts of life, when fully carried out, serve to make a population moral and happy.

All of these propositions, and many others too, were familiar to me thirty years ago, as in the number of the tenets of Liberalism, and, while I gave into none of them except No. 12, and perhaps No. 11, and partly No. 1, before I began to publish, so afterwards I wrote against most of them in some part of other of my Anglican works.

If it is necessary to refer to a work, not simply my own, but of the Tractarian school, which contains a similar protest, I should name the *Lyra Apostolica*. This volume, which by accident has been left unnoticed, except incidentally, in my Narrative, was collected together from the pages of the *British Magazine*, in which its contents originally appeared, and published in a separate form, immediately after Hurrell Froude's death in 1836. Its signatures, α, β, γ, δ, ε, ζ, denote respectively as authors, Mr. Bowden, Mr. Hurrell Froude, Mr. Keble, Mr. Newman, Mr. Robert Wilberforce, and Mr. Isaac Williams.

There is one poem on 'Liberalism,' beginning 'Ye cannot halve the Gospel of God's grace;' which bears out the account of Liberalism as above given; and another upon 'the Age to come,' defining from its own point of view the position and prospects of Liberalism.

I need hardly say that the above Note is mainly historical. How far the Liberal party of 1830–40 really held the above eighteen Theses, which I attributed to them, and how far and in what sense I should oppose those Theses now, could scarcely be explained without a separate Dissertation.

Note B. On Page 41

ECCLESIASTICAL MIRACLES

The writer, who gave occasion for the foregoing Narrative, was very severe with me for what I had said about Miracles in the Preface to the Life of St. Walburga. I observe therefore as follows: –

Catholics believe that miracles happen in any age of the Church, though not for the same purposes, in the same number, or with the same evidence, as in Apostolic times. The Apostles wrought them in evidence of their divine mission; and with this object they have been sometimes wrought by Evangelists of countries since, as even Protestants allow. Hence we hear of

them in the history of St. Gregory in Pontus, and St. Martin in
Gaul; and in their case, as in that of the Apostles, they were both
numerous and clear. As they are granted to Evangelists, so are
they granted, though in less measure and evidence, to other holy
men; and as holy men are not found equally at all times and in all
places, therefore miracles are in some places and times more than
in others. And since, generally, they are granted to faith and
prayer, therefore in a country in which faith and prayer abound,
they will be more likely to occur, than where and when faith and
prayer are not; so that their occurrence is irregular. And further,
as faith and prayer obtain miracles, so still more commonly do
they gain from above the ordinary interventions of Providence;
and, as it is often very difficult to distinguish between a providence and a miracle, and there will be more providences than
miracles, hence it will happen that many occurrences will be
called miraculous, which, strictly speaking, are not such, that is,
not more than providential mercies, or what are sometimes called
'*grazie*' or 'favours.'

Persons, who believe all this, in accordance with Catholic
teaching, as I did and do, they, on the report of a miracle, will of
necessity, the necessity of good logic, be led to say, first, 'It *may*
be,' and secondly, 'But I must have *good evidence* in order to
believe it.'

1. It *may* be, because miracles take place in all ages; it must be
clearly *proved*, because perhaps after all it may be only a providential mercy, or an exaggeration, or a mistake, or an imposture.
Well, this is precisely what I had said, which the writer, who has
given occasion to this Volume, considered so irrational. I had
said, as he quotes me, 'In this day, and under our present
circumstances, we can only reply, that there is no reason why
they should not be.' Surely this is good logic, *provided* that
miracles *do* occur in all ages; and so again I am logical in saying,
'There is nothing, *primâ facie*, in the miraculous accounts in
question, to repel a *properly taught* or religiously disposed mind.'
What is the matter with this statement? My assailant does not
pretend to say *what* the matter is, and he cannot; but he expresses
a rude, unmeaning astonishment. Accordingly, in the passage
which he quotes, I observe, 'Miracles are the kind of facts proper
to ecclesiastical history, just as instances of sagacity or daring,

personal prowess, or crime, are the facts proper to secular history.' What is the harm of this?

2. But, though a miracle be conceivable, it has to be *proved*. *What* has to be proved? (1) That the event occurred as stated, and is not a false report or an exaggeration. (2) That it is clearly miraculous, and not a mere providence or answer to prayer within the order of nature. What is the fault of saying this? The inquiry is parallel to that which is made about some extraordinary fact in secular history. Supposing I hear that King Charles II. died a Catholic, I am led to say: It *may* be, but what is your *proof*?

In my *Essay on Miracles* of the year 1826, I proposed three questions about a professed miraculous occurrence: 1. is it antecedently *probable*? 2. is it in its *nature* certainly miraculous? 3. has it sufficient *evidence*? To these three heads I had regard in my Essay of 1842; and under them I still wish to conduct the inquiry into the miracles of Ecclesiastical History.

So much for general principles; as to St. Walburga, though I have no intention at all of denying that numerous miracles have been wrought by her intercession, still, neither the Author of her Life, nor I, the Editor, felt that we had grounds for binding ourselves to the belief of certain alleged miracles in particular. I made, however, one exception; it was the medicinal oil which flows from her relics. Now as to the *verisimilitude*, the *miraculousness*, and the *fact*, of this medicinal oil.

1. The *verisimilitude*. It is plain there is nothing extravagant in this report of her relics having a supernatural virtue; and for this reason, because there are such instances in Scripture, and Scripture cannot be extravagant. For instance, a man was restored to life by touching the relics of the Prophet Eliseus. The sacred text runs thus: – And Elisha died, and they buried him. And the bands of the Moabites invaded the land at the coming in of the year. And it came to pass, as they were burying a man, that, behold, they spied a band of men; and they cast the man into the sepulchre of Elisha. And, when the man was let down, *and touched the bones of Elisha, he revived*, and stood upon his feet.' Again, in the case of an inanimate substance, which had touched a living Saint: 'And God wrought *special miracles* by the hands of Paul; so that *from his body* were brought unto the sick *handkerchiefs*

or aprons, and *the diseases departed from them*.' And again in the case of a pool: 'An *Angel went down* at a certain season into the pool, and troubled the water; whosoever then first, after the troubling of the water, stepped in, *was made whole whatsoever disease* he had.' 2 Kings [4 Kings] xiii. 20, 21. Acts xix. 11, 12. John v. 4. Therefore there is nothing *extravagant* in the *character* of the miracle.

2. Next, the *matter of fact*: – *is* there an oil flowing from St. Walburga's tomb, which is medicinal? To this question I confined myself in my Preface. Of the accounts of medieval miracles, I said that there was no *extravagance* in their *general character*, but I could not affirm that there was always *evidence* for them. I could not simply accept them as *facts*, but I could not reject them in their *nature*; – they *might* be true, for they were not impossible; but they were *not proved* to be true, because there was not trustworthy testimony. However, as to St. Walburga, I repeat, I made *one* exception, the fact of the medicinal oil, since for that miracle there was distinct and successive testimony. And then I went on to give a chain of witnesses. It was my duty to state what those witnesses said in their very words; so I gave the testimonies in full, tracing them from the Saint's death. I said, 'She is one of the principal Saints of her age and country.' Then I quoted Basnage, a Protestant, who says, 'Six writers are extant, who have employed themselves in relating the deeds or miracles of Walburga.' Then I said that her 'renown was not the mere natural *growth* of ages, but begins with the very century of the Saint's death.' Then I observed that only two miracles seem to have been 'distinctly reported of her as occurring in her lifetime; and they were handed down apparently by tradition.' Also, that such miracles are said to have commenced about A.D. 777. Then I spoke of the medicinal oil as having testimony to it in 893, in 1306, after 1450, in 1615, and in 1620. Also, I said that Mabillon seems not to have believed some of her miracles; and that the earliest witness had got into trouble with his Bishop. And so I left the matter, as a question to be decided by evidence, not deciding any thing myself.

What was the harm of all this? but my Critic muddled it together in a most extraordinary manner, and I am far from sure that he knew himself the definite categorical charge which he intended it to convey against me. One of his remarks is, 'What has become of the holy oil for the last 240 years, Dr. Newman does not say,' p. 391. Of course I did not, because I did not know; I gave the evidence as I found it; he assumes that I had a point to prove, and then asks why I did not make the evidence larger than it was.

I can tell him more about it now: the oil still flows; I have had some of it in my possession; it is medicinal still. This leads to the third head.

3. Its *miraculousness*. On this point, since I have been in the Catholic Church, I have found there is a difference of opinion. Some persons consider that the oil is the natural produce of the rock, and has ever flowed from it; others, that by a divine gift it flows from the relics; and others, allowing that it now comes naturally from the rock, are disposed to hold that it was in its origin miraculous, as was the virtue of the pool of Bethsaida.

This point must be settled of course before the virtue of the oil can be ascribed to the sanctity of St. Walburga; for myself, I neither have, nor ever have had, the means of going into the question; but I will take the opportunity of its having come before me, to make one or two remarks, supplemental of what I have said on other occasions.

1. I frankly confess that the present advance of science tends to make it probable that various facts take place, and have taken place, in the order of nature, which hitherto have been considered by Catholics as simply supernatural.

2. Though I readily make this admission, it must not be supposed in consequence that I am disposed to grant at once, that every event was natural in point of fact, which *might* have taken place by the laws of nature; for it is obvious, no Catholic can bind the Almighty to act only in one and the same way, or to the observance always of His own laws. An event which is possible in the way of nature, is certainly possible too to Divine Power without the sequence of natural cause and effect at all. A conflagration, to take a parallel, may be the work of an incendiary, or the result of a flash of lightning; nor would a jury think it safe to find a man guilty of arson, if a dangerous thunderstorm was raging at the very time when the fire broke out. In like manner, upon the hypothesis that a miraculous dispensation is in

operation, a recovery from diseases to which medical science is equal, may nevertheless in matter of fact have taken place, not by natural means, but by a supernatural interposition. That the Lawgiver always acts through His own laws, is an assumption, of which I never saw proof. In a given case, then, the possibility of assigning a human cause for an event does not *ipso facto* prove that it is not miraculous.

3. So far, however, is plain, that, till some *experimentum crucis* can be found, such as to be decisive against the natural cause or the supernatural, an occurrence of this kind will as little convince an unbeliever that there has been a divine interference in the case, as it will drive the Catholic to admit that there has been no interference at all.

4. Still there is this gain accruing to the Catholic cause from the larger views we now possess of the operation of natural causes, viz. that our opponents will not in future be so ready as hitherto, to impute fraud and falsehood to our priests and their witnesses, on the ground of their pretending or reporting things that are incredible. Our opponents have again and again accused us of false witness, on account of statements which they now allow are either true, or may have been true. They account indeed for the strange facts very differently from us; but still they allow that facts they were. It is a great thing to have our characters cleared; and we may reasonably hope that, the next time our word is vouched for occurrences which appear to be miraculous, our facts will be investigated, not our testimony impugned.

5. Even granting that certain occurrences, which we have hitherto accounted miraculous, have not absolutely a claim to be so considered, nevertheless they constitute an argument still in behalf of Revelation and the Church. Providences, or what are called *grazie*, though they do not rise to the order of miracles, yet, if they occur again and again in connexion with the same persons, institutions, or doctrines, may supply a cumulative evidence of the fact of a supernatural presence in the quarter in which they are found. I have already alluded to this point in my Essay on Ecclesiastical Miracles, and I have a particular reason, as will presently be seen, for referring here to what I said in the course of it.

*

In that Essay, after bringing its main argument to an end, I append to it a review of 'the evidence for particular alleged miracles.' 'It does not strictly fall within the scope of the Essay,' I observe, 'to pronounce upon the truth or falsehood of this or that miraculous narrative, as it occurs in ecclesiastical history; but only to furnish such general considerations, as may be useful in forming a decision in particular cases,' p. cv. However, I thought it right to go farther and 'to set down the evidence for and against certain miracles as we meet with them,' ibid. In discussing these miracles separately, I make the following remarks, to which I have just been referring.

After discussing the alleged miracle of the Thundering Legion, I observe: − 'Nor does it concern us much to answer the objection, that there is nothing strictly miraculous in such an occurrence, because sudden thunder clouds after drought are not unfrequent; for, I would answer, Grant me such miracles ordinarily in the early Church, and I will ask no other; grant that, upon prayer benefits are vouchsafed, deliverances are effected, unhoped-for results obtained, sicknesses cured, tempests laid, pestilences put to flight, famines remedied, judgments inflicted, and there will be no need of analyzing the causes, whether supernatural or natural, to which they are to be referred. They may, or they may not, in this or that case, follow or surpass the laws of nature, and they may do so plainly or doubtfully, but the common sense of mankind will call them miraculous; for by a miracle is popularly meant whatever be its formal definition, an event which impresses upon the mind the immediate presence of the Moral Governor of the world. He may sometimes act through nature, sometimes beyond or against it; but those who admit the fact of such interferences, will have little difficulty in admitting also their strictly miraculous character, if the circumstances of the case require it, and those who deny miracles to the early Church will be equally strenuous against allowing her the grace of such intimate influence (if we may so speak) upon the course of divine Providence, as is here in question, even though it be not miraculous.' − p. cxxi.

And again, speaking of the death of Arius: 'But after all, was it a miracle? for, if not we are labouring at a proof of which nothing comes. The more immediate answer to this question has already been suggested several times. When a Bishop with his flock prays night and day against a heretic, and at length begs of God to take him away, and when he *is* suddenly taken away, almost at the moment of his triumph, and that by a death awfully significant, from its likeness to one recorded in Scripture, is it not trifling to ask whether such an occurrence comes up to the definition of a miracle? The question is not whether it is formally a miracle, but whether it is an event, the like of which persons, who deny that miracles continue, will consent that the Church should be considered still able to perform. If they are willing to allow to the Church such extraordinary protection, it is for them to draw the line to the satisfaction of people in general, between these and strictly miraculous events; if, on the other hand, they deny their occurrence in the times of the Church, then there is sufficient reason for our appealing here to the history of Arius in proof of the affirmative.' – p. clxxii.

These remarks, thus made upon the Thundering Legion and the death of Arius, must be applied, in consequence of investigations made since the date of my Essay, to the apparent miracle wrought in favour of the African confessors in the Vandal persecution. Their tongues were cut out by the Arian tyrant, and yet they spoke as before. In my Essay I insisted on this fact as being strictly miraculous. Among other remarks (referring to the instances adduced by Middleton and others in disparagement of the miracle, viz. of 'a girl born without a tongue, who yet talked as distinctly and easily, as if she had enjoyed the full benefit of that organ,' and of a boy who lost his tongue at the age of eight or nine, yet retained his speech, whether perfectly or not,) I said, 'Does Middleton mean to say, that, if certain of men lost their tongues *at the command of a tyrant* for the *sake of their religion*, and then spoke *as plainly* as before, nay *if only one person was so mutilated* and so gifted, it would not be a miracle?' – p. ccx. And I enlarged upon the minute details of the fact as reported to us by eye-witnesses and contemporaries. 'Out of the seven writers adduced, six are contemporaries; three, if not four, are eye-witnesses of the miracles. One reports from an eye-witness, and one testifies to a fervent record at the burial-place of the subjects of it. All seven were living, or had been staying, at one or other of the two places which are mentioned as their abode. One is a Pope, a second a Catholic Bishop, a third a Bishop of a schismatical party, a fourth an emperor, a fifth a soldier, a politician, and a suspected infidel, a sixth a statesman and courtier, a seventh a rhetorician and philosopher. "He cut out the tongues by the roots," says Victor, Bishop of Vito; "I perceived the tongues entirely gone by the roots," says Aeneas; "as low down as the throat," says Procopius; "at the roots," says Justinian and St. Gregory; "he spoke like an educated man, without impediment," says Victor of Vito; "with articulateness," says Aeneas; "better than before;" "they talked without any impediment," says Procopius; "speaking with perfect voice," says Marcellinus; "they spoke perfectly, even to the end," says the second Victor; "the words were formed, full, and perfect," says St. Gregory.' – p. ccviii.

However, a few years ago an Article appeared in *Notes and Queries* (No. for May 22, 1858), in which various evidence was adduced to show that the tongue is not necessary for articulate speech.

1. Col. Churchill, in his *Lebanon*, speaking of the cruelties of Djezzar Pacha, in extracting to the root the tongues of some Emirs, adds, 'It is a curious fact, however, that the tongues grow again sufficiently for the purposes of speech.'

2. Sir John Malcolm, in his *Sketches of Persia*, speaks of Zâb, Khan of Khisht, who was condemned to lose his tongue. 'This mandate,' he says, 'was imperfectly executed, and the loss of half this member deprived him of speech. Being afterwards persuaded that its being cut close to the root would enable him to speak so as to be understood, he submitted to the operation; and the effect has been, that his voice, though indistinct and thick, is yet intelligible to persons accustomed to converse with him. . . . I am not an anatomist, and I cannot therefore give a reason, why a man, who could not articulate with half a tongue, should speak when he had none at all; but the facts are as stated.'

3. And Sir John McNeill says, 'In answer to your inquiries about the powers of speech retained by persons who have had their tongues cut out, I can state from personal observation, that several persons whom I knew in Persia, who had been subjected

to that punishment, spoke so intelligibly as to be able to transact important business. . . . The conviction in Persia is universal, that the power of speech is destroyed by merely cutting off the tip of the tongue; and is to a useful extent restored by cutting off another portion as far back as a perpendicular section can be made of the portion that is free from attachment at the lower surface. . . . I never had to meet with a person who had suffered this punishment, who could not speak so as to be quite intelligible to his familiar associates.'

I should not be honest, if I professed to be simply converted, by these testimonies, to the belief that there was nothing miraculous in the case of the African confessors. It is quite as fair to be sceptical on one side of the question as on the other; and if Gibbon is considered worthy of praise for his stubborn incredulity in receiving the evidence for this miracle, I do not see why I am to be blamed, if I wish to be quite sure of the full appositeness of the recent evidence which is brought to its disadvantage. Questions of fact cannot be disproved by analogies or presumptions; the inquiry must be made into the particular case in all its parts, as it comes before us. Meanwhile, I fully allow that the points of evidence brought in disparagement of the miracle are *primâ facie* of such cogency, that, till they are proved to be irrelevant, Catholics are prevented from appealing to it for controversial purposes.

Note C. On Page 145

SERMON ON WISDOM AND INNOCENCE

The professed basis of the charge of lying and equivocation made against me, and, in my person, against the Catholic clergy, was, as I have already noticed in the Preface, a certain Sermon of mine on *Wisdom and Innocence*, being the 20th in a series of 'Sermons on Subjects of the Day,' written, preached, and published while I was an Anglican. Of this Sermon my accuser spoke thus in his Pamphlet: –

'It is occupied entirely with the attitude of "the world" to "Christians" and "the Church." By the world appears to be signified, especially, the Protestant public of these realms; what Dr. Newman means by Christians, and the Church, he has not left in doubt; for in the preceding Sermon he says: "But if the truth must be spoken, what are the humble monk and the holy nun, and other regulars, as they are called, but Christians after the very pattern given us in Scripture, &c." . . . This is his definition of Christians. And in the Sermon itself, he sufficiently defines what he means by "the Church," in two notes of her character, which he shall give in his own words: "What, for instance, though we grant that sacramental confession and the celibacy of the clergy do tend to consolidate the body politic in the relation of rulers and subjects, or, in other words, to aggrandize the priesthood? for how can the Church be one body without such relation?"' – Pp. 8, 9.

He then proceeded to analyze and comment on it at great length, and to criticize severely the method and tone of my Sermons generally. Among other things, he said: –

'What, then, did the Sermon *mean*? Why was it preached? To insinuate that a Church which had sacramental confession and a celibate clergy was the only true Church? Or to insinuate that the admiring young gentlemen who listened to him stood to their fellow-countrymen in the relation of the early Christians to the heathen Romans? Or that Queen Victoria's Government was to the Church of England what Nero's or Dioclesian's was to the Church of Rome? It may have been so. I know that men used to suspect Dr. Newman, – I have been inclined to do so myself, – of writing a whole Sermon, not for the sake of the text or of the matter, but for the sake of one single passing hint – one phrase, one epithet, one little barbed arrow, which, as he swept magnificently past on the stream of his calm eloquence, seemingly unconscious of all presences, save those unseen, he delivered unheeded, as with his finger-tip, to the very heart of an initiated hearer, never to be withdrawn again. I do not blame him for that. It is one of the highest triumphs of oratoric power, and may be employed honestly and fairly by any person who has the skill to do it honestly and fairly; but then, Why did he entitle his Sermon "Wisdom and Innocence"?

'What, then, could I think that Dr. Newman *meant*? I found a preacher bidding Christians imitate, to some undefined point, the "arts" of the basest of animals, and of men, and of the devil himself. I found him, by a strange perversion of Scripture, insinuating that St. Paul's conduct and manner were such as naturally to bring down on him the reputation of being a crafty deceiver. I found him – horrible to say it – even hinting the same of one greater than St. Paul. I found him denying or explaining away the existence of that Priestcraft, which is a notorious fact to every honest student of history, and justifying (as far as I can understand him) that double-dealing by which prelates, in the middle age, too often played off alternately the sovereign against the people, and the people against the sovereign, careless which was in the right, so long as their own power gained by the move. I found him actually using of such (and, as I thought, of himself and his party likewise) the words "They yield outwardly; to assent inwardly were to betray the faith. Yet they are called deceitful and double-dealing, because they do as much as they can, and not more than they may." I found him telling Christians that they will always seem "artificial," and, "wanting in openness and manliness;" that they will always be "a mystery" to the world, and that the world will always think them rogues; and bidding them glory in what the world (i.e. the rest of their countrymen), disown, and say with Mawworm, "I like to be despised."

'Now, how was I to know that the preacher, who had the reputation of being the most acute man of his generation, and of having a specially intimate acquaintance with the weaknesses of the human heart, was utterly blind to the broad meaning and the plain practical result of a Sermon like this, delivered before fanatic and hot-headed young men, who hung upon his every word? that he did not foresee that they would think that they obeyed him by becoming affected, artificial, sly, shifty, ready for concealments and equivocations?' &c. &c. – Pp. 14–16.

My accuser asked in this passage what did the Sermon *mean*, and why was it preached. I will here answer this question; and with this view will speak, first of the *matter* of the Sermon, then of its *subject*, then of its *circumstances*.

1. It was one of the last six Sermons which I wrote when I was an Anglican. It was one of the five Sermons I preached in St. Mary's between Christmas and Easter, 1843, the year when I gave up my Living. The MS. of the Sermon is destroyed; but I

believe, and my memory too bears me out, as far as it goes, that the sentence in question about Celibacy and Confession, of which this writer would make so much, *was not preached at all*. The Volume, in which this Sermon is found, was published *after* that I had given up St. Mary's, when I had no call on me to restrain the expression of any thing which I might hold: and I stated an important fact about it in the Advertisement, in these words: –

'In preparing [these Sermons] for publication, *a few words and sentences* have in several places been *added*, which will be found to express more *of private or personal opinion*, than it was expedient to introduce into the *instruction* delivered in Church to a parochial Congregation. Such introduction, however, seems unobjectionable in the case of compositions, which are *detached* from the sacred place and service to which they once belonged, and *submitted to the reason* and judgment of the general reader.'

This Volume of Sermons then cannot be criticized at all as *preachments*; they are *essays*; essays of a man who, at the time of publishing them, was *not* a preacher. Such passages, as that in question, are just the very ones which I added *upon* my publishing them; and, as I always was on my guard in the pulpit against saying anything which looked towards Rome, I shall believe that I did not preach the obnoxious sentence till some one is found to testify that he heard it.

At the same time I cannot conceive why the mention of Sacramental Confession, or of Clerical Celibacy, had I made it, was inconsistent with the position of an Anglican Clergyman. For Sacramental Confession and Absolution actually form a portion of the Anglican Visitation of the Sick; and though the 32nd Article says that 'Bishops, priests, and deacons, are not *commanded* by God's law either to vow the state of single life or to abstain from marriage,' and 'therefore it is *lawful* for them to marry,' this proposition I did not dream of denying, nor is it inconsistent with St. Paul's doctrine, which I held, that it is '*good* to abide even as he,' i.e. in celibacy.

But I have more to say on this point. This writer says, 'I know that men used to suspect Dr. Newman, – I have been inclined to do so myself, – of *writing a whole Sermon, not for the sake of the text or of the matter*, but for the sake of one simple passing hint, – one phrase, one epithet.' Now observe; can there be a plainer testimony borne to the practical character of my Sermons at St. Mary's than this gratuitous insinuation? Many a preacher of Tractarian doctrine has been accused of not letting his parishioners alone, and of teasing them with his private theological notions. The same report was spread about me twenty years ago as this writer spreads now, and the world believed that my Sermons at St. Mary's were full of red-hot Tractarianism. Then strangers came to hear me preach, and were astonished at their own disappointment. I recollect the wife of a great prelate from a distance coming to hear me, and then expressing her surprise to find that I preached nothing but a plain humdrum Sermon. I recollect how, when on the Sunday before Commemoration one year, a number of strangers came to hear me, and I preached in my usual way, residents in Oxford, of high position, were loud in their satisfaction that on a great occasion, I had made a simple failure, for after all there was nothing in the Sermon to hear. Well, but they were not going to let me off, for all my commonsense view of duty. Accordingly they got up the charitable theory which this Writer revives. They said that there was a double purpose in those plain addresses of mine, and that my Sermons were never so artful as when they seemed commonplace; that there were sentences which redeemed their apparent simplicity and quietness. So they watched during the delivery of a Sermon, which to them was too practical to be useful, for the concealed point of it, which they could at least imagine, if they could not discover. 'Men used to suspect Dr. Newman,' he says, 'of writing a *whole* Sermon, *not* for the sake of *the text or of the matter*, but for the sake of one single passing hint, . . . *one* phrase, *one* epithet, *one* little barbed arrow, which, as he *swept magnificently* past on the stream of his calm eloquence, *seemingly* unconscious of all presences, save those unseen, he delivered unheeded,' &c. To all appearance, he says, I was 'unconscious of all presences.' He is not able to deny that the '*whole* Sermon' had the *appearance* of being '*for the sake* of the text and matter;' therefore he suggests that perhaps it wasn't.

2. And now as to the subject of the Sermon. The Sermons of which the Volume consists are such as are, more or less,

exceptions to the rule which I ordinarily observed, as to the subjects which I introduced into the pulpit of St. Mary's. They are not purely ethical or doctrinal. They were for the most part caused by circumstances of the day or of the moment, and they belong to various years. One was written in 1832, two in 1836, two in 1838, five in 1840, five in 1841, four in 1842, seven in 1843. Many of them are engaged on one subject, viz. in viewing the Church in its relation to the world. By the world was meant, not simply those multitudes which were not in the Church, but the existing body of human society, whether in the Church or not, whether Catholics, Protestants, Greeks, or Mahometans, theists or idolaters, as being ruled by principles, maxims, and instincts of their own, that is, of an unregenerate nature, whatever their supernatural privileges might be, greater or less, according to their form of religion. This view of the relation of the Church to the world as taken apart from questions of ecclesiastical politics, as they may be called, is often brought out in my Sermons. Two occur to me at once; No. 3 of my *Plain Sermons*, which was written in 1829, and No. 15 of my Third Volume of *Parochial*, written in 1835. On the other hand, by Church I meant, – in common with all writers connected with the Tract Movement, whatever their shades of opinion, and with the whole body of English divines, except those of the Puritan or Evangelical School, – the whole of Christendom, from the Apostles' time till now, whatever their later divisions into Latin, Greek, and Anglican. I have explained this view of the subject above at pp. 77–9 of this Volume. When then I speak, in the particular Sermon before us, of the members, or the rulers, or the action of 'the Church,' I mean neither the Latin, nor the Greek, nor the English, taken by itself, but of the whole Church as one body: of Italy as one with England, of the Saxon or Norman as one with the Caroline Church. *This* was specially the one Church, and the points in which one branch or one period differed from another were not and could not be Notes of the Church, because Notes necessarily belong to the whole of the Church every where and always.

This being my doctrine as to the relation of the Church to the world, I laid down in the Sermon three principles concerning it, and there left the matter. The first is, that Divine Wisdom had framed for its action laws, which man, if left to himself, would have antecedently pronounced to be the worst possible for its success, and which in all ages have been called by the world, as they were in the Apostles' days, 'foolishness;' that man ever relies on physical and material force, and on carnal inducements, or as Mahomet with his sword and his houris, or indeed almost as that theory of religion, called, since the Sermon was written, 'muscular Christianity;' but that our Lord, on the contrary, has substituted meekness for haughtiness, passiveness for violence, and innocence for craft: and that the event has shown the high wisdom of such an economy, for it has brought to light a set of natural laws, unknown before, by which the seeming paradox that weakness should be stronger than might, and simplicity than worldly policy, is readily explained.

Secondly, I said that men of the world, judging by the event, and not recognizing the secret causes of the success, viz. a higher order of natural laws, – natural, though their source and action were supernatural, (for 'the meek inherit the earth,' by means of a meekness which comes from above,) – these men, I say, concluded, that the success which they witnessed must arise from some evil secret which the world had not mastered, – by means of magic, as they said in the first ages, by cunning as they say now. And accordingly they thought that the humility and inoffensiveness of Christians, or of Churchmen, was a mere pretence and blind to cover the real causes of that success, which Christians could explain and would not; and that they were simply hypocrites.

Thirdly, I suggested that shrewd ecclesiastics, who knew very well that there was neither magic nor craft in the matter, and, from their intimate acquaintance with what actually went on within the Church, discerned what were the real causes of its success, were of course under the temptation of substituting reason for conscience, and, instead of simply obeying the command, were led to do good that good might come, that is, to act *in order* to secure success, and not from a motive of faith. Some, I said, did yield to the temptation more or less, and their motives became mixed; and in this way the world in a more subtle shape had got into the Church; and hence it had come to pass, that, looking at its history from first to last, we could not possibly draw the line between good and evil there, and say either that every thing was to be defended, or certain things to be condemned. I expressed the difficulty, which I supposed to be inherent in the Church, in the following words. I said, '*Priestcraft has ever been considered the badge*, and its imputation is a kind of Note of the Church: and *in part indeed truly*, because the presence of powerful enemies, and the sense of their own weakness, *has sometimes tempted Christians to the abuse, instead of the use of Christian wisdom, to be wise without being harmless*; but partly, nay, for the most part, not truly, but slanderously, and merely because the world called their wisdom craft, when it was found to be a match for its own numbers and power.'

Such is the substance of the Sermon: and as to the main drift of it, it was this; that I was, there and elsewhere, scrutinizing the course of the Church as a whole, as if philosophically, as an historical phenomenon, and observing the laws on which it was conducted. Hence the Sermon, or Essay as it more truly is, is written in a dry and unimpassioned way: it shows as little of human warmth of feeling as a Sermon of Bishop Butler's. Yet, under that calm exterior there was a deep and keen sensitiveness, as I shall now proceed to show.

3. If I mistake not, it was written with a secret thought about myself. Every one preaches according to his frame of mind, at the time of preaching. One heaviness especially oppressed me at that season, which this Writer, twenty years afterwards, has set himself with a good will to renew: it arose from the sense of the base calumnies which were heaped upon me on all sides. It is worth observing that this Sermon is exactly contemporaneous with the report spread by a Bishop (*vid. supr.* p. 168), that I had advised a clergyman converted to Catholicism to retain his Living. This report was in circulation in February 1843, and my Sermon was preached on the 19th. In the trouble of mind into which I was thrown by such calumnies as this, I gained, while I reviewed the history of the Church, at once an argument and a consolation. My argument was this: if I, who knew my own innocence, was so blackened by party prejudice, perhaps those high rulers and those servants of the Church, in the many ages which intervened between the early Nicene times and the present,

who were laden with such grievous accusations, were innocent also; and this reflection served to make me tender towards those great names of the past, to whom weaknesses or crimes were imputed, and reconciled me to difficulties in ecclesiastical proceedings, which there were no means now of properly explaining. And the sympathy thus excited for them, re-acted on myself, and I found comfort in being able to put myself under the shadow of those who had suffered as I was suffering, and who seemed to promise me their recompense, since I had a fellowship in their trial. In a letter to my Bishop at the time of Tract 90, part of which I have quoted, I said that I had ever tried to 'keep innocency;' and now two years had passed since then, and men were louder and louder in heaping on me the very charges, which this Writer repeats out of my Sermon, of 'fraud and cunning,' 'craftiness and deceitfulness,' 'double-dealing,' 'priest-craft,' of being 'mysterious, dark, subtle, designing,' when I was all the time conscious to myself, in my degree, and after my measure, of 'sobriety, self-restraint, and control of word and feeling.' I had had experience how my past success had been imputed to 'secret management;' and how, when I had shown surprise at that success, that surprise again was imputed to 'deceit;' and how my honest heartfelt submission to authority had been called, as it was called in a Bishop's charge abroad, 'mystic humility;' and how my silence was called an 'hypocrisy;' and my faithfulness to my clerical engagements a secret correspondence with the enemy. And I found a way of destroying my sensitiveness about these things which jarred upon my sense of justice, and otherwise would have been too much for me, by the contemplation of a large law of the Divine Dispensation, and felt myself more and more able to bear in my own person a present trial, of which in my past writings I had expressed an anticipation.

For thus feeling and thus speaking this Writer compares me to 'Mawworm.' 'I found him telling Christians,' he says, 'that they will always seem "artificial," and "wanting in openness and manliness;" that they will always be "a mystery" to the world; and that the world will always think them rogues; and bidding them glory in what the world (that is, the rest of their fellow-countrymen) disown, and say with Mawworm, "I like to be despised." Now how was I to know that the preacher ... was utterly blind to the broad meaning and the plain practical result of a Sermon like this delivered before fanatic and hot-headed young men, who hung upon his every word?' – Fanatic and hot-headed young men, who hung on my every word! If he had undertaken to write a history, and not a romance, he would have easily found out, as I have said above, that from 1841 I had severed myself from the younger generation of Oxford, that Dr. Pusey and I had then closed our theological meetings at his house, that I had brought my own weekly evening parties to an end, that I preached only by fits and starts at St. Mary's, so that the attendance of young men was broken up, that in those very weeks from Christmas till over Easter, during which this Sermon was preached, I was but five times in the pulpit there. He would have found, that it was written at a time when I was shunned rather than sought, when I had great sacrifices in anticipation, when I was thinking much of myself; that I was ruthlessly tearing myself away from my own followers, and that, in the musings of that Sermon, I was at the very utmost only delivering a testimony in my behalf for time to come, not sowing my rhetoric broadcast for the chance of present sympathy.

Again, he says: 'I found him actually using of such [prelates], (and, as I thought, of himself and his party likewise,) the words "They yield outwardly; to assent inwardly were to betray the faith. Yet they are called deceitful and double-dealing, because they do as much as they can, not more than they may"'. This too is a proof of my duplicity! Let this writer, in his dealings with some one else, go just a little further than he has gone with me; and let him get into a court of law for libel; and let him be convicted; and let him still fancy that his libel, though a libel, was true, and let us then see whether he will not in such a case 'yield outwardly,' without assenting internally; and then again whether we should please him, if we called him 'deceitful and double-dealing,' because 'he did as much as he could, not more than he ought to do.' But Tract 90 will supply a real illustration of what I meant. I yielded to the Bishops in outward act, viz. in not defending the Tract, and in closing the Series; but, not only did I not assent inwardly to any condemnation of it, but I opposed myself to the proposition of a condemnation on the part of authority. Yet I was then by the public called 'deceitful and double-dealing,' as this Writer calls me now, 'because I did as much as I felt I could do, and not more than I felt I could honestly do.' Many were the publications of the day and the private letters, which accused me of shuffling, because I closed the Series of Tracts, yet kept the Tracts on sale, as if I ought to comply not only with what my Bishop asked, but with what he did not ask, and perhaps did not wish. However, such teaching, according to this Writer, was likely to make young men 'suspect, that truth was not a virtue for its own sake, but only for the sake of the spread of "Catholic opinions," and the "salvation of their own souls;" and that cunning was the weapon which heaven had allowed to them to defend themselves against the persecuting Protestant public.' – p. 16.

And now I draw attention to a further point. He says, 'How was I to know that the preacher ... did not foresee, that [fanatic and hot-headed young men] would think that they obeyed him, by becoming affected, artificial, sly, shifty, ready for concealments and *equivocations*?' 'How should he know!' What! I suppose that we are to think every man a knave till he is proved not to be such. Know! had he no friend to tell him whether I was 'affected' or 'artificial' myself? Could he not have done better than impute *equivocations* to me, at a time when I was in no sense answerable for the *amphibologia* of the Roman casuists? Had he a single fact which belongs to me personally or by profession to couple my name with equivocation in 1843? 'How should he know' that I was not sly, smooth, artificial, non-natural! he should know by that common manly frankness, by which we put confidence in others, till they are proved to have forfeited it; he should know it by my own words in that very Sermon, in which I say it is best to be natural, and that reserve is at best but an unpleasant necessity. For I say there expressly: –

'I do not deny that there is something very engaging in a frank and unpretending manner; some persons have it more than others; in *some persons it is a great grace*. But it must be recollected that I am speaking of *times of persecution and oppression* to Christians, such as the text foretells; and then surely frankness will become nothing else than indignation at the oppressor, and vehement speech, if it is permitted. Accordingly, as persons have deep feelings, so they will find the necessity of self-control, lest they should say what they ought not.'

He sums up thus: –

'If [Dr. Newman] would . . . persist (as in this Sermon) in dealing with matters dark, offensive, doubtful, sometimes actually forbidden, at least according to the notions of the great majority of English Churchmen; if he would always do so in a tentative, paltering way, seldom or never letting the world know how much he believed, how far he intended to go; if, in a word, his method of teaching was a suspicious one, what wonder if the minds of men were filled with suspicions of him?' – p. 17.

Now, in the course of my Narrative, I have frankly admitted that I was tentative in such of my works as fairly allowed of the introduction into them of religious inquiry; but he is speaking of my *Sermons*; where, then, is his proof that in my *Sermons* I dealt in matters dark, offensive, doubtful, actually forbidden? He must show that I was tentative in my *Sermons*; and he has the range of eight volumes to gather evidence in. As to the ninth, my *University Sermons*, of course I was tentative in them; but not because 'I would seldom or never let the world know how much I believed, or how far I intended to go;' but because *University Sermons* are commonly, and allowably, of the nature of disquisitions, as preached before a learned body; and because in deep subjects, which had not been fully investigated, I said as much as I believed, and about as far as I saw I could go; and a man cannot do more; and I account no man to be a philosopher who attempts to do more.

Note D. On Page 193

SERIES OF SAINTS' LIVES OF 1843–4

I have here an opportunity of preserving, what otherwise would be lost, the Catalogue of English Saints which I formed, as preparatory to the Series of their Lives which was begun in the above years. It is but a first Essay, and has many obvious imperfections; but it may be useful to others as a step towards a complete hagiography for England. For instance St. Osberga is omitted; I suppose because it was not easy to learn any thing about her. Boniface of Canterbury is inserted, though passed over by the Bollandists on the ground of the absence of proof of a *cultus* having been paid to him. The Saints of Cornwall were too numerous to be attempted. Among the men of note, not Saints, King Edward II. is included from piety towards the founder of Oriel College. With these admissions I present my Paper to the reader.

Preparing for Publication, in Periodical Numbers, in small 8vo, The Lives of the English Saints, Edited by the Rev. John Henry Newman, B.D., Fellow of Oriel College.

It is the compensation of the disorders and perplexities of these latter times of the Church that we have the history of the foregoing. We indeed of this day have been reserved to witness a disorganization of the City of God, which it never entered into the minds of the early believers to imagine: but we are witnesses also of its triumphs and of its luminaries through those many ages which have brought about the misfortunes which at present overshadow it. If they were blessed who lived in primitive times, and saw the fresh traces of their Lord, and heard the echoes of Apostolic voices, blessed too are we whose special portion it is to see that same Lord revealed in His Saints. The wonders of His grace in the soul of man, its creative power, its inexhaustible resources, its manifold operation, all this we know, as they knew it not. They never heard the names of St. Gregory, St. Bernard, St. Francis, and St. Louis. In fixing our thoughts then, as in an undertaking like the present, on the History of the Saints, we are but availing ourselves of that solace and recompense of our peculiar trials which has been provided for our need by our Gracious Master.

And there are special reasons at this time for recurring to the Saints of our own dear and glorious, most favoured, yet most erring and most unfortunate England. Such a recurrence may serve to make us love our country better, and on truer grounds, than heretofore; to teach us to invest her territory, her cities and villages, her hills and springs, with sacred associations; to give us an insight into her present historical position in the course of the

Divine Dispensation; to instruct us in the capabilities of the English character; and to open upon us the duties and the hopes to which that Church is heir, which was in former times the Mother of St. Boniface and St. Ethelreda.

Even a selection or specimens of the Hagiology of our country may suffice for some of these high purposes; and in so wide and rich a field of research it is almost presumptuous in one undertaking to aim at more than such a partial exhibition. The list that follows, though by no means so large as might have been drawn up, exceeds the limits which the Editor proposes to his hopes, if not to his wishes; but, whether it is allowed him to accomplish a larger or smaller portion of it, it will be his aim to complete such subjects or periods as he begins before bringing it to a close. It is hardly necessary to observe that any list that is producible in this stage of the undertaking can but approximate to correctness and completeness in matters of detail, and even in the names which are selected to compose it.

He has considered himself at liberty to include in the Series such saints as have been born in England, though they have lived and laboured out of it; and such, again, as have been in any sufficient way connected with our country, though born out of it; for instance, Missionaries or Preachers in it, or spiritual or temporal rulers, or founders of religious institutions or houses.

He has also included in the Series a few eminent or holy persons, who, though not in the Sacred Catalogue, are recommended to our religious memory by their fame, learning, or the benefits they have conferred on posterity. These have been distinguished from the Saints by printing their names in italics.

It is proposed to page all the longer Lives separately; the shorter will be thrown together in one. They will be published in monthly issues of not more than 128 pages each; and no regularity, whether of date or of subject, will be observed in the order of publication. But they will be so numbered as to admit ultimately of a general chronological arrangement.

The separate writers are distinguished by letters subjoined to each Life, and it should be added, to prevent misapprehension, that, since under the present circumstances of our Church, they are necessarily of various, though not divergent, doctrinal opinions, no one is answerable for any composition but his own. At the same time, the work professing an historical and ethical character, questions of theology will be, as far as possible, thrown into the back ground.

J. H. N.

Littlemore, Sept. 9, 1843.

Calendar of English Saints

JANUARY

1	Elvan, B. and Medwyne, C.	27	Bathildis, Queen.
2	Martyrs of Lichfield.	28	
3	Melorus, M.	29	Gildas, A.
4		30	
5	Edward, K. C.	31	Adamnan, Mo. Serapion,
6	Peter, A.		M.
7	Cedd, B.		
8	Pega, V. Wulsin, B.		
9	Adrian, A. Bertwald, Archb.		

FEBRUARY

10	Sethrida, V.	1	
11	Egwin, B.	2	Laurence, Archb.
12	Benedict Biscop, A. Aelred, A.	3	Wereburga, V.
13	Kentigern, B.	4	Gilbert, A. Liephard, B. M.
14	Beuno, A.	5	
15	Ceolulph, K. Mo.	6	Ina, K. Mo.
16	Henry, Hermit. Fursey, A.	7	Augulus, B. M. Richard, K.
17	Mildwida, V.	8	Elfleda, A. Cuthman, C.
18	Ulfrid or Wolfrid, M.	9	Theliau, B.
19	Wulstan, B. Henry, B.	10	Trumwin, B.
20		11	
21		12	Ethelwold, B. of Lindisfarne. Cedmon, Mo.
22	Brithwold, B.		
23	Boisil, A.		
24	Cadoc, A.	13	Ermenilda, Q. A.
25		14	
26	Theoritgida, V.	15	Sigefride, B.

16	Finan, B.		16	
17			17	Withburga, V.
18			18	Edward, K. M.
19			19	Alcmund, M.
20	Ulric, H.		20	Cuthbert, B. Herbert, B.
21			21	
22			22	
23	Milburga, V.		23	Aedelwald, H.
24	Luidhard, B. Ethelbert of Kent, K.		24	Hildelitha, A.
25	Walburga, V. A.		25	Alfwold of Sherborne, B. and William, M.
26			26	
27	Alnoth, H. M.		27	
28	Oswald, B.		28	
29			29	Gundleus, H.
			30	Merwenna, A.
			31	

MARCH

1	David Archb. Swibert, B.		APRIL	
2	Chad, B. Willeik, C. Joavan, B.		1	
3	Winwaloe, A.		2	
4	Owin, Mo.		3	Richard, B.
5			4	
6	Kineburga, &c., and Tibba, VV. Balther, C. and Bilfrid, H.		5	
			6	
			7	
7	Easterwin, A. William, Friar.		8	
8	Felix, B.		9	Frithstan, B.
9	Bosa, B.		10	
10			11	Guthlake, H.
11			12	
12	Elphege, B. Paul de Leon, B.C.		13	Caradoc, H.
			14	*Richard of Bury, B.*
			15	Paternus, B.
13			16	
14	Robert, H.		17	Stephen, A.
15	Eadgith, A.		18	

19	Elphege, Archb.	20	Ethelbert, K. M.
20	Adelhare, M. Cedwalla, K.	21	Godric, H.
21	Anselm, Archb. Doctor.	22	Winewald, A. Berethun, A.
22			*Henry, K.*
23	George, M.	23	
24	Mellitus, Archb. Wilfrid,	24	Ethelburga, Q.
	Archb. Egbert, C.	25	Aldhelm, B.
25		26	Augustine, Archb.
26		27	Bede, D. Mo.
27		28	*Lanfranc, Archb.*
28		29	
29	Wilfrid II. Archb.	30	Walston, C.
30	Erconwald, B. Suibert, B.	31	Jurmin, C.
	Maud, Q.		

MAY		JUNE	
1	Asaph, B. Ultan, A. Brioc, B.C.	1	Wistan, K. M.
2	Germanus, M.	2	
3		3	
4		4	Petroc, A.
5	Ethelred, K. Mo.	5	Boniface, Archb. M.
6	Eadbert, A.	6	Gudwall, B.
7	John, Archb. of Beverley.	7	Robert, A.
8		8	William, Archb.
9		9	
10		10	Ivo, B. and Ithamar, B.
11	Fremund, M.	11	
12		12	Eskill, B.M.
13		13	
14		14	Elerius, A.
15		15	Edburga, V.
16	Simon Stock, H.	16	
17		17	Botulph, A. John, Fr.
18	Elgiva, Q.	18	
19	Dunstan, Archb. B. *Alcuin, A.*	19	
		20	Idaberga, V.

| 22 | Alban, and Amphibalus, MM. | 18 | Edburga and Edgitha of Aylesbury, VV. Frederic, B. M. |

22 Alban, and Amphibalus, MM.
23 Ethelreda, V. A.
24 Bartholomew, H.
25 Adelbert, C.
26
27 John, C. of Moutier.
28
29 *Margaret, Countess of Richmond.*
30

JULY

1 Julius, Aaron, MM. Rumold, B. Leonorus, B.
2 Oudoceus, B. Swithun, B.
3 Gunthiern, A.
4 Odo, Archb.
5 Modwenna, V. A.
6 Sexburga, A.
7 Edelburga, V. A. Hedda, B. Willibald, B. Ercongota, V.
8 Grimbald, and Edgar, K.
9 *Stephen Langton, Archb.*
10
11
12
13 Mildreda, V. A.
14 Marchelm, C. Boniface, Archb.
15 Deusdedit, Archb. Plech elm, B. David, A. and Editha of Tamworth, Q. V.
16 Helier, H. M.
17 Kenelm, K. M.

18 Edburga and Edgitha of Aylesbury, VV. Frederic, B. M.
19
20
21
22
23
24 Wulfud and Ruffin, MM. Lewinna, V. M.
25
26
27 Hugh, M.
28 Sampson, B.
29 Lupus, B.
30 Tatwin, Archb. and Ermenigitha, V.
·31 Germanus, B. and Neot, H.

AUGUST

1 Ethelwold, B. of Winton.
2 Etheldritha, V.
3 Walthen, A.
4
5 Oswald, K. M. Thomas, Mo. M. of Dover.
6
7
8 Colman, B.
9
10
11 *William of Waynfleet, B.*
12
13 Wigbert, A. Walter, A.
14 Werenfrid, C.
15

16		16	Ninian, B. Edith, daughter of Edgar, V.
17			
18	Helen, Empress.	17	Socrates and Stephen, MM.
19		18	
20	Oswin, K. M.	19	Theodore, Archb.
21	Richard, B. of Andria.	20	
22	Sigfrid, A.	21	Hereswide, Q. *Edward II. K.*
23	Ebba, V.A.		
24		22	
25	Ebba, V. A. M.	23	
26	Bregwin, Archb. *Bradwardine, Archb.*	24	
		25	Ceolfrid, A.
27	Sturmius, A.	26	
28		27	*William of Wykeham, B.*
29	Sebbus, K.	28	Lioba, V. A.
30		29	*B. Richard of Hampole, H.*
31	Eanswida, V. A. Aidan, A. B. Cuthburga, Q. V.	30	Honorius, Archb.

OCTOBER

		1	Roger, B.
	SEPTEMBER	2	Thomas of Hereford, B.
1		3	Ewalds (two) MM.
2	William, B. of Roschid. William, Fr.	4	
		5	*Walter Stapleton, B.*
3		6	Ywy, C.
4		7	Ositha, Q. V. M.
5		8	Ceneu, V.
6	Bega, A.	9	Lina, V. and *Robert Grostete, B.*
7	Alcmund, A. Tilhbert, A.		
8		10	Paulinus, Archb. John, C. of Bridlington.
9	Bertelin, H. Wulfhilda or Vulfridis, A.	11	Ediburga, V. A.
10	Otger, C.	12	Edwin, K.
11	*Robert Kilwardby, Archb.*	13	
12		14	Burchard, B.
13		15	Tecla, V. A.
14	*Richard Fox, B.*	16	Lullus, Archb.
15			

17 Ethelred, Ethelbright,
       MM.
18 *Walter de Merton, B.*
19 Frideswide, V. and
       Ethbin, A.
20
21 Ursula, V. M.
22 Mello, B. C.
23
24 Magloire, B.
25 *John of Salisbury, B.*
26 Eata, B.
27 Witta, B.
28 *B. Alfred.*
29 Sigebert, K. Elfreda, A.
30
31 Foillan, B. M.

NOVEMBER

1
2
3 Wenefred, V. M. Rumwald,
       C.
4 Brinstan, B. Clarus, M.
5 Cungar, H.
6 Iltut, A. and Winoc, A.
7 Willebrord, B.
8 Willehad, B. Tyssilio, B.
9
10 Justus, Archb.
11
12 Lebwin, C.
13 Eadburga of Menstrey, A.
14 Dubricius, B. C.
15 Malo, B.
16 Edmund, B.
17 Hilda, A. Hugh, B.

18
19 Ermenburga, Q.
20 Edmund, K. M. Humbert,
       B. M. Acca, B.
21
22 Paulinus, A.
23 Daniel, B. C.
24
25
26
27
28 Edwold, M.
29
30

DECEMBER

1
2 Weede, V.
3 Birinus, B. Lucius, K. and
       Sola, H.
4 Osmund, B.
5 Christina, V.
6
7
8 *John Peckham, Archb.*
9
10
11 Elfleda, A.
12 Corentin, B. C.
13 Ethelburga, Q. wife of
       Edwin.
14
15
16
17
18 Winebald, A.
19

20		26	Tathai, C.
21	Eadburga, V. A.	27	Gerald, A. B.
22		28	
23		29	Thomas, Archb. M.
24		30	
25		31	

N.B. *St. William, Austin-Friar, Ingulphus*, and *Peter of Blois* have not been introduced into the above Calendar, their days of death or festival not being as yet ascertained.

Chronological Arrangement

SECOND CENTURY

182	Dec. 3.	Lucius, K. of the British.
	Jan. 1.	Elvan, B. and Medwyne, C. envoys from St. Lucius to Rome.

FOURTH CENTURY

300	Oct. 22.	Mello, B.C. of Rouen.
303	Apr. 23.	George, M. under Dioclesian. Patron of England.
—	June 22.	Alban and Amphibalus, MM.
—	July 1.	Julius and Aaron, MM. of Caerleon.
304	Jan. 2.	Martyrs of Lichfield.
—	Feb. 7.	Augulus, B.M. of London.
328	Aug. 18.	Helen, Empress, mother of Constantine.
388	Sept. 17.	Socrates and Stephen, MM. perhaps in Wales.
411	Jan. 3.	Melorus, M. in Cornwall.

FIFTH CENTURY

432	Sept. 16.	Ninian, B. Apostle of the Southern Picts.
429	July 31.	Germanus, B.C. of Auxerre.
	July 29.	Lupus, B.C. of Troyes.
502	May 1.	Brioc, B.C., disciple of St. Germanus.
490	Oct. 8.	Ceneu, or Keyna, V., sister-in-law of Gundleus.
492	Mar. 29.	Gundleus, Hermit, in Wales.
	July 3.	Gunthiern, A., in Brittany.
453	Oct. 21.	Ursula, V.M. near Cologne.
bef. 500	Dec. 12.	Corentin, B.C. of Quimper.

FIFTH AND SIXTH CENTURIES

Welsh Schools

444–522	Nov. 14.	Dubricius, B.C., first Bishop of Llandaff.
520	Nov. 22.	Paulinus, A. of Whitland, tutor of St. David and St. Theliau.
445–544	Mar. 1.	David, Archb. of Menevia, afterwards called from him.
abt. 500	Dec. 26.	Tathai, C., master of St. Cadoc.
480	Jan. 24.	Cadoc, A., son of St. Gundleus, and nephew of St. Keyna.
abt. 513	Nov. 6.	Iltut, A., converted by St. Cadoc.
545	Nov. 23.	Daniel, B.C., first Bishop of Bangor.
aft. 559	Apr. 18.	Paternus, B.A., pupil of St. Iltut.
573	Mar. 12.	Paul, B.C., of Leon, pupil of St. Iltut.
	Mar. 2.	Ioavan, B., pupil of St. Paul.
599	July 28.	Sampson, B., pupil of St. Iltut, cousin of St. Paul de Leon.
565	Nov. 15.	Malo, B., cousin of St. Sampson.
575	Oct. 24.	Magloire, B., cousin of St. Malo.
583	Jan. 29.	Gildas, A., pupil of St. Iltut.
	July 1.	Leonorus, B., pupil of St. Iltut.
604	Feb. 9.	Theliau, B. of Llandaff, pupil of St. Dubricius.
560	July 2.	Oudoceus, B., nephew to St. Theliau.
500–580	Oct. 19.	Ethbin, A., pupil of St. Sampson.
516–601	Jan. 13.	Kentigern, B. of Glasgow, founder of Monastery of Elwy.

SIXTH CENTURY

529	Mar. 3.	Winwaloe, A., in Brittany.
564	June 4.	Petroc., A., in Cornwall.
	July 16.	Helier, Hermit, M., in Jersey.
	June 27.	John, C. of Moutier, in Tours.
590	May 1.	Asaph, B. of Elwy, afterwards called after him.
abt. 600	June 6.	Gudwall, B. of Aleth in Brittany.
	Nov. 8.	Tyssilio, B. of St. Asaph.

SEVENTH CENTURY

Part I

600	June 10.	Ivo, or Ivia, B. from Persia.
596	Feb. 24.	Luidhard, B. of Senlis, in France.
616	Feb. 24.	Ethelbert, K. of Kent.
608	May 26.	Augustine, Archb. of Canterbury, Apostle of England.

624	Apr. 24.	Mellitus, Archb. of Canterbury,	
619	Feb. 2.	Laurence, Archb. of Canterbury,	Companions
608	Jan. 6.	Peter, A. at Canterbury,	of St.
627	Nov. 10.	Justus, Archb. of Canterbury,	Augustine.
653	Sept. 30.	Honorius, Archb. of Canterbury,	
662	July 15.	Deusdedit, Archb. of Canterbury.	

SEVENTH CENTURY

Part II

642	Oct. 29.	Sigebert, K. of the East Angles.
646	Mar. 8.	Felix, B. of Dunwich, Apostle of the East Angles.
650	Jan. 16.	Fursey, A., preacher among the East Angles.
680	May 1.	Ultan, A., brother of St. Fursey.
655	Oct. 31.	Foillan, B. M., brother of St. Fursey, preacher in the Netherlands.
680	June 17.	Botulph, A., in Lincolnshire or Sussex.
671	June 10.	Ithamar, B. of Dorchester.
650	Dec. 3.	Birinus, B. of Dorchester.
705	July 7.	Hedda, B. of Dorchester.
717	Jan. 11.	Egwin, B. of Worcester.

SEVENTH CENTURY

Part III

690	Sept. 19.	Theodore, Archb. of Canterbury.
709	Jan. 9.	Adrian, A. in Canterbury.
709	May 25.	Aldhelm, B. of Sherborne, pupil of St. Adrian.

SEVENTH CENTURY

Part IV

630	Nov. 3.	Winefred, V. M. in Wales.
642	Feb. 4	Liephard, M.B., slain near Cambray.
660	Jan 14.	Beuno, A., kinsman of St. Cadocus and St. Kentigern.
673	Oct. 7.	Osgitha, Q.V.M., in East Anglia during a Danish inroad.
630	June 14.	Elerius, A. in Wales.
680	Jan. 27.	Bathildis, Q., wife of Clovis II., king of France.
687	July 24.	Lewinna, V.M., put to death by the Saxons.
700	July 18.	Edberga and Edgitha, VV. of Aylesbury.

SEVENTH CENTURY

Part V

644	Oct. 10.	Paulinus, Archb. of York, companion of St. Augustine.
633	Oct. 12.	Edwin, K. of Northumberland.
	Dec. 13.	Ethelburga, Q., wife to St. Edwin.
642	Aug. 5.	Oswald, K.M., St. Edwin's nephew.
651	Aug. 20.	Oswin, K.M., cousin to St. Oswald.
683	Aug. 23.	Ebba, V.A. of Coldingham, half-sister to St. Oswin.
689	Jan. 31.	Adamnan, Mo. of Coldingham.

SEVENTH CENTURY

Part VI – Whitby

650	Sept. 6.	Bega, V.A., foundress of St. Bee's, called after her.
681	Nov. 17.	Hilda, A. of Whitby, daughter of St. Edwin's nephew.
716	Dec. 11.	Elfleda, A. of Whitby, daughter of St. Oswin.
680	Feb. 12.	Cedmon. Mo. of Whitby.

SEVENTH AND EIGHTH CENTURIES

Part I

	Sept. 21.	Hereswida, Q., sister of Hilda, wife of Annas, who succeeded Egric, Sigebert's cousin.
654	Jan. 10.	Sethrida, V.A. of Faremoutier, St. Hereswida's daughter by a former marriage.
693	Apr. 30.	Erconwald, A.B., son of Annas and St. Hereswida, Bishop of London, Abbot of Chertsey, founder of Barking.
677	Aug. 29.	Sebbus, K., converted by St. Erconwald.
	May 31.	Jurmin, C., son of Annas and St. Hereswida.
650	July 7.	Edelburga, V.A. of Faremoutier, natural daughter of Annas.
679	June 23.	Ethelreda, Etheldreda, Etheltrudis, or Awdry, V.A., daughter of Annas and St. Hereswida.
	Mar. 17.	Withburga, V., daughter of Annas and St. Hereswida.
699	July 6.	Sexburga, A., daughter of Annas and St. Hereswida.
660	July 7.	Ercongota, or Ertongata, V.A. of Faremoutier, daughter of St. Sexburga.
699	Feb. 13.	Ermenilda, Q.A., daughter of St. Sexburga, wife of Wulfere.
aft. 675	Feb. 3.	Wereburga, V., daughter of St. Ermenilda and Wulfere, patron of Chester.
abt. 680	Feb. 27	Alnoth, H.M., bailiff to St. Wereburga.

640	Aug. 31.	Eanswida, V.A., sister-in-law of St. Sexburga, grand-daughter to St. Ethelbert.
668	Oct. 17	Ethelred and Ethelbright, MM., nephews of St. Eanswida.
	July 30.	Ermenigitha, V., niece of St. Eanswida.
676	Oct. 11.	Edilberga, V.A. of Barking, daughter of Annas and St. Hereswida.
678	Jan. 26.	Theoritgida, V., nun of Barking
aft. 713	Aug. 31.	Cuthberga, Q.V., of Barking, sister of St. Ina.
700	Mar. 24.	Hildelitha, A. of Barking.
728	Feb. 6.	Ina, K. Mo. of the West Saxons.
740	May 24.	Ethelburga, Q., wife of St. Ina, nun at Barking.

SEVENTH AND EIGHTH CENTURIES

Part II

652	June 20.	Idaburga, V.
696	Mar. 6.	Kineburga, Q.A.
701	——	Kinneswitha, V. } Daughters of King Penda.
	——	Chidestre, V.
692	Dec. 2.	Weeda, V.A.
696	Mar. 6.	Tibba, V., their kinswoman.
	Nov. 3.	Rumwald, C., grandson of Penda.
680	Nov. 19.	Ermenburga, Q., mother to the three following.
	Feb. 23.	Milburga, V.A. of Wenlock, } Grand-daughters of
	July 13.	Mildreda, V. A. of Menstrey, Penda.
676	Jan 17.	Milwida, or Milgitha, V.
750	Nov. 13.	Eadburga, A. of Menstrey.

SEVENTH AND EIGHTH CENTURIES

Part III

670	July 24.	Wulfad and Ruffin, MM., sons of Wulfere, Penda's son, and of St. Erminilda.
672	Mar. 2.	Chad, B. of Lichfield.
664	Jan. 7.	Cedd, B. of London.
688	Mar. 4.	Owin, Mo. of Lichfield.
689	Apr. 20	Cedwalla, K. of West Saxons.
690–725	Nov. 5.	Cungar, H., in Somersetshire.
700	Feb. 10.	Trumwin, B. of the Picts.
705	Mar. 9.	Bosa, Archb. of York.
709	Apr. 24.	Wilfrid, Archb. of York.
721	May 7.	John of Beverley, Archb. of York.
743	Apr. 29	Wilfrid II., Archb. of York
733	May 22.	Berethun, A. of Deirwood, disciple of St. John of Beverley.
751	May 22.	Winewald, A. of Deirwood.

SEVENTH AND EIGHTH CENTURIES

Part IV – Missions

729	Apr. 24.	Egbert, C., master to Willebrord.
693	Oct. 3.	Ewalds (two), MM. in Westphalia.
690–736	Nov. 7.	Willebrord, B. of Utrecht, Apostle of Friesland.
717	Mar. 1.	Swibert, B., Apostle of Westphalia.
727	Mar. 2	Willeik, C., successor to St. Swibert.
705	June 25.	Adelbert, C., grandson of St. Oswald, preacher in Holland.
705	Aug. 14.	Werenfrid, C., preacher in Friesland.
720	June 21.	Engelmund, A., preacher in Holland.
730	Sept. 10.	Otger, C. in Low Countries.
732	July 15.	Plechelm, B., preacher in Guelderland.
750	May 2.	Germanus, B.M. in the Netherlands.
760	Nov. 12.	Lebwin, C. in Overyssel, in Holland.
760	July 14.	Marchelm, C., companion of St. Lebwin, in Holland.
697–755	June 5.	Boniface, Archb., M. of Mentz. Apostle of Germany.
712	Feb. 7.	Richard, K. of the West Saxons.

704–790	July 7.	Willibald, B. of Aichstadt, in Franconia,	⎫
730–760	Dec. 18.	Winebald, A. of Heidenheim, in Suabia,	Children of St. Richard.
779	Feb. 25.	Walburga, V. A. of Heidenheim,	⎭
aft. 755	Sept. 28.	Lioba, V.A. of Bischorsheim,	
750	Oct. 15.	Tecla, V.A. of Kitzingen, in Franconia,	⎫
788	Oct. 16.	Lullus, Archb. of Mentz,	
abt. 747	Aug. 13.	Wigbert, A. of Fritzlar and Ortdorf, in Germany,	Companions of St. Boniface.
755	Apr. 20.	Adelhare, B.M. of Erford, in Franconia,	
780	Aug. 27.	Sturmius, A. of Fulda,	
786	Oct. 27.	Witta, or Albuinus, B. of Buraberg, in Germany,	
791	Nov. 8.	Willehad, B. of Bremen, and Apostle of Saxony,	
791	Oct. 14.	Burchard, B. of Wurtzburg, in Franconia,	
790	Dec. 3	Sola, H., near Aichstadt, in Franconia,	⎭
775	July 1.	Rumold, B., Patron of Mechlin.	
807	Apr. 30.	Suibert, B. of Verden in Westphalia.	

SEVENTH AND EIGHTH CENTURIES

Part V – Lindisfarne and Hexham

670	Jan. 23.	Boisil, A. of Melros, in Scotland.
651	Aug. 31.	Aidan, A.B. of Lindisfarne.
664	Feb. 16.	Finan, B. of Lindisfarne.
676	Aug. 8.	Colman, B. of Lindisfarne.
685	Oct. 26.	Eata, B. of Hexham.
687	Mar. 20.	Cuthbert, B. of Lindisfarne.
	Oct. 6.	Ywy, C. disciple of St. Cuthbert.
690	Mar. 20.	Herbert, H. disciple of St. Cuthbert.
698	May 6.	Eadbert, B. of Lindisfarne.
700	Mar. 23.	Aedelwald, H. successor of St. Cuthbert, in his hermitage.
740	Feb. 12.	Ethelwold, B. of Lindisfarne.
740	Nov. 20.	Acca, B. of Hexham.
764	Jan. 15.	Ceolulph, K. Mo. of Lindisfarne.
756	Mar. 6.	Balther, H. at Lindisfarne.
	,,	Bilfrid, H. Goldsmith at Lindisfarne.
781	Sept. 7.	Alchmund, B. of Hexham.
789	Sept. 7.	Tilhbert, B. of Hexham.

SEVENTH AND EIGHTH CENTURIES

Part VI – Wearmouth and Yarrow

703	Jan. 12.	Benedict Biscop, A. of Wearmouth.
685	Mar. 7.	Easterwin, A. of Wearmouth.
689	Aug. 22.	Sigfrid, A. of Wearmouth.
716	Sept. 25.	Ceofrid, A. of Yarrow.
734	May 27.	Bede, Doctor, Mo. of Yarrow.
804	May 19.	B. Alcuin, A. in France.

EIGHTH CENTURY

710	May 5.	Ethelred, K. Mo. King of Mercia, Monk of Bardney.
719	Jan. 8.	Pega, V., sister of St. Guthlake.
714	April 11.	Guthlake, H. of Croyland.
717	Nov. 6.	Winoc, A. in Brittany.
730	Jan. 9.	Bertwald, Archb. of Canterbury.
732	Dec. 27.	Gerald, A.B. in Mayo.
734	July 30.	Tatwin, Archb. of Canterbury.
750	Oct. 19.	Frideswide, V. patron of Oxford.
762	Aug. 26.	Bregwin, Archb. of Canterbury.
700–800	Feb. 8.	Cuthman, C. of Stening in Sussex.
bef. 800	Sept. 9.	Bertelin, H. patron of Stafford.

EIGHTH AND NINTH CENTURIES

793	May 20.	Ethelbert, K.M. of the East Angles.
834	Aug. 2.	Etheldritha, or Alfreda, V., daughter of Offa, king of Mercia, nun at Croyland.
819	July 17.	Kenelm, K.M. of Mercia.
849	June 1.	Wistan, K.M. of Mercia.
838	July 18.	Frederic, Archb. M. of Utrecht.
894	Nov. 4.	Clarus, M. in Normandy.

NINTH CENTURY

Part I – Danish Slaughters, &c.

819	Mar. 19	Alcmund, M., son of Eldred, king of Northumbria, Patron of Derby.
870	Nov. 20.	Edmund, K.M. of the East Angles.
862	May 11.	Fremund, H.M. nobleman of East Anglia.
870	Nov. 20.	Humbert, B.M. of Elmon in East Anglia.
867	Aug. 25.	Ebba, V.A.M. of Coldingham.

NINTH CENTURY

Part II

862	July 2.	Swithun, B. of Winton.
870	July 5.	Modwenna, V.A. of Pollesworth in Warwickshire.
	Oct. 9.	Lina, V. nun at Pollesworth.
871	Mar. 15.	Eadgith, V.A. of Pollesworth, sister of King Ethelwolf.
900	Dec. 21.	Eadburga, V.A. of Winton, daughter of King Ethelwolf.
880	Nov. 28.	Edwold, H., brother of St. Edmund.

NINTH AND TENTH CENTURIES

883	July 31.	Neot, H. in Cornwall.
903	July 8.	Grimbald, A. at Winton.
900	Oct. 28.	B. *Alfred*, K.
929	April 9.	Frithstan, B. of Winton.
934	Nov. 4.	Brinstan, B. of Winton.

TENTH CENTURY

Part I

960	June 15.	Edburga, V., nun at Winton, granddaughter of Alfred.
926	July 15.	Editha, Q.V., nun of Tamworth, sister to Edburga.

921	May 18.	Algyfa, or Elgiva, Q., mother of Edgar.
975	July 8.	Edgar, K.
978	Mar. 18.	Edward, K.M. at Corfe Castle.
984	Sept. 16.	Edith, V., daughter of St. Edgar and St. Wulfhilda.
990	Sept. 9.	Wulfhilda, or Vulfrida, A. of Wilton.
980	Mar. 30.	Merwenna, V.A. of Romsey.
990	Oct. 29.	Elfreda, A. of Romsey.
1016	Dec. 5.	Christina of Romsey, V., sister of St. Margaret of Scotland.

TENTH CENTURY

Part II

961	July 4.	Odo, Archb. of Canterbury, Benedictine Monk.
960–992	Feb. 28.	Oswald, Archb. of York, B. of Worcester, nephew to St. Odo.
951–1012	Mar. 12.	Elphege the Bald, B. of Winton.
988	May 19.	Dunstan, Archb. of Canterbury.
973	Jan. 8.	Wulsin, B. of Sherbourne.
984	Aug. 1.	Ethelwold, B. of Winton.
1015	Jan. 22.	Brithwold, B. of Winton.

TENTH AND ELEVENTH CENTURIES

Missions

950	Feb. 15.	Sigfride, B., apostle of Sweden.
1016	June 12.	Eskill, B.M. in Sweden, kinsman of St. Sigfride.
1028	Jan. 18.	Wolfred, M. in Sweden.
1050	July 15.	David, A., Cluniac in Sweden.

ELEVENTH CENTURY

1012	April 19.	Elphege, M. Archb. of Canterbury.
1016	May 30.	Walston, C. near Norwich.
1053	Mar. 35.	Alfwold, B. of Sherborne.
1067	Sept. 2.	William, B. of Roschid in Denmark.
1066	Jan. 5.	Edward, K. C.
1099	Dec. 4.	Osmund, B. of Salisbury.

ELEVENTH AND TWELFTH CENTURIES

1095	Jan. 19.	Wulstan, B. of Worcester.
1089	May 28.	*Lanfranc, Archb. of Canterbury.*
1109	Apr. 21.	Anselm, Doctor, Archb. of Canterbury.
1170	Dec. 29.	Thomas, Archb. M. of Canterbury.
1200	Nov. 17.	Hugh, B. of Lincoln, Carthusian Monk.

TWELFTH CENTURY

Part I

1109		*Ingulphus, A. of Croyland.*
1117	Apr. 30.	B. *Maud, Q.* Wife of Henry I.
1124	Apr. 13.	Caradoc, H. in South Wales.
1127	Jan. 16.	Henry, H. in Northumberland.
1144	Mar. 25.	William, M. of Norwich.
1151	Jan. 19.	Henry, M.B. of Upsal.
1150	Aug. 13.	Walter, A. of Fontenelle, in France.
1154	June 8.	William, Archb. of York.
1170	May 21.	Godric, H. in Durham.
1180	Oct. 25.	*John of Salisbury, B. of Chartres.*
1182	June 24.	Bartholomew, C., monk at Durham.
1189	Feb. 4.	Gilbert, A. of Sempringham.
1190	Aug. 21.	Richard, B. of Andria.
1200		*Peter de Blois, Archd. of Bath.*

TWELFTH CENTURY

Part II – Cistertian Order

1134	Apr. 17.	Stephen, A. of Citeaux.
1139	June 7.	Robert, A. of Newminster in Northumberland.
1154	Feb. 20.	Ulric, H. in Dorsetshire.
1160	Aug. 3.	Walthen, A. of Melrose.
1166	Jan. 12.	Aelred, A. of Rieval.

THIRTEENTH CENTURY

Part I

1228	July 9.	*Stephen Langton, Archb. of Canterbury.*
1242	Nov. 16.	Edmund, Archb. of Canterbury.
1253	Apr. 3.	Richard, B. of Chichester.
1282	Oct. 2.	Thomas, B. of Hereford.
1294	Dec. 3.	*John Peckham, Archb. of Canterbury.*

THIRTEENTH CENTURY

Part II – Orders of Friars

1217	June 17.	John, Fr., Trinitarian.
1232	Mar. 7.	William, Fr., Franciscan.
1240	Jan. 31.	Serapion, Fr., M. Redemptionist.
1265	May 16.	Simon Stock, H., General of the Carmelites.
1279	Sept. 11.	*Robert Kilwardby, Archb. of Canterbury Fr. Dominican.*

THIRTEENTH CENTURY

Part III

1239	Mar. 14.	Robert H. at Knaresboro'.
1241	Oct. 1.	Roger, B. of London.
1255	July 27.	Hugh, M. of Lincoln.
1295	Aug. 5.	Thomas, Mo., M. of Dover.
1254	Oct. 9.	*Robert Grosseteste, B. of Lincoln.*
1270	July 14.	Boniface, Archb. of Canterbury.
1278	Oct. 18.	*Walter de Merton, B. of Rochester.*

FOURTEENTH CENTURY

1326	Oct. 5.	*Stapleton, B. of Exeter.*
1327	Sept. 21.	*Edward K.*
1349	Sept. 29.	*B. Richard, H. of Hampole.*
1345	Apr. 14.	*Richard of Bury, B. of Lincoln.*
1349	Aug. 26.	*Bradwardine, Archb. of Canterbury, the Doctor Profundus.*
1358	Sept. 2.	William, Fr., Servite.
1379	Oct. 10.	John, C. of Bridlington.
1324–1404	Sept. 27.	*William of Wykeham, B. of Winton.*
1400		William, Fr. Austin.

FIFTEENTH CENTURY

1471	May 22.	*Henry, K. of England.*
1486	Aug. 11.	*William of Wanefleet, B. of Winton.*
1509	June 29.	*Margaret, Countess of Richmond.*
1528	Sept. 14.	*Richard Fox, B. of Winton.*

Note E. On Page 205

THE ANGLICAN CHURCH

I have been bringing out my mind in this Volume on every subject which has come before me; and therefore I am bound to state plainly what I feel and have felt, since I was a Catholic, about the Anglican Church. I said, in a former page, that, on my conversion, I was not conscious of any change in me of thought or feeling, as regards matters of doctrine; this, however, was not the case as regards some matters of fact, and, unwilling as I am to give offence to religious Anglicans, I am bound to confess that I felt a great change in my view of the Church of England. I cannot tell how soon there came on me, – but very soon, – an extreme astonishment that I had ever imagined it to be a portion of the Catholic Church. For the first time, I looked at it from without, and (as I should myself say) saw it as it was. Forthwith I could not get myself to see in it any thing else, than what I had so long fearfully suspected, from as far back as 1836, – a mere national institution. As if my eyes were suddenly opened, so I saw it – spontaneously, apart from any definite act of reason or any argument; and so I have seen it ever since. I suppose, the main cause of this lay in the contrast which was presented to me by the Catholic Church. Then I recognized at once a reality which was quite a new thing with me. Then I was sensible that I was not making for myself a Church by an effort of thought; I needed not to make an act of faith in her; I had not painfully to force myself into a position, but my mind fell back upon itself in relaxation and in peace, and I gazed at her almost passively as a great objective fact. I looked at her; – at her rites, her ceremonial, and her precepts; and I said, 'This *is* a religion;' and then, when I looked back upon the poor Anglican Church, for which I had laboured so hard, and upon all that appertained to it, and thought of our various attempts to dress it up doctrinally and esthetically, it seemed to me to be the veriest of nonentities.

Vanity of vanities, all is vanity! How can I make a record of what passed within me, without seeming to be satirical? But I speak plain, serious words. As people call me credulous for acknowledging Catholic claims, so they call me satirical for disowning Anglican pretensions; to them it *is* credulity, to them it *is* satire; but it is not so in me. What they think exaggeration, I think truth. I am not speaking of the Anglican Church with any disdain, though to them I seem contemptuous. To them of course it is 'Aut Caesar aut nullus,' but not to me. It may be a great creation, though it be not divine, and this is how I judge of it. Men, who abjure the divine right of kings would be very indignant, if on that account they were considered disloyal. And so I recognize in the Anglican Church a time-honoured institution, of noble historical memories, a monument of ancient wisdom, a momentous arm of political strength, a great national organ, a source of vast popular advantage, and, to a certain point, a witness and teacher of religious truth. I do not think that, if what I have written about it since I have been a Catholic, be equitably considered as a whole, I shall be found to have taken any other view than this; but that it is something sacred, that it is an oracle of revealed doctrine, that it can claim a share in St. Ignatius or St. Cyprian, that it can take the rank, contest the teaching, and stop the path of the Church of St. Peter, that it can call itself 'the Bride of the Lamb,' this is the view of it which simply disappeared from my mind on my conversion, and which it would be almost a miracle to reproduce. 'I went by, and lo! it was gone; I sought it, but its place could no where be found;' and nothing can bring it back to me. And, as to its possession of an episcopal succession from the time of the Apostles, well, it may have it, and, if the Holy See ever so decide, I will believe it, as being the decision of a higher judgment than my own; but, for myself, I must have St. Philip's gift, who saw the sacerdotal character on the forehead of a gaily-attired youngster, before I can by my own wit acquiesce in it, for antiquarian arguments are altogether unequal to the urgency of visible facts. Why is it that I must pain dear friends by saying so, and kindle a sort of resentment against me in the kindest of hearts? but I must, though to do it be not only a grief to me, but most impolitic at the moment. Any how, this is my mind; and, if to have it, if to have betrayed it, before now, involuntarily by my words or my deeds, if on a fitting occasion, as now, to have avowed it, if all this be a proof of the justice of the charge brought against me by my accuser of having 'turned round upon my Mother-Church with contumely and slander,' in this sense but in no other sense, do I plead guilty to it without a word in extenuation.

In no other sense surely; the Church of England has been the instrument of Providence in conferring great benefits on me; – had I been born in Dissent, perhaps I should never have been baptized; had I been born an English Presbyterian, perhaps I should never have known our Lord's divinity; had I not come to Oxford, perhaps I never should have heard of the visible Church, or of Tradition, or other Catholic doctrines. And as I have received so much good from the Anglican Establishment itself, can I have the heart or rather the want of charity, considering that it does for so many others, what it has done for me, to wish to see it overthrown? I have no such wish while it is what it is, and while we are so small a body. Not for its own sake, but for the sake of the many congregations to which it ministers, I will do nothing against it. While Catholics are so weak in England, it is doing our work; and, though it does us harm in a measure, at present the balance is in our favour. What our duty would be at another time and in other circumstances, supposing, for instance, the Establishment lost its dogmatic faith, or at least did not preach it, is another matter altogether. In secular history we read of hostile nations having long truces, and renewing them from time to time, and that seems to be the position which the Catholic Church may fairly take up at present in relation to the Anglican Establishment.

Doubtless the National Church has hitherto been a serviceable breakwater against doctrinal errors, more fundamental than its own. How long this will last in the years now before us, it is impossible to say, for the Nation drags down its Church to its own level; but still the National Church has the same sort of influence over the Nation that a periodical has upon the party which it represents, and my own idea of a Catholic's fitting attitude towards the National Church in this its supreme hour, is that of assisting and sustaining it, if it be in our power, in the interest of dogmatic truth. I should wish to avoid every thing (except indeed under the direct call of duty, and this is a material exception,) which went to weaken its hold upon the public mind, or to unsettle its establishment, or to embarrass and lessen its maintenance of those great Christian and Catholic principles and doctrines which it has up to this time successfully preached.

Note F. On Page 239

THE ECONOMY

For the Economy, considered as a rule of practice, I shall refer to what I wrote upon it in 1830–32, in my History of the Arians. I have shown above, pp. 43, 44, that the doctrine in question had in the early Church a large signification, when applied to the divine ordinances: it also had a definite application to the duties of Christians, whether clergy or laity, in preaching, in instructing or catechizing, or in ordinary intercourse with the world around them; and in this aspect I have here to consider it.

As Almighty God did not all at once introduce the Gospel to the world, and thereby gradually prepared men for its profitable reception, so, according to the doctrine of the early Church, it was a duty, for the sake of the heathen among whom they lived, to observe a great reserve and caution in communicating to them the knowledge of 'the whole counsel of God.' This cautious dispensation of the truth, after the manner of a discreet and vigilant steward, is denoted by the word 'economy.' It is a mode of acting which comes under the head of Prudence, one of the four Cardinal Virtues.

The principle of the Economy is this; that out of various courses, in religious conduct or statement, all and each *allowable antecedently and in themselves*, that ought to be taken which is most expedient and most suitable at the time for the object in hand.

Instances of its application and exercise in Scripture are such as the following: – 1. Divine Providence did but gradually impart to the world in general, and to the Jews in particular, the knowledge of His will: – He is said to have 'winked at the times of ignorance among the heathen;' and He suffered in the Jews divorce 'because of the hardness of their hearts.' 2. He has allowed Himself to be represented as having eyes, ears, and hands, as having wrath, jealousy, grief, and repentance. 3. In like manner, our Lord spoke harshly to the Syro-Phoenician woman, whose daughter He was about to heal, and made as if He would go further, when the two disciples had come to their journey's end. 4. Thus too Joseph 'made himself strange to his brethren,' and Elisha kept silence on request of Naaman to bow in the house of Rimmon. 5. Thus St. Paul circumcised Timothy, while he cried out 'Circumcision availeth not.'

It may be said that this principle, true in itself, yet is dangerous, because it admits of an easy abuse, and carries men away into what becomes insincerity and cunning. This is undeniable; to do evil that good may come, to consider that the means, whatever they are, justify the end, to sacrifice truth to expedience, unscrupulousness, recklessness, are grave offences. These are abuses of the Economy. But to call them *economical* is to give a fine name to what occurs every day, independent of any knowledge of the *doctrine* of the Economy. It is the abuse of a rule which nature suggests to every one. Every one looks out for the 'mollia tempora fandi,' and for 'mollia verba' too.

Having thus explained what is meant by the Economy as a rule of social intercourse between men of different religious, or, again, political, or social views, next I will go on to state what I said in the Arians.

I say in that Volume first, that our Lord has given us the *principle* in His own words, — 'Cast not your pearls before swine;' and that He exemplified it in His teaching by parables; that St. Paul expressly distinguishes between the milk which is necessary to one set of men, and the strong meat which is allowed to others, and that, in two Epistles. I say, that the Apostles in the Acts observe the same rule in their speeches, for it is a fact, that they do not preach the high doctrines of Christianity, but only 'Jesus and the Resurrection' or 'repentance and faith.' I also say, that this is the very reason that the Fathers assign for the silence of various writers in the first centuries on the subject of our Lord's divinity. I also speak of the catechetical system practised in the early Church, and the *disciplina arcani* as regards the doctrine of the Holy Trinity, to which Bingham bears witness; also of the defence of this rule by Basil, Cyril of Jerusalem, Chrysostom, and Theodoret.

But next the question may be asked, whether I have said any thing in my Volume *to guard* the doctrine, thus laid down, from the abuse to which it is obviously exposed: and my answer is easy. Of course, had I had any idea that I should have been exposed to such hostile misrepresentations, as it has been my lot to undergo on the subject, I should have made more direct avowals than I have done of my sense of the gravity and the danger of that abuse. Since I could not foresee when I wrote, that I should have been wantonly slandered, I only wonder that I have anticipated the charge as fully as will be seen in the following extracts.

For instance, speaking of the Disciplina Arcani, I say: – (1) 'The elementary information given to the heathen or catechumen was *in no sense undone* by the subsequent secret teaching, which was in fact but the *filling up of a bare but correct outline*,' p. 58, and I contrast this with the conduct of the Manichaeans 'who represented the initiatory discipline as founded on a *fiction* or hypothesis, which was to be forgotten by the learner as he made progress in the *real* doctrine of the Gospel.' (2) As to allegorizing, I say that the Alexandrians erred, whenever and as far as they proceeded 'to *obscure* the primary meaning of Scripture, and to *weaken the force of historical facts* and express declarations,' p. 69. (3) And that they were 'more open to *censure*,' when, on being '*urged by objections* to various passages in the history of the Old Testament, as derogatory to the divine perfections or to the Jewish Saints, they had *recourse to an allegorical explanation by way of answer*,' p. 71. (4) I add, '*It is impossible to defend such a procedure*, which seems to imply a *want of faith* in those who had recourse to it;' for 'God has given us *rules of right and wrong*', *ibid.* (5) Again, I say, – The *abuse of the Economy* in *the hands of unscrupulous reasoners*, is obvious. *Even the honest* controversialist or teacher will find it very difficult to represent, *without misrepresenting*, what it is yet his duty to present to his hearers with caution or reserve. Here the obvious rule to guide our practice is, to be careful ever to maintain *substantial truth* in our use of the economical method,' pp. 79, 80. (6) And so far from concurring at all hazards with Justin, Gregory, or Athanasius, I say, 'It *is plain* [they] *were justified or not* in their Economy, *according* as they did or did not *practically mislead their opponents*', p. 80. (7) I proceed, 'It is so difficult to hit the mark in these perplexing cases, that it is not wonderful, should these or other Fathers have failed at times, and said more or less than was proper,' *ibid*.

The Principle of the Economy is familiarly acted on among us every day. When we would persuade others, we do not begin by treading on their toes. Men would be thought rude who introduced their own religious notions into mixed society, and were devotional in a drawing-room. Have we never thought lawyers tiresome who did *not* observe this polite rule, who came down for the assizes and talked law all through dinner? Does the same argument tell in the House of Commons, on the hustings, and at Exeter Hall? Is an educated gentleman never worsted at an election by the tone and arguments of some clever fellow, who, whatever his shortcomings in other respects, understands the common people?

As to the Catholic Religion in England at the present day, this only will I observe, – that the truest expedience is to answer right out, when you are asked; that the wisest economy is to have no management; that the best prudence is not to be a coward; that the most damaging folly is to be found out shuffling; and that the first of virtues is to 'tell truth, and shame the devil.'

Note G. On Page 247

LYING AND EQUIVOCATION

Almost all authors, Catholic and Protestant, admit, that *when a just cause is present*, there is some kind or other of verbal misleading, which is not sin. Even silence is in certain cases virtually such a misleading, according to the Proverb, 'Silence gives consent.' Again, silence is absolutely forbidden to a Catholic, as a mortal sin, under certain circumstances, e.g. to keep silence, when it is a duty to make a profession of faith.

Another mode of verbal misleading, and the most direct, is actually saying the thing that is not; and it is defended on the principle that such words are not a lie, when there is a 'justa causa,' as killing is not murder in the case of an executioner.

Another ground of certain authors for saying that an untruth is not a lie where there is a just cause, is, that veracity is a kind of justice, and therefore, when we have no duty of justice to tell truth to another, it is no sin not to do so. Hence we may say the thing that is not, to children, to madmen, to men who ask impertinent questions, to those whom we hope to benefit by misleading.

Another ground, taken in defending certain untruths, *ex justâ causâ*, as if not lies, is, that veracity is for the sake of society, and that, if in no case whatever we might lawfully mislead others, we should actually be doing society great harm.

Another mode of verbal misleading is equivocation or a play upon words; and it is defended on the theory that to lie is to use words in a sense which they will not bear. But an equivocator uses them in a received sense, though there is another received sense, and therefore, according to this definition, he does not lie.

Others say that all equivocations are, after all, a kind of lying, – faint lies or awkward lies, but still lies; and some of these disputants infer, that therefore we must not equivocate, and others that equivocation is but a half-measure, and that it is better to say at once that in certain cases untruths are not lies.

Others will try to distinguish between evasions and equivocations; but though there are evasions which are clearly not equivocations, yet it is very difficult scientifically to draw the line between the one and the other.

To these must be added the unscientific way of dealing with lies: – viz. that on a great or cruel occasion a man cannot help telling a lie, and he would not be a man, did he not tell it, but still it is very wrong, and he ought not to do it, and he must trust that the sin will be forgiven him, though he goes about to commit it ever so deliberately, and is sure to commit it again under similar circumstances. It is a necessary frailty, and had better not be thought about before it is incurred, and not thought of again, after it is well over. This view cannot for a moment be defended, but, I suppose, it is very common.

I think the historical course of thought upon the matter has been this: the Greek Fathers thought that, when there was a *justa causa*, an untruth need not be a lie. St. Augustine took another view, though with great misgiving; and, whether he is rightly interpreted or not, is the doctor of the great and common view that all untruths are lies, and that there can be *no* just cause of untruth. In these later times, this doctrine has been found difficult to work, and it has been largely taught that, though all untruths are lies, yet that certain equivocations, when given in a just cause, are not untruths.

Further, there have been and all along through these later ages, other schools, running parallel with the above mentioned, one of which says that equivocations, &c. after all *are* lies, and another which says that there are untruths which are not lies.

And now as to the 'just cause,' which is the condition, *sine quâ non*. The Greek Fathers make it such as these, self-defence, charity, zeal for God's honour, and the like.

St. Augustine seems to deal with the same 'just causes' as the Greek fathers, even though he does not allow of their availableness as depriving untruths, spoken on such occasions, of their sinfulness. He mentions defence of life and of honour, and the safe custody of a secret. Also the great Anglican writers, who have followed the Greek Fathers, in defending untruths when there is the 'just cause,' consider that 'just cause' to be such as the preservation of life and property, defence of law, the good of others. Moreover, their moral rights, e.g. defence against the inquisitive, &c.

St. Alfonso, I consider, would take the same view of the 'justa causa' as the Anglican divines; he speaks of it as 'quicunque finis *honestus*, ad servanda bona spiritui vel corpori utilia;' which is very much the view which they take of it, judging by the instances which they give.

In all cases, however, and as contemplated by all authors, Clement of Alexandria, or Milton, or St. Alfonso, such a causa is, in fact, extreme, rare, great, or at least special. Thus the writer in the *Mélanges Théologiques* (Liège, 1852–3, p. 453) quotes Lessius: 'Si absque justa causa fiat, est abusio orationis contra virtutem veritatis, et civilem consuetudinem, etsi proprie non sit mendacium.' That is, the virtue of truth, and the civil custom, are the *measure* of the just cause. And so Voit, 'If a man has used a reservation (restrictione non purè mentali) without a *grave* cause, he has sinned gravely.' And so the author himself, from whom I quote, and who defends the Patristic and Anglican doctrine that there *are* untruths which are not lies, says, 'Under the name of mental reservation theologians authorize many lies, *when there is for them a grave reason* and proportionate,' i.e. to their character – p. 459. And so St. Alfonso, in another Treatise, quotes St. Thomas to the effect, that if from one cause two immediate effects follow, and, if the good effect of that cause is *equal in value* to the bad effect (bonus *aequivalet* malo), then nothing hinders the speaker's intending the good and only permitting the evil. From which it will follow that, since the evil to society from lying is very great, the just cause which is to make it allowable, must be very great also. And so Kenrick: 'It is confessed by all Catholics that, in the common intercourse of life, all ambiguity of language is to be avoided; but it is debated whether such ambiguity is *ever* lawful. Most theologians answer in the affirmative, supposing a *grave cause* urges, and the [true] mind of the speaker can be collected from the adjuncts, though in fact it be not collected.'

However, there are cases, I have already said, of another kind, in which Anglican authors would think a lie allowable; such as when a question is *impertinent*. Of such a case Walter Scott, if I mistake not, supplied a very distinct example, in his denying so long the authorship of his novels.

What I have been saying shows what different schools of opinion there are in the Church in the treatment of this difficult doctrine; and, by consequence, that a given individual, such as I am, *cannot* agree with all of them, and has a full right to follow which of them he will. The freedom of the Schools, indeed, is one of those rights of reason, which the Church is too wise really to interfere with. And this applies not to moral questions only, but to dogmatic also.

It is supposed by Protestants that, because St. Alfonso's writings have had such high commendation bestowed upon them by authority, therefore they have been invested with a quasi-infallibility. This has arisen in good measure from Protestants not knowing the force of theological terms. The words to which they refer are the authoritative decision that 'nothing in his works has been found *worthy of censure*,' 'censurâ dignum;' but this does not lead to the conclusions which have been drawn from it. Those words occur in a legal document, and cannot be interpreted except in a legal sense. In the first place, the sentence is negative; nothing in St. Alfonso's writings is positively approved; and, secondly, it is not said that there are no faults in what he has written, but nothing which comes under the ecclesiastical *censura*, which is something very definite. To take and interpret them, in the way commonly adopted in England, is the same mistake, as if one were to take the word *Apologia* in the English sense of apology, or *Infant* in law to mean a little child.

1. Now first as to the meaning of the above form of words viewed as a proposition. When a question on the subject was asked of the fitting authorities at Rome by the Archbishop of Besançon, the answer returned to him contained this condition, viz. that those words were to be interpreted, 'with due regard to the mind of the Holy See concerning the approbation of writings of the servants of God, ad effectum Canonizationis.' This is intended to prevent any Catholic taking the words about St. Alfonso's works in too large a sense. Before a Saint is canonized, his works are examined, and a judgment pronounced upon them. Pope Benedict XIV. says, 'The *end* or *scope* of this judgment is, that it may appear, whether the doctrine of the servant of God, which he has brought out in his writings, is free from any soever *theological censure*.' And he remarks in addition, 'It never can be said that the doctrine of a servant of God is *approved* by the Holy See, but at most it can [only] be said that it is not disapproved (non reprobatam) in case that the Revisers had reported that there is nothing found by them in his works, which is adverse to the decrees of Urban VIII., and that the judgment of the Revisers has been approved by the sacred Congregation, and confirmed by the Supreme Pontiff.' The Decree of Urban VIII. here referred to is, 'Let works be examined, whether they contain errors against faith or good morals (bonos mores), or any new doctrine, or a doctrine foreign and alien to the common sense and custom of the Church.' The author from whom I quote this (M. Vandenbroeck, of the diocese of Malines) observes, 'It is therefore clear, that the approbation of the works

of the Holy Bishop touches not the truth of every proposition, adds nothing to them, nor even gives them by consequence a degree of intrinsic probability.' He adds that it gives St. Alfonso's theology an extrinsic probability, from the fact that, in the judgment of the Holy See, no proposition deserves to receive a censure; but that 'that probability will cease nevertheless in a particular case, for any one who should be convinced, whether by evident arguments, or by a decree of the Holy See, or otherwise, that the doctrine of the Saint deviates from the truth.' He adds, 'From the fact that the approbation of the works of St. Alfonso does not decide the truth of each proposition, it follows, as Benedict XIV. has remarked, that we may combat the doctrine which they contain; only, since a canonized saint is in question, who is honoured by a solemn *culte* in the Church, we ought not to speak except with respect, nor to attack his opinions except with temper and modesty.'

2. Then, as to the meaning of the word *censura*: Benedict XIV. enumerates a number of 'Notes' which come under that name; he says, 'Out of propositions which are to be noted with theological censure, some are heretical, some erroneous, some close upon error, some savouring of heresy,' and so on; and each of these terms has its own definite meaning. Thus by 'erroneous' is meant, according to Viva, a proposition which is not *immediately* opposed to a revealed proposition, but only to a theological *conclusion* drawn from premisses which are *de fide*; 'savouring of heresy' is a proposition, which is opposed to a theological conclusion not evidently drawn from premisses which are *de fide*, but most probably and according to the common mode of theologizing; – and so with the rest. Therefore when it was said by the Revisers of St. Alfonso's works that they were not 'worthy of *censure*,' it was only meant that they did not fall under these particular Notes.

But the answer from Rome to the Archbishop of Besançon went further than this; it actually took pains to declare that any one who pleased might follow other theologians instead of St. Alfonso. After saying that no Priest was to be interfered with who followed St. Alfonso in the Confessional, it added, 'This is said, however, without on that account judging that they are reprehended who follow opinions handed down by other approved authors.'

And this too I will observe, – that St. Alfonso made many changes of opinion himself in the course of his writings; and it could not for an instant be supposed that we were bound to every one of his opinions, when he did not feel himself bound to them in his own person. And, what is more to the purpose still, there are opinions, or some opinion, of his which actually have been proscribed by the Church since, and cannot now be put forward or used. I do not pretend to be a well-read theologian myself, but I say this on the authority of a theological professor of Breda, quoted in the *Mélanges Théol.* for 1850–1. He says: 'It may happen, that, in the course of time, errors may be found in the works of St. Alfonso and be proscribed by the Church, *a thing which in fact has already occurred.*'

In not ranging myself then with those who consider that it is justifiable to use words in a double sense, that is, to equivocate, I put myself under the protection of such authors as Cardinal Gerdil, Natalis Alexander, Contenson, Concina, and others. Under the protection of these authorities, I say as follows: –

Casuistry is a noble science, but it is one to which I am led, neither by my abilities nor my turn of mind. Independently, then, of the difficulties of the subject, and the necessity, before forming an opinion, of knowing more of the arguments of theologians upon it than I do, I am very unwilling to say a word here on the subject of Lying and Equivocation. But I consider myself bound to speak; and therefore, in this strait, I can do nothing better, even for my own relief, than submit myself, and what I shall say, to the judgment of the Church, and to the consent, so far as in this matter there be a consent, of the Schola Theologorum.

Now in the case of one of those special and rare exigencies or emergencies, which constitute the *justa causa* of dissembling or misleading, whether it be extreme as the defence of life, or a duty as the custody of a secret, or of a personal nature as to repel an impertinent inquirer, or a matter too trivial to provoke question, as in dealing with children or madmen, there seem to be four courses: –

1. *To say the thing that is not.* Here I draw the reader's attention to the words *material* and *formal.* 'Thou shalt not kill;' *murder* is

the *formal* transgression of this commandment, but *accidental homicide* is the *material* transgression. The *matter* of the act is the same in both cases; but in the *homicide*, there is nothing more than the act, whereas in *murder* there must be the intention, &c., which constitutes the formal sin. So, again, an executioner commits the material act, but not that formal killing which is a breach of the commandment. So a man, who, simply to save himself from starving, takes a loaf which is not his own, commits only the material, not the formal act of stealing, that is, he does not commit a sin. And so a baptized Christian, external to the Church, who is in invincible ignorance, is a material heretic, and not a formal. And in like manner, if to say the thing which is not be in special cases lawful, it may be called a *material lie*.

The first mode then which has been suggested of meeting those special cases, in which to mislead by words has a sufficient occasion, or has a *just cause*, is by a material lie.

The second mode is by an *aequivocatio*, which is not equivalent to the English word 'equivocation,' but means sometimes a *play upon words*, sometimes an *evasion*: we must take these two modes of misleading separately.

2. *A play upon words.* St. Alfonso certainly says that a play upon words is allowable; and, speaking under correction, I should say that he does so on the ground that lying is *not* a sin against justice, that is, against our neighbour, but a sin against God. God has made words the signs of ideas, and therefore if a word denotes two ideas, we are at liberty to use it in either of its senses: but I think I must be incorrect in some respect in supposing that the Saint does not recognise a lie as an injustice, because the Catechism of the Council, as I have quoted it at p. 249, says, 'Vanitate et mendacio fides ac veritas tolluntur, arctissima vincula *societatis humanae*; quibus sublatis, sequitur summa vitae *confusio*, ut *homines nihil a daemonibus differre videantur*.'

3. *Evasion*; – when, for instance, the speaker diverts the attention of the hearer to another subject; suggests an irrelevant fact or makes a remark, which confuses him and gives him something to think about; throws dust into his eyes; states some truth, from which he is quite sure his hearer will draw illogical and untrue conclusion, and the like.

The greatest school of evasion, I speak seriously, is the House of Commons; and necessarily so, from the nature of the case. And the hustings is another.

An instance is supplied in the history of St. Athanasius: he was in a boat on the Nile, flying persecution; and he found himself pursued. On this he ordered his men to turn his boat round, and ran right to meet the satellites of Julian. They asked him, 'Have you seen Athanasius?' and he told his followers to answer, 'Yes, he is close to you.' *They* went on their course as if they were sure to come up to him, while *he* ran back into Alexandria, and there lay hid till the end of the persecution.

I gave another instance above, in reference to a doctrine of religion. The early Christians did their best to conceal their Creed on account of the misconceptions of the heathen about it. Were the question asked of them, 'Do you worship a Trinity?' and did they answer, 'We worship one God, and none else;' the inquirer might, or would, infer that they did not acknowledge the Trinity of Divine Persons.

It is very difficult to draw the line between these evasions and what are commonly called in English *equivocations*; and of this difficulty, again, I think, the scenes in the House of Commons supply us with illustrations.

4. The fourth method is *silence*. For instance, not giving the *whole* truth in a court of law. If St. Alban, after dressing himself in the Priest's clothes, and being taken before the persecutor, had been able to pass off for his friend, and so gone to martyrdom without being discovered; and had he in the course of examination answered all questions truly, but not given the whole truth, the most important truth, that he was the wrong person, he would have come very near to telling a lie, for a half-truth is often a falsehood. And his defence must have been the *justa causa*, viz. either that he might in charity or for religion's sake save a priest, or again that the judge had no right to interrogate him on the subject.

Now, of these four modes of misleading others by the tongue, when there is a *justa causa* (supposing there can be such), – (1) a material lie, that is, an untruth which is not a lie, (2) an equivocation, (3) an evasion, and (4) silence, – First, I have no difficulty whatever in recognizing as allowable the method of *silence*.

Secondly, But, if I allow of *silence*, why not of the method of *material lying*, since half of a truth *is* often a lie? And, again, if all killing be not murder, nor all taking from another stealing, why must all untruths be lies? Now I will say freely that I think it difficult to answer this question, whether it be urged by St. Clement or by Milton; at the same time, I never have acted, and I think, when it came to the point, I never should act upon such a theory myself, except in one case, stated below. This I say for the benefit of those who speak hardly of Catholic theologians, on the ground that they admit text-books which allow of equivocation. They are asked, how can we trust you, when such are your views? but such views, as I already have said, need not have any thing to do with their own practice, merely from the circumstance that they are contained in their text-books. A theologian draws out a system; he does it partly as a scientific speculation: but much more for the sake of others. He is lax for the sake of others, not of himself. His own standard of action is much higher than that which he imposes upon men in general. One special reason why religious men, after drawing out a theory, are unwilling to act upon it themselves, is this: that they practically acknowledge a broad distinction between their reason and their conscience; and that they feel the latter to be the safer guide, though the former may be the clearer, nay even though it be the truer. They would rather be in error with the sanction of their conscience, than be right with the mere judgment of their reason. And again here is this more tangible difficulty in the case of exceptions to the rule of Veracity, that so very little external help is given us in drawing the line, as to when untruths are allowable and when not; whereas that sort of killing which is not murder, is most definitely marked off by legal enactments, so that it cannot possibly be mistaken for such killing as *is* murder. On the other hand the cases of exemption from the rule of Veracity are left to the private judgment of the individual, and he may easily be led on from acts which are allowable to acts which are not. Now this remark does *not* apply to such acts as are related in Scripture, as being done by a particular inspiration, for in such cases there *is* a command. If I had my own way, I would oblige society, that is, its great men, its lawyers, its divines, its literature, publicly to acknowledge as such, those instances of untruth which are not lies, as for instance untruths in war; and then there could be no perplexity to the individual Catholic, for he would not be taking the law into his own hands.

Thirdly, as to playing upon words, or equivocation, I suppose it is from the English habit, but, without meaning any disrespect to a great Saint, or wishing to set myself up, or taking my conscience for more than it is worth, I can only say as a fact, that I admit it as little as the rest of my countrymen: and, without any reference to the right and the wrong of the matter, of this I am sure, that, if there is one thing more than another which prejudices Englishmen against the Catholic Church, it is the doctrine of great authorities on the subject of equivocation. For myself, I can fancy myself thinking it was allowable in extreme cases for me to lie, but never to equivocate. Luther said, 'Pecca fortiter.' I anathematize his formal sentiment, but there is a truth in it, when spoken of material acts.

Fourthly, I think *evasion*, as I have described it, to be perfectly allowable; indeed, I do not know, who does not use it, under circumstances; but that a good deal of moral danger is attached to its use; and that, the cleverer a man is, the more likely he is to pass the line of Christian duty.

But it may be said, that such decisions do not meet the particular difficulties for which provision is required; let us then take some instances.

1. I do not think it right to tell lies to children, even on this account, that they are sharper than we think them, and will soon find out what we are doing; and our example will be a very bad training for them. And so of equivocation: it is easy of imitation, and we ourselves shall be sure to get the worst of it in the end.

2. If an early Father defends the patriarch Jacob in his mode of gaining his father's blessing, on the ground that the blessing was divinely pledged to him already, that it was his, and that his father and brother were acting at once against his own rights and the divine will, it does not follow from this that such conduct is a pattern to us, who have no supernatural means of determining *when* an untruth becomes a *material*, and not a *formal* lie. It seems to me very dangerous, be it ever allowable or not, to lie or equivocate in order to preserve some great temporal or spiritual

benefit; nor does St. Alfonso here say any thing to the contrary, for he is not discussing the question of danger or expedience.

3. As to Johnson's case of a murderer asking you which way a man had gone, I should have anticipated that, had such a difficulty happened to him, his first act would have been to knock the man down, and to call out for the police; and next, if he was worsted in the conflict, he would not have given the ruffian the information he asked, at whatever risk to himself. I think he would have let himself be killed first. I do not think that he would have told a lie.

4. A secret is a more difficult case. Supposing something has been confided to me in the strictest secrecy, which could not be revealed without great disadvantage to another, what am I to do? If I am a lawyer, I am protected by my profession. I have a right to treat with extreme indignation any question which trenches on the inviolability of my position; but, supposing I was driven up into a corner, I think I should have a right to say an untruth, or that, under such circumstances, a lie would be *material*, but it is almost an impossible case, for the law would defend me. In like manner, as a priest, I should think it lawful to speak as if I knew nothing of what passed in confession. And I think in these cases, I do in fact possess that guarantee, that I am not going by private judgment, which just now I demanded; for society would bear me out, whether as a lawyer or as a priest, in holding that I had a duty to my client or penitent, such, that an untruth in the matter was not a lie. A common type of this permissible denial, be it *material lie* or *evasion*, is at the moment supplied to me: – an artist asked a Prime Minister, who was sitting to him, 'What news, my Lord, from France?' He answered, '*I do not know*; I have not read the Papers.'

5. A more difficult question is, when to accept confidence has not been a duty. Supposing a man wishes to keep the secret that he is the author of a book, and he is plainly asked on the subject. Here I should ask the previous question, whether any one has a right to publish what he dare not avow. It requires to have traced the bearings and results of such a principle, before being sure of it; but certainly, for myself, I am no friend of strictly anonymous writing. Next, supposing another has confided to you the secret of his authorship: – there are persons who would

have no scruple at all in giving a denial to impertinent questions asked them on the subject. I have heard a great man in his day at Oxford, warmly contend, as if he could not enter into any other view of the matter, that, if he had been trusted by a friend with the secret of his being author of a certain book, and he were asked by a third person, if his friend was not (as he really was) the author of it, he ought, without any scruple and distinctly, to answer that he did not know. He had an existing duty towards the author; he had none towards his inquirer. The author had a claim on him; an impertinent questioner had none at all. But here again I desiderate some leave, recognized by society, as in the case of the formulas 'Not at home,' and 'Not guilty,' in order to give me the right of saying what is a *material* untruth. And moreover, I should here also ask the previous question, Have I any right to accept such a confidence? have I any right to make such a promise? and, if it be an unlawful promise, is it binding when it cannot be kept without a lie? I am not attempting to solve these difficult questions, but they have to be carefully examined. And now I have said more than I had intended on a question of casuistry.

SUPPLEMENTAL MATTER

I

LETTERS AND PAPERS OF THE AUTHOR USED IN THE
COURSE OF THIS WORK

Cardinal Newman's Works

1. SERMONS

VOLS.

1–8   PAROCHIAL AND PLAIN SERMONS. 8 vols. Crown 8vo. 5s. each. (*Longmans*)

9   SERMONS ON SUBJECTS OF THE DAY. Crown 8vo. 5s. (*Longmans.*)

10   UNIVERSITY SERMONS. Crown 8vo. 5s. (*Longmans.*)

11   SERMONS TO MIXED CONGREGATIONS. (*Burns and Oates.*)

12   OCCASIONAL SERMONS. (*Burns and Oates.*)

2. TREATISES

13   ON THE DOCTRINE OF JUSTIFICATION. Crown 8vo. 5s. (*Longmans.*)

14   ON THE DEVELOPMENT OF CHRISTIAN DOCTRINE. Cabinet Edition, crown 8vo. 6s. Cheap Edition, 3s. 6d. (*Longmans.*)

15   ON THE IDEA OF A UNIVERSITY. Crown 8vo. 7s. (*Longmans.*)

16   AN ESSAY IN AID OF A GRAMMAR OF ASSENT. 7s. 6d. (*Longmans.*)

3. ESSAYS

VOLS.

17 TWO ESSAYS ON MIRACLES. 1. Of Scripture. 2. Of Ecclesiastical History. Cabinet Edition, crown 8vo. 6s. Cheap Edition, 3s. 6d. (*Longmans.*)

18 DISCUSSIONS AND ARGUMENTS. 1. How to accomplish it. 2. The Antichrist of the Fathers. 3. Scripture and the Creed. 4. Tamworth Reading-Room. 5. Who's to blame? 6. An Argument for Christianity. Crown 8vo. 6s. (*Longmans.*)

19, 20 ESSAYS CRITICAL AND HISTORICAL. 2 vols. 1. Poetry, 2. Rationalism. 3. Apostolical Tradition. 4. De la Mennais. 5. Palmer on Faith and Unity. 6. St. Ignatius. 7. Prospects of the Anglican Church. 8. The Anglo-American Church. 9. Countess of Huntingdon. 10. Catholicity of the Anglican Church. 11. The Antichrist of Protestants. 12. Milman's Christianity. 13. Reformation of the Eleventh Century. 14. Private Judgment. 15. Davison. 16. Keble. Cabinet Edition, crown 8vo. 12s. Cheap Edition, 7s. (*Longmans.*)

4. HISTORICAL

21–23 HISTORICAL SKETCHES. 3 vols. 1. The Turks. 2. Cicero. 3. Apollonius. 4. Primitive Christianity. 5. Church of the Fathers. 6. St. Chrysostom. 7. Theodoret. 8. St. Benedict. 9. Benedictine Schools. 10. Universities. 11. Northmen and Normans. 12. Medieval Oxford. 13. Convocation of Canterbury. Crown 8vo. 6s. each. (*Longmans.*)

5. THEOLOGICAL

24 THE ARIANS OF THE FOURTH CENTURY. Cabinet Edition, crown 8vo. 6s. Cheap Edition, 3s. 6d. (*Longmans.*)

25, 26 ANNOTATED TRANSLATION OF ATHANASIUS. 2 vols. Crown 8vo. 15s. (*Longmans.*)

VOLS.

27   TRACTS. 1. Dissertatiunculae. 2. On the Text of
the Seven Epistles of St. Ignatius.
3. Doctrinal Causes of Arianism.
4. Apollinarianism. 5. St. Cyril's Formula.
6. Ordo de Tempore. 7. Douay Version of
Scripture. (*Burns and Oates.*)

6. POLEMICAL

28, 29   THE VIA MEDIA OF THE ANGLICAN CHURCH. 2
vols. with Notes. Vol. I. Prophetical Office of the
Church. Vol. II. Occasional Letters and Tracts.
Crown 8vo. 6s. each. (*Longmans.*)

30, 31   CERTAIN DIFFICULTIES FELT BY ANGLICANS IN
CATHOLIC TEACHING CONSIDERED. 2 vols. Vol. I.
Twelve Lectures. Vol. II. Letters to Dr. Pusey
concerning the Bl. Virgin, and to the Duke of
Norfolk in Defence of the Pope and Council.
Vol. 1, 7s. 6d.; Vol. 2, 5s. 6d. (*Longmans.*)

32   PRESENT POSITION OF CATHOLICS IN ENGLAND.
Crown 8vo. 7s. 6d. (*Longmans.*)

33   APOLOGIA PRO VITÂ SUÂ. Cabinet Edition, crown
8vo. 6s. Cheap Edition, 3s. 6d. (*Longmans.*)

7. LITERARY

34   VERSES ON VARIOUS OCCASIONS. Cabinet Edition,
crown 8vo. 6s. Cheap Edition, 3s. 6d. (*Longmans.*)

35   LOSS AND GAIN. (*Burns and Oates.*)

36   CALLISTA. Cabinet Edition, crown 8vo. 6s. Cheap
Edition, 3s. 6d. (*Longmans.*)

37   THE DREAM OF GERONTIUS. 16mo. 6d. sewed,
1s. cloth. (*Longmans.*)

III

LETTER OF APPROBATION AND ENCOURAGEMENT FROM THE BISHOP OF THE DIOCESE OF BIRMINGHAM, DR. ULLATHORNE

'Bishop's House, June 2, 1864.

'My dear Dr. Newman, –

'It was with warm gratification that, after the close of the Synod yesterday, I listened to the Address presented to you by the clergy of the diocese, and to your impressive reply. But I should have been little satisfied with the part of the silent listener, except on the understanding with myself that I also might afterwards express to you my own sentiments in my own way.

'We have now been personally acquainted, and much more than acquainted, for nineteen years, during more than sixteen of which we have stood in special relation of duty towards each other. This has been one of the singular blessings which God has given me amongst the cares of the Episcopal office. What my feelings of respect, of confidence, and of affection have been towards you, you know well, nor should I think of expressing them in words. But there is one thing that has struck me in this day of explanations, which you could not, and would not, be disposed to do, and which no one could do so properly or so authentically as I could, and which it seems to me is not altogether uncalled for, if every kind of erroneous impression that some persons have entertained with no better evidence than conjecture is to be removed.

'It is difficult to comprehend how, in the face of facts, the notion should ever have arisen that during your Catholic life, you have been more occupied with your own thoughts than with the service of religion and the work of the Church. If we take no other work into consideration beyond the written productions which your Catholic pen has given to the world, they are enough for the life's labour of another. There are the Lectures on Anglican Difficulties, the Lectures on Catholicism in England, the great work on the Scope and End of University Education, that on the Office and Work of Universities, the Lectures and Essays on University Subjects, and the two Volumes of Sermons; not to speak of your contributions to the Atlantis, which you founded, and to other periodicals; then there are those beautiful offerings to Catholic literature, the Lectures on the Turks, Loss and Gain, and Callista, and though last, not least, the Apologia, which is destined to put many idle rumours to rest, and many unprofitable surmises; and yet all these productions represent but a portion of your labour, and that in the second half of your period of public life.

'These works have been written in the midst of labour and cares of another kind, and of which the world knows very little. I will specify four of these undertakings, each of a distinct character, and any one of which would have made a reputation for untiring energy in the practical order.

'The first of these undertakings was the establishment of the congregation of the Oratory of St. Philip Neri – that great ornament and accession to the force of English Catholicity. Both the London and the Birmingham Oratory must look to you as their founder and as the originator of their characteristic excellences; whilst that of Birmingham has never known any other presidency.

'No sooner was this work fairly on foot than you were called by the highest authority to commence another, and one of yet greater magnitude and difficulty, the founding of a University in Ireland. After the Universities had been lost to the Catholics of these kingdoms for three centuries, every thing had to be begun from the beginning: the idea of such an institution to be inculcated, the plan to be formed that would work, the resources to be gathered, and the staff of superiors and professors to be brought together. Your name was then the chief point of attraction which brought these elements together. You alone know what difficulties you had to conciliate and what to surmount, before the work reached that state of consistency and promise, which enabled you to return to those responsibilities in England which you had never laid aside or suspended. And here, excuse me if I give expression to a fancy which passed through my mind.

'I was lately reading a poem, not long published, from the MSS. De Rerum Natura, by Neckham, the foster-brother of Richard the Lion-hearted. He quotes an old prophecy, attributed to Merlin, and with a sort of wonder, as if recollecting that England owed so much of its literary learning to that country; and the prophecy says that after long years Oxford will pass into Ireland – "Vada boum suo tempore transibunt in Hiberniam." When I read this, I could not but indulge the pleasant fancy that in the days when the Dublin University shall arise in material splendour, an allusion to this prophecy might form a poetic element in the inscription on the pedestal of the statue which commemorates its first Rector.

'The original plan of an Oratory did not contemplate any parochial work, but you could not contemplate so many souls in want of pastors without being prompt and ready at the beck of authority to strain all your efforts in coming to their help. And this brings me to the third and the most continuous of those labours to which I have alluded. The mission in Alcester Street, its church and schools, were the first work of the Birmingham Oratory. After several years of close and hard work, and a considerable call upon the private resources of the Fathers who had established this congregation, it was delivered over to other hands, and the Fathers removed to the district of Edgbaston, where up to that time nothing Catholic had appeared. Then arose under your direction the large convent of the Oratory, the church expanded by degrees into its present capaciousness, a numerous congregation has gathered and grown in it; poor schools and other pious institutions have grown up in connexion with it, and, moreover, equally at your expense and that of your brethren, and, as I have reason to know, at much inconvenience, the Oratory has relieved the other clergy of Birmingham all this while by constantly doing the duty in the poor-house and gaol of Birmingham.

'More recently still, the mission and the poor school at Smethwick owe their existence to the Oratory. And all this while the founder and father of these religious works has added to his other solicitudes the toil of frequent preaching, of attendance in the confessional, and other parochial duties.

'I have read on this day of its publication the seventh part of the Apologia, and the touching allusion in it to the devotedness of the Catholic clergy to the poor in seasons of pestilence reminds me that when the cholera raged so dreadfully at Bilston, and the two priests of the town were no longer equal to the number of cases to which they were hurried day and night, I asked you to lend me two fathers to supply the place of other priests whom I wished to send as a further aid. But you and Father St. John preferred to take the place of danger which I had destined for others, and remained at Bilston till the worst was over.

'The fourth work which I would notice is one more widely known. I refer to the school for the education of the higher classes, which at the solicitation of many friends you have founded and attached to the Oratory. Surely after reading this bare enumeration of work done, no man will venture to say that Dr. Newman is leading a comparatively inactive life in the service of the Church.

'To spare, my dear Dr. Newman, any further pressure on those feelings with which I have already taken so large a liberty, I will only add one word more for my own satisfaction. During our long intercourse there is only one subject on which, after the first experience, I have measured my words with some caution, and that has been where questions bearing on ecclesiastical duty have arisen. I found some little caution necessary, because you were always so prompt and ready to go even beyond the slightest intimation of my wish or desires.

'That God may bless you with health, life, and all the spiritual good which you desire, you and your brethren of the Oratory, is the earnest prayer now and often of,

'My dear Dr. Newman,

'Your affectionate friend and faithful servant in Christ,
'+ W. B. ULLATHORNE.'

IV

LETTERS OF APPROBATION AND ENCOURAGEMENT FROM CLERGY AND LAITY

It requires some words of explanation why I allow myself to sound my own praises so loudly, as I am doing by adding to my Volume the following Letters, written to me last year by large bodies of my Catholic brethren, Priests and Laymen, in the course or on the conclusion of the publication of my *Apologia*. I have two reasons for doing so.

1. It seems hardly respectful to them, and hardly fair to myself, to practise self-denial in a matter, which after all belongs to others as well as to me. Bodies of men become authorities by the fact of being bodies, over and above the personal claims of the individuals who constitute them. To have received such unusual Testimonials in my favour, as I have to produce, and then to have let both those Testimonials and the generous feelings which dictated them be wasted, and come to nought, would have been

a rudeness of which I could not bear to be guilty. Far be it from me to show such ingratitude to those who were especially 'friends in need.' I am too proud of their approbation not to publish it to the world.

2. But I have a further reason. The belief obtains extensively in the country at large, that Catholics, and especially the Priest-hood, disavow the mode and form, in which I am accustomed to teach the Catholic faith, as if they were not generally recognized, but something special and peculiar to myself; as if, whether for the purposes of controversy, or from the traditions of an earlier period of my life, I did not exhibit Catholicism pure and simple, as the bulk of its professors manifest it. Such testimonials, then, as now follow, from as many as 558 priests, that is, not far from half of the clergy of England, secular and religious, from the Bishop and clergy of a diocese at the Antipodes, and from so great and authoritative a body as the German Congress assembled last year at Würzburg, scatter to the winds a suspicion, which it is not less painful, I am persuaded, to numbers of those Protestants who entertain it, than it is injurious to me who have to bear it.

I — THE DIOCESE OF WESTMINSTER

The following Address was signed by 110 of the Westminster clergy, including all the Canons, the Vicars-General, a great number of secular priests, and five Doctors in theology; Fathers of the Society of Jesus, Fathers of the Order of St. Dominic, of St. Francis, of the Oratory, of the Passion, of Charity, Oblates of St. Charles, and Marists.

'London, March 15, 1864.

Very Reverend and Dear Sir,

We, the undersigned Priests of the Diocese of Westminster, tender to you our respectful thanks for the service you have done to religion, as well as to the interests of literary morality, by your Reply to the calumnies of [a popular writer of the day.]

We cannot but regard it as a matter of congratulation that your assailant should have associated the cause of the Catholic

Priesthood with the name of one so well fitted to represent its dignity, and to defend its honour, as yourself.

We recognize in this latest effort of your literary power one further claim, besides the many you have already established, to the gratitude and veneration of Catholics, and trust that the reception which it has met with on all sides may be the omen of new successes which you are destined to achieve in the vindication of the teaching and principles of the Church.

We are,

Very Reverend and Dear Sir,

Your faithful and affectionate Servants in Christ.'

(*The Subscriptions follow.*)

'To the Very Rev.

John Henry Newman, D.D.'

II — THE ACADEMIA OF CATHOLIC RELIGION

'London, April 19, 1864.

Very Rev. and Dear Sir,

The Academia of Catholic Religion, at their meeting held to-day, under the Presidency of the Cardinal Archbishop, have instructed us to write to you in their behalf.

As they have learned, with great satisfaction, that it is your intention to publish a defence of Catholic Veracity, which has been assailed in your person, they are precluded from asking you that that defence might be made by word of mouth, and in London, as they would otherwise have done.

Composed, as the Academia is, mainly of Laymen, they feel that it is not out of their province to express their indignation that your opponent should have chosen, while praising the Catholic Laity, to do so at the expense of the Clergy, between whom and themselves, in this as in all other matters, there exists a perfect identity of principle and practice.

It is because, in such a matter, your cause is the cause of all Catholics, that we congratulate ourselves on the rashness of the opponent that has thrown the defence of that cause into your hands.

We remain,

Very Reverend and Dear Sir,

Your very faithful Servants,

'JAMES LAIRD PATTERSON, $\Big\}$ *Secretaries*
EDW. LUCAS,

To the Very Rev. John Henry Newman, D.D.,
        Provost of the Birmingham Oratory.'

The above was moved at the meeting by Lord PETRE and seconded by the Hon. CHARLES LANGDALE.

III – THE DIOCESE OF BIRMINGHAM

In this Diocese there were in 1864, according to the Directory of the year, 136 Priests.

'June 1, 1864.

'Very Reverend and Dear Sir,

'In availing ourselves of your presence at the Diocesan Synod to offer you our hearty thanks for your recent vindication of the honour of the Catholic Priesthood, We, the Provost and Chapter of the Cathedral, and the Clergy, Secular and Regular, of the Diocese of Birmingham, cannot forego the assertion of a special right, as your neighbours and colleagues, to express our veneration and affection for one whose fidelity to the dictates of conscience, in the use of the highest intellectual gifts, has won even from opponents unbounded admiration and respect.

'To most of us you are personally known. Of some, indeed, you were, in years long past, the trusted guide, to whom they owe more than can be expressed in words; and all are conscious that the ingenuous fulness of your answer to a false and unprovoked accusation, has intensified their interest in the labours and trials of your life. While, then, we resent the indignity to which you have been exposed, and lament the pain and annoyance which the manifestation of yourself must have cost you, we cannot but rejoice that, in the fulfilment of a duty, you have allowed neither the unworthiness of your assailant to shield him from rebuke, nor the sacredness of your inmost motives to deprive that rebuke of the only form which could at once complete his discomfiture, free your own name from the obloquy which prejudice had cast upon it, and afford invaluable aid to honest seekers after Truth.

'Great as is the work which you have already done, Very Reverend Sir, permit us to express a hope that a greater yet remains for you to accomplish. In an age and in a country in which the very foundations of religious faith are exposed to assault, we rejoice in numbering among our brethren one so well qualified by learning and experience to defend that priceless deposit of Truth, in obtaining which you have counted as gain the loss of all things most dear and precious. And we esteem ourselves happy in being able to offer you that support and encouragement which the assurance of our unfeigned admiration and regard may be able to give you under your present trials and future labours.

'That you may long have strength to labour for the Church of God and the glory of His Holy Name is, Very Reverend and Dear Sir, our heartfelt and united prayer.'

(*The Subscriptions follow.*)

'To the Very Rev. John Henry Newman, D.D.'

IV – THE DIOCESE OF BEVERLEY

The following Address, as is stated in the first paragraph, comes from more than 70 Priests: –

'Hull, May 9, 1864.

'Very Rev. and Dear Dr. Newman,

'At a recent meeting of the clergy of the Diocese of Beverley, held in York, at which upwards of seventy priests were present, special attention was called to your correspondence with [a popular writer]; and such was the enthusiasm with which your name was received – such was the admiration expressed of the dignity with which you had asserted the claims of the Catholic Priesthood in England to be treated with becoming courtesy and respect – and such was the strong and all-pervading sense of the invaluable service which you had thus rendered, not only to faith and morals, but to good manners so far as regarded religious controversy in this country, that I was requested, as Chairman, to become the voice of the meeting, and to express to you as strongly and as earnestly as I could, how heartily the whole of the clergy of this diocese desire to thank you for services to religion as well-timed as they are in themselves above and beyond all commendation, services which the Catholics of England will never cease to hold in most grateful remembrance. God, in His infinite wisdom and great mercy, has raised you up to stand prominently forth in the glorious work of re-establishing in this country the holy faith which in good old times shed such lustre upon it. We all lament that, in the order of nature, you have so few years before you in which to fight against false teaching that good fight in which you have been so victoriously engaged of late. But our prayers are that you may long be spared, and may possess to the last all your vigour, and all that zeal for the advancement of our holy faith, which imparts such a charm to the productions of your pen.

'I esteem it a great honour and a great privilege to have been deputed, as the representative of the clergy of the Diocese of Beverley, to tender you the fullest expression of our most grateful thanks, and the assurance of our prayers for your health and eternal happiness.

   'I am,

     'Very Rev. and Dear Sir,

       'With sentiments of profound respect,

        'Yours most faithfully in Christ,

          'M. TRAPPES.

'The Very Rev. Dr. Newman.'

V AND VI - THE DIOCESES OF LIVERPOOL AND SALFORD

The Secular Clergy of Liverpool amounted in 1864 to 103, and of Salford to 76.

         'Preston, July 27, 1864.

'Very Rev. and Dear Sir,

'It may seem, perhaps, that the Clergy of Lancashire have been slow to address you; but it would be incorrect to suppose that they have been indifferent spectators of the conflict in which you have been recently engaged. This is the first opportunity that has presented itself, and they gladly avail themselves of their annual meeting in Preston to tender to you the united expression of their heartfelt sympathy and gratitude.

'The atrocious imputation, out of which the late controversy arose, was felt as a personal affront by them, one and all, conscious as they were, that it was mainly owing to your position as a distinguished Catholic ecclesiastic, that the charge was connected with your name.

'While they regret the pain you must needs have suffered, they cannot help rejoicing that it has afforded you an opportunity of rendering a new and most important service to their holy religion. Writers, who are not overscrupulous about the truth themselves, have long used the charge of untruthfulness as an ever ready weapon against the Catholic Clergy. Partly from the frequent repetition of this charge, partly from a consciousness that, instead of undervaluing the truth, they have ever prized it above every earthly treasure, partly, too, from the difficulty of obtaining a hearing in their own defence, they have generally passed it by in silence. They thank you for coming forward as their champion: your own character required no vindication. It was their battle more than your own that you fought. They know and feel how much pain it has caused you to bring so prominently forward your own life and motives, but they now congratulate you on the completeness of your triumph, as admitted alike by friend and enemy.

'In addition to answering the original accusation, you have placed them under a new obligation, by giving to all, who read the English language, a work which, for literary ability and the lucid exposition of many difficult and abstruse points, forms an invaluable contribution to our literature.

'They fervently pray that God may give you health and length of days, and, if it please Him, some other cause in which to use for His glory the great powers bestowed upon you.

'Signed on behalf of the Meeting,

'THOS. PROVOST COOKSON

'The Very Rev. J. H. Newman.'

VII – THE DIOCESE OF HEXHAM

The Secular Priests on Mission in 1864 in this Diocese were 64.

'Durham, Sept. 22, 1864.

'My Dear Dr. Newman,

'At the annual meeting of the Clergy of the Diocese of Hexham and Newcastle, held a few days ago at Newcastle-upon-Tyne, I was commissioned by them to express to you their sincere sympathy, on account of the slanderous accusations, to which you have been so unjustly exposed. We are fully aware that these foul calumnies were intended to injure the character of the whole body of the Catholic Clergy, and that your distinguished name was singled out, in order that they might be more effectually propagated. It is well that these poisonous shafts were thus aimed, as no one could more triumphantly repel them. The "Apologia pro Vitâ suâ" will, if possible, render still more illustrious the name of its gifted author, and be a lasting monument of the victory of truth, and the signal overthrow of an arrogant and reckless assailant.

'It may appear late for us now to ask to join in your triumph, but as the Annual Meeting of the Northern Clergy does not take place till this time, it is the first occasion offered us to present our united congratulations, and to declare to you, that by none of your brethren are you more esteemed and venerated, than by the Clergy of the Diocese of Hexham and Newcastle.

'Wishing that Almighty God may prolong your life many more years for the defence of our holy religion and the honour of your brethren,

'I am, dear Dr. Newman,
'Yours sincerely in Jesus Christ,
'RALPH PROVOST PLATT, V.G.
'The Very Rev. J. H. Newman.'

VIII – THE CONGRESS OF WÜRZBURG

'September 15, 1864.
'Sir,

'The undersigned, President of the Catholic Congress of Germany assembled in Würzburg, has been commissioned to express to you, Very Rev. and Dear Sir, its deep-felt gratitude for your late able defence of the Catholic Clergy, not only of England, but of the whole world, against the attacks of its enemies.

'The Catholics of Germany unite with the Catholics of England in testifying to you their profound admiration and sympathy, and pray that the Almighty may long preserve your valuable life.

'The above Resolution was voted by the Congress with acclamation.

'Accept, Very Rev. and Dear Sir, the expression of the high consideration with which I am

'Your most obedient servant,
'(Signed) ERNEST BARON MOIJ DE SONS.
'The Very Rev. J. H. Newman.'

IX - THE DIOCESE OF HOBART TOWN

'Hobart Town, Tasmania, November 22, 1864.
'Very Rev. and Dear Sir,

'By the last month's post we at length received your admirable book, entitled, *Apologia pro Vitâ suâ*, and the pamphlet, *What then does Dr. Newman mean?*

'By this month's mail, we wish to express our heartfelt gratification and delight for being possessed of a work so triumphant in maintaining truth, and so overwhelming in confounding arrogance and error, as the "Apologia."

'No doubt, your adversary, resting on the deep-seated prejudice of our fellow-countrymen in the United Kingdom, calculated upon establishing his own fame as a keen-sighted polemic, as a shrewd and truth-loving man, upon the fallen reputation of one, who, as he would demonstrate, – yes, that he would, – set little or no value on truth, and who, therefore, would deservedly sink into obscurity, henceforward rejected and despised!

'Aman of old erected a gibbet at the gate of the city, on which an unsuspecting and an unoffending man, one marked as a victim, was to be exposed to the gaze and derision of the people, in order that his own dignity and fame might be exalted; but a divine Providence ordained otherwise. The history of the judgment that fell upon Aman, has been recorded in Holy Writ, it is to be presumed, as a warning to vain and unscrupulous men, even in our days. There can be no doubt, a moral gibbet, full "fifty cubits high," had been prepared some time, on which you were to be exposed, for the pity at least, if not for the scorn and derision of so many, who had loved and venerated you through life!

'But the effort made in the forty-eight pages of the redoubtable pamphlet, *What then does Dr. Newman Mean?* – the production of a bold, unscrupulous man, with a coarse mind, and regardless of inflicting pain on the feelings of another, has failed, – marvellously failed, – and he himself is now exhibited not only in our fatherland, but even at the Antipodes, in fact wherever the English language is spoken or read, as a shallow pretender, one quite incompetent to treat of matters of such undying interest as those he presumed to interfere with.

'We fervently pray the Almighty, that you may be spared to His Church for many years to come, – that to Him alone the glory of this noble work may be given, – and to you the reward in eternal bliss!

'And from this distant land we beg to convey to you, Very Rev. and Dear Sir, the sentiments of our affectionate respect, and deep veneration.'

> (*The Subscritions follow, of the Bishop, Vicar-General and eighteen Clergy.*)

'The Very Rev. Dr. Newman,
&c. &c. &c.'

ADDITIONAL NOTES

Note on Page 31

CORRESPONDENCE WITH ARCHBISHOP WHATELY IN 1834

On application of the Editor of Dr. Whately's Correspondence, the following four letters were sent to her for publication: they are here given entire. It will be observed that they are of the same date as my letter to Dr. Hampden at p. 68.

I

'Dublin, October 25, 1834.

'My dear Newman,

'A most shocking report concerning you has reached me, which indeed carries such an improbability on the face of it that you may perhaps wonder at my giving it a thought; and at first I did not, but finding it repeated from different quarters, it seems to me worth contradicting for the sake of your character. Some Oxford undergraduates, I find, openly report that when I was at Oriel last spring you absented yourself from chapel on purpose to avoid receiving the Communion along with me; and that you yourself declared this to be the case.

'I would not notice every idle rumour; but this has been so confidently and so long asserted that it would be a satisfaction to me to be able to declare its falsity as a fact, from your authority. I did indeed at once declare my utter unbelief; but then this has only the weight of my opinion; though an opinion resting I think on no insufficient grounds. I did not profess to rest my disbelief on our long, intimate, and confidential friendship, which would make it your right and your duty – if I did any thing to offend you or any thing you might think materially wrong – to remonstrate with me; – but on your general character; which I was persuaded would have made you incapable, even had no such close connexion existed between us, of conduct so unchristian and inhuman. But, as I said, I should like for your sake to be able to contradict the report from your own authority.

'Ever yours very truly,
'R. WHATELY.'

2

'Oriel College, October 28, 1834

'My dear Lord,

'My absence from the Sacrament in the College Chapel on the Sunday you were in Oxford, was occasioned solely and altogether by my having it on that day in St. Mary's; and I am pretty sure, if I may trust my memory, that I did not even know of your Grace's presence there, till after the Service. Most certainly such knowledge would not have affected my attendance. I need not say, this being the case, that the report of my having made any statement on the subject is quite unfounded; indeed, your letter of this morning is the first information I have had in any shape of the existence of the report.

'I am happy in being thus able to afford an explanation as satisfactory to you, as the kind feelings which you have ever entertained towards me could desire; – yet, on honest reflection, I cannot conceal from myself, that it was generally a relief to me, to see so little of your Grace, when you were at Oxford: and it is a greater relief now to have an opportunity of saying so to yourself. I have ever wished to observe the rule, never to make a public charge against another behind his back, and, though in the course of conversation and the urgency of accidental occurrences it is sometimes difficult to keep to it, yet I trust I have not broken it, especially in your own case: i.e. though my most intimate friends know how deeply I deplore the line of ecclesiastical policy adopted under your archiepiscopal sanction, and though in society I may have clearly shown that I have an opinion one way rather than the other, yet I have never in my intention, never (as I believe) at all, spoken of your Grace in a serious way before strangers; – indeed mixing very little in general society, and not overapt to open myself in it, I have had little temptation to do so. Least of all should I so forget myself as to take undergraduates into my confidence in such a matter.

'I wish I could convey to your Grace the mixed and very painful feelings, which the late history of the Irish Church has raised in me: – the union of her members with men of heterodox views, and the extinction (without ecclesiastical sanction) of half her Candlesticks, the witnesses and guarantees of the Truth and trustees of the Covenant. I willingly own that both in my secret judgment and my mode of speaking concerning you to my friends, I have had great alternations and changes of feeling, – defending, then blaming your policy, next praising your own self and protesting against your measures, according as the affectionate remembrances which I had of you rose against my utter aversion of the secular and unbelieving policy in which I considered the Irish Church to be implicated. I trust I shall never be forgetful of the kindness you uniformly showed me during your residence in Oxford: and anxiously hope that no duty to Christ and His Church may ever interfere with the expression of my sense of it. However, on the present opportunity, I am conscious to myself, that I am acting according to the dictates both of duty and gratitude, if I beg your leave to state my persuasion, that the perilous measures in which your Grace has acquiesced are but the legitimate offspring of those principles, difficult to describe in few words, with which your reputation is especially associated; principles which bear upon the very fundamentals of all argument and investigation, and affect almost every doctrine and every maxim by which our faith or our conduct is to be guided. I can feel no reluctance to confess, that, when I first was noticed by your Grace, gratitude to you and admiration of your powers wrought upon me; and, had not something from within resisted, I should certainly have adopted views on religious and social duty, which seem to my present judgment to be based in the pride of reason and to tend towards infidelity, and which in your own case nothing but your Grace's high religious temper and the unclouded faith of early piety has been able to withstand.

'I am quite confident, that, however you may regard this judgment, you will give me credit, not only for honesty, but for a deeper feeling in thus laying it before you.

'May I be suffered to add, that your name is ever mentioned in my prayers, and to subscribe myself

'Your Grace's very sincere friend and servant,

'J. H. NEWMAN.'

3

'Dublin, November 3, 1834,'

'My dear Newman,

'I cannot forbear writing again to express the great satisfaction I feel in the course I adopted; which has, eventually, enabled me to contradict a report which was more prevalent and more confidently upheld than I could have thought possible: and which, while it was perhaps likely to hurt my character with some persons, was injurious to yours in the eyes of the best men. For what idea must any one have had of religion – or at least of your religion – who was led to think there was any truth in the imputation to you of such uncharitable arrogance!

'But it is a rule with me, not to cherish, even on the strongest assertions, any belief or even suspicion, to the prejudice of any one whom I have any reason to think well of, till I have carefully inquired, and dispassionately heard both sides. And I think if others were to adopt the same rule, I should not myself be quite so much abused as I have been.

'I am well aware indeed that one cannot expect all, even good men, to think alike on every point, even after they shall have heard both sides; and that we may expect many to judge, after all, very harshly of those who do differ from them: for, God help us! what will become of men if they receive no more mercy than they show to each other! But at least, if the rule were observed, men would not condemn a brother on mere vague popular rumours about principles (as in my case) "difficult to describe in few words," and with which his "reputation is associated." My own reputation I know is associated, to a very great degree, with what are in fact calumnious imputations, originated in exaggerated, distorted, or absolutely false statements, for which even those who circulate them, do not, for the most part, pretend to have any ground except popular rumour: like the Jews at Rome; "as for this way, we know that it is every where spoken against."

'For I have ascertained that a very large proportion of those who join in the outcry against my works, confess, or even boast, that they have never read them. And in respect of the measure you advert to – the Church Temporalities Act – (which of course I shall not now discuss), it is curious to see how many of those who load me with censure for acquiescing in it, receive with open arms, and laud to the skies, the Primate; who was consulted on the measure – as was natural, considering his knowledge of Irish affairs, and his influence – long before me; and gave his consent to it; differing from Ministers only on a point of detail, whether the revenues of six Sees, or of ten, should be alienated.

'Of course, every one is bound ultimately to decide according to his own judgment; nor do I mean to shelter myself under his example: but only to point out what strange notions of justice those have, who acquit with applause the leader, and condemn the follower in the same individual transaction.

'Far be it from any servant of our Master, to feel surprise or anger at being thus treated: it is only an admonition to me to avoid treating others in a similar manner; and not to "judge another's servant," at least without a fair hearing.

'You do me no more than justice, in feeling confident that I shall give you credit both for "honesty and for a deeper feeling" in freely laying your opinions before me: and besides this, you might have been no less confident, from your own experience, that, long since – whenever it was that you changed your judgment respecting me – if you had freely and calmly remonstrated with me on any point where you thought me going wrong, I should have listened to you with that readiness and candour and deference, which as you well know, I always showed, in the times when "we took sweet counsel together, and walked in the house of God as friends;" – when we consulted together about so many practical measures, and about almost all the principal points in my publications.

'I happen to have before me a letter from you just eight years ago, in which, after saying that "there are few things you wish more sincerely than to be known as a friend of mine," and attributing to me, in the warmest and most flattering terms, a much greater share in the forming of your mind than I could presume to claim, you bear a testimony, in which I do most heartily concur, to the *freedom* at least of our *intercourse*, and the readiness and respect with which you were listened to. Your words are: "Much as I owe to Oriel in the way of mental improvement, to none, as I think, do I owe so much as to yourself. I know who it was first gave me heart to look about me after my election, and taught me to think correctly, and – strange office for an instructor – to rely upon myself. Nor can I forget that it has been at your kind suggestion, that I have since been led to employ myself in the consideration of several subjects, which I cannot doubt have been very beneficial to my mind."

'If in all this I was erroneous, – if I have misled you, or any one else, into "the pride of reason," or any other kind of pride, –

or if I have entertained, or led others into, any wrong opinions, I can only say I sincerely regret it. And again I rejoice if I have been the means of contributing to form in any one that "high religious temper and unclouded faith" of which I not only believe, with you, that they are able to withstand tendencies towards infidelity, but also, that *without* them, no correctness of abstract opinions is worth much. But what I meant to point out, is, that there was plainly nothing to preclude you from offering friendly admonition (when your view of my principles changed), with a full confidence of being at least patiently and kindly listened to.

'I for my part could not bring myself to find relief in escaping the society of an old friend, – with whom I had been accustomed to frank discussion, – on account of my differing from him as to certain principles, whether through a change of *his* views, or (much more) of *my own*, – till at least I had made full trial of private and affectionate remonstrance and free discussion. Even a "man that is a heretic" we are told, even a ruler of a Church is not to reject, till after repeated admonitions.

'But though your regard for me does not show itself such as I think mine would have been under similar circumstances, I will not therefore reject what remains of it. Let us pray for each other that it may please God to enlighten whichever of us is, on any point, in error, and recall him to the truth; and that at any rate we may hold fast that charity, without which all knowledge, and all faith, that could remove mountains, will profit us nothing.

'I fear you will read with a jaundiced eye, – if you venture to read it at all – any publication of mine; but "for auld lang syne" I take advantage of a frank to enclose you my last two addresses to my clergy.

'Very sincerely yours,
'RD. WHATELY.'

4

'Oriel, November 11, 1834.
'My dear Lord,
'The remarks contained in your last letter do not come upon me by surprise, and I can only wish that I may be as able to explain myself to you, as I do with a clear and honest conscience to myself. Your Grace will observe that the letter of mine from which you make an extract, was written when I *was* in habits of

intimacy with you, in which I have not been of late years. It does not at all follow, because I could then speak freely to you, that I might at another time. Opportunity is the chief thing in such an office as delivering to a superior an opinion about himself. Though I never concealed my opinion from you, I have never been forward. I have spoken when place and time admitted, when my opinion was asked, when I was called to your side and was made your counsellor. No such favourable circumstances have befallen me of late years, – if I must now state in explanation what in truth has never occurred to me in *this fulness*, till now I am called to reflect upon my own conduct and to account for an apparent omission. I have spoken the first opportunity you have given me; and I am persuaded good very seldom comes of *volunteering* a remonstrance.

'Again, I cannot doubt for an instant that you have long been aware in a measure that my opinions differed from your Grace's. You knew it when at Oxford, for you often found me differing from you. You must have felt it, at the time you left Oxford for Dublin. You must have known it from hearsay in consequence of the book I have published. What indeed can account for my want of opportunities to speak to you freely my mind, but the feeling on your part, (which, if existing, is nothing but a fair reason,) that my views are different from yours?

'And that difference is certainly of no recent date. I tacitly allude to it in the very letter you quote – in which, I recollect well that the words "strange office for an instructor – *to rely upon myself*," were intended to convey to you that, much as I valued (and still value) your great kindness and the advantage of your countenance to me at that time, yet even then I did not fall in with the line of opinions which you had adopted. In them I never acquiesced. Doubtless I may have used at times sentiments and expressions, which I should not now use; but I believe these had no root in my mind, and as such they were mere idle words which I ought ever to be ashamed of, because they *were* idle. But the opinions to which I especially alluded in my former letter as associated by the world with your Grace's name under the title of "Liberal," (but not, as you suppose, received by me on the world's authority,) are those which may be briefly described as the Anti-superstition notions; and to these I do not recollect ever assenting. Connected with these I would instance the undervaluing of Antiquity, and resting on one's own reasonings, judgments, definitions, &c., rather than authority and precedent; and I think

I gave very little in to this; – for a very short time too (if at all), in to the notion that the State, as such, had nothing to do with religion. On the other hand, whatever I held then deliberately, I believe I hold now; though perhaps I may not consider them as points of such prominent importance, or with precisely the same bearing as I did then: – as the abolition of the Jewish Sabbath, the unscripturalness of the doctrine of imputed righteousness (i.e. our Lord's active obedience) – the mistakes of the so-called Evangelical system, the independence of the Church; the genius of the Gospel as a Law of Liberty, and the impropriety of forming geological theories from Scripture. Of course every one changes in opinion between twenty and thirty; doubtless, I have changed; yet I am not conscious that I have so much *changed*, as made up my mind on points on which I had no opinion. E.g. I had no opinion about the Catholic Question till 1829. No one can truly say I was ever *for* the Catholics; but I was not against them. In fact I did not enter into the state of the question at all.

'Then as to my change of judgment as to the character of your Grace's opinions, it is natural that, when two persons pursue different lines from the same point, they should not discover their divergence for a long while; especially if there be any kind feeling in the one towards the other. It was not for a very long time that I discovered that your opinions were (as I now think them) but part of intellectual views, so different from your own inward mind and character, so peculiar in themselves, and (if you will let me add) so dangerous. For a long time I thought them to be but different; for a longer, to be but in parts dangerous; but their full character in this respect came on me almost on a sudden. I heard at Naples the project of destroying the Irish Sees, and at first indignantly rejected the notion, which some one suggested, that your Grace had acquiesced in it. I thought I recollected correctly your Grace's opinion of the inherent rights of the Christian Church, and I thought you never would allow men of this world so to insult it. When I returned to England, all was over. I was silent on the same principle that you are silent about it in your letter; that it was not the time for speaking; and I only felt, what I hinted at when I wrote last, a bitter grief, which prompted me, when the act was irretrievable, to hide myself from you. However, I have spoken, with whatever pain to myself, the first opportunity you have given me.

'I might appeal to my conscience without fear in proof of the delight it would give me at this time to associate my name with yours, and to stand forward as your friend and defender, however humble. I should hope you know me enough to be sure, that, however great my faults are, I have no fear of man such as to restrain me, if I could feel I had a call that way. But may God help me, as I will ever strive to fulfil my first duty, the defence of His Church, and of the doctrine of the old Fathers, in opposition to all the innovations and profanities which are rising round us.

'My dear Lord,

'Ever yours most sincerely and gratefully,

'J. H. NEWMAN.

'P.S. I feel much obliged by your kindness in sending me your Addresses to your clergy, which I value highly for your Grace's sake.'

Note on Page 94

EXTRACT OF A LETTER FROM THE REV. E. SMEDLEY, EDITOR OF THE 'ENCYCLOPAEDIA METROPOLITANA'

When I urged on one occasion an 'understanding' I had had with the publishers of the 'Encyclopaedia,' he answered, June 5, 1828, 'I greatly dislike the word "understanding," which is always *misunderstood*, and which occasions more mischief than any other in our language, unless it be its cousin-german "delicacy."'

Note on Page 171

EXTRACT OF A LETTER OF THE LATE REV. FRANCIS A. FABER, OF SAUNDERTON

A letter of Mr F. Faber's to a friend has just now (March, 1878) come into my hands, in which he says, 'I have had a long correspondence with Newman on the subject of my uncle's saying he was "a concealed Roman Catholic" long before he left us. It ends in my uncle making an *amende*.'

Note on Pages 178–80

I have said above, 'Dr. Russell had, perhaps, more to do with my conversion than any one else. He called on me in passing through Oxford in the summer of 1843; and I think I took him over some of the buildings of the University. He called again another summer, on his way from Dublin to London. I do not recollect that he said a word on the subject of religion on either occasion. He sent me at different times several letters. . . . He also gave me one or two books; Veron's *Rule of Faith and some Treatises of the Wallenburghs* was one; a volume of St. Alfonso Liguori's sermons was another. . . . At a later date Dr. Russell sent me a large bundle of penny or halfpenny books of devotion,' &c.

On this passage I observe first that he told me, on one occasion of my seeing him since the publication of the *Apologia*, that I was so far in error, that he had called on me at Oxford once only, not twice. He was quite positive on the point; it was when he was, I believe, on his way to Rome to escape a bishopric.

Secondly, my own mistake has led to some vagueness or inaccuracy in the statements made by others. In a friendly notice of Dr. Russell upon his death, it is said, in the *Times*: –

'Personally he was unknown to the leaders of the movement, but his reputation stood high in Oxford. He was often applied to for information and suggestion on the points arising in the Tractarian controversy. Through a formal call made by him on Dr. Newman a correspondence arose, which resulted in the final determination of the latter to join the Roman Catholic Church.'

On this I remark – (1) that in 1841–5, Dr. Russell was not well known in Oxford, and it cannot be said that then "his reputation stood high" there; (2) that he never was "applied to for information" by any one of us, as far as my knowledge goes; and (3) that his call on me in 1841 (3?) was in no sense "formal"; I had not expected it; I think he introduced himself, though he may have had a letter from Dr. Wiseman; and no "correspondence" arose in consequence. He may perhaps have sent me three letters, independent of each other, in five years; and, as far as I know, he was unaware of his part in my conversion, till he saw my notice of it in the "Apologia."

Note on Page 209

EXTRACT OF A LETTER FROM THE REV. JOHN KEBLE TO THE AUTHOR

'Nov. 18, 1844. – I hope I shall not annoy you if I copy out for you part of a letter which I had the other day from Judge Coleridge: –

'"I was struck with part of a letter from A. B., expressing a wish that Newman should know how warmly he was loved, honoured, and sympathized with by large numbers of Churchmen, so that he might not feel solitary, or, as it were, cast out. What think you of a private address, carefully guarded against the appearance of making him the head of a party, but only assuring him of gratitude, veneration, and love?" &c., &c.

'I thought I would just let you understand how such a person as Coleridge feels.'

Note on Page 213

EXTRACT FROM THE 'TIMES' NEWSPAPER ON THE AUTHOR'S VISIT TO OXFORD IN FEBRUARY, 1878

'The Very Rev. Dr. Newman has this week revisited Oxford for the first time since 1845. He has been staying with the Rev. S. Wayte, President of Trinity College, of which society Dr. Newman was formerly a scholar, and has recently been elected an Honorary Fellow. On Tuesday evening Dr. Newman met a number of old friends at dinner at the President's lodgings, and on the following day he paid a long visit to Dr. Pusey at Christ Church. He also spent a considerable time at Keble College, in which he was greatly interested. In the evening Dr. Newman dined in Trinity College Hall at the high table, attired in his academical dress, and the scholars were invited to meet him afterwards. He returned to Birmingham on Thursday morning.'

Note on Page 266

THE MEDICINAL OIL OF ST. WALBURGA

I have received the following on the subject of the oil of St. Walburga from a German friend, the Rev. Corbinian Wandinger, which is a serviceable addition to what is said upon it in Note B. He says: –

'In your "Apologia" 2nd Edition, p. 302, you say you neither have, nor ever have had, the means of going into the question of the miraculousness of the oil of St. Walburga. By good chance, there has arisen a contest not long ago between two papers, a catholic and a free-thinking one, about this very question, from which I collected materials. Afterwards I asked Professor Suttner, of Eichstädt, if the defender of the miraculousness might be fully and in every point trusted, and I was answered he might, since he was nobody else but the parson of St. Walburga, Rev. Mr. Brudlacher.

'You know all the older literature of the oil of St. Walburga, therefore I restrict myself to statements of a later date than 1625.

'First of the attempts to explain the oil as a natural produce of the rock.

'Some thought of ordinary rock-oil. But the slightest experiment proves that origin, properties, and effect of the oil of St. Walburga and petroleum have nothing common with each other.

'Others thought of a salt-rock, and of solution of the salt particles. But the marble slab from which the oil drops is of Jura-chalk, and in the whole Jura is not a single particle of salt to be found, and the liquor itself does not in the least savour of salt; besides that, if this were the case, the stone must have crumbled into pieces long since, whilst it is quite massive still.

'Others thought of humour in the air, or the so-called sweating of the stones. But why does the slab which bears the holy relics alone sweat? and, why do all others beside, above, beneath it, in and out of the altar-cave, though being of the same nature, remain perfectly dry? Why should it sweat, the whole church being so dry that not a single humid spot of a hand's breadth is visible? Why does this slab not sweat except within a certain period, that is from October 12, the anniversary of depositing, to February 25, the day of the death of St. Walburga? And why does it remain dry at every other time, even at the most humid temperature of the air possible, and in the wettest years, for instance, 1866? Besides, what other stone, and be it in the deepest cave, will sweat during four or five months a quantity of liquor from six to ten Mass (a Mass = 1.07 French Litres)? If these naturalists are asked all this, then they, too, are at the end of their wits.

'To this point I add two facts which may be proved beyond any doubt; the one by unquestionable historical records, the other by still living eye-witnesses. When under Bishop Friedrich von Parsberg the interdict was inflicted on the city of Eichstädt, during all the year 1239 not a single drop of liquor became visible on the coffin-plate of St. Walburga. The contrary fact was stated on June 7, 1835. The cave was opened on this day by chance, passengers longing to see it. To their astonishment they found the stone so profusely dropping with oil, that the golden vase fixed underneath was full to the brim, whereas at this season never had been observed there any fluid. Some weeks later arrived the long-wished-for royal decree which sanctioned the reopening of the convent of St. Walburga; it was signed on that very 7th of June, 1835, by his Majesty King Louis I.

'Moreover, let one try to gather water which is dropping from sweating stone, or glass, or metal, and let him see if it will be pure and limpid, or rather muddy, filthy, and cloudy. The oil of St. Walburga on the contrary, is and remains so limpid and crystal, that a bottle, which had been filled and officially sealed at the reopening of the cave after the Swedish invasion, 1645, preserves to this day the oil so very clear and clean as if it had been filled yesterday; an occurrence never to be observed even on the purest spring-water, according to the testimony of the royal circuit-physician (K. Bezirksarz).

'To this testimony of a naturalist may be added that of a much higher authority. The renowned naturalist, Von Oken, surely an unquestionable expert, came one day, while he was Professor in the University of Munich, to Eichstädt on the special purpose to investigate this extraordinary phenomenon. The cave was opened to him, he received every information he wished for, and having seen and examined everything, he pronounced publicly without any reluctance that he could not explain the matter in a natural way. He took of the liquor to Munich in order to subject it to a chemical analysis, and declared then by writing the result of his researches to be that he could take it neither for natural water, nor oil, and that, in general, he was not able to explain the phenomenon as being in accordance with the laws of nature.

'Let me add the testimony of a historical authority. Mr Sax, counsellor of the government (K. Regierungsrath), in his history of the diocese and city of Eichstädt, after he has spoken of the origin, the properties, and the effect of the oil of St. Walburga, concludes that "they are of such a singular kind, that they not only exceed far the province of extraordinary nature-phenomena, but that they, in spite of the constant discrediting and slandering by bullying free-thinkers, preserved the great confidence of the catholic people even in far distant countries."

'Now of the miracles. There are related by the people many thousands, but, of course, few of them are attested. In the Pastoral paper of Eichstädt, 1857, page 207, I read that Anton Ernest, Bishop of Brünn, in Moravia, announces, under Nov. 1, 1857, to the Bishop of Eichstädt, the recovery of a girl in the establishment of the sisters of charity from blindness, and sends, in order to attest the fact, the following document, which I am to translate literally: –

'"In the name of the indivisible Trinity. We, Anton Ernest, by God's and the Holy See's grace, Bishop of Brünn. After we had received, first by the curate of the establishment of the Daughters of Christian Charity in this place, and then also from other quarters, the notice that a girl in the aforesaid establishment had regained the use of her eyes miraculously in the very moment when she had a vial, containing oil of St. Walburga, offered to her, brought to her mouth and kissed, we thought it to be our duty to research scrupulously into the fact, and to put it beyond all doubt in the way of a special commission, by hearing of witnesses and a trial at the place of the fact, if there be truth, and how much of it, in the supposed miraculous healing.

'"About the report of this commission and the adjoined testimony of the physician, we have then, as prescribes the Holy Council of Trent (Sess. 25), collected the judgments of our theologians and other pious men; and as these all were quite in accordance, and the fact itself with all its circumstances lay before us quite clear and open, we have, after invocation of assistance of the Holy Ghost, pronounced, judged, and decided as follows: –

'"The instantaneous removal of the most pertinacious eyelid-cramp (Augenlied-krampf), which Matilda Makara during many months had hindered in the use of her eyes and kept in blindness, and the simultaneous recurrence of the full eye-sight, phlogistic appearances still remaining in the eyes, which occurred when Matilda Makara on Nov. 7, 1856, had a vial with the oil of St. Walburga brought, full of confidence, to her mouth and kissed, must be acknowledged to be a fact which, besides the order of nature, has been effected by God's grace, and is therefore a miracle.

'"And that the memory of this Divine favour may be preserved, that to God eternal thanks may be given, the confidence of the faithful may be incited and nourished, this devotion to the great wonder-worker St. Walburga may be promoted, we order that this aforegoing decision shall be affixed in the chapel of the Daughters of Christian Charity in this place, that it shall be preserved for all times to come, and that the 7th Nov. shall be celebrated as a holiday every year in this aforesaid establishment.

'"Given in our Episcopal Residence at Brünn,

'"Nov. 1, 1857,

'"(L.S.)   ANTON ERNEST, Bishop."

'A second record about St. Walburga I find in the Eichstädt Pastoral paper, 1858, page 192, from which I take the following: "The Superioress of the Convent of St. Walburga had received in summer 1858 the notice of a miraculous cure written by the Superioress of the Convent of St. Leonard-sur-Mer, Sussex. At request for an authenticated report, John Bamber, chaplain of the Convent of the Holy Infant at St. Leonard-sur-Mer, wrote about the following: 'Sister Walburga had been ill fifteen months, of which five bedridden. The physician pronounced the malady to be incurable. Large exterior tumour, frequent (thrice or four times a day) vomitings were caused by the diseased pylorus. The matter was hopeless, when the Superioress on April 27 thought of using the oil of St. Walburga. The chaplain brought it on the tongue of the sick sister, and in the same moment she had a burning feeling which seemed to her to descend, and to affect especially the sick part. In a few minutes the inner smart ceased, the tumour fell off, she felt recovered. Next morning she rose, assisted at the holy mass, communicated, ate with good appetite. She was quite recovered, but somewhat feeble, as people always are after a great disease. The physician, a Protestant, abode by his opinion the malady to be incurable, acknowledged, however, the healing. His words were: "I believe the healing to be effected by the oil of St Walburga, but how, I don't know." As a Protestant he refused to give testimony that the operation of the oil had been miraculous.

'The report is authenticated by Thomas, Bishop of Southwark.

'Freising, Bayern,
'September 13, 1873.'

Note on Page 282

BONIFACE OF CANTERBURY

When I made the above reference in 1865 to Boniface of Canterbury, I was sure I had seen among my books some recent authoritative declaration on the subject of his *cultus* in opposition to the Bollandists; but I did not know where to look for it. I have now found in our Library (Concess. Offic. t. 2) what was in my mind. It consists of five documents proceeding from the Sacred Congregration of Rites, with the following title: –

'Emo ac Revmo Domino Card Lambruschini Relatore, Taurinen. Approbationis cultûs ab immemorabili tempore praestiti B. Bonifacio à Subaudiâ Archiepiscopi Cantuarien. Instante serenissimo Rege Sardiniae Carolo Alberto Romae, 1838.'

Also Dr. Grant, Bishop of Southwark, has kindly supplied me with the following extract from the Correspondance de Rome, 24 November, 1851, adding 'St. Boniface of Canterbury or of Savoy was beatified *aequipollenter* by Gregory XVI.:'–

'Le B. Boniface de Savoie, xi de ce nom, petit-fils d'Humbert iii, Archevêque de Cantorbéry. Confirmation de son culte, également à la demande du Roi Charles Albert, 7 Sept. 1838. D'abord moine parmi les Chartreux, puis Archevêque de Cantorbéry, consacré par Innocent IV. au Concile Général de Lyons; il occupa le siège 25 ans. Mort en 1270 pendant un voyage en Savoie. Son corps porté à Haucatacombe; concours des populations; miracles; son corps retrouvé intact trois siècles après sa mort. Son nom dans les livres liturgiques. Sa fête célébrée sans aucune interruption. Sur la relation de Card. Lambruschini, la S. C. des Rites le 1 Sept. 1838, décida qu'il constait de cas exceptionnel aux décrets d'Urbain VIII. p. 410.'

APPENDICES

APPENDIX A

Mr. Kingsley and Dr. Newman

A CORRESPONDENCE ON THE QUESTION 'WHETHER DR. NEWMAN TEACHES THAT TRUTH IS NO VIRTUE?'

ADVERTISEMENT

To prevent misconception, I think it necessary to observe, that, in my Letters here published, I am far indeed from implying any admission of the truth of Mr. Kingsley's accusations against the Catholic Church, although I have abstained from making any formal protest against them. The object which led to my writing at all, has also led me, in writing, to turn my thoughts in a different direction.

J. H. N.

January 31, 1864

I

Extract from a Review of Froude's *History of England*, vols. vii and viii, in *Macmillan's Magazine* for January, 1864, signed 'C.K.'

Pages 216, 217

'The Roman religion had, for some time past, been making men not better men, but worse. We must face, we must conceive honestly for ourselves, the deep demoralization which had been brought on in Europe by the dogma that the Pope of Rome had the power of creating right and wrong; that not only truth and falsehood, but morality and immorality, depended on his setting his seal to a bit of parchment. From the time that indulgences were hawked about in his name, which would insure pardon for any man, "*etsi matrem Dei violavisset*," the world in general began to be of that opinion. But the mischief was older and deeper than those indulgences. It lay in the very notion of the dispensing power. A deed might be a crime, or no crime at all – like Henry the Eighth's marriage of his brother's widow – according to the will of the Pope. If it suited the interest or caprice of the old man of Rome *not* to say the word, the doer of a certain deed would be burned alive in hell for ever. If it suited him, on the other hand, to say it, the doer of the same deed would go, sacramentis munitus, to endless bliss. What rule of morality, what eternal law of right and wrong, could remain in the hearts of men born and bred under the shadow of so hideous a deception?

'And the shadow did not pass at once, when the Pope's authority was thrown off. Henry VIII. evidently thought that if the Pope could make right and wrong, perhaps he could do so likewise. Elizabeth seems to have fancied, at one weak moment, that the Pope had the power of making her marriage with Leicester right, instead of wrong.

'Moreover, when the moral canon of the Pope's will was gone, there was for a while no canon of morality left. The average morality of Elizabeth's reign was not so much low, as capricious, self-willed, fortuitous; magnificent one day in virtue, terrible the next in vice. It was not till more than one generation had grown up and died with the Bible in their hands, that Englishmen and Germans began to understand (what Frenchmen and Italians did not understand) that they were to be judged by the everlasting laws of a God who was no respecter of persons.

'So, again, of the virtue of truth. Truth, for its own sake, had never been a virtue with the Roman clergy. Father Newman informs us that it need not, and on the whole ought not to be; that cunning is the weapon which Heaven has given to the saints wherewith to withstand the brute male force of the wicked world which marries and is given in marriage. Whether his notion be doctrinally correct or not, it is at least historically so.

'Ever since Pope Stephen forged an epistle from St. Peter to Pepin, King of the Franks, and sent it with some filings of the saint's holy chains, that he might bribe him to invade Italy, destroy the Lombards, and confirm to him the "Patrimony of St. Peter;" ever since the first monk forged the first charter of his monastery, or dug the first heathen Anglo-Saxon out of his barrow, to make him a martyr and a worker of miracles, because his own minster did not "draw" as well as the rival minster ten miles off; – ever since this had the heap of lies been accumulating, spawning, breeding fresh lies, till men began to ask themselves whether truth was a thing worth troubling a practical man's head about, and to suspect that tongues were given to men, as claws to cats and horns to bulls, simply for purposes of offence and defence.'

II

DR. NEWMAN to MESSRS. MACMILLAN AND CO.

The Oratory, Dec. 30, 1863

Gentlemen,

I do not write to you with any controversial purpose, which would be preposterous; but I address you simply because of your special interest in a Magazine which bears your name.

That highly respected name you have associated with a Magazine, of which the January number has been sent to me by this morning's post, with a pencil mark calling my attention to page 217.

There, apropos of Queen Elizabeth, I read as follows: –

'Truth, for its own sake, had never been a virtue with the Roman clergy. Father Newman informs us that it need not, and on the whole ought not to be; that cunning is the weapon which Heaven has given to the saints wherewith to withstand the brute male force of the wicked world which marries and is given in marriage. Whether his notion be doctrinally correct or not, it is at least historically so.'

There is no reference at the foot of the page to any words of mine, much less any quotation from my writings, in justification of this statement.

I should not dream of expostulating with the writer of such a passage, nor with the editor who could insert it without appending evidence in proof of its allegations. Nor do I want any reparation from either of them. I neither complain of them for their act, nor should I thank them if they reversed it. Nor do I even write to you with any desire of troubling you to send me an answer. I do but wish to draw the attention of yourselves, as gentlemen, to a grave and gratuitous slander, with which I feel confident you will be sorry to find associated a name so eminent as yours.

I am, Gentlemen,
Your obedient Servant,
(Signed) JOHN H. NEWMAN

III

The REV. CHARLES KINGSLEY to DR. NEWMAN

Eversley Rectory, January 6, 1864

Reverend Sir,

I have seen a letter of yours to Mr. Macmillan, in which you complain of some expressions of mine in an article in the January number of Macmillan's Magazine.

That my words were just, I believed from many passages of your writings; but the document to which I expressly referred was one of your Sermons on 'Subjects of the Day,' No. XX., in the volume published in 1844, and entitled 'Wisdom and Innocence.'

It was in consequence of that Sermon, that I finally shook off the strong influence which your writings exerted on me; and for much of which I still owe you a deep debt of gratitude.

I am most happy to hear from you that I mistook (as I understand from your letter) your meaning; and I shall be most happy, on your showing me that I have wronged you, to retract my accusation as publicly as I have made it.

I am, Reverend Sir,
Your faithful Servant,
(Signed) CHARLES KINGSLEY

IV

DR. NEWMAN to the REV. CHARLES KINGSLEY

The Oratory, Birmingham,
January 7, 1864

Reverend Sir,

I have to acknowledge your letter of the 6th, informing me that you are the writer of an article in Macmillan's Magazine, in which I am mentioned, and referring generally to a Protestant sermon of mine, of seventeen pages, published by me, as Vicar of St. Mary's, in 1844, and treating of the bearing of the Christian towards the world, and of the character of the reaction of that bearing upon him; and also, referring to my works *passim*; in justification of your statement, categorical and definite, that 'Father Newman informs us that truth for its own sake need not, and on the whole ought not to be, a virtue with the Roman clergy'.

I have only to remark, in addition to what I have already said with great sincerity to Messrs. Macmillan and Co., in the letter of which you speak, and to which I refer you, that, when I wrote to them, no person whatever, whom I had ever seen or heard of, had occurred to me as the author of the statement in question. When I received your letter, taking upon yourself the authorship, I was amazed.

I am, Reverend Sir,
Your obedient Servant,
(Signed) JOHN H. NEWMAN

V

DR. NEWMAN to X. Y., ESQ.*

The Oratory, January 8, 1864

Dear Sir,

I thank you for the friendly tone of your letter of the 5th just received, and I wish to reply to it with the frankness which it invites. I have heard from Mr. Kingsley, avowing himself, to my extreme astonishment, the author of the passage about which I wrote to Messrs. Macmillan. No one, whose name I had ever heard, crossed my mind as the writer in their Magazine: and, had any one said that it was Mr. Kingsley, I should have laughed in his face. Certainly, I saw the initials at the end; but, you must recollect, I live out of the world; and, I must own, if Messrs. Macmillan will not think the confession rude, that, as far as I remember, I never before saw even the outside of their Magazine. And so of the Editor: when I saw his name on the cover, it conveyed to me absolutely no idea whatever. I am not defending myself, but merely stating what was the fact; and as to the article, I said to myself, 'Here is a young scribe, who is making himself a cheap reputation by smart hits at safe objects.'

All this will make you see, not only how I live out of the world, but also how wanton I feel it to have been in the parties concerned thus to let fly at me. Were I in active controversy with the Anglican body, or any portion of it, as I have been before now, I should consider untrue assertions about me to be in a certain sense a rule of the game, as times go, though God forbid that I should indulge in them myself in the case of another. I have never been very sensitive of such attacks; rarely taken notice of them. Now, when I have long ceased from controversy, they continue: they have lasted incessantly from the year 1833 to this day. They do not ordinarily come in my way: when they do, I let them pass through indolence. Sometimes friends send me specimens of them; and sometimes they are such as I am bound to answer, if I would not compromise interests which are dearer to me than life. The January number of the Magazine was sent to

---

* A gentleman who interposed between Mr. Kingsley and Dr. Newman.

me, I know not by whom, friend or foe, with the passage on which I have animadverted, emphatically, not to say indignantly, scored against. Nor can there be a better proof that there was a call upon me to notice it, than the astounding fact that you can so calmly (excuse me) 'confess plainly' of yourself, as you do, 'that you had read the passage, and did not even think that I or any of my communion would think it unjust.'

Most wonderful phenomenon! An educated man, breathing English air, and walking in the light of the nineteenth century, thinks that neither I nor any members of my communion feel any difficulty in allowing that 'Truth for its own sake need not, and on the whole ought not to be, a virtue with the Roman clergy;' nay, that they are not at all surprised to be told that 'Father Newman had informed' the world, that such is the standard of morality acknowledged, acquiesced in, by his co-religionists! But, I suppose, in truth, there is nothing at all, however base, up to the high mark of Titus Oates, which a Catholic may not expect to be believed of him by Protestants, however honourable and hard-headed. However, dismissing this natural train of thought, I observe on your avowal as follows; and I think what I shall say will commend itself to your judgment as soon as I say it.

I think you will allow then, that there is a broad difference between a virtue, considered in itself as a principle or rule, and the application or limits of it in human conduct. Catholics and Protestants, in their view of the substance of the moral virtues, agree, but they carry them out variously in detail; and in particular instances, and in the case of particular actors or writers, with but indifferent success. Truth is the same in itself and in substance to Catholic and Protestant; so is purity: both virtues are to be referred to that moral sense which is the natural possession of us all. But when we come to the question in detail, whether this or that act in particular is conformable to the rule of truth, or again to the rule of purity; then sometimes there is a difference of opinion between individuals, sometimes between schools, and sometimes between religious communions. I, on my side, have long thought, even before I was a Catholic, that the Protestant system, as such, leads to a lax observance of the rule of purity; Protestants think that the Catholic system, as such, leads to a lax observance of the rule of truth. I am very sorry that they should think so, but I cannot help it; I lament their mistake, but I bear it as I may. If Mr. Kingsley had said no more than this, I should not have felt it necessary to criticize such an ordinary remark. But, as I should be committing a crime, heaping dirt upon my soul, and storing up for myself remorse and confusion of face at a future day, if I applied my abstract belief of the latent sensuality of Protestantism, on *à priori* reasoning, to individuals, to living persons, to authors and men of name, and said (not to make disrespectful allusion to the living) that Bishop Van Mildert, or the Rev. Dr. Spry, or Dean Milner, or the Rev. Charles Simeon 'informs us that chastity for its own sake need not be, and on the whole ought not to be, a virtue with the Anglican clergy,' and then, when challenged for the proof, said, '*Vide* Van Mildert's Bampton Lectures and Simeon's Skeleton Sermons *passim*;' and, as I should only make the matter still worse, if I pointed to flagrant instances of paradoxical divines or of bad clergymen among Protestants, as, for instance, to that popular London preacher at the end of last century who advocated polygamy in print; so, in like manner, for a writer, when he is criticizing definite historical facts of the sixteenth century, which stand or fall on their own merits, to go out of his way to have a fling at an unpopular name, living but 'down,' and boldly to say to those who know no better, who know nothing but what he tells them, who take their tradition of historical facts from him, who do not know *me*, – to say of *me*, 'Father Newman *informs* us that Truth for its own sake *need not be, and on the whole ought not to be*, a virtue with the Roman clergy,' and to be thus brilliant and antithetical (save the mark!) in the very cause of Truth, is a proceeding of so special a character as to lead me to exclaim, after the pattern of the celebrated saying, 'O Truth, how many lies are told in thy name!'

Such being the state of the case, I think I shall carry you along with me when I say, that, if there is to be any explanation in the Magazine of so grave an inadvertence, it concerns the two gentlemen who are responsible for it, of what complexion that explanation shall be. For me, it is not I who ask for it; I look on mainly as a spectator, and shall praise or blame, according to my best judgment, as I see what they do. Not that, in so acting, I am implying a doubt of all that you tell me of them; but 'handsome is, that handsome does.' If they set about proving their point, or, should they find that impossible, if they say so, in either case I shall call them *men*. But, – bear with me for harbouring a suspicion which Mr. Kingsley's letter to me has inspired, – if they propose merely to smooth the matter over by publishing to the world that I have 'complained,' or that 'they yield to my letters, expostulations, representations, explanations,' or that 'they are quite ready to be convinced of their mistake, if I will convince them,' or that 'they have profound respect for me, but really they are not the only persons who have gathered from my writings what they have said of me,' or that 'they are unfeignedly surprised that I should visit in their case what I have passed over in the case of others,' or that 'they have ever had a true sense of my good points, but cannot be expected to be blind to my faults,' if this be the sum total of what they are to say, and they ignore the fact that the *onus probandi* of a very definite accusation lies upon them, and that they have no right to throw the burden upon others, then, I say with submission, they had better let it all alone, as far as I am concerned, for a half-measure settles nothing.

January 10. I will add, that any letter addressed to me by Mr. Kingsley, I account public property; not so, should you favour me with any fresh communication yourself.

I am, Dear Sir,

Yours faithfully,

(Signed) JOHN H. NEWMAN

VI

The REV. CHARLES KINGSLEY to DR. NEWMAN

Eversley Rectory, January 14, 1864

Reverend Sir,

I have the honour to acknowledge your answer to my letter.

I have also seen your letter to Mr X. Y. On neither of them shall I make any comment, save to say, that, if you fancy that I have attacked you because you were, as you please to term it, 'down,' you do me a great injustice; and also, that the suspicion expressed in the latter part of your letter to Mr X. Y., is needless.

The course, which you demand of me, is the only course fit for a gentleman; and, as the tone of your letters (even more than their language) make me feel, to my very deep pleasure, that my opinion of the meaning of your words was a mistaken one, I shall send at once to Macmillan's Magazine the few lines which I inclose.

You say, that you will consider my letters as public. You have every right to do so.

I remain, Reverend Sir,

Yours faithfully,

(Signed) C. KINGSLEY

VII

[*This will appear in the next number*]

'TO THE EDITOR OF *MACMILLAN'S MAGAZINE*

'Sir,

'In your last number I make certain allegations against the teaching of the Rev. Dr. Newman, which were founded on a Sermon of his, entitled "Wisdom and Innocence," (the sermon will be fully described, as to* . . .).

'Dr. Newman has, by letter, expressed in the strongest terms, his denial of the meaning which I have put upon his words.

'No man knows the use of words better than Dr. Newman; no man, therefore, has a better right to define what he does, or does not, mean by them.

'It only remains, therefore, for me to express my hearty regret

---

* Here follows a word or half-word, which neither I nor any one else to whom I have shown the MS can decypher. I have at pp. 368–9 filled in for Mr. Kingsley what I understood him to mean by 'fully'.   J. H. N.

at having so seriously mistaken him; and my hearty pleasure at finding him on the side of Truth, in this, or any other, matter.

(Signed) CHARLES KINGSLEY'

VIII

DR. NEWMAN to the REV. CHARLES KINGSLEY

The Oratory, January 17, 1864

Reverend Sir,

Since you do no more than announce to me your intention of inserting in Macmillan's Magazine the letter, a copy of which you are so good as to transcribe for me, perhaps I am taking a liberty in making any remarks to you upon it. But then, the very fact of your showing it to me seems to invite criticism; and so sincerely do I wish to bring this painful matter to an immediate settlement, that, at the risk of being officious, I avail myself of your courtesy to express the judgment which I have carefully formed upon it.

I believe it to be your wish to do me such justice as is compatible with your duty of upholding the consistency and quasi-infallibility which is necessary for a periodical publication; and I am far from expecting any thing from you which would be unfair to Messrs. Macmillan and Co. Moreover, I am quite aware, that the reading public, to whom your letter is virtually addressed, cares little for the wording of an explanation, provided it be made aware of the fact that an explanation has been given.

Nevertheless, after giving your letter the benefit of both these considerations, I am sorry to say I feel it my duty to withhold from it the approbation which I fain would bestow.

Its main fault is, that, quite contrary to your intention, it will be understood by the general reader to intimate, that I have been confronted with definite extracts from my works, and have laid before you my own interpretations of them. Such a proceeding I have indeed challenged, but have not been so fortunate as to bring about.

But besides, I gravely disapprove of the letter as a whole. The grounds of this dissatisfaction will be best understood by you, if I place in parallel columns its paragraphs, one by one, and what I conceive will be the popular reading of them.

This I proceed to do.

I have the honour to be,

Reverend Sir,

Your obedient Servant,

(Signed) JOHN H. NEWMAN

Mr. Kingsley's Letter	*Unjust, but too probable, popular rendering of it*
1. Sir, – In your last number I made certain allegations against the teaching of the Rev. Dr. Newman, which were founded on a Sermon of his, entitled 'Wisdom and Innocence,' preached by him as Vicar of St. Mary's, and published in 1844.	
2. Dr. Newman has, by letter, expressed in the strongest terms his denial of the meaning which I have put upon his words.	2. I have set before Dr. Newman, as he challenged me to do, extracts from his writings, and he has affixed to them what he conceives to be their legitimate sense, to the denial of that in which I understood them.
3. No man knows the use of words better than Dr. Newman; no man, therefore, has a better right to define what he does, or does not, mean by them.	3. He has done this with the skill of a great master of verbal fence, who knows, as well as any man living, how to insinuate a doctrine without committing himself to it.

4. It only remains, therefore, for me to express my hearty regret at having so seriously mistaken him, and my hearty pleasure at finding him on the side of truth, in this or any other matter.

4. However, while I heartily regret that I have so seriously mistaken the sense which he assures me his words were meant to bear, I cannot but feel a hearty pleasure also, at having brought him, for once in a way, to confess that after all truth is a Christian virtue.

IX

REV. CHARLES KINGSLEY to DR. NEWMAN

Eversley Rectory, January 18, 1864

Reverend Sir,

I do not think it probable that the good sense and honesty of the British Public will misinterpret my apology, in the way in which you expect.

Two passages in it, which I put in in good faith and good feeling, may, however, be open to such a bad use, and I have written to Messrs. Macmillan to omit them; viz. the words, 'No man knows the use of words better than Dr. Newman;' and those, 'My hearty pleasure at finding him in the truth (*sic*) on this or any other matter.'

As to your Art. 2, it seems to me, that, by referring publicly to the Sermon on which my allegations are founded, I have given, not only you, but every one an opportunity of judging of their injustice. Having done this, and having frankly accepted your assertion that I was mistaken, I have done as much as one English gentleman can expect from another.

I have the honour to be,
Reverend Sir,
Your obedient Servant,
(Signed) CHARLES KINGSLEY

X

DR. NEWMAN to MESSRS. MACMILLAN & CO.

The Oratory, January 22, 1864

Gentlemen,

Mr. Kingsley, the writer of the paragraph to which I called your attention on the 30th of last month, has shown his wish to recall words, which I considered a great affront to myself, and a worse insult to the Catholic priesthood. He has sent me the draft of a Letter which he proposes to insert in the February number of your Magazine; and, when I gave him my criticisms upon it, he had the good feeling to withdraw two of its paragraphs.

However, he did not remove that portion of it, to which, as I told him, lay my main objection.

That portion ran as follows: –

'Dr. Newman has by letter expressed in the strongest terms his denial of the meaning which I have put upon his words.'

My objection to this sentence, which (with the addition of a reference to a Protestant sermon of mine, which he says formed the ground of his assertion, and of an expression of regret at having mistaken me) constitutes, after the withdrawal of the two paragraphs, the whole of his proposed letter, I thus explained to him: –

'Its [the proposed letter's] main fault is, that, quite contrary to your intention, it will be understood by the general reader to intimate, that I have been confronted with definite extracts from my works, and have laid before you my own interpretation of them. Such a proceeding I have indeed challenged, but have not been so fortunate as to bring about.'

In answer to this representation, Mr. Kingsley wrote to me as follows: –

'It seems to me, that, by referring publicly to the sermon, on which my allegations are founded, I have given, not only you, but every one, an opportunity of judging of their injustice. Having done this, and having frankly accepted your assertion that I was mistaken, I have done as much as one English gentleman can expect from another.'

I received this reply the day before yesterday. It disappointed me, for I had hoped that, with the insertion of a letter from him in your Magazine for February, there would have been an end of the whole matter. However, I have waited forty-eight hours, to give time for his explanation to make its full, and therefore its legitimate impression on my mind. After this interval, I find my judgment of the passage just what it was.

Moreover, since sending to Mr. Kingsley that judgment, I have received a letter from a friend at a distance, whom I had consulted, a man about my own age, who lives out of the world of theological controversy and contemporary literature, and whose intellectual habits especially qualify him for taking a clear and impartial view of the force of words. I put before him the passage in your January number, and the writer's proposed letter in February,* and I asked him whether I might consider the letter sufficient for its purpose, without saying a word to show him the leaning of my own mind. He answers:

'In answer to your question, whether Mr. Kingsley's proposed reparation is sufficient, I have no hesitation in saying, Most decidedly not. Without attempting to quote any passage from your writings which justifies in any manner the language which he has used in his review, he leaves it to be inferred that the representation, which he has given of your statements and teaching in the sermon to which he refers, is the fair and natural and primary sense of them, and that it is only by your declaring that you did not mean what you really and in effect said, that he finds that he had made a false charge.'

This opinion thus given came to me, I repeat, *after* I had sent to Mr. Kingsley the letter of objection, of which I have quoted a portion above. You will see that, though the two judgments are independent of each other, they in substance coincide.

It only remains for me then to write to you again; and, in writing to you now, I do no more than I did on the 30th of December. I bring the matter before you, without requiring from you any reply.

I am, Gentlemen,
Your obedient Servant,
(Signed) JOHN H. NEWMAN

* Viz. as it is given above, pp. 366–7.   J. H. N.

XI

LETTER OF EXPLANATION FROM MR. KINGSLEY, AS IT STANDS IN MACMILLAN'S MAGAZINE FOR FEBRUARY, 1864, P. 368

To the Editor of Macmillan's Magazine

Sir,

In your last number I made certain allegations against the teaching of Dr. John Henry Newman, which I thought were justified by a Sermon of his, entitled 'Wisdom and Innocence' (Sermon 20 of 'Sermons bearing on Subjects of the Day'). Dr. Newman has by letter expressed, in the strongest terms, his denial of the meaning which I have put upon his words. It only remains, therefore, for me to express my hearty regret at having so seriously mistaken him.

Yours faithfully,

(Signed)   CHARLES KINGSLEY

Eversley, January 14, 1864

XII

REFLECTIONS ON THE ABOVE

I shall attempt a brief analysis of the foregoing correspondence; and I trust that the wording which I shall adopt will not offend against the gravity due both to myself and to the occasion. It is impossible to do justice to the course of thought evolved in it without some familiarity of expression.

Mr. Kingsley begins then by exclaiming, – 'O the chicanery, the wholesale fraud, the vile hypocrisy, the conscience-killing tyranny of Rome! We have not far to seek for an evidence of it. There's Father Newman to wit: one living specimen is worth a hundred dead ones. He, a Priest writing of Priests, tells us that lying is never any harm.'

I interpose: 'You are taking a most extraordinary liberty with my name. If I have said this, tell me when and where.'

Mr. Kingsley replies: 'You said it, Reverend Sir, in a Sermon which you preached, when a Protestant, as Vicar of St. Mary's, and published in 1844; and I could read you a very salutary lecture on the effects which that Sermon had at the time on my own opinion of you.'

I make answer: 'Oh . . . *Not*, it seems, as a Priest speaking of Priests; – but let us have the passage.'

Mr. Kingsley relaxes: 'Do you know, I like your *tone*. From your *tone* I rejoice, greatly rejoice, to be able to believe that you did not mean *what you said*.'

I rejoin: '*Mean* it! I maintain I never *said* it, whether as a Protestant or as a Catholic.'

Mr. Kingsley replies: 'I waive that point.'

I object: 'Is it possible! What? waive the main question! I either said it or I didn't. You have made a monstrous charge against me; direct, distinct, public. You are bound to prove it as directly, as distinctly, as publicly; – or to own you can't.'

'Well,' says Mr. Kingsley, 'if you are quite sure you did not say it, I'll take your word for it; I really will.'

My *word*! I am dumb. Somehow I thought that it was my *word* that happened to be on trial. The *word* of a Professor of lying, that he does not lie!

But Mr. Kingsley re-assures me: 'We are both gentlemen,' he says: 'I have done as much as one English gentleman can expect from another.'

I begin to see: he thought me a gentleman at the very time that he said I taught lying on system. After all, it is not I, but it is Mr. Kingsley who did not mean what he said. 'Habemus confitentem reum.'

So we have confessedly come round to this, preaching without practising; the common theme of satirists from Juvenal to Walter Scott! 'I left Baby Charles and Steenie laying his duty before him', says King James of the reprobate Dalgarno: 'O Geordie, jingling Geordie, it was grand to hear Baby Charles laying down the guilt of dissimulation, and Steenie lecturing on the turpitude of incontinence.'

While I feel then that Mr. Kingsley's February explanation is miserably insufficient in itself for his January enormity, still I feel also that the Correspondence, which lies between these two acts of his, constitutes a real satisfaction to those principles of historical and literary justice to which he has given so rude a shock.

Accordingly, I have put it into print, and make no further criticism on Mr. Kingsley.

J. H. N.

APPENDIX B

'What, Then, Does Dr. Newman Mean?'

A REPLY TO A PAMPHLET LATELY PUBLISHED BY DR.
NEWMAN

by

The Reverend Charles Kingsley

It is not more than a hyperbole to say, that, in certain
cases, a lie is the nearest approach to truth.

NEWMAN, *Sermons on the Theory of Religious Belief*, (page
343)

Dr. Newman has made a great mistake. He has published a
correspondence between himself and me, with certain 'Reflexions'
and a title-page, which cannot be allowed to pass without a
rejoinder.

Before commenting on either, I must give a plain account of
the circumstances of the controversy, which seem to have been
misunderstood in several quarters. In the January number of
Macmillan's Magazine, I deliberately and advisedly made use of
these words: –

'Truth, for its own sake, had never been a virtue with the
Roman clergy. Father Newman informs us that it need not, and,
on the whole, ought not to be; that cunning is the weapon which
Heaven has given to the saints wherewith to withstand the brute
male force of the wicked world which marries and is given in
marriage.' This accusation I based upon a considerable number
of passages in Dr. Newman's writings, and especially on a sermon

entitled 'Wisdom and Innocence,' and preached by Dr. Newman as Vicar of St. Mary's, and published as No. XX. of his 'Sermons on Subjects of the Day.'

Dr. Newman wrote, in strong but courteous terms, to Messrs. Macmillan and Co. complaining of this language as a slander. I at once took the responsibility on myself, and wrote to Dr. Newman.

I had been informed (by a Protestant) that he was in weak health, that he wished for peace and quiet, and was averse to controversy; I therefore felt some regret at having disturbed him; and this regret was increased by the moderate and courteous tone of his letters, though they contained, of course, much from which I differed. I addressed to him the following letter, of which, as I trust every English gentleman will feel, I have no reason to be ashamed: –

Reverend Sir,

I have seen a letter of yours to Mr. Macmillan, in which you complain of some expressions of mine in an article in the January number of *Macmillan's Magazine*.

That my words were just, I believed from many passages of your writings; but the document to which I expressly referred was one of your sermons on 'Subjects of the Day,' No. XX. in the volume published in 1844, and entitled 'Wisdom and Innocence.'

It was in consequence of that sermon that I finally shook off the strong influence which your writings exerted on me, and for much of which I still owe you a deep debt of gratitude.

I am most happy to hear from you that I mistook (as I understand from your letter) your meaning; and I shall be most happy, on your showing me that I have wronged you, to retract my accusation as publicly as I have made it.

I am, Rev. Sir,

Your faithful servant,

CHARLES KINGSLEY

I received a very moderate answer from Dr. Newman, and a short correspondence ensued, which ended in my inserting in the February number of *Macmillan's Magazine* the following apology: –

TO THE EDITOR OF MACMILLAN'S MAGAZINE

Sir,

In your last number I made certain allegations against the teaching of Dr. John Henry Newman, which I thought were justified by a sermon of his, entitled 'Wisdom and Innocence' (Sermon XX. of 'Sermons bearing on Subjects of the Day'). Dr. Newman has, by letter, expressed in the strongest terms his denial of the meaning which I have put upon his words. It only remains, therefore, for me to express my hearty regret at having so seriously mistaken him.

Yours faithfully,
CHARLES KINGSLEY

My object had been throughout to avoid war, because I thought Dr Newman wished for peace. I therefore dropped the question of the meaning of 'many passages of his writings,' and confined myself to the sermon entitled 'Wisdom and Innocence,' simply to give him an opportunity of settling the dispute on that one ground.

But whether Dr. Newman lost his temper, or whether he thought that he had gained an advantage over me, or whether he wanted a more complete apology than I chose to give, whatever, I say, may have been his reasons, he suddenly changed his tone of courtesy and dignity for one of which I shall only say that it shows sadly how the atmosphere of the Romish priesthood has degraded his notions of what is due to himself; and when he published (as I am much obliged to him for doing) the whole correspondence, he appended to it certain reflexions, in which he attempted to convict me of not having believed the accusation which I had made.

There remains for me, then, nothing but to justify my mistake, as far as I can.

I am, of course, precluded from using the sermon entitled 'Wisdom and Innocence' to prove my words. I have accepted Dr. Newman's denial that it means what I thought it did; and Heaven forbid that I should withdraw my word once given, at whatever disadvantage to myself. But more. I am informed by those from whose judgment on such points there is no appeal, that *'en hault courage'* and strict honour, I am also precluded, by the terms of my explanation, from using any other of Dr.

Newman's past writings to prove my assertion. I have declared
Dr. Newman to have been an honest man up to the 1st of
February, 1864. It was, as I shall show, only Dr. Newman's fault
that I ever thought him to be anything else. It depends entirely
on Dr. Newman whether he shall sustain the reputation which he
has so recently acquired. If I give him thereby a fresh advantage
in this argument, he is most welcome to it. He needs, it seems to
me, as many advantages as possible. But I have a right, in self-
justification, to put before the public so much of that sermon,
and of the rest of Dr. Newman's writings, as will show why I
formed so harsh an opinion of them and him, and why I still consider that sermon (whatever may be its meaning) as most dangerous and misleading. And I have a full right to do the same by those
'many passages of Dr. Newman's writings' which I left alone at first,
simply because I thought that Dr. Newman wished for peace.

First, as to the sermon entitled 'Wisdom and Innocence.' It
must be remembered always that it is not a Protestant, but a
Romish sermon. It is occupied entirely with the attitude of 'the
world' to 'Christians' and 'the Church.' By the world appears to
be signified, especially, the Protestant public of these realms.
What Dr. Newman means by Christians, and the Church, he has
not left in doubt; for in the preceding sermon (XIX. p. 328) he
says: 'But, if the truth must be spoken, what are the humble
monk, and the holy nun, and other regulars, as they are called,
but Christians after the very pattern given us in Scripture? What
have they done but this – continue in the world the Christianity
of the Bible? Did our Saviour come on earth suddenly, as He
will one day visit, in whom would He see the features of the
Christians He and His apostles left behind them, but in them?
Who but these give up home and friends, wealth and ease, good
name and liberty of will, for the kingdom of heaven? Where shall
we find the image of St. Paul, or St. Peter, or St. John, or of Mary
the mother of Mark, or of Philip's daughters, but in those who,
whether they remain in seclusion, or are sent over the earth, have
calm faces, and sweet plaintive voices, and spare frames, and
gentle manners, and hearts weaned from the world, and wills
subdued; and for their meekness meet with insult, and for their
purity with slander, and for their gravity with suspicion, and for
their courage with cruelty. . . .' This is his definition of Christians.

And in the sermon itself he sufficiently defines what he means by 'the Church' in two 'notes' of her character, which he shall give in his own words (Sermon XX. p. 346): – 'What, for instance, though we grant that sacramental confession and the celibacy of the clergy do tend to consolidate the body politic in the relation of rulers and subjects, or, in other words, to aggrandise the priesthood? for how can the Church be one body without such relation? . . .

Monks and nuns the only perfect Christians; sacramental confession and the celibacy of the clergy notes of the Church; the laity in relation to the clergy of subjects to rulers. What more? If I, like others, on the strength of Dr. Newman's own definitions, gave to his advice to Christians concerning 'wisdom,' 'prudence,' 'silence,' the meaning which they would have in the mouth of a Romish teacher – St. Alfonso da Liguori, for instance – whom can Dr. Newman blame for the mistake, save himself?

But to the sermon itself; the text of which is from Matthew x. 16. It begins by stating that the Church has been always helpless and persecuted, in proportion to its purity. Dr. Newman then asks, how Christians are to defend themselves if they might not fight? and answers, 'They were allowed the arms, that is, the arts, of the defenceless.' He shows how the weaker animals are enabled to defend themselves by various means, among which he enumerates 'natural cunning, which enables them to elude or even to destroy their enemies.' He goes on to show how the same holds good in our own species, in the case of 'a captive, effeminate race;' of 'slaves;' of 'ill-used and oppressed children;' of the 'subjects of a despot.' 'They exercise the inalienable right of self-defence in such methods as they best may; only, since human nature is unscrupulous, guilt or innocence is all the same to them, if it works their purpose.'

He goes on to point out the analogy between these facts and the conduct fit for Christians. 'The servants of Christ are forbidden to defend themselves by violence; but they are not forbidden other means: direct means are not allowed, but others are even commanded. For instance, foresight, 'beware of men;' avoidance, 'when they persecute you in one city, flee into another:' prudence and skill, as in the text, 'Be ye wise as serpents.'

The mention of the serpent reminds him of the serpent in

Paradise; and he says, 'Considering that the serpent was chosen by the enemy of mankind as the instrument of his temptations in Paradise, it is very remarkable that Christ should choose it as the pattern of wisdom for His followers. It is as if He appealed to the whole world of sin, and to the bad arts by which the feeble gain advantages over the strong. It is as if He set before us the craft and treachery, the perfidy of the slave, and bade us extract a lesson even from so great an evil. It is as if the more we are forbidden violence, the more we are exhorted to prudence; as if it were our bounden duty to rival the wicked in endowments of mind, and to excel them in their exercise.'

Dr. Newman then goes on to assert, that 'if there be one reproach more than another which has been cast upon' the Church, 'it is that of fraud and cunning.' He quotes the imputations of craftiness and deceitfulness thrown upon St. Paul, and even of 'deceit' upon our Lord himself. He then says that 'Priestcraft has ever been considered the badge, and its imputation is a kind of note, of the Church.' He asserts that the accusation has been, save in a few exceptions, unfounded; and that 'the words "craft" and "hypocrisy" are but the version of "wisdom" and "harmlessness" in the language of the world.' 'It is remarkable, however, that not only is harmlessness the corrective of wisdom, securing it against the corruption of craft and deceit, as stated in the text: but innocence, simplicity, implicit obedience to God, tranquillity of mind, contentment, these and the like virtues are in themselves a sort of wisdom; I mean, they produce the same results as wisdom, because God works for those who do not work for themselves; and thus they especially incur the charge of craft at the hands of the world, because they pretend to so little, yet effect so much. This circumstance admits dwelling on.'

He then goes on to mention seven heads: –

'First, sobriety, self-restraint, control of word and feeling, which religious men exercise, have about them an appearance of being artificial, because they are not natural; and of being artful, because artificial;' and adds shortly after, that 'those who would be holy and blameless, the sons of God, find so much in the world to unsettle and defile them, that they are necessarily forced upon a strict self-restraint, lest they should receive injury from such intercourse with it as is unavoidable; and this self-restraint is the first thing which makes holy persons seem wanting in openness and manliness.' Next he points out that 'religious men are a mystery to the world; and being a mystery, they will in mere self-defence be called by the world mysterious, dark, subtle, designing.' Next, that 'it is very difficult to make the world understand the difference between an outward obedience and an inward assent.' He then instances the relations between the early Christians and the heathen magistrates; and adds, that 'when religious men outwardly conform, on the score of duty, to the powers that be, the world is easily led into the mistake that they have renounced their opinions, as well as submitted their actions; and it feels or affects surprise, to find that their opinions remain; and it considers, or calls this, an inconsistency, or a duplicity:' with more to the same purpose.

Next, the silent resignation of Christians is set forth as a cause of the world's suspicion; and 'so is their confidence, in spite of their apparent weakness, their cause will triumph.'

Another cause of the world's suspicion is, the unexpected success of religious men.

Another, that the truth has in itself the power of spreading, with instruments, 'making the world impute' to secret management that uniformity, which is nothing but the echo of the One Living and True Word.

Another, that when Christians prosper, contrary to their own expectations, 'it looks like deceit to show surprise, and to disclaim the work themselves.'

And lastly, because God works for Christians, and they are successful, when they only mean to be dutiful. 'But what duplicity does the world think it, to speak of conscience, or honour, or propriety, or delicacy, or to give other tokens of personal motives, when the event seems to show that a calculation of results has been the actuating principle at bottom. It is God who designs, but His servants seem designing. . . .'

Dr. Newman then goes on to point out how 'Jacob is thought worldly wise in his dealings with Laban, whereas he was a "plain man," simply obedient to the angel'. . . . 'Moses is sometimes called sagacious and shrewd in his measures or his law, as if wise acts might not come from the source of wisdom.' . . . 'Bishops have been called hypocritical in submitting and yet opposing themselves to the civil power, in a matter of plain duty, if a popular movement was the consequence; and then hypocritical again, if they did their best to repress it. And, in like manner, theological doctrines or ecclesiastical usages are styled politic if they are but salutary; as if the Lord of the Church, who has willed her sovereignty, might not effect it by secondary causes. What, for instance, though we grant that sacramental confession and the celibacy of the clergy do tend to consolidate the body politic in the relation of rulers and subjects, or, in other words, to aggrandise the priesthood? For how can the Church be one body without such relation; and why should not He, who has decreed that there should be unity, take measures to secure it?'

The reason of these suspicions on the part of the world is then stated to be, that 'men do not like to hear of the interposition of Providence in the affairs of the world; and they invidiously ascribe ability and skill to His agents, to escape the thought of an Infinite Wisdom and an Almighty Power . . .'.

The sermon then closes with a few lines of great beauty, in that style which has won deservedly for Dr. Newman the honour of being the most perfect orator of this generation; but they have no reference to the question in hand, save the words, 'We will glory in what they disown.'

I have tried conscientiously to give a fair and complete digest of this, to me, very objectionable and dangerous sermon. I have omitted no passage in which Dr. Newman guards himself against the conclusions which I drew from it; and none, I verily believe, which is required for the full understanding of its general drift. I have abstained from all comment as I went on, in order not to prejudice the minds of my readers. But I must now turn round and ask, whether the mistake into which Dr. Newman asserts me to have fallen was not a very reasonable one; and whether the average of educated Englishmen, in reading that sermon, would not be too likely to fall into the same? I put on it, as I thought, the plain and straightforward signification. I find I am wrong; and nothing is left for me but to ask, with some astonishment, What, then, did the sermon mean? Why was it preached? To insinuate that a Church which had sacramental confession and a celibate clergy was the only true Church? Or to insinuate that the admiring young gentlemen who listened to him stood to their fellow-countrymen in the relation of the early Christians to the heathen Romans? Or that Queen Victoria's Government was to the Church of England what Nero's or Diocletian's was to the Church of Rome? It may have been so. I know that men used to suspect Dr. Newman – I have been inclined to do so myself – of writing a whole sermon, not for the sake of the text or of the matter, but for the sake of one single passing hint – one phrase, one epithet, one little barbed arrow which, as he swept magnificently past on the stream of his calm eloquence, seemingly unconscious of all presences, save those unseen, he delivered unheeded, as with his fingertip, to the very heart of an initiated hearer, never to be withdrawn again. I do not blame him for that. It is one of the highest triumphs of oratoric power, and may be employed honestly and fairly, by any person who has the skill to do it honestly and fairly. But then – Why did he entitle his sermon 'Wisdom and Innocence'?

What, then, could I think that Dr. Newman meant? I found a preacher bidding Christians imitate, to some undefined point, the 'arts' of the basest of animals and of men, and even of the Devil himself. I found him, by a strange perversion of Scripture, insinuating that St. Paul's conduct and manner were such as naturally to bring down on him the reputation of being a crafty deceiver. I found him – horrible to have to say it – even hinting the same of One greater than St. Paul. I found him denying or explaining away the existence of that priestcraft which is a notorious fact to every honest student of history; and justifying (as far as I can understand him) that double-dealing by which prelates, in the middle age, too often played off alternately the sovereign against the people and the people against the sovereign, careless which was in the right, as long as their own power gained by the move. I found him actually using of such (and, as I thought, of himself and his party likewise) the words, 'They yield outwardly; to assent inwardly were to betray the faith. Yet they are called deceitful and double-dealing, because they do as much as they can, and not more than they may.' I found him telling Christians that they will always seem 'artificial', and 'wanting in openness and manliness;' that they will always be 'a mystery' to the world, and that the world will always think them rogues; and bidding them glory in what the world (*i.e.* the rest of their fellow-countrymen) disown, and say with Mawworm, 'I like to be despised.'

Now how was I to know that the preacher, who had the reputation of being the most acute man of his generation, and of having a specially intimate acquaintance with the weaknesses of the human heart, was utterly blind to the broad meaning and the plain practical result of a sermon like this, delivered before fanatic and hot-headed young men, who hung over his every word? That he did not foresee that they would think that they obeyed him, by becoming affected, artificial, sly, shifty, ready for concealments and equivocations? That he did not foresee that they, hearing his words concerning priestcraft and double-dealing, and being engaged in the study of the Mediaeval Church, would consider the same chicanery allowed to them which they found practised but too often by the Mediaeval Church? or even go to the Romish casuists, to discover what amount of cunning did or did not come under Dr. Newman's one passing warning against craft and deceit? In a word, that he did not foresee that the natural result of the sermon on the minds of his disciples would be, to make them suspect that truth was not a virtue for its own sake, but only for the sake of the spread of 'catholic opinions,' and the 'salvation of their own souls;' and that cunning was the weapon which Heaven had allowed to them to defend themselves against the persecuting Protestant public?

All England stood round in those days, and saw that this would be the outcome of Dr. Newman's teaching. How was I to know that he did not see it himself?

And as a fact, his teaching had this outcome. Whatever else it did, it did this. In proportion as young men absorbed it into themselves, it injured their straightforwardness and truthfulness. The fact is notorious to all England. It spread misery and shame into many an English home. The net practical result of Dr. Newman's teachings on truthfulness cannot be better summed up than by one of his own disciples, Mr. Ward, who, in his 'Ideal of a Christian Church,' page 382, says thus: –

'Candour is rather an intellectual than a moral virtue, and by no means either universally or distinctively characteristic of the saintly mind.'

Dr. Newman ought to have told his disciple, when he wrote those words, that he was on the highroad to the father of lies; and he ought to have told the world, too, that such was his opinion; unless he wished it to fall into the mistake into which I fell – namely, that he had wisdom enough to know the practical result of his words, and therefore meant what they seemed to say.

Dr. Newman has nothing to blame for that mistake, save his own method. If he would (while a member of the Church of England) persist (as in this sermon) in dealing with matters dark, offensive, doubtful, sometimes actually forbidden, at least according to the notions of the great majority of English Churchmen; if he would always do so in a tentative, paltering way, seldom or never letting the world know how much he believed, how far he intended to go; if, in a word, his method of teaching was a suspicious one, what wonder if the minds of men were filled with suspicions of him? What wonder if they said of him (as he so naïvely, in one of his letters, expresses his fear that they will say again), 'Dr. Newman has the skill of a great master of verbal fence, who knows, as well as any man living, how to insinuate a doctrine without committing himself to it?' If he told the world, as he virtually does in this sermon, 'I know that my conduct looks like cunning; but it is only the "arts" of the defenceless:' what wonder if the world answered, 'No. It is what it seems. That is just what we call cunning; a habit of mind which, once indulged, is certain to go on from bad to worse, till the man becomes – like too many of the mediaeval clergy who indulged in it – utterly untrustworthy.' Dr. Newman, I say, has no one to blame but himself. The world is not so blind but that it will soon find out an honest man if he will take the trouble of talking and acting like one. No one would have suspected him to be a dishonest man, if he had not perversely chosen to assume a style which (as he himself confesses) the world always associates with dishonesty.

When, therefore, Dr. Newman says (p. 363 of his pamphlet) that 'he supposes, in truth, there is nothing at all, however base, up to the high mark of Titus Oates, which a Catholic may not expect to be believed of him by Protestants, however honourable and hard-headed,' he is stating a mere phantom of his own brain.

It is not so. I do not believe it ever was so. In the days when Jesuits were inciting fanatics to assassinate Queen Elizabeth, and again in the days of Gunpowder Plot, there was deservedly a very strong feeling against Romish priests, and against a few laymen who were their dupes; and it was the recollection of that which caused the 'Titus Oates' tragedy, which Dr. Newman so glibly flings in our teeth, omitting (or forgetting) that Oates' villany would have been impossible without the preceding villanies of Popish fanatics, and that he was unmasked, condemned, and punished by the strong and great arm of British law. But there was never, I believe, even in the worst times, any general belief that Catholics, simply as such, must be villains.

There is none now. The Catholic laity of these realms are just as much respected and trusted as the Protestants, when their conduct justifies that respect and trust, as it does in the case of all save a few wild Irish; and so are the Romish priests, as long as they show themselves good and honest men, who confine themselves to the care of their flock. If there is (as there is) a strong distrust of certain Catholics, it is restricted to the proselytizing priests among them; and especially to those who, like Dr. Newman, have turned round upon their mother-Church (I had almost said their mother-country) with contumely and slander. And I confess, also, that this public dislike is very rapidly increasing, for reasons which I shall leave Dr. Newman and his advisers to find out for themselves.

I go on now to other works of Dr. Newman, from which (as I told him in my first letter) I had conceived an opinion unfavourable to his honesty.

I shall be expected to adduce, first and foremost, the too-notorious No. 90 of 'Tracts for the Times.' I shall not do so. On reading that tract over again, I have been confirmed in the opinion which I formed of it at first, that, questionable as it was, it was not meant to be consciously dishonest; that some few sayings in it were just and true; that many of its extravagances were pardonable, as the natural fruit of a revulsion against the popular cry of those days, which called on clergymen to interpret the Articles only in their Calvinistic sense, instead of including under them (as their wise framers intended) not only the Calvinistic, but the Anglican form of thought. There were pages in it which shocked me, and which shock me still. I will instance the commentaries on the 5th, on the 7th, on the 9th, and on the 12th Articles; because in them Dr. Newman seemed to me trying to make the Articles say the very thing which (I believe) the Articles were meant not to say. But I attributed to him no intentional dishonesty. The fullest licence of interpretation should be given to every man who is bound by the letter of a document. The *animus imponentium* should be heard of as little as possible, because it is almost certain to become merely the *animus interpretantium*. And more: Every excuse was to be made for a man struggling desperately to keep himself in what was, in fact, his right place, to remain a member of the Church of England, where Providence had placed him, while he felt himself irresistibly attracted towards Rome. But I saw in that tract a fearful danger for the writer. It was but too probable, that if he continued to demand of that subtle brain of his, such *tours de force* as he had all but succeeded in performing, when he tried to show that the Article against 'the sacrifice of masses' 'did not speak against the mass itself,' he would surely end in one or other of two misfortunes. He would either destroy his own sense of honesty – *i.e.* conscious truthfulness – and become a dishonest person; or he would destroy his common sense – *i.e.* unconscious truthfulness, and become the slave and puppet seemingly of his own logic, really of his own fancy, ready to believe anything, however preposterous, into which he could, for the moment, argue himself. I thought, for years past, that he had become the former; I now see that he has become the latter.

I beg pardon for saying so much about myself. But this is a personal matter between Dr. Newman and me, and I say what I say simply to show, not Dr. Newman, but my fellow-Protestants, that my opinion of him was not an 'impulsive' or 'hastily-formed one.' I know his writings of old, and now. But I was so far just to him, that No. 90, which made all the rest of England believe him a dishonest man, had not the same effect on me.

But again –

I found Dr. Newman, while yet (as far as could be now discovered) a member of the Church of England, aiding and abetting the publication of certain 'Lives of the English Saints,' of which I must say, that no such public outrage on historic truth, and on plain common sense, has been perpetrated in this generation. I do not intend to impute to any of the gentlemen who wrote these lives – and more than one of whom, I believe, I knew personally – the least deliberate intention to deceive. They said what they believed; at least, what they had been taught to believe that they ought to believe. And who had taught them? Dr. Newman can best answer that question. He had, at least, that power over them, and in those days over hundreds more, which genius can always command. He might have used it well. He might have made those 'Lives of Saints,' what they ought to have been, books to turn the hearts of the children to the Fathers, and to make the present generation acknowledge and respect the true sanctity which there was, in spite of all mistakes, in those great men of old – a sanctity founded on true virtue and true piety, which required no tawdry super-structure of lying and ridiculous wonders. He might have said to the author of the 'Life of St. Augustine,' when he found him, in the heat and haste of youthful fanaticism, outraging historic truth and the law of evidence: 'This must not be. Truth for its own sake is a more precious thing than any purpose, however pious and useful, which we may have in hand.' But when I found him allowing the world to accept, as notoriously sanctioned by him, such statements as are found in that life, was my mistake a hasty, or far-fetched, or unfounded one, when I concluded that he did not care for truth for its own sake, or teach his disciples to regard it as a virtue? I found that 'Life of St. Augustine' saying, that though the pretended visit of St. Peter to England wanted historic evidence, 'yet it has undoubtedly been received as a pious opinion by the Church at large, as we learn from some often-quoted words of St. Innocent I. (who wrote A.D. 416), that St. Peter was instrumental in the conversion of the West generally. And this sort of argument, though it ought to be kept quite distinct from documentary and historic proof, and will form no substitute for such proof with those who stipulate for something like legal accuracy in inquiries of this nature, will not be without its effect upon devout minds, accustomed to rest in the thought of God's watchful guardianship over His church.' . . . And much more in the same tone, which is worthily, and consistently summed up by the question: 'On what evidence do we put faith in the existence of St. George, the patron of England? Upon such, assuredly, as an acute critic or skilful pleader might easily scatter to the winds; the belief of prejudiced or credulous witnesses; the unwritten record of empty pageants and bauble decorations. On the side of scepticism might be exhibited a powerful array of suspicious legends and exploded acts. Yet, after all, what Catholic is there but would count it a profaneness to question the existence of St. George?'

When I found Dr. Newman allowing his disciples – members, even then, of the Protestant Church of England – in page after page, in Life after Life, to talk nonsense of this kind, which is not only sheer Popery, but saps the very foundation of historic truth, was it so wonderful that I conceived him to have taught and thought like them?

But more. I found, that although the responsibility of these Saints' Lives was carefully divided and guarded by anonymousness, and by Dr. Newman's advertisement in No. 1, that the different lives would be 'published by their respective authors on their own responsibility,' yet that Dr. Newman had, in what I must now consider merely a moment of amiable weakness, connected himself formally with one of the most offensive of these Lives, and with its most ridiculous statements. I speak of the 'Life of St. Walburga.' There is, in all the Lives, the same tendency to repeat childish miracles, to waive the common laws of evidence, to say to the reader, 'You must believe all or nothing.' But some of them, the writers, for instance, of Vol. IV., which contains, among others, a charming life of St. Neot – treat the stories openly as legends and myths, and tell them as they stand, without asking the reader, or themselves, to believe them altogether. The method is harmless enough, if the legends had stood alone; but dangerous enough, when they stand side by side with stories told in earnest, like that of St. Walburga. In that, not only has the writer expatiated upon some of the most nauseous superstitions of the middle age, but Dr. Newman has, in a preface signed with his initials, solemnly set his seal to the same.

The writer – an Oxford scholar, and, as far as I know, then a professed member of the Church of England – dares to tell us of such miracles as these: –

How a little girl, playing with a ball near the monastery, was punished for her over-fondness for play, by finding the ball stick to her hand, and, running to St. Walburga's shrine to pray, had the ball immediately taken off.

How a woman who would spin on festival-days in like manner found her distaff cling to her hand, and had to beg of St. Walburga's bone, before she could get rid of it.

How a man who came into the church to pray, 'irreverently kept his rough gauntlets, or gloves, on his hands, as he joined them in the posture of prayer.' How they were miraculously torn off, and then, when he repented, 'restored by a miracle.' 'All these', says the writer, 'have the character of a gentle mother correcting the idleness and faults of careless and thoughtless children with tenderness.'

'But the most remarkable and lasting miracle, attesting the holy Walburga's sanctity, is that which reckons her among the saints who are called "Elaeophori", or "unguentiferous", becoming, almost in a literal sense, olive-trees in the courts of God. These are they from whose bones a holy oil distils. That oil of charity and gentle mercy which graced them while alive, and fed in them the flame of universal love at their death, still permeates their bodily remains.' After quoting the names of male saints who have possessed this property, the author goes on to detail how this holy oil fell, in drops, sometimes the size of a hazel-nut, sometimes of a pea, into the silver bowl beneath the stone slab. How, when the state of Aichstadt was laid under an interdict, the holy oil ceased, 'until the Church regained its rights,' and so forth, and so forth; and then, returning to his original image, metaphor, illustration, proof, or whatever else it may be called by reasoners such as he and Dr. Newman, he says that the same flow of oil or dew is related of this female saint and that – women whose souls, like that of Walburga, were touched 'with true compassion; whose bosom, like hers, melted by divine love, was filled with the milk of human kindness,' &c. I can quote no more. I really must recollect that my readers and I are living in the nineteenth century.

And to all this stuff and nonsense, more materialist than the dreams of any bone-worshipping Buddhist, Dr. Newman puts a preface, in which he says of the question whether the 'miracles recorded in these narratives' (*i.e.* in the whole series, this being only No. II.), especially those contained in the life of St. Walburga, 'are to be received as matter of fact;' that 'in this day, and under our present circumstances, we can only reply, that there is no reason why they should not be. They are the kind of facts proper to ecclesiastical history, just as instances of sagacity or daring, personal prowess, or crime, are the facts proper to secular history.' Verily, his idea of 'secular history' is almost as degraded as his idea of 'ecclesiastical.'

He continues: 'There is nothing, then, *primâ facie*, in the miraculous accounts in question to repel a properly-taught or religiously-disposed mind:' only, it has the right of rejecting or accepting them according to the evidence. No doubt; for (as he himself confesses) Mabillon, like many sensible Romanists, has found some of these miracles too strong for his 'acute nostril', and has, therefore, been reproved by Basnage for 'not fearing for himself, and warning the reader.'

But what evidence Dr. Newman requires, he makes evident at once. He, at least, will 'fear for himself,' and swallow the whole as it comes.

'As to the miracles ascribed to St. Walburga, it must be remembered that she is one of the principal saints of her age and country;' and then he goes on to quote the authorities for these miracles. They begin nearly 100 years after her death, with one Wolfhard, a monk. Then follows, more than 400 years after, Philip, Bishop of Aichstadt, the disinterested witness who tells the story of the holy oil ceasing during the interdict, who tells the world how, 'From her virgin limbs, *maxime pectoralibus*, flows this sacred oil, which, by the grace of God and the intercession of the blessed Virgin Walburga, illuminates the blind, makes the deaf hear', &c., and of which he says that he himself once drank a whole cup, and was cured forthwith. Then come the nuns of this same place, equally disinterested witnesses, after the invention of printing; then one Rader, in 1615; and one Gretser, in 1620. But what has become of the holy oil for the last 240 years, Dr. Newman does not say.

In his 'Lectures on the present position of Catholics in England, addressed to the brothers of the Oratory,' in 1851, he has again used the same line of sophism. Argument I cannot call it, while such a sentence as this is to be found: – (p. 295) 'Is the tower of London shut against sight-seers, because the coats of mail or pikes there may have half legendary tales connected with them? Why, then, may not the country people come up in joyous companies, singing and piping, to see the holy coat at Treves?' To see, forsooth! To worship, Dr. Newman would have said, had he known (as I take for granted he does not) the facts of that imposture. He himself, meanwhile, seems hardly sure of the authenticity of the holy coat. He (p. 298) 'does not see why it may not have been what it professes to be.' It may 'have been' so, no doubt, but it certainly is not so now; for the very texture and material of the thing prove it to be spurious. However, Dr. Newman 'firmly believes that portions of the true Cross are at Rome and elsewhere, that the crib of Bethlehem is at Rome,' &c. And more than all; he thinks it 'impossible to withstand the evidence which is brought for the liquefaction of the blood of St. Januarius, at Naples, and for the motion of the eyes of the pictures of the Madonna in the Roman States.'

How art thou fallen from heaven, O Lucifer, son of the Morning!

But when I read these outrages upon common sense, what wonder if I said to myself, 'This man cannot believe what he is saying?'

I believe I was wrong. I have tried, as far as I can, to imagine to myself Dr. Newman's state of mind; and I see now the possibility of a man's working himself into that pitch of confusion, that he can persuade himself, by what seems to him logic, of anything whatsoever which he wishes to believe; and of his carrying self-deception to such perfection that it becomes a sort of frantic honesty, in which he is utterly unconscious, not only that he is deceiving others, but that he is deceiving himself.

But I must say, If this be 'historic truth,' what is historic falsehood? If this be honesty, what is dishonesty? If this be wisdom, what is folly?

I may be told, But this is Roman Catholic doctrine. You have no right to be angry with Dr. Newman for believing it. I answer, this is not Roman Catholic doctrine, any more than belief in miraculous appearances of the Blessed Virgin, or the miracle of the stigmata, on which two matters I shall say something hereafter. No Roman Catholic, as far as I am aware, is bound to believe these things. Dr. Newman has believed them of his own free will. He is anxious, it would seem, to show his own credulity. He has worked his mind, it would seem, into that morbid state, in which nonsense is the only food for which it hungers. Like the sophists of old, he has used reason to destroy reason. I had thought that, like them, he had preserved his own reason, in order to be able to destroy that of others. But I was unjust to him, as he says. While he tried to destroy others' reason, he was at least fair enough to destroy his own. That is all that I can say. Too many prefer the charge of insincerity to that of insipience – Dr. Newman seems not to be of that number.

But more. In connexion with this said life of St. Walburga, Dr. Newman has done a deed, over which I might make merry, if that were my wish. But I am not a wit, like Dr. Newman.

In page 77, we find the following wonderful passage: 'Illuminated men . . . to them the evil influence of Satanic power is horribly discernible . . . and the only way to express their keen perception of it is to say, that they see upon the countenances of the slaves of sin, the marks, and lineaments, and stamp of the evil one; and they smell with their nostrils the horrible fumes which arise from their vices and uncleansed hearts, driving good angels from them in dismay, and attracting and delighting devils. It is said of the holy Sturme, a disciple and companion of Winfred, that in passing a horde of unconverted Germans, as they were bathing and gambolling in a stream, he was so overpowered by the intolerable scent which arose from them, that he nearly fainted away. And no doubt such preternatural discernments are sometimes given to saints' – and a religious reason is given for it which I shall not quote. I should be ashamed to use the sacred name in the same page with such materialist nonsense.

Now this 'no doubt' seemed as convincing to Dr. Newman as to the author. The fly which his disciple had heedlessly cast over the turbid waters of his brain was too fine to be resisted; and he rose at it, heavily but surely, and has hooked himself past remedy. For into his lectures, given before the Catholic University of Ireland, published in 1859, he has inserted, at page 96, on the authority of 'an Oxford writer,' the whole passage which relates to St. Sturme, word for word.

I thought, when I was in my former mind as to Dr. Newman, that he had gone out of his way to tell this fable, in order to intimate to the young gentlemen who had the blessing of his instructions, that they need care nothing for 'truth for its own sake,' in the investigation of a miracle, but take it on any anonymous authority, provided only it made for the Catholic faith. And when I saw that I was wrong, I was sorely puzzled as to why my old friend St. Sturme (against whom I do not say a word) had thus been dragged unceremoniously into a passage on National Literature, which had nothing whatsoever to do with him. But I am not bound to find motives for Dr. Newman's eccentricities.

But now comes the worst part of the matter. Dr. Newman has been taken in. There is no miracle. There never was any in the original document. There is none in Mabillon who quotes it. It is a sheer invention of the ardent Oxford writer.

The story appears first in the Life of St. Sturme, by his contemporary and friend St. Eigils. It may be found in Pertz's 'Monumenta Critica;' and a most charming sketch of mediaeval missionary life it is; all the more so because one can comfortably believe every word of it, from its complete freedom (as far as I recollect) from signs and wonders.

The original passage sets forth how St. Sturme rides on his donkey, and wishing for a place where to found Fulda Abbey, came to a ford where the Sclavonians (not Germans, as the Oxford writer calls them) were bathing, on the way to the fair at Mentz, '*whose naked bodies the animal on which he rode fearing, began to tremble, and the man of God himself shuddered (exhorruit) at their evil smell.*' They mocked him, and went about to hurt him; but Divine providence kept them back, and he went on in safety.

That is all. There is not a hint of a miracle. A horde of dirty savages, who had not, probably, washed for a twelve-month, smelt very strong, and St. Sturme had a nose. As for his 'nearly fainting away,' that is a 'devout imagination.'

Really, if Dr. Newman or the 'Oxford writer' had been monks of more than one Roman Catholic nation, one might have excused their seeing something quite miraculous in any man's being shocked at his fellow-creatures' evil smell; but in Oxford gentlemen, accustomed to the use of soap and water, it is too bad.

Besides, to impute a miracle in this case, is clearly to put the saint, in virtue, below his own donkey; for while the saint was only shocked at the odour, the donkey did what the saint should have done (in imitation of many other saints before and since), and expressed his horror at the impropriety of the *déshabille* of the 'miscreants.' Unless we are to understand a miracle – and why not? – in the donkey's case likewise; not indeed expressed, but understood as a matter of course by 'properly taught and religiously-disposed minds;' and piously hold that the virtue of the saint (which seems, from monkish writings, to be some kind of gas or oil) diffused itself through the saddle into the inmost recesses of the donkey's frame, and imbued him for the moment, through the merits of St. Sturme, with a preternatural and angelic modesty?

Which if we shall believe, we shall believe something not a whit more ridiculous than many a story told in these hapless volumes.

What can I say, again, of Dr. Newman's 'Lectures on Anglican Difficulties', published in 1850, save what I have said already? That if I, like hundreds more, have mistaken his meaning and intent, he must blame not me, but himself. If he will indulge in subtle paradoxes, in rhetorical exaggerations; if, whenever he touches on the question of truth and honesty, he will take a perverse pleasure in saying something shocking to plain English notions, he must take the consequences of his own eccentricities.

He tells us, for instance, in Lecture VIII. that the Catholic Church 'holds it better for sun and moon to drop from heaven, for the earth to fail, and for all the many millions on it to die of starvation in extremest agony, as far as temporal affliction goes, than that one soul, I will not say should be lost, but should commit one single venial sin, should tell one wilful untruth, or should steal one poor farthing without excuse.' And this in the face of those permissions to deception, which may be seen formalized and detailed in the works of the Romish casuists, and especially in those of the great Liguori, whose books have received the public and solemn sanction of the Romish see. In one only way can Dr. Newman reconcile this passage with the teaching of his Church; namely, by saying that the licence given to equivocation, even on oath, is so complete, that to tell a downright lie is the most superfluous and therefore most wanton of all sins.

But how will he reconcile it with the statement with which we meet a few pages on, that the Church 'considers consent, though quick as thought, to a single unchaste wish as indefinitely more heinous than any lie that can possibly be fancied; that is when viewed, of course, in itself, and apart from its causes, motives, and consequences?' Heaven forbid that any man should say that such consent is anything save a great and mortal sin: but how can we reconcile this statement with the former one, save by the paradox, that it is a greater crime to sin like an animal, than like the Devil the Father of Lies?

Indeed, the whole teaching of this lecture and the one following it concerning such matters is, I confess, so utterly beyond my comprehension, that I must ask, in blank astonishment, What does Dr. Newman mean? He assures us so earnestly and indignantly that he is an honest man, believing what he says, that we in return are bound, in honour and humanity, to believe him; but still – What does he mean?

He says: 'Take a mere beggar woman, lazy, ragged, and filthy, and not over-scrupulous of truth – (I do not say she has arrived at perfection) – but if she is chaste, sober, and cheerful, and goes to her religious duties (and I am not supposing at all an impossible case), she will, in the eyes of the Church, have a prospect of heaven, quite closed and refused to the State's pattern-man, the just, the upright, the generous, the honourable, the conscientious, if he be all this, not from a supernatural power (I do not determine whether this is likely to be the fact, but I am contrasting views and principles) – not from a supernatural power, but from mere natural virtue.' (Lecture viii. p. 207.)

I must ask again, What does Dr. Newman mean by this astounding passage? What I thought that he meant, when I first read it, some twelve years ago, may be guessed easily enough. I said, This man has no real care for truth. Truth for its own sake is no virtue in his eyes, and he teaches that it need not be. I do not say that now: but this I say, that Dr. Newman, for the sake of exalting the magical powers of his Church, has committed himself unconsciously to a statement which strikes at the root of all morality. If he answer, that such is the doctrine of his Church concerning 'natural virtues,' as distinguished from 'good works performed by God's grace,' I can only answer, So much the worse for his Church. The sooner it is civilized off the face of the earth, if this be its teaching, the better for mankind. For as for his theory that it may be a 'natural virtue', I value it as little as I trust every honest Englishman will do. I hold it to be utterly antiscriptural; to border very closely (in theological language) on the Pelagian heresy. Every good gift and every perfect gift comes down from God above. Without Him no man does a right deed, or thinks a right thought; and when Dr. Newman says otherwise, he is doing his best (as in this passage) to make the 'State's pattern-man' an atheist, as well as to keep the beggarwoman a lying barbarian. What Dr. Newman may have meant to teach by these words, I cannot say; but what he has taught practically is patent. He has taught the whole Celtic Irish population, that as long as they are chaste (which they cannot well help being, being married almost before they are men and women) and sober (which they cannot well help being, being too poor to get enough whisky to make them drunk), and 'go to their religious duties' – an expression on which I make no comment – they may look down upon the Protestant gentry who send over millions to feed them in famine; who found hospitals and charities to which they are admitted freely; who try to introduce among them capital, industry, civilization, and, above all, that habit of speaking the truth, for want of which they are what they are and are likely to remain such, as long as they have Dr. Newman for their teacher – that they may look down, I say, on the Protestant gentry as cut off from God, and without hope of heaven, because they do their duty by mere 'natural virtue.'

And Dr. Newman has taught them, too, in the very same page,* that they may confess 'to the priest thefts which would sentence the penitent to transportation if brought into a court of justice; but which the priest knows too' (and it is to be remembered that the priest is bound to conceal his knowledge of the

* P. 207.

crime), 'in the judgment of the Church, might be pardoned on the man's private contrition, without any confession at all.'

If I said that Dr. Newman has, in this page, justified, formally and deliberately, some of the strongest accusations brought by the Exeter Hall party against the Irish priests, I should be answered (and possibly with temporary success) by some of those ingenious special pleadings with which, in spite of plain fact and universal public opinion, black is made to appear, if not white, yet still grey enough to do instead. But this I will say, that if the Roman Catholic hierarchy in these realms had had any sense of their own interests (as far as standing well with the British nation is concerned), they would, instead of sending the man who wrote those words to teach in an Irish Catholic university, have sent him to their furthest mission among the savages of the South Seas.

The next lecture, the ninth, contains matter more liable still to be mistaken; and equally certain, mistaken or not, to shock common sense. It is called, 'The Religious Character of Catholic Countries no Prejudice to the Sanctity of the Church.' By the religious character, we find, is meant what we should call the irreligious character – the tendency to profanity, blasphemy, imposture, stealing, lying. These are not my accusations, but Dr. Newman's. He details them all with charming *naïveté*, and gives (as we shall see) most picturesque and apposite instances. But this, he holds 'is no prejudice to the sanctity of the Church,' because the Church considers that 'faith and works are separable,' and that all these poor wretches, though they have not works, have at least faith, 'caused directly by a supernatural influence from above,' and are, therefore, unless I have lost utterly the clue to the intent of Dr. Newman's sophistries, *ipso facto* infinitely better off than Protestants. What he means by the separableness of faith and works is clear enough. A man, he says, 'may be gifted with a simple, undoubting, cloudless, belief that Christ is in the Blessed Sacrament, and yet commit the sacrilege of breaking open the tabernacle, and carrying off the consecrated particles for the sake of the precious vessel containing them.'

At which most of my readers will be inclined to cry: 'Let Dr. Newman alone, after that. What use in arguing with a man who has argued himself into believing that? He had a human reason once, no doubt: but he has gambled it away, and left no common ground on which he and you, or we either, can meet him.'

True: so true, that I never would have written these pages, save because it was my duty to show the world, if not Dr. Newman, how the mistake of his not caring for truth arose; and specially how this very lecture fostered that mistake. For in it, after using the blasphemy and profanity which he confesses to be so common in Catholic countries, as an argument for, and not against, the 'Catholic Faith,' he takes a seeming pleasure in detailing instances of dishonesty on the part of Catholics, as if that were the very form of antinomianism which was most strongly and perpetually present to his mind, and which needed most to be palliated and excused. 'The feeble old woman, who first genuflects before the Blessed Sacrament, and then steals her neighbour's handkerchief or prayer-book, who is intent on his devotions' – she is very wrong, no doubt: but 'she worships, and she sins: she kneels because she believes; she steals because she does not love. She may be out of God's grace; she is not altogether out of His sight.'

Heaven forbid that we should deny those words. That, at least, is a doctrine common to Romanist and to Protestant: but while Dr. Newman, with a kind of desperate audacity, will dig forth such scandals as notes of the 'Catholic Church,' he must not wonder at his motive for so doing being mistaken.

His next instance is even more wanton and offensive, and so curious that I must quote it at length: –

'You come out again and mix in the idle and dissipated throng, and you fall in with a man in a palmer's dress, selling false relics, and a credulous circle of customers buying them as greedily, as though they were the supposed French laces and India silks of a pedlar's basket. One simple soul has bought of him a cure for the rheumatism or ague, which might form a case of conscience. It is said to be a relic of St. Cuthbert, but only has virtue at sunrise, and when applied with three crosses to the head, arms, and feet. You pass on to encounter a rude son of the Church, more like a showman than a religious, recounting to the gaping multitude some tale of a vision of the invisible world, seen by Brother Augustine of the Friar Minors, or by a holy Jesuit preacher who died in the odour of sanctity, and sending round his bag to collect pence for the souls in purgatory; and of some appearance of Our Lady (the like of which has really been before and since), but on no authority except popular report, and in no shape but that which popular caprice has given it. You go forward, and you find preparations proceeding for a great pageant or mystery; it is a high festival, and the incorporated trades have each undertaken their special religious celebration. The plumbers and glaziers are to play the Creation; the barbers the call of Abraham; and at night is to be the grandest performance of all, the Resurrection and Last Judgment, played by the carpenters, masons, and blacksmiths. Heaven and hell are represented, – saints, devils, and living men; and the *chef d'œuvre* of the exhibition is the display of fireworks to be let off as the *finale.* "How unutterably profane!" again you cry. Yes, profane to you, my dear brother – profane to a population which only half believes; not profane to those who believe wholly, who one and all have a vision within which corresponds with what they see, which resolves itself into, or rather takes up into itself, the external pageant, whatever be the moral condition of each individual composing the mass. They gaze, and in drinking in the exhibition with their eyes they are making one continuous and intense act of faith' (Lecture IX. 236, 237).

The sum of which is, that for the sake of the 'one continuous and intense act of faith' which the crowd is performing, 'the rude son of the Church, more like a showman than a religious' – in plain English, the brutal and lying monk, is allowed to continue his impostures without interruption; and the moral which Dr. Newman draws is, that though his miraculous appearance of our Lady may be a lie, yet 'the like thereof has been before and since.'

After which follows a passage – of which I shall boldly say, that I trust that it will arouse in every English husband, father, and brother, who may read these words, the same feelings which it roused in me; and express my opinion, that it is a better compliment to Dr. Newman to think that he did not believe what he said, than to think that he did believe it: –

'You turn to go home, and in your way you pass through a retired quarter of the city. Look up at those sacred windows; they belong to the Convent of the Perpetual Adoration, or to the poor Clares, or to the Carmelites of the Reform of St. Theresa, or to the Nuns of the Visitation. Seclusion, silence, watching, adoration, is their life day and night. The Immaculate Lamb of God is ever before the eyes of the worshippers; or, at least, the invisible mysteries of faith ever stand out, as if in bodily shape, before their mental gaze. Where will you find such a realized heaven upon earth? Yet that very sight has acted otherwise on the mind of a weak sister; and the very keenness of her faith and wild desire of approaching the object of it has led her to fancy or to feign that she has received that singular favour vouchsafed only to a few elect souls; and she points to God's wounds, as imprinted on her hand, and feet, and side, though she herself has been instrumental in their formation' (Lecture IX. 237, 238).

There are occasions on which courtesy or reticence is a crime, and this one of them. A poor girl, cajoled, flattered, imprisoned, starved, maddened, by such as Dr. Newman and his peers, into that degrading and demoralising disease, hysteria, imitates on her own body, from that strange vanity and deceit which too often accompany the complaint, the wounds of our Lord; and all that Dr. Newman has to say about the matter is, to inform us that the gross and useless portent is 'a singular favour vouchsafed only to a few elect souls.' And this is the man who, when accused of countenancing falsehood, puts on first a tone of plaintive and startled innocence, and then one of smug self-satisfaction – as who should ask, 'What have I said? What have I done? Why am I upon my trial?' On his trial? If he be on his trial for nothing else, he is on his trial for those words; and he will remain upon his trial as long as Englishmen know how to guard the women whom God has committed to their charge. If the British public shall ever need informing that Dr. Newman wrote that passage, I trust there will be always one man left in England to inform them of the fact, for the sake of the ladies of this land.

Perhaps the most astounding specimens of Dr. Newman's teaching are to be found, after all, in the two sermons which end his 'Discourses addressed to Mixed Congregations,' published in 1849; 'The Glories of Mary for the sake of her Son;' and 'On the fitness of the Glories of Mary.' Of the mis-quotations of Scripture, of the sophisms piled on sophisms, of these two sermons, I have no room wherein to give specimens. All I ask is, that they should be read; read by every man who thinks it any credit to himself to be a rational being. But two culminating wonders of these two sermons I must point out. The first is the assertion that the Blessed Virgin 'had been inspired, the first of woman-kind, to dedicate her virginity to God.' As if there had not been Buddhist nuns (if not others) centuries before Christianity. As if (allowing the argument that they dedicated their virginity to a false God) there were the slightest historic proof that the Blessed Virgin dedicated hers before the Incarnation. The second is in a sermon which professes to prove logically the 'fitness' of the Immaculate Conception, and is filled (instead of logic) with traditions which are utterly baseless. I allude to the assertion that 'the world' – *i.e.* all who do not belong to the Romish Church – 'blasphemes' Mary. I make no comment. All I ask, again, of my readers is, to read these two sermons.

But what, after all, does Dr. Newman teach concerning truth? What he taught in 1843, and what he (as far as I can see) teaches still, may be seen in his last sermon in a volume entitled 'Chiefly on the Theory of Religious Belief,' called a sermon 'On the Theory of Developments in Religious Doctrine.' I beg all who are interested in this question to read that sermon (which I had overlooked till lately); and to judge for themselves whether I exaggerate when I say that it tries to undermine the grounds of all rational belief for the purpose of substituting blind supersti-tion. As examples: – speaking of 'certain narratives of martyr-doms,' and 'alleged miracles,' he says (p. 345): 'If the alleged facts did not occur, they ought to have occurred, if I may so speak.' Historic truth is thus sapped; and physical truth fares no better. 'Scripture says (p. 350) that the sun moves, and that the earth is stationary; and science that the earth moves, and the sun is comparatively at rest. How can we determine which of these statements is the very truth, till we know what motion is? If our idea of motion be but an accident of our present senses neither proposition is true, and both are true; neither true philosophi-cally, both true for certain purposes in the system in which they are respectively found; and physical science will have no better meaning when it says that the earth moves, than plain astronomy when it says that the earth is still.'

Quorsum haec? What is the intent of this seemingly sceptic

method, pursued through page after page? To tell us that we can know nothing certainly, and therefore must take blindly what 'The Church' shall choose to teach us. For the Church, it would seem, is not bound to tell us, indeed cannot tell us, the whole truth. We are to be treated like children, to whom (at least to those with whom Dr. Newman has come in contact) it is necessary to (p. 343) 'dispense and "divide" the word of truth, if we would not have it changed, as far as they are concerned, into a word of falsehood.' 'And so, again, as regards savages, or the ignorant, or weak, or narrow-minded, our representations must take a certain form, if we are to gain admission into their minds at all, and to reach them.'

This method of teaching by half-truths Dr. Newman calls 'economy;' and justifies it (if I understand his drift), by the instances of 'mythical representations,' legends, and so forth, 'which, if they did not occur, ought to have occurred.' 'Many a theory or view of things,' – he goes on – (p. 345) 'on which an institution is founded, or a party held together, is of the same kind. Many an argument, used by zealous and earnest men, has this economical character, being not the very ground on which they act (for they continue in the same course, though it be refuted), yet, in a certain sense, a representation of it, a proximate description of their feelings in the shape of argument, on which they can rest, to which they can recur when perplexed, and appeal when they are questioned.' After which startling words, Dr. Newman says – and it is really high time – 'In this reference to accommodation or economy in human affairs, I do not meddle with the question of casuistry, viz. which of such artifices, as it may be called, are innocent, or where the "line is to be drawn."'

A hasty reader might say, that herein is an open justification of equivocation and dishonest reticence. But he would be mistaken. The whole sermon is written in so tentative a style, that it would be rash and wrong to say that Dr. Newman intends to convey any lesson by it, save that the discovery of truth is an impossibility. Only once, and in a note, he speaks out. P. 342.

'Hence it is not more than an hyperbole to say that, in certain cases, a lie is the nearest approach to truth. This seems the meaning, for instance, of St. Clement, when he says "He (the

Christian) both thinks and speaks the truth, unless when, at any time, in the way of treatment, as a physician toward his patients, so for the welfare of the sick he will be false, or will tell a falsehood, as the sophists speak." '

If St. Clement said that, so much the worse for him. He was a great and good man. But he might have learned from his Bible that no lie was of the truth, and that it is ill stealing the devil's tools to do God's work withal.

Be that as it may. What Dr. Newman teaches is clear at last, and I see how deeply I have wronged him. So far from thinking truth for its own sake to be no virtue, he considers it a virtue so lofty, as to be unattainable by man, who must therefore, in certain cases, take up with what-it-is-no-more-than-a-hyperbole-to-call lies; and who, if he should be so lucky as to get any truth into his possession, will be wise in 'economizing' the same, and 'dividing it,' so giving away a bit here and a bit there, lest he should waste so precious a possession.

That this is Dr. Newman's opinion at present, there can be no manner of doubt. What he has persuaded himself to believe about St. Walburga's oil, St. Sturme's nose, St. Januarius' blood, and the winking Madonna's eyes, proves sufficiently that he still finds, in certain cases, what-it-is-no-more-than-a-hyperbole-to-call lies, the nearest approach which he can make to truth; while, as to the right of economizing and dividing truth, I shall shortly bring forward two instances of his having done so to such an extent, that very little of poor truth remains after the dismemberment.

And yet I do not call this conscious dishonesty. The man who wrote that sermon was already past the possibility of such a sin. It is simple credulity, the child of scepticism. Credulity, frightened at itself, trying to hide its absurdity alike from itself and from the world by quibbles and reticences which it thinks prudent and clever; and, like the hunted ostrich, fancying that because it thrusts its head into the sand, its whole body is invisible.

And now, I have tried to lead my readers along a path to which some of them, I fear, have objected.

They have fallen, perhaps, into the prevailing superstition that cleverness is synonymous with wisdom. They cannot believe that (as is too certain) great literary, and even barristerial ability, may co-exist with almost boundless silliness: but I can find no other explanation of the phenomena than that which I have just given. That Dr. Newman thinks that there is no harm in 'economy,' and 'dividing the truth,' is evident; for he has employed it again in his comments on the correspondence. He has employed twice, as the most natural and innocent thing possible, those 'arts of the defenceless' which require so much delicacy in the handling, lest 'liberal shepherds give a grosser name,' and call them cunning, or even worse.

I am, of course, free to make my own comments on them, as on all other words of Dr. Newman's printed since the 1st of February, 1864, on which day my apology was published. I shall certainly take the sense of the British public on the matter. Though Dr. Newman may be 'a mystery' to them, as he says 'religious men' always are to the world, yet they possess quite common sense enough to see what his words are, even though his intention be, as it is wont to be, obscure.

They recollect the definitions of the 'Church' and 'Christians,' on the ground of which I called Sermon XX. a Romish sermon?

Dr. Newman does not apply to it that epithet. He called it, in his letter to me of the 7th of January (published by him), a 'Protestant' one. I remarked that, but considered it a mere slip of the pen. Besides, I have now nothing to say to that letter. It is to his 'Reflexions' in page 372 which are open ground to me, that I refer. In them he deliberately repeats the epithet 'Protestant:' only he, in an utterly imaginary conversation, puts it into my mouth, 'which you preached when a Protestant.' I call the man who preached that sermon a Protestant? I should have sooner called him a Buddhist. At that very time he was teaching his disciples to scorn and repudiate that name of Protestant, under which, for some reason or other, he now finds it convenient to take shelter. If he forgets, the world does not, the famous article in the *British Critic* (the then organ of his party), of three years before – July, 1841 – which, after denouncing the name of Protestant, declared the object of the party to be none other than the 'Unprotestantising' the English Church.

But Dr. Newman convicts himself. In the sermon before, as I have shown, monks and nuns are spoken of as the only true Bible Christians, and in the sermon itself a celibate clergy is made a note of the Church. And yet Dr. Newman goes on to say that he was not then 'a priest, speaking of priests.' Whether he were a priest himself matters little to the question; but if he were not speaking of priests, and those Romish ones, when he spoke of a celibate clergy, of whom was he speaking? But there is no use in wasting words on this 'economical' statement of Dr. Newman's. I shall only say that there are people in the world whom it is very difficult to help. As soon as they are got out of one scrape, they walk straight into another.

But Dr. Newman has made, in my opinion, another and a still greater mistake. He has committed, on the very title-page of his pamphlet, an 'economy' which some men will consider a very serious offence. He has there stated that the question is, 'Whether Dr. Newman teaches that truth is no virtue.' He has repeated this misrepresentation in a still stronger form at page 372, where he has ventured to represent me as saying 'Dr. Newman tells us that lying is never any harm.' He has economized the very four words of my accusation, which make it at least a reasonable one; namely – '*For its own sake*.'

I never said what he makes me say, or anything like it. I never was inclined to say it. Had I ever been, I should be still more inclined to say it now.

But Dr. Newman has shown 'wisdom' enough of that serpentine type which is his professed ideal in what he has done, and has been so economic of truth, and 'divided' the truth so thoroughly, that really there is very little of it left.

For while no one knew better than he the importance of the omission, none knew better that the public would not do so; that they would never observe it; that, if I called their attention to it, they would smile, and accuse me of word-splitting and raising metaphysical subtleties. Yes, Dr. Newman is a very economical person. So, when I had accused him and the Romish clergy of teaching that 'truth is no virtue, for its own sake,' he simply economized the last four words, and said that I accused him and them of teaching that 'truth is no virtue.'

This, in Dr. Newman, the subtle dialectician, is, indeed, an 'enormity,' as he chooses to call my accusation of him. No one better knows the value of such limitations. No one has, sometimes fairly, sometimes unfairly, made more use of them. No man, therefore, ought to have been more careful of doing what he has done.

Dr. Newman tries, by cunning sleight-of-hand logic, to prove that I did not believe the accusation when I made it. Therein he is mistaken. I did believe it, and I believed, also, his indignant denial. But when he goes on to ask, with sneers, Why I should believe his denial, if I did not consider him trustworthy in the first instance? – I can only answer, I really do not know. There is a great deal to be said for that view, now that Dr. Newman has become (one must needs suppose) suddenly, and since the 1st of February, 1864, a convert to the economic views of St. Alfonso da Liguori and his compeers. I am henceforth in doubt and fear, as much as an honest man can be, concerning every word Dr. Newman may write. How can I tell that I shall not be the dupe of some cunning equivocation, of one of the three kinds laid down as permissible by the blessed St. Alfonso da Liguori and his pupils even when confirmed with an oath, because 'then we do not deceive our neighbour, but allow him to deceive himself'?* – The whole being justified by the example of Christ, 'who answered, "I go not up to this feast," *subintelligendo*, "openly."' 'For,' say the casuists, 'if there were no such restrictions (on the telling of truth), there would be no means of concealing secrets, which one could not open without loss or inconvenience; but this would be no less pernicious to human society than a lie itself.' It is admissible, therefore, to use words and sentences which have a double signification, and leave the hapless hearer to take which of them he may choose. What proof have I, then, that by '*mean* it! I never *said* it!' Dr. Newman does not signify, 'I did not say it: but I did mean it'?

Or again, how can I tell that I may not in this pamphlet have made an accusation, of the truth of which Dr. Newman is perfectly conscious; but that as I, a heretic Protestant, have no business to make it, he has a full right to deny it? For what says Neyraguet, after the blessed St. Alfonso da Liguori? That 'a criminal or witness, being interrogated by a judge contrary to law, may swear that he knows not of the crime; meaning, that he

---

* I quote from Scavini, tom. ii. page 232, of the Paris edition, and from Neyraguet, p. 141, two compendiums of Liguori which are (or were lately) used, so I have every reason to believe – one at Oscott, the other at Maynooth.

knows not of a crime of which he may be lawfully questioned.'

These are hard words. If Dr. Newman shall complain of them, I can only remind him of the fate which befel the stork caught among the cranes, even though the stork had not done all he could to make himself like a crane, as Dr. Newman has, by 'economizing' on the very title-page of his pamphlet.

I know perfectly well that truth – 'veracity', as they call it – is a virtue with the Romish moralists; that it is one of the cardinal virtues, the daughters of justice, like benevolence, courtesy, gratitude, and so forth; and is proved to be such because there is a *naturalis honestas* in it, and also that without it society could not go on. Lying, on the other hand, though not one of the seven 'capital' sins, which are pride, avarice, luxury (unchastity), gluttony, anger, envy, and acedia (lukewarmness), is yet held to be always a sin, when direct. It is proved to be such from Scripture, from the fathers, and from natural reason, because 'truth is an essential perfection of the Divine nature.' So far well. But a lie is a venial sin, if it 'neither hurts our neighbour or God gravely, or causes a grave scandal;' as no lie told in behalf of the Catholic faith can well do, though one wise Pope laid it down that it was a sin to tell a lie, even for the sake of saving a soul. But though it were a sin, the fact of its being a venial one seems to have gained for it, as yet, a very slight penance. Meanwhile, as a thousand venial sins can never make one mortal one, a man may be a habitual liar all his life long, without falling into mortal sin. Moreover, though 'formal simulation,' when 'one signifies by outward act something different to what he has in his mind,' is illicit, as a lie, yet 'material simulation,' or stratagem, is not so. 'For when one does something, not intending the deception of another, but some end of his own, then it is allowable on cause; although, from other circumstances, men might conjecture that the act was done for another end. So Joshua fled lawfully, not meaning fear, but that he might draw the enemy further from the city of Hai.' From which one can gather, that Romish casuists allow the same stratagems to man against his neighbours, in peaceable society, which Protestant public opinion allows (and that with a growing compunction) only to officers in war, against the enemies of their country. Considering this fact, and the permission of equivocation, even on oath, it is somewhat at difficult to expect that the Romish moralists, at least, hold truth to be a virtue for its own sake, or to deny that they teach cunning to be the weapons of the weak against the strong.

Yes – I am afraid that I must say it once more – Truth is not honoured among these men for its own sake. There are, doubtless, pure and noble souls among them, superior, through the grace of God, to the official morality of their class: but in their official writings, and in too much of their official conduct, the great majority seem never, for centuries past, to have perceived that truth is the capital virtue, the virtue of all virtues, without which all others are hollow and rotten; and with which there is hope for a man's repentance and conversion, in spite of every vice, if only he remains honest. They have not seen that facts are the property not of man, to be 'economized' as man thinks fit, but of God, who ordereth all things in heaven and earth; and that therefore not only every lie, but every equivocation, every attempt at deception, is a sin, not against man, but against God; they have not seen that no lie is of the truth, and that God requires truth, not merely in outward words, but in the inward parts; and that therefore the first and most absolute duty of every human being is to speak and act the exact truth; or if he wish to be silent, to be silent, courageously and simply, and take the risk, trusting in God to protect him, as long as he remains on God's side in the universe, by scorning to sully his soul by stratagem or equivocation. Had they seen this; had they not regarded truth as a mere arbitrary command of God, which was not binding in doubtful cases, they would never have dared to bargain with God as to how little truth He required of men; and to examine and define (to the injury alike of their own sense of honour, and that of their hearers) how much deception He may be reasonably supposed to allow.

Is this last Dr. Newman's view of truth? I hope not. I hope that he, educated as an English gentleman and Oxford scholar, is at variance with the notions formally allowed by the most popular and influential modern Doctor of his Church. But that there is some slight difference between his notions of truth and ours he has confessed – in a letter to 'X. V. Esqre,'* which he has

* ['X.V.' for 'X.Y.', so in first and third editions of Kingsley's pamphlet.]

printed in his 'Correspondence'. For there he says (p. 363): 'I think that you will allow that there is a broad difference between a virtue, considered as a principle or rule, and the applications and limits of it in human conduct. Catholics and Protestants, in their view of the substance of the moral virtues, agree; but they carry them out variously in detail.' He then gives us to understand, that this is the case as to truth; that Catholics differ from Protestants as to 'whether this or that act in particular is conformable to the rule of truth.'

I beg to say, that in these words Dr. Newman has made another great mistake. He has calumniated, as far as my experience goes, the Catholic gentry of these realms. I am proud to say, as far as I have had the honour and pleasure of their acquaintance, that there is no difference whatsoever, of detail or other, between their truthfulness and honour, and the truthfulness and honour of the Protestant gentry among whom they live, respected and beloved, in spite of all religious differences, simply because they are honest gentlemen and noble ladies. But if Dr. Newman will limit his statement to the majority of the Romish priesthood, and to those hapless Irish Celts over whom they rule, then we will willingly accept it as perfectly correct. There is a very wide difference in practical details between their notions of truth and ours; and what that difference is, I have already pointed out. It is notorious enough in facts and practice. It may be seen at large by any one who chooses to read the Romish Moral Theologians. And if Dr. Newman, as a Catholic priest, includes himself in his own statement, that is his act, not mine.

And so I leave Dr. Newman, only expressing my fear, that if he continues to 'economize' and 'divide' the words of his adversaries as he has done mine, he will run great danger of forfeiting once more his reputation for honesty.

CHARLES KINGSLEY

APPENDIX C

Apologia pro Vita Sua

BEING A REPLY TO A PAMPHLET ENTITLED 'WHAT, THEN, DOES DR. NEWMAN MEAN?'

'Commit thy way to the Lord, and trust in Him, and He
will do it. And He will bring forth thy justice as the light,
and thy judgment as the noon-day.'

By John Henry Newman, D.D.

PART I

Mr. Kingsley's Method of Disputation

I cannot be sorry to have forced Mr. Kingsley to bring out in
fulness his charges against me. It is far better that he should
discharge his thoughts upon me in my lifetime, than after I am
dead. Under the circumstances I am happy in having the opportunity of reading the worst that can be said of me by a writer who
has taken pains with his work and is well satisfied with it. I
account it a gain to be surveyed from without by one who hates
the principles which are nearest to my heart, has no personal
knowledge of me to set right his misconceptions of my doctrine,
and who has some motive or other to be as severe with me as he
can possibly be.

And first of all, I beg to compliment him on the motto in his
Title-page; it is felicitous. A motto should contain, as in a
nutshell, the contents, or the character, or the drift, or the *animus*
of the writing to which it is prefixed. The words which he has

taken from me are so apposite as to be almost prophetical. There cannot be a better illustration than he thereby affords of the aphorism which I intended them to convey. I said that it is not more than an hyperbolical expression to say that in certain cases a lie is the nearest approach to truth. Mr. Kingsley's pamphlet is emphatically one of such cases as are contemplated in that proposition. I really believe, that his view of me is about as near an approach to the truth about my writings and doings, as he is capable of taking. He has done his worst towards me; but he has also done his best. So far well; but, while I impute to him no malice, I unfeignedly think, on the other hand, that, in his invective against me, he as faithfully fulfils the other half of the proposition also.

This is not a mere sharp retort upon Mr. Kingsley, as will be seen, when I come to consider directly the subject, to which the words of his motto relate. I have enlarged on that subject in various passages of my publications; I have said that minds in different states and circumstances cannot understand one another, and that in all cases they must be instructed according to their capacity, and, if not taught step by step, they learn only so much the less; that children do not apprehend the thoughts of grown people, nor savages the instincts of civilization, nor blind men the perceptions of sight, nor pagans the doctrines of Christianity, nor men the experiences of Angels. In the same way, there are people of matter-of-fact, prosaic minds, who cannot take in the fancies of poets; and others of shallow, inaccurate minds, who cannot take in the ideas of philosophical inquirers. In a Lecture of mine I have illustrated this phenomenon by the supposed instance of a foreigner, who, after reading a commentary on the principles of English Law, does not get nearer to a real apprehension of them than to be led to accuse Englishmen of considering that the Queen is impeccable and infallible, and that the Parliament is omnipotent. Mr. Kingsley has read me from beginning to end in the fashion in which the hypothetical Russian read Blackstone; not, I repeat, from malice, but because of his intellectual build. He appears to be so constituted as to have no notion of what goes on in minds very different from his own, and moreover to be stone-blind to his ignorance. A modest man or a philosopher would have scrupled to treat with scorn and scoffing, as Mr.

Kingsley does in my own instance, principles and convictions, even if he did not acquiesce in them himself, which had been held so widely and for so long, – the beliefs and devotions and customs which have been the religious life of millions upon millions of Christians for nearly twenty centuries, – for this in fact is the task on which he is spending his pains. Had he been a man of large or cautious mind, he would not have taken it for granted that cultivation must lead every one to see things precisely as he sees them himself. But the narrow-minded are the more prejudiced by very reason of their narrowness. The Apostle bids us 'in malice be children, but in understanding be men.' I am glad to recognize in Mr. Kingsley an illustration of the first half of this precept; but I should not be honest, if I ascribed to him any sort of fulfilment of the second.

I wish I could speak as favourably either of his drift or of his method of arguing, as I can of his convictions. As to his drift, I think its ultimate point is an attack upon the Catholic Religion. It is I indeed, whom he is immediately insulting, – still, he views me only as a representative, and on the whole a fair one, of a class or caste of men, to whom, conscious as I am of my own integrity, I ascribe an excellence superior to mine. He desires to impress upon the public mind the conviction that I am a crafty, scheming man, simply untrustworthy; that, in becoming a Catholic, I have just found my right place; that I do but justify and am properly interpreted by the common English notion of Roman casuists and confessors; that I was secretly a Catholic when I was openly professing to be a clergyman of the Established Church; that so far from bringing, by means of my conversion, when at length it openly took place, any strength to the Catholic cause, I am really a burden to it, – an additional evidence of the fact, that to be a pure, german, genuine Catholic, a man must be either a knave or a fool.

These last words bring me to Mr. Kingsley's method of disputation, which I must criticize with much severity; – in his drift he does but follow the ordinary beat of controversy, but in his mode of arguing he is actually dishonest.

He says that I am either a knave or a fool, and (as we shall see by and by) he is not quite sure which, probably both. He tells his readers that on one occasion he said that he had fears I should 'end in one or other of two misfortunes.' 'He would either,' he continues, 'destroy his own sense of honesty, i.e. conscious truthfulness – and become a dishonest person; or he would destroy his common sense, i.e. unconscious truthfulness, and become the slave and puppet seemingly of his own logic, really of his own fancy. . . . I thought for years past that he had become the former; I now see that he has become the latter.' pp. 387. Again, 'When I read these outrages upon common sense, what wonder if I said to myself, "This man cannot believe what he is saying"?' p. 392. Such has been Mr. Kingsley's state of mind till lately, but now he considers that I am possessed with a spirit of 'almost boundless silliness,' of 'simple credulity, the child of scepticism,' of 'absurdity' (pp. 404–05), of a 'self-deception which has become a sort of frantic honesty' (p. 392). And as to his fundamental reason for this change, he tells us, he really does not know what it is (p. 407). However, let the reason be what it will, its upshot is intelligible enough. He is enabled at once, by this professed change of judgment about me, to put forward one of these alternatives, yet to keep the other in reserve; – and this he actually does. He need not commit himself to a definite accusation against me, such as requires definite proof and admits of definite refutation; for he has two strings to his bow; – when he is thrown off his balance on the one leg, he can recover himself by the use of the other. If I demonstrate that I am not a knave, he may exclaim, 'Oh, but you are a fool!' and when I demonstrate that I am not a fool, he may turn round and retort, 'Well, then, you are a knave.' I have no objection to reply to his arguments in behalf of either alternative, but I should have been better pleased to have been allowed to take them one at a time.

But I have not yet done full justice to the method of disputation, which Mr. Kingsley thinks it right to adopt. Observe this first: – He means by a man who is 'silly' not a man who is to be pitied, but a man who is to be *abhorred*. He means a man who is not simply weak and incapable, but a moral leper; a man who, if not a knave, has every thing bad about him except knavery; nay, rather, has together with every other worst vice, a spice of knavery to boot. *His* simpleton is one who has become such, in judgment for his having once been a knave. *His* simpleton is not a born fool, but a self-made idiot, one who has drugged and abused himself into a shameless depravity; one, who, without any misgiving or remorse, is guilty of drivelling superstition, of reckless violation of sacred things, of fanatical excesses, of passionate inanities, of unmanly audacious tyranny over the weak, meriting the wrath of fathers and brothers. This is that milder judgment, which he seems to pride himself upon as so much charity; and, as he expresses it, he 'does not know' why. This is what he really meant in his letter to me of January 14, when he withdrew his charge of my being dishonest. He said, 'The *tone* of your letters, even more than their language, makes me feel, *to my very deep pleasure*,' – what? that you have gambled away your reason, that you are an intellectual sot, that you are a fool in a frenzy. And in his Pamphlet, he gives us this explanation why he did not say this to my face, viz. that he had been told that I was 'in weak health,' and was 'averse to controversy,' p. 376. He 'felt some regret for having disturbed me.'

But I pass on from these multiform imputations, and confine myself to this one consideration, viz. that he has made any fresh imputation upon me at all. He gave up the charge of knavery; well and good: but where was the logical necessity of his bringing another? I am sitting at home without a thought of Mr. Kingsley; he wantonly breaks in upon me with the charge that I had '*informed*' the world 'that Truth for its own sake *need not* and on the whole *ought not to be* a virtue with the Roman clergy.' When challenged on the point he cannot bring a fragment of evidence in proof of his assertion, and he is convicted of false witness by the voice of the world. Well, I should have thought that he had now nothing whatever more to do. 'Vain man!' he seems to make answer, 'what simplicity in you to think so! If you have not broken one commandment, let us see whether we cannot convict you of the breach of another. If you are not a swindler or forger, you are guilty of arson or burglary. By hook or by crook you shall not escape. Are *you* to suffer or *I*? What does it matter to you who are going off the stage, to receive a slight additional daub upon a character so deeply stained already? But think of me, the immaculate lover of Truth, so observant (as I have told you p. 377) of "*hault courage* and strict honour," – and (*aside*) – "and not as this publican" – do you think I can let you go scot free instead of myself? No; *noblesse oblige*. Go to the shades, old man, and boast that Achilles sent you thither.'

But I have not even yet done with Mr. Kingsley's method of disputation. Observe secondly: – when a man is said to be a knave or a fool, it is commonly meant that he is *either* the one *or* the other; and that, – either in the sense that the hypothesis of his being a fool is too absurd to be entertained; or, again, as a sort of contemptuous acquittal of one, who after all has not wit enough to be wicked. But this is not at all what Mr. Kingsley proposes to himself in the antithesis which he suggests to his readers. Though he speaks of me as an utter dotard and fanatic, yet all along, from the beginning of his Pamphlet to the end, he insinuates, he proves from my writings, and at length in his last pages he openly pronounces, that after all he was right at first, in thinking me a conscious liar and deceiver.

Now I wish to dwell on this point. It cannot be doubted, I say, that, in spite of his professing to consider me as a dotard and driveller, on the ground of his having given up the notion of my being a knave, yet it is the very staple of his Pamphlet that a knave after all I must be. By insinuation, or by implication, or by question, or by irony, or by sneer, or by parable, he enforces again and again a conclusion which he does not categorically enunciate.

For instance (1) P. 383. 'I know that men *used to suspect Dr. Newman*, I have been inclined to do so myself, of writing a whole sermon . . . for the sake of one single passing hint, one phrase, one epithet, one little barbed arrow which . . . he delivered unheeded, as with his finger tip, to the very heart of an initiated hearer, *never to be withdrawn again.*'

(2) P. 384. 'How *was* I to know that the preacher, who had the reputation of being the most *acute* man of his generation, and of having a specially intimate acquaintance with the weaknesses of the human heart, was utterly blind to the broad meaning and the plain practical result of a sermon like this, delivered before fanatic and hot-headed young men, who hung upon his every word? That he did not *foresee* that they would think that they obeyed him, *by becoming affected, artificial, sly, shifty, ready for concealments and equivocations?*'

(3) P. 385. 'No one *would have* suspected him to be a dishonest

man, if he had not perversely chosen *to assume a style* which (as he himself confesses) the world always associates with dishonesty.'

(4) P. 395. '*If* he will indulge in subtle paradoxes, in rhetorical exaggerations; if, *whenever he touches on the question of truth and honesty*, he will take a perverse pleasure in saying something shocking to plain English notions, he *must take the consequences of his own eccentricities.*'

(5) Pp. 398–9. 'At which most of my readers will be inclined to cry: "Let Dr. Newman alone, after that. . . . He had a human reason once, no doubt: but he has gambled it away.' . . . True: so true, &c.'

(6) P. 399. He continues: 'I should never have written these pages, save because it was my duty to show the world, if not Dr. Newman, how the mistake (!) of his *not caring* for truth *arose.*'

(7) P. 401. 'And this is the man, who when accused of countenancing falsehood, puts on first a tone of *plaintive* (!) and startled innocence, and then one of smug self-satisfaction – as who should ask, "What have I said? What have I done? Why am I on my trial?"'

(8) P. 404. 'What Dr. Newman teaches is clear at last, and *I see now how deeply I have wronged him*. So far from thinking truth for its own sake to be no virtue, *he considers it a virtue so lofty as to be unattainable by man.*'

(9) P. 406. 'There is no use in wasting words on this "economical" statement of Dr. Newman's. I shall only say that there are people in the world whom it is very difficult to *help*. As soon as they are got out of one scrape, they walk straight into another.'

(10) P. 406. 'Dr. Newman has shown "wisdom" enough of that *serpentine* type which is his professed ideal. . . . Yes, Dr. Newman is a very economical person.'

(11) P. 407. 'Dr. Newman *tries*, by *cunning sleight-of-hand logic*, to prove that I did not believe the accusation when I made it.'

(12) P. 408. 'These are hard words. If Dr. Newman shall complain of them, I can only remind him of the fate which befel the stork caught among the cranes, *even though* the stork had *not* done all he could to make himself like a crane, *as Dr. Newman has*, by "economising" on the very title-page of his pamphlet.'

These last words bring us to another and far worse instance of these slanderous assaults upon me, but its place is in a subsequent page.

Now it may be asked of me, 'Well, why should not Mr. Kingsley take a course such as this? It was his original assertion that Dr. Newman was a professed liar, and a patron of lies; he spoke somewhat at random; granted; but now he has got up his references and he is proving, not perhaps the very thing which he said at first, but something very like it, and to say the least quite as bad. He is now only aiming to justify morally his original assertion; why is he not at liberty to do so?'

Why should he *not* now insinuate that I am a liar and a knave! he had of course a perfect right to make such a charge, if he chose; he might have said, 'I was virtually right, and here is the proof of it,' but this he has not done, but on the contrary has professed that he no longer draws from my works, as he did before, the inference of my dishonesty. He says distinctly, p. 392, 'When I read these outrages upon common sense, what wonder if I said to myself, "This man cannot believe what he is saying?" *I believe I was wrong.*' And in p. 396, 'I said, This man has no real care for truth. Truth for its own sake is no virtue in his eyes, and he teaches that it need not be. *I do not say that now.*' And in p. 404, 'I do not call this conscious dishonesty; the man who wrote that sermon *was already past the possibility* of such a sin.'

Why should he *not*! because it is on the ground of my not being a knave that he calls me a fool; adding to the words just quoted, '[My readers] have fallen perhaps into the prevailing superstition that cleverness is synonymous with wisdom. They cannot believe that (as is too certain) great literary and even barristerial ability may co-exist with almost boundless silliness.'

Why should he *not*! because he has taken credit to himself for that high feeling of honour which refuses to withdraw a concession which once has been made; though, (wonderful to say!) at the very time that he is recording this magnanimous resolution, he lets it out of the bag that his relinquishment of it is only a profession and a pretence; for he says, p. 377: 'I have accepted Dr. Newman's denial that [the Sermon] means what I thought it did; and *heaven forbid*' (oh!) 'that I should withdraw my word once given, *at whatever disadvantage to myself.*' Disadvantage! but nothing can be advantageous to him which is *untrue*; therefore in proclaiming that the concession of my honesty is a disadvantage to him, he thereby implies unequivocally that there is some probability still, that I am *dis*honest. He goes on, 'I am informed by those from whose judgment on such points there is no appeal, that '*en hault courage*,' and strict honour, I am also *precluded*, by the *terms* of my explanation, from using any other of Dr. Newman's past writings to prove my assertion.' And then, 'I have declared Dr. Newman to have been an honest man up to the 1st of February, 1864; it was, as I shall show, only Dr. Newman's fault that I ever thought him to be any thing else. It depends entirely on Dr. Newman whether he shall *sustain* the reputation which he has so recently acquired,' (by diploma of course from Mr. Kingsley.) 'If I give him thereby a fresh advantage in this argument, he is *most welcome* to it. He needs, it seems to me, *as many advantages as possible.*'

What a princely mind! How loyal to his rash promise, how delicate towards the subject of it, how conscientious in his interpretation of it! I have no thought of irreverence towards a Scripture Saint, who was actuated by a very different spirit from Mr. Kingsley's, but somehow since I read his Pamphlet words have been running in my head, which I find in the Douay version thus; 'Thou hast also with thee Semei the son of Gera, who cursed me with a grievous curse when I went to the camp, but I swore to him, saying, I will not kill thee with the sword. Do not thou hold him guiltless. But thou art a wise man and knowest what to do with him, and thou shalt bring down his grey hairs with blood to hell.'

Now I ask, Why could not Mr. Kingsley be open? If he intended still to arraign me on the charge of lying, why could he not say so as a man? Why must he insinuate, question, imply, and use sneering and irony, as if longing to touch a forbidden fruit, which still he was afraid would burn his fingers, if he did so? Why must he 'palter in a double sense,' and blow hot and cold in one breath? He first said he considered me a patron of lying; well, he changed his opinion; and as to the logical ground of this change, he said that, if any one asked him what it was, he could only answer that *he really did not know*. Why could not he change back again, and say he did not know why? He had quite a right to do so; and then his conduct would have been so far straightforward and unexceptionable. But no; – in the very act of professing to believe in my sincerity, he takes care to show the world that it is a profession and nothing more. That very proceeding which at p. 383 he lays to my charge, (whereas I detest it,) of avowing one thing and thinking another, that proceeding he here exemplifies himself; and yet, while indulging in practices as offensive as this, he ventures to speak of his sensitive admiration of 'hault courage and strict honour!' 'I forgive you, Sir Knight,' says the heroine in the Romance, 'I forgive you as a Christian.' 'That means,' said Wamba, 'that she does not forgive him at all.' Mr. Kingsley's word of honour is about as valuable as in the jester's opinion was the Christian charity of Rowena. But here we are brought to a further specimen of Mr. Kingsley's method of disputation, and having duly exhibited it, I shall have done with him.

It is his last, and he has intentionally reserved it for his last. Let it be recollected that he professed to absolve me from his original charge of dishonesty up to February I. And further, he implies that, *at the time when he was writing*, I had not *yet* involved myself in any fresh acts suggestive of that sin. He says that I have had a great *escape* of conviction, that he hopes I shall take warning, and act more cautiously. 'It depends entirely', he says, 'on *Dr. Newman, whether* he shall *sustain* the reputation which he has so recently acquired' (p. 378). Thus, in Mr. Kingsley's judgment, I was *then*, when he wrote these words, *still* innocent of dishonesty, for a man cannot sustain what he actually has not got; *only he could not be sure of my future*. Could not be sure! Why at this very time he had already noted down valid proofs, as he thought them, that I *had* already forfeited the character which he contemptuously accorded to me. He had cautiously said '*up to* February 1st,' *in order* to reserve the Title-page and last three pages of my Pamphlet, which were not published till February 12th, and out of these four pages, which he had *not* whitewashed, he had *already* forged charges against me of dishonesty at the very time that he implied that as yet there was nothing against me. When he gave me that plenary condonation, as it seemed to be, he had already done his best that I should never enjoy it. He knew well at p. 377, what he meant to say at pp. 407 and 408. At best indeed I was only out upon ticket of leave; but that ticket

was a pretence; he had made it forfeit when he gave it. But he
did not say so at once, first, because between p. 377 and p. 407
he meant to talk a great deal about my idiotcy and my frenzy,
which would have been simply out of place, had he proved me
too soon to be a knave again; and next, because he meant to
exhaust all those insinuations about my knavery in the past,
which 'strict honour' did not permit him to countenance, in
order thereby to give colour and force to his direct charges of
knavery in the present, which 'strict honour' *did* permit him to
handsel. So in the fifth act he gave a start, and found to his
horror that, in my miserable four pages, I had committed the
'enormity' of an 'economy,' which in matter of fact he had got
by heart before he began the play. Nay, he suddenly found
two, three, and (for what he knew) as many as four profligate
economies in that Title-page and those Reflections, and he uses
the language of distress and perplexity at this appalling discovery.

Now why this *coup de théâtre*? The reason soon breaks on us.
Up to February 1, he could not categorically arraign me for
lying, and therefore could not involve me, (as was so necessary
for his case,) in the popular abhorrence which is felt for the
casuists of Rome: but, as soon as ever he could openly and
directly pronounce (saving his 'hault courage and strict honour')
that I am guilty of three or four new economies, then at once I
am made to bear, not only my own sins, but the sins of other
people also, and, though I have been condoned the knavery of
my antecedents, I am guilty of the knavery of a whole priesthood
instead. So the hour of doom for Semei is come, and the wise
man knows what to do with him; – he is down upon me with the
odious names of 'St. Alfonso da Liguori,' and 'Scavini' and
'Neyraguet,' and 'the Romish moralists,' and their 'compeers and
pupils,' and I am at once merged and whirled away in the gulph
of notorious quibblers, and hypocrites, and rogues.

But we have not even yet got at the real object of the stroke,
thus reserved for his *finale*. I really feel sad for what I am obliged
now to say. I am in warfare with him, but I wish him no ill; – it
is very difficult to get up resentment towards persons whom one
has never seen. It is easy enough to be irritated with friends or
foes, *vis-à-vis*; but, though I am writing with all my heart against
what he has said of me, I am not conscious of personal unkindness

towards himself. I think it necessary to write as I am writing, for my own sake, and for the sake of the Catholic Priesthood; but I wish to impute nothing worse to Mr. Kingsley than that he has been furiously carried away by his feelings. But what shall I say of the upshot of all this talk of my economies and equivocations and the like? What is the precise *work* which it is directed to effect? I am at war with him; but there is such a thing as legitimate warfare: war has its laws; there are things which may fairly be done, and things which may not be done. I say it with shame and with stern sorrow; – he has attempted a great transgression; he has attempted (as I may call it) to *poison the wells*. I will quote him and explain what I mean.

'Dr. Newman tries, by cunning sleight-of-hand logic, to prove that I did not believe the accusation when I made it. Therein he is mistaken. I did believe it, and I believed also his indignant denial. But when he goes on to ask with sneers, why I should believe his denial, if I did not consider him trustworthy in the first instance? I can only answer, I really do not know. There is a *great deal* to be said for *that* view, *now that* Dr. Newman has become (one must needs suppose) *suddenly* and *since* the 1st of February, 1864, a convert to the *economic* views of St. Alfonso da Liguori and his compeers. I am *henceforth* in doubt and *fear*, as much as any honest man can be, *concerning every word* Dr. Newman may write. *How can I tell that I shall not be the dupe of some cunning equivocation*, of one of the three kinds laid down as permissible by the blessed Alfonso da Liguori and his pupils, even when confirmed by an oath, because "then we do not deceive our neighbour, but allow him to deceive himself?" ... It is admissible, therefore, to use words and sentences which have a double signification, and leave the hapless hearer to take which of them he may choose. *What proof have I, then, that by "mean it? I never said it!" Dr. Newman does not signify*, I did not say it, but I did mean it?' – P. 407.

Now these insinuations and questions shall be answered in their proper places; here I will but say that I scorn and detest lying, and quibbling, and double-tongued practice, and slyness, and cunning, and smoothness, and cant, and pretence, quite as much as any Protestants hate them; and I pray to be kept from the snare of them. But all this is just now by the bye; my present subject is Mr. Kingsley; what I insist upon here, now that I am bringing this portion of my discussion to a close, is this unmanly attempt of his, in his concluding pages, to cut the ground from under my feet; – to poison by anticipation the public mind against me, John Henry Newman, and to infuse into the imaginations of my readers, suspicion and mistrust of everything that I may say in reply to him. This I call *poisoning the wells*.

'I am henceforth in *doubt and fear*,' he says, 'as much as any *honest* man can be, *concerning every word* Dr. Newman may write. *How can I tell that I shall not be the dupe of some cunning equivocation? . . .* What proof have I, that by "mean it? I never said it!" Dr. Newman does not signify, "I did not say it, but I did mean it?"'

Well, I can only say, that, if his taunt is to take effect, I am but wasting my time in saying a word in answer to his foul calumnies; and this is precisely what he knows and intends to be its fruit. I can hardly get myself to protest against a method of controversy so base and cruel, lest in doing so, I should be violating my self-respect and self-possession; but most base and most cruel it is. We all know how our imagination runs away with us, how suddenly and at what a pace; – the saying, 'Caesar's wife should not be suspected,' is an instance of what I mean. The habitual prejudice, the humour of the moment, is the turning-point which leads us to read a defence in a good sense or a bad. We interpret it by our antecedent impressions. The very same sentiments, according as our jealousy is or is not awake, or our aversion stimulated, are tokens of truth or of dissimulation and pretence. There is a story of a sane person being by mistake shut up in the wards of a Lunatic Asylum, and that, when he pleaded his cause to some strangers visiting the establishment, the only remark he elicited in answer was, 'How naturally he talks! you would think he was in his senses.' Controversies should be decided by the reason; is it legitimate warfare to appeal to the misgivings of the public mind and to its dislikings? Any how, if Mr. Kingsley is able thus to practise upon my readers, the more I succeed, the less will be my success. If I am natural, he will tell them, 'Ars est celare artem;' if I am convincing, he will suggest that I am an able logician; if I show warmth, I am acting the indignant innocent; if I am calm, I am thereby detected as a smooth hypocrite; if I clear up difficulties, I am too plausible and perfect to be true. The more triumphant are my statements, the more certain will be my defeat.

So will it be if Mr. Kingsley succeeds in his manoeuvre; but I do not for an instant believe that he will. Whatever judgment my readers may eventually form of me from these pages, I am confident that they will believe me in what I shall say in the course of them. I have no misgiving at all, that they will be ungenerous or harsh with a man who has been so long before the eyes of the world; who has so many to speak of him from personal knowledge; whose natural impulse it has ever been to speak out; who has ever spoken too much rather than too little; who would have saved himself many a scrape, if he had been wise enough to hold his tongue; who has ever been fair to the doctrines and arguments of his opponents; who has never slurred over facts and reasonings which told against himself; who has never given his name or authority to proofs which he thought unsound, or to testimony which he did not think at least plausible; who has never shrunk from confessing a fault when he felt that he had committed one; who has ever consulted for others more than for himself; who has given up much that he loved and prized and could have retained, but that he loved honesty better than name, and Truth better than dear friends.

And now I am in a train of thought higher and more serene than any which slanders can disturb. Away with you, Mr. Kingsley, and fly into space. Your name shall occur again as little as I can help, in the course of these pages. I shall henceforth occupy myself not with you, but with your charges.

PART II

True mode of meeting Mr. Kingsley

What shall be the special imputation, against which I shall throw myself in these pages, out of the thousand and one which my accuser directs upon me? I mean to confine myself to one, for there is only one about which I much care, – the charge of

Untruthfulness. He may cast upon me as many other imputations as he pleases, and they may stick on me, as long as they can, in the course of nature. They will fall to the ground in their season.

And indeed I think the same of the charge of Untruthfulness, and I select it from the rest, not because it is more formidable, but because it is more serious. Like the rest, it may disfigure me for a time, but it will not stain: Archbishop Whately used to say, 'Throw dirt enough, and some will stick;' well, will stick, but not stain. I think he used to mean 'stain', and I do not agree with him. Some dirt sticks longer than other dirt; but no dirt is immortal. According to the old saying, Praevalebit Veritas. There are virtues indeed, which the world is not fitted to judge about or to uphold, such as faith, hope, and charity: but it can judge about Truthfulness; it can judge about the natural virtues, and Truthfulness is one of them. Natural virtues may also become supernatural; Truthfulness is such; but that does not withdraw it from the jurisdiction of mankind at large. It may be more difficult in this or that particular case for men to take cognizance of it, as it may be difficult for the Court of Queen's Bench at Westminster to try a case fairly, which took place in Hindoostan; but that is a question of capacity, not of right. Mankind has the right to judge of Truthfulness in the case of a Catholic, as in the case of a Protestant, of an Italian, or of a Chinese. I have never doubted, that in my hour, in God's hour, my avenger will appear, and the world will acquit me of untruthfulness, even though it be not while I live.

Still more confident am I of such eventual acquittal, seeing that my judges are my own countrymen. I think, indeed, Englishmen the most suspicious and touchy of mankind; I think them unreasonable and unjust in their seasons of excitement; but I had rather be an Englishman (as in fact I am) than belong to any other race under heaven. They are as generous, as they are hasty and burly; and their repentance for their injustice is greater than their sin.

For twenty years and more I have borne an imputation, of which I am at least as sensitive, who am the object of it, as they can be, who are only the judges. I have not set myself to remove it, first, because I never have had an opening to speak, and, next, because I never saw in them the disposition to hear. I have wished to appeal from Philip drunk to Philip sober. When shall I pronounce him to be himself again? If I may judge from the tone of the public press, which represents the public voice, I have great reason to take heart at this time. I have been treated by contemporary critics in this controversy with great fairness and gentleness, and I am grateful to them for it. However, the decision of the time and mode of my defence has been taken out of my hands; and I am thankful that it has been so. I am bound now as a duty to myself, to the Catholic cause, to the Catholic Priesthood, to give account of myself without any delay, when I am so rudely and circumstantially charged with Untruthfulness. I accept the challenge; I shall do my best to meet it, and I shall be content when I have done so.

I confine myself then, in these pages, to the charge of Untruthfulness; and I hereby cart away, as so much rubbish, the impertinences, with which the Pamphlet of Accusation swarms. I shall not think it necessary here to examine, whether I am 'worked into a pitch of confusion,' or have 'carried self-deception to perfection,' or am 'anxious to show my credulity,' or am 'in a morbid state of mind,' or 'hunger for nonsense as my food,' or 'indulge in subtle paradoxes' and 'rhetorical exaggerations,' or have 'eccentricities' or teach in a style 'utterly beyond' my Accuser's 'comprehension,' or create in him 'blank astonishment,' or 'exalt the magical powers of my Church,' or have 'unconsciously committed myself to a statement which strikes at the root of all morality,' or 'look down on the Protestant gentry as without hope of heaven,' or 'had better be sent to the furthest' Catholic 'mission among the savages of the South seas,' than 'to teach in an Irish Catholic University,' or have 'gambled away my reason,' or adopt 'sophistries,' or have published 'sophisms piled upon sophisms,' or have in my sermons 'culminating wonders,' or have a 'seemingly sceptical method,' or have 'barristerial ability' and 'almost boundless silliness,' or 'make great mistakes,' or am 'a subtle dialectician,' or perhaps have 'lost my temper,' or 'misquote Scripture,' or am 'anti-scriptural,' or 'border very closely on the Pelagian heresy.' – Pp. 392, 393, 395, 396, 397, 398, 399, 401, 402, 403, 404, 405, 406, 377, 401, 397.

These are all impertinences; and the list is so long that I am almost sorry to have given them room which might be better used. However, there they are, or at least a portion of them; and having noticed them thus much, I shall notice them no more.

Coming then to the subject, which is to furnish the staple of my publication, the question of my Truthfulness, I first direct attention to the passage which the Act of Accusation contains at p. 378 and p. 405. I shall give my reason presently, why I begin with it.

My accuser is speaking of my Sermon on Wisdom and Innocence, and he says, 'It must be *remembered always* that it is not a Protestant, but a Romish sermon.' – P. 378.

Then at p. 405 he continues, 'Dr. Newman does not apply to it that epithet. He called it in his letter to me of the 7th of January, (published by him,) a "Protestant" one. I remarked that, but considered it a mere slip of the pen. Besides, I have now nothing to say to that letter. It is to his "Reflections," in p. 373, which are open ground to me, that I refer. In them he deliberately repeats the epithet "Protestant:" only he, in an utterly imaginary conversation, puts it into my mouth, "which you preached when a Protestant." I call the man who preached that Sermon a Protestant? I should have sooner called him a Buddhist. *At that very time he was teaching his disciples to scorn* and repudiate that name of Protestant, under which, for some reason or other, he *now finds it convenient to take shelter.* If *he* forgets, the world does not, the famous article in the British Critic (the then organ of his party) of three years before, July 1841, which, after denouncing the name of Protestant, declared the object of the party to be none other than the "*unprotestantising*" the English Church.'

In this passage my accuser asserts or implies, 1. that the Sermon, on which he originally grounded his slander against me in the January No. of the Magazine, was really and in matter of fact a 'Romish' Sermon; 2. that I ought in my Pamphlet to have acknowledged this fact; 3. that I didn't. 4. That I actually called it instead a Protestant Sermon. 5. That at the time when I published it, twenty years ago, I should have denied that it was a Protestant Sermon. 6. By consequence, I should in that denial have avowed that it was a 'Romish' Sermon; 7. and therefore, not only, when I was in the Established Church, was I guilty of the dishonesty of preaching what at the time I knew to be a 'Romish' Sermon, but now too, in 1864, I have committed the additional dishonesty of calling it a Protestant Sermon. If my accuser does not mean this, I submit to such reparation as I owe him for my mistake, but I cannot make out that he means any thing else.

Here are two main points to be considered; 1. I in 1864 have called it a Protestant Sermon. 2. He in 1844 and now has styled it a Popish Sermon. Let me take these two points separately.

1. Certainly, when I was in the English Church, I *did* disown the word 'Protestant', and that, even at an earlier date than my Accuser names; but just let us see whether this fact is any thing at all to the purpose of his accusation. Last January 7th I spoke to this effect: 'How can you prove that *Father* Newman informs us of a certain thing about the Roman Clergy', by referring to a *Protestant* Sermon of the Vicar of St. Mary's? My Accuser answers me thus: 'There's a quibble! why, *Protestant* is *not* the word which you would have used when at St. Mary's, and yet you use it now!' Very true; I do; but what on earth does this matter to my *argument*? how does this word 'Protestant,' which I used, tend in any degree to make my argument a quibble? What word *should* I have used twenty years ago instead of 'Protestant?' 'Roman' or 'Romish?' by no manner of means.

My accuser indeed says that 'it must always be remembered that it is not a Protestant *but* a Romish Sermon.' He implies, and, I suppose, he thinks, that not to be a Protestant is to be a Roman; he may say so, if he pleases, but so did not say that large body who have been called by the name of Tractarians, as all the world knows. The movement proceeded on the very basis of denying that position which my Accuser takes for granted that I allowed. It ever said, and it says now, that there is something *between* Protestant and Romish; that there is a 'Via Media' which is neither the one nor the other. Had I been asked twenty years ago, what the doctrine of the Established Church was, I should have answered, 'Neither Romish *nor* Protestant, *but* "Anglican" or "Anglo-catholic."' I should never have granted that the

Sermon was Romish; I should have denied, and that with an internal denial, quite as much as I do now, that it was a Roman or Romish Sermon. Well then, substitute the word 'Anglican' or 'Anglo-catholic' for 'Protestant' in my question, and see if the argument is a bit the worse for it, – thus: 'How can you prove that *Father* Newman informs us a certain thing about the Roman Clergy, by referring to an *Anglican* or *Anglo-catholic* Sermon of the Vicar of St. Mary's?' The cogency of the argument remains just where it was. What have I gained in the argument, what has he lost, by my having said, not 'an Anglican Sermon', but 'a Protestant Sermon?' What dust then is he throwing into our eyes!

For instance: in 1844 I lived at Littlemore; two or three miles distant from Oxford; and Littlemore lies in three, perhaps in four, distinct parishes, so that of particular houses it is difficult to say, whether they are in St. Mary's, Oxford, or in Cowley, or in Iffley, or in Sandford, the line of demarcation running even through them. Now, supposing I were to say in 1864, that 'twenty years ago I did not live in Oxford, *because* I lived out at Littlemore, in the parish of Cowley;' and if upon this there were letters of mine produced dated Littlemore, 1844, in one of which I said that 'I lived, not in Cowley, but at Littlemore, in St. Mary's parish,' how would that prove that I contradicted myself, and that therefore after all I must be supposed to have been living in Oxford in 1844? The utmost that would be proved by the discrepancy, such as it was, would be, that there was some confusion either in me, or in the state of the fact as to the limits of the parishes. There would be no confusion about the place or spot of my residence. I should be saying in 1864, 'I did not live in Oxford twenty years ago, because I lived at Littlemore in the Parish of Cowley.' I should have been saying in 1844, 'I do not live in Oxford, because I live in St. Mary's, Littlemore.' In either case I should be saying that my *habitat* in 1844 was *not* Oxford, but Littlemore; and I should be giving the same reason for it. I should be proving an *alibi*. I should be naming the same place for the *alibi*; but twenty years ago I should have spoken of it as St. Mary's, Littlemore, and to-day I should have spoken of it as Littlemore in the Parish of Cowley.

And so as to my Sermon; in January, 1864, I called it a

Protestant Sermon, and not a Roman; but in 1844 I should, if asked, have called it an *Anglican* Sermon, and not a Roman. In both cases I should have denied that it was Roman, and that on the ground of its being something else; though I should have called that something else, then by one name, now by another. The doctrine of the *Via Media* is a *fact*, whatever name we give to it; I, as a Roman Priest, find it more natural and usual to call it Protestant: I, as an Oxford Vicar, thought it more exact to call it Anglican; but, whatever I then called it, and whatever I now call it, I mean one and the same object by my name, and therefore not another object, – viz. not the Roman Church. The argument, I repeat, is sound, whether the *Via Media* and the Vicar of St. Mary's be called Anglican or Protestant.

This is a specimen of what my Accuser means by my 'Economies;' nay, it is actually one of those special two, three, or four, committed after February 1, which he thinks sufficient to connect me with the shifty casuists and the double-dealing moralists, as he considers them, of the Catholic Church. What a 'Much ado about nothing!'

2. But, whether or no he can prove that I in 1864 have committed any logical fault in calling my Sermon on Wisdom and Innocence a Protestant Sermon, he is and has been all along, most firm in the belief himself that a Romish Sermon it is; and this is the point on which I wish specially to insist. It is for this cause that I made the above extract from his Pamphlet, not merely in order to answer him, though, when I had made it, I could not pass by the attack on me which it contains. I shall notice his charges one by one by and by; but I have made this extract here in order to insist and to dwell on this phenomenon – viz. that he does consider it an undeniable fact, that the Sermon is 'Romish,' – meaning by 'Romish' not 'savouring of Romish doctrine' merely, but 'the work of a real Romanist, of a conscious Romanist.' This belief it is which leads him to be so severe on me, for now calling it 'Protestant.' He thinks that, whether I have committed any logical self-contradiction or not, I am very well aware that, when I wrote it, I ought to have been elsewhere, that I was a conscious Romanist, teaching Romanism; – or if he does not believe this himself, he wishes others to think so, which

comes to the same thing; certainly I prefer to consider that he thinks so himself, but, if he likes the other hypothesis better, he is welcome to it.

He believes then so firmly that the Sermon was a 'Romish Sermon,' that he pointedly takes it for granted, before he has adduced a syllable of proof of the matter of fact. He *starts* by saying that it is a fact to be 'remembered.' 'It *must* be *remembered always*,' he says, 'that it is not a Protestant, but a Romish Sermon,' p. 378. Its Romish parentage is a great truth for the memory, not a thesis for inquiry. Merely to refer his readers to the Sermon is, he considers, to secure them on his side. Hence it is that, in his letter of January 18, he said to me, 'It seems to me, that, by *referring* publicly to the Sermon on which my allegations are founded, I have given every one *an opportunity of judging of their injustice*,' that is, an opportunity of seeing that they are transparently just. The notion of there being a *Via Media*, held all along by a large party in the Anglican Church, and now at least not less than at any former time, is too subtle for his intellect. Accordingly, he thinks it was an allowable figure of speech, – not more, I suppose, than an 'hyperbole,' – when referring to a Sermon of the Vicar of St. Mary's in the Magazine, to say that it was the writing of a Roman Priest; and as to serious arguments to prove the point, why, they may indeed be necessary, as a matter of form, in an Act of Accusation, such as his Pamphlet, but they are superfluous to the good sense of any one who will only just look into the matter himself.

Now, with respect to the so-called arguments which he ventures to put forward in proof that the Sermon is Romish, I shall answer them, together with all his other arguments, in the latter portion of this Reply; here I do but draw the attention of the reader, as I have said already, to the phenomenon itself, which he exhibits, of an unclouded confidence that the Sermon is the writing of a virtual member of the Roman communion, and I do so because it has made a great impression on my own mind, and has suggested to me the course that I shall pursue in my answer to him.

I say, he takes it for granted that the Sermon is the writing of a virtual or actual, of a conscious Roman Catholic; and is impatient at the very notion of having to prove it. Father Newman and the Vicar of St. Mary's are one and the same: there has been no change of mind in him; what he believed then he believes now, and what he believes now he believed then. To dispute this is frivolous; to distinguish between his past self and his present is subtlety, and to ask for proof of their identity is seeking opportunity to be sophistical. This writer really thinks that he acts a straightforward honest part, when he says 'A Catholic Priest informs us in his Sermon on Wisdom and Innocence preached at St. Mary's,' and he thinks that I am the shuffler and quibbler when I forbid him to do so. So singular a phenomenon in a man of undoubted ability has struck me forcibly, and I shall pursue the train of thought which it opens.

It is not he alone who entertains, and has entertained, such an opinion of me and my writings. It is the impression of large classes of men; the impression twenty years ago and the impression now. There has been a general feeling that I was for years where I had no right to be; that I was a 'Romanist' in Protestant livery and service; that I was doing the work of a hostile Church in the bosom of the English Establishment, and knew it, or ought to have known it. There was no need of arguing about particular passages in my writings, when the fact was so patent, as men thought it to be.

First it was certain, and I could not myself deny it, that I scouted the name 'Protestant.' It was certain again, that many of the doctrines which I professed were popularly and generally known as badges of the Roman Church, as distinguished from the faith of the Reformation. Next, how could I have come by them? Evidently, I had certain friends and advisers who did not appear; there was some underground communication between Stonyhurst or Oscott and my rooms at Oriel. Beyond a doubt, I was advocating certain doctrines, not by accident, but on an understanding with ecclesiastics of the old religion. Then men went further, and said that I had actually been received into that religion, and withal had leave given me to profess myself a Protestant still. Others went even further, and gave it out to the world, as a matter of fact, of which they themselves had the proof in their hands, that I was actually a Jesuit. And when the opinions which I advocated spread, and younger men went further than I, the feeling against me waxed stronger and took a wider range.

And now indignation arose at the knavery of a conspiracy such as this: – and it became of course all the greater, in consequence of its being the received belief of the public at large, that craft and intrigue, such as they fancied they beheld with their own eyes, were the very instruments to which the Catholic Church has in these last centuries been indebted for her maintenance and extension.

There was another circumstance still, which increased the irritation and aversion felt by the large classes, of whom I have been speaking, as regards the preachers of doctrines, so new to them and so unpalatable; and that was, that they developed them in so measured a way. If they were inspired by Roman theologians, (and this was taken for granted,) why did they not speak out at once? Why did they keep the world in such suspense and anxiety as to what was coming next, and what was to be the upshot of the whole? Why this reticence, and half-speaking, and apparent indecision? It was plain that the plan of operations had been carefully mapped out from the first, and that these men were cautiously advancing towards its accomplishment, as far as was safe at the moment; that their aim and their hope was to carry off a large body with them of the young and the ignorant; that they meant gradually to leaven the minds of the rising generation, and to open the gate of that city, of which they were the sworn defenders, to the enemy who lay in ambush outside of it. And when in spite of the many protestations of the party to the contrary, there was at length an actual movement among their disciples, and one went over to Rome, and then another, the worst anticipations and the worst judgments which had been formed of them received their justification. And, lastly, when men first had said of me, 'You will see, *he* will go, he is only biding his time, he is waiting the word of command from Rome,' and, when after all, after my arguments and denunciations of former years, at length I did leave the Anglican Church for the Roman, then they said to each other, 'It is just as we said: I told you so.'

This was the state of mind of masses of men twenty years ago, who took no more than an external and common-sense view of what was going on. And partly the tradition, partly the effect of that feeling, remains to the present time. Certainly I consider that, in my own case, it is the great obstacle in the way of my being favourably heard, as at present, when I have to make my defence. Not only am I now a member of a most un-English communion, whose great aim is considered to be the extinction of Protestantism and the Protestant Church, and whose means of attack are popularly supposed to be unscrupulous cunning and deceit, but besides, how came I originally to have any relations with the Church of Rome at all? did I, or my opinions, drop from the sky? how came I, in Oxford, *in gremio Universitatis*, to present myself to the eyes of men in that full-blown investiture of Popery? How could I dare, how could I have the conscience, with warnings, with prophecies, with accusations against me, to persevere in a path which steadily advanced towards, which ended in, the religion of Rome? And how am I now to be trusted, when long ago I was trusted, and was found wanting?

It is this which is the strength of the case of my Accuser against me; – not his arguments in themselves, which I shall easily crumble into dust, but the bias of the court. It is the state of the atmosphere; it is the vibration all around which will more or less echo his assertion of my dishonesty; it is that prepossession against me, which takes it for granted that, when my reasoning is convincing it is only ingenious, and that when my statements are unanswerable, there is always something put out of sight or hidden in my sleeve; it is that plausible, but cruel conclusion to which men are so apt to jump, that when much is imputed, something must be true, and that it is more likely that one should be to blame, than that many should be mistaken in blaming him; – these are the real foes which I have to fight, and the auxiliaries to whom my Accuser makes his court.

Well, I must break through this barrier of prejudice against me, if I can; and I think I shall be able to do so. When first I read the Pamphlet of Accusation, I almost despaired of meeting effectively such a heap of misrepresentation and such a vehemence of animosity. What was the good of answering first one point, and then another, and going through the whole circle of its abuse; when my answer to the first point would be forgotten, as soon as I got to the second? What was the use of bringing out half a hundred separate principles or views for the refutation of the separate counts in the Indictment, when rejoinders of this sort would but confuse and torment the reader by their number and their diversity? What hope was there of condensing into a pamphlet of a readable length, matter which ought freely to expand itself into half a dozen volumes? What means was there, except the expenditure of interminable pages, to set right even one of that series of 'single passing hints', to use my Assailant's own language, which, 'as with his finger tip, he had delivered' against me?

All those separate charges of his had their force in being illustrations of one and the same great imputation. He had a positive idea to illuminate his whole matter, and to stamp it with a form, and to quicken it with an interpretation. He called me a *liar*, – a simple, a broad, an intelligible, to the English public a plausible arraignment; but for me, to answer in detail charge one by reason one, and charge two by reason two, and charge three by reason three, and so to proceed through the whole string both of accusations and replies, each of which was to be independent of the rest, this would be certainly labour lost as regards any effective result. What I needed was a corresponding antagonist unity in my defence, and where was that to be found? We see, in the case of commentators on the prophecies of Scripture, an exemplification of the principle on which I am insisting; viz. how much more powerful even a false interpretation of the sacred text is than none at all; – how a certain key to the visions of the Apocalypse, for instance, may cling to the mind – (I have found it so in my own case), – mainly because they are positive and objective, in spite of the fullest demonstration that they really have no claim upon our belief. The reader says, 'What else can the prophecy mean?' just as my Accuser asks, 'What, then, does Dr. Newman mean?' . . . I reflected, and I saw a way out of my perplexity.

Yes, I said to myself, his very question is about my *meaning*; 'What does Dr. Newman mean?' It pointed in the very same direction as that into which my musings had turned me already. He asks what I *mean*; not about my words, not about my arguments, not about my actions, as his ultimate point, but about that living intelligence, by which I write, and argue, and act. He asks about my Mind and its Beliefs and its Sentiments; and he shall be answered; – not for his own sake, but for mine, for the sake of the Religion which I profess, and of the Priesthood in which I am unworthily included, and of my friends and of my foes, and of that general public which consists of neither one nor the other, but of well-wishers, lovers of fair play, sceptical cross-questioners, interested inquirers, curious lookers-on, and simple strangers, unconcerned yet not careless about the issue.

My perplexity did not last half an hour. I recognized what I had to do, though I shrank from both the task and the exposure which it would entail. I must, I said, give the true key to my whole life; I must show what I am that it may be seen what I am not, and that the phantom may be extinguished which gibbers instead of me. I wish to be known as a living man, and not as a scarecrow which is dressed up in my clothes. False ideas may be refuted indeed by argument, but by true ideas alone are they expelled. I will vanquish, not my Accuser, but my judges. I will indeed answer his charges and criticisms on me one by one, lest any one should say that they are unanswerable, but such a work shall not be the scope nor the substance of my reply. I will draw out, as far as may be, the history of my mind; I will state the point at which I began, in what external suggestion or accident each opinion had its rise, how far and how they were developed from within, how they grew, were modified, were combined, were in collision with each other, and were changed; again how I conducted myself towards them, and how, and how far, and for how long a time, I thought I could hold them consistently with the ecclesiastical engagements which I had made and with the position which I filled. I must show, – what is the very truth, – that the doctrines which I held, and have held for so many years, have been taught me (speaking humanly) partly by the suggestions of Protestant friends, partly by the teaching of books, and partly by the action of my own mind: and thus I shall account for that phenomenon which to so many seems so wonderful, that I should have left 'my kindred and my father's house' for a Church from which once I turned away with dread; – so wonderful to them! as if forsooth a Religion which has flourished through so many ages, among so many nations, amid such varieties of social life, in such contrary classes and conditions of men, and after so many revolutions, political and civil, could not subdue the reason and overcome the heart, without the aid of fraud and the sophistries of the schools.

What I had proposed to myself in the course of half an hour, I determined on at the end of ten days. However, I have many difficulties in fulfilling my design. How am I to say all that has to be said in a reasonable compass? And then as to the materials of my narrative; I have no autobiographical notes to consult, no written explanations of particular treatises or of tracts which at the time gave offence, hardly any minutes of definite transactions or conversations, and few contemporary memoranda, I fear, of the feelings or motives under which from time to time I acted. I have an abundance of letters from friends with some copies or drafts of my answers to them, but they are for the most part unsorted, and, till this process has taken place, they are even too numerous and various to be available at a moment for my purpose. Then, as to the volumes which I have published, they would in many ways serve me, were I well up in them; but though I took great pains in their composition, I have thought little about them, when they were at length out of my hands, and, for the most part, the last time I read them has been when I revised their proof sheets.

Under these circumstances my sketch will of course be incomplete. I now for the first time contemplate my course as a whole; it is a first essay, but it will contain, I trust, no serious or substantial mistake, and so far will answer the purpose for which I write it. I purpose to set nothing down in it as certain, for which I have not a clear memory, or some written memorial, or the corroboration of some friend. There are witnesses enough up and down the country to verify, or correct, or complete it; and letters moreover of my own in abundance, unless they have been destroyed.

Moreover, I mean to be simply personal and historical: I am not expounding Catholic doctrine, I am doing no more than explaining myself, and my opinions and actions. I wish, as far as I am able, simply to state facts, whether they are ultimately determined to be for me or against me. Of course there will be room enough for contrariety of judgment among my readers, as to the necessity, or appositeness, or value, or good taste, or religious prudence of the details which I shall introduce. I may be accused of laying stress on little things, of being beside the mark, of going into impertinent or ridiculous details, of sounding my own praise, of giving scandal; but this is a case above all others, in which I am bound to follow my own lights and to speak out my own heart. It is not at all pleasant for me to be egotistical; nor to be criticized for being so. It is not pleasant to reveal to high and low, young and old, what has gone on within me from my early years. It is not pleasant to be giving to every shallow or flippant disputant the advantage over me of knowing my most private thoughts, I might even say the intercourse between myself and my Maker. But I do not like to be called to my face a liar and a knave: nor should I be doing my duty to my faith or to my name, if I were to suffer it. I know I have done nothing to deserve such an insult; and if I prove this, as I hope to do, I must not care for such incidental annoyances as are involved in the process.

APPENDIX

Answer in detail to Mr. Kingsley's Accusations

In proceeding now, according to the engagement with which I entered upon my undertaking, to examine in detail the Pamphlet which has been written against me, I am very sorry to be obliged to say, that it is as slovenly and random and futile in its definite charges, as it is iniquitous in its method of disputation. And now I proceed to show this without any delay; and shall consider in order,

1. My Sermon on the Apostolical Christian.
2. My Sermon on Wisdom and Innocence.
3. The Anglican Church.
4. The Lives of the English Saints.

    5. Ecclesiastical Miracles.
    6. Popular Religion.
    7. The Economy.
    8. Lying and Equivocation.

1   My Sermon on 'The Apostolical Christian', being the 19th of 'Sermons on Subjects of the Day'

This writer says, 'What Dr. Newman means by Christians . . . he has not left in doubt;' and then, quoting a passage from this Sermon which speaks of 'the humble monk and the holy nun' being 'Christians after the very pattern given us in Scripture,' he observes, 'This is his *definition* of Christians.'–p. 378.

This is not the case. I have neither given a definition, nor implied one, nor intended one; nor could I, either now or in 1843–4, or at any time, allow of the particular definition he ascribes to me. As if all Christians must be monks or nuns!

What I have said is, that monks and nuns are patterns of Christian perfection; and that Scripture itself supplies us with this pattern. Who can deny this? Who is bold enough to say that St. John Baptist, who, I suppose, is a Scripture Character, is not a pattern-monk; and that Mary, who 'sat at our Lord's feet,' was not a pattern-nun? and 'Anna too, who served God with fastings and prayers night and day?' Again, what is meant but this by St. Paul's saying, 'It is good for a man not to touch a woman?' and, when speaking of the father or guardian of a young girl, 'He that giveth her in marriage doeth well; but he that giveth her not in marriage doeth better?' And what does St. John mean but to praise virginity, when he says of the hundred forty and four thousand on Mount Sion, 'These are they which were not defiled with women, for they are virgins'? And what else did our Lord mean, when He said, 'There be eunuchs who have made themselves eunuchs for the kingdom of heaven's sake. He that is able to receive it, let him receive it'?

He ought to know his logic better: I have said that 'monks and nuns find their pattern in Scripture': he adds, *Therefore* I hold all Christians are monks and nuns.

This is Blot *one*.

Now then for Blot *two*.

'Monks and nuns the *only* perfect Christians . . . what more' – p. 379.

A second fault in logic. I said no more than that monks and nuns were perfect Christians: he adds, *Therefore* 'monks and nuns are the *only* perfect Christians.' Monks and nuns are *not* the only perfect Christians; I never thought so or said so, now or at any other time.

P. 405. 'In the Sermon . . . monks and nuns are spoken of as the *only true* Bible Christians.' This, again, is not the case. What I said is, that 'monks and nuns are Bible Christians:' it does not follow, nor did I mean, that 'all Bible Christians are monks and nuns.' Bad logic again. Blot *three*.

2   My Sermon on 'Wisdom and Innocence', being the 20th of 'Sermons on Subjects of the Day'

This writer says, p. 378, about my Sermon 20, 'By the world appears to be signified, especially, the Protestant public of these realms.'

He also asks, pp. 382-3, 'Why was it preached? . . . to insinuate, that the admiring young gentlemen, who listened to him, stood to their fellow-countrymen in the relation of the early Christians to the heathen Romans? or that Queen Victoria's Government was to the Church of England, what Nero's or Diocletian's was to the Church of Rome? It may have been so.'

May or may not, it wasn't. He insinuates, what not even with his little finger does he attempt to prove. Blot *four*.

He asserts, p. 379, that I said in the Sermon in question, that 'Sacramental Confession and the celibacy of the clergy are "notes" of the Church.' And, just before, he puts the word 'notes' in inverted commas, as if it was mine. That is, he garbles. It is *not* mine. Blot *five*.

He says that I '*define* what I mean by the Church in two "notes" of her character.' I do not define, or dream of defining.

1. He says that I teach that the celibacy of the clergy enters

into the *definition* of the Church. I do no such thing; that is the blunt truth. Define the Church by the celibacy of the clergy! why, let him read I Tim. iii.; there he will find that bishops and deacons are spoken of as married. How, then, could I be the dolt to say or imply that the celibacy of the clergy was a part of the definition of the Church? Blot *six*.

And again in pp. 405-6, 'In the Sermon a celibate clergy is made a note of the Church.' Thus the untruth is repeated. Blot *seven*.

2. And now for Blot *eight*. Neither did I say that 'Sacramental confession' was 'a note of the Church.' Nor is it. Nor could I with any cogency have brought this as an argument against the Church of England, for the Church of England has retained Confession, nay, Sacramental Confession. No fair man can read the form of Absolution in the Anglican Prayer in the Visitation of the Sick, without seeing that that Church does sanction and provide for Confession and Absolution. If that form does not contain the profession of a grave Sacramental act, words have no meaning. The form is almost in the words of the Roman form; and, by the time that this Clergyman has succeeded in explaining it away, he will have also got skill enough to explain away the Roman form; and if he did but handle my words with that latitude with which he interprets his own formularies, he would prove that, instead of my being superstitious and frantic, I was the most Protestant of preachers and the most latitudinarian of thinkers. It would be charity in him, in his reading of my words, to use some of that power of evasion, of which he shows himself such a master in his dealing with his own Prayer Book. Yet he has the assurance at pp. 382-3 to ask, 'Why was the Sermon preached? to insinuate that a Church which had sacramental confession and a celibate clergy was the only true Church?'

'Why?' I will tell the reader, *why*; and with this view will speak, first of the contents of the Sermon, then of its subject, then of its circumstances.

1. It was one of the last six Sermons which I wrote when I was an Anglican. It was one of the five Sermons I preached in St. Mary's between Christmas and Easter, 1843, the year when I gave up my Living. The MS. of the Sermon is destroyed; but I

believe, and my memory too bears me out, as far as it goes, that
the sentence in question about Celibacy and Confession *was not
preached at all*. The Volume, in which this Sermon is found, was
published *after* that I had given up St. Mary's, when I had no call
on me to restrain the expression of any thing which I might
hold: and I state an important fact about it in the Advertisement,
which this truth-loving writer *suppresses*. Blot *nine*.

My words, which stared him in the face, are as follows:— 'In
preparing [these Sermons] for publication, *a few words and sentences*
have in several places been *added* which will be found to express
more *of private or personal opinion*, than it was expedient to
introduce into the *instruction* delivered in Church to a parochial
Congregation. Such introduction, however, seems unobjectionable in the case of compositions, which are *detached* from the
sacred place and service to which they once belonged, and
submitted to the reason and judgment of the general reader.'

This Volume of Sermons then cannot be criticized at all as
preachments; they are *essays*; essays of a man who, at the time of
publishing them, was *not* a preacher. Such passages, as that in
question, are just the very ones which I added *upon* my publishing
them. I always was on my guard in the pulpit of saying any thing
which looked towards Rome; and therefore all his rhetoric about
my 'disciples,' 'admiring young gentlemen who listened to me,'
'fanatic and hot-headed young men, who hung upon my every
word,' becomes simple rubbish.

I have more to say on this point. This writer says, p. 383, 'I
know that men used to suspect Dr Newman, – I have been
inclined to do so myself, – of *writing a whole Sermon, not for the
sake of the text or of the matter*, but for the sake of one simple
passing hint, – one phrase, one epithet.' Can there be a plainer
testimony borne to the practical character of my Sermons at St.
Mary's than this gratuitous insinuation? Many a preacher of
Tractarian doctrine has been accused of not letting his parishioners alone, and of teasing them with his private theological
notions. You would gather from the general tone of this Writer
that that was my way. Every one who was in the habit of hearing
me, knows that it wasn't. This Writer either knows nothing
about it, and then he ought to be silent; or he does know, and
then he ought to speak the truth. Others spread the same report

twenty years ago as he does now, and the world believed that my Sermons at St. Mary's were full of red-hot Tractarianism. Then strangers came to hear me preach, and were astonished at their own disappointment. I recollect the wife of a great prelate from a distance coming to hear me, and then expressing her surprise to find that I preached nothing but a plain humdrum Sermon. I recollect how, when on the Sunday before Commemoration one year, a number of strangers came to hear me, and I preached in my usual way, residents in Oxford, of high position, were loud in their satisfaction that on a great occasion, I had made a simple failure, for after all there was nothing in the Sermon to hear. Well, but they were not going to let me off, for all my common-sense view of duty. Accordingly, they got up the charitable theory which this Writer revives. They said that there was a double purpose in those plain addresses of mine, and that my Sermons were never so artful as when they seemed common-place; that there were sentences which redeemed their apparent simplicity and quietness. So they watched during the delivery of a Sermon, which to them was too practical to be useful, for the concealed point of it, which they could at least imagine, if they could not discover. 'Men used to suspect Dr Newman,' he says, 'of writing a *whole* Sermon, *not* for the sake of *the text or of the matter*, but for the sake of . . . *one* phrase, *one* epithet, *one* little barbed arrow, which, as he *swept magnificently* past on the stream of his calm eloquence, *seemingly* unconscious of all presences, save those unseen, he delivered unheeded,' &c., p. 383. To all appear-ance, he says, I was 'unconscious of all presences;' so this kind Writer supplies the true interpretation of this unconsciousness. He is not able to deny that 'the *whole* Sermon' had the *appearance* of being '*for the sake* of the text and matter;' therefore he suggests that perhaps it wasn't. And then he emptily talks of the 'magnifi-cent sweep of my eloquence,' and my 'oratoric power.' Did he forget that the Sermon of which he thus speaks can be read by others as well as him? Now, the sentences are as short as Aristotle's, and as grave as Bishop Butler's. It is written almost in the condensed style of Tract 90. Eloquence there is none. I put this down as Blot *ten*.

2. And now as to the subject of the Sermon. The series of which

the Volume consists are such Sermons as are, more or less, exceptions to the rule which I ordinarily observed, as to the subjects which I introduced into the pulpit of St. Mary's. They are not purely ethical or doctrinal. They were for the most part caused by circumstances of the day or of the time, and they belong to various years. One was written in 1832, two in 1836, two in 1838, five in 1840, five in 1841, four in 1842, seven in 1843. Many of them are engaged on one subject, viz. in viewing the Church in its relation to the world. By the world was meant, not simply those multitudes which were not in the Church, but the existing body of human society, whether in the Church or not, whether Catholics, Protestants, Greeks, or Mahometans, theists or idolaters, as being ruled by principles, maxims, and instincts of their own, that is, of an unregenerate nature, whatever their supernatural privileges might be, greater or less, according to their form of religion. This view of the relation of the Church to the world as taken apart from questions of ecclesiastical politics, as they may be called, is often brought out in my Sermons. Two occur to me at once; No. 3 of my Plain Sermons, which was written in 1829, and No. 15 of my Third Volume, written in 1835. Then, on the other hand, by Church I meant, – in common with all writers connected with the Tract Movement, whatever their shades of opinion, and with the whole body of English divines, except those of the Puritan or Evangelical School, – the whole of Christendom, from the Apostles' time till now, whatever their later divisions into Latin, Greek, and Anglican. I have explained this view of the subject above at pp. 77–9 of this Volume. When then I speak, in the particular Sermon before us, of the members, or the rulers, or the action of 'the Church,' I mean neither the Latin, nor the Greek, nor the English, taken by itself, but of the whole Church as one body: of Italy as one with England, of the Saxon or Norman as one with the Caroline Church. *This* was specially the one Church, and the points in which one branch or one period differed from another were not and could not be Notes of the Church, because Notes necessarily belonged to the whole of the Church every where and always.

This being my doctrine as to the relation of the Church to the world, I laid down in the Sermon three principles concerning it, and there left the matter. The first is, that Divine Wisdom had framed for its action, laws which man, if left to himself, would have antecedently pronounced to be the worst possible for its success, and which in all ages have been called by the world, as they were in the Apostles' days, 'foolishness;' that man ever relies on physical and material force, and on carnal inducements, – as Mahomet with his sword and his houris, or indeed almost as that theory of religion, called, since the Sermon was written, 'muscular Christianity;' but that our Lord, on the contrary, has substituted meekness for haughtiness, passiveness for violence, and innocence for craft: and that the event has shown the high wisdom of such an economy, for it has brought to light a set of natural laws, unknown before, by which the seeming paradox that weakness should be stronger than might, and simplicity than worldly policy, is readily explained.

Secondly, I said that men of the world, judging by the event, and not recognizing the secret causes of the success, viz. a higher order of natural laws, – natural, though their source and action were supernatural, (for 'the meek inherit the earth,' by means of a meekness which comes from above,) – these men, I say, concluded, that the success which they witnessed must arise from some evil secret which the world had not mastered, – by means of magic, as they said in the first ages, by cunning as they say now. And accordingly they thought that the humility and inoffen-siveness of Christians, or of Churchmen, was a mere pretence and blind to cover the real causes of that success, which Christians could explain and would not; and that they were simply hypocrites.

Thirdly, I suggested that shrewd ecclesiastics, who knew very well that there was neither magic nor craft in the matter, and, from their intimate acquaintance with what actually went on within the Church, discerned what were the real causes of its success, were of course under the temptation of substituting reason for conscience, and, instead of simply obeying the com-mand, were led to do good that good might come, that is, to act *in order* to their success, and not from a motive of faith. Some, I said, did yield to the temptation more or less, and their motives became mixed; and in this way the world in a more subtle shape has got into the Church; and hence it has come to pass, that, looking at its history from first to last, we cannot possibly draw the line between good and evil there, and say either that every thing is to be defended, or some things to be condemned. I expressed the difficulty, which I supposed to be inherent in the Church, in the following words. I said, '*Priestcraft has ever been considered the badge*, and its imputation is a kind of Note of the Church; and *in part indeed truly*, because the presence of powerful enemies, and the sense of their own weakness, *has sometimes tempted Christians to the abuse, instead of the use of Christian wisdom, to be wise without being harmless*; but partly, nay, for the most part, not truly, but slanderously, and merely because the world called their wisdom craft, when it was found to be a match for its own numbers and power.' This passage he has partly garbled, partly omitted. Blot *eleven*.

Such is the substance of the Sermon: and as to the main drift of it, it was this; that I was, there and elsewhere, scrutinizing the course of the Church as a whole, as if philosophically, as an historical phenomenon, and observing the laws on which it was conducted. Hence the Sermon, or Essay as it more truly is, is written in a dry and unimpassioned way: it shows as little of human warmth of feeling, I repeat, as a Sermon of Bishop Butler's. Yet, under that calm exterior there was a deep and keen sensitiveness, as I shall now proceed to show.

3. If I mistake not, it was written with a secret thought about myself. Every one preaches according to his frame of mind, at the time of preaching. One heaviness especially oppressed me at that season, which this Writer, twenty years afterwards, has set himself with a good will to renew: it arose from the sense of the base calumnies which were thrown upon me on all sides. In this trouble of mind I gained, while I reviewed the history of the Church, at once an argument and a consolation. My argument was this: if I, who knew my own innocence, was so blackened by party prejudice, perhaps those high rulers and those servants of the Church, in the many ages which intervened between the early Nicene times and the present, who were laden with such grievous accusations, were innocent also; and this reflection served to make me tender towards those great names of the past, to whom weaknesses or crimes were imputed, and reconciled me to difficul-

ties in ecclesiastical proceeding, which there were no means now of properly explaining. And the sympathy thus excited for them, re-acted on myself, and I found comfort in being able to put myself under the shadow of those who had suffered as I was suffering, and who seemed to promise me their recompense, since I had a fellowship in their trial. In a letter to my Bishop at the time of Tract 90, part of which I have quoted, I said that I had ever tried to 'keep innocency;' and now two years had passed since then, and men were louder and louder in heaping on me the very charges, which this Writer repeats out of my Sermon, of 'fraud and cunning,' 'craftiness and deceitfulness,' 'double-dealing,' 'priestcraft,' of being 'mysterious, dark, subtle, designing,' when I was all the time conscious to myself, in my degree, and after my measure, of 'sobriety, self-restraint, and control of word and feeling.' I had had experience how my past success had been imputed to 'secret management;' and how, when I had shown surprise at that success, that surprise again was imputed to 'deceit;' and how my honest heartfelt submission to authority had been called, as it was called in a colonial Bishop's charge, 'mystic humility;' and how my silence was called an 'hypocrisy,' and my faithfulness to my clerical engagements a secret correspondence with the enemy. And I found a way of destroying my sensitiveness about these things which jarred upon my sense of justice, and otherwise would have been too much for me, by the contemplation of a large law of the Divine Dispensation, and found myself more and more able to bear in my own person a present trial, of which in my past writings I had expressed an anticipation.

For thus feeling and thus speaking this Writer has the charitableness and the decency to call me 'Mawworm.' 'I found him telling Christians,' he says, 'that they will always seem "artificial," and "wanting in openness and manliness;" that they will always be "a mystery" to the world; and that the world will always think them rogues; and bidding them glory in what the world (that is, the rest of their fellow-countrymen) disown, and say with Mawworm, "I like to be despised." . . . How was I to know that the preacher . . . was utterly blind to the broad meaning and the plain practical result of a Sermon like this delivered before fanatic and hot-headed young men, who hung upon his every word?' – pp. 383-4. Hot-headed young men! why, man, you are writing a Romance. You think the scene is Alexandria or the Spanish main, where you may let your imagination play revel to the extent of inveracity. It is good luck for me that the scene of my labours was not at Moscow or Damascus. Then I might be one of your ecclesiastical Saints, of which I sometimes hear in conversation, but with whom, I am glad to say, I have no personal acquaintance. Then you might ascribe to me a more deadly craft than mere quibbling and lying; in Spain I should have been an Inquisitor, with my rack in the background; I should have had a concealed dagger in Sicily; at Venice I should have brewed poison; in Turkey I should have been the Sheik-el-Islam with my bowstring; in Khorassan I should have been a veiled Prophet. 'Fanatic young men!' Why he is writing out the list of a Dramatis Personae; 'guards, conspirators, populace,' and the like. He thinks I was ever moving about with a train of Capulets at my heels. 'Hot-headed fanatics, who hung on my every word!' If he had taken to write a history, and not a play, he would have easily found out, as I have said, that from 1841 I had severed myself from the younger generation of Oxford, that Dr. Pusey and I had then closed our theological meetings at his house, that I had brought my own weekly evening parties to an end, that I preached only by fits and starts at St. Mary's, so that the attendance of young men was broken up, that in those very weeks from Christmas till over Easter, during which this Sermon was preached, I was but five times in the pulpit there. He would have known, that it was written at a time when I was shunned rather than sought, when I had great sacrifices in anticipation, when I was thinking much of myself; that I was ruthlessly tearing myself away from my own followers, and that, in the musings of that Sermon, I was at the very utmost only delivering a testimony in my behalf for time to come, not sowing my rhetoric broadcast for the chance of present sympathy. Blot *twelve*.

I proceed: he says at p. 383, 'I found him actually using of such [prelates], (and, as I thought, of himself and his party likewise,) the words "They yield outwardly; to assent inwardly were to betray the faith. Yet they are called deceitful and double-dealing, because they do as much as they can, not more than they may."' This too is a proof of my duplicity! Let this writer go with some one else, just a little further than he has gone with me; and let him get into a court of law for libel; and let him be convicted; and let him still fancy that his libel, though a libel, was true, and let us then see whether he will not in such a case 'yield outwardly,' without assenting internally; and then again whether we should please him, if we called him 'deceitful and double-dealing,' because 'he did as much as he could, not more than he ought to do.' But Tract 90 will supply a real illustration of what I meant. I yielded to the Bishops in outward act, viz. in not defending the Tract, and in closing the Series; but, not only did I not assent inwardly to any condemnation of it, but I opposed myself to the proposition of a condemnation on the party of authority. Yet I was then by the public called 'deceitful and double-dealing,' as this Writer calls me now, 'because I did as much as I felt I could do, and not more than I felt I could honestly do.' Many were the publications of the day and the private letters which accused me of shuffling, because I closed the Series of Tracts, yet kept the Tracts on sale, as if I ought to comply not only with what my Bishop asked, but with what he did not ask, and perhaps did not wish. However, such teaching, according to this Writer, was likely to make young men suspect, that truth was not a virtue for its own sake, but only for the sake of 'the spread of Catholic opinions,' and the 'salvation of their own souls,' and that 'cunning was the weapon which heaven had allowed to them to defend themselves against the persecuting Protestant public.' – p. 384. Blot *thirteen*.

And now I draw attention to another point. He says at p. 384, 'How was I to know that the preacher . . . did not foresee, that [fanatic and hot-headed young men] would think that they obeyed him, by becoming affected, artificial, sly, shifty, ready for concealments and *equivocations*?' 'How should he know!' What! I suppose that we are to think every man a knave till he is proved not to be such. Know! had he no friend to tell him whether I was 'affected' or 'artificial' myself? Could he not have done better than impute *equivocations* to me, at a time when I was in no sense answerable for the *amphibologia* of the Roman casuists? Has he a single fact which belongs to me personally or by profession to couple my name with equivocation in 1843? 'How should he know' that I was not sly, smooth, artificial, non-natural! he should know by that common manly frankness, if he had it, by which we put confidence in others, till they are proved to have forfeited it; he should know it by my own words in that very Sermon, in which I say it is best to be natural, and that reserve is at best but an unpleasant necessity. I say, 'I do not deny that there is something very engaging in a frank and unpretending manner; some persons have it more than others; in *some persons it is a great grace*. But it must be recollected that I am speaking of *times of persecution and oppression* to Christians, such as the text foretells; and then surely frankness will become nothing else than indignation at the oppressor, and vehement speech, if it is permitted. Accordingly, as persons have deep *feelings*, so they will find the necessity of self-control, lest they should say what they ought not.' He omits these words. I call, then, this base insinuation that I taught equivocation, Blot the *fourteenth*.

Lastly, he sums up thus: 'If [Dr. Newman] would . . . persist (as in this Sermon) in dealing with matters dark, offensive, doubtful, sometimes actually forbidden, at least according to the notions of the great majority of English Churchmen; if he would always do so in a tentative, paltering way, seldom or never letting the world know how much he believed, how far he intended to go; if, in a word, his method of teaching was a suspicious one, what wonder if the minds of men were filled with suspicions of him?' – p. 385.

Now first he is speaking of my Sermons; where, then, is his proof that in my Sermons I dealt in matters dark, offensive, doubtful, actually forbidden? he has said nothing in proof that I had not been able flatly to deny.

'Forbidden according to the notions of the great majority of English Churchmen.' I should like to know what opinions, beyond those which relate to the Creed, *are* held by the 'majority of English Churchmen:' – are his own? is it not perfectly well known, that 'the great majority' think of him and his views with a feeling which I will not describe, because it is not necessary for my argument? So far is certain, that he has not the majority with him.

'In a tentative, paltering way.' The word 'paltering' I reject, as vague; as to 'tentative,' he must show that I was tentative in my Sermons; and he has eight volumes to look through. As to the ninth, my University Sermons, of course I was 'tentative;' but not because 'I would seldom or never let the world know how much I believed, or how far I intended to go;' but because in deep subjects, which had not been fully investigated, I said as much as I believed, and about as far as I saw I could go; and a man cannot do more; and I account no man to be a philosopher who attempts to do more. How long am I to have the office of merely negativing assertions which are but supported by former assertions, in which John is ever helping Tom, and the elephant stands upon the tortoise? This is Blot *fifteen*.

3   *The Anglican Church*

This Writer says: – 'If there is, as there is, a strong distrust of certain Catholics, it is restricted to the proselytizing priests among them; and especially to those, who, like Dr. Newman, have turned round upon their mother Church, (I had almost said their mother country,) with contumely and slander.' – p. 386.

No one has a right to make a charge, without at least an attempt to prove what he says; but this Writer is consistent with himself. From the time that he first spoke of me in the Magazine, *when* has he ever even professed to give evidence of any sort for any one of his charges, from his own sense of propriety, and without being challenged on the point? After the sentence which I have been quoting, and another like it, he coolly passes on to Tract 90! Blot *sixteen*; but I shall dwell on it awhile, for its own sake.

Now I have been bringing out my mind in this Volume on every subject which has come before me; and therefore I am bound to state plainly what I feel and have felt, since I was a Catholic, about the Anglican Church. I said, in a former page, that, on my conversion, I was not conscious of any change in me of thought or feeling, as regards matters of doctrine; this, however, was not the case as regards some matters of fact, and, unwilling as I am to give offence to religious Anglicans, I am bound to confess that I felt a great change in my view of the Church of England. I cannot tell how soon there came on me, – but very soon, – an extreme astonishment that I had ever imagined it to be a portion of the Catholic Church. For the first time, I looked at it from without, and (as I should myself say) saw it as it was. Forthwith I could not get myself to see in it any thing else, than what I had so long fearfully suspected, from as far back as 1836, – a mere national institution. As if my eyes were suddenly opened, so I saw it – spontaneously, apart from any definite act of reason or any argument; and so I have seen it ever since. I suppose, the main cause of this lay in the contrast which was presented to me by the Catholic Church. Then I recognized at once a reality which was quite a new thing with me. Then I was sensible that I was not making for myself a Church by an effort of thought; I needed not to make an act of faith in her; I had not painfully to force myself into a position, but my mind fell back upon itself in relaxation and in peace, and I gazed at her almost passively as a great objective fact. I looked at her; – at her rites, her ceremonial, and her precepts; and I said, 'This *is* a religion;' and then, when I looked back upon the poor Anglican Church, for which I had laboured so hard, and upon all that appertained to it, and thought of our various attempts to dress it up doctrinally and esthetically, it seemed to me to be the veriest of nonentities. Vanity of vanities, all is vanity! How can I make a record of what passed within me, without seeming to be satirical? But I speak plain, serious words. As people call me credulous for acknowledging Catholic claims, so they call me satirical for disowning Anglican pretensions; to them it *is* credulity, to them it *is* satire; but it is not so in me. What they think exaggeration, I think truth. I am not speaking of the Anglican Church in any disdain, though to them I seem contemptuous. To them of course it is 'Aut Caesar aut nullus', but not to me. It may be a great creation, though it be not divine, and this is how I judge of it. Men, who abjure the divine right of kings, would be very indignant, if on that account they were considered disloyal. And so I recognize in the Anglican Church a time-honoured institution, of noble historical memories, a monument of ancient wisdom, a momentous arm of political strength, a great national organ, a source of vast popular advantage, and, to a certain point, a witness and teacher of religious truth. I do not think that, if what I have written about it since I have been a Catholic, be equitably considered as a whole, I shall be found to have taken any other view than this; but that it is something sacred, that it is an oracle of revealed doctrine, that it can claim a share in St. Ignatius or St. Cyprian, that it can take the rank, contest the teaching, and stop the path of the Church of St. Peter, that it can call itself 'the Bride of the Lamb,' this is the view of it which simply disappeared from my mind on my conversion, and which it would be almost a miracle to reproduce. 'I went by, and lo! it was gone; I sought it, but its place could no where be found;' and nothing can bring it back to me. And, as to its possession of an episcopal succession from the time of the Apostles, well, it may have it, and, if the Holy See ever so decided, I will believe it, as being the decision of a higher judgment than my own; but, for myself, I must have St. Philip's gift, who saw the sacerdotal character on the forehead of a gaily-attired youngster, before I can by my own wit acquiesce in it, for antiquarian arguments are altogether unequal to the urgency of visible facts. Why is it that I must pain dear friends by saying so, and kindle a sort of resentment against me in the kindest of hearts? but I must, though to do it be not only a grief to me, but most impolitic at the moment. Any how, this is my mind; and, if to have it, if to have betrayed it, before now, involuntarily by my words or my deeds, if on a fitting occasion, as now, to have avowed it, if all this be a proof of the justice of the charge brought against me of having 'turned round upon my Mother-Church with contumely and slander', in this sense, but in no other sense, do I plead guilty to it without a word in extenuation.

In no other sense surely; the Church of England has been the instrument of Providence in conferring great benefits on me; had I been born in Dissent, perhaps I should never have been baptized; had I been born an English Presbyterian, perhaps I should never have known our Lord's divinity; had I not come to Oxford, perhaps I never should have heard of the visible Church, or of Tradition, or other Catholic doctrines. And as I have received so much good from the Anglican Establishment itself, can I have the heart, or rather the want of charity, considering that it does for so many others, what it has done for me, to wish to see it overthrown? I have no such wish while it is what it is, and while we are so small a body. Not for its own sake, but for the sake of the many congregations to which it ministers, I will do nothing against it. While Catholics are so weak in England, it is doing our work; and, though it does us harm in a measure, at present the balance is in our favour. What our duty would be at another time and in other circumstances, supposing, for instance, the Establishment lost its dogmatic faith, or at least did not preach it, is another matter altogether. In secular history we read of hostile nations having long truces, and renewing them from time to time, and that seems to be the position the Catholic Church may fairly take up at present in relation to the Anglican Establishment.

Doubtless the National Church has hitherto been a serviceable breakwater against doctrinal errors, more fundamental than its own. How long this will last in the years now before us, it is impossible to say, for the Nation drags down its Church to its own level; but still the National Church has the same sort of influence over the Nation that a periodical has upon the party which it represents, and my own idea of a Catholic's fitting attitude towards the National Church in this its supreme hour, is that of assisting and sustaining it, if it be in our power, in the interest of dogmatic truth. I should wish to avoid every thing, except under the direct call of duty, which went to weaken its hold upon the public mind, or to unsettle its establishment, or to embarrass and lessen its maintenance of those great Christian and Catholic principles and doctrines which it has up to this time successfully preached.

I say, 'except under the call of duty;' and this exception, I am obliged to admit, is not a slight one; it is one which necessarily places a bar to any closer relation between it and ourselves, than that of an armed truce. For, in the first place, it stands to reason that even a volume, such as this has been, exerts an influence adverse to the Establishment, – at least in the case of many minds; and this I cannot avoid, though I have sincerely attempted to keep as wide of controversy in the course of it, as ever I could. And next I cannot deny, what must be ever a very sore point with Anglicans, that, if any Anglican comes to me after careful thought and prayer, and with deliberate purpose, and says, 'I believe in the Holy Catholic Church, and that your Church and yours alone is it, and I demand admittance into it,' it would be the greatest of sins in me to reject such a man, as being a distinct contravention of our Lord's maxim, 'Freely ye have received, freely give.'

I have written three volumes which may be considered controversial; Loss and Gain in 1847; Lectures on Difficulties felt by Anglicans in submitting to the Catholic Church in 1850; and Lectures on the present Position of Catholics in England in 1851. And though I have neither time nor need to go into the matter minutely, a few words will suffice for some general account of what has been my object and my tone in these works severally.

Of these three, the Lectures on the 'Position of Catholics' have nothing to do with the Church of England, as such; they are directed against the Protestant or Ultra-Protestant Tradition on the subject of Catholicism since the time of Queen Elizabeth, in which parties indeed in the Church of England have largely participated, but which cannot be confused with Anglican teaching itself. Much less can that Tradition be confused with the doctrine of the Laudian or of the Tractarian School. I owe nothing to Protestantism; and I spoke against it even when I was an Anglican, as well as in these Catholic Lectures. If I spoke in them against the Church Established, it was because, and so far as, at the time when they were delivered, the Establishment took a violent part against the Catholic Church, on the basis of the Protestant Tradition. Moreover, I had never as an Anglican been a lover of the actual Establishment; Hurrell Froude's Remains, in which it is called an 'incubus' and 'Upas Tree,' will stand in evidence, as for him, so for me; for I was one of the Editors. What I said even as an Anglican, it is not strange that I said when I was not. Indeed I have been milder in my thoughts of the Establishment ever since I have been a Catholic than before, and for an obvious reason; – when I was an Anglican, I viewed it as representing a higher doctrine than its own; and now I view it as keeping out a lower and more dangerous.

Then as to my Lectures on Anglican Difficulties. Neither were these formally directed against the National Church. They were addressed to the 'Children of the Movement of 1833,' to impress upon them, that, whatever was the case with others, their duty at least was to become Catholics, since Catholicism was the real scope and issue of that Movement. 'There is but one thing,' I say, 'that forces me to speak ... It will be a miserable thing for you and for me, if I have been instrumental in bringing you but half-way, if I have co-operated in removing your invincible ignorance, but am able to do no more.' – p. 5. Such being the drift of the Volume, the reasoning directed against the Church of England goes no further than this, that it had no claims whatever on such of its members as were proceeding onwards with the Movement into the Catholic Church.

Lastly, as to Loss and Gain: it is the story, simply ideal, of the conversion of an Oxford man. Its drift is to show how little there is in Anglicanism to satisfy and retain a young and earnest heart. In this Tale, all the best characters are sober Church-of-England people. No Tractarians proper are introduced: and this is noted in the Advertisement: 'No *proper* representative is intended in this Tale, of the religious opinions, which had lately so much influence in the University of Oxford.' There *could* not be such in the Tale, without the introduction of friends, which was impossible in its very notion. But, since the scene was to be laid during the very years, and at the head-quarters, of Tractarianism, some expedient was necessary in order to meet what was a great difficulty. My expedient was the introduction of what may be called Tractarians *improper*; and I took them the more readily, because, though I knew that such there were, I knew none of them personally. I mean such men as I used to consider of 'the gilt-gingerbread school,' from whom I expected little good, persons whose religion lay in ritualism or architecture, and who 'played at Popery' or at Anglicanism. I repeat I knew no such men, because it is one thing to desire fine churches and ceremonies, (which of course I did myself,) and quite another thing to desire these and nothing else; but at that day there was in some quarters, though not in those where I had influence, a strong movement in the esthetic direction. Doubtless I went too far in my apprehension of such a movement: for one of the best, and most devoted and hard-working Priests I ever knew was the late Father Hutchison, of the London Oratory, and I believe it was architecture that directed his thoughts towards the Catholic

Church. However, I had in my mind an external religion which was inordinate; and, as the men who were considered instances of it, were personally unknown to me, even by name, I introduced them, under imaginary representatives, in Loss and Gain, and that, in order to get clear of Tractarians proper; and of the three men, whom I have introduced, the Anglican is the best. In like manner I introduced two 'gilt-gingerbread' young ladies, who were ideal, absolutely, utterly, without a shred of concrete existence about them; and I introduced them with the remark that they were 'really kind charitable persons,' and '*by no means* put forth as *a type* of a class,' that 'among such persons were to be found the gentlest spirits and the tenderest hearts,' and that 'these sisters had open hands, if they had not wise heads,' but that 'they did not know much of matters ecclesiastical, and they knew less of themselves.'

It has been said, indeed, I know not to what extent, that I introduced my friends or partisans into the Tale; this is utterly untrue. Only two cases of this misconception have come to my knowledge, and I at once denied each of them outright; and I take this opportunity of denying generally the truth of all other similar charges. No friend of mine, no one connected in any way with the Movement, entered into the composition of any one of the characters. Indeed, putting aside the two instances which have been distinctly brought before me, I have not even any sort of suspicion who the persons are, whom I am thus accused of introducing.

Next, this writer goes on to speak of Tract 90; a subject of which I have treated at great length in a former passage of this narrative, and, in consequence, need not take up again now.

4   Series of Lives of the English Saints

I have given the history of this publication above at pp. 191–3. It was to have consisted of almost 300 Lives, and I was to have been the Editor. It was brought to an end, before it was well begun, by the act of friends who were frightened at the first Life printed, the Life of St. Stephen Harding. Thus I was not responsible except for the first two numbers; and the Advertisements distinctly declared this. I had just the same responsibility about the other Lives, that my assailant had, and not a bit more. However, it answers his purpose to consider me responsible.

Next, I observe, that his delusion about 'hot-headed fanatic young men' continues: here again I figure with my strolling company. 'They said,' he observes, 'what they believed; at least, what they had been taught to believe that they ought to believe. And who had taught them? Dr. Newman can best answer that question,' p. 388. Well, I will do what I can to solve the mystery.

Now as to the juvenile writers in the proposed series. One was my friend Mr. Bowden, who in 1843 was a man of 46 years old; he was to have written St. Boniface. Another was Mr. Johnson, a man of 42; he was to have written St. Aldhelm. Another was the author of St. Augustine: let us hear something about him from this writer: –

'Dr. Newman,' he says, 'might have said to the Author of the Life of St. Augustine, when he found him, in *the heat and haste of youthful fanaticism*, outraging historic truth and the law of evidence, "This must not be."' – p. 388.

Good. This juvenile was past 40, – well, say 39. Blot *seventeen*. 'This must not be.' This is what I ought to have said, it seems! And then, you see, I have not the talent, and never had, of some people, for lecturing my equals, much less men twenty years older than myself.

But again, the author of St. Augustine's Life distinctly says in his Advertisement, '*No one but himself* is responsible for the way in which these materials have been used.' Blot *eighteen*.

Thirty-three Lives were actually published. Out of the whole number this writer notices *three*. Of these one is 'charming;' therefore I am not to have the benefit of it. Another 'outrages historic truth and the law of evidence;' therefore 'it was notoriously sanctioned by Dr. Newman.' And the third was 'one of the most offensive,' and Dr. Newman must have formally connected himself with it in 'a moment of amiable weakness.' – pp. 388–9. What even-handed justice is here! Blot *nineteen*.

But to return to the juvenile author of St. Augustine: – 'I found,' says this writer, 'the Life of St. Augustine saying, that, though the pretended visit of St. Peter to England wanted *historic evidence*, "yet it has undoubtedly been received as a *pious opinion* by the Church at large, as we learn from the often-quoted words of St. Innocent I. (who wrote A.D. 416) that St. Peter was instrumental in the conversion of the West generally."' – p. 388. He brings this passage against me (with which, however, I have nothing more to do than he has) as a great misdemeanour; but let us see what his criticism is worth. 'And this sort of argument,' continues the passage, 'though it ought to be kept *quite distinct from* documentary and historic proof, will *not be without its effect* on devout minds,' &c. I should have thought this a very sober doctrine, viz. that we must not confuse together two things quite distinct from each other, criticism and devotion, proof and opinion, – that a *devout* mind will hold *opinions* which it cannot demonstrate by 'historic *proof*.' What, I ask, is the harm of saying this? Is *this* my Assailant's definition of opinion, 'a thing which *can* be proved?' I cannot answer for him, but I can answer for men in general. Let him read Sir David Brewster's 'More Worlds than One,' – this principle, which is so shocking to my assailant, is precisely the argument of Sir David's book; he tells us that the plurality of worlds *cannot* be *proved*, but *will* be *received* by religious men. He asks, p. 229, '*If* the stars are *not* suns, for what conceivable *purpose* were they created?' and then he lays down dogmatically, p. 254, 'There is no *opinion*, *out of* the region of *pure demonstration*, more universally *cherished* than the doctrine of the Plurality of worlds.' And in his Title-page he styles this 'opinion' 'the *creed* of the philosopher and the *hope* of the Christian.' If Brewster may bring devotion into Astronomy, why may not my friend bring it into History? and that the more, when he actually declares that it ought to be kept *quite distinct* from history, and by no means assumes that he is an historian because he is a hagiographer; whereas, somehow or other, Sir David does seem to me to show a zeal greater than becomes a *savant*, and to assume that he himself is a theologian because he is an astronomer. This writer owes Sir David as well as me an apology. Blot *twenty*.

He ought to wish his original charge against me in the Magazine dead and buried; but he has the good sense and good taste to revive it again and again. This is one of the places which he has chosen for it. Let him then, just for a change, substitute Sir David Brewster for me in his sentence; Sir David has quite as much right to the compliment as I have, as far as this Life of St. Augustine is concerned. Then he will be saying, that, because Sir David teaches that the belief in more worlds than one is a pious opinion, and not a demonstrated fact, he 'does not care for truth for its own sake, or teach men to regard it as a virtue', p. 388. Blot *twenty-one*.

However, he goes on to give in this same page one other evidence of my disregard of truth. The author of St. Augustine's Life also asks the following question: '*On what evidence* do we put faith in the existence of St. George, the patron of England? Upon such, assuredly, as an acute *critic or skilful pleader* might easily scatter to the winds; the belief of prejudiced or credulous witnesses, the unwritten record of empty pageants and bauble decorations. On the side of scepticism might be exhibited a powerful array of suspicious legends and exploded acts. Yet, *after all, what Catholic is there but would count it a profaneness to question the existence of St. George?*' On which my assailant observes, 'When I found Dr. Newman allowing his disciples ... in page after page, in Life after Life, to talk nonsense of this kind which is not only sheer Popery, *but saps the very foundation of historic truth*, was it so wonderful that I conceived him to have taught and thought like them?' p. 389, that is, to have taught lying.

Well and good; here again take a parallel; not St. George, but Lycurgus.

Mr. Grote says: 'Plutarch begins his biography of Lycurgus with the following ominous words: "Concerning the lawgiver Lycurgus, we can assert *absolutely nothing*, which is not controverted. There are different stories in respect to his birth, his travels, his death, and also his mode of proceeding, political as well as legislative: least of all is the time in which he lived agreed on." And this exordium *is but too well borne out* by the unsatisfactory nature of the accounts which we read, not only in Plutarch himself, but in those other authors, out of whom we are obliged to make up our idea of the memorable Lycurgian system.' – Greece, vol. ii. p. 455. But Bishop Thirlwall says, 'Experience proves that *scarcely any amount of variation*, as to the time or circumstances of a fact, in the authors who record it, *can be a sufficient ground* for doubting its reality.' – Greece, vol. i. p. 332.

Accordingly, my assailant is virtually saying of the latter of these two historians, 'When I found the Bishop of St. David's talking nonsense of this kind, which saps the very foundation of historic truth', was it 'hasty or far-fetched' to conclude 'that he did not care for truth for its own sake, or teach his disciples to regard it as a virtue?' p. 388. Nay, further, the Author of St. Augustine is no more a disciple of mine, than the Bishop of St. David's is of my Assailant's, and therefore the parallel will be more exact if I accuse this Professor of History of *teaching* Dr. Thirlwall not to care for truth, as a virtue, for its own sake. Blot *twenty-two*.

It is hard on me to have this dull, profitless work, but I have pledged myself; – so now for St. Walburga.

Now will it be believed that this Writer suppresses the fact that the miracles of St. Walburga are treated by the author of her Life as mythical? yet that is the tone of the whole composition. This Writer can notice it in the Life of St. Neot, the first of the three Lives which he criticizes; these are his words: 'Some of them, the writers, for instance, of Volume 4, which contains, among others, a charming life of St. Neot, treat the stories openly as legends and myths, and tell them as they stand, without asking the reader, or themselves, to believe them altogether. The method is harmless enough, if the legends had stood alone; but dangerous enough, when they stand side by side with stories told in earnest, like that of St. Walburga.' – p. 389.

Now, first, that the miraculous stories *are* treated, in the Life of St. Walburga, as legends and myths. Throughout, the miracles and extraordinary occurrences are spoken of as 'said' or 'reported;' and the suggestion is made that, even though they occurred, they might have been after all natural. Thus, in one of the very passages which my Assailant quotes, the author says, 'Illuminated men feel the privileges of Christianity, and to them the evil influence of Satanic power is horribly discernible, like the Egyptian darkness which could be felt; and *the only way to express* their keen perception of it is *to say*, that they *see* upon the countenances of the slaves of sin, the marks, and lineaments, and stamp of the evil one; and [that] they *smell* with their nostrils the horrible fumes that arise from their *vices* and uncleansed *heart*,' &c. p. 78. This introduces St. Sturme and the gambolling Germans; what does it mean but that 'the intolerable scent' was nothing physical, or strictly miraculous, but the horror, parallel to physical distress, with which the Saint was affected, from his knowledge of the state of their souls? My assailant is a lucky man, if mental pain has never come upon him with a substance and a volume, as forcible as if it were bodily.

And so in like manner, the Author of the Life says, as this writer actually has quoted him, 'a story *was told and believed*,' p. 94. 'One evening, *says her history*', p. 87. 'Another incident *is thus related*,' p. 88. 'Immediately, *says* Wülfhard,' p. 91. 'A vast number of other cases are *recorded*,' p. 92. And there is a distinct intimation that they may be myths, in a passage which this Assailant himself quotes, 'All these have the *character* of a gentle mother correcting the idleness and faults of careless and thoughtless children with tenderness.' – p. 95. I think the criticism which he makes upon this Life is one of the most wanton passages in his Pamphlet. The Life is beautifully written, full of poetry, and, as I have said, bears on its very surface the profession of a legendary and mythical character. Blot *twenty-three*.

In saying all this, I have no intention whatever of implying that miracles did not illustrate the Life of St. Walburga; but neither the Author nor I have bound ourselves to the belief of certain instances in particular. My Assailant, in the passage which I just now quoted from him, made some distinction, which was apparently intended to save St. Neot, while it condemned St. Walburga. He said that legends are 'dangerous enough, when they stand side by side with stories told in earnest like St. Walburga.' He will find he has here Dr. Milman against him, as he has already had Sir David Brewster, and the Bishop of St. David's. He accuses me of having 'outraged historic truth and the law of evidence,' because friends of mine have considered that, though opinions need not be convictions, nevertheless that legends may be connected with history: now, on the contrary, let us hear the Dean of St. Paul's: –

'*History*, to be *true*, must condescend to speak the language of *legend*; the *belief* of the times is *part* of the *record* of the times; and, though there may occur what may baffle its more calm and searching philosophy, *it must not disdain* that which was the primal, almost universal, motive of human life.' – Latin. Christ., vol. i, p. 388. Dr. Milman's decision justifies me in putting this down as Blot *twenty-four*.

However, there is one miraculous account for which this writer makes me directly answerable, and with reason; and with it I shall conclude my reply to his criticisms on the 'Lives of the English Saints.' It is the medicinal oil which flows from the relics of St. Walburga.

Now, as I shall have occasion to remark under my next Head, these two questions among others occur, in judging of a miraculous story; viz. whether the matter of it is extravagant, and whether it is a fact. And first, it is plain there is nothing extravagant in this report of the relics having a supernatural virtue; and for this reason, because there are such instances in Scripture, and Scripture cannot be extravagant. For instance, a man was restored to life by touching the relics of the Prophet Eliseus. The sacred text runs thus: – 'And Elisha died, and they buried him. And the bands of the Moabites invaded the land at the coming in of the year. And it came to pass, as they were burying a man, that, behold, they spied a band of men; and they cast the man into the sepulchre of Elisha. And, when the man was let down, *and touched the bones of Elisha, he revived*, and stood upon his feet.' Again, in the case of an inanimate substance, which had touched a living Saint: 'And God wrought *special miracles* by the hands of Paul; so that *from his body* were brought unto the sick *handkerchiefs or aprons*, and *the diseases departed from them*.' And again in the case of a pool: '*An Angel went down* at a certain season into the pool, and troubled the water; whosoever then first, after the troubling of the water, stepped in, *was made whole of whatsoever disease* he had.' 2 Kings [4 Kings] xiii. 20, 21. Acts xix. 11, 12. John v. 4. Therefore there is nothing *extravagant* in the *character* of the miracle.

The main question then (I do not say the only remaining question, but the main question) is the *matter of fact*: – *is* there an oil flowing from St. Walburga's tomb, which is medicinal? To

this question I confined myself in the Preface to the Volume. Of
the accounts of medieval miracles, I said that there was no
extravagance in their *general character*, but I could not affirm that
there was always *evidence* for them. I could not simply accept
them as *facts*, but I could not reject them in their *nature*; they
might be true, for they were not impossible: but they were *not
proved* to be true, because there was not trustworthy testimony.
However, as to St. Walburga, I made *one* exception, the fact of
the medicinal oil, since for that miracle there was distinct and
successive testimony. And then I went on to give a chain of
witnesses. It was my duty to state what those witnesses said in
their very words; and I did so; they were in Latin, and I gave
them in Latin. One of them speaks of the 'sacrum oleum'
flowing 'de membris ejus virgineis, maximè tamen pectoralibus;'
and I so printed it; – if I had left it out, this sweet-tempered
Writer would have accused me of an 'economy.' I gave the
testimonies in full, tracing them from the Saint's death. I said,
'She is one of the principal Saints of her age and country.' Then
I quoted Basnage, a Protestant, who says, 'Six writers are extant,
who have employed themselves in relating the deeds or miracles
of Walburga.' Then I said that her 'renown was not the mere
natural *growth* of ages, but begins with the very century of the
Saint's death.' Then I observed that only two miracles seem to
have been 'distinctly reported of her as occurring in her lifetime;
and they were handed down apparently by tradition.' Also, that
they are said to have commenced about A.D. 777. Then I spoke
of the medicinal oil as having testimony to it in 893, in 1306,
after 1450, in 1615, and in 1620. Also, I said that Mabillon seems
not to have believed some of her miracles; and that the earliest
witness had got into trouble with his Bishop. And so I left it, as
a question to be decided by evidence, not deciding any thing
myself.

What was the harm of all this? but my Critic has muddled it
together in a most extraordinary manner, and I am far from sure
that he knows himself the definite categorical charge which he
intends it to convey against me. One of his remarks is, 'What has
become of the holy oil for the last 240 years, Dr. Newman does
not say,' p. 391. Of course I did not, because I did not know; I
gave the evidence as I found it; he assumes that I had a point to

prove, and then asks why I did not make the evidence larger than it was. I put this down as Blot *twenty-five*.

I can tell him more about it now; the oil still flows; I have had some of it in my possession; it is medicinal; some think it is so by a natural quality, others by a divine gift. Perhaps it is on the confines of both.

5   *Ecclesiastical Miracles*

What is the use of going on with this Writer's criticism upon me, when I am confined to the dull monotony of exposing and oversetting him again and again, with a persistence, which many will think merciless, and few will have the interest to read? Yet I am obliged to do so, lest I should seem to be evading difficulties.

Now as to Miracles. Catholics believe that they happen in any age of the Church, though not for the same purposes, in the same number, or with the same evidence, as in Apostolic times. The Apostles wrought them in evidence of their divine mission; and with this object they have been sometimes wrought by Evangelists of countries since, as even Protestants allow. Hence we hear of them in the history of St. Gregory in Pontus, and St. Martin in Gaul; and in their case, as in that of the Apostles, they were both numerous and clear. As they are granted to Evangelists, so are they granted, though in less measure and evidence, to other holy men; and as holy men are not found equally at all times and in all places, therefore miracles are in some places and times more than in others. And since, generally, they are granted to faith and prayer, therefore in a country in which faith and prayer abound, they will be more likely to occur, than where and when faith and prayer are not; so that their occurrence is irregular. And further, as faith and prayer obtain miracles, so still more commonly do they gain from above the ordinary interventions of Providence; and, as it is often very difficult to distinguish between a providence and a miracle, and there will be more providences than miracles, hence it will happen that many occurrences will be called miraculous, which, strictly speaking, are not such, and not more than providential mercies, or what are sometimes called 'graces' or 'favours.'

Persons, who believe all this, in accordance with Catholic

teaching, as I did and do, they, on the report of a miracle, will of necessity, the necessity of good logic, be led to say, first, 'It *may* be,' and secondly, 'But I must have *good evidence* in order to believe it.' It *may* be, because miracles take place in all ages; it must be clearly *proved*, because perhaps after all it may be only a providential mercy, or an exaggeration, or a mistake, or an imposture. Well, this is precisely what I have said, which this Writer considers so irrational. I have said, as he quotes me, p. 391, 'In this day, and under our present circumstances, we can only reply, that there is no reason why they should not be.' Surely this is good logic, *provided* that miracles *do* occur in all ages; and so again is it logical to say, 'There is nothing, *primâ facie*, in the miraculous accounts in question, to repel a *properly taught* or religiously disposed mind.' What is the matter with this statement? My assailant does not pretend to say *what* the matter is, and he cannot; but he expresses a rude, unmeaning astonishment. Next, I stated *what* evidence there is for the miracles of which I was speaking; what is the harm of that? He observes, 'What evidence Dr. Newman requires, he makes evident at once. He at least will fear for himself, and swallow the whole as it comes.' – p. 391. What random abuse is this, or, to use *his own words* of me just before, what 'stuff and nonsense'! What is it I am 'swallowing'? 'the whole' what? the evidence? or the miracles? I have swallowed neither, nor implied any such thing. Blot *twenty-six*.

But to return: I have just said that a Catholic's state of mind, of logical necessity, will be, 'It *may* be a miracle, but it has to be *proved*.' *What* has to be proved? 1. That the event occurred as stated, and is not a false report or an exaggeration. 2. That it is clearly miraculous, and not a mere providence or answer to prayer within the order of nature. What is the fault of saying this? The inquiry is parallel to that which is made about some extraordinary fact in secular history. Supposing I hear that King Charles II. died a Catholic, I should say, 1. It *may* be. 2. What is your *proof*? Accordingly, in the passage which this writer quotes, I observe, 'Miracles are the kind of facts proper to ecclesiastical history, just as instances of sagacity or daring, personal prowess, or crime, are the facts proper to secular history.' What is the harm of this? But this writer says, 'Verily his [Dr. Newman's] idea of secular history is almost as degraded as his idea of ecclesiastical,' p. 391, and he ends with this muddle of an *Ipse dixit*! Blot *twenty-seven*.

In like manner, about the Holy Coat at Treves, he says of me, 'Dr. Newman . . . seems *hardly sure* of the authenticity of the Holy Coat.' Why *need* I be, more than I am sure that Richard III. murdered the little princes? If I have not *means* of making up my mind one way or the other, surely my most logical course is '*not* to be sure.' He continues, 'Dr. Newman "does not see *why it may not have been* what it professes to be."' Well, is not that just what this Writer would say of a great number of the facts recorded in secular history? is it not what he would be obliged to say of much that is told us about the armour and other antiquities in the Tower of London? To this I alluded in the passage from which he quotes; but he has *garbled* that passage, and I must show it. He quotes me to this effect: 'Is the Tower of London shut against sight-seers because the coats of mail or pikes there may have half-legendary tales connected with them? why then may not the country people come up in joyous companies, singing and piping, to *see* the holy coat at Treves?' On this he remarks, 'To *see*, forsooth! to *worship*, Dr. Newman would have said, had he known (as I take for granted he does not) the facts of that imposture.' Here, if I understand him, he implies that the people came up, not only to see, but to worship, and that I have slurred over the fact that their coming was an act of religious homage, that is, what *he* would call 'worship.' Now, will it be believed that, so far from concealing this, I had carefully stated it in the sentence immediately preceding, and *he suppresses it*? I say, 'The world pays civil honour to it [a jewel said to be Alfred's] on the probability; we pay *religious honour* to relics, if so be, on the probability. Is the Tower of London,' I proceed, 'shut,' &c. Blot *twenty-eight*.

These words of mine, however, are but one sentence in a long argument, conveying the Catholic view on the subject of ecclesiastical miracles; and, as it is carefully worked out, and very much to the present point, and will save me doing over again what I could not do better or more fully now, if I set about it, I shall make a very long extract from the Lecture in which it occurs, and so bring this Head to an end.

The argument, I should first observe, which is worked out, is this, that Catholics set out with a definite religious tenet as a first principle, and Protestants with a contrary one, and that on this account it comes to pass that miracles are credible to Catholics and incredible to Protestants.

'We affirm that the Supreme Being has wrought miracles on earth ever since the time of the Apostles; Protestants deny it. Why do we affirm, why do they deny? We affirm it on a first principle, they deny it on a first principle; and on either side the first principle is made to be decisive of the question. ... Both they and we start with the miracles of the Apostles; and then their first principle or presumption against our miracles is this, "What God did once, He is *not* likely to do again;" while our first principle or presumption for our miracles is this; "What God did once, He *is* likely to do again." They say, It cannot be supposed He will work *many* miracles; we, It cannot be supposed He will work *few*.

'The Protestant, I say, laughs at the very idea of miracles or supernatural powers as occurring at this day; his first principle is rooted in him; he repels from him the idea of miracles; he laughs at the notion of evidence; one is just as likely as another; they are all false. Why? because of his first principle, There are no miracles since the Apostles. Here, indeed, is a short and easy way of getting rid of the whole subject, not by reason, but by a first principle which he calls reason. Yes, it *is* reason, granting his first principle is true; it is not reason, supposing his first principle is false.

'There is in the Church a vast tradition and testimony about miracles; how is it to be accounted for? If miracles *can* take place, then the *fact* of the miracle will be a natural explanation of the *report*, just as the fact of a man dying accounts satisfactorily for the news that he is dead; but the Protestant cannot so explain it, because he thinks miracles cannot take place; so he is necessarily driven, by way of accounting for the report of them, to impute that report to fraud. He cannot help himself. I repeat it; the whole mass of accusations which Protestants bring against us under this head, Catholic credulity, imposture, pious frauds, hypocrisy, priestcraft, this vast and varied superstructure of imputation, you see, all rests on an assumption, on an opinion of theirs, for which they offer no kind of proof. What then, in fact, do they say more than this, *If* Protestantism be true, you Catholics are a most awful set of knaves? Here, at least, is a most sensible and undeniable position.

'Now, on the other hand, let me take our own side of the question, and consider how we ourselves stand relatively to the charge made against us. Catholics, then, hold the mystery of the Incarnation; and the Incarnation is the most stupendous event which ever can take place on earth; and after it and henceforth, I do not see how we can scruple at any miracle on the mere ground of its being unlikely to happen. . . . When we start with assuming that miracles are not unlikely, we are putting forth a position which lies embedded, as it were, and involved in the great revealed fact of the Incarnation. So much is plain on starting; but more is plain too. Miracles are not only not unlikely, but they are positively likely; and for this simple reason, because for the most part, when God begins, He goes on. We conceive, that when He first did a miracle, He began a series; what He commenced, He continued: what has been, will be. Surely this is good and clear reasoning. To my own mind, certainly, it is incomparably more difficult to believe that the Divine Being should do one miracle and no more, than that He should do a thousand; that He should do one great miracle only, than that He should do a multitude of lesser besides. . . . If the Divine Being does a thing once, He is, judging by human reason, likely to do it again. This surely is common sense. If a beggar gets food at a gentleman's house once, does he not send others thither after him? If you are attacked by thieves once, do you forthwith leave your windows open at night? . . . Nay, suppose you yourselves were once to see a miracle, would you not feel the occurrence to be like passing a line? would you, in consequence of it, declare, "I never will believe another if I hear of one?" would it not, on the contrary, predispose you to listen to a new report? . . .

'When I hear the report of a miracle, my first feeling would be of the same kind as if it were a report of any natural exploit or event. Supposing, for instance, I heard a report of the death of some public man; it would not startle me, even if I did not at once credit it, for all men must die. Did I read of any great feat of valour, I should believe it, if imputed to Alexander or Coeur de Lion. Did I hear of any act of baseness, I should disbelieve it, if imputed to a friend whom I knew and loved. And so in like manner were a miracle reported to me as wrought by a Member of Parliament, or a Bishop of the Establishment, or a Wesleyan preacher, I should repudiate the notion: were it referred to a saint, or the relic of a saint, or the intercession of a saint, I should not be startled at it, though I might not at once believe it. And I certainly should be right in this conduct, supposing my First Principle be true. Miracles to the Catholic are historical facts, and nothing short of this; and they are to be regarded and dealt with as other facts; and as natural facts, under circumstances, do not startle Protestants, so supernatural, under circumstances, do not startle the Catholic. They may or may not have taken place in particular cases; he may be unable to determine which; he may have no distinct evidence; he may suspend his judgment, but he will say "It is very possible;" he never will say "I cannot believe it."

'Take the history of Alfred; you know his wise, mild, benefi-cent, yet daring character, and his romantic vicissitudes of for-tune. This great king has a number of stories, or, as you may call them, legends told of him. Do you believe them all? no. Do you, on the other hand, think them incredible? no. Do you call a man a dupe or a blockhead for believing them? no. Do you call an author a knave or a cheat who records them? no. You go into neither extreme, whether of implicit faith or of violent reproba-tion. You are not so extravagant; you see that they suit his character, they may have happened: yet this is so romantic, that has so little evidence, a third is so confused in dates or in geography, that you are in matter of fact indisposed towards them. Others are probably true, others certainly. Nor do you force every one to take your view of particular stories; you and your neighbour think differently about this or that in detail, and agree to differ. There is in the museum at Oxford, a jewel or trinket said to be Alfred's; it is shown to all comers; I never heard the keeper of the museum accused of hypocrisy or fraud for showing, with Alfred's name appended, what he might or might not himself believe to have belonged to that great king; nor did I ever see any party of strangers who were looking at it with awe, regarded by any self-complacent bystander with scornful compassion. Yet the curiosity is not to a certainty Alfred's. The world pays civil honour to it on the probability; we pay religious honour to relics, if so be, on the probability. Is the Tower of London shut against sight-seers, because the coats of mail and pikes there may have half-legendary tales connected with them? why then may not the country people come up in joyous companies, singing and piping, to see the Holy Coat at Treves? There is our Queen again, who is so truly and justly popular; she roves about in the midst of tradition and romance; she scatters myths and legends from her as she goes along; she is a being of poetry, and you might fairly be sceptical whether she had any personal existence. She is always at some beautiful, noble, bounteous work or other, if you trust the papers. She is doing alms-deeds in the Highlands; she meets beggars in her rides at Windsor; she writes verses in albums, or draws sketches, or is mistaken for the housekeeper by some blind old woman, or she runs up a hill as if she were a child. Who finds fault with these things? he would be a cynic, he would be white-livered, and would have gall for blood, who was not struck with this graceful, touching evidence of the love her subjects bear her. Who could have the head, even if he had the heart, who could be so cross and peevish, who could be so solemn and perverse, as to say that some of these stories *may* be simple lies, and all of them might have stronger evidence than they carry with them? Do you think she is displeased at them? Why then should He, the Great Father, who once walked the earth, look sternly on the unavoidable mistakes of His own subjects and children in their devotion to Him and His? Even granting they mistake some cases in particular, from the infirmity of human nature and the contingencies of evidence, and fancy there is or has been a miracle here and there when there is not, though a tradition, attached to a picture, or to a shrine, or a well, be very doubtful, though one relic be sometimes mistaken for another, and St. Theodore stands for St. Eugenius or St. Agathocles, still, once take into account our First Principle, that He is likely to continue miracles among us, which is as good as the Protestant's, and I do not see why He should feel much displeasure with us on account of this, or should cease to work wonders in our behalf. In the Protestant's view, indeed, who assumes that miracles never are, our thaumatology is one great falsehood; but that is *his* First Principle, as I have said so often, which he does not prove but assume. If *he*, indeed, upheld *our* system, or *we* held *his* principle, in either case he or we should be impostors; but though we should be partners to a fraud if we thought like Protestants, we surely are not if we think like Catholics.

'Such then is the answer I make to those who would urge against us the multitude of miracles recorded in our Saints' Lives and devotional works, for many of which there is little evidence, and for some next to none. We think them true in the same sense in which Protestants think the history of England true. When they say *that*, they do not mean to say that there are no mistakes, but no mistakes of consequence, none which alter the general course of history. Nor do they mean they are equally sure of every part; for evidence is fuller and better for some things than for others. They do not stake their credit on the truth of Froissart or Sully, they do not pledge themselves for the accuracy of Doddington or Walpole, they do not embrace as an Evangelist Hume, Sharon Turner, or Macaulay. And yet they do not think it necessary, on the other hand, to commence a religious war against all our historical catechisms, and abstracts, and dictionaries, and tales, and biographies, through the country; they have no call on them to amend and expurgate books of archaeology, antiquities, heraldry, architecture, geography, and statistics, to rewrite our inscriptions, and to establish a censorship on all new publications for the time to come. And so as regards the miracles of the Catholic Church; if, indeed, miracles never can occur, then, indeed, impute the narratives to fraud; but till you prove they are not likely, we shall consider the histories which have come down to us true on the whole, though in particular cases they may be exaggerated or unfounded. Where, indeed, they can certainly be proved to be false, there we shall be bound to do our best to get rid of them; but till that is clear, we shall be liberal enough to allow others to use their private judgment in their favour, as we use ours in their disparagement. For myself, lest I appear in any way to be shrinking from a determinate judgment on the claims of some of those miracles and relics, which Protestants are so startled at, and to be hiding particular questions in what is vague and general, I will avow distinctly, that, *putting out of the question* the *hypothesis of unknown laws of nature* (which is an evasion from the force of any proof), I think it impossible to *withstand the evidence* which is brought for the liquefaction of the blood of St. Januarius at Naples, and for the motion of the eyes of the pictures of the Madonna in the Roman States. I *see no reason to doubt* the material of the Lombard crown at Monza; and I *do not see why* the Holy Coat at Treves may not have been what it professes to be. I *firmly believe* that portions of the True Cross are at Rome and elsewhere, that the Crib of Bethlehem is at Rome, and the bodies of St. Peter and St. Paul also. . . . Many men when they hear an educated man so speak, will at once impute the avowal to insanity, or to an idiosyncrasy, or to imbecility of mind, or to decrepitude of powers, or to fanaticism, or to hypocrisy. They have a right to say so, if they will; and we have a right to ask them why they do not say it of those who bow down before the Mystery of mysteries, the Divine Incarnation?'

In my Essay on Miracles of the year 1826, I proposed three questions about a professed miraculous occurrence, 1. is it antecedently *probable*? 2. is it in its *nature* certainly miraculous? 3. has it sufficient *evidence*? These are the three heads under which I still wish to conduct the inquiry into the miracles of Ecclesiastical History.

6 *Popular Religion*

This Writer uses much rhetoric against a Lecture of mine, in which I bring out, as honestly as I can, the state of countries which have long received the Catholic Faith, and hold it by the force of tradition, universal custom, and legal establishment; a Lecture in which I give pictures, drawn principally from the middle ages, of what, considering the corruption of the human race generally, that state is sure to be, – pictures of its special sins and offences, *sui generis*, which are the result of that Faith when it is separated from Love or Charity, or of what Scripture calls a 'dead faith,' of the Light shining in darkness, and the truth held in unrighteousness. The nearest approach which this Writer is able to make towards stating what I have said in this Lecture, is to state the very reverse. Observe: we have already had some instances of the haziness of his ideas concerning the 'Notes of the Church.' These Notes are, as any one knows who has looked into the subject, certain great and simple characteristics, which He who founded the Church has stamped upon her in order to draw both the reason and the imagination of men to her, as being really a divine work, and a religion distinct from all other religious communities; the principal of these Notes being that she is Holy, One, Catholic, and Apostolic, as the Creed says. Now, to use his own word, he has the incredible 'audacity' to say, that I have declared, not the divine characteristics of the Church, but the sins and scandals in her, to be her Notes, – as if I made God the Author of evil. He says distinctly, 'Dr. Newman, with a kind of desperate audacity, *will* dig forth such *scandals* as *Notes* of the Catholic Church.' This is what I get at his hands for my honesty. Blot *twenty-nine*.

Again, he says, '[Dr. Newman uses] the blasphemy and profanity which he confesses to be so common in Catholic countries, as an argument *for*, and not *against* the "Catholic Faith."' – p. 399. That is, because I admit that profaneness exists in the Church, therefore I consider it a token of the Church. Yes, certainly, just as our national form of cursing is an evidence of the being of a God, and as a gallows is the glorious sign of a civilized country, – but in no other way. Blot *thirty*.

What is it that I really say? I say as follows: Protestants object that the communion of Rome does not fulfil satisfactorily the expectation which we may justly form concerning the True Church, as it is delineated in the four Notes, enumerated in the Creed; and among others, e.g. in the Note of sanctity; and they point, in proof of what they assert, to the state of Catholic countries. Now, in answer to this objection, it is plain what I might have done, if I had not had a conscience. I might have denied the fact. I might have said, for instance, that the middle ages were as virtuous, as they were believing. I might have

denied that there was any violence, any superstition, any immorality, any blasphemy during them. And so as to the state of
countries which have long had the light of Catholic truth, and
have degenerated. I might have admitted nothing against them,
and explained away every thing which plausibly told to their
disadvantage. I did nothing of the kind; and what effect has this
had upon this estimable critic? 'Dr. Newman takes a seeming
pleasure,' he says, 'in detailing instances of dishonesty on the
part of Catholics.' – p. 399. Blot *thirty-one*. Any one who knows
me well, would testify that my 'seeming pleasure,' as he calls it,
at such things, is just the impatient sensitiveness, which relieves
itself by means of a definite delineation of what is so hateful to it.

However, to pass on. All the miserable scandals of Catholic
countries, taken at the worst, are, as I view the matter, no
argument against the Church itself; and the reason which I give
in the Lecture is, that, according to the proverb, Corruptio
optimi est pessima. The Jews could sin in a way no other
contemporary race could sin, for theirs was a sin against light;
and Catholics can sin with a depth and intensity with which
Protestants cannot sin. There will be more blasphemy, more
hatred of God, more of diabolical rebellion, more of awful
sacrilege, more of vile hypocrisy in a Catholic country than any
where else, because there is in it more of sin against light. Surely,
this is just what Scripture says, 'Woe unto thee, Chorazin! woe
unto thee, Bethsaida!' And, again, surely what is told us by
religious men, say by Father Bresciani, about the present unbelieving party in Italy, fully bears out the divine text: 'If, after they
have escaped the pollutions of the world . . . they are again
entangled therein and overcome, the latter end is worse with
them than the beginning. For it had been better for them not to
have known the way of righteousness, than, after they have
known it, to turn from the holy commandments delivered unto
them.'

And what is true of those who thus openly oppose themselves
to the truth, as it was true of the Evil One in the beginning, will
in an analogous way be true in the case of all sin, be it of a
heavier or lighter character, which is found in a Catholic country:
– sin will be strangely tinged or dyed by religious associations or
beliefs, and will exhibit the tragical inconsistencies of the excess

of knowledge over love, or of much faith with little obedience. The mysterious battle between good and evil will assume in a Catholic country its most frightful shape, when it is not the collision of two distinct and far-separated hosts, but when it is carried on in hearts and souls, taken one by one, and when the eternal foes are so intermingled and interfused that to human eyes they seem to coalesce into a multitude of individualities. This is in course of years, the real, the hidden condition of a nation, which has been bathed in Christian ideas, whether it be a young vigorous race, or an old and degenerate; and it will manifest itself socially and historically in those characteristics, sometimes grotesque, sometimes hideous, sometimes despicable, of which we have so many instances, medieval and modern, both in this hemisphere and in the western. It is, I say, the necessary result of the intercommunion of divine faith and human corruption.

But it has a light side as well as a dark. First, much which seems profane, is not in itself profane, but in the subjective view of the Protestant beholder. Scenic representations of our Lord's Passion are not profane to a Catholic population; in like manner, there are usages, customs, institutions, actions, often of an indifferent nature, which will be necessarily mixed up with religion in a Catholic country, because all things whatever are so mixed up. Protestants have been sometimes shocked, most absurdly as a Catholic rightly decides, at hearing that Mass is sometimes said for a good haul of fish. There is no sin here, but only a difference from Protestant customs. Other phenomena of a Catholic nation are at most mere extravagances. And then as to what is really sinful, if there be in it fearful instances of blasphemy or superstition, there are also special and singular fruits and exhibitions of sanctity; and, if the many do not seem to lead better lives for all their religious knowledge, at least they learn, as they can learn nowhere else, how to repent thoroughly and to die well.

The visible state of a country, which professes Catholicism, need not be the measure of the spiritual result of that Catholicism, at the Eternal Judgment Seat; but no one could say that that visible state was a Note that Catholicism was divine.

All this I attempted to bring out in the Lecture of which I am speaking; and that I had some success, I am glad to infer from the message of congratulation upon it, which I received at the time, from a foreign Catholic layman, of high English reputation, with whom I had not the honour of a personal acquaintance. And having given the key to the Lecture, which the Writer so wonderfully misrepresents, I pass on to another head.

7   *The Economy*

For the subject of the Economy, I shall refer to my discussion upon it in my History of the Arians, after one word about this Writer. He puts into his Title-page these words from a Sermon of mine: 'It is not more than an hyperbole to say, that, in certain cases, a lie is the nearest approach to truth.' This Sermon he attacks; but I do not think it necessary to defend it here, because any one who reads it, will see that he is simply incapable of forming a notion of what it is about. It treats of subjects which are entirely out of his depth; and, as I have already shown in other instances, and observed in the beginning of this Volume, he illustrates in his own person the very thing that shocks him, viz. that the nearest approach to truth, in given cases, is a lie. He does his best to make something of it, I believe; but he gets simply perplexed. He finds that it annihilates space, robs him of locomotion, almost scoffs at the existence of the earth, and he is simply frightened and cowed. He can but say 'the man who wrote that sermon was already past the possibility of conscious dishonesty,' p. 404. Perhaps it is hardly fair, after such a confession on his part of being fairly beat, to mark down a blot; however, let it be Blot *thirty-two*.

Then again, he quotes from me thus: 'Many a theory or view of things, on which an institution is founded, or a party held together, is of the same kind (economical). Many an argument, used by zealous and earnest men, has this economical character, being not the very ground on which they act (for they continue in the same course, though it be refuted) yet in a certain sense, a representation of it, a proximate description of their feelings, in the shape of argument, on which they can rest, to which they can recur when perplexed, and appeal when they are questioned.' He calls these 'startling words,' p. 403. Yet here again he illustrates their truth; for in his own case, he has acted on them in this very controversy with the most happy exactness. Surely he referred to my Sermon on Wisdom and Innocence, when called on to prove me a liar, as 'a proximate description of his feelings about me, in the shape of argument,' and he has 'continued in the same course, though it has been refuted.' Blot *thirty-three*.

Then, as to 'a party being held together by a mythical representation,' or economy. Surely 'Church and King,' 'Reform,' 'Non-intervention,' are such symbols; or let this Writer answer Mr. Kinglake's question in his 'Crimean War,' 'Is it true that . . . great armies were gathering, and that for the sake of the *Key* and the *Star* the peace of the nations was brought into danger?' Blot *thirty-four*.

In the beginning of this work, pp. 427–32, I refuted his gratuitous accusation against me at p. 405, founded on my calling one of my Anglican Sermons a Protestant one: so I have nothing to do but to register it here as Blot *thirty-five*.

Then he says that I committed an economy in placing in my original title-page, that the question between him and me, was whether 'Dr. Newman teaches that Truth is no virtue.' It was a 'wisdom of the serpentine type,' since I did not add, 'for its own sake.' Now observe: First, as to the matter of fact, in the course of my Letters, which bore that Title-page, I printed the words 'for its own sake,' *five* times over. Next, pray, what kind of a virtue is that, which is *not* done for its own sake? So this, after all, is this Writer's idea of virtue! a something that is done for the sake of something *else*; a sort of expedience! He is honest, it seems, simply *because* honesty is 'the best policy,' and on that score it is that he thinks himself virtuous. Why, 'for its own sake' enters into the very idea or definition of a virtue. Defend me from such virtuous men, as this Writer would inflict upon us! Blot *thirty-six*.

These Blots are enough just now; so I proceed to a brief sketch of what I held in 1833 upon the Economy, as a rule of practice. I wrote this two months ago; perhaps the composition is not quite in keeping with the run of this Appendix; and it is short; but I think it will be sufficient for my purpose: –

The doctrine of the *Economia*, had, as I have shown, pp. 43–6, a large signification when applied to the divine ordinances; it also had a definite application to the duties of Christians, whether clergy or laity, in preaching, in instructing or catechizing, or in ordinary intercourse with the world around them.

As Almighty God did not all at once introduce the Gospel to the world, and thereby gradually prepared men for its profitable reception, so, according to the doctrine of the early Church, it was a duty, for the sake of the heathen among whom they lived, to observe a great reserve and caution in communicating to them the knowledge of 'the whole counsel of God.' This cautious dispensation of the truth, after the manner of a discreet and vigilant steward, is denoted by the word 'economy.' It is a mode of acting which comes under the head of Prudence, one of the four Cardinal Virtues.

The principle of the Economy is this; that out of various courses, in religious conduct or statement, all and each *allowable antecedently and in themselves*, that ought to be taken which is most expedient and most suitable at the time for the object in hand.

Instances of its application and exercise in Scripture are such as the following: – 1. Divine Providence did but gradually impart to the world in general, and to the Jews in particular, the knowledge of His will: – He is said to have 'winked at the times of ignorance among the heathen;' and He suffered in the Jews divorce 'because of the hardness of their hearts.' 2. He has allowed Himself to be represented as having eyes, ears, and hands, as having wrath, jealousy, grief and repentance. 3. In like manner, our Lord spoke harshly to the Syro-Phoenician woman, whose daughter He was about to heal, and made as if He would go further, when the two disciples had come to their journey's end. 4. Thus too Joseph 'made himself strange to his brethren,' and Elisha kept silence on request of Naaman to bow in the house of Rimmon. 5. Thus St. Paul circumcised Timothy, while he cried out 'Circumcision availeth not.'

It may be said that this principle, true in itself, yet is dangerous, because it admits of an easy abuse, and carries men away into what becomes insincerity and cunning. This is undeniable; to do evil that good may come, to consider that the means, whatever they are, justify the end, to sacrifice truth to expedience, unscrupulousness, recklessness, are grave offences. These are abuses of the Economy. But to call them *economical* is to give a fine name to what occurs every day, independent of any knowledge of the *doctrine* of the Economy. It is the abuse of a rule which nature suggests to every one. Every one looks out for the 'mollia tempora fandi,' and 'mollia verba' too.

Having thus explained what is meant by the Economy as a rule of social intercourse between men of different religious, or, again, political, or social views, next I go on to state what I said in the Arians.

I say in that Volume first, that our Lord has given us the *principle* in His own words, – 'Cast not your pearls before swine;' and that He exemplified it in His teaching by parables; that St. Paul expressly distinguishes between the milk which is necessary to one set of men, and the strong meat which is allowed to others, and that, in two Epistles. I say, that the Apostles in the Acts observe the same rule in their speeches, for it is a fact, that they do not preach the high doctrines of Christianity, but only 'Jesus and the resurrection' or 'repentance and faith.' I also say, that this is the very reason that the Fathers assign for the silence of various writers in the first centuries on the subject of our Lord's divinity. I also speak of the catechetical system practised in the early Church, and the *disciplina arcani* as regards the doctrine of the Holy Trinity, to which Bingham bears witness; also of the defence of this rule by Basil, Cyril of Jerusalem, Chrysostom, and Theodoret.

And next the question may be asked, whether I have said any thing in my Volume *to guard* the doctrine, thus laid down, from the abuse to which it is obviously exposed: and my answer is easy. Of course, had I had any idea that I should have been exposed to such hostile misrepresentations, as it has been my lot to undergo on the subject, I should have made more direct avowals than I have done of my sense of the gravity and the danger of that abuse. Since I could not foresee when I wrote, that I should have been wantonly slandered, I only wonder that I have anticipated the charge as fully as will be seen in the following extracts.

For instance, speaking of the Disciplina Arcani, I say: – (1) 'The elementary information given to the heathen or catechumen was *in no sense undone* by the subsequent secret teaching, which was in fact but the *filling up of a bare but correct outline*,' p. 58, and I contrast this with the conduct of the Manichaeans 'who represented the initiatory discipline as founded on a *fiction* or hypothesis, which was to be forgotten by the learner as he made progress in the *real* doctrine of the Gospel.' (2) As to allegorizing, I say that the Alexandrians erred, whenever and as far as they proceeded 'to *obscure* the primary meaning of Scripture, and to *weaken the force of historical facts* and express declaration,' p. 69. (3) And that they were 'more open to *censure*,' when, on being '*urged by objections* to various passages in the history of the Old Testament, as derogatory to the divine perfections or to the Jewish Saints, they had *recourse to an allegorical explanation by way of answer*,' p. 71. (4) I add, '*It is impossible to defend such a procedure*, which seems to imply a *want of faith* in those who had recourse to it;' for 'God has given us *rules of right and wrong*,' *ibid.* (5) Again, I say, – 'The *abuse of the Economy* in *the hands of unscrupulous reasoners*, is obvious. *Even the honest* controversialist or teacher will find it very difficult to represent, *without misrepresenting*, what it is yet his duty to present to his hearers with caution or reserve. Here the obvious rule to guide our practice is, to be careful ever to maintain *substantial truth* in our use of the economical method,' pp. 79, 80. (6) And so far from concurring at all hazards with Justin, Gregory, or Athanasius, I say, 'It *is plain* [they] *were justified or not* in their Economy, *according* as they did or did not *practically mislead their opponents*,' p. 80. (7) I proceed, 'It is so difficult to hit the mark in these perplexing cases, that it is not wonderful, should these or other Fathers have failed at times, and said more or less than was proper,' *ibid.*

The Principle of the Economy is familiarly acted on among us every day. When we would persuade others, we do not begin by treading on their toes. Men would be thought rude who introduced their own religious notions into mixed society, and were devotional in a drawing-room. Have we never thought lawyers tiresome who came down for the assizes and talked law all through dinner? Does the same argument tell in the House of Commons, on the hustings, and at Exeter Hall? Is an educated gentleman never worsted at an election by the tone and arguments of some clever fellow, who, whatever his shortcomings in other respects, understands the common people?

As to the Catholic Religion in England at the present day, this only will I observe, – that the truest expedience is to answer right out, when you are asked; that the wisest economy is to have no management; that the best prudence is not to be a coward; that the most damaging folly is to be found out shuffling; and that the first of virtues is to 'tell truth, and shame the devil.'

8   Lying and Equivocation

This writer says, 'Though [a lie] be a sin, the fact of its being a venial one seems to have gained for it as yet a very slight penance.' – p. 408. Yet he says also that Dr Newman takes 'a perverse pleasure in eccentricities,' because I say that 'it is better for sun and moon to drop from heaven than that one soul should tell one wilful untruth.' – p. 395. That is, he first accuses us without foundation of making light of a lie; and, when he finds that we don't, then he calls us inconsistent. I have noticed these words of mine, and two passages besides, which he quotes, above at pp. 221–3. Here I will but observe on the subject of venial sin generally, that he altogether forgets our doctrine of Purgatory. This punishment may last till the day of judgment; so much for duration; then as to intensity, let the image of fire, by which we denote it, show what we think of it. Here is the expiation of venial sins. Yet Protestants, after the manner of this Writer, are too apt to play fast and loose; to blame us because we hold that sin may be venial, and to blame us again when we tell them what we think will be its punishment. Blot *thirty-seven*.

At the end of his Pamphlet he makes a distinction between the Catholic clergy and gentry in England, which I know the latter consider to be very impertinent; and he makes it apropos of a passage in one of my original letters in January. He quotes me as saying that 'Catholics differ from Protestants, as to whether this or that act in particular is conformable to the rule of truth,' p. 410; and then he goes on to observe, that I have 'calumniated the

Catholic gentry,' because 'there is no difference whatever, of detail or other, between their truthfulness and honour, and the truthfulness and honour of the Protestant gentry among whom they live.' But again he has garbled my words; they run thus:

'Truth is the same in itself and in substance, to Catholic and Protestant; so is purity; both virtues are to be referred to that moral sense which is the natural possession of us all. But, when we come to the question in detail, whether this or that act in particular is conformable to the rule of truth, or again to the rule of purity, then *sometimes* there is a difference of opinion *between individuals, sometimes between schools*, and *sometimes* between religious communions.' I knew indeed perfectly well, and I confessed that '*Protestants* think that the Catholic system, as such, leads to a lax observance of the rule of truth,' but I added, 'I am very sorry that they should think so,' and I never meant myself to grant that all Protestants were on the strict side, and all Catholics on the lax. Far from it; there is a stricter party as well as a laxer party among Catholics, there is a laxer party as well as a stricter party among Protestants. I have already spoken of Protestant writers who in certain cases allow of lying, I have also spoken of Catholic writers who do not allow of equivocation; when I wrote 'a difference of opinion between individuals,' and 'between schools,' I meant between Protestant and Protestant, and particular instances were in my mind. I did not say then, or dream of saying, that Catholics, priests and laity, were lax on the point of lying, and that Protestants were strict, any more than I meant to say that all Catholics were pure, and all Protestants impure; but I meant to say that, whereas the rule of Truth is one and the same both to Catholic and Protestant, nevertheless some Catholics were lax, some strict, and again some Protestants were strict, some lax; and I have already had opportunities of recording my own judgment on which side this Writer is *himself*, and therefore he may keep his forward vindication of 'honest gentlemen and noble ladies,' who, in spite of their priests, are still so truthful, till such time as he can find a worse assailant of them than I am, and they no better champion of them than himself. And as to the Priests of England, those who know them, as he does *not*, will pronounce them no whit inferior in this great virtue to the gentry, whom he says that he *does*; and I cannot say more. Blot *thirty-eight*.

Lastly, this Writer uses the following words, which I have more than once quoted, and with a reference to them I shall end my remarks upon him. 'I am henceforth,' he says, 'in doubt and fear, as much *as an honest man can be*, concerning every word Dr. Newman may write. How can I tell that I shall not be the dupe of some cunning equivocation, of one of the three kinds, laid down as permissible by the blessed St. Alfonso da Liguori and his pupils, even when confirmed with an oath . . .?'

I will tell him why he need not fear; because he has *left out* one very important condition in the statement of St. Alfonso, – and very applicable to my own case, even if I followed St. Alfonso's view of the subject. St. Alfonso says 'ex justâ causâ;' but our 'honest man,' as he styles himself, has *omitted these words*; which are a key to the whole question. Blot *thirty-nine*. Here endeth our 'honest man.' Now for the subject of Lying.

Almost all authors, Catholic and Protestant, admit, that *when a just cause is present*, there is some kind or other of verbal misleading, which is not sin. Even silence is in certain cases virtually such a misleading, according to the Proverb, 'Silence gives consent.' Again, silence is absolutely forbidden to a Catholic, as a mortal sin, under certain circumstances, e.g. to keep silence, instead of making a profession of faith.

Another mode of verbal misleading, and the most direct, is actually saying the thing that is not; and it is defended on the principle that such words are not a lie, when there is a 'justa causa,' as killing is not murder in the case of an executioner.

Another ground of certain authors for saying that an untruth is not a lie where there is a just cause, is, that veracity is a kind of justice, and therefore, when we have no duty of justice to tell truth to another, it is no sin not to do so. Hence we may say the thing that is not, to children, to madmen, to men who ask impertinent questions, to those whom we hope to benefit by misleading.

Another ground taken in defending certain untruths, *ex justâ causâ*, as if not lies, is that veracity is for the sake of society, and, if in no case we might lawfully mislead others, we should actually be doing society great harm.

Another mode of verbal misleading is equivocation or a play

upon words; and it is defended on the view that to lie is to use words in a sense which they will not bear. But an equivocator uses them in a received sense, though there is another received sense, and therefore, according to this definition, he does not lie.

Others say that all equivocations are, after all, a kind of lying, faint lies or awkward lies, but still lies; and some of these disputants infer, that therefore we must not equivocate, and others that equivocation is but a half-measure, and that it is better to say at once that in certain cases untruths are not lies.

Others will try to distinguish between evasions and equivocations; but they will be answered, that, though there are evasions which are clearly not equivocations, yet that it is difficult scientifically to draw the line between them.

To these must be added the unscientific way of dealing with lies, viz. that on a great or cruel occasion a man cannot help telling a lie, and he would not be a man, did he not tell it, but still it is wrong and he ought not to do it, and he must trust that the sin will be forgiven him though he goes about to commit it. It is a frailty, and had better not be anticipated, and not thought of again, after it is once over. This view cannot for a moment be defended, but, I suppose, it is very common.

And now I think the historical course of thought upon the matter has been this: the Greek Fathers thought that, when there was a *justa causa*, an untruth need not be a lie. St. Augustine took another view though with great misgiving; and, whether he is rightly interpreted or not, is the doctor of the great and common view that all untruths are lies, and that there can be *no* just cause of untruth. In these later times, this doctrine has been found difficult to work, and it has been largely taught that, though all untruths are lies, yet that certain equivocations, when there is a just cause, are not untruths.

Further, there have been and all along through these later ages, other schools, running parallel with the above mentioned, one of which says that equivocations, &c. after all *are* lies, and another which says that there are untruths which are not lies.

And now as to the 'just cause,' which is the condition, *sine quâ non.* The Greek Fathers make them such as these, self-defence, charity, zeal for God's honour, and the like.

St. Augustine seems to deal with the same 'just causes' as the Greek Fathers, even though he does not allow of their availableness as depriving untruths, spoken with such objects, of their sinfulness. He mentions defence of life and of honour, and the safe custody of a secret. Also the Anglican writers, who have followed the Greek Fathers, in defending untruths when there is the 'just cause,' consider that just cause to be such as the preservation of life and property, defence of law, the good of others. Moreover, their moral rights, e.g. defence against the inquisitive, &c.

St. Alfonso, I consider, would take the same view of the 'justa causa' as the Anglican divines; he speaks of it as 'quicunque finis *honestus*, ad servanda bona spiritui vel corpori utilia;' which is very much the view which they take of it, judging by the instances which they give.

In all cases, however, and as contemplated by all authors, Clement of Alexandria, or Milton, or St. Alfonso, such a causa is, in fact, extreme, rare, great, or at least special. Thus the writer in the Mélanges Théologiques (Liège, 1852–3, p. 453) quotes Lessius: 'Si absque justa causa fiat, est abusio orationis contra virtutem veritatis, et civilem consuetudinem, etsi proprie non sit mendacium.' That is, the virtue of truth, and the civil custom are the *measure* of the just cause. And so Voit, 'If a man has used a reservation (restrictione non purè mentali) without a *grave* cause, he has sinned gravely.' And so the author himself, from whom I quote, and who defends the Patristic and Anglican doctrine that there *are* untruths which are not lies, says, 'Under the name of mental reservation theologians authorize many lies, *when there is for them a grave reason* and proportionate' i.e. to their character. – p. 459. And so St. Alfonso, in another Treatise, quotes St. Thomas to the effect, that, if from one cause two immediate effects follow, and, if the good effect of that cause is *equal in value* to the bad effect (bonus *aequivalet* malo), then nothing hinders that the good may be intended and the evil permitted. From which it will follow that, since the evil to society from lying is very great, the just cause which is to make it allowable, must be very great also. And so Kenrick: 'It is confessed by all Catholics that, in the common intercourse of life, all ambiguity of language is to be avoided; but it is debated whether such ambiguity is ever lawful. Most theologians answer in the affirmative, supposing a *grave cause* urges, and the [true] mind of the speaker can be collected from the adjuncts, though in fact it be not collected.'

However, there are cases, I have already said, of another kind, in which Anglican authors would think a lie allowable; such as when a question is *impertinent*. Accordingly, I think the best word for embracing all the cases which would come under the 'Justa causa,' is, not 'extreme,' but 'special,' and I say the same as regards St. Alfonso; and therefore, above in pp. 242 and 243, whether I speak of St. Alfonso or Paley, I should have used the word 'special,' or 'extraordinary,' not 'extreme.'

What I have been saying shows what different schools of opinion there are in the Church in the treatment of this difficult doctrine; and, by consequence, that a given individual, such as I am, *cannot* agree with all, and has a full right to follow which he will. The freedom of the Schools, indeed, is one of those rights of reason, which the Church is too wise really to interfere with. And this applies not to moral questions only, but to dogmatic also.

It is supposed by Protestants that, because St. Alfonso's writings have had such high commendation bestowed upon them by authority, therefore they have been invested with a quasi-infallibility. This has arisen in good measure from Protestants not knowing the force of theological terms. The words to which they refer are the authoritative decision that 'nothing in his works has been found *worthy of censure*,' 'censurâ dignum;' but this does not lead to the conclusions which have been drawn from it. Those words occur in a legal document, and cannot be interpreted except in a legal sense. In the first place, the sentence is negative; nothing in St. Alfonso's writings is positively approved; and secondly it is not said that there are no faults in what he has written, but nothing which comes under the ecclesiastical *censurâ*, which is something very definite. To take and interpret them, in the way commonly adopted in England, is the same mistake, as if one were to take the word 'Apologia' in the English sense of apology, or 'Infant' in law to mean a little child.

1. Now first as to the meaning of the form of words viewed as

a proposition. When they were brought before the fitting authorities at Rome by the Archbishop of Besançon, the answer returned to him contained the condition that those words were to be interpreted, 'with due regard to the mind of the Holy See concerning the approbation of writings of the servants of God, ad effectum Canonizationis.' This is intended to prevent any Catholic taking the words about St. Alfonso's works in too large a sense. Before a Saint is canonized, his works are examined and a judgment pronounced upon them. Pope Benedict XIV. says, 'The *end* or *scope* of this judgment is, that it may appear, whether the doctrine of the servant of God, which he has brought out in his writings, is free from any soever *theological censure*.' And he remarks in addition, 'It never can be said that the doctrine of a servant of God is *approved* by the Holy See, but at most it can [only] be said that it is not disapproved (non reprobatam) in case that the Revisers had reported that there is nothing found by them in his works, which is adverse to the decrees of Urban VIII., and that the judgment of the Revisers has been approved by the sacred Congregation, and confirmed by the Supreme Pontiff.' The Decree of Urban VIII. here referred to is, 'Let works be examined, whether they contain errors against faith or good morals (bonos mores), or any new doctrine, or a doctrine foreign and alien to the common sense and custom of the Church.' The author from whom I quote this (M. Vandenbroeck, of the diocese of Malines) observes, 'It is therefore clear, that the approbation of the works of the Holy Bishop touches not the truth of every proposition, adds nothing to them, nor even gives them by consequence a degree of intrinsic probability.' He adds that it gives St. Alfonso's theology an extrinsic probability, from the fact that, in the judgment of the Holy See, no proposition deserves to receive a censure; but that 'that probability will cease nevertheless in a particular case, for any one who should be convinced, whether by evident arguments, or by a decree of the Holy See, or otherwise, that the doctrine of the Saint deviates from the truth.' He adds, 'From the fact that the approbation of the works of St. Alfonso does not decide the truth of each proposition, it follows, as Benedict XIV. has remarked, that we may combat the doctrine which they contain; only, since a canonized saint is in question, who is honoured by a solemn *culte* in the Church, we ought not to speak except with respect, nor to attack his opinions except with temper and modesty.'

2. Then, as to the meaning of the word *censura*: Benedict XIV. enumerates a number of 'Notes' which come under that name; he says, 'Out of propositions which are to be noted with theological censure, some are heretical, some erroneous, some close upon error, some savouring of heresy,' and so on; and each of these terms has its own definite meaning. Thus by 'erroneous' is meant, according to Viva, a proposition which is not *immediately* opposed to a revealed proposition, but only to a theological *conclusion* drawn from premises which are *de fide*; 'savouring of heresy,' when a proposition is opposed to a theological conclusion not evidently drawn from premises which are *de fide*, but most probably and according to the common mode of theologizing, and so with the rest. Therefore when it was said by the Revisers of St. Alfonso's works that they were not 'worthy of *censure*,' it was only meant that they did not fall under these particular Notes.

But the answer from Rome to the Archbishop of Besançon went further than this; it actually took pains to declare that any one who pleased might follow other theologians instead of St. Alfonso. After saying that no Priest was to be interfered with who followed St. Alfonso in the Confessional, it added, 'This is said, however, without on that account judging that they are reprehended who follow opinions handed down by other approved authors.'

And this too, I will observe, that St. Alfonso made many changes of opinion himself in the course of his writings; and it could not for an instant be supposed that we were bound to every one of his opinions, when he did not feel himself bound to them in his own person. And, what is more to the purpose still, there are opinions, or some opinion, of his which actually has been proscribed by the Church since, and cannot now be put forward or used. I do not pretend to be a well-read theologian myself, but I say this on the authority of a theological professor of Breda, quoted in the Mélanges Théol. for 1850–1. He says: 'It may happen, that, in the course of time, errors may be found in the works of St. Alfonso and be proscribed by the Church, *a thing which in fact has already occurred.*'

In not ranging myself then with those who consider that it is justifiable to use words in a double sense, that is, to equivocate, I put myself, first, under the protection of Cardinal Gerdil, who, in a work lately published at Rome, has the following passage, which I owe to the kindness of a friend:

Gerdil

'In an oath one ought to have respect to the intention of the party swearing, and the intention of the party to whom the oath is taken. Whoso swears binds himself in virtue of the words, not according to the sense he retains in his own mind, but in *the sense according to which he perceives that they are understood by him to whom the oath is made*. When the mind of the one is discordant with the mind of the other, if this happens by deceit or cheat of the party swearing, he is bound to observe the oath according to the right sense (sana mente) of the party receiving it; but, when the discrepancy in the sense comes of misunderstanding, without deceit of the party swearing, in that case he is not bound, except to that to which he had in mind to wish to be bound. It follows hence, that *whoso uses mental reservation or equivocation in the oath*, in order to deceive the party to whom he offers it, *sins most grievously*, and is always bound to observe the oath *in the sense in which he knew that his words were* taken by the other party, according to the decision of St. Augustine, "They are perjured, who, having kept the words, have deceived the expectations of those to whom the oath was taken." He who swears externally, without the inward intention of swearing, commits a most grave sin, and remains all the same under the obligation to fulfil it. . . . In a word, all that is contrary to good faith, is iniquitous, and by introducing the name of God the iniquity is aggravated by the guilt of sacrilege.'

Natalis Alexander

'They certainly lie, who utter the words of an oath, and without the will to swear or bind themselves; or who *make use of mental reservations and equivocations* in swearing, since they signify by words what they have not in mind, contrary to the end for which language was instituted, viz. as signs of ideas. Or they mean something else than the words signify in themselves, and the common custom of speech, and the circumstances of persons and business-matters; and thus they abuse words which were instituted for the cherishing of society.'

Contenson

'Hence is apparent how worthy of condemnation is the temerity of those half-taught men, who give a colour to lies and *equivocations* by the words and instances of Christ. Than whose doctrine, which is an art of deceiving, nothing can be more pestilent. And that, both because what you do not wish done to yourself, you should not do to another; now the patrons of equivocations and mental reservations would not like to be themselves deceived by others, &c. . . . and also because St. Augustine, &c. . . . In truth, as there is no pleasant living with those whose language we do not understand, and, as St. Augustine teaches, a man would more readily live with his dog than with a foreigner, less pleasant certainly is our converse with those who make use of frauds artificially covered, over-reach their hearers by deceits, address them insidiously, observe the right moment, and catch at words to their purpose, by which truth is hidden under a covering; and so on the other hand nothing is sweeter than the society of those, who both love and speak the naked truth, . . . without their mouth professing one thing and their mind hiding another, or spreading before it the cover of double words. Nor does it matter that they colour their lies with the name of *equivocations or mental reservations*. For Hilary says, "The sense, not the speech, makes the crime."'

Concina allows of what I shall presently call *evasions*, but nothing beyond, if I understand him; but he is most vehement against mental reservation of every kind, so I quote him.

Concina

'That mode of speech, which some theologians call pure mental reservation, others call reservation not simply mental; that language which to me is lying, to the greater part of recent authors is only amphibological ... I have discovered that nothing is adduced by more recent theologians for the lawful use of *amphibologies* which has not been made use of already by the ancients, whether philosophers or some Fathers, in defence of lies. Nor does there seem to me other difference when I consider their respective grounds, except that the ancients frankly called those modes of speech lies, and the more recent writers, not a few of them, call them amphibological, equivocal, and *material.*'

In another place he quotes Caramuel, so I suppose I may do so too, for the very reason that his theological reputation does not place him on the side of strictness. Concina says, 'Caramuel himself, who bore away the palm from all others in relaxing the evangelical and natural law, says,

Caramuel

"I have an innate aversion to mental reservations. If they are contained within the bounds of piety and sincerity, then they are not necessary; ... but if [otherwise] they are the destruction of human society and sincerity, and are to be condemned as pestilent. Once admitted, they open the way to all lying, all perjury. And the whole difference in the matter is, that what yesterday was called a lie, changing, not its nature and malice, but its name, is to-day entitled 'mental reservation;' and this is to sweeten poison with sugar, and to colour guilt with the appearance of virtue."

St. Thomas

'When the sense of the party swearing, and of the party to whom he swears, is not the same, if this proceeds from the deceit of the former, the oath ought to be kept according to the right sense of the party to whom it is made. But if the party swearing does not make use of deceit, then he is bound according to his own sense.'

St. Isidore

'With whatever artifice of words a man swears, nevertheless God who is the witness of his conscience, so takes the oath as he understands it, to whom it is sworn. And he becomes twice guilty, who both takes the name of God in vain, and deceives his neighbour.'

St. Augustine

'I do not question that this is most justly laid down, that the promise of an oath must be fulfilled, not according to the words of the party taking it, but according to the expectation of the party to whom it is taken, of which he who takes it is aware.'

And now, under the protection of these authorities, I say as follows: –

Casuistry is a noble science, but it is one to which I am led, neither by my abilities nor my turn of mind. Independently, then, of the difficulties of the subject, and the necessity, before forming an opinion, of knowing more of the arguments of theologians upon it than I do, I am very unwilling to say a word here on the subject of Lying and Equivocation. But I consider myself bound to speak; and therefore, in this strait, I can do nothing better, even for my own relief, than submit myself and what I shall say to the judgment of the Church, and to the consent, so far as in this matter there be a consent, of the Schola Theologorum.

Now, in the case of one of those special and rare exigencies or emergencies, which constitute the *justa causa* of dissembling or misleading, whether it be extreme as the defence of life, or a duty as the custody of a secret, or of a personal nature as to repel an impertinent inquirer, or a matter too trivial to provoke question, as in dealing with children or madmen, there seem to be four courses: –

1. *To say the thing that is not.* Here I draw the reader's attention to the words *material* and *formal*. 'Thou shalt not kill;' *murder* is the *formal* transgression of this commandment, but *accidental homicide* is the *material* transgression. The *matter* of the act is the same in both cases; but in the *homicide* there is nothing more than the act, whereas in murder there must be the intention, &c. which constitutes the formal sin. So, again, an executioner commits the material act, but not that formal killing which is a breach of the commandment. So a man, who, simply to save

himself from starving, takes a loaf which is not his own, commits only the material, not the formal act of stealing, that is, he does not commit a sin. And so a baptized Christian, external to the Church, who is in invincible ignorance, is a material heretic, and not a formal. And in like manner, if to say the thing which is not be in special cases lawful, it may be called a *material lie*.

The first mode then which has been suggested of meeting those special cases, in which to mislead by words has a sufficient object, or has a *just cause* is by a material lie.

The second mode is by an *aequivocatio* which is not equivalent to the English word 'equivocation', but means sometimes a *play upon words*, sometimes an *evasion*.

2. *A play upon words*. St. Alfonso certainly says that a play upon words is allowable; and, speaking under correction, I should say that he does so on the ground that lying is *not* a sin against justice, that is, against our neighbour, but a sin against God; because words are the signs of ideas, and therefore if a word denotes two ideas, we are at liberty to use it in either of its senses: but I think I must be incorrect here in some respect, because the Catechism of the Council, as I have quoted it at p. 249, says, 'Vanitate et mendacio fides ac veritas tolluntur, arctissima vincula *societatis humanae*; quibus sublatis, sequitur summa vitae confusio, ut *homines nihil a daemonibus differre videantur*.'

3. *Evasion*; – when, for instance, the speaker diverts the attention of the hearer to another subject; suggests an irrelevant fact or makes a remark, which confuses him and gives him something to think about; throws dust into his eyes; states some truth, from which he is quite sure his hearer will draw an illogical and untrue conclusion, and the like. Bishop Butler seems distinctly to sanction such a proceeding, in a passage which I shall extract below.

The greatest school of evasion, I speak seriously, is the House of Commons; and necessarily so, from the nature of the case. And the hustings is another.

An instance is supplied in the history of St. Athanasius: he was in a boat on the Nile, flying persecution; and he found himself pursued. On this he ordered his men to turn his boat round, and ran right to meet the satellites of Julian. They asked him, Have you seen Athanasius? and he told his followers to answer, 'Yes, he is close to you.' *They* went on their course, and *he* ran into Alexandria, and there lay hid till the end of the persecution.

I gave another instance above, in reference to a doctrine of religion. The early Christians did their best to conceal their Creed on account of the misconceptions of the heathen about it. Were the question asked of them, 'Do you worship a Trinity?' and did they answer, 'We worship one God, and none else;' the inquirer might, or would, infer that they did not acknowledge the Trinity of Divine Persons.

It is very difficult to draw the line between these evasions, and what are commonly called in English *equivocations*; and of this difficulty, again, I think, the scenes in the House of Commons supply us with illustrations.

4. The fourth method is *silence*. For instance, not giving the *whole* truth in a court of law. If St. Alban, after dressing himself in the Priest's clothes, and being taken before the persecutor, had been able to pass off for his friend, and so gone to martyrdom without being discovered; and had he in the course of examination answered all questions truly, but not given the whole truth, the most important truth, that he was the wrong person, he would have come very near to telling a lie, for a half-truth is often a falsehood. And his defence must have been the *justa causa*, viz. either that he might in charity or for religion's sake save a priest, or again that the judge had no right to interrogate him on the subject.

Now, of these four modes of misleading others by the tongue, when there is a *justa causa* (supposing there can be such), – a material lie, that is an untruth which is not a lie, an equivocation, an evasion, and silence, – First, I have no difficulty whatever in recognizing as allowable the method of *silence*.

Secondly, But, if I allow of *silence*, why not of the method of *material lying*, since half of a truth *is* often a lie? And, again, if all killing be not murder, nor all taking from another stealing, why must all untruths be lies? Now I will say freely that I think it difficult to answer this question, whether it be urged by St. Clement or by Milton; at the same time, I never have acted, and I think, when it came to the point, I never should act upon such a theory myself, except in one case, stated below. This I say for the benefit of those who speak hardly of Catholic theologians, on the ground that they admit text-books which allow of equivocation. They are asked, how can we trust you, when such are your views? but such views, as I already have said, need not have any thing to do with their own practice, merely from the circumstance that they are contained in their text-books. A theologian draws out a system; he does it partly as a scientific speculation: but much more for the sake of others. He is lax for the sake of others, not of himself. His own standard of action is much higher than that which he imposes upon men in general. One special reason why religious men, after drawing out a theory, are unwilling to act upon it themselves, is this: that they practically acknowledge a broad distinction between their reason and their conscience; and that they feel the latter to be the safer guide, though the former may be the clearer, nay even though it be the truer. They would rather be wrong with their conscience, than right with their reason. And again here is this more tangible difficulty in the case of exceptions to the rule of Veracity, that so very little external help is given us in drawing the line, as to when untruths are allowable and when not; whereas that sort of killing which is not murder, is most definitely marked off by legal enactments, so that it cannot possibly be mistaken for such killing as *is* murder. On the other hand the cases of exemption from the rule of Veracity are left to the private judgment of the individual, and he may easily be led on from acts which are allowable to acts which are not. Now this remark does *not* apply to such acts as are related in Scripture, as being done by a particular inspiration, for in such cases there *is* a command. If I had my own way, I would oblige society, that is, its great men, its lawyers, its divines, its literature, publicly to acknowledge, as such, those instances of untruth which are not lies, as for instance, untruths in war; and then there could be no danger in them to the individual Catholic, for he would be acting under a rule.

Thirdly, as to playing upon words, or equivocation, I suppose it is from the English habit, but, without meaning any disrespect to a great Saint, or wishing to set myself up, or taking my conscience for more than it is worth, I can only say as a fact, that I admit it as little as the rest of my countrymen: and, without any reference to the right and the wrong of the matter, of this I am sure, that, if there is one thing more than another which prejudices Englishmen against the Catholic Church, it is the doctrine of great authorities on the subject of equivocation. For myself, I can fancy myself thinking it was allowable in extreme cases for me to lie, but never to equivocate. Luther said, 'Pecca fortiter.' I anathematize the formal sentiment, but there is a truth in it, when spoken of material acts.

Fourthly, I think *evasion*, as I have described it, to be perfectly allowable; indeed, I do not know, who does not use it, under circumstances; but that a good deal of moral danger is attached to its use; and that, the cleverer a man is, the more likely he is to pass the line of Christian duty.

But it may be said, that such decisions do not meet the particular difficulties for which provision is required; let us then take some instances.

1. I do not think it right to tell lies to children, even on this account, that they are sharper than we think them, and will soon find out what we are doing; and our example will be a very bad training for them. And so of equivocation: it is easy of imitation, and we ourselves shall be sure to get the worst of it in the end.

2. If an early Father defends the patriarch Jacob in his mode of gaining his father's blessing, on the ground that the blessing was divinely pledged to him already, that it was his, and that his father and brother were acting at once against his own rights and the divine will, it does not follow from this that such conduct is a pattern to us, who have no supernatural means of determining *when* an untruth becomes a *material*, and not a *formal* lie. It seems to me very dangerous, be it allowable or not, to lie or equivocate in order to preserve some great temporal or spiritual benefit, nor does St. Alfonso here say any thing to the contrary, for he is not discussing the question of danger or expedience.

3. As to Johnson's case of a murderer asking you which way a man had gone, I should have anticipated that, had such a difficulty happened to him, his first act would have been to knock the man down, and to call out for the police; and next, if he was worsted in the conflict, he would not have given the ruffian the information he asked, at whatever risk to himself. I

think he would have let himself be killed first. I do not think that he would have told a lie.

4. A secret is a more difficult case. Supposing something has been confided to me in the strictest secrecy, which could not be revealed without great disadvantage to another, what am I to do? If I am a lawyer, I am protected by my profession. I have a right to treat with extreme indignation any question which trenches on the inviolability of my position; but, supposing I was driven up into a corner, I think I should have a right to say an untruth, or that, under such circumstances, a lie would be *material*, but it is almost an impossible case, for the law would defend me. In like manner, as a priest, I should think it lawful to speak as if I knew nothing of what passed in confession. And I think in these cases, I do in fact possess that guarantee, that I am not going by private judgment, which just now I demanded; for society would bear me out, whether as a lawyer or as a priest, that I had a duty to my client or penitent, such, that an untruth in the matter was not a lie. A common type of this permissible denial, be it *material lie* or *evasion*, is at the moment supplied to me: an artist asked a Prime Minister, who was sitting to him, 'What news, my Lord, from France?' He answered, '*I do not know*; I have not read the Papers.'

5. A more difficult question is, when to accept confidence has not been a duty. Supposing a man wishes to keep the secret that he is the author of a book, and he is plainly asked on the subject. Here I should ask the previous question, whether any one has a right to publish what he dare not avow. It requires to have traced the bearings and results of such a principle, before being sure of it; but certainly, for myself, I am no friend of strictly anonymous writing. Next, supposing another has confided to you the secret of his authorship: there are persons who would have no scruple at all in giving a denial to impertinent questions asked them on the subject. I have heard a great man in his day at Oxford, warmly contend, as if he could not enter into any other view of the matter, that, if he had been trusted by a friend with the secret of his being author of a certain book, and he were asked by a third person, if his friend was not (as he really was) the author of it, he ought without any scruple and distinctly to answer that he did not know. He had an existing duty towards

the author; he had none towards his inquirer. The author had a claim on him; an impertinent questioner had none at all. But here again I desiderate some leave, recognized by society, as in the case of the formulas 'Not at home,' and 'Not guilty,' in order to give me the right of saying what is a *material* untruth. And moreover, I should here also ask the previous question, Have I any right to accept such a confidence? have I any right to make such a promise? and, if it be an unlawful promise, is it binding at the expense of a lie? I am not attempting to solve these difficult questions, but they have to be carefully examined.

As I put into print some weeks ago various extracts from authors relating to the subject which I have been considering, I conclude by inserting them here, though they will not have a very methodical appearance.

For instance, St. Dorotheus: 'Sometimes the *necessity* of some matter urges (incumbit), which, unless you somewhat conceal and dissemble it, will turn into a greater trouble.' And he goes on to mention the case of saving a man who has committed homicide from his pursuers: and he adds that it is not a thing that can be done often, but once in a long time.

St. Clement in like manner speaks of it only as a necessity, and as a necessary medicine.

Origen, after saying that God's commandment makes it a plain duty to speak the truth, adds, that a man, 'when necessity urges,' may avail himself of a lie, as medicine, that is, to the extent of Judith's conduct towards Holofernes; and he adds that that necessity may be the obtaining of a great good as Jacob hindered his father from giving the blessing to Esau against the will of God.

Cassian says, that the use of a lie, in order to be allowable, must be like the use of hellebore, which is itself poison, unless a man has a fatal disease on him. He adds, 'Without the condition of an extreme necessity, it is a present ruin.'

St. John Chrysostom defends Jacob on the ground that his deceiving his father was not done for the sake of temporal gain, but in order to fulfil the providential purpose of God; and he says, that, as Abraham was not a murderer, though he was minded to kill his son, so an untruth need not be a lie. And he adds, that often such a deceit is the greatest possible benefit to a man who is deceived, and therefore allowable. Also St. Hilary, St. John Climacus, &c., in Thomassin, Concina, the *Mélanges*, &c.

Various modern Catholic divines hold this doctrine of the 'material lie' also. I will quote three passages in point.

Cataneo: 'Be it then well understood, that the obligation to veracity, that is, of conforming our words to the sentiments of our mind, is founded principally upon the necessity of human intercourse, for which reason they (i.e. words) ought not and cannot be lawfully opposed to this end, so just, so necessary, and so important, without which, the world would become a Babylon of confusion. And this would in a great measure be really the result, as often as a man should be unable to defend secrets of high importance, and other evils would follow, even worse than confusion, in their nature destructive of this very intercourse between man and man for which speech was instituted. Every body must see the advantage a hired assassin would have, if supposing he did not know by sight the person he was commissioned to kill, I being asked by the rascal at the moment he was standing in doubt with his gun cocked, were obliged to approve of his deed by keeping silence, or to hesitate, or lastly to answer "Yes, that is the man." [Then follow other similar cases.] In such and similar cases, in which your sincerity is unjustly assailed, when no other way more prompt or more efficacious presents itself, and when it is not enough to say, "I do not know," let such persons be met openly with a downright resolute "No" without thinking upon any thing else. For such a "No" is conformable to the universal opinion of men, who are the judges of words, and who certainly have not placed upon them obligations to the injury of the Human Republic, nor even entered into a compact to use them in behalf of rascals, spies, incendiaries, and thieves. I repeat that such a "No" is conformable to the universal mind of man, and with this mind your own mind ought to be in union and alliance. Who does not see the manifest advantage which highway robbers would derive, were travellers when asked if they had gold, jewels, &c., obliged either to invent tergiversations or to answer "Yes, we have"? Accordingly in such circumstances that "No" which you utter [see Card. Pallav. lib. iii. c. xi. n. 23, de Fide, Spe, &c.] remains deprived of its proper meaning, and is like a piece of coin, from which by the command of the government the current value has been withdrawn, so that by using it you become in no sense guilty of lying.'

Bolgeni says, 'We have therefore proved satisfactorily, and with more than moral certainty, that an *exception* occurs to the general law of not speaking untruly, viz. when it is impossible to observe a certain other precept, more important, *without* telling a lie. Some persons indeed say, that in the cases of impossibility which are above drawn out, what is said is *not* a lie. But a man who thus speaks confuses ideas and denies the essential characters of things. What is a lie? It is "locutio contra mentem;" this is its common definition. But in the cases of impossibility, a man speaks *contra mentem*; that is clear and evident. Therefore he tells a lie. Let us distinguish between the lie and the sin. In the above cases, the man really tells a lie, but this lie is not a sin, by reason of the existing impossibility. To say that in those cases no one has a right to ask, that the words have a meaning according to the common consent of men, and the like, as is said by certain authors in order in those cases to exempt the lie from sin, this is to commit oneself to frivolous excuses, and to subject oneself to a number of retorts, when there is the plain reason of the above-mentioned fact of impossibility.'

And the Author in the *Mélanges Théologiques*: 'We have then gained this truth, and it is a conclusion of which we have not the smallest doubt, that if the intention of deceiving our neighbour is essential to a lie, it is allowable in certain cases to say what we know to be false, as, e.g. to escape from a great danger. . . .

'But, let no one be alarmed, it is never allowable to lie; in this we are in perfect agreement with the whole body of theologians. The only point in which we differ from them is in what we mean by a lie. They call that a lie which is not such in our view, or rather, if you will, what in our view is only a material lie they account to be both formal and material.'

Now to come to Anglican authorities.

Taylor: 'Whether it can in any case be lawful to tell a lie? To this I answer, that the Holy Scriptures of the Old and New Testament do indefinitely and severely forbid lying. Prov. xiii. 5; xxx. 8. Ps. v. 6. John viii. 44. Col. iii. 9. Rev. xxi. 8. 27. Beyond these things, nothing can be said in condemnation of lying.

'*But then* lying is to be understood to be *something said or written to the hurt of our neighbour*, which cannot be understood otherwise than to differ from the mind of him that speaks. "A lie is petulantly or from a desire of hurting, to say one thing, or to signify it by gesture, and to think another thing:"* so Melanchthon, "To lie is to deceive our neighbour to his hurt." For *in this sense* a lie is naturally or *intrinsically* evil; that is, to speak a lie *to our neighbour* is naturally evil ... *not* because it is different from an eternal truth. ... A lie is an *injury* to our neighbour. ... There is in mankind a universal *contract* implied in all their intercourses. ... *In justice* we are bound to speak, so as that our neighbour do not lose his *right*, which by our speaking we give him to the truth, that is, in our heart. And of a lie, *thus defined*, which is *injurious* to our neighbour, so long as his *right* to truth remains, it is that St. Austin affirms it to be simply unlawful, and that it can in no case be permitted, nisi forte regulas quasdam daturus es. ... If a lie be *unjust*, it can never become lawful; but, *if it can be separate from injustice* then it may be *innocent*. Here then I consider,

'This right, though it be regularly and commonly belonging to all men, yet it may be *taken away* by a superior right intervening; or it may be lost, or it may be hindered, or it may cease, upon a greater reason.

'Therefore upon this account it was lawful for the children of Israel to borrow jewels of the Egyptians, *which supposes a promise of restitution, though they intended not to pay them back again*. God gave commandment so to spoil them, and the Egyptians were divested of their *rights*, and *were to be used like enemies*.

'*It is lawful to tell a lie to children or to madmen*; because they, having no powers of judging, have no *right* to truth; but then, *the lie must be charitable and useful*. ... If a lie be told, it must be such as is *for their good* ... and so do physicians to their patients. ... This and the like were so usual, so permitted to physicians, that it grew to a proverb, "You lie like a doctor;"† which yet was always to be understood in the way of charity, and with honour to the profession. ... To tell a lie for charity, to save a man's life,

---

* 'Mendacium est petulanter, aut cupiditate nocendi, aliud loqui, seu gestu significare, et aliud sentire.'
† Mentiris ut medicus.

the life of a friend, of a husband, of a prince, of a useful and a public person, hath not only been done at all times, but commended by great and wise and good men. . . . Who would not save his father's life . . . at the charge of a *harmless lie*, from the rage of persecutors or tyrants? . . . When the telling of a truth will certainly be the cause of evil to a man, though he have right to truth, yet it must not be given to him to his harm. . . . *Every* truth is no more *justice*, than every restitution of a straw to the right owner is a duty. "Be not over-righteous," says Solomon. . . . If it be objected, that we must not tell a lie for God, therefore much less for our brother, I answer, that it does not follow; for God needs not a lie, *but our brother does*. . . . *Deceiving* the enemy by the stratagem of actions or *words*, is *not properly lying*; for this supposes a conversation, of law or peace, trust or *promise* explicit or implicit. A lie is a deceiving of a *trust or confidence*.' – Taylor, vol. xiii. pp. 351–371, ed. Heber.

It is clear that Taylor thought that veracity was one branch of justice; a social virtue; under the second table of the law, not under the first; only binding, when those to whom we speak have a claim of justice upon us, which ordinarily all men have. Accordingly, in cases where a neighbour has no claim of justice upon us, there is no opportunity of exercising veracity, as, for instance, when he is mad, or is deceived by us for his own advantage. And hence, in such cases, a lie is *not really* a lie, as he says in one place, 'Deceiving the enemy is *not properly* lying.' Here he seems to make that distinction common to Catholics; viz. between what they call a *material* act and a *formal* act. Thus Taylor would maintain, that to say the thing that is not to a madman, has the *matter* of a lie, but the man who says it as little tells a formal lie, as the judge, sheriff, or executioner murders the man whom he certainly kills by forms of law.

Other English authors take precisely the same view, viz. that veracity is a kind of justice, – that our neighbour generally has a *right* to have the truth told him; but that he may forfeit that right, or lose it for the time, and then to say the thing that is not to him is no sin against veracity, that is, no lie. Thus Milton says,* 'Veracity is a virtue, by which we speak true things to him

* The Latin original is given at the end of the Appendix.

to whom it is equitable, and concerning what things it is suitable for the *good of our neighbour*. . . . All dissimulation is not wrong, for it is not necessary for us always openly to bring out the truth; that only is blamed which is *malicious*. . . . I do not see why that cannot be said of lying which can be said of homicide and other matters, which are not weighed so much by the *deed* as by *the object and end of acting. What man in his senses will deny* that there are those whom we have the best of grounds for considering that we ought to deceive, – as boys, madmen, the sick, the intoxicated, enemies, men in error, thieves? . . . Is it a point of conscience not to deceive them? . . . I would ask, by which of the commandments is a lie forbidden? You will say, by the ninth. Come, read it out, and you will agree with me. For whatever is here forbidden comes under the head of injuring one's neighbour. If then any lie does *not* injure one's neighbour, certainly it is not forbidden by this commandment. It is on this ground that, by the judgment of theologians, we shall acquit so many holy men of lying. Abraham, who said to his servants that he would return with his son; . . . the wise man understood that it did not matter to his servants to know [that his son would not return], and that it was at the moment expedient for himself that they should not know. . . . Joseph would be a man of many lies if the common definition of lying held; [also] Moses, Rahab, Ehud, Jael, Jonathan.' Here again veracity is due only on the score of *justice* towards the person whom we speak with; and, if he has *no claim* upon us to speak the truth, we *need* not speak the truth to him.

And so, again, Paley: '*A lie is a breach of promise*; for whoever seriously addresses his discourse to another tacitly promises to speak the truth, because he knows that the truth is expected. Or the *obligation* of veracity may be made out from the direct ill consequences of lying to social happiness. . . . There are *falsehoods* which are not *lies; that is, which are not criminal*.' (Here, let it be observed, is the same distinction as in Taylor between *material* and *formal* untruths.) '1. When no one is deceived. . . . 2. When the person to whom you speak has no *right* to know the truth, or, more properly, when little or no inconveniency results from the want of confidence in such cases, as *where you tell a falsehood to a madman* for his own advantage; to a robber, to conceal your property; to an assassin, to defeat or divert him from his purpose. ... It is upon this principle that, by the laws of war, it is allowable to deceive an enemy by feints, false colours, spies, false intelligence.... Many people indulge, in serious discourse, a habit of fiction or exaggeration.... So long as ... their narratives, though false, are *inoffensive*, it may seem a superstitious regard to truth to censure them *merely for truth's sake*.' Then he goes on to mention reasons *against* such a practice, adding, 'I have seldom known any one who deserted truth in trifles that could be trusted in matters of importance.' – Works, vol. iv. p. 123.

Dr. Johnson, who, if any one, has the reputation of being a sturdy moralist, thus speaks: –

'We talked', says Boswell, 'of the casuistical question, – whether it was allowable at any time to depart from *truth*.' Johnson. 'The general rule is, that truth should never be violated; because it is of the utmost importance to the comfort of life, that we should have a full security by mutual faith; and occasional inconveniences should be willingly suffered, that we may preserve it. There must, however, be some exceptions. If, for instance, a murderer should ask you which way a man is gone, you may tell him what is not true, because you are under a previous obligation not to betray a man to a murderer.' Boswell. 'Supposing the person who wrote Junius were asked whether he was the author, might he deny it?' Johnson. 'I don't know what to say to this. If you were *sure* that he wrote Junius, would you, if he denied it, think as well of him afterwards? Yet it may be urged, that what a man has no right to ask, you may refuse to communicate; and there is no other effectual mode of preserving a secret, and an important secret, the discovery of which may be very hurtful to you, but a flat denial; for if you are silent, or hesitate, or evade, it will be held equivalent to a confession. But stay, sir; here is another case. Supposing the author had told me confidentially that he had written Junius, and I were asked if he had, I should hold myself at liberty to deny it, as being under a previous promise, express or implied, to conceal it. Now what I ought to do for the author, may I not do for myself? But I deny the lawfulness of telling a lie to a sick man for fear of alarming him. You have no business with consequences; you are to tell the truth. Besides, you are not sure what effect your telling him that he is in danger may have; it may bring his distemper to a crisis, and that may cure him. Of all lying I have the greatest abhorrence of this, because I believe it has been frequently practised on myself.' – Boswell's Life, vol. iv. p. 277.

There are English authors who allow of mental reservation and equivocation; such is Jeremy Taylor.

He says, 'In the same cases in which it is lawful to tell a lie, in the same cases it is lawful to use a mental reservation.' – Ibid. p. 374.

He says, too, 'When the things are true in *several senses*, the not explicating in *what sense* I mean the words is not a criminal reservation. . . . But 1. this liberty is not to be used by inferiors, but by superiors only; 2. not by those that are interrogated, but by them which speak voluntarily; 3. not by those which speak of duty, but which speak of grace and kindness.' – Ibid. p. 378.

Bishop Butler, the first of Anglican authorities, writing in his grave and abstract way, seems to assert a similar doctrine in the following passage: –

'Though veracity, as well as justice, is to be our rule of life, it must be added, otherwise a snare will be laid in the way of some plain men, that the use of common forms of speech generally understood, cannot be falsehood; and, in general, that there can be no designed falsehood without designing to deceive. It must likewise be observed, that, *in numberless cases, a man may be under the strictest obligations to what he foresees will deceive, without his intending it.* For *it is impossible not to foresee*, that the words and actions of men in different ranks and employments, and of different educations, *will perpetually be mistaken by each other*; and it cannot but be so, whilst they will judge with the utmost careless-ness, as they daily do, *of what they are not perhaps enough informed to be competent judges of*, even though they considered it with great attention.' – *Nature of Virtue*, fin. These last words seem in a measure to answer to the words in Scavini, that an equivocation is permissible, because 'then we do not deceive our neighbour, but allow him to deceive himself.' In thus speaking, I have not the slightest intention of saying any thing disrespectful to Bishop Butler; and still less of course to St. Alfonso.

And a third author, for whom I have a great respect, as

different from the above two as they are from each other, bears testimony to the same effect in his 'Comment on Scripture,' Thomas Scott. He maintains indeed that Ehud and Jael were divinely directed in what they did; but they could have no divine direction for what was in itself wrong.

Thus on Judges iii. 15–21:

'"And Ehud said, I have a secret errand unto thee, O king; I have a message from God unto thee, and Ehud thrust the dagger into his belly." Ehud, indeed', says Scott, 'had a secret errand, a message from God unto him; *but it was of a far different nature than Eglon expected.*'

And again on Judges iv. 18–21:

'"And Jael said, Turn in, my lord, fear not. And he said to her, When any man doth inquire, Is there any man here? thou shalt say, No. Then Jael took a nail, and smote the nail into his temple." Jael,' says Scott, 'is not said to have promised Sisera that she would deny his being there; she would give him shelter and refreshment, but not utter a falsehood to oblige him.'

Notes

The following are the originals of some of the passages translated under this last Head: –

Gerdil

'Nel giuramento si dee riguardare l'intenzione di chi giura, e l'intenzione di quello a cui si presta il giuramento. Chicunque giura si obbliga in virtù delle parole non secondo il senso ch'egli si ritiene in mente, ma nel senso secondo cui egli cognosce che sono intese da quello a cui si fa il giuramento. Allorchè la mente dell'uno è discordante dalla mente dell'altro, se ciò avviene per dolo e inganno del giurante, questi è obbligato ad osservare il giuramento secondo la sana mente di chi la ha ricevuto; ma quando la discrepanza nel senso proviene da mala intelligenza senza dolo di chi giura, in quel caso egli non è obbligato se non a ciò che avea in mente di volersi obbligare. Da ciò segue che chiunque usa restrizione mentale o equivocazione nel giuramento per ingannare la parte cui egli lo presta, pecca gravissimamente, ed è sempre obbligato ad osservare il giuramento nel senso in cui egli sapea che le sue parole erano prese dall'altro, secondo la decisione di S. Agostino (epist. 224) "Perjuri sunt qui servatis verbis, expectationem eorum quibus juratum est deceperunt." Chi giura esternamente senza interna intenzione di giurare, commette gravissimo peccato, e rimane con tutto ciò nell'obbligo di adimperlo. . . . In somma tutto che è contrario alla buona fede, è iniquo, e facendovi intervenire il nome di Dio si aggrava l'iniquità colla reità del sacrilegio.' – Opusc. Theolog. Rom. 1851, p. 28.

Natalis Alexander

'Perjurium est mendacium juramento firmatum. Illos vero mentiri compertum est, qui juramenti verba proferunt, et jurare vel obligare se nolunt, aut qui restrictiones mentales et aequivocationes jurando adhibent, siquidem verbis significant quod in mente non habent, contra finem propter quem institutae sunt voces, ut videlicet sint signa conceptuum. Vel aliud volunt quàm verba significent secundum se et secundum communem loquendi morem, et personarum ac negotiorum circumstantias; atque ita verbis ad societatem fovendam institutis abutuntur.' – Theol. Lib. iv. c. iv. Art. 3. Reg. II.

Contenson

'Atque ex his apparet quam damnanda sit eorum semidoctorum temeritas, qui mendacia et aequivocationes verbis et exemplis Christi praecolorant. Quorum doctrinâ, quae ars fallendi est, nihil pestilentius esse potest. Tum quia quod tibi non vis fieri, alteri ne feceris; sed aequivocationum, ac restrictionum mentalium patroni aequo animo non paterentur se ab aliis illudi: ergo illud oecumenicum naturae principium nulli ignotum, omnibus quamlibet barbaris implantatum violant. Tum quia urget argumentum Augustinus, etc. . . . Sanè sicut aegrè cum illis convivimus, quorum linguam non intelligimus; et authore Augustino, lib. 19, de Civit. "Libentiùs vivit homo cum cane suo, quam cum homine alieno": aegriùs certè cum illis conversamur qui fraudes

artificio tectas adhibent, audientes circumveniunt dolis, insidiis
eos petunt, tempus observant, verbaque idonea aucupantur,
quibus veritas veluti quodam involucro obtegitur: sicut è contra
nihil eorum convictu suavius, qui ab omni simulandi studio
longe absentes, sincero animo, candido ingenio, aperta voluntate
praediti sunt, oderunt artes, nudam veritatem tam amant, quam
loquuntur: quorum denique manus linguae, lingua cordi, cor
rationi, ratio Deo congruit, et tota vita unius faciei est, unius
et coloris: nec aliud os prae se fert, aliud animus celat, et
verborum duplicium velo obtendit. Certe tolerabilior erat Baby-
lonica confusio, in qua invicem loquentes se minimè intellige-
bant, eorum convictu, qui non se intelligunt, nisi ut sese mutuo
decipiant.

'Nec obest quod nomine aequivocationum, vel restrictionum
mentalium mendacia fucent. Nam ut ait Hilarius lib. 2. de
Trinit., "Sensus, non sermo, fit crimen. O ubi simplicitas
Christiana, quae regulâ illâ Legislatoris sui Christi contenta est:
Sit sermo vester, Est est, Non non!" O ubi est mulier illa virilis
totam Probabilistarum aequivocationibus veniam dantium na-
tionem confusura! quae referente Hieronymo *epist.* 49, nec ad
gravissimos torturarum et dirae mortis cruciatus vitandos
aequivocationum usum septies icta advocavit.' – Theol. vii. p.
30.

Concina

'Cardo disputationis Augustinianae, in duobus recensitis libris,
potissimum in eo vertitur, ut rationes praebeantur pro veritatis
occultatione in negotiis summi momenti . . . Augustinus nulla
reperire remedia potuit praeter haec: Primum est silentium . . .
Alterum est aperta et invicta significatio. . . . Nullam aliam viam
occultandi veritatem agnovit, – non restrictiones internas, non
materiales locutiones, non verborum amphibolias, non alia junio-
rum inventa.' – Theol. T. iii. p. 278. Lib. v. in Decal. Diss. 3. c.
5. prop. 2d.

'. . . Haec autem omnium scopulorum, et difficultatum origo:
quia cum non possit rectae disputationi locus esse, nisi id pateat
de quo est disputandum; certas et claras notiones aequivocationum, amphibologiarum, et mentalium restrictionum praefinire

minime possumus, attentis recentiorum distinctiunculis, effugiis, et thecnis, quae rem hanc maxime implicatam efficiunt. Has ambages ut evitarem, cursum inceptum abrumpere, telamque redordiri, atque retexere decrevi: idque consilii cepi, ut primum omnium de mendacio sermonem institutam. Illud namque commodi mihi peracta controversiae tractatio attulit, ut deprehenderim, nihil a recentioribus Theologis pro licito amphibologiarum usu efferri quod prius ab antiquis tum Philosophis, tum Patribus aliquibus usurpatum non fuerit in mendaciorum patrocinium. Nec aliud discrimen mihi utrorumque fundamenta perpendenti occurrit, nisi quod antiqui eas locutiones quas recentiorum Theologorum non pauci amphibologicas, aequivocas, et *materiales* vocant, ingenua sinceritate mendacia appellaverint.' – Diss. iii. De Juram. Dol. etc.

Caramuel

'. . . Est mihi', inquit, 'innata aversio contra restrictiones mentales. Si enim continentur inter terminos pietatis, et sinceritatis, necessariae non sunt. Nam omnia quae ipsae praestare possunt, praestabunt consignificantes circumstantiae. Quod si tales dicantur, ut etiam ibi admittendae sint, ubi desunt circumstantiae significantes (ignoscant mihi earumdem auctores, et propugnatores) tollunt humanam societatem, et securitatem, et tamquam pestiferae damnandae sunt. Quoniam semel admissae aperiunt omni mendacio, omni perjurio viam. Et tota differentia in eo erit ut quod heri vocabatur mendacium, naturam, et malitiam non mutet, sed nomen, ita ut hodie jubeatur Restrictio mentalis nominari; quod est virus condire saccharo, et scelus specie virtutis colorare.' – Apud Concinam Theol. Diss. iii. De Juram. Dol. etc.

S. Thomas

'Quando non est eadem jurantis intentio, et ejus cui jurat, si hoc proveniat ex dolo jurantis, debet juramentum servari secundum sanum intellectum ejus, cui juramentum praestatur. Si autem jurans dolum non adhibeat, obligatur secundum intentionem jurantis.' – Apud Nat. Alex.

S. Isidorus

'Quacunque arte verborum quisquis juret, Deus tamen qui conscientiae testis est, ita hoc accipit, sicut ille, cui juratur, intelligit. Dupliciter autem reus fit, qui et Dei nomen in vanum assumit, et proximum dolo capit.' – Apud Nat. Alex.

S. Augustinus

'Illud sanè rectissime dici non ambigo, non secundum verba jurantis, sed secundum expectationem illius cui juratur, quam novit ille qui jurat, fidem jurationis impleri. Nam verba difficillimè comprehendunt, maxime breviter, sententiam cujus a jurante fides exigitur. Unde perjuri sunt, qui servatis verbis, expectationem eorum, quibus juratum est, deceperunt: et perjuri non sunt, qui etiam verbis non servatis, illud quod ab eis cum jurarent expectatum est, impleverunt.' – Apud Natal. Alex.

Cattaneo

'Sappiasi dunque, che l'obbligo della veracità, cioè, di conformare le parole ai sentimenti dell'animo nostro, egli è principalmente fondato nella necessità del commercio umano; onde elle non devono giammai nè possono lecitamente opporsi a questo fine, si giusto, si necessario, e si importante; tolto il quale, diverebbe il mondo una Babilonia di confusione. E ciò accaderebbe in gran parte, ogni qual volta non si potessero custodire, ne difendere i segreti d'alta importanza, e ne seguissero altri mali anche peggiori, distruttivi di lor natura di questo stesso commercio, per cui è stato istituito il parlare. Ognun vede, quanto tornerebbe in acconcio ad un mandatario, se non conoscendo la persona, che deve uccidere, io da lui interrogato, mentre il traditore sta dubbioso coll'archibugio già alzato, dovessi, o approvar col silenzio, o titubare, o rispondergli, "Si egli è il tale." ... In somiglianti casi, ne quali viene ingiustamente assalita la vostra sincerità, quando non sovvenga altro mezzo più pronto, e più efficace, e quando non basti dire "no'l so"; piantisi pure in faccia a costoro un "No" franco e risoluto, senza pensar ad altro. Imperocchè un tal "no" egli à conforme alla mente universale degli uomini, i quali sono arbitri delle parole, e certamente non le hanno obligate a danno della Republica umana, nè hanno già mai pattuito di usarle in prò di furbi, di spie, d'incendiarii, di masnadieri, e di ladri. Torno a dire, che quel No egli à conforme alla mente universale degli uomini, e a questa mente deve esser unita e collegata anche la vostra. Chi non vede l'utile manifesto, che ne trarrebbero gli assassini di strada, se i passaggieri interrogati se abbian seco oro, o gemme dovissero, o tergiversare, o rispondere, "si che l'abbiamo"; adunque, in tali congiunture, quel "No", che voi proferite (Card. Pallav., lib. iii. c. xi. n. 23 de fide, spe, &c.) resta privo del suo significato e resta appunto agguisa di una moneta, a cui per volere del Principio, sia stato tolto il valore, con cui prima correva; onde in niun modo voi siete reo di menzogna.' Lezione xliv. Prima Parte.

Bolgeni

'Abbiamo dunque bene, e con certezza più che morale, provata una eccezione da porsi alla legge generale di non mentire, cioè, quando non si possa osservare qualche altro precetto più importante se non col dir bugia. Dicono alcuni che nei casi della impossibilità sopra esposta non è bugia, quello che si dice. Ma chi dice così, confonde le idee, e nega l'essenza della cose. Che cosa è la bugia? *Est locutio contra mentem*: così la definiscono tutti. *Atqui* nei casi della impossibilità sovra esposta si parla *contra mentem*: ciò è chiaro ed evidente. Dunque si dice bugia. Distinguiamo la bugia dal peccato. Nei casi detti si dice realmente bugia; ma questa *bugia* non è *peccato* per ragione della impossibilità. Il dire che in quei casi niuno ha diritto d'interrogare; che le parole significano secondo la convenzione comune fra gli uomini; e cose simili, che da alcuni Autori si dicono per esimere da peccato la bugia in quei casi: questo è un attaccarsi a ragioni frivole, e soggette a molte repliche quando si ha la ragione evidente della citata impossibilità.' – Il Possesso, c. 48.

Author in the Mélanges Théologiques

'Il reste donc acquis, et nous n'avons pas le moindre doute sur la vérité de cette conclusion, que si l'intention de tromper le prochain, est essentielle au mensonge, il sera permis de dire ce qu'on sait être faux, en certain cas, comme pour éviter un grand danger. . . . Au reste, que personne ne s'effraie, il ne sera jamais permis de mentir, et en cela nous sommes d'accord avec tous les théologiens: nous nous eloignons d'eux en ce seul point qu'ils appellent *mensonge*, ce qui ne l'est pas pour nous, ou si l'on veut, ils regardent comme mensonge formel et matériel ce qui pour nous est seulement un mensonge matériel.' – Mélanges Théologiques, vime Série, p. 442.

Milton

'*Veracitas* est Virtus qua ei cui aequum est, et quibus de rebus convenit ad bonum proximi, vera dicimus. Psal. xv. 2. Prov. xii. 21, 17; xx. 6. Zech. viii. 16. Eph. iv. 25.

'Huic opponitur dissimulatio vitiosa. Nam omnis non improbatur: non enim semper vera palam expromere necesse habemus; ea tantum reprehenditur quae malitiosa est.

'Secundo opponitur mendacium. Psal. v. 7. xii. 2, 3. Prov. xiii. 5; xix. 5. Joan viii. 44. Apoc. xxii. 15. Mendacio itaque ne Dei quidem causa est utendum. Job xiii. 7.

Mendacium vulgo definitur, quo *falsum anima fallendi verbis factisve significatur*. Sed quoniam saepe usu venit, ut non solum vera dissimulare aut reticere, sed etiam fallendi animo falsa dicere, utile ac salutare proximo sit, danda opera est, ut mendacium quid sit melius definiamus. Neque enim video cur non idem de mendacio, quod de homicidio aliisque rebus, de quibus infra dicetur, nunc dici possit, quae non tam facto, quam objecto et fine agendi ponderanda sunt. Esse enim quos jure optimo fallendos putemus, quis sanus negaverit? quid enim pueros, quid furentes, quid aegrotos, quid ebrios, quid hostes, quid fallentes, quid latrones? (certe juxta illud tritum, *Cui nullum est jus, ei nulla fit injuria*:) an illos ne fallamus religio erit? per hanc tamen definitionem ne illos quidem dictis aut factis fallere licebit. Certe si gladium, aliamve rem quam apud me sanus deposuerit, eidem furenti non reddiderim, cur veritatem non depositam, ei ad quem veritas minime pertineat, male usuro expromam? Enimvero si quidquid cuicunque interroganti respondetur fallendi animo, mendacium est censendum, profecto sanctis viris et prophetis nihil familiarius erat quam mentiri.

'Quid si igitur mendacium hoc modo definiamus? *Mendacium* est cum *quis dolo malo aut veritatem depravat, aut falsum dicit ei, quicunque is sit, cui dicere veritatem ex officio debuerat.* Sic diabolus serpens primus erat mendax, Gen. iii. 4. et Cain, cap. iv. 9. et Sara, cap. xviii. 15. angelis enim merito offensis non satisfecit ingenua confessione: et Abrahamus, cap. xii. 13. et cap. xx. illud enim de Sara tanquam sorore figmentum, ut ipse didicisse poterat in Aegypto, quamvis incolumitatem vitae sibi proposuerat solam, homines tamen inscientes in errorem et alieni cupiditatem induxit: et Davides fugiens, 1 Sam. xxi. 3. debebat enim non celasse Abimelecum quo loco res suae apud regem essent, neque tantum periculum hospiti creare: sic Ananias et Sapphira, Act. v., mentiti sunt.

'Ex hac definitione, 1mo, haud secus atque ex altera, patet, parabolas, hyperbolas, apologos, ironias mendacia non esse: haec enim omnia non fallendi sed erudiendi studio adhibentur. 1 Regum xviii. 27. et xxii. 15. 2do, si fallendi vocem significatione debita sumamus, neminem quidem fallere poterimus, quin eum eadem opera laedamus. Quem igitur nullo modo laedimus, sed vel juvamus, vel ab injuria aut inferenda aut patienda prohibemus, eum certe ne falso quidem millies dicto revera fallimus, sed vero potius beneficio necopinantem afficimus, 3^{tio}, dolos et stratege- mata in bello, modo absit perfidia aut perjurium, non esse mendacia omnes concedunt: quae concessio alteram definitionem plane destruit. Vix enim ullae insidiae aut doli in bello strui possunt, quin palam idque summo fallendi studio dicantur multa quae falsissima sunt: unde per illam definitionem mendacio ab- solvi nequeunt. Hanc igitur potius ob causam licere strategemata dicendum erit, etiam cum mendacio conjuncta, eo quod, si quis est cui verum dicere officii nostri non sit, nihil certe interest an illi, quoties expedit, etiam falsum dicamus: nec video cur hoc in bello magis quam in pace liceat, praesertim quoties injuriam aut periculum a nobismetipsis aut a proximo salutari et probo quodam mendacio depellere licet.

'Quae igitur testimonia scripturae contra mendacium proferun- tur, de eo intelligenda sunt mendacio, quod aut Dei gloriam aut nostrum proximive bonum imminuere videatur. Hujusmodi sunt, praeter ea quae supra citavimus, Lev. xix. Ps. ci. 7. Prov. vi. 16, 17. Jer. ix. 5. His atque aliis hujusmodi locis veritatem dicere jubemur: at cui? non hosti, non furioso, non violento, non sicario; sed proximo, quîcum scilicet pax et justa societas nobis intercedit. Jam vero si veritatem soli proximo dicere jubemur, profecto iis qui nomen proximi non merentur, ne falsum quidem, quoties opus est, dicere vetamur. Qui aliter sentit, ex eo libens quaererem, quonam decalogi praecepto prohibeatur mendacium? respondebit certissime, nono. Age, recitet modo, et mecum sentiet: quidquid enim hic prohibetur, id proximum laedere ostenditur; siquod igitur mendacium non laedit proximum, sub hoc certe mandato nequaquam prohibetur.

'Hinc tot sanctissimos viros theologorum fere judicio mendacii reos merito absolvemus: Abrahamum, Gen. xxii. 5. cum dixit servis suis se reversurum cum filio; fallendi tamen animo, nequid illi suspicarentur; cum ipse persuasus esset mactatum ibi filium se relicturum; nam nisi ita sibi persuasisset, quid hoc magnopere tentationis erat? sed intellexit vir sapiens nihil interesse servorum hoc ut scirent, sibi expedire in praesentia ne scirent. Rebeccam et Jacobum, Gen. xxvii., prudenti enim astutia et cautione aditum sibi muniebant ad jus illud haereditatis quod alter vili vendiderat; ad jus, inquam, et oraculo et redemptione jam suum. At patri imposuit: immo potius errori patris, qui amore praepostero in Esauum ferebatur, tempestive occurrit. Josephum, Gen. xlii. 7, etc. multorum sane mendaciorum hominem, si vulgari illa definitione stetur: quam multa enim dixit non vera, eo animo ut fratres falleret? dolo tamen fratribus non malo, sed utilissimo. Obstetrices Hebraeas, Exod. i. 19, etc., comprobante etiam Deo; fefellerant enim Pharaonem, non laeserant tamen, sed beneficio potius affecerant, dum male faciendi facultatem ademerunt. Mosen, Exod. iii., etiam a Deo jussum iter tridui a Pharaone petere, quasi ad rem divinam faciendam in deserto; eo licet consilio petentem ut Pharaoni verba daret; non causam enim pro causa, vel fictam saltem pro vera profectionis afferebat. Universum populum Israeliticum, Exod. xi. et xii., ab eodem Deo jussum aurum, vasa, vestemque pretiosam ab Aegyptiis mutuam petere; et pollicitum sine dubio reddere: fallendi tamen animo; quidni enim et Dei hostes et hospitii violatores et spoliatores jamdiu suos? Raabbam, Jos. ii. 4, 5. splendide mentitam, nec sine fide; fallebat enim quos Deus falli voluit, populares licet suos, et magistratus: quos voluit ille salvos conservabat; civile officium religioni recte posthabuit. Ehudem, qui duplici mendacio Eglonem fefellit, Judic. iii. 19, 20. nec injuria tamen, quippe hostem; idque Dei non injussu. Jaelem, quae confugientem ad se Siseram blanditiis perdidit, Judic. iv. 18, 19. hostem licet Dei magis quam suum: quamquam id non mendacio, sed pia fraude factum vult Junius, quasi quidquam interesset. Jonathanem, dum rogatus ab amico Davide causam ejus absentiae fictam refert patri, 1 Sam. xx. 6, 28. malebat enim innocentis saluti quam patris crudelitati officiosum se esse; et majoris erat momenti ad charitatem ut innocentis amici consuleretur vitae, interposito licet mendacio, quam ut patri ad maleficium exequendum veritatis inutili confessione mos gereretur. Hos atque alios tot viros sanctissimos vulgari illa definitione mendacii condemnatos, vetuli ex limbo quodam patrum disquisitio haec veritatis accuratior educit.'

EDITOR'S NOTES

EDITOR'S NOTES

PREFACE

1. *St. Alfonso da Liguori* (1696–1787), doctor of the Church and founder of the Redemptorist order, was an important target for anti-Catholic polemic, not only because he was considered the standard Roman Catholic authority on moral theology but also because of his exuberant devotion to the Virgin Mary.

2. *Oakeley's* Frederick Oakeley (1802–80), a fellow of Balliol, became minister of Margaret Street chapel, London, where he introduced ritualistic Tractarianism. He was, along with W. G. Ward, the leader of the younger, more extreme Romanizing Tractarians. Converted to Rome in 1845, he became a priest and published *Historical Notes on the Tractarian Movement* in 1865.

3. *economies* The early Christian principle of economy or reserve, according to which the mysteries of Christianity should not be openly exposed to the gaze of the unbelieving or uninstructed, was advocated for the sake of reverence by the Tractarians, much to the suspicion of their opponents.

4. *'Ars . . . artem'* It is art to conceal art.

5. *Whately* See ch. I, ed. n. 27.

6. *Praevalebit Veritas* Truth will prevail.

7. *scouted* Derided.

8. *Stonyhurst* Jesuit college in Lancashire.

9. *Oscott* See ch. IV, ed. n. 105.

10. *in . . . Universitatis* In the bosom of the University.

11. *'my . . . house'* Genesis 12: 1.

CHAPTER I

1. *'Secretum . . . mihi'* My secret is my own. Isaiah 24: 16. Frequently used as a maxim on humility by St Philip Neri (1515–95), the founder of the Oratory, the English branch of which Newman established in Birmingham in 1848.

2. *Remnants of Time* The Improvement of the Mind, with a discourse on Education, and the Remnants of Time, employed in prose and verse (1741),

sec. xvii, by Isaac Watts (1674–1748), the hymn-writer and Nonconformist minister.

3. *the village*   Ham, near Richmond, Surrey. Grey Court House, the family country home for the first six years of Newman's life, still stands.

4. *the school*   Ealing School (no longer in existence) near London, where Newman was a boarder from the age of seven to nearly sixteen.

5. *My brother*   Francis William (1805–97), professor of Latin at University College, London, was Newman's younger brother, who abandoned Evangelical Christianity for unbelief and became a well-known proponent of various secular causes.

6. *Warwick Street Chapel*   Off Regent Street, then the Catholic chapel of the Bavarian embassy, which Newman's diary (*LD* i. 7) records he visited on 27 January 1811, a visit which may explain the picture of the rosary he apparently drew a couple of weeks later.

7. *Littlemore*   A village close to Oxford and then part of the parish of the university church of St Mary the Virgin of which Newman was vicar (1828–43). He built a church for the village in 1836, and in 1842 moved to a row of cottages which he had bought and where he lived a quasi-monastic community life with a group of associates until his reception into the Roman Catholic Church in 1845.

8. *Radcliffe's*   Ann Radcliffe (1764–1823), the author of *The Mysteries of Udolpho* (1794) and other Gothic novels.

9. *Porter's*   Either Jane Porter (1776–1850) or her sister Anna Maria (1780–1832), both writers of popular historical romances.

10. *Paine's*   Thomas Paine (1737–1809), the deist and author of *The Age of Reason; Being an Investigation of True and Fabulous Theology* (1795, 1811), which contains his attack on the Old Testament.

11. *Miracles*   David Hume (1711–76), the sceptical Scottish philosopher and author of the anti-Christian *Philosophical Essays concerning Human Understanding* (1748), which contains the essay 'Of Miracles'.

12. *1816*   Actually, from the beginning of August to 21 December when the autumn term ended. Instead of leaving school at the end of the summer term, Newman had been obliged to stay on through the summer holidays and for another term because of the closure of his father's bank in the economic crisis after the Napoleonic wars, when his father was forced to become a manager of a brewery in Alton, Hampshire. During August he suffered the first of the 'three great illnesses' of his life, 'the first, keen terrible one, when I was a boy of 15, and it made me a Christian – with experiences before and after, awful, and known only to God'. (*AW* 150, 268.)

13. *fell*   In spite of all the Evangelical influences, five years later in 1821 Newman doubted whether his had been a genuinely Evangelical

conversion: '. . . my own feelings, as far as I remember, were so different from any account I have ever read . . .' And again five years later, once more writing in his private journal, he noted that his conversion had not been emotionally *'violent'* in the 'special' Evangelical manner, 'but a returning to, a renewing of, principles, under the power of the Holy Spirit, which I had *already* felt, and in a measure acted on, when young'. (*A W* 79, 166, 172.)

14. *Walter Mayers* (1790–1828), an Evangelical master at Ealing School, became curate of Over Worton, Oxfordshire, where Newman was to preach his first sermon and where he preached the funeral sermon of his mentor.

15. *Romaine's* William Romaine (1714–95), a member of the extreme Calvinist Evangelical wing of the Church of England and famous as a preacher, eloquently expounded the doctrine of final perseverance in *The Triumph of Faith* (1795), according to which the elect are predestined to be saved.

16. *Thomas Scott* (1747–1821) recounted the story of his conversion from Unitarianism to (Calvinist) Christianity in *The Force of Truth* (1779), his autobiography, which, with its insistence on the importance of conscience as a guide to truth, greatly influenced Newman and which may have served as a model for the *Apologia*. His commentary on the Bible (4 vols., 1788–92) became the standard authority for Evangelicals. His *Essays on the Most Important Subjects in Religion* appeared in 1793. He was vicar of Aston Sandford, near Oxford, from 1801 till death.

17. *Daniel Wilson* (1778–1858), the Evangelical minister of St John's chapel, Bedford Row, Bloomsbury, from 1812 to 1824, became bishop of Calcutta in 1832 and was a strong opponent of the Oxford movement.

18. *Jones* William Jones (1726–1800), curate of Nayland, Suffolk, a high-church theologian and author of *The Catholic Doctrine of the Trinity proved by above an Hundred short and clear Arguments, expressed in the terms of the Holy Scripture* (1756).

19. *Athanasian Creed*, probably dating from the late fourth or fifth century, sets out the doctrines of the Trinity and incarnation in a series of brief propositions. Enjoined as a profession of faith in the Thirty-nine Articles, it was included in the Book of Common Prayer.

20. *Antinomianism*, the early heretical doctrine that Christians are freed by grace from the moral law, was revived by the Protestant reformers' insistence on justification by faith alone and was characteristic of Calvinists.

21. *justified* According to the Protestant reformers, to be regenerate or

to be born again is the same as being justified by faith in Christ's atonement; whereas the Catholic teaching is that regeneration or new life comes through baptism but that justification or being acceptable to God depends on works as well as faith.

22. *Law's*   William Law (1686–1761), Non-juror, whose *Serious Call to a Devout and Holy Life* (1729) was widely read in the eighteenth century, influencing both Dr Johnson and the two Wesleys.

23. *History*   Joseph Milner (1744–97), one of the founders of Evangelicalism in the Church of England, author of the five-volume *History of the Church of Christ* (1794–1809).

24. *Prophecies*   Thomas Newton (1704–82), bishop of Bristol, author of the widely influential *Dissertation on the Prophecies, which have been remarkably fulfilled, and at this time are fulfilling in the world* (3 vols., 1754–8).

25. *predicted*   Daniel 7: 7ff.; 2 Thessalonians 2: 3ff.; 1 John 2: 18, 22; Apocalypse 17–18.

26. *1822*   Newman was an undergraduate at Trinity College, Oxford from 1817 to 1820. In 1822 he was elected a fellow of Oriel College, which had become the leading academic college at Oxford and whose leading dons were called 'Noetics', an Aristotelian term meaning those who use their minds.

27. *Whately*   Richard Whately (1787–1863) had to resign his fellowship on marrying in 1821, when he accepted the living of Halesworth, Suffolk. In 1831 he resigned the Drummond chair of political economy, to which he had been appointed in 1829, to become archbishop of Dublin. The book for which he is chiefly remembered is his pioneering *Elements of Logic* (1826), which Newman at this time helped him to write.

28. *Hawkins*   Edward Hawkins (1789–1882), elected a fellow of Oriel in 1813 and provost in 1828, was appointed vicar of the university church of St Mary's in 1823.

29. *curacy*   Newman was ordained deacon in June 1824 and worked as a curate in St Clement's parish until Easter 1826.

30. *provoked*   Newman had voted for Hawkins in the election for provost, which he soon came to regret because of what he considered Hawkins's high-handed manner, and particularly because the provost opposed Newman's attempts to tighten up undergraduate discipline. Hostilities came to a head with a plan by Newman to reform the tutorial system on more pastoral and personal lines, a disagreement that ended in Newman's enforced resignation as a tutor.

31. *Sumner*   John Bird Sumner (1780–1862) became archbishop of Canterbury in 1848. He published *Apostolical Preaching Considered in an Examination of St Paul's Epistles* in 1815.

32. *White* Joseph Blanco White (1775–1841), a former Catholic priest in Spain, born of Irish and Spanish parents, came to England in 1810 and became an Anglican clergyman. In 1826 he entered Oriel and became a member of the senior common room. He eventually moved from Anglicanism to Unitarianism.

33. *sermon* Preached on 31 May 1818, it was published in 1819 as *A Dissertation upon the Use and Importance of Unauthoritative Tradition as an Introduction to the Christian Doctrines*.

34. *Society* Newman joined the British and Foreign Bible Society, which had been founded by Evangelicals in 1804, in 1824 and resigned in 1830.

35. *James* William James (1787–1861) was elected a fellow of Oriel in 1809.

36. *Apostolical Succession* is the doctrine that bishops are the successors of the first Apostles in an uninterrupted line.

37. *Analogy* The Analogy of Religion, Natural and Revealed, to the Constitution and Course of Nature (1736) by Joseph Butler (1692–1752), bishop of Durham.

38. *Origen* See ed. n. 89 to this chapter.

39. *Article* 'Poetry, with Reference to Aristotle's Poetics' was published in January 1829 in the first number of the short-lived *London Review*, which was edited by Blanco White, and later reprinted in *Ess.* i. 1–26.

40. *correspondence* See Additional Notes.

41. *anti-Erastian* Erastianism, the heresy that the State controls the Church, takes its name from Thomas Erastus (1524–83).

42. *Froude* Richard Hurrell Froude (1803–36), the brother of the historian James Anthony Froude, was educated at Oriel and elected a fellow in 1826. Because of the onset of tuberculosis, he left for the West Indies in 1834, but returned the next year without recovering his health to his father's house in Devon, where he died in 1836.

43. *tenets* Newman suspected Whately of holding the Sabellian heresy, according to which there were not really three persons in the Trinity, but rather the persons only existed relatively to us as aspects of God. Whately also denied original sin in the orthodox sense.

44. *Arianizing* The Arians of the fourth century denied the full divinity of Christ as being of one substance with God the Father. The reference is to the Easter sermon preached by Newman in Oriel chapel, which argued for the subordination of the Son to the Father on the lines followed by the early Eastern fathers.

45. *Defensio Fidei Nicaenae* (1685) by George Bull (1634–1710), bishop of St David's, maintained against the seventeenth-century Jesuit

scholar Petavius that the doctrine of the Trinity was already developed before the Council of Nicaea (325), so that the Nicene creed is only the natural key to interpreting the ante-Nicene Fathers.

46. *Remains*   *Remains of the Late Reverend Richard Hurrell Froude, M. A.*, a collection of his sermons, letters, journals, and papers, edited by Newman and Keble in two parts (4 vols., 1838–9), caused a sensation because of Froude's hostility to the Protestant reformers and his Catholic sentiments. See pt. I, vol. i, p. 245.

47. *language*   See 'The Life of Apollonius Tyaneus; with a comparison of the miracles of scripture and those related elsewhere, as regards their respective object, nature, and evidence', published in the *Encyclopaedia Metropolitana* of 1826, and reprinted in two separate parts as 'The Life of Apollonius of Tyana' in *HS* i. 302–31 and 'The Miracles of Scripture' in *Mir.* 1–94.

48. *Middleton*   Conyers Middleton (1683–1750) in *A Free Inquiry into the Miraculous Powers which are Supposed to have Subsisted in the Christian Church from the Earliest Ages through Several Successive Centuries* (1749) denied the possibility of miracles after the time of the Apostles.

49. *bereavement*   In November 1827 Newman collapsed from nervous exhaustion while examining at Oxford. On 5 January 1828 his youngest sister Mary died suddenly.

50. *affair*   Sir Robert Peel (1788–1850), then Home Secretary in the Tory government of the Duke of Wellington, had been forced to accept Catholic emancipation because of the threat of civil war in Ireland if Daniel O'Connell was refused a seat in parliament. Having originally opposed the measure because of its implicit threat to the establishment of the Church of England, Peel now resigned as MP for the University of Oxford, which was still exclusively Anglican, but agreed to be nominated by his supporters for re-election – unsuccessfully, in the event.

51. *the Petition* was presented annually.

52. *Convocation*   The legislative assembly of the university.

53. '*two-bottle-orthodox*'   Newman explained this reference in a note to the French edition of the *Apologia*: ' . . . amongst ecclesiastics who enjoy great revenues and have not much to do (such as the members of the Cathedral chapters), many have long since deteriorated in the pursuit of their personal advantage. Those who held high positions in great towns have been led to adopt the habits of a great position and of external display, and have boasted a formal orthodoxy which was cold and almost entirely devoid of interior life. These self-indulgent pastors have for a long time been nick-named "two-bottle orthodox", as though their greatest religious zeal manifested itself in the drinking of port wine to the health of

"the Church and King".' (*Apologia*, ed. Wilfrid Ward (London, 1913), xxvi–vii.)

54. *Keble* John Keble (1792–1866), who came from a high Anglican background, was elected a fellow of Oriel in 1811, but left Oxford in 1823 to become a country clergyman. After the phenomenal success of *The Christian Year* (see ed. n. 70 to this chapter) he became non-resident professor of poetry at Oxford.

55. *verses* 'A Thanksgiving', *VV* 45.

56. *Copleston* Edward Copleston (1776–1849) was provost of Oriel from 1814 to 1827, when he became bishop of Llandaff.

57. '*Nunquam . . . solus*' Never less alone than when alone. Cf. Cicero, *Officiis*, III. i. 1; *De Re Publica*, I. xvii. 27.

58. *Pusey* Edward Bouverie Pusey (1800–82), elected a fellow of Oriel in 1823, was appointed Regius Professor of Hebrew in 1828. After Newman's conversion to Rome, he became the leader of the Oxford movement.

59. *Essays* Apart from the articles already referred to in ed. nn. 39 and 47 to this chapter, Newman also contributed the 'Personal and Literary Character of Cicero' (1824) to the *Encyclopaedia Metropolitana*; this was reprinted in *HS* i. 239–300.

60. *Sermon* 'The Philosophical Temper, first enjoined by the Gospel' (1826), *US* 1–15.

61. *persons* Samuel Rickards (1796–1865), fellow of Oriel 1819–22, vicar of Stowlangtoft, Suffolk from 1832, was a close friend of Newman and his family, but soon became alarmed by the Tractarian movement and broke off relations. Henry Arthur Woodgate (1801–74), fellow of St John's till 1837 when he was appointed rector of Belbroughton, near Birmingham, became friendly with Newman in 1825; and on reading this reference to himself wrote to resume the friendship.

62. *probationer Fellows* were not confirmed in their fellowships until the end of their first year, after which they could retain their fellowships for life unless they married.

63. *Robert Isaac Wilberforce* (1802–57), the second son of William Wilberforce the Evangelical philanthropist, was elected a fellow of Oriel in 1826 and in 1828 became a tutor along with Froude and Newman, whose attempt to reform the college tutorial system he strongly supported. A leading Tractarian theologian, he became a Catholic in 1854, but died shortly before his ordination.

64. *Tower* The room in the tower above Oriel gate was where candidates for fellowships were examined orally and where they were later summoned to receive the news of their election.

65. *day* Newman was elected a fellow on 12 April 1822.

66. *John William Bowden* (1798–1844), Newman's closest undergraduate friend at Trinity, was a keen lay supporter of the Tractarian movement, for which he wrote some of the *Tracts for the Times*, until his premature death. He was a commissioner of stamps.

67. *Milman*   Henry Hart Milman (1791–1868), dean of St Paul's from 1849, was a liberal Anglican historian (see ch. III, ed. n. 110).

68. *residence*   In fact, Keble did not leave Oriel till 1823.

69. *Remains*   Pt. I, vol. i, p. 438.

70. *Christian Year* (1827), a phenomenally successful collection of poems for Sundays and other important liturgical days and occasions, was firmly based on the spirituality of the Book of Common Prayer.

71. *article*   The ninth article of the Apostles' creed contains the doctrine of the spiritual communion in Christ of all Christians, whether living or dead.

72. *Berkeley*   George Berkeley (1685–1753), the idealist philosopher, maintained in *A Treatise Concerning the Principles of Human Knowledge* (1710) that material things only really exist in so far as they are perceived by spiritual beings, and that the world itself only substantially exists in the mind of God.

73. *saying*   Attributed to a soldier before the battle of Blenheim.

74. *Psalm*   32: 8, 9.

75. *Poem*   *The Christian Year* (Oxford, 1827), 148.

76. *Miller*   John Miller (1787–1858), fellow of Worcester and a close friend of Keble, delivered the 1817 Bampton lectures at Oxford on *The Adaptation of Holy Scripture to the Real State of Human Nature*.

77. *found*   Especially in the not yet published *An Essay in Aid of a Grammar of Assent* (1870).

78. *Essay*   'Essay on the Miracles recorded in Ecclesiastical History' was written in 1842 as a preface to Newman's partial translation of Fleury's *Ecclesiastical History*, reprinted separately in 1843 as 'An Essay on the Miracles recorded in the Ecclesiastical History of the Early Ages', and later reprinted as 'The Miracles of Early Ecclesiastical History, compared with those of Scripture, as regards their Nature, Credibility, and Evidence' in *Mir.* 1–94.

79. *maxim*   In *The Religion of Protestants a Safe Way to Salvation* (1638) by William Chillingworth (1602–44). See op. cit. (London, 1719), 81.

80. *Real Presence*   The Catholic doctrine that Christ is really, as opposed to symbolically, present in the consecrated bread and wine of the eucharist.

81. *Reform Bill* of 1832 extended the franchise and was the beginning of modern parliamentary democracy.

82. *St. Ignatius* (*c.*35–*c.*107), either the second or third bishop of Antioch after St Peter, was martyred at Rome. On his way there he

wrote seven epistles to different churches which are especially important for their teaching on the episcopacy.

83. *St. Justin* (*c*.100–*c*.165), the convert philosopher and lay apologist.

84. *1830* In March 1831 Newman was invited by Hugh James Rose (see ch. II, ed. n. 4) to contribute a history of the general councils of the church to a new library of theological works of which Rose was co-editor with Archdeacon William Rowe Lyall (1788–1857). The understanding was that the book would be a kind of introduction to the work on the Thirty-nine Articles that Newman had proposed himself.

85. *The Arians of the Fourth Century* was published by Rivington in 1833, having been turned down for the theological library by Lyall on the grounds that it was a history of the Arian heresy rather than of the councils, that it was too specialized for the general reader, and that Newman's theological views, particularly on tradition, seemed more Roman Catholic than Protestant. The historical originality of Newman's first book lay in ascribing the origins of the Arian heresy to Antioch rather than Alexandria and to Aristotelian rather than Platonic influence; its theological topicality lay in the parallel it openly drew between Arianism and contemporary religious liberalism.

86. *117* The reference is to the pagination of the first edition, but it is a slip or misprint for 217.

87. *works* Newman took Bull's *Defensio Fidei Nicaenae* as his 'key' to his study of the Fathers at this time.

88. *Athanasius* (296–373), St, bishop from 328, played a prominent role at the Council of Nicaea, the creed of which he so vigorously defended against the Arians that he suffered exile for a good part of his episcopate.

89. *Origen* (*c*.185–*c*.254), whose chief exegetical work was his edition of the Old Testament or *Hexapla*, was defended by Newman against the later charge of heterodoxy on the ground that his theological speculations were on points of faith not yet defined and of secondary importance.

90. *Dionysius* the Great (d. *c*.264), bishop of Alexandria and a pupil of Origen, whom he succeeded as head of the catechetical school at Alexandria in *c*.233 and as bishop in 247.

91. *Clement* of Alexandria (*c*.150–*c*.215), St, became head of the catechetical school in 190. He applied the ideas of Greek philosophy, which he defended as coming from God, to the Christian revelation.

92. *'thoughts . . . given'* Keble, *The Christian Year*, xxvii, 'Third Sunday in Lent'.

93. *'at . . . manners'*   Hebrews 1: 1.

94. *Sermon*   'The Powers of Nature', *PS* ii. 361–2, 364.

95. *Children*   Shadrach, Meschach, and Abednego. Daniel 3.

96. δαιμόνια   Spirits.

97. *Daniel*   10: 13.

98. *Apocalypse*   1: 20.

99. *Samuel Francis Wood* (1810–43) was a pupil of Newman at Oriel, and became a strong Tractarian.

100. *Angels*   See Genesis 6: 2, where the accepted reading is 'sons of God', not angels. However, the early patristic tradition, reflecting a reading to be found in the Septuagint and following the later Jewish interpretation, held that these sons of God were in fact angels.

101. *'Hippoclides . . . care'*   A proverbial saying. When Cleisthenes the tyrant told Hippoclides, the favoured suitor for his daughter's hand, 'You have danced away your wife' because he had stood on his head and used his arms for legs at the nuptial feast, Hippoclides immediately replied, 'Hippoclides doesn't care.' See Herodotus, vi. 126–9.

102. *Arians*   *Ari.* 65ff.

103. *Revolution*   At the end of July 1830 Charles X, the last of the Bourbons, was dethroned in favour of the 'Citizen King', Louis-Philippe.

104. *Reform*   The great Reform Bill was finally passed in June 1832 by Earl Grey's Whig administration which had come to power in November 1830. On moving the second reading of the bill in October 1831, Grey had appealed to the bishops not to vote against it, although he had commended them for having already decided they must set their house in order by removing ecclesiastical abuses like pluralism. In the event, the bishops voted overwhelmingly against the bill, fearful that a reformed parliament including non-Anglicans would interfere with the established Church, as a result of which Grey's words were taken out of context and quoted against them.

105. *Blomfield*   Charles James Blomfield (1786–1857), bishop of London from 1828 to 1856, was an active supporter of church reform.

106. *Non-jurors* were those who refused to swear allegiance to William and Mary in 1689 because of the oath they had already taken to James II, effectively forming a separate church which lasted till the early nineteenth century. Maintaining the high-church tradition of the Carolines, they were the precursors of the Tractarians who admired their resistance to Erastianism.

107. *Ryder*   Henry Dudley Ryder (1777–1836), bishop of Lichfield from

1824, was the first Evangelical to be raised to the episcopate when he became bishop of Gloucester in 1815.

108. *Mystery* i.e. of the Trinity.

109. *'Incessu . . . Dea'* By her step she was revealed as a goddess. (*Aeneid*, i. 405.)

110. *'Look . . . that'* Shakespeare, *Hamlet*, III. iv. 53.

111. *duties* In June 1830 Newman had been given an ultimatum by the provost, that if he did not revert to the old tutorial methods he would not be given any more students. Since Newman refused, he was forced gradually to relinquish his tutorship.

112. *Father* Robert Hurrell Froude (1770–1859), a high churchman, was archdeacon of Totnes and rector of Dartington, Devon.

113. *Lyra Apostolica*, published in 1836, was a collection of poems, nearly two-thirds of which were by Newman, which appeared first in the *British Magazine* (1833–6), edited by Rose. Hoping to build on what Keble had accomplished in *The Christian Year*, Newman and Froude intended the poems to be an effective contribution to spreading the ideas of the Oxford movement. Other contributors were Keble, Isaac Williams, J. W. Bowden, and R. I. Wilberforce. Most of Newman's own poems were republished in *VV*.

114. *verses* 'Angelic Guidance', dated 3 December 1832, *VV* 73.

115. *Dean* Canon Lanzon, dean of the cathedral.

116. *Santini* Fortunato Santini (1778–1862), a composer and authority on church music.

117. *Wiseman* Nicholas Wiseman (1802–65), of Spanish–Irish parentage, was rector of the English College from 1828 to 1840, when he became first coadjutor to the vicar apostolic of the Midland district and then in the same year vicar apostolic of the central district and president of Oscott College. He followed the Tractarian movement closely, established Newman and his companions at Maryvale, the old Oscott college, in 1845, and helped Newman found the English Oratory at Birmingham. In 1850 Wiseman became cardinal archbishop of Westminster.

118. *Priest* Newman made the request 'when half light headed'. See *AW* 135.

119. *Tenebrae* On Good Friday, 5 April 1833, Newman attended the old pre-Vatican II holy week service of tenebrae (darkness), so called because the candles were extinguished gradually during the singing of the office, which was characterized by the chanting of the fourth penitential psalm, the 'Miserere'. The special attraction would have been Allegri's famous setting of that psalm, no copies of which were allowed to leave the Vatican.

120. *'All . . . divine'* Byron, *Bride of Abydos*, I. i.

121. *Bill*   A bill to suppress ten out of the twenty-two sees of the established Church of Ireland, as well as to make the clergy pay tax, was brought into parliament in February and carried in June 1833.

122. *preacherships*   The banqueting house of Inigo Jones, which survived the destruction by fire of the royal palace at Whitehall, was converted into a chapel, and George III established preacherships there under the direction of the bishop of London as dean of the royal chapels. Soon after becoming bishop, Blomfield decided to replace the twenty-four preachers selected equally from Oxford and Cambridge with only one or two preachers from each university.

123. *Arnold*   Thomas Arnold (1795–1842) was elected a fellow of Oriel in 1815 and became the great reforming headmaster of Rugby in 1828. In his letters of the time Newman satirized Arnold's *Principles of Church Reform* (1833) which advocated that the Church of England should become a truly comprehensive national church by admitting all religious believers except Jews, Roman Catholics and Quakers.

124. *conversation*   One evening, while he was in Rome (2 March–9 April 1833), Newman dined with the Froudes and Anthony Grant, a fellow of New College, who wrote an account of the conversation after dinner to a mutual friend of his and Arnold, which the friend sent on to Arnold. Edward Neale, a pupil of Newman at Oriel, had joined the party and was talking with Newman about some passages in Niebuhr's history of Rome which seemed to imply a religious scepticism. According to Grant's account, Neale remarked that 'Arnold considered him to be a Christian', to which Newman replied, 'But Arnold must first show (or prove, I forget which) that he is one himself.' Arnold complained through Grant, to whom Newman wrote that while he could not remember using the words, it was true that he did regard Arnold's 'ecclesiastical principles' as 'unscriptural, unchristian, and open to ecclesiastical censure'. (*LD* iv. 105–8.)

125. *began*   On 16 March 1833 Newman sent two instalments to Rose for the projected *Lyra Apostolica* section of the *British Magazine*.

126. *Bunsen*   Baron von Christian C. J. Bunsen (1791–1860), the Prussian theological scholar and ambassador to the Holy See (1823–39). In 1841 he was sent as a special envoy to London, when he played a leading role in the establishment of the Anglo-Prussian bishopric of Jerusalem (see ch. III).

127. *words*   Cf. Homer, *Iliad*, xviii. 125.

128. '*Exoriare aliquis!*'   Arise, some (avenger)! Virgil, *Aeneid*, iv. 625. From Dido's great soliloquy on hearing that Aeneas has deserted her.

129. *Thalaba*   Robert Southey's romantic poem *Thalaba the Destroyer*

(1801) tells the story of how a young Arab called Thalaba, with faith as his tribesman, avenges his father by destroying the evil powers who murdered him.

130. *leave*   Froude and Newman first called on Wiseman on 3 April, and then again on 6 April, when they learned to their dismay that there was no prospect of reunion with Rome without full acceptance of all the teachings of the Council of Trent. Newman seems to have spoken much less dramatically than on the second occasion (see next paragraph) when he used virtually the same words. As he recalled a few years later, the words on this occasion, 'though sincerely said . . . were not deeply pointedly? said, but in answer to the question how long we stayed there, I said that we had work at home'. (*A W* 136.)

131. *Sicily*   Newman and the Froudes left Rome on 9 April, when they parted company as the Froudes were returning to England, while Newman wanted to revisit Sicily which, with its Greek and Roman remains, had fascinated him on his first brief visit in February. He had to wait in Naples till 19 April for a sailing and arrived in Messina on the 21st. He took with him a Neapolitan servant called Gennaro who had been a sailor on board the *Victory* at the Battle of Trafalgar.

132. *Leonforte*   On 22 April they set off on foot southwards, visiting Taormini, Mt Etna and Catania, from where they took a boat to Syracuse. Blown off course by the sirocco, they had to spend the night in a cove before returning to Catania, by which time Newman was already feeling feverish symptoms. After spending a night at Adernò, they reached Leonforte on 2 May; the next day Newman had to stay in bed seriously ill with the gastric or typhoid fever, of which there was an epidemic. At the time Newman thought it was a punishment for his sins (see ed. n. 133 to this chapter), but a year later he was sure it was an attempt by the devil to prevent his doing the work he was called to do, i.e. the Oxford movement. He came later to see it as one of the 'three great illnesses' of his life, the others being those of 1816 and 1827, which were also decisive turning-points for him. (*A W* 121–2, 268.)

133. *directions*   'I gave him a direction to write to, if I died (Froude's) but I said "I do not think I shall" – "I have not sinned against light" or "God has still work for me to do." I think the latter.' However, as Newman recorded earlier in the wonderfully vivid account of 'My Illness in Sicily', which he wrote up in 1834–5 and 1840, already while he was in bed at Leonforte, 'I felt and kept saying to myself "I have not sinned against light."' He explains there that in his feverish state he was reproaching himself for 'self will' over the

Oriel tutorship and for insisting on returning to Sicily against the Froudes' wishes and also in general for not living up to the high ideals he preached: 'Yet still I said to myself "I have not sinned against light."' (*A W* 125–6.)

134. *Castro-Giovanni*   Refusing to accept that he was seriously ill, Newman had insisted on leaving Leonforte for Palermo on 6 May; but only with great difficulty managed to reach Castro-Giovanni that evening.

135. *May*   Newman left Castro-Giovanni on 25 May and reached Palermo on the 27th.

136. *inn*   I.e. at an inn *en route* to Palermo. For the incident, see *A W* 136.

137. *impatience*   Newman does not record the effect of personal experience of Roman Catholicism on his imagination, but it is indicated by the opening lines of a poem he wrote in Palermo on the Church of Rome, supposedly the Antichrist, as 'The Good Samaritan': 'Oh that thy creed were sound! / For thou dost soothe the heart, thou Church of Rome, / By thy unwearied watch and varied round / Of service, in thy Saviour's holy home.' (*V V* 153.)

138. *last*   On 13 June, having left Gennaro to return to his wife and family in Naples.

139. *lines*   'The Pillar of the Cloud', written on 16 June, usually known by its opening words, had already become a highly popular hymn in Newman's time.

140. *last*   Having been held up at Palermo, then on the voyage, and again at Lyons, which he reached on 30 June but was unable to leave till 2 July because his ankles were so swollen – Newman became convinced that 'some unseen power, good or bad, was resisting my return'; but he was also sure that this 'severe lesson of patience' came as a test from God (*LD* iii. 310). After a night in Paris, he set off for Dieppe next evening via Rouen, and took a steamship for Brighton; arriving in London on the night of the 8th, he finally reached his mother's house at Rose Hill, Oxford at about 7 o'clock on the evening of the 9th. There he found his brother Francis, who had been involved for the last three years in a mission to Persia led by one of the founders of the Plymouth Brethren, having in 1830 resigned his fellowship at Balliol because of his refusal to subscribe to the Thirty-nine Articles.

141. *Sermon*   Keble had been appointed by the vice-chancellor to preach at the customary service in St Mary the Virgin for the summer assizes in Oxford. He did so against the background of the bill to reform the Church of Ireland, and insisted that the Church was of divine origin rather than a department of the State.

CHAPTER II

1. *Palmer*   William Palmer (1803–85), a graduate of Trinity College, Dublin, became a fellow of Worcester in 1831.

2. *Palmer of Magdalen* (1811–79), elected a fellow of Magdalen in 1832, went as a tutor to the new university of Durham where he became a Tractarian under the influence of H. J. Rose, but returned to Magdalen in 1836. He became very interested in the Eastern Orthodox Church, but his attempts to gain recognition of the Anglican Church as a branch of the Catholic Church were rebuffed by the Russian Church which refused him the right of intercommunion and the Greek Church which insisted on his unconditional rebaptism as a prerequisite of membership. Eventually in 1855 he became a Catholic in Rome where he spent the rest of his life. As his literary executor, Newman in 1882 edited with a preface his *Notes of a Visit to the Russian Church in the Years 1840, 1841*.

3. *Arthur Perceval* (1799–1853), a graduate of Oriel, became rector of East Horsley, Surrey in 1824 and in 1826 chaplain to George IV, and subsequently to William IV and Victoria.

4. *Rose*   Hugh James Rose (1795–1838), a graduate of Trinity College, Cambridge, went to Germany in 1824, where he studied the new rationalist biblical criticism, which he attacked on his return in 1825 as select preacher at Cambridge, his sermons being published as *The State of the Protestant Religion in Germany* (1825). In 1830 he became rector of Hadleigh, Suffolk, where a meeting with Froude, Palmer and Perceval from 25 to 29 July 1833 was really the beginning of what became known as the Oxford movement. Newman dedicated to him the fourth volume of *PS*.

5. *Pro Ecclesia Dei*   For the Church of God.

6. *letter*   Of 17 March 1834; Rose's reply of 24 March elicited an apology from Newman on 30 March. See *LD* iv. 206–7, 223–5.

7. *the penny post* did not in fact come into operation till 1840.

8. *Gloucestershire*   Keble was curate of Southrop, near Fairford, until 1836 when he became vicar of Hursley in Hampshire.

9. *Tracts*   The first by Newman appeared in September 1833, 'Thoughts on the Ministerial Commission, respectfully addressed to the clergy'. Newman wrote or edited a third of the *Tracts for the Times*, of which nearly a quarter were reprints and anthologies of works by Anglican divines.

10. *Hampden*   See ed. n. 53 to this chapter.

11. *Edinburgh Review*   xxxv (October 1821), 254.

12. *letter*   Of 20 July 1834, published in *A Letter to the Rev. Thomas*

Arnold, D.D., by the Hon. and Rev. A. P. Perceval, BCL (London, 1841), 39–40.

13. *è cathedrâ*   From the chair (of a bishop), i.e. with authority.

14. *series*   There were five, appearing on 24, 31 October; 7, 11, 14 November 1833; they were privately reprinted in 1871.

15. *'Temperance Societies'*   Principally, the British and Foreign Temperance Society, founded in 1831. Newman's hostility was based on his suspicion of the growing secularization of morality, which he thought should be based on religious faith.

16. *seventeenth*   I.e. the catholicizing Caroline divines, the most famous being Lancelot Andrewes, rather than the Protestant reformers.

17. *high*   I.e. the so-called 'high-and-dry' party which upheld the traditions of the Church of England, but for conservative rather than doctrinal reasons.

18. *man*   Solomon in Proverbs 26: 5.

19. *Tract 15*   'On the Apostolical Succession in the English Church', Newman's revised and completed version of a draft by Palmer of Worcester.

20. *Apostolica*   Originally called 'Zeal before Love' (20 November 1832), it was retitled 'Zeal and Love' in *VV* 64.

21. *Sermons*   'The Religion of the Day' (26 August 1832), *PS* i. 320.

22. *passage*   *Ari.* 234–5.

23. *dignitary*   See *Ess.* i. 279–80, where Newman denies he was speaking of 'persecution', but 'of the duty of *cross-examining*, pressing hard *in argument*, and forcing into *consequences*, the originator of an heretical opinion . . . since a heresiarch, instead of hiding his heresy from himself under ambiguous phrases, should have its full *consequences*, its fullest developed malignity, wrought out in his own instance, instead of its running its course through other minds, and growing by degree into its full proportions after perhaps his death'. (*Ess.* i. 279 n.)

24. *Arius* (*c*.250–*c*.336), a priest of Alexandria, was condemned at the Council of Nicaea (335) for holding that the Son of God was not God by nature but created by God.

25. *burned*   Later Newman felt that he had conceded too much, 'for there is nothing whatever . . . about civil punishment in the passage in question. The notice of Arius's *banishment* occurs in a subsequent part of my volume, which throughout discountenances civil penalties for religious opinions as leading to hypocritical conformity.' (*Ess.* i. 280 n.)

26. *one*   Charles Girdlestone (1797–1881), fellow of Balliol 1818–26, who offered Newman (through Pusey) his first curacy at St Clement's, Oxford in 1824, wrote on 6 November 1833, criticizing the circular

'Suggestions for the Formation of an Association of the Church' (partly written by Newman), a copy of which Newman had sent him on 1 November, saying: 'Surely the Church will shortly be delivered from its captivity under wicked men, who are worse than Chushanrishathaim . . . we shall be truly glad of your co-operation . . . but, if you will not, we will march past you.' (*LD* iv. 79.)

27. *Othniel* delivered the Jews who were enslaved for eight years for disobeying God. Judges 3: 7–9.

28. *dealings* On the ground that Francis after his return from Persia 'was *originating* schism . . . that he was a *teacher* and *organizer* of a *new* sect [the Plymouth Brethren]. This he gave over about 1838 – and then I at once changed my conduct and went to see him.' (*LD* v. 351 n. 1.)

29. *Paul* Romans 16: 17.

30. *Hampden* See ed. n. 53 to this chapter.

31. *Vol. iii. p. 131* The Life of the Rev. Joseph Blanco White Written by Himself with Portions of his Correspondence, ed. J. H. Thom (3 vols., London, 1845).

32. *Laud* William Laud (1573–1645), high-church archbishop of Canterbury under Charles I. A seven-volume edition of his theological writings, arguing for the Anglican middle way between Rome and Protestantism, was published (1847–60) in the Library of Anglo-Catholic Theology.

33. *Bramhall* John Bramhall (1594–1663), bishop of Derry, and after the Restoration archbishop of Armagh, supported Charles I and Laudian Anglicanism through his theological writings which were published in five volumes (1842–5) as part of the Library of Anglo-Catholic Theology.

34. *Stillingfleet* Edward Stillingfleet (1635–99), bishop of Worcester, was a Latitudinarian whose *Irenicum* (1659) downplayed episcopacy but who asserted the independence of the Church from the State.

35. *Epistles* See 'The Theology of St Ignatius' (originally published as a review article in 1839) in *Ess.* i. 222–62.

36. *Tract 11* 'The Visible Church'.

37. *Service* Penitential service for Ash Wednesday, the Latin word meaning 'threatening'.

38. *passage* The Epistle to the Magnesians, iii.

39. *jure ecclesiastico* Of church law.

40. *jure divino* Of divine law.

41. *Vicariate* See ch. I, ed. n. 117. Until the restoration of the hierarchy in 1840, the Roman Catholic Church in England had only vicars apostolic.

42. *Bagot* Richard Bagot (1782–1854), bishop of Oxford 1829–45, was critically sympathetic towards the Tractarians.

43. *stanza* The last stanza of the poem for 5 November, 'Gunpowder Treason'.

44. *St. Gregory I.* (*c*.540–604), Pope Gregory the Great, sent St Augustine in 597 to convert England, but he also strongly affirmed papal authority and other 'Popish' beliefs.

45. *the Council of Trent* met from 1545 to 1563 to counter the Protestant Reformation.

46. *St. Philip* See ch. I, ed. n. 1. For his opposition to the carnival, see 'The Mission of St Philip', *OS* 240.

47. *Records, No. 24* 'St Vincent of Lerins on the Test of Heresy', p. 7. For this passage from the *Records of the Church*, which were extracts from the Fathers, see *Tracts for the Times*, vol. ii.

48. *catena* a chain or collection of passages.

49. *Bernard Gilpin* (1517–83), the 'Apostle of the North', denounced clerical abuses but was deeply disturbed by the doctrinal changes of the English Reformation and the spoliation of church property. For this quotation see Tract 15, 'On the Apostolical Succession in the English Church', 10, in *Tracts for the Times*, vol. i.

50. *Preface The Catechetical Lectures of S. Cyril, Archbishop of Jerusalem* (1838), xi, the second volume of *Library of Fathers of the Holy Catholic Church, anterior to the division of the East and West* (50 vols., Oxford, 1838–85).

51. τῷ . . . φέρων Putting his trust in the finish. Sophocles, *Electra*, 735. Orestes held back his chariot at the Delphic games while the other chariots crashed into each other.

52. *attack* The agitation to remove the requirement to subscribe to the Thirty-nine Articles at Oxford and Cambridge came to a head in March 1834 with the introduction of a bill to admit Dissenters.

53. *Hampden* Renn Dickson Hampden (1793–1868), fellow of Oriel, became a tutor after the enforced resignation of Newman and his supporters. His appointment by the Whig Prime Minister Lord Melbourne as Regius Professor of Divinity in 1836 caused a storm of protest.

54. *letter* Of 28 November (*LD* iv. 371).

55. *sun* Phaeton, the son of Helios, was famous for his unlucky driving of the sun-chariot. 'By Phaeton I meant liberalism in Religion – by the Sun the Secular Power, the National Government viewed in its Action.' (*LD* XXX. 8.)

56. *broken* The House of Lords threw out not only the first bill against religious tests in the summer of 1834, but a similar bill in July 1835. Convocation at Oxford also decisively rejected in 1835 the proposal to remove subscription to the Articles as a condition of matriculation.

57. *friend* See *LD* xvii. 492. Benjamin Harrison (1808–87) was elected a
    student (i.e. fellow) of Christ Church in 1828 and was the author of
    four of the *Tracts for the Times*. Conservative ecclesiastically, he
    became domestic chaplain to Archbishop Howley of Canterbury in
    1843, and was later canon of Canterbury and archdeacon of
    Maidstone.

58. *verse . . . Nazianzen   VV* 152. St Gregory Nazianzen (*c*.329–90),
    bishop of Constantinople, one of the great Eastern Fathers who
    most influenced Newman, was ordained a priest against his will and
    preferred a solitary ascetic life to episcopal duties.

59. *British Critic* Newman became editor in January 1838. Two years
    before he had helped to save the review which was running at a
    loss by promising unpaid contributions from himself and the other
    members of the movement who had long wanted a specifically
    Tractarian review of their own. They withdrew their support when
    the editor James S. Boone (1799–1859) accepted articles they disap-
    proved of, whereupon Boone resigned.

60. *writer* Charles Webb Le Bas, 'Newman and Faber on Justification',
    British Critic, xxiv (July 1838), 82–119. See Moz. ii. 294. *Lectures on
    Justification* was published on 30 March 1838.

61. *article* Edward Churton, 'Revival of Jesuitism. Political View',
    British Critic, xxv (January 1839), 143–86. Newman criticized its
    'irreverence principally' in its strictures on 'the Eutychianism of the
    Roman system', which he thought could be 'taken as Nestorianiz-
    ing'. In 1875 Newman also noted his 'disinclination to oppose the
    devotions of the Immaculate Conception and the Sacred Heart'
    which Churton had attacked. (*LD* vi. 354–5.)

62. *friend* In April 1835 Newman offered Charles P. Golightly (1807–
    85), a graduate of Oriel, the curacy of Littlemore which was in the
    parish of St Mary the Virgin, and where a church began to be built
    in July 1835, which was completed a year later. But Golightly, who
    had warned Newman he might not altogether approve of his views
    on baptismal regeneration, never took up the appointment after
    Pusey had complained in the spring of 1836 about a sermon he had
    preached against Pusey's tract on baptism. Golightly was to be in
    the forefront of opposition to Tract 90.

63. *Editors* The project to publish a translation with notes of the
    twenty-volume *Histoire Ecclésiastique* (1691–1720) by Charles Fleury
    (1640–1725) began in the summer of 1839, commencing with the
    Council of Constantinople in 381 and ending in 456 (3 vols., 1842–
    4). The editors included, for example, George Buckle, the evolution-
    ary scientist.

64. ὁ μέγας The great.

65. *On Fasting*   Tract 18, 'Thoughts on the Benefits of the System of Fasting, Enjoined by our Church'.

66. *On Baptism*   'Scriptural Views of Holy Baptism' (1835), Tracts 67, 68, 69.

67. *started*   In August 1836 Pusey, with Newman, began to plan an English edition of the Fathers.

68. *connexions*   Pusey's paternal grandfather was the first Viscount Folkestone, his father inherited the family estate at Pusey, Berkshire, his older brother was an influential MP, and he himself married the sister of Lord Porchester, later the third Earl of Carnarvon.

69. *Sir Robert Inglis* (1786–1855) successfully stood against Peel in the 1829 by-election at Oxford (see ch. I, ed. n. 50), which he continued to represent as a Tory until 1854.

70. *initials*   Up to 1834 there was a 'distance between the Oriel party (Froudites) and Pusey', so that 'when Pusey wrote Tract 18, he bargained with me that he might put his initials at the end of it, that he might separate himself from the movement party. . . . we always considered that that had been the very reason why the movement was called "Puseyism", because Pusey was the only writer whose name presented itself to the general public.' (*LD* xxviii. 346.)

71. *Catenas*   Tract 74, 'Catena Patrum. No. I. Testimony of Writers in the later English Church to the Doctrine of the Apostolical Succession', and Tract 76, 'Catena Patrum. No. II. Testimony of Writers in the Later English Church to the Doctrine of Baptismal Regeneration'.

72. *appointment*   See ed. n. 53 to this chapter.

73. *Lectures on the Principal Doctrines and Practices of the Catholic Church* (1836) were delivered in 1835 and 1836, and were reviewed by Newman in the *British Critic* (October 1836). They led to the conversion of A. W. Pugin, the Gothic revival architect.

74. *work*   In July and August 1834 Newman completed Tracts 38 and 40 on the 'Via Media' (*VM* i. 19–48). At the beginning of September Newman was asked by Benjamin Harrison (see ed. n. 57 to this chapter) to take over a controversy about the theology of the Tracts that he was having in the French Catholic newspaper *L'Univers* with a priest called Jean-Nicolas Jager (1790–1868). His first letter was completed and translated before Christmas, and the first part of his second letter was sent off at the end of July 1835, but the controversy came to an end and the second part was never published. See *John Henry Newman and the Abbé Jager: A Controversy on Scripture and Tradition (1834–1836)*, ed. Louis Allen (London:

Oxford University Press, 1975). The lectures were delivered between 16 May and 11 July 1836 in the Adam de Brome chapel in St Mary's. The resulting book, most of which went through several drafts, was published on 11 March 1837, and was included by Newman in the uniform edition of his works as *VM* i.

75. *Tract 71* 'On the Controversy with the Romanists', reprinted in *VM* ii. 93–141 as 'On the Mode of Conducting the Controversy with Rome'.

76. *title* William Palmer (of Worcester) argued in *A Treatise on the Church of Christ* (1838) for the 'branch theory' according to which the Anglican, along with the Roman and Orthodox Churches, is a branch of the Catholic Church.

77. *Perrone* Giovanni Perrone (1794–1876), the leading Jesuit theologian at the Roman College. For the reference, see his standard work *Praelectiones Theologicae* (9 vols., 1835–42), *Tract de Loc. Theol.* 189 n. For a much less flattering reference to Newman's lectures, see op. cit. 339 n. However, in later editions Perrone saluted Newman as a distinguished convert. When Newman was studying for the Catholic priesthood in Rome in 1846–7, he sought Perrone's approval of his views on faith and reason and especially of his theory of doctrinal development which had come under suspicion.

78. *Lanzknechts* Mercenary soldiers.

79. *appointment* See ed. n. 53 to this chapter.

80. *Tract 90* See ed. n. 110 to this chapter.

81. *Via Media* Middle way, i.e. between Protestantism and Roman Catholicism.

82. *Andrewes* Lancelot Andrewes (1555–1626), the saintly bishop of Winchester and the father of Anglo-Catholicism, whose *Preces Privatae*, a manual of devotions in Greek and Latin, was translated by Newman in Tract 88. A patristic scholar, controversialist and preacher whose sermons are of high literary quality, he is a kind of forerunner of the Tractarian Newman.

83. *Hammond* Henry Hammond (1605–60), fellow of Magdalen, chaplain to Charles I, best known for his *Practical Catechism* (1644).

84. *Wilson* Thomas Wilson (1663–1755), bishop of Sodor and Man, famous for his devotional writings, including *Sacra Privata* (1781), which Newman published in 1838 with a preface.

85. *in solido* Completely.

86. *Howley* William Howley (1766–1848), archbishop of Canterbury from 1828, in his opposition to the Church Temporalities Act of 1833 could be said to resemble his predecessor St Thomas à Becket who paid with his life for opposing the king, Henry II.

87. *ex animo* From the heart.

88. *paragraph* Pusey maintained the Fathers could show the Roman Church the way back to true Christianity.

89. *paradox* Luther held that faith alone, without love, justifies, and yet he regarded faith as 'implying all at once, love, gratitude, devotion, belief, holiness, repentance, hope, dutifulness, and all other graces'. (*Jfc.* 7.)

90. *Melanchthon's* Philip Melanchthon (1497–1560), Lutheran theologian. 'To say we are justified by faith only was in that Reformer's mouth a lively mode of speech . . . for saying that we are justified neither by faith nor by works, but by God only . . . And since when thus explained it was most true, and was a protest against errors, which then were said to be widely spread in the Church, it was adopted by our Reformers . . .' (*Jfc.* 244–5.)

91. *Sermons* Sermons, *Chiefly on the Theory of Religious Belief, preached before the University of Oxford* (1843); published in enlarged edition as *US.*

92. *Pamphlet A Letter Addressed to the Rev. the Margaret Professor of Divinity, on Mr R. Hurrell Froude's Statements concerning the Holy Eucharist, and other Matters Theological and Ecclesiastical,* reprinted in *VM* ii. 195–257.

93. *Church of the Fathers* appeared in the *British Magazine* as articles between 1833 and 1836. Published with additions and omissions in one volume in 1840, they were reprinted in *HS* i. 333–46, under the title 'Primitive Christianity'.

94. *Life Life and Pontificate of Gregory VII* (1840). Newman's review in the *British Critic* of April 1841 was reprinted in *Ess.* ii. 249–335, under the title 'Reformation of the Eleventh Century', together with a short sketch of Bowden's life.

95. *Tract 75* 'On the Roman Breviary as embodying the Substance of the Devotional Services of the Church Catholic', 24 June 1836. The breviary or divine office contains the liturgy of the hours of the day.

96. *younger men* During 1838 Samuel Wood and Robert Williams, former pupils of Newman at Oriel, began a translation which they abandoned in November 1838 in deference to misgivings expressed by some of the Tractarians, including Keble.

97. *friend* Frederic Rogers (1811–89), one of Newman's pupils and then a fellow of Oriel, became Newman's closest friend at Oxford until Newman's revelation of his doubts about the Church of England. He became permanent under-secretary of state for the colonies and was created Lord Blachford.

98. *Translation* Newman began work in summer 1841 on *Select Treatises of S. Athanasius, Archbishop of Alexandria in Controversy with the Arians, translated with notes and indices* (pt. I, 1842; pt. II, 1844) for

the Library of the Fathers. It was reprinted in 1881 in a considerably revised version as *Ath*. i, ii.

99. *words   The Works of . . . John Bramhall, D.D.* (Dublin, 1677), 141; cited in *VM* i. xii.

100. *passage   Diff*. i. 96–8.

101. *Charge* of 14 August. Bishop Bagot commended the high doctrine of the Church in the Tracts but voiced disquiet about their divisive effect and the possibility of their encouraging extremism.

102. *Pamphlet   A Letter to the Right Reverend Father in God, Richard, Lord Bishop of Oxford, on Occasion of No. 90, in the Series called the Tracts for the Times* (1841), reprinted in *VM* ii. 395–424 (see p. 398).

103. *Articles   The Thirty-nine Articles, the official formularies of the Church of England, are more Protestant than the relatively Catholic liturgy of the Book of Common Prayer.

104. *Pius IV*. (1499–1565), pope from 1559, imposed in 1564 a profession of faith, based on the recently concluded Council of Trent, on all holders of ecclesiastical office.

105. *seventeenth*   On predestination.

106. *in medias res*   Into the middle of things.

107. *Homilies*   Two books of sermons intended for disaffected and un-educated clergy, the first of which was published in 1547 and the second in 1563.

108. *imponens*   Imposing.

109. *Zuinglians*   Followers of Ulrich Zwingli (1484–1531), Swiss Protes-tant reformer.

110. *Tract 90*   'Remarks on Certain Passages in the Thirty-nine Articles' (1841), reprinted in *VM* ii. 259–356 (see p. 345).

111. *interpretation*   Newman later found himself unable to defend his interpretation of Article 31 which attacks the doctrine of the sacrifice of the Mass. See *VM* ii, 351–6.

112. *Paul* insists that justifying faith must show itself in good works. See Galatians 5: 6, 14; 6: 2; Romans 8: 2, 4; 13: 8–10.

113. *James*   2: 14–26.

114. *'the Pillar . . . Truth'*   Timothy 3: 15.

115. *'Let . . . days*   Colossians 2: 16.

116. *'He . . . him'*   John 8: 7.

117. *occupation . . . gone*   Cf. Shakespeare, *Othello*, III. iii. 357.

118. *Hook*   Walter Farquhar Hook (1798–1875), well-known high-church vicar of Leeds, defended Newman in *A Letter to the Bishop of Ripon on the State of Parties in the Church of England* (1841).

119. *Palmer*   The learned Palmer of Worcester, who had distanced him-self early on from the movement, actually congratulated Newman now on having written the most valuable of the tracts.

120. *letter* See ed. n. 102 to this chapter. In the letter, published on 31 March, Newman acknowledged that the bishop of Oxford objected to Tract 90 and wished the Tracts to be discontinued.

121. *man* Edward Smedley (1788–1836). See Additional Notes.

122. *Houghton* Richard Monckton Milnes (1809–85), a Cambridge 'Apostle', entered parliament in 1837 and was created Baron Houghton in 1863. His pamphlet *One Tract More, by a Layman* was published in 1841.

CHAPTER III

1. '*infandum dolorem*' Unspeakable grief. Aeneas recounts to Dido the fall of Troy. Virgil, *Aeneid*, ii. 3.

2. *declared* A Letter Addressed to the Rev. R. W. Jelf, D.D., Canon of Christ Church, in Explanation of the Ninetieth Tract in the Series called The Tracts for the Times (1841), reprinted in *VM* ii. 365–93 (see p. 379).

3. *comprecation* I.e. a praying with rather than a direct invocation of. Bramhall, *Works*, 418.

4. *all but Transubstantiation* I.e. the real presence of Christ in the consecrated elements as opposed to the Tridentine doctrine that the 'accidents' of the bread and wine remain while the substance changes into the body and blood of Christ. For the relevant passages (in English translation) from Andrewes's *Responsio ad Apologiam Cardinalis Bellarmini* (1610), see P. E. More and F. L. Cross, edd., *Anglicanism: The Thought and Practice of the Church of England illustrated from the Religious Literature of the Seventeenth Century* (London, 1935), 465.

5. *Hooker* Richard Hooker (1553–1600), the foremost apologist for Anglicanism after the Elizabethan settlement, upheld the doctrine of the real presence while refusing to define the precise manner of it in *Treatise on the Laws of Ecclesiastical Polity*, V. lxvii (*Works*, ed. John Keble (Oxford, 1836), ii. 452).

6. *Hammond* For Hammond's view that the infallibility of general councils, while not an article of faith, falls into the realm of pious belief, see *The Miscellaneous Theological Works of Henry Hammond, D.D.* (Oxford, 1849), ii. 350.

7. *Bull* See *The Works of George Bull, D.D.* (Oxford, 1846), ii. 52–3.

8. *Thorndike* Herbert Thorndike (1598–1672), high Anglican theologian, whose chief work is *An Epilogue to the Tragedy of the Church of England* (1659). For his view of penance, see *Works* (Oxford, 1844–54), iv. 203–6.

9. *Pearson* John Pearson (1613–86), bishop of Chester, patristic scholar.

See his popular work (1659) *An Exposition of the Creed* (London, 1887), 530.

10. *Article* 'State of Religious Parties', *British Critic*, xxv (Apr. 1839), 396–426, reprinted as 'Prospects of the Anglican Church' in *Ess.* i. 263–308.

11. *not altogether mine* In an appended note to its 1871 reprint Newman corrected himself: 'Now, on going through it carefully for re-publication, I am quite clear, first, that it is from first to last my writing; and secondly, that what I have borrowed from the papers of my friend is the topic, which I have worked out and illustrated between pp. 283 [284] and 292 [293], and on which I have ap-pended a note at p. 287 [288], pointing out the difference between it and the view of doctrine which was habitual to my own mind.' (*Ess.* i 308.) Whereas Newman believed in 'doctrinal development, or the evolution of doctrines out of certain original and fixed *dogmatic truths*, which are held inviolate from first to last, and the more firmly established and illustrated by the very process of enlargement', in this section of the article he gave 'utterance to a theory, not mine, of a certain *metamorphosis* and recasting of doc-trines into new shapes . . . those old and new shapes being foreign to each other, and connected only as symbolizing or realizing certain immutable but nebulous *principles*' (p. 288).

12. *writer* Baden Powell (1796–1860), Savilian professor of geometry at Oxford, a liberal Anglican, in *Tradition Unveiled; or, an exposition of the pretensions and tendency of authoritative teaching in the church* (London, 1839), 4.

13. *Another* Edward Bickersteth (1786–1850), a strong Evangelical clergyman, in *Remarks on the Dangers of the Church of Christ* (London, 1839), 15.

14. *Another* Identified only as 'the scoffing author of the Via Media' in *Ess.* i 264.

15. *Another* C. S. Bird, *The Oxford Tract System considered with reference to the Principle of Reserve in Preaching* (London, 1838), 5–6.

16. *Another* Isaac Taylor (1787–1865), lay theologian and author of *The Natural History of Enthusiasm* (1829), in *Ancient Christianity and the Doctrines of the Oxford Tracts* (2 vols., London, 1839–40), i. xi, which attacks the Tractarians' alleged credulity and super-stition.

17. *Another* Identified only as 'a well-known Scotch Magazine', *Ess.* i. 266.

18. *Another* James Grant (1802–79), Calvinist journalist, in *Travels in Town* (London, 1839), ii. 127.

19. *bishop* Sumner (see ch. I, ed. n. 31) in *A Charge Delivered to the Clergy*

of the Diocese of Chester and the Triennial Visitation in 1838 (London, 1838), 2.

20. *authors*   I.e. the Romantics.

21. *Alexander Knox* (1757–1831), reclusive Irish lay theologian, anticipated the Tractarian view of the Church of England as Catholic, not Protestant. For the quotation here, see his *Remains* (4 vols., London, 1834–7), i. 51, 61 (letter of 4 June 1816).

22. *clergyman*   Thomas Sikes, rector of Guilsborough, a leader of the high-church party who died in 1834. The words were spoken in conversation with Newman's curate and friend W. J. Copeland 'about the year 1833'. Moz. ii. 483–4.

23. *Churton*   Edward Churton (1800–74), rector of Crayke in Suffolk, a theologian sympathetic to Tractarianism who had left Oxford before the movement began.

24. *Germany*   Pusey studied 1825–7 at Göttingen, Berlin, and Bonn under liberal Protestant theologians, including Schleiermacher, as a result of which he published *An Historical Enquiry into the Probable Causes of the Rationalist Character lately predominant in the Theology of Germany* (2 pts., 1828, 1830).

25. *Arabic MSS.*   Pusey spent six years on the final part of the catalogue of Arabic manuscripts in the Bodleian Library, which was printed in 1835.

26. *Dodsworth*   William Dodsworth (1798–1861), a Cambridge graduate who abandoned Evangelicalism for Tractarianism, becoming a Roman Catholic in 1851, published a series of periodical articles as *The Second Advent of Our Lord Jesus Christ, with an appendix on Jesus Christ as the Destroyer of Antichrist* (1835).

27. *Oakeley*   Oakeley (see preface, ed. n. 2) acknowledged his adhesion to the Oxford movement in the preface to his *Sermons, preached chiefly in the Chapel Royal, at Whitehall* (Oxford, 1839), lv–vi.

28. *Series*   *Plain Sermons, by Contributors to the 'Tracts for the Times'* (10 vols., 1839–48), the fifth volume of which (1843) was by Newman and constitutes *PS* vii and viii.

29. *Kebles*   John and his younger brother Thomas (1793–1875), vicar of Bisley, Gloucestershire. Newman only mentions Thomas in the footnote he added to the article when he reprinted it in *Ess.* i (see p. 280 n.). But he seems to be in some doubt here, having just referred, three paragraphs earlier, to 'two or three . . . writers'.

30. *Isaac Williams* (1802–65), fellow of Trinity College, Oxford, a curate of Newman at St Mary's, whose Tracts 80 and 87 (1838, 1840) 'On Reserve in Communicating Religious Knowledge' gained much notoriety for the movement. The Tractarians failed in 1842 to secure his election as professor of poetry in succession to Keble.

31. *"Fortes . . . adjuvat"*   Fortune favours the bold. Latin proverb.

32. *Liberalism*   In a later note on the passage in the article, Newman admitted that in fact 'these formularies have not excluded it from the Anglican Church'. *Ess.* i. 294 n.

33. *stags*   In Virgil, *Eclogues*, i. 59, the shepherd Tityrus declares, 'sooner shall the stags graze in air . . . than . . .'

34. *Hildebrand*   Gregory VII (1021–85), pope from 1073, the great reformer of clerical discipline and defender of the Church's independence of the State.

35. *Loyola*   St Ignatius Loyola (1491 or 1495–1556), founder of the Jesuits.

36. *Bellarmine*   St Robert Bellarmine (1542–1621), Italian Jesuit, the leading theologian of the Counter-Reformation.

37. *Lloyd*   Charles Lloyd (1784–1829), Regius Professor of divinity at Oxford and from 1827 bishop of Oxford, in 'View of the Roman Catholic Doctrines', *British Critic*, xxii (October 1825), 94–149.

38. *Vincentius of Lerins* (d. *c*.434) gave his famous test for distinguishing heresy from orthodoxy in his *Commonitorium*, ii. 3 – 'that is to be received as Apostolic which has been taught "always, everywhere, and by all."' (*VM* i. 51.)

39. *paper*   Reprinted as 'How to Accomplish it' in *DA* 1–43.

40. *July 1841*   'Private Judgment', *British Critic*, xxx (July 1841), 100–134; reprinted in *Ess.* ii. 336–74. For the two passages quoted here and later, see pp. 365, 367.

41. *St. Cyprian* (d. 258), bishop of Carthage, in *De Catholicae Ecclesiae Unitate*, iv.

42. *St. Augustine* of Hippo (354–430) in Epistle 49. The schism of Donatus, who rejected the validity of a sacrament performed by an unworthy minister, began in Carthage in 311 and lasted a hundred years.

43. *argument*   St Cyril (*c*.315–*c*.386), bishop of Jerusalem, in *Catecheses*, xviii. 12.

44. *Cup*   Since about the twelfth century until the Second Vatican Council (1962–5) communion in the Roman Church was given only under the form of bread.

45. *1838*   In 'Palmer's *Treatise on the Church of Christ*', *British Critic*, xxiv (October 1838), 347–72; reprinted as 'Palmer's View of Faith and Unity' in *Ess.* i. 179–221. For the so-called 'doctrine of Fundamentals' referred to here, see *Ess.* i. 209–10.

46. *British Critic*, xxvii. 40–88, 'Catholicity of the English Church'; reprinted as 'The Catholicity of the Anglican Church' in *Ess.* ii. 1–111 (see p. 6).

47. *July, 1841*   See ed. n. 40 to this chapter (see p. 367).

48. *conclusion*   *VM* i. 331-2.

49. *Commemoration*   Annual celebration in memory of the founders and benefactors at the end of the summer term at Oxford.

50. *Monophysites* held that the incarnate Christ had only one nature, the divine absorbing the human. See ed. n. 52 to this chapter.

51. *work   Lectures on Certain Difficulties felt by Anglicans in submitting to the Catholic Church* (1850), reprinted as *Diff.* i (see pp. 372-3).

52. *Eutychians* were extreme Monophysites who held that Christ had one divine person and nature which completely swallowed up his humanity. Eutyches was abbot of a monastery near Constantinople, where he was condemned at a council in 448 for his heretical views. This was overturned by the so-called 'Robber' council at Ephesus (449), at which Dioscorus, bishop of Alexandria and a friend of Eutyches, presided by appointment of the Emperor Theodosius, who was also friendly to Eutyches, and which broke up in disorder without the pope's legates being able to make their voice heard. In 451 the Council of Chalcedon accepted the teaching of Pope St Leo that Christ was not only *of* but *in* two natures, with the acclamation 'Peter has thus spoken through Leo' (*Dev.* 309). The Monophysites of Egypt refused to accept the decision of the council and insisted that they were orthodox in following St Athanasius and St Cyril who had maintained 'one nature incarnate', while at the same time disowning Eutyches as an extremist.

53. *Petavius*   See ch. 1, ed. n. 45. For his view of Eutyches as a silly old man, see his *De Incarnatione*, I. lxiii-viii, in *Opus de Theologicis Dogmatibus* (Paris, 1644-50).

54. *passage   Diff.* i. 387-8.

55. *Leo*   See ed. n. 52 to this chapter.

56. *Sooner . . . hand*   Psalms 137: 5.

57. *wither . . . God*   1 Kings 13: 1-4. Jeroboam, king of Israel, had his hand withered when he stretched it out against a prophet from Judah who prophesied against the king's altar of idolatry at Bethel.

58. *Cranmers*   Thomas Cranmer (1489-1556), first Anglican archbishop of Canterbury, was largely responsible for the Prayer Book and the Thirty-nine Articles.

59. *Ridleys*   Nicholas Ridley (*c.*1500-55), bishop of London, one of the leading Protestant reformers.

60. *Latimers*   Hugh Latimer (*c.*1490-1555), bishop of Worcester, popular Protestant preacher and confidant of Cranmer.

61. *Jewels*   John Jewel (1522-71), bishop of Salisbury, apologist for the Elizabethan settlement.

62. *Ussher*   James Ussher (1581–1656), archbishop of Armagh, loyal to Charles I.

63. *Taylor*   Jeremy Taylor (1613–67), chaplain to Archbishop Laud, author of famous devotional works.

64. *Barrow*   Isaac Barrow (1630–77), Isaac Newton's predecessor as professor of mathematics at Cambridge, became chaplain to Charles II and later master of Trinity. His chief theological work was his *Treatise on the Pope's Supremacy* (1680).

65. *friends*   Actually Robert Williams (1811–90) (see below), a former Oriel pupil, who became a Conservative MP and abandoned Tractarianism for Evangelicalism after Newman's conversion to Rome. See Ker, 182.

66. *article*   'The Anglican Claim of Apostolical Succession', *Dublin Review*, vii (August 1839), 139–80.

67. *words*   Wiseman translated the sentence from *Contra Epistolam Parmeniani*, iii. 3, as 'the entire world judges *with security*, that they are not good, who separate themselves from the entire world, in whatever part of the entire world' (pp. 153–4). Newman's own (free) translation of the key words is 'The universal Church is in its judgments secure of truth.' (*Ess*. ii. 101.)

68. *'Turn . . . Whittington'*   Richard Whittington (d. 1423) was ill-treated by the cook under whom he served as a scullion, and while running away thought he heard Bow bells ringing the jingle 'Turn again, Whittington, / Lord mayor of London', whereupon he returned to his master and became three times lord mayor of London.

69. *'Tolle . . . lege'*   Take up, read (*Confessions*, viii. 12). Augustine, while weeping over his sins, heard a child's voice repeating these words, which he took to mean that he should open the Bible, whereupon his eyes alighted on St Paul's Epistle to the Romans, 13: 13–14, and he was converted.

70. *friends*   See p. 165.

71. *hand . . . wall*   Cf. Daniel 5: 5 for God's warning to Belshazzar of his imminent downfall.

72. *heavens*   For the opening of the heavens see Ezekiel 1: 1, Matthew 3: 16, Mark 1: 10, Acts 7: 56.

73. *ends*   *PS* viii. 32.

74. *'When . . . back'*   'Discipline', reprinted in *VV* 187 as 'Semita Justorum'.

75. *memorandum*   *A W* 5.

76. *'he . . . Lord'*   1 Samuel 3: 7.

77. *Leo*   See ed. n. 52 to this chapter.

78. *Gradus ad Parnassum*   The standard Latin verse thesaurus, originally

compiled by the German Paul Aler (1656–1727). The papal titles referred to are 'Vicar of Christ', 'sacred interpreter', 'bearer of the sceptre'.

79. *Daniel*   7: 7.

80. *letter*   See *Apo.* 127.

81. *volumes*   *A Preservative against Popery in several Select Discourses upon the Principal Heads of Controversy between Protestants and Papists: being written and published by the most eminent Divines of the Church of England chiefly in the Reign of King James II2*, ed. Edward Gibson (3 vols. 1738).

82. *Letter*   *A Letter addressed to the Rev. R. W. Jelf, D.D., canon of Christ Church, in Explanation of no. 90, in the series called the Tracts for the Times* (1841), reprinted in *VM* ii. 365–93 (see p. 369).

83. *words*   In a letter of 1 November 1835 (*LD* v. 56). Froude died on 28 February 1836.

84. *O'Connell*   Daniel O'Connell (1775–1847), who was instrumental in winning Catholic emancipation, agreed in 1835 to support the Whig (and Radical) opposition to the Tory government and to abandon his campaign for the repeal of the Union (of Great Britain and Ireland) in exchange for the undertaking that a Whig administration would abolish the tithes Irish Catholics had to pay for the established Church of Ireland as well as other reforms.

85. *Spencer*   George Spencer (1799–1864), younger son of Earl Spencer, was an Anglican clergyman who converted to Rome in 1830 and became a priest. He began a campaign of prayer for Anglicans among continental Catholics. For his meeting with Newman on 8 January 1840 and Newman's letter of 9 February, see Ker 191–2.

86. *'in . . . apostatae'*   In the position of an apostate.

87. *"The voice . . . Esau"*   Genesis 27: 22.

88. *British Critic*   See ed. n. 46 to this chapter. (*Ess.* ii. 71–3.)

89. *Ximenes*   Francisco Ximénez de Cisneros (1436–1517), Franciscan cardinal archbishop of Toledo, who revived the Mozarabic rite and was responsible for the Complutensian Polyglot, the first polyglot edition of the whole Bible, which he began in 1502 at the university of Alcalá (which he had founded).

90. *Borromeo*   St Charles Borromeo (1538–84), archbishop of Milan, prominent figure at the Council of Trent and foremost in the implementation of its reforming decrees.

91. *Pascal*   Blaise Pascal (1623–62), French mathematician and theologian, whose *Pensées* is a classic of Christian apologetics.

92. *"have . . . faith"*   Cf. 2 Corinthians 1: 24.

93. *news*   See ed. n. 85 to this chapter.

94. *occurrences* J. B. Morris of Exeter College, who had been looking after St Mary's in Newman's absence, had preached on both fasting and transubstantiation, as a result of which the vice-chancellor complained to the bishop of Oxford and stopped attending St Mary's. Moreover, Newman's curate, J. R. Bloxam, who in the summer had visited Alton Towers, the home of the Roman Catholic earl of Shrewsbury, was reported as having bowed at the elevation of the Host (although in fact he had simply been in the gallery saying his prayers).

95. *Bellarmine* In *De Notis Ecclesiae* in *Roberti Cardinalis Bellarmini Opera Omnia* (Naples, 1856–72), ii. 139.

96. *Article* See ed. n. 46 to this chapter.

97. *experimentum crucis* Crucial test.

98. *Beveridge* William Beveridge (1637–1708), high-church bishop of St Asaph, author of *Exposition of the Thirty-Nine Articles* (1710). Walter Mayers at the end of 1816 had given Newman a copy of Beveridge's *Private Thoughts upon Religion* (1709) together with his *Private Thoughts upon a Christian Life* (1709), which Newman later noted he did not mention in the *Apologia* because Beveridge had no theological influence on him – 'But no book was more dear to me, or exercised a more powerful influence over my devotion and my habitual thoughts.' (*LD* i. 30.)

99. *Letter* See ed. n. 82 to this chapter. For the quotation see *VM* ii. 385.

100. *Jelf* Richard Jelf (1798–1871), fellow of Oriel and canon of Christ Church, had a reputation for impartiality.

101. *Littlemore* See ch. I, ed. n. 7.

102. *letter* Of 26 October 1840. See Ker, 200–201.

103. *began* In 1834 Newman began an evening service, followed by a lecture, every Wednesday, daily morning prayer, and later a communion service on saints' days. A weekly early communion service did not begin until 1837. See Ker, 103, 145.

104. *late* Ashurst Turner Gilbert (1786–1870), vice-chancellor from 1836 to 1840, and bishop of Chichester from 1842. Ironically, his blind daughter Elizabeth never forgot the sound of Newman's voice as he read from the Bible in church.

105. *the present* See ed. n. 94 to this chapter. Philip Wynter (1794–1871) was vice-chancellor from 1840 to 1844.

106. *Exeter Hall* The London meeting-place for Evangelicals, including Nonconformists hostile to the established Church.

107. *Rogers* See ch. II, ed. n. 97.

108. *answered* 6 November 1840. See Ker, 201–2.

109. *'hoisting . . . petard'* Shakespeare, *Hamlet*, III. iv. 206.

110. *book*   *History of Christianity to the Abolition of Paganism in the Roman Empire* (1840), reviewed by Newman in January 1841 in the *British Critic* (reprinted in *Ess.* ii. 186–248).

111. *curate*   William John Copeland (1804–85), fellow of Trinity, became Newman's curate at Littlemore in 1840. A renewal of their friendship in 1861 aided Newman with the *Apologia* as he turned to old Anglican friends for their help in confirming his history of the movement. It was Copeland, too, who edited the collected edition of *Parochial and Plain Sermons* in 1868, thus enabling Newman to begin the republication of his Anglican works.

112. *another friend*   Maria Rosina Giberne (1802–85), sister-in-law of Walter Mayers and herself a former Evangelical, became a Catholic in 1845 and a nun in 1863. See Ker, 222, 224.

113. *Letter*   See ch. II, ed. n. 102.

114. *one*   Ambrose Lisle Phillipps (1809–78), an early convert to Catholicism and an enthusiastic ecumenist. See Ker, 224–5.

115. *Volume*   *Diff.* i. 378–87. The semi-Arians or Eusebians, who were favoured by the Emperor Constantine as avoiding the extremes of both Arius and Athanasius, held that the Son is of a like rather than the same substance as the Father.

116. *friend*   Maria Giberne. See Ker, 233.

117. *stranger*   The copy or draft of the letter in the Birmingham Oratory archives does not contain the name.

118. *Bishopric*   The appointment was to be made alternately by the British and Prussian governments.

119. *King*   Frederick William IV (1795–1861).

120. *Archbishop*   William Howley (1766–1848), archbishop of Canterbury from 1828.

121. *Jacobite*   Syrian Monophysites, named after their founder Jacob Baradaeus (*c.*500–578).

122. *Nestorian*   heresy, named after Nestorius (d. *c.*451), held that Christ had two separate divine and human persons.

123. *British Critic*, xxx. 100–134, 'Private Judgment', reprinted in *Ess.* ii. 336–74 (see pp. 365–6).

124. *Jew*   Michael Solomon Alexander (1799–1845), an ex-rabbi.

125. *Epistle*   The Evangelicals who supported the scheme openly referred to the projected Jewish church as the church 'of the circumcision', apparently in disregard of St Paul's warning to the converted Galatians that justification comes of faith, not of the circumcision of the Mosaic law.

126. *Confession of Augsburg*   Lutheran profession of faith drawn up by Melanchthon in 1530.

127. *observed*   *SD* 340–41.

CHAPTER IV

1. *Torres Vedras* A town near Lisbon where Sir Arthur Wellesley (later duke of Wellington) established his lines of defence, behind which he retreated in 1810 before successfully counter-attacking, a turning-point in the Peninsular War.

2. *Article* 'The Catholicity of the Anglican Church'; see *Ess.* ii. 59, 69–70.

3. *Meletius* St Meletius (d. 381) became bishop of Antioch in 360 during the Arian crisis; but because he had formerly been a semi-Arian he came under suspicion and was replaced by another bishop who was recognized by Rome and Alexandria, although not by the East. Meletius was eventually restored as bishop and canonized as a saint. His sanctity, then, 'outweighed his separation from Rome and Alexandria, and proves that saints may be matured in a state which Romanists of this day would fain call schism.' (*Ess.* ii. 65.)

4. *say* *VM* ii. 269–71.

5. *said* *VM* ii. 421.

6. '*Samaria*' When the ten tribes of Israel revolted against the house of David and separated from the tribe of Judah and Jerusalem, Samaria became the capital.

7. *Sermons*, xxi–v, *SD* 308–80.

8. *point* See ed. n. 6 to this chapter.

9. *Elias and Eliseus* Elija and Elisha.

10. *Carmel* See 1 Kings 18 for Elijah's triumph over the prophets of Baal, when God consumed his sacrifice with fire.

11. *Shunammite* The woman of Shunam who gave Elisha hospitality in return for which she was enabled to conceive a son although her husband was old. See 2 Kings 4.

12. *Wilkes* Samuel Charles Wilks (1789–1872) edited the organ of the Evangelical 'Clapham sect' from 1816 until 1850. For the *Christian Observer*'s attack and Newman's response (reprinted in *VM* ii. 143–94), see *LD* vi. 9 n. 1.

13. *Church* Richard William Church (1815–90), fellow of Oriel, who as a proctor ensured that Tract 90 was not condemned in Convocation in 1845, became dean of St Paul's and is best known for his history, *The Oxford Movement, 1833–1845* (1891).

14. *Moberly* George Moberly (1803–85), fellow of Balliol and a sympathizer of the Tractarian movement, became bishop of Salisbury.

15. *Charles Marriott* (1811–58), fellow of Oriel, became a close collaborator of Pusey after Newman's conversion and was chiefly responsible for the Library of the Fathers.

16. *Barter* William Brudenell Barter (1788–1858), fellow of Oriel,

publicly defended Tract 90, while expressing reservations about the Tracts.

17. *a man* Probably two, according to Pusey. See H. P. Liddon, *Life of Edward Bouverie Pusey* (London, 1893), ii. 232 n. 1.

18. *in posse* Possible.

19. *Socinianism* denies the divinity of Christ, and therefore the eucharist as a sacrament.

20. *Ken's* Thomas Ken (1637–1711), the high-church bishop of Bath and Wells and leading Non-juror.

21. *century* Eighteenth-century Anglicanism was characterized by Latitudinarianism.

22. *the Ecclesiastical Commission* was set up by parliament in 1836 to manage and redistribute the revenues of the Church of England.

23. *catachrestically* By improper use of words.

24. *churchman* W. F. Hook. See *Corr.* 100.

25. *diocesan* J. B. Sumner, who became bishop of Chester in 1828, was violently hostile to the Tractarians.

26. *reply* For Newman's letter of 26 January 1842, see Ker, 242–4.

27. *Henry* William Wilberforce (1807–73), youngest son of William Wilberforce, a pupil of Newman at Oriel, took Anglican holy orders but became a Catholic in 1850. He remained one of Newman's closest friends.

28. *signal* As a canon of the Westminster chapter, Oakeley took a prominent part in an address sent on 15 March 1864 to Newman by over half the clergy of the diocese expressing support in his controversy with Kingsley. His strong defence of Newman contrasted with the lack of sympathy that now existed between Newman and the other leader of the younger, more aggressive Tractarian party, W. G. Ward, whose Ultramontane Catholicism was consistent with his earlier Tractarian extremism.

29. *one* 'The Reverence due to the Virgin Mary', *PS* ii. 127–38.

30. *one* *Letter addressed . . . to . . . Jelf*, *VM* ii. 386–7.

31. *Ambrose* *De Fide ad Gratianum Augustum*, I. v. 42. It is not by logic that it has pleased God to save his people.

32. *Ward* William George Ward (1812–82), fellow of Balliol, was condemned by convocation in February 1845 for his extreme, romanizing *Ideal of the Christian Church*. He was received into the Catholic Church a few weeks before Newman. A lay theologian, he turned the *Dublin Review* into an organ of extreme Ultramontanism. See also ed. n. 28 to this chapter.

33. *'Di . . . hostis'* It is the gods that terrify me, and Jupiter my foe. Virgil, *Aeneid*, xii. 895, where Turnus denies he is afraid of Aeneas's fierce words.

34. *motto*   Where the lapse? What have I done?

35. *Heads*   Richard Jenkyns, master of Balliol, and Benjamin Symons, warden of Wadham, went to watch the building works. (*LD* xiv. 52.)

36. *conversion*   Newman had admitted William Lockhart (1820–92) to the Littlemore community on the understanding that he would wait three years before making a final decision about Rome. Lockhart's conversion in August 1843 was especially scandalous because he had been teaching in the parish school.

37. *you*   Ambrose St John (1815–75), student (i.e. fellow) of Christ Church, was Wilberforce's curate until August 1843 when he came to live at Littlemore. Received into the Catholic Church a few days before Newman, he joined the Birmingham Oratory and became Newman's closest confidant.

38. *in . . . partem*   In bad part.

39. *clergyman*   Bernard Smith (1815–1903), rector of Leadenham under Bishop Kaye of Lincoln, became a Catholic on 15 December 1842. Kaye (1783–1853) had been Regius Professor of divinity at Cambridge where he revived patristic studies; as a bishop he was energetic in introducing reforms and raising the standard of the clergy; he was also known for his calm and caution in dealing with church controversies.

40. *Editor*   Of the *English Churchman*. Newman's letters were dated 23 and 27 February 1843.

41. *wrote*   On 2 March 1843.

42. *informant*   Smith's brother-in-law who had misunderstood a remark of Smith's mother.

43. *Sermon*   'The Parting of Friends', *SD* 395–409.

44. *Faber*   George Stanley Faber (1773–1854), master of Sherburn Hospital, Durham, an Evangelical controversialist. The reference seems to be to his *Letters on Tractarian Secessions to Popery* (1846).

45. *nephew*   Francis Atkinson Faber (1804–76), a Tractarian and elder brother of Father Faber of the London Oratory, was rector of Saunderton, Bucks. from 1845.

46. *sans phrase*   Plainly, straight out.

47. *set . . . grapes*   Cf. Ezekiel 18: 3.

48. *layman*   See ch. III, ed. n. 114.

49. ἄνομος   Lawless.

50. *"approving . . . Christ"*   2 Corinthians 6: 4.

51. *Russell*   Charles William Russell (1812–80), then professor of church history, and from 1857 president, of St Patrick's College, Maynooth, the national seminary of Ireland.

52. *Faith*   *Règle de la foi catholique* (1649) by François Veron (*c*.1575–

1625), which carefully distinguished what was of faith and what was not, was noted for its ecumenical spirit.

53. *Treatises*   *Tractatus generales de controversiis fidei* and *Tractatus speciales* by Adrian (d. 1669) and Pierre (d. 1675) de Wallenburch, Dutch Catholic apologists.

54. *in . . . naturâ*   In the nature of things.

55. *Exercises*   The *Spiritual Exercises* (probably written 1522–3) consist of a series of meditations, the special characteristic of which is the combination of the senses, imagination, and intellect in directing the will towards God.

56. *account*   *Dev.* 431–6.

57. *mention*   *DA* 19.

58. *introduced*   Cf. *Ari.* 36–7.

59. *Sermon*   'The Theory of Developments in Religious Doctrine', *US* 312–51.

60. *friend*   Catherine Froude (1809 or 10–78), who became a Catholic in 1857, was the wife of William Froude (1810–79), the fourth son of Archdeacon Froude and a distinguished naval architect, who remained a close friend of Newman in spite of his agnosticism about which they corresponded.

61. *Retractation*   Under the title 'Oxford and Rome' it appeared as a letter (dated 12 December 1842) in the *Conservative Journal* of 28 January 1843. It was anonymous but appeared with the editorial comment that the identity of the author was obvious. Reprinted in *VM* ii. 427–33.

62. *Valeat quantum*   For what it may be worth.

63. *William's*   See ed. n. 60 to this chapter.

64. *Tradition*   'A Relation of the Conference between William Laud . . . and Mr Fisher the Jesuit', *Works* (Oxford, 1849), xvi. 70–131.

65. *friend*   John Keble.

66. *Lives of the English Saints*, 14 vols. (London, 1844–5).

67. *a publisher*   Francis Rivington (1805–85), whose firm published *Tracts for the Times*.

68. *Life of St Stephen Harding* (d. 1134), founder of the Cistercian order, by John Dobrée Dalgairns (1818–76), one of the younger Tractarians who joined the Littlemore community and then the Birmingham Oratory, which he left in 1856 for the London Oratory, where he succeeded Father Faber as superior.

69. *author*   James Anthony Froude (1818–94), youngest of the brothers, the distinguished historian, whose subsequent religious scepticism has sometimes been attributed to the work he did on one of the *Lives of the English Saints*.

70. *T.'s* James Toovey (1813–93), London bookseller, who published the *Lives of the English Saints*.

71. *considered* By Charles Kingsley in *What, Then, Does Dr Newman Mean?* See *Apo.* 384.

72. *Johnson* Manuel Johnson (1805–59), first cousin of J. W. Bowden, was appointed Radcliffe Observer in 1839. His house was a meeting-place for Tractarians.

73. *A. B.* William Lockhart.

74. *friend* R. W. Church.

75. *Volume* *SD*. See ed. n. 7 to this chapter.

76. *Goldsmid* Nathaniel Goldsmid (1807–60), a lawyer sympathetic to the Tractarians, who became a Catholic in 1850.

77. *Scott Kenilworth*, xli, quoting Exodus 22: 19; 34: 26.

78. *'Victrix . . . Catoni'* The victorious cause won the favour of the gods but the vanquished Cato's. Lucan, *Pharsalia*, i. 128. In other words, the just cause lost.

79. *request* Newman's successor at St Mary's, C. P. Eden, made it clear that he would not permit him to continue officiating at Littlemore.

80. *words* I shall die alone. *Pensées*, ii. 211.

81. *lady* Maria Spencer Ruscombe Poole (1815–81) became a Catholic in 1845 and later a nun. She described her conversion in 'The Modern Pilgrim's Progress, or the History of Puseyism in a Dream', *Rambler*, xi (February 1853), 122–35.

82. *Manning* Henry Edward Manning (1808–92), archdeacon of Chichester, became a Catholic in 1851 and archbishop of Westminster in 1865. The extreme Ultramontanism he espoused in opposition to Newman is implicitly criticized in ch. V.

83. *charge* Of 23 May 1842.

84. *friend* James Bowling Mozley (1813–78), fellow of Magdalen, later Regius Professor of Divinity, a keen Tractarian, two of whose brothers married two of Newman's sisters, while his sister Anne edited the authorized *Letters and Correspondence of John Henry Newman* (1891). For Newman's letter of 1 September 1843, see Ker, 279.

85. *Memorial* The idea of erecting by subscription a monument to Cranmer, Ridley and Latimer, who had been burned at the stake in Broad Street, was mooted in the autumn of 1838; it was provoked apparently by the publication of Hurrell Froude's *Remains* and intended as a test of loyalty of the Tractarians to the Church of England.

86. *authorities* In June 1843 Pusey was suspended by the university from preaching for two years because of a sermon on the eucharist preached in May in Christ Church Cathedral.

87. *Dodsworth* For Newman's letter of 28 June 1843 to William

Dodsworth (1798–1861), a London Tractarian clergyman who became a Catholic in 1850, see Ker, 277.

88. *friend*   W. G. Ward. See Moz. ii. 351.

89. *Scott*   James Robert Hope (1812–73), fellow of Merton, became a Catholic in 1851. A close friend of Newman, he made a fortune as a parliamentary lawyer for the railway companies and in 1853 inherited Abbotsford, the home of Sir Walter Scott, whose granddaughter he had married, consequently changing his surname to Hope Scott.

90. *letter*   Of 2 November 1843.

91. *friend*   J. W. Bowden.

92. *wrote*   According to his diary he sent a letter (not apparently extant) on 19 September 1844.

93. *friend*   Ambrose St John.

94. *Zoar*   The little town where Lot took shelter and which God spared in answer to his prayer. Genesis 19: 18–22.

95. *Moab and Ammon*   The sons of Lot by his daughters, whose land was barred to the Israelites by God. Deuteronomy 2: 9, 19.

96. *friend*   Manning, on 24 November 1844.

97. *lady*   See ch. III, ed. n. 112.

98. *Psalmist*   Psalms 86: 17.

99. *measures*   See Additional Notes, *Apo.* 348.

100. *Quarterly*   J. B. Mozley, 'Recent Proceedings at Oxford', *Christian Remembrancer*, xlvii (April, 1845), 517–71.

101. *Badeley*   Edward Lowth Badeley (1803–68), ecclesiastical lawyer, who became a Catholic in 1851, played a critical role in the writing of the *Apologia* by advising Newman not to accept Kingsley's first half-hearted apology or his subsequent offer partially to amend it, as well as by expressing his strong approval for Newman's satirical comments in the original pamphlet he published containing the correspondence.

102. *One*   J. D. Dalgairns. See ed. n. 68 to this chapter.

103. *Father Dominic* Barberi (1712–1849), Italian Passionist missionary who established the order in England and was beatified in 1963.

104. *Acton*   Charles Januarius Acton (1803–47), great-uncle of the historian Lord Acton, held important offices in the Papal States.

105. *Oscott*   St Mary's College was founded in 1794 as a school and seminary at Old Oscott (renamed Maryvale by Newman), outside Birmingham, the college having moved in 1839 to another site two miles away. It was to Old Oscott that Newman and his companions moved after leaving Littlemore.

106. *Rome*   Newman studied for the priesthood at the College of Propaganda from November 1846 to June 1847.

107. *Birmingham*   On 1 February 1848 Newman formally established the English Oratory at Old Oscott or Maryvale. It moved to Alcester Street, Birmingham in February 1849, and in February 1852 to Edgbaston, then just outside the city.

108. *friend*   Ambrose St John.

109. *"Obliviscere . . . tui"*   Forget your people and your father's house. Psalms 44: 10.

110. *Observatory*   See ed. n. 72 to this chapter.

111. *Copeland*   See ch. III, ed. n. 111.

112. *Buckle*   George Buckle (1820–1900), the translator of one volume of Fleury's history, became a fellow of Oriel in 1848.

113. *Pattison*   Mark Pattison (1813–84), fellow and later rector of Lincoln, who became a prominent university reformer, came under Newman's influence as an undergraduate at Oriel, but by 1848 had abandoned Tractarianism, and subsequently orthodox Christianity.

114. *Lewis*   David Lewis (1814–95), fellow of Jesus, was Newman's curate at St Mary's from 1842–3. He became a Catholic in 1846 and translated the works of St Teresa of Avila and St John of the Cross.

115. *Ogle*   James Adey Ogle (1792–1857), a mathematician, became Regius Professor of Medicine in 1851.

CHAPTER V

1. *Macaulay*   In his 1840 review of Ranke's *History of the Popes*; see *Works* (London, 1879), vi. 458.

2. *scroll*   Ezekiel 2: 9–10.

3. *words*   Ephesians 2: 12.

4. *credenda*   Things to be believed.

5. *said*   *Diff.* i. 240. For Kingsley's criticism, see *Apo.* 372.

6. *'Ye . . . again'*   John 3: 7.

7. *statement*   *Diff.* i. 249–50. For Kingsley's ridicule of the passage, see *Apo.* 373.

8. *'The . . . you'*   Matthew 21: 31.

9. *'whoso . . . heart'*   Matthew 5: 28.

10. *seat*   The doctrine that infallibility in solemn definitions is exercised by the pope as well as by a general council was defined in 1870 at the First Vatican Council.

11. *St. Thomas*   Aquinas (1225–74), the 'Angelic Doctor', whose *Summa Theologica* remains the most authoritative theological work for the Roman Catholic Church.

12. *'does grow'*   Cf. *Gustavus Vasa: A Tragedy*, iii. 7, by Henry Brooke (1703–83).

13. *St. Paul*   2 Corinthians 10: 8.

14. *Pelagianism*   The fifth-century English heretic Pelagius denied original sin and held that through free will and without grace man can be saved.

15. *Manichaeism*, named after the Persian Mani or Manes (third century), which arose as a heresy particularly in North Africa in the fourth and fifth centuries, taught a dualism between good and evil, the spirit being from God and the flesh from Satan.

16. *Jansenism*   The heresy named after Cornelius Jansenius (1585–1638), bishop of Ypres, which maintained the total corruption of man and an extreme moral rigorism.

17. *definition*   By Pope Pius IX.

18. *St. Bernard* (1090–1153), abbot of Clairvaux, the great Cistercian theologian. 'To many [the doctrine] seemed to imply that the Blessed Virgin did not die in Adam, that she did not come under the penalty of the fall, that she was not redeemed ... If controversy had in earlier days so cleared the subject as to make it plain to all, that the doctrine meant nothing else than that in fact in her case the general sentence on mankind was not carried out, and that, by means of the indwelling in her of divine grace from the first moment of her being (and this is all the decree of 1854 has declared), I cannot believe that the doctrine would have ever been opposed ...' (*Diff*. ii. 49.)

19. *Sermon*   'The Theory of Developments in Religious Doctrine', *US* 335–6. For Kingsley's criticism, see *Apo*. 402–4.

20. *pomoeria*   The open spaces free of buildings inside and outside the walls of a town, i.e. its outer boundaries.

21. *poet*   Shakespeare, *Measure for Measure*, II. ii. 107–9.

22. *Apostle*   2 Corinthians 4: 7.

23. *Theophilus* (d. 412), patriarch of Alexandria from 385 till 412, condemned Origenism at the Synod of Alexandria in 401, and treated its adherents harshly. He was also responsible for sending St John Chrysostom into exile, which ended in his death.

24. *Vigilius* (d. 555) opposed the Monophysites, by whose support, as well as by other corrupt and unjust means, he was elected pope in 537; he also assented to the condemnation of Origenism.

25. *party*   An unmistakable reference to the Ultramontanes who accused Newman of disloyalty to the papacy and who were insisting on an extreme version of the doctrine of papal infallibility, for the definition of which they were busily lobbying.

26. *periodical*   The *Liberal*, which Shelley and Leigh Hunt helped found, lasted for four numbers in 1822–3.

27. *school*   See Note A, 'Liberalism'.

28. *words*   *Contra Epistolam Manichaei quam vocant Fundamenti*, I. ii.

29. *poet*   William Cowper, 'The Needless Alarm', 132.

30. *acts*   Particularly Pope Pius IX's 'Munich Brief' of December 1863, which rejected the intellectual freedom claimed for Catholic thinkers and scientists at a recent congress of liberal scholars and theologians held at Munich.

31. '*Fear ... peace*   Exodus 14: 13–14.

32. *Galileo* (1564–1642) was condemned for teaching the Copernican as opposed to the Ptolemaic theory of astronomy.

33. '*exceptio ... regulam*'   The exception proves the rule.

34. *point*   See ch. III, ed. n. 52.

35. *Tertullian* (*c*.160–*c*.225), the father of Latin theology, eventually joined the Montanist sect.

36. *Hilary* (*c*.315–67), St, bishop of Poitiers, called the 'Athanasius of the West' because of his opposition to Arianism, in his commentaries on the psalms and St Matthew's gospel.

37. *Ambrose* (*c*.339–97), St, bishop of Milan, one of the four great doctors of the Latin Church, closely studied Origen's scriptural commentaries.

38. *Jerome* (*c*.340–420), St, was responsible for the Vulgate or Latin version of the Bible.

39. *Eusebius* (*c*.260–*c*.340), bishop of Caesarea, called the father of church history, was a semi-Arian.

40. *Malchion* (third century), a presbyter of Antioch, exposed the heretical monarchianism of Paul of Samosata (third century), bishop of Antioch, at the Council of Antioch (*c*.270).

41. *St. Anselm* (1033–1109), archbishop of Canterbury, famous for his ontological argument for the existence of God, maintained the Western teaching on the procession of the Spirit from the Father and the Son as against the Eastern doctrine of the procession from the Father only at the Council of Bari (1098), called by Pope Urban II.

42. *St. Bonaventura* (1221–74), Franciscan doctor of the Church, one of the greatest medieval schoolmen.

43. *Salmeron*   Alphonsus Salmeron (1515–85), Jesuit theologian, one of the original companions of St Ignatius Loyola.

44. *Zosimus* (d.418), St, pope 417–18, at first defended Pelagius on the basis of a misleading profession of faith, and was ready to accept that his friend and follower Coelestius, who had been condemned by the previous pope, Innocent I, was not guilty of heresy.

45. *Berengarius* of Tours (*c*.1010–88), scholastic theologian, seemed sometimes to imply that he believed in a merely symbolic, and at other times in the real presence of Christ in the eucharist, but Pope Gregory VII accepted his retraction and refused to allow him to be condemned as a heretic.

46. *own*   The Roman Catholic hierarchy was restored to England in 1850.

47. *Arians*   See Note F.

48. *Sermons*   'The Theory of Developments in Religious Doctrine', *US* 340–42 (see *Apo.* 402–4).

49. *writer*   Isaac Williams in Tracts 80 and 87. See ch. III, ed. n. 30.

50. *'Cast . . . swine'*   Matthew 7: 6.

51. *Disciplina Arcani*   Discipline of the secret. A term first used apparently in the seventeenth century.

52. *Clement*   *Stromateis*, vii. 8,9.

53. *Old Hall Green*   St Edmund's College, Ware, Hertfordshire.

54. *Ushaw*   College, near Durham.

55. *Bishop*   William Bernard Ullathorne (1806–89), bishop of Birmingham, an 'old Catholic'.

56. *fever*   Brought by Irish immigrants during the famine years after 1845.

57. *bishop*   William Riddell (1807–47), vicar apostolic of the Northern district.

58. *cholera*   Newman himself went in September 1849 to help the priests at Bilston, Staffordshire during an outbreak.

59. *If . . . miserable*   1 Corinthians 15: 19.

60. *It . . . way*   Baruch 3: 22–3.

61. *Liguori*   *Theologia Moralis* (1753, 1755), iv. 2. See *Apo.* 407–10.

62. *Taylor*   *The Rule of Conscience*, III. ii. 5, in *The Whole Works*, ed. R. Heber (15 vols., London, 1839), xiii. 355. See also *Apo.* 501–3, 506

63. *Milton*   *De Doctrina Christiana* (posthumously, 1825), II. xiii. See also *Apo.* 503–4, 513–16.

64. *Paley*   William Paley (1743–1805), famous for his *Evidences of Christianity* (1794), in *Principles of Moral and Political Philosophy* (1785), III. v. See also *Apo.* 504–5.

65. *Johnson*   James Boswell, *Life of Johnson*, ed. G. Birkbeck Hill, rev. L. F. Powell (Oxford: Clarendon Press, 1934), iv. 305.

66. *Scavini*   Pietro Scavini's *Theologia Moralis Universa* was a highly popular nineteenth-century exposition of St Alphonso's moral theology, which went through many editions.

67. *Hey*   John Hey (1734–1815), Cambridge Latitudinarian theologian, in spite of subscribing to the Thirty-nine Articles, regarded the differences between Anglicans and Unitarians as more or less verbal in his *Lectures in Divinity* (1796).

68. *Burnett*   Gilbert Burnet (1643–1715), bishop of Salisbury and author of *History of my own Times*, published in 1699 his Latitudinarian *Exposition of the Thirty-nine Articles*.

69. *writer*   John Hill Burton, *Life and Correspondence of David Hume* (2 vols., Edinburgh, 1846), ii. 437ff.

70. *Life*   *The Life of St Alphonsus Maria de Liguori*, compiled from the

published memoirs of the saint by one of the Redemptorist fathers (Baltimore, 1855), 29–30.

71. *Gerdil* Hyacinthe Sigismonde Gerdil (1718–1802), theologian and philosopher. See the quotation in *Apo.* 490 from *Opusculi Teologici Inediti* (Rome, 1864), 28–9.

72. *Natalis Alexander* (1639–1724), French Dominican theologian. See *Apo.* 508 for the original Latin quotation from his *Theologia Dogmatica et Moralis* (Cologne, 1698).

73. *notices* Pt. III, ch. ix.

74. *Oratorian* P. G. Bacci, *The Life of St Philip Neri, Apostle of Rome*, tr. F. W. Faber (2 vols., London, 1847), i. 293.

75. *St. John* See ch. IV, ed. n. 37.

76. *Mills* (1823–1903) became a Catholic in 1846 and joined the Birmingham Oratory in 1848, where he remained for the rest of his life.

77. *Bittleston* (1818–86) became a Catholic in 1849 and in 1850 joined the Oratory, which he left in 1879 to become a diocesan priest.

78. *Caswall* (1814–78), well known as a translator and writer of hymns, became a Catholic in 1847 and two years later joined the Oratory after the death of his wife.

79. *Neville* (1824–1905) became a Catholic in 1851, when he joined the Oratory. In Newman's last years he became his secretary and after his death his literary executor.

80. *Ryder* (1837–1907), whose convert father had been a pupil of Newman's at Oriel, joined the Oratory in 1856 and was superior after Newman's death.

PENGUIN ONLINE

READ MORE IN PENGUIN

In every corner of the world, on every subject under the sun, Penguin represents quality and variety – the very best in publishing today.

For complete information about books available from Penguin – including Puffins, Penguin Classics and Arkana – and how to order them, write to us at the appropriate address below. Please note that for copyright reasons the selection of books varies from country to country.

In the United Kingdom: Please write to *Dept. EP, Penguin Books Ltd, Bath Road, Harmondsworth, West Drayton, Middlesex UB7 0DA*

In the United States: Please write to *Consumer Services, Penguin Putnam Inc., 405 Murray Hill Parkway, East Rutherford, New Jersey 07073-2136.* VISA and MasterCard holders call 1-800-631-8571 to order Penguin titles

In Canada: Please write to *Penguin Books Canada Ltd, 10 Alcorn Avenue, Suite 300, Toronto, Ontario M4V 3B2*

In Australia: Please write to *Penguin Books Australia Ltd, 487 Maroondah Highway, Ringwood, Victoria 3134*

In New Zealand: Please write to *Penguin Books (NZ) Ltd, Private Bag 102902, North Shore Mail Centre, Auckland 10*

In India: Please write to *Penguin Books India Pvt Ltd, 11 Community Centre, Panchsheel Park, New Delhi 110017*

In the Netherlands: Please write to *Penguin Books Netherlands bv, Postbus 3507, NL-1001 AH Amsterdam*

In Germany: Please write to *Penguin Books Deutschland GmbH, Metzlerstrasse 26, 60594 Frankfurt am Main*

In Spain: Please write to *Penguin Books S. A., Bravo Murillo 19, 1°B, 28015 Madrid*

In Italy: Please write to *Penguin Italia s.r.l., Via Vittorio Emanuele 45la, 20094 Corsico, Milano*

In France: Please write to *Penguin France, 12, Rue Prosper Ferradou, 31700 Blagnac*

In Japan: Please write to *Penguin Books Japan Ltd, Iidabashi KM-Bldg, 2-23-9 Koraku, Bunkyo-Ku, Tokyo 112-0004*

In South Africa: Please write to *Penguin Books South Africa (Pty) Ltd, P.O. Box 751093, Gardenview, 2047 Johannesburg*